CORPORATE SYSTEMS CENTER

HARD DRIVE

BIBLE

EDITION VIII

CSC

Eighth Edition
July, 1996

Martin Bodo
Author

Harold Moorehead
Editor, Photographer

Jody Coil
Production Manager

Janné Masingale
Typographer

DEDICATION

To my father, Joseph Bodo, who sparked my interest in electronics at an early age.

ABOUT THE AUTHOR

Martin Bodo is the founder and president of Corporate Systems Center. An avid computer enthusiast since his early teens, he holds a degree in Physics from the University of Santa Clara.

SPECIAL THANKS TO

The entire CSC staff who have helped write, edit, sell, and distribute the **Hard Drive Bible** to over 40,000 satisfied customers.

ACKNOWLEDGEMENTS

We would like to thank all of the manufacturers who provided us with data for this publication. Without their cooperation, production of this book would not have been possible.

Maxtor Technical Support Department
Maxtor Service Center
Quantum Technical Support Department
Western Digital Technical Support Department
Jim Plelps   - Rodime Inc.
Bill Rudock   - Seagate Technology
Mike Mori   - Sycard Technologies

90000

9 780964 150317

International Standard Book Number: 0-9641503-1-X

CSC's corporate headquarters is located in Sunnyvale, California. This location puts CSC at the epicenter of the latest developments in data storage technology.

About CSC

CSC was founded in 1986 by our president, Martin Bodo. Since then, we've grown consistently by providing the best customer service in the industry. Our mission is to offer quality data storage products available and to back them up with professional service and support.

Our in-house technical service center provides free lifetime technical support for hardware customers.

We're proud to employ the most technically qualified individuals in the data storage industry.

Corporate Systems Center proudly services the entire digital data storage market, from manufacturers to end users.

PCI WIDE SCSI-III CONTROLLER

UNIVERSAL SCSI CONTROLLER

- ASPI™, DOS, OS/2™, Windows '95 and NT™ drivers included
- An ideal match for fast Pentiums and Windows '95
- Supports both Wide and Narrow SCSI drives
- FLASH BIOS option permits upgrade to SCSI-III software features
- Automatic termination eliminates data errors

You asked for it – we built it. The PCI bus is a perfect performance match for Wide SCSI-III. Take advantage of these new standards and get twice the data rates of SCSI-II. Connect up to fifteen Wide drives to your fileserver and get double the performance of standard SCSI-II drives. This card is ideal for disk intensive fileservers and Audio Visual workstations which operate several drives concurrently.

You want maximum system performance with the fewest headaches. Now, existing, inexpensive SCSI-II drives can share the bus with Fast & Wide SCSI-III. Get it all – compatibility, ease of installation, and FastCache™ performance with Fast & Wide SCSI-III transfer rates.

Drive transfer rate: 20MB/sec; Bus transfer rate: 133MB/sec. Call us today for a free price comparison guide including Fast & Wide SCSI-III hard disk drives and other storage devices.

CSC FASTCACHE™ PCMCIA CONTROLLER

CSC'S FASTCACHE™ PCMCIA SCSI-II

- Fastest PCMCIA controller available
- ASPI™ Compliant. CD-ROM and hard disk drivers included
- 3.3MB/sec Sustained Data Transfer Rate; 10MB/sec Burst Rate
- Full, high performance Windows '95 and OS/2 Warp™ drivers are included
- Supports Windows 3.x, Windows for Workgroups, DOS, and OS/2
- Includes Cable and Software – Compare and Save

Upgrade your notebook to Fast SCSI-II. The CSC FastCache™ PC Card slips into your PCMCIA slot and brings your notebook all the power of CD-ROM, DAT, optical, and Fast SCSI-II hard drives. This controller is ASPI compliant and includes free CD-ROM and hard disk drivers.

Using PCMCIA is the only way to add CD-ROM with acceptable performance. The PCMCIA Fastcache Card is fully format compatible with most other SCSI cards, so you can share peripherals with your desktop. Made in the U.S.A. Call today and connect any SCSI device to your notebook.

CSC FASTCACHE™ X10 FLOPPY

ADVANCED FEATURES

- Accelerates floppy performance up to 10 times

- Transfers data instantly using 1.5MB cache

- Duplicates disks in less than 15 seconds

- Complete kit includes drive and controller

- Now includes motorized disk eject

You purchased high end Pentium performance. The video and SCSI accelerators work great. But you could die frustrated waiting for the floppy drive.

Slip the new FastCache X10 into your system and hold on. A separate microprocessor and 1.5MB RAM cache now control your floppy. You can boot faster from a floppy than from a hard drive. Your floppy drive is finally useful. Transfer data instantly. Duplicate disks in seconds, not minutes. Install large applications instantly. The CSC FastCache X10 runs applications up to 10 times faster than normal drives.

The FastCache X10 is designed for people who can't afford to wait. Try it risk free for 15 days. Call us today.

AK47 ISA SCSI-II CONTROLLER

ADVANCED FEATURES

- True FAST SCSI-II 10MB/sec burst transfer rate

- Sustained transfer rates reach 3-4MB/sec - depending on processor and ISA bus speeds

- On board floppy controller supports 4 drives, including 2.88MB units and "fast floppy tapes"

- Includes floppy cables, internal SCSI cable, update and ASPI, Windows '95 and Windows NT™ driver software

- Easy plug and play installation in any standard 16 bit slot

- Free software upgrades from the CSC BBS

Connect any IBM compatible system to the world of CD-ROM and Fast SCSI-II drives. You'll get maximum SCSI disk system performance without headaches. CSC's proprietary "hyper-FIFO" design and industry standard drivers make this card compatible where others fail.

Strong termination and power protection eliminate cabling problems and offer maximum reliability, even with up to 7 drives attached. The optional caching drivers accelerate CD-ROM performance to hard disk speeds.

Flash BIOS lets you add additional SCSI features with free software updates from the CSC BBS.

UNIVERSAL DRIVE DUPLICATOR

COPIES TO AND FROM ANY DRIVE:

- SCSI-I, SCSI-II, or SCSI-III disk drives
- CD-ROM players and CD-R recorders
- Erasable Optical Cartridges
- DOS and 32 bit NT compatible files, even on file servers
- IDE, MFM, RLL, or ESDI drives
- Now supports SCSI tape drives

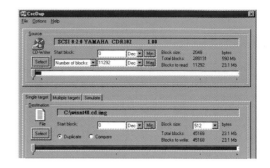

Easily copy an entire hard drive or CD-ROM. Using standard drives, you can instantly copy an entire disk, including operating systems, directories, files, simply …everything. Make fast backup copies of CD-ROM software using CD-R drives. Instantly format drives for PCs, Sun, SGI, and UNIX workstations.

Dealers and system builders can save hours of time by preinstalling software on one drive and then using that drive as a master for rapid duplication. Users can back up and restore data from CD disk, M/O optical disks, or even DOS compatible files.

CSC's new menu driven duplication software saves MIS professionals hours every day. Fully install standard configurations over a network using the DOS file compatibility mode to create master image files on your server.

Any data is fair game for the FastCache duplicator. Data is precisely duplicated on a byte by byte basis. Exact copies result.

WINDOWS '95 TAPE BACK UP

MAXIMIZE YOUR SCSI PERFORMANCE

- Universal SCSI device support including 4mm, DAT, 8mm, Exabyte, ¼", DLT, autoloaders and others not supported under Microsoft backup
- Easy to use - Fast menu driven interface shows files on disk and tape
- Automatic selection of files which require backup
- True 32 bit performance and reliability

You made the right choice with Windows '95. Now get powerful multitasking tape backup and restore protection. FastCache™ backup is your high performance backup and restore solution. Get full compatibility with SCSI devices not supported by Microsoft Backup™. Protect your data from accidental deletion and system crashes with fast, efficient backups.

Installation is automatic. Backup operation has never been simpler. A clean graphical user interface shows files on tape and disk for easy selection.

SCSI MECHANIC™ FOR WINDOWS '95 AND NT

MAXIMIZE YOUR SCSI PERFORMANCE

- Low level format drives, optical cartridges & tapes – reassign defective sectors manually or automatically

- Verify drive performance and data integrity

- Clone drives – including Windows '95 and NT operating systems

- Read manufacturers' information and mode settings

- Easily change drive modes and cache settings

Windows '95 and NT are great operating systems. But it's tough to manage servers and workstations without good SCSI utilities. Get the new Windows '95 SCSI utility pack from CSC. All the features Microsoft left out are now yours.

Control disk drive "mode pages" to increase efficiency and change cache parameters. Read the manufacturers' information and mode settings. Verify drive performance and data integrity with efficient surface scans. Clone entire hard drives - including Windows '95 and NT operating systems and files. Automatically reassign bad sectors for data security.

This true 32 bit software is designed specifically for Windows '95 and NT. Call CSC today and maximize your Windows '95 SCSI performance.

CD-ROM DUPLICATOR

QUICKLY COPY CD-ROMS

- Sustained reading speed 4X - 600KB/sec

- Sustained writing speed 4X - 600KB/sec

- Both drives operate concurrently for top performance

- System includes controller, drives, software and blank disk

- PCI controller, cables and terminator are included

Use your PC to copy CD-ROM disks in minutes. Make software backups on rugged, permanent media. Produce disks quickly and economically for distribution. No mastering software or multimedia experience is required.

Everything you need is included. You get a complete external system with two matched drives: a 4X/6X CD-ROM reader/writer and an A/V certified 700MB SCSI drive. The CSC FastCache duplication software and controller take advantage of both, operating them simultaneously to automatically duplicate disks in minutes. You can even transfer CD images to and from hard disks or optical cartridges.

Plug the controller card in any Pentium PCI slot, connect the external unit, and you'll be up and running out of the box. Software and hardware are matched for compatibility and top performance.

DISK ARRAY ENCLOSURES

SCSI SERVER TOWER

- Holds up to 8 SCSI drives
- Solid steel case with dual cooling fans and microfiltering
- Ideal for LAN servers
- Up to 2 SCSI ports and up to 8 ID switches, optional
- Holds any combination of half or full height 5.25" drives
- Custom cabling to meet your specifications

CSC is now delivering the ultimate SCSI enclosure. Up to eight half height SCSI hard, CD-ROM, optical, and tape drives can be configured to your specifications.

Whether you need a network storage subsystem, an external SCSI drive case, or a full-blown disk array, CSC has it. We'll custom build it complete with the drives of your choice for free, when drives and tower are purchased together.

A professionally designed micro-filtered air cooling system featuring dual forced air fans protects sensitive optical and tape drives.

CD-ROM TOWERS

NETWORK CD TOWER

- Access data immediately with seven drives on line simultaneously
- Ideal for Novell, OS/2, Banyan, and NT network servers
- Includes dual cooling fans for long term reliability
- Full SCSI-II command set for software compatibility
- Heavy duty enclosure and 300 watt power supply

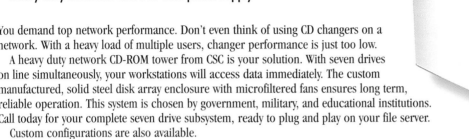

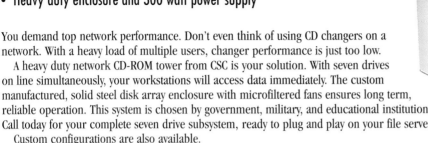

You demand top network performance. Don't even think of using CD changers on a network. With a heavy load of multiple users, changer performance is just too low.

A heavy duty network CD-ROM tower from CSC is your solution. With seven drives on line simultaneously, your workstations will access data immediately. The custom manufactured, solid steel disk array enclosure with microfiltered fans ensures long term, reliable operation. This system is chosen by government, military, and educational institutions. Call today for your complete seven drive subsystem, ready to plug and play on your file server.

Custom configurations are also available.

TABLE OF CONTENTS

TABLE OF CONTENTS

TABLE OF CONTENTS

TABLE OF CONTENTS

TABLE OF CONTENTS

TABLE OF CONTENTS

TABLE OF CONTENTS

TABLE OF CONTENTS

TABLE OF CONTENTS

HISTORY OF DISK DRIVES

The magnetic recording technology used in today's disk drives can be traced back to around 500 B.C. when the mineral magnetite was discovered. Magnetite is the naturally occuring magnetic material that was first used in compasses. Alchemists in the first century B.C. discovered the first magnetic compasses when they noticed that loadstones hung from a string always pointed the same way.

Several hundred years later, the connection between electricity and magnetism was discovered. Early scientists noticed a that a compass needle was deflected when it was put near a wire carrying electric current. It was in this era that magnetic technology was pioneered by experimental geniuses like Danish physicist Hans Christian Oersted and English scientist Michael Faraday who discovered the principles of electromagnetic induction.

The first practical magnetic recording device was the Telegraphone patented in 1898 by Danish telephone engineer and inventor Vlademar Poulsen. The Telegraphone was a crude audio recorder using a stretched magnetized wire. The Telegraphone attracted considerable curiosity when it was first exhibited at the Exposition Universelle in Paris in 1900. The few words that the Austrian emperor Franz Josef spoke into it at that exhibition are believed to be the earliest surviving magnetic recording.

As World War I approached, the German war effort assumed leadership in magnetic recording technology. The German firm AEG was the first to use plastic strips (tape) for magnetic recording. The Germans put magnetic recording to its first military application on submarines. Secret communications were recorded on crude reel to reel tape recorders at slow speeds. The tapes were then played back and retransmitted at high speeds to prevent Allied interception. The receiving station used another tape recorder to reconstruct the messages. By World War II the Germans had perfected the recording technology and manufactured high quality reel-to-reel tape recorders called Magnetophons. These tape recorders were nearly identical to today's high quality audio tape recorders.

In 1945 an American Signal Corps soldier, John T. Mullin, sent two of these captured machines home to San Francisco. The analysis of these units by American engineers at Ampex Corporation in Redwood City lead to the development of the Ampex Model 200 in 1948. The Model 200 was the first magnetic recorder to be manufactured in volume and used commercially. The American Broadcasting Corporation had

Magnetophon Recorder

provided some of the financing for the Ampex recorder project, and was the first to use them in broadcasting the Bing Crosby Show in 1948. This same technology is used in today's high resolution audio, video and digital tape drives.

Reel to reel tape recorders and Hollerith punch cards were the main storage devices used in early computers. Paper Holerith cards and paper tapes were used to perform initial program loading when early computers were first powered up. Paper tapes were popularized by the Teletype Corporation who added paper tape readers and punches to many of their Teletype terminals. Paper tape remained popular for over 20 years, lasting until the early 1970's. It took the convenience and erasability of floppy disks to eliminate paper tapes.

In 1952, IBM, realizing the need for a random access method of data retrieval with faster access than magnetic tapes, sent Reynold B. Johnson to San Jose, California to head up a magnetic recording research team. Johnson was convinced that a disk based system was the way to go, but other engineers advised him to abandon the project. Following his intuition, Johnson designed the first commercially successful digital disk drive. In 1956, IBM announced the Model 350 RAMAC (Random Access Method of Accounting and Control). It was a quantum leap in disk technology for its time. The RAMAC stored 5 megabytes of data on fifty 24-inch disks, spinning at 1200 RPM, and had an access time of 600 milliseconds. The resulting data transfer rate was .10 Mbits per second. Compare that to the 25 to 80Mbits per second data rates typical today! The popular name for this huge stack of disks at IBM was the "baloney slicer".

In 1955, realizing that magnetic recording density was severely limited by the number of linear stripes (tracks) on the tape, two brilliant engineers at Ampex Corporation, Charles Ginsburg and Ray Dolby, developed the helical scan recording system. Their ingenious scanning system uses a tiny spinning magnetic head with tape wrapped around it in a spiral. This design packed recording tracks much more tightly onto the tape than was previously possible. The helical scan recording technique provides an extremely high recording density with a single small head. Helical scan recording is now used in every video recorder (VCR), Digital Audio Tape drives (DATs), and all high capacity tape backup drives. I have read with respect several documents authored by Ginsburg and Dolby at Ampex. These engineers deserve more credit for their brilliant invention of the mechanisms and recording techniques copied in every modern VCR.

The Baloney Slicer!

In 1961, IBM pushed disk data storage ahead by announcing the 1301 Disk Storage unit that used aerodynamically shaped recording heads that "flew" above the surfaces of the spinning disks. This enabled roughly 10 times as much information to be packed in each square inch of disk surface. This head design would eventually become the "Winchester disk drive".

The next year, IBM announced the 1311 Disk Pack unit which helped speed the end of the punched card era by providing removable and interchangeable "disk packs" containing six disks protected by a transparent plastic "cake cover." Each disk pack could store roughly as much data as 25,000 punched cards. Magnetic disks were finally becoming a practical storage medium for computers.

During 1964, my parents made the mistake of conceiving Martin Bodo. Little did they know how much trouble I would eventually cause them. My early fascination with computers would ultimately place Corporate Systems Center (CSC) at the forefront of magnetic data storage technology.

In 1967, IBM assigned David L. Noble to head a research team to develop a convenient storage medium to store and ship microcode. In

1969 several engineers left the project to join Memorex. Memorex soon became an industry leader in magnetic media technologies, disk drive manufacturing, and magnetic media production.

In 1970, IBM announced the 3330 Disk Storage Facility which was the first disk storage product to use an electrical feedback system called a "track-following servo" to control a "voice coil" motor that could quickly position recording heads at desired positions over the disk. This combination provided better response time, higher track density, and more reliable operation than was previously attainable. Twenty years ahead of its time, this closed loop track following servo technology would eventually be used in every large capacity disk drive.

In 1971, the first "diskette" was produced by IBM as an ICPL (Initial Control Program Load) device. It was called the Minnow and was an 8-inch read-only model that stored 81,664 bytes. It caused paper tapes to become obsolete almost overnight.

While IBM and others were developing disk technology at home in America, Japanese companies like Sony and Japan Victor Corporation (JVC) were making rapid advances in consumer VCR technology. By the early 1980's, the Japanese had a lead in helical scan tape drive manufacturing technology that the US could never overcome.

In 1973, the first read-write floppy disk, the Igar (IBM 33FD), which stored an incredible (for it's time) 242,944 bytes - started shipping to customers. The original code name of the read-write disk was Figaro, but the initial f and final o were removed as a symbolic removal of "fat" and "overhead". Memorex was the first company after IBM to produce floppy disk products and soon became a strong competitor in this field.

Also in 1973, IBM announced the 3340 Disk Storage Unit, which featured an ultra light-weight recording head that could "land" on and "take off" from a lubricated disk while it was still spinning. This eliminated the need for a mechanism to raise the heads off the disk surface before stopping; substantially reducing the cost of manufacturing. The 3340 also contained two spindles, each with a storage capacity of 30 million characters. Referring to this arrangement as a "30-30", engineers were reminded of the famous rifle and called their creation a "Winchester" file. This term became an industry standard to

IBM 33FD Floppy Drive

identify this "floating head" design.

In 1975, IBM announced the 3350 Direct Access Storage Device, which marked an extension of Winchester technology and a return from the removable disk pack to fixed disks, permitting higher recording densities and lower cost per bit for on-line storage. The 3350 could store data at a density of more than 3 million bits per square inch, an increase of more than 1500 times the density of the RAMAC. By this time, competitors were catching up. Several companies, including Shugart, Magnetic Peripherals Incorporated, and PerSci were about to introduce competitive floppy disk drives.

In 1976, the success of the 33FD floppy disk led to the development of the 43FD using a dual-head drive, that could store 568,320 bytes. This was followed a year later by the double-density, double-sided, 53FD using MFM encoding and a capacity of 1,212,416 bytes. By 1977, nineteen companies were manufacturing floppy disk drives in the United States and MFM had become the encoding method of choice.

In 1979 Seagate Technology was founded and was the first company to mass produce an affordable hard disk drive (the 5 Megabyte ST506). Seagate has become the largest independent manufacturer of hard drives, having shipped over 50 million units to date.

I was a runny-nosed high school sophomore in 1979. While IBM was inventing thin-film recording heads, I was content with my first 5.25" 160K floppy drive. I was hooked, but I didn't know it.

The data storage industry exploded in the early 1980's with the help of brilliant engineers who had business sense. Alan Shugart made the floppy disk the standard for data interchange and floppy drive sales soared. By 1982, hard disk drive sales had exploded and form factors were shrinking from 14" disks to 8" disks. The 5.25" form factor made popular by Seagate's ST506 was now an industry standard.

When I graduated from college in 1986, I made a living by modifying Alan Shugart's Model 712, 5.25" 10 megabyte hard drives so they would hold 20MB. I was starting to understand the equation for success in the hard drive industry. It was simple: "Provide the Most Megs in the Smallest Size for the Least Bucks". I saw an opportunity for a company that would initially provide repair services for disk drives. CSC was born in 1986.

In 1989, IBM announced the 3390 Direct Access Storage Device, which could store as much as 21.5 billion characters in each storage unit -- the same capacity as its predecessor, the 3380 Model K, but at an increased density that required only one-third the floor space. Gosh, it weighed only 800 pounds!

As sales of Apple Computer's Macintosh line of personal computers began to grow, the industry was introduced to the idea of using the Small Computer Systems Interface (SCSI) as a standard port for desktop PC peripherals. SCSI at this point was basically a glorified 8 bit parallel port. But SCSI would eventually grow into one of the most popular standards for both low performance PC and higher performance workstation disk drives! Like the IBM-PC, SCSI caught on like crazy because it was hardware with software standards included.

In 1990, Conner Peripherals in partnership with Compaq computers created and made popular both the IDE interface and the 3.5" hard drive form factor. An enormous volume market for IDE drives grew in the next few years as IBM compatible desktop systems grew in popularity.

By 1990, there was not one American company left producing helical

Early Conner IDE Drive

scan tape recording mechanisms. The Japanese conquest in consumer electronics was about to pay off. Soon, all helical scan digital tape recording mechanisms for computer technology would come from Asia. In addition, the American loss of consumer audio manufacturing technology would cost US companies dearly. All digital CD-ROM disk drives based on this technology would now come from Japan and the Orient.

In 1991, we designed our first caching disk controllers at CSC. These cards would eventually sell by the thousands, as the size of CSC continued to double yearly.

In 1991, IBM created another first in drive technology, the MR head. IBM's 9340 drive became the first IBM disk to use magneto-resistive recording-head technology, and IBM could now boast of bit densities of >100Mbits per square inch.

In 1992, improvements in mechanical alignment and media boosted the capacity of standard diskettes to 2.88MB and "ZIP" diskettes to 100MB. Maxtor Corporation announced the "Magic" MXT series of disk 3.5" disk drives with capacities over 1GB and access times under 8ms. 5.25" disk drives were available in 1994 with over 8GB of formatted capacity.

As we write the update to the Hard Drive Bible, it is now 1996. It's hard to predict the future, but I'll be glad to share a few thoughts on the data storage industry.

Compaq will soon ship Floptical drives with 120 MB capacity in a standard 3.5" form factor. I'm not sure what industry standards will develop, but other than "floptical" drives, I don't see much future for the floppy disk industry. Read the chapter on CD-ROM for more insight. CD-ROM and recordable CD-R drives revolutionizing software distribution.

The hard disk industry, on the other hand, is moving faster than ever. Volumes are huge while only a few manufacturing companies are staying profitable because of the intense competition. Technology is advancing faster than ever. My friends and I used to talk about "mini-mono" disk heads. Then it was "micro-sliders" and even "nano-sliders". Today we had a nerd's lunch and talked about "pico-sliders" that fly at 4 millionths of an inch above the disk. As far as I'm concerned, that should be called "contact recording"!

Will hard drive sales continue to grow? To be honest, there are some potential challengers for hard drives. Optical, and Flash technologies are improving. You can bet our friends at Intel hope Flash will kill hard drives. But our friends in Japan working on DVD optical disk drives feel that optical drives will win out in the long run. My opinion is unchanged. For the last ten years, I've had people tell me that something better will replace hard drives. Every time there's a technical advance in Flash or optical drive, there's a corresponding advance in magnetic disk drive technology. Hard drives are here to stay. As magnetic, optical, and semiconductor technologies advance together, hard drives continue to offer more storage for less money, with a better access time. Each technology has it's distinct advantages, but the magnetic recording technology used in hard drives is simple, mature and easy to manufacture. Hard drives will remain practical for several more years at least.

In 1996, a major disk drive merger took place between Seagate and Conner Peripherals. I take my hat off to Alan Shugart, CEO of Seagate Technologies for that accomplishment. Seagate has a broad line of products from 8" drives to PCMCIA FLASH memory. They're quick on their feet and poised for the future.

But the majority of disk drive manufacturers continue to loose money! This is the largest potential problem facing the data storage industry: price competition. Severe price competition is forcing many companies to abandon research efforts and concentrate on high volume, low-tech products. Only the lean, high tech companies will survive the competition.

Some feel that magnetic recording technology has begun to give way to optical technologies. I agree that optical technology has now become affordable and reliable enough to replace magnetic drives in some selected applications. In the past few years, optical recording techniques pioneered by the Japanese in consumer products have developed to the point where optical drives are manufactured at reasonable costs. Many companies like Hitachi, Sony, Ricoh, and MaxOptix do a brisk business selling fast, reliable, low cost optical drives. I feel that the compelling advantage behind optical media is removability. Cartridge hard drives and hard drives with removable HDA's are not as large or convenient as optical media. The market for erasable optical drives will continue to grow, but hard drives will remain the best choice for non-removable applications.

BASIC DRIVE OPERATION

All disk drives perform three basic functions. They spin, seek, and transfer data. The disks inside a hard drive are mounted and rotated by a motor normally located in the center of the disks called the spindle motor. The read/write heads are held and moved in a head carriage that usually also holds the preamplifier electronics. Disks and heads are stacked vertically on the spindle motor, and the head stack assembly is positioned on-track by a servo system.

Raw read data flows from the preamplifier and is encoded and decoded by the drive electronics. The heads read and write this "encoded" data to the disks (media). Data encoding and decoding circuitry is designed to pack as much information as possible into the smallest area. Read/write circuits move the encoded data to and from the magnetic recording heads. When writing, the heads convert the electric currents from read/write circuits into highly concentrated magnetic fields. These magnetic fields are stored in miniature magnetic groups called "domains" on the surface of the disk. When reading, the magnetic domains stored on the media are converted into electric currents as the heads pass by a second time, operating in reverse to read data. The heads convert the changing magnetic fields from the disk into electric currents as the read data is recovered.

The sections below describe the operation and purpose of the basic components of a disk drive: the spindle motor, head carriage, the servo system, heads and media, and the data encoding circuitry.

Spindle Motors

The motor used to rotate the disks in a drive is called a spindle motor. Disk drives use many different types of spindle motors. The type used determines the spin-up time of the disk and torque as well as the heat dissipation inside the drive. A motor with a high start-up torque is necessary since the extremely flat heads and disks used in modern drives tend to stick together when power is removed and the heads land on the disk. At the same time, the spindle motor must operate efficiently with a minimum power consumption. Heat dissipated inside a disk drive causes the mechanical parts in the actuator and disk assembly to expand. Because modern drives require extremely precise mechanical alignment, it is essential that thermal expansion caused by spindle motor power dissipation be kept to a minimum. Some early drive designs were plagued with stiction or heat problems caused by inadequate spindle motors. Newer designs have resolved

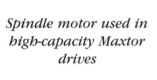

Spindle motor used in high-capacity Maxtor drives

these problems by providing spindle motors with higher start-up torques and lower power consumption. All modern drives use microprocessor controlled spindle motor drive circuitry that uses pulse width modulation to minimize power consumption once the drive reaches operating speed.

In high capacity disk drives the quality of the bearings used in the spindle motor assembly is becoming increasingly important. As the concentric tracks in a drive are pushed closer and closer together in an effort to gain higher storage capacities, spindle bearing "runout" becomes a consideration. The smallest amount of wobble in a modern disk assembly can throw a head assembly slightly off track, resulting in reduced data integrity. Drive manufacturers have gone to great lengths to find affordable spindle motor bearings that offer the lowest amount of runout while still providing long life.

Early hard drives spun at 60 revolutions per second (3600 RPM) because synchronous motors were used that locked to the 60 Hz AC line frequency. Some newer designs now offer "fast spin" speeds of up to 8000 RPM. At these higher spin speeds, improved spindle motor bearing quality and balancing is essential. Faster response servo systems are also required to track data at higher spindle speeds.

Head Carriage

The mechanical engineer asked to design a modern head carriage is faced with a difficult task: design a perfectly balanced mechanism to hold the heads firmly and rigidly using existing bearing and actuator technology. And management wants it for free! The head carriage must have the lowest moving mass possible, enabling it to be moved hundreds of time a second.

Head carriage with linear actuator

The head carriage pictured uses a linear actuator. The advantage of this type of actuator is that the heads always stay parallel to the recording track. The disadvantages are more complexity and moving parts (higher cost) and higher mass than a rotary actuator.

The head carriage to the right is typical of a modern rotary actuator. This actuator system has become standard in modern hard disk drives for two main reasons. Rotary actuators are cheap and reliable. Typically only two ball bearings are needed at the top and bottom of the actuator.

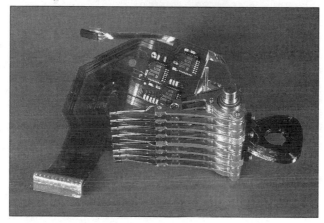

Head carriage with rotary actuator

Media and Heads

The ultimate limiting factors in the push for higher and higher data densities in today's drives are the heads and media. Hard disk media was originally manufactured by spin depositing iron oxide (rust) particles on machined aluminum disks. Modern disks are made of annealed aluminum that is sputtered and plated with magnetic coatings, then polished and coated with rugged lubricated coatings. Disk media is classified by the amount of magnetic field in Oersteds (Oe) required to produce enough magnetic dipole reversals in the disk coating to be detected by a magnetic head. Earlier media was easily magnetized using fields of 600 Oe or less. Newer high density media requires fields of 1800 Oe or more to achieve sufficient magnetic penetration.

Head technologies have also evolved over the years. As head gaps become smaller, the size of the magnetic coils used must shrink accordingly. New heads must handle higher write currents and be more sensitive when reading. Head gap sizes are constantly shrinking. Due to this, the drive industry is moving toward the thin film and magneto-resistive heads of the future and away from monolithic heads of yesterday. Head flying heights are now just a few millionths of an inch to enable efficient magnetic coupling with miniscule gap widths.

5.25" Plated media

Stepper Motor Servo Systems

Stepper motors are rotary actuators that rapidly move in small discrete steps (usually .8 to 4 degrees per step). Stepper motors provide a simple, reliable positioning system that is easy to use and inexpensive to manufacture. The stepper motor shaft is usually connected to a small metal band that converts the rotary shaft motion into a linear or rotary motion of the head carriage. Stepper motors are ideal positioners for floppy drives due to their low cost.

A low cost stepper motor servo system has two major disadvantages. The mass of the rotor in a stepper motor is generally high. Using stepper motors as actuators in disk drives produces low access times because the heavy rotor inside the stepper motor must be moved along with the head carriage.

The number of concentric tracks recorded per inch on a disk drive is referred to as the "track density". The second disadvantage in a stepper motor servo system is a limitation on track density. High track densities are difficult to achieve with stepper motor servo systems because most stepper motors move only in large discrete steps. The electronics required to "fine tune" the position of a stepper motor servo system are expensive to manufacture. It is easier to adjust the position of a voice coil and keep the heads on track than it is to fine tune a stepper motor.

The future of stepper motors remains in low cost open-loop servo system, like floppy disk drives. They have become yesterday's technology, and there's no reason to use them in hard disk drives today.

Voice Coil Servo Systems

It's hard to imagine a mechanism that can move to any position over an inch in less than 1/100th of a second and come to a complete stop within 0.0001" of its target. Modern voice coil actuators are capable of doing this over 1,000,000,000 times. The voice coil servo system is the key component in all newer high performance disk drives. A voice coil actuator is simply a coil of copper wire attached to the head carriage. This coil is surrounded by high energy permanent magnets that are attached to the HDA base casting. To move the head carriage

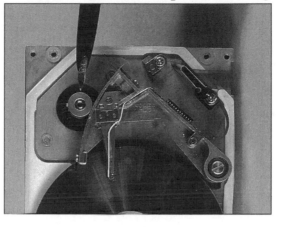

Stepper Motor Server

and "seek" to a track, the control electronics apply a current to the voice coil. The current applied induces a magnetic field in the coil that attracts or repels the stationary permanent magnets. The amount of torque induced to move the head carriage is directly proportional to the amount of current applied to the voice coil.

Many drives use an ASIC control chip in the voice coil servo system that contains a D/A converter. The output of the D/A converter usually drives a MOSFET power amplifier that provides the current required by the voice coil. The circuitry that moves the head from track to track is simple compared to the circuitry that decodes the servo information recorded on the drive. In order to control the voice coil, the servo electronics must know precisely where the head is positioned on the drive. The positioning information fed back to the electronics to control the voice coil positioner is called "servo feedback". Several different servo schemes are used to provide position feedback information to the drive electronics and "close" the servo loop.

Some large capacity drives use a "dedicated" voice coil servo feedback system. When you see a drive in the drive table with an odd number of read/write heads, it probably uses a dedicated servo system. In a dedicated system, the entire surface of one disk is reserved for use by the servo system. Position information is recorded on the reserved (dedicated) disk so that the drive electronics can determine the exact position and velocity of the head carriage.

Assuming that the head carriage holds the entire head stack rigidly together, the position of the read/write heads will track along with the dedicated servo head. A dedicated servo system offers fast positioning and is simple to design. One of the only disadvantages to this system is that since only one head is used for servo, a dedicated servo system has difficulty compensating for thermal warpage of the head stack assembly.

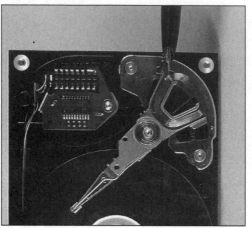

Voice Coil Servo

A more popular voice coil servo feedback system is called an "embedded" servo. An embedded servo system works in a manner similar to the dedicated system except for the physical location of the servo position information. The embedded system interleaves servo and data information by placing servo positioning bursts between the data recorded on the disk. Embedded servo systems have advantages and disadvantages over dedicated servo systems. Advantages of an embedded system include the ability to accurately position each individual head by sensing the position information directly under that head. A dedicated servo system positions all of the heads together. Disadvantages of an embedded servo system are increased servo electronics complexity (which translates to higher cost), and the requirement for seek and settling delays when switching between heads.

Some drives employ a "hybrid" servo system that combines both a dedicated servo for fast coarse positioning, and an embedded servo to finely position the head on track. Hybrid servo systems offer the best access and positioning of any system, but their cost is also the highest. One disadvantage this system shares with dedicated servo systems is that an entire surface is used for servo. This dedicated surface could have been used to store more data.

Keeping it Clean

When a drive is running, Winchester heads "fly" or "float" on a cushion of air. There is virtually no wear on the disk surface when the drive is running and the heads are stationary. Almost all the wear on a drive occurs when the drive is turned off and the heads "land" and touch the disk.

All modern voice coil servo drives use an electronic or mechanical mechanism to move the heads away from the data area of the disk to a "landing zone" when power is removed. Better drives also use a mechanical latch mechanism to park and lock the heads in the landing zone.

As the media wears in a drive, microscopic particles flake off from the disk surface. A quality hard drive designed for long life contains a circulating air system that catches these particles in a filter.

Most disk drives have filtered vents that permit outside air to enter and exit the HDA. These vents help if a pressure differential develops between the HDA and the ambient air. Some newer drive designs (notably Conner and Maxtor drives) have eliminated the outside air vents.

Drive Filter and Latch Components

Data Encoding and Decoding

Data encoding is the technique used to convert a stream of binary data into a varying current that drives a magnetic head. The varying current in the head produces magnetic flux reversals in the head. These flux reversals orient the molecular magnetic dipole moments of the media. The media is thus "magnetized" in a pattern that stores the data. The magnetic head has a maximum frequency limitation that determines how close the magnetic flux reversals can be placed on the disk while still maintaining acceptable reliability. There is also a minimum frequency limitation imposed by the drive electronics.

The difference between the minimum and maximum frequency limitations is called the recording bandwidth. One goal in manufacturing disk drives is to provide the highest data recording rate possible. A higher data recording rate translates to higher capacity per track and higher data transfer speeds. The magnetic recording bandwidth of a drive is limited by several factors including head and media design and positioning accuracy.

The goal in designing data encoding and decoding circuitry then becomes one of placing the maximum amount of data bits within a fixed recording bandwidth while maintaining acceptable reliability.

Disk drive data encoder circuitry removes the need to place clock information on the track by combining the data bits to be recorded with as few clock signals as possible. The decoder circuitry regenerates the clock from the recorded signal and synchronizes the clock to the decoded data. The encoder and decoder circuitry in a drive are usually combined into a chip called an "ENDEC".

Encoding and Decoding Codes

The following encoding and decoding codes are used in disk drives:

NRZ (Non-Return to Zero)

This code was originally used in telecommunications and its encoding and decoding are simple to understand. Instead of discrete pulses for each data bit, the signal rises or falls only when a one (1) bit in the incoming data stream is followed by a zero (0) bit or when a zero (0) bit is followed by a one (1) bit.

This coding technique has a serious flaw because certain data patterns can be generated which will result in a fixed logic state output (i.e. the output of the encoder will be static, stuck at zero or one). The "worst-case" condition can violate the minimum recording bandwidth of the drive electronics. In practice, this would rarely happen, but it's a serious strike against NRZ coding.

PE (Phase Encoded)

This coding is used in credit cards and instrument recorders. It is reliable and also simple to understand. The direction of a flux reversal in the middle of each cell indicates whether the encoded bit is either a zero or a one. This effectively shifts the phase of the output signal each time there is an NRZ type transition between zeros and ones.

FM (Frequency Modulation)

This coding technique was used in the earlier floppy drives (including 8" drives). These older drives were called single density "SD" drives. The FM method of encoding is basically equivalent to the PE method. FM coding is no longer used in disk drives.

MFM (Modified Frequency Modulation)

MFM is by far the easiest modern coding technique to implement. This encoding is used in all modern floppy drives and many small capacity hard drives. MFM doubles the data capacity of FM encoding without increasing the recording bandwidth (MFM floppy drives are called Double Density). It works by eliminating the clock pulses in FM encoding and replacing them with data bits. Clock pulses are still used, but they are written only when a one (1) data bit is not present in both the preceding and the current data cell.

To decode MFM data, a data separator must generate a clock signal based on several flux transitions. In order to maintain a low error rate, the speed of data flowing into the encoder must remain

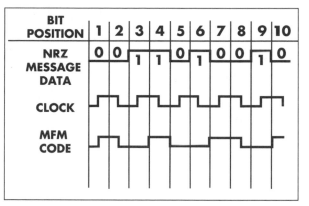

MFM Encodingz

steady, and the decoder must lock onto this stream. In practice, the rotational speed of hard and floppy drives is easily controlled within the tolerances required for reliable MFM recording. An electronic compensating circuit called a Phase Locked Loop (or PLL) is used to lessen the effects of spindle speed variations.

RLL (Run Length Limited Encoding)

This encoding scheme was first used in 14" drives from IBM, CDC, and DEC. It is now used in almost all high capacity 3.5" and 5.25" hard drives. Common RLL coding techniques are RLL 1,7 and RLL 2,7. 1,7 and 2,7 refer to the maximum number of consecutive zeros in the code. RLL 2,7 offers a 50% improvement in data transfer rate and data recording density as compared with MFM within the same fixed recording bandwidth.

The easiest way to understand RLL encoding is to examine the encoding tree below. Bits are encoded by following the tree, starting at the root. When you reach the end of a branch, the stream of bits at that branch correspond to the encoded data to be written to the drive.

RLL encoding has two main disadvantages. The first is that RLL requires significantly more complex encoding and decoding circuitry than MFM. This has been overcome in

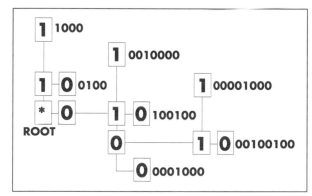

RLL 2,7 Encoding Tree

part by single ENDEC chips from companies like SSI, VTC and National Semiconductor. The second disadvantage with RLL encoding is that a small defect can produce a long stream of data errors. To combat this, drive manufacturers are improving the design of read/write heads and media and lowering the flying height of these heads to improve signal to noise ratios. Longer, improved error correcting codes and retry algorithms are also used with RLL encoded drives.

Spindle motors are now driven by crystal controlled microprocessors to improve rotational speed accuracy. The quality of the heads, media, and spindle control circuits used to manufacture today's hard disk drives are more than adequate for reliable RLL encoding.

Future Codes

Many other coding and encoding techniques have been developed that offer higher data rates and recording densities than RLL within the same fixed recording bandwidth. All of these codes are more susceptible to timing jitter and large error bursts than RLL coding. At present, nearly all ESDI, SCSI, and IDE drives use RLL coding. We expect that RLL will continue to be the most commonly used coding in magnetic mass storage devices for the next few years. The recent advent of PRML techniques to improve read channel performance is causing a gradual shift away from RLL.

INTERFACE STANDARDS

With every new developing technology comes the problem of standardization. The data storage industry has been influenced by standards from manufacturers and various groups including:

ANSI

American National Standards Institute
11 West 42nd Street, 13th Floor
New York, New York 10036-8002
(212)642-4900   (212)398-0023 Fax

NAB

National Association of Broadcasters
1771 North Street, N.W.
Washington, DC 20036-2891
(202)429-5300   (202)429-5343 Fax

IBM

First in standards for drives and computers
IBM Personal Computer Division
Route 100
Somers, NY 10589
(800) 772-2227

IRCC

International Radio Consultive Committee

IRIG

Interrange Instrumentation Group

Shugart Associates

Pioneer in floppy disk drives

Seagate Technology

Pioneer in hard disk drives
Seagate Technology
920 Disc Drive
Scotts Valley, CA 95067
(408)438-6550   (408)438-6356 Fax

Some of the popular standards that have evolved are listed below:

"IDE" or "ATA" Interface

With the emergence of IBM compatible PCs as a hardware standard, drive manufacturers have integrated much of the IBM controller hardware onto their disk drives. These drives are called "Intelligent Drive Electronics" or "Integrated Drive Electronics" (IDE) drives. This interface is often referred to as the "ATA" or "IBM Task File" compatible interface. Drives with an older 8-bit IDE interface were originally called "XT Interface" drives, while drives with a 16-bit interface are often called "AT Interface" drives. By imbedding an AT controller card into the drive, a significant manufacturing cost savings occurs. Many parts (including line drivers and even a microprocessor) can be eliminated.

Older "XT Interface" drives used a BIOS ROM on the paddleboard and could not be interchanged with "AT Interface" drives. An XT Interface controller and drive may be used in an AT class computer if the CMOS is set to "no drive installed".

Conner Peripherals and Compaq Computer were among the first companies to ship AT compatible IDE drives in volume. Since then, acceptance of the IDE interface based on their original design has grown.

Since the imbedded controller on an IDE drive is optimized to run efficiently with the drive it is attached to, IDE interface drives often operate with improved performance over their comparable MFM or RLL counterparts. Some sacrifices were made in MFM/RLL controller and drive design to ensure compatibility with a large range of drives. Imbedded controllers are usually faster due to optimization.

It is clear that IDE drives have rapidly replaced the original MFM and RLL drives used in early IBM-AT compatible applications. Since most new disk drives use zoned recording techniques to increase drive capacity, all of these drives must use imbedded controllers. The only practical interface alternatives for imbedded controllers on small disks are IDE or SCSI.

One disadvantage of the original IDE interface was the 528MB limitiation. This limitation has been overcome with the industry standard "EIDE" or Enhanced IDE interface. See the Enhanced IDE chapter for more information on how the EIDE interface will continue to be improved in the future.

Another minor problem with the IDE interface is hardware incompatibility. Some IDE drives may be incompatible with each other. This is generally due to different buffering or decoding. See the Enhanced IDE Chapter for more information on IDE drives.

ST-506/ST-412 Interface

Seagate Technology is the world's largest manufacturer of hard drives. Their first ST506 five megabyte full-height 5.25" disk drive was one of the first hard drives manufactured in volume. This drive used a 5 Mbit/second MFM encoded interface. The standard interface copied from this drive was used in all "ST-506 compatible" MFM and RLL drives.

MFM and RLL Encoding

Modified Frequency Modulation (MFM) encoding was first patented by Ampex Corporation in 1963. MFM encoding is often called "double density" and is used to code data on floppy and hard drives. MFM is an attractive coding scheme mainly because it is simple to encode and decode. MFM is now the standard coding technique for floppy disk drives and some small capacity hard disk drives.

Run Length Limited (RLL) encoding is a group coding technique that provides an increase in data density over MFM encoding. In RLL encoding, streams of data are grouped together and each group of data produces a recording pattern that depends on the bits that came before it. RLL encoding eliminates high frequency flux transitions and permits an increased data density within a fixed recording bandwidth.

The most common RLL coding (RLL 2,7) provides a 50% improvement in recording density over MFM coding. For example, a drive that stores 1000MB of data at 5Mbit/sec MFM data rate can be made to store 1500MB of data using RLL encoding. The data transfer rate increases by 50% using RLL 2,7, while the recording bandwidth stays the same.

Other RLL codings can provide even higher recording densities. RLL 3,9 (commonly called ARRL) provides a 100% improvement in recording density. Longer codes can provide even greater increases. Because RLL coding does not require an increased read/write channel bandwidth when compared to MFM encoding, RLL is now a popular coding technique used to increase capacity in many hard disk drives. Modern IDE and SCSI drives use RLL encoding. For a more detailed description of how RLL data is coded and decoded, see the previous chapter.

Since RLL encoding provides higher data density in the same recording bandwidth, the data capture window is reduced. To accurately reproduce data in this smaller capture window, RLL encoding requires an improved data separator, an accurate read channel, and better PLL circuitry. The rotational speed of the disk drive must also remain more constant. Simply put, there is less margin for error using RLL encoding.

ESDI Interface

The Enhanced Small Device Interface (ESDI) was basically an improved, high speed ST-506 interface. This interface was pioneered by Maxtor. The combination of a 34-pin control cable and a 20-pin data cable from the ST-506 interface are retained, but the ESDI interface features improved actuator commands and data transfer rates.

The ESDI interface uses a data separator located on the disk drive itself. Older ST-506 designs used a data separator on the controller card instead. Moving the data separator to the drive improved compatibility and made the ESDI interface independent of data rate. Providing the maximum data transfer rate of the controller is not exceeded, any speed ESDI drive can be connected to any controller. ESDI drives were manufactured with rates up to 28 Mbits/sec.

ESDI is not particularly well suited to zoned recording, and is really only useful for fixed disks. ESDI was once a useful, fast interface for hard disks, but SCSI has won out in popularity. The attraction of being able to daisy chain peripherals like CD-ROM and SCSI tape drives has ultimately driven the industry away from ESDI and toward SCSI and EIDE/ATAPI.

SCSI Interface

The Small Computer Systems Interface (SCSI) first became popular as the interface used for Apple Macintosh peripherals. Actually, SCSI has been used for quite some time in workstation applications and is rapidly gaining popularity in the PC marketplace. SCSI offers the ability to daisy chain up to fifteen devices (hard, optical, tape, etc.) to a single controller with a single cable.

SCSI is basically a high-speed bidirectional 8-bit parallel interface that has been standardized in terms of both hardware and software by ANSI. The SCSI bus allows addition of up to 15 devices using a daisy-chained cable. Unfortunately though, most manufacturers of SCSI peripherals adhere to the basic ANSI hardware specifications; while the level of SCSI software compatibility varies from manufacturer to manufacturer. A newer ANSI standard, SCSI-II was announced in an attempt to standardize the SCSI software interface. The ANSI SCSI-II specification added features like disconnect/reconnect, and messaging while maintaining downward compatibility with SCSI-I devices. A recent copy of the SCSI specification may be obtained from ANSI or at www.corpsys.com. The SCSI-III specification is now under development.

Good termination and shielding allow a "single wide" SCSI bus to operate at speeds in excess of 10MB/sec. Since most existing SCSI peripherals only sustain data rates of around 4-5MB/sec, the SCSI interface has the data bandwidth to handle higher speed drives in the future.

The new SCSI-II standards for Wide SCSI and Fast SCSI offer a wider bus and sustained transfer rates up to 40MB/sec. These new versions of SCSI offer more than adequate throughput for any storage device that might appear in the near future.

The SCSI interface offers the flexibility and room for future expansion, but brings with it all the problems of a developing technology.

WIDE SCSI

Currently, the terms "wide SCSI" and "double wide SCSI" are used to refer to a SCSI interface with a 16 bit wide data path. This interface uses a 68 pin connector, and the electrical handshaking and data transfer system is identical to the more common 8 bit "single wide" SCSI bus. The ANSI SCSI specification provides a method for negotiating with peripherals to determine if they offer "wide SCSI" capabilities. Theoretically, the wide SCSI bus is downward compatible with standard "single wide" SCSI devices.

FAST SCSI

"FAST SCSI" refers to a SCSI handshaking system that reduces hardware overhead during data transfers. Peripherals that support this feature will transfer data at higher burst rates if they are connected to a controller that also supports FAST SCSI. If either the peripheral or the controller does not support FAST SCSI, the burst data transfer rate is unaffected.

Ultra SCSI

The "Ultra SCSI" industry standard is an attempt to accelerate SCSI peripherals by changing SCSI timing and handshake specifications. To keep up with the more critical and noise sensitive requirements of Ultra SCSI, cable lengths must be reduced and termination becomes more critical. In most systems, Wide SCSI provides a more practical performance boost than Ultra SCSI.

SMD Interface

The Storage Module Device (SMD) interface is the most popular interface for the 8" drives used in mainframe, minicomputer, and workstation applications. Variations include an improved data transfer rate (HSMD). SMD drives are gradually being replaced by SCSI in most applications. Bridge controllers are now available to adapt newer ESDI and SCSI drives to the SMD interface.

IPI Interface

The Intelligent Peripheral Interface (IPI) is a mainframe disk drive interface standard used mainly on 8" and 14" drives. It is popular in IBM and Sun workstation and minicomputer applications. Many drives are available with dual IPI ports.

QIC-02 Interface

This QIC-02 interface is a software standard for tape drives. Most PC based 1/4" tape controllers use a QIC-02 command set.

QIC-40 Interface

This interface uses an standard floppy controller to store data on minicartridge data tapes. Although they are relatively slow, these drives are popular in PC applications due to their low cost. Drives are now available with up to 400MB (800MB compressed) capacities and data transfer rates up to 2Mbit/sec.

QIC-36 Interface

This now obsolete 50-pin tape drive interface standard was pioneered by companies like Wangtec and Archive. The pinout is listed in the Pinout Section. If you run across a QIC-36 drive, you'll need a controller card which is QIC-02 software compatible to make it work.

SA-400 Interface

As with Seagate and the ST-506 Interface, the SA-400 interface is named after the originator of the first mass produced floppy disk drive. Shugart Associates manufactured the SA-400 in 1978 and it was the first disk drive to gain wide acceptance. The interface used a simple 34-pin cable with the 17 odd numbered pins connected to ground for noise reduction and shielding.

This 34-pin interface was modified to create the ST-506 hard disk drive interface discussed earlier in this section. The pinout of the interface used in modern floppy disk drives is shown in the Pinout Section. Although additional functions have been added since the original SA-400 drive (mainly DISK_CHANGE, SPEED_SELECT, and DRIVE_READY), this pinout is still affectionately referred to as the SA-400 interface.

Future Standards

Currently the most popular disk drive interface for small capacity hard drives is the EIDE (or ATAPI) standard. In the immediate future, the PC market will continue to be dominated by IDE drives.

The most popular interface for high performance, large capacity drives in now SCSI. As SCSI software standards evolve, and the costs of SCSI drives and controllers drop, much of the EIDE market will be displaced by SCSI.

In workstations and high-end PC applications, it seems clear that SCSI is the interface of the future. For example, all of the popular optical and DAT drives use the SCSI interface. We look forward to the time when small computer peripheral interfacing is simplified as manufacturers all begin to conform to the new SCSI-III and future SCSI-IV standards.

PRML TECHNOLOGY

PRML Technology

PRML is an acronym for Partial Response Maximum Likelyhood. PRML is a new solution to an old problem. Since disk drives were first designed, there has been a push to pack the largest amount of data possible into the smallest possible disk area. To understand PRML, first look at the problem PRML is designed to overcome.

As data is packed closer and closer on the magnetic media, the recorded bits tend to blur together. The blurring is mainly caused by "bit shift" and by the unavoidable introduction of noise in the read channel.

PRML read channels differ from conventional analog read channels in the way they detect and separate recorded data. Analog read channels typically look at the position of the recorded peaks and use only the peak position information to recover the recorded data. PRML channels digitize the height of each peak and compare it to an average peak value. Once the PRML read channel has established values for the size and shape of the peak, it adds this information to the values of peaks which are read subsequently. The PRML circuit looks at the combination of the bit read and the subsequent bits, and then decides which interpretation of bits will produce the least amount of errors. If a weak or slightly shifted bit is detected (using an error checking code), the PRML read channel can determine what the weak bit should have been by analyzing it in combination with its neighboring bits.

The net effect is that bits can be placed closer together on the magnetic recording media. This means increased disk capacities without significantly increased costs.

So how soon will PRML technology actually affect the performance of available hard drives? Sooner than you might expect. Mid range dri-ves will be the first to take advantage of the new technology. Cirrus Logic and VTC are currently shipping silicon that fully implements PRML. IBM, Quantum and others have PRML drives in production. The current bottleneck seems to be data rate. Analog read channels are still much faster than their available PRML counter-parts. When this gap closes, expect PRML to add 30% to 50% more to existing disk drive capacities!

PRML Encoding

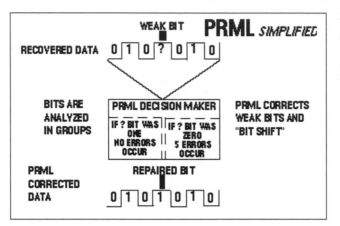

ENHANCED IDE

The Enhanced IDE standard originally proposed by Western Digital provides a solution to IDE's three biggest problems: capacity, performance, and expandability. The original IDE drives developed by Conner and Compaq were designed to be compatible with IBM's early MFM controller card used in the original IBM AT's. When this "register level" compatibility was copied, some limitations went along with it.

The original IDE interface had a total drive capacity limitation of 528MB. This constraint came from the original IBM MFM controller design that supported a maximum of 1024 cylinders, 16 heads, and 63 sectors per track. The original MFM controller used 10 bits to address the cylinder count, 4 bits to select the head, and 6 bits to select the sector number (that started with #1). This means that all existing PC applications which write directly to the IBM compatible disk controller registers have a total of 20 bits available to control the logical block address of an IDE disk drive. Since a sector number of zero is disallowed in the IDE interface, a total of 1,032,192 blocks can be addressed. With a standard block size of 512 bytes per sector, original IDE was limited to a 528MB maximum capacity.

ORIGINAL (NON-ENHANCED) IDE LIMITATIONS

Heads - 16 Maximum (Numbered 0 through 15)
Sectors - 63 Maximum (Numbered 1 through 63)
Cylinders - 1024 Maximum (Numbered 0 through 1023)
Total Blocks - 1,032,192
Maximum Capacity - 528 MB with 512 byte sectors

To bypass this limitation, the new Enhanced IDE standard uses a 28 bit logical block address which can address a total of 26,8435,456 blocks. This provides a maximum drive capacity of over 13 Gigabytes, which is enough for the near future. A standard IBM compatible BIOS has it's own capacity limitations. BIOS is limited to 1024 cylinders, 256 heads, and 255 sectors per track. This results in a BIOS maximum capacity of 8.4GB.

IBM AT COMPATIBLE BIOS LIMITATIONS

Heads - 256 Maximum (Numbered 0 though 255)
Sectors - 63 Maximum (Numbered 1 through 63)
Cylinders - 1024 Maximum (Numbered 0 through 1023)
Total Blocks - 16,515,072
Maximum Capicity - 8.4GB with 512 byte sectors

Without a device driver, the maximum capacity of the proposed enhanced IDE standard is 8.4GB. This is not currently an issue for hard disks, but for larger capacity drives, like helical scan tape backup units, it would be a limitation if other workarounds were not provided. One way to bypass this may be to switch to a larger block size for these larger devices, such as the 2048 byte per sector block size used in CD-ROM drives. Another is through the ATAPI system described below.

The original IDE standard was also limited in terms of performance. This was mainly due to the speed of 16 bit programmed (PIO) data transfers. SCSI host adapters can transfer data faster than IDE by using bus mastering processes programmed memory moves, or Direct Memory Access. IDE drives must wait for the CPU to move data, two bytes at a time. An instruction execution and an I/O cycle are required as each pair of bytes to be moved from the IDE registers into main memory. This PIO process is significantly slower than other methods. When the original MFM drives were introduced, these slower data rates were adequate, but with higher performance drives they are a serious bottleneck.

The original IDE interface supports a maximum of two drives. Removable drives, Optical drives, Tape Drives, and CD-ROM drives were not provided for in the original IBM AT. Western Digital's proposed solution to this in Enhanced IDE is called ATAPI. ATAPI stands for ATA Packet Interface, and its design is suspiciously similar to SCSI.

In fact, ATAPI appears to have been copied from SCSI so that existing manufacturers of SCSI drives could easily convert their drives to run on Enhanced IDE systems. ATAPI provides support for tape, optical, and CD-ROM drives through a packet messaging system.

Enhanced IDE hard drives are now available from several manufacturers in capacities over 2GB. ATAPI CD-ROM drives have become low cost, standard units.

SCSI COMMAND REFERENCE

When we asked CSC customers what they wanted added to the Sixth Edition Hard Drive Bible, the answer was unanimous. You asked for a complete SCSI command set specification. Although printing the entire ANSI specification is beyond the scope of this book, this chapter details the most common SCSI commands and their command blocks.

The following commands are supported by nearly all SCSI drives:

COMMAND	OP CODE (HEX)
FORMAT UNIT	04
INQUIRY	12
MODE SELECT	15
MODE SENSE	1A
READ	08*
READ CAPACITY	25
READ EXTENDED	28*
READ LONG	3E*
REASSIGN BLOCKS	07
RELEASE	17
REQUEST SENSE	03
REZERO UNIT	01
SEEK	0B
SEEK EXTENDED	2B
START DIAGNOSTICS	1D
START/STOP UNIT	1B
TEST UNIT READY	00
VERIFY	2F
WRITE	0A*
WRITE EXTENDED	2A*
WRITE LONG	3F*

Note:
99% of the active time on the SCSI bus is spent executing these commands. Most average systems execute 8 or more read commands for each write command.

Format Unit - Op Code 04$_H$

The FORMAT UNIT command ensures that the media is formatted so that all initiator addressable data blocks can be addressed. The medium is certified and control structures are created for the management of the medium and defects.

Note that successful completion

BIT BYTE	7	6	5	4	3	2	1	0
0	Operation Code 04$_H$							
1	LUN			FmtDat	CmpLst	Defect List Format		
2	Reserved							
3	Interleave (MSB)							
4	Interleave (LSB)							
5	VU		Reserved				Flag	Link

of a FORMAT UNIT command does not necessarily mean that data has been erased.

Inquiry - Op Code 12$_H$

The INQUIRY command requests that information regarding parameters of the target to be sent to the initiator.

BIT BYTE	7	6	5	4	3	2	1	0
0	Operation Code 12$_H$							
1	LUN			Reserved				
2	Reserved							
3	Reserved							
4	Allocation Length							
5	VU		Reserved				Flag	Link

Mode Select - Op Code 15$_H$

The MODE SELECT command provides a means for the initiator to change the drive's operating parameters.

BIT BYTE	7	6	5	4	3	2	1	0
0	Operation Code 15$_H$							
1	LUN			Reserved				SP
2	Reserved							
3	Reserved							
4	Parameter List Length							
5	VU		Reserved				Flag	Link

Mode Sense - Op Code 1A$_H$

The MODE SENSE command provides a means for the drive to report its medium or peripheral to the initiator. This command is a complementary command to the MODE SELECT command.

BIT BYTE	7	6	5	4	3	2	1	0
0	Operation Code 1A$_H$							
1	LUN			Reserved				
2	PCF		Page Code					
3	Reserved							
4	Allocation Length							
5	VU		Reserved				Flag	Link

Read - Op Code 08$_H$

The READ command requests that the drive transfer data to the initiator.

Bit/Byte Definition:

Logical Block Address - Specifies the logical block where the read operation will begin.

BIT BYTE	7	6	5	4	3	2	1	0
0	Operation Code 08H							
1	LUN			Logical Block Address (MSB)				
2	Logical Block Address							
3	Logical Block Address (LSB)							
4	Transfer Length							
5	VU		Reserved				Flag	Link

Transfer Length - Specifies the number of contiguous logical blocks of data to transfer. A transfer length of zero indicates that 256 logical blocks will be transferred. Any other value indicates the number of logical blocks that will be transferred.

Read Capacity - Op Code 25$_H$

The READ CAPACITY command provides a means for the initiator to request information regarding the capacity of the drive.

BIT BYTE	7	6	5	4	3	2	1	0
0	Operation Code 25$_H$							
1	LUN			Reserved				RclAdr
2	Logical Block Address (MSB)							
3	Logical Block Address							
4	Logical Block Address							
5	Logical Block Address (LSB)							
6	Reserved							
7	Reserved							
8	VU		Reserved					PMI
9	VU		Reserved				Flag	Link

Read Extended - Op Code 12$_H$

The READ EXTENDED command requests that the drive transfer data to the initiator.

Logical Block Address - Specifies the logical block where the read operation will begin.

Transfer Length - Specifies the number of contiguous logical blocks of data to transfer. A transfer length of zero indicates that 256 logical blocks will be transferred. Any other value indicates the number of logical blocks that will be transferred.

BIT BYTE	7	6	5	4	3	2	1	0
0	Operation Code 12$_H$							
1	LUN			Reserved				RelAdr
2	Logical Block Address (MSB)							
3	Logical Block Address							
4	Logical Block Address							
5	Logical Block Address (LSB)							
6	Reserved							
7	Transfer Length (MSB)							
8	Transfer Length (LSB)							
9	VU		Reserved				Flag	Link

Read Long - Op Code 3E$_H$

The READ LONG command will transfer the specified sector of data and ECC bytes to the initiator. The drive will not correct the data field or the ECC bytes. This command is intended for diagnostic purposes.

The number of bytes transferred to the initiator will be the sector size plus the mnumber of bytes contained in the ECC field.

BIT BYTE	7	6	5	4	3	2	1	0
0	Operation Code 3E$_H$							
1	LUN			Reserved				RelAdr
2	Logical Block Address (MSB)							
3	Logical Block Address							
4	Logical Block Address							
5	Logical Block Address (LSB)							
6	Reserved							
7	Reserved							
8	01$_H$							
9	VU		Reserved				Flag	Link

Reassign Blocks - Op Code 07$_H$

The REASSIGN BLOCKS command requests the drive to reassign the defective logical blocks to an area on the drive's media reserved for this purpose

The initiator transfers a defect list that contains the logical block addresses to be reassigned. The drive will reassign the physical media used for each logical block address in the list. The data contained in the logical blocks specified in the defect list may be altered, but the data in all other logical blocks on the medium will be preserved.

Specifying a logical block to be reassigned that was previously

BIT BYTE	7	6	5	4	3	2	1	0
0	Operation Code 07$_H$							
1	LUN			Reserved				
2	Reserved							
3	Reserved							
4	Reserved							
5	VU		Reserved				Flag	Link

reassigned will cause that block to be reassigned again. Thus, over the life of the medium, a logical block can be assigned to a multiple physical addresses until no more spare locations remain.

Reassign Blocks Defect List

The REASSIGN BLOCKS defect list contains a four byte header followed by one or more defect descriptors. The length of each defect descriptor is four bytes.

Defect List Length - Specifies the total length in bytes of the defect descriptors that follow. The defect list length is equal to four times the number of defect descriptors.

REASSIGN BLOCKS Defect List	
BYTE	Defect List Header
0	Reserved
1	Reserved
2	Defect List Length (MSB)
3	Defect List Length (LSB)

The defect descriptor specifies the four byte defect logical block address that contains the defect. The defect descriptors must be in ascending order.

DEFECT DESCRIPTOR(S)
BYTE
0	Defect Logical Block Address (MSB)
1	Defect Logical Block Address
2	Defect Logical Block Address
3	Defect Logical Block Address (LSB)

If the drive has insufficient capacity to reassign all of the defective logical blocks, the command will terminate with a CHECK CONDITION status and the sense key set to MEDIUM ERROR. The logical block address of the first logical block not reassigned will be returned in the information bytes of the sense data.

Release - Op Code 17$_H$

The RELEASE command is used to release a previously reserved drive. It is not an error for an initiator to attempt to release a reservation that is not currently active.

BIT BYTE	7	6	5	4	3	2	1	0
0	Operation Code 17$_H$							
1	LUN			3rd Pty	Third Party Device ID			Extent
2	Reservation Identification							
3	Reserved							
4	Reserved							
5	VU		Reserved				Flag	Link

Request Sense - Op Code 03$_H$

The REQUEST SENSE command requests that the target transfer sense data to the initiator.

The sense data is valid for a CHECK CONDITION status returned on a prior command. The sense data is preserved by the drive for the initiator receiving the CHECK CONDITION status until a REQUEST SENSE command or any other is issued to the drive. Sense data is cleared upon receipt of any subsequent command to the drive from the initiator receiving the CHECK CONDITION.

The REQUEST SENSE command will return the CHECK CONDITION status only to report fatal errors for this command. For example.

* The target receives a non-zero reserved bit in the command descriptor block.
* An unrecovered parity error occurs on the data bus.
* A target malfunction prevents the return of sense data.

BIT BYTE	7	6	5	4	3	2	1	0
0	Operation Code 03$_H$							
1	LUN			Reserved				
2	Reserved							
3	Reserved							
4	Allocation Length							
5	VU		Reserved				Flag	Link

Rezero Unit - Op Code 01$_H$

The REZERO UNIT command requests that the drive position the actuator to cylinder zero.

BIT BYTE	7	6	5	4	3	2	1	0
0	Operation Code 01$_H$							
1	LUN			Reserved				
2	Reserved							
3	Reserved							
4	Reserved							
5	VU		Reserved				Flag	Link

Seek - Op Code 0B$_H$

The SEEK command requests that the drive position itself to the specified logical block.

BIT BYTE	7	6	5	4	3	2	1	0
0	Operation Code 0B$_H$							
1	LUN			Logical Block Address (MSB)				
2	Logical Block Address							
3	Logical Block Address (LSB)							
4	Reserved							
5	VU		Reserved				Flag	Link

Seek Extended - Op Code 2B$_H$

The SEEK EXTENDED command requests that the drive position itself to the specified logical block.

BIT BYTE	7	6	5	4	3	2	1	0
0	Operation Code 2B$_H$							
1	LUN			Reserved				
2	Logical Block Address (MSB)							
3	Logical Block Address							
4	Logical Block Address							
5	Logical Block Address (LSB)							
6	Reserved							
7	Reserved							
8	Reserved							
9	VU		Reserved				Flag	Link

Send Diagnostic - Op Code 1D$_H$

The SEND DIAGNOSTIC command requests that the drive perform diagnostic tests on itself. There are no additional parameters for this command.

BIT BYTE	7	6	5	4	3	2	1	0
0	Operation Code 1D$_H$							
1	LUN			Reserved		Slf Test	Dev of 1	Unit of 1
2	Reserved							
3	Parameter List Length (MSB)							
4	Parameter List Length (LSB)							
5	VU		Reserved				Flag	Link

Start/Stop Unit - Op Code 1B$_H$

The START/STOP UNIT command requests that the drive either start the spin motor and position the read/write heads to cylinder zero or stop the spin motor and position the read/write heads in the landing zone.

BIT BYTE	7	6	5	4	3	2	1	0
0	Operation Code 1BH							
1	LUN			Reserved				Immed
2	Reserved							
3	Reserved							
4	Reserved							Start
5	VU		Reserved				Flag	Link

Test Unit Ready - Op Code 00$_H$

The TEST UNIT READY command provides a means to check if the drive is ready. This is not a request for a self-test. If the drive will accept a medium-access command without returning a CHECK CONDITION status then this command will return a GOOD status.

BIT BYTE	7	6	5	4	3	2	1	0
0	Operation Code 00H							
1	LUN			Reserved				
2	Reserved							
3	Reserved							
4	Reserved							
5	VU		Reserved				Flag	Link

Verify - Op Code 2F$_H$

BIT BYTE	7	6	5	4	3	2	1	0
0	Operation Code 2F$_H$							
1	LUN			Reserved			BytChk	RelAdr
2	Logical Block Address (MSB)							
3	Logical Block Address							
4	Logical Block Address							
5	Logical Block Address (LSB)							
6	Reserved							
7	Verification Length (MSB)							
8	Verification Length (LSB)							
9	VU		Reserved				Flag	Link

The VERIFY command requests that the drive verify the data on the medium.

Write - Op Code 0A$_H$

BIT BYTE	7	6	5	4	3	2	1	0
0	Operation Code 0A$_H$							
1	LUN			Logical Block Address (MSB)				
2	Logical Block Address							
3	Logical Block Address (LSB)							
4	Transfer Length							
5	VU		Reserved				Flag	Link

The WRITE command requests that the drive write the data transferred by the initiator to the medium.

Write Extended - Op Code 2A$_H$

BIT BYTE	7	6	5	4	3	2	1	0
0	Operation Code 2A$_H$							
1	LUN			Reserved				RelAdr
2	Logical Block Address (MSB)							
3	Logical Block Address							
4	Logical Block Address							
5	Logical Block Address (LSB)							
6	Reserved							
7	Transfer Length (MSB)							
8	Transfer Length (LSB)							
9	VU		Reserved				Flag	Link

The WRITE EXTENDED command requests that the drive write the data transferred by the initiator to the medium.

Write Long - Op Code 3F_H

The WRITE LONG command will transfer a sector of data and ECC bytes to the drive. The bytes transferred to the drive are written in the data field and the ECC bytes for the particular sector specified in the logical block address. This command is intended for diagnostic purposes.

The number of bytes transferred to the drive will be the sector size plus the number of bytes contained in the ECC field.

BIT BYTE	7	6	5	4	3	2	1	0
0	Operation Code 3F$_H$							
1	LUN			Reserved				RelAdr
2	Logical Block Address (MSB)							
3	Logical Block Address							
4	Logical Block Address							
5	Logical Block Address (LSB)							
6	Reserved							
7	Reserved							
8	01$_H$							
9	VU		Reserved				Flag	Link

WHAT IS SCSI-III?

SCSI Buzzwords

The American National Standards Institute (abbreviated ANSI) organizes committees of industry representatives who work together and form standards for computer interfaces. These standards are designed so that peripheral products from different manufacturers will operate together with little or no custom configuration.

The ultimate goal of ANSI SCSI committees is the creation of true "plug and play" interface standards. They want SCSI to support *ALL* of the drives in your system: HARD, CD-ROM, TAPE, OPTICAL and even printers! They're making progress, but the standards are constantly changing. Here's a brief explanation of the more popular terms:

SCSI-III

SCSI-III is the popular name for the newest standard document that is currently being completed by ANSI. The SCSI-III document will include several new interface standards, including "fiber channel" which uses an optical fiber to transmit data at increased speeds. You can download more information and SCSI specifications from the CSC BBS at (408) 541-8455.

We will be adding the SCSI spec documents to our Web site at: WWW.CORPSYS.COM soon.

The current SCSI-II standard document is the only SCSI document that has been completed and accepted by the industry at the time of this writing. The SCSI-II specification includes the following connector standards that are now in widespread use throughout the hard disk drive industry.

FAST SCSI - How it all started

The original SCSI-I standard dates back to 1986. ANSI named the specification "ANSI X3.31-1986", and a standard was born. The first SCSI products transferred data at rates from 1.5 to 5MB/sec over a standard 50 pin connector. As more devices began to share the bus, and as hard disk performance increased, the 5MB/sec maximum transfer specification became a bottleneck. "Fast SCSI" came to the rescue. Timing specifications were adjusted as synchronous transfers were added so that 10 MB/sec could be transferred over the 8 bit interface.

Narrow SCSI

The term "Narrow SCSI" is now used to refer to SCSI devices that transfer data over a "narrow" 8 bit 50 pin connector up to 10MB/sec. Most currently manufactured SCSI-II devices support "fast SCSI" and transfer data up to 10 MB/sec. Several manufacturers are working on variations of narrow SCSI that increase transfer rates over 10 MB/sec. One proposed standard is "Ultra SCSI", which uses the 50 pin narrow SCSI interface but makes changes to timing and handshaking to increase burst transfer performance up to 20MB/sec. For "Ultra SCSI" to work, both the controller and drive must fully support the faster timing and handshaking. "Ultra SCSI" drives are more susceptible to termination and noise problems, and require shorter cables than standard 10 MB/sec SCSI-II drives.

WIDE SCSI

The term "SCSI-III" is often used to refer to WIDE SCSI. This isn't exactly correct. WIDE SCSI is the correct name of the popular 16-bit wide interface that doubles data transfer rates to 20MB/sec. Wide SCSI drives use 68 pin and separate power connectors. Wide SCSI provides a reliable performance boost for workstations and file servers. The difference between narrow (50 pin) and wide (68 pin) SCSI performance is particularly noticeable when using multitasking operating systems like Novell or Windows NT. Proposed standards exist to increase the transfer rates up to 40MB/sec using a 32-bit cable. Wide SCSI drives are reliable and robust. The only disadvantage to using WIDE is the added bulk and expense of the cables.

SCA

Another popular SCSI drive interface is "SCA", which stands for Single Connector Assembly. SCA connectors carry both the SCSI data and power to the drive in a single connector. SCA is used in newer file servers, disk arrays, and workstations. 80 pin, 16 bit Wide SCSI is the most common SCA, but narrow connectors are also available. SCA connectors are rugged and designed for "hot plug" operation.

Fiber Channel - The future of SCSI?

Fiber channel is an optical interface proposed but not finalized in the new SCSI-III standard. Current fiber channel technology operates at 12.5-25MB/sec data transfer rates. Much higher transfer rates are possible as the technology develops. Fiber channel cables are unaffected by termination, electrical noise, length, and other limitations that make conventional SCSI cabling difficult.

Note: 1MB/sec = 8-10 Mbit/sec

Both Sun Microsystems and Silicon Graphics use fiber channel interfaces to their disk arrays. In early 1996, list prices for fiber channel disk arrays started around $16,000. Inside the disk arrays, standard SCA or Wide SCSI cables are used to interface with the drives. Disk drives with optical fiber interfaces have not yet become affordable or available in quantity. Fiber channel will certainly have an effect on the SCSI industry, but it will be years before it's in widespread use.

Another potential alternative is Apple Computer's proposed "Fire Wire" standard. "Fire Wire" offers fiber channel data transfer rates over lower cost, easy to connect 6 pin cables. Time will tell if Apple's idea will catch on.

Downward Compatibility?

Can SCSI-II and SCSI-III devices share the same controller? How about narrow and wide drives? The answer is yes - sometimes. To properly share narrow and wide drives on a PC, you'll want a controller card that has both connectors - narrow 50 pin and wide 68 pin.

If you're using a workstation with a 68 pin wide connector, you'll need a 50 pin to 68 pin adaptor cable to use both wide and narrow drives simultaneously. Adapter cables can cause termination problems for reasons that we won't discuss here. Use them only as a last resort.

The ideal solution is a controller with three connectors (2 wide and one narrow) and automatic termination. CSC manufactures a three connector PCI card that's supported by Win '95 and NT.

What SCSI flavor should I buy?

All standards are subject to change until the industry approves and accepts them. Whatever you choose, make sure it's upgradable for future expansion. A card with FLASH ROM or removable EPROM like CSC's PCI cards will let you add software features as SCSI standards advance.

For file servers and workstations, your best performance choice today is Wide SCSI. In the PC environment, we recommend SCSI over IDE for performance, flexibility, and the ability to add high performance peripherals.

SCA HOT PLUG

Technically, SCA isn't a separate interface. It's really just another way to use SCSI. SCA stands for "Single Connector Assembly", and SCA drives use a single 8 pin connector which carries both power and data. SCA was originally desinged for use in disk arrays, but it's finding its way into workstations and high end PC environments.

SCA drives are often mounted in a carrier which permits them to be easily removed for service, replacement, or to exchange data. Military and Government institutions with strong data security requirements like the removability of SCA. Since hard drives are relatively fragile devices, we don't recommend you remove your drive for transport in your briefcase.

SCA drive in carrier (as used in SUN workstations)

But if you're running a mission critical network system, SCA provides great serviceability along with Wide SCSI performance.

Since an SCA drive includes everything a SCSI drive contains, simple adapters are available to connect thes drives to either Narrow or Wide systems. A SCA adaptor from CSC is pictured to the right.

SCA Adapter (available from CSC)

PCI INTERFACE

The PCI bus has rapidly overtaken older industry standards like EISA, and VESA. PCI uses a solid hardware and sofware specification to ensure compatability with different cards *and* different CPU chips. PCI stands for "Peripheral Computer Interface", and is used with processors ranging from Intel's Pentium Pro to DEC's fast Alpha Chip. Apple loves how it accelerates the Motorola Power PC processors.

PCI offers two main advantages. First, it's fast. Real fast. A true 133MB/sec transfer rate is realistic. This transfer feeds data faster than most microprocessors and memory systems can digest. There's no disk drive that can sustain transfer rates anywhere near what the PCI bus can handle.

The second advantage of PCI is "plug and play". PCI boards install easily without setting jumpers or switches. Automatic configuration of interrupts, memory and I/O address space are performed by the host processor when the system first starts up. There's almost no potential for an interrupt or address conflict.

PCI self configuration is made possible by a hardware resource switching system that operates under software control. On power up, the host processor first checks to see what hardware requirements each adaptor card will have. These requirements may include memory address space, I/O address space, hardware interrupts, and even DMA transfer capability. The processor then starts assigning resources to each PCI slot. To be "PCI compatible", the adapter card and its driver software must support any address, interrupt, or I/O location that is assigned to it. So the processor forces each card to take a "place in line" by assigning hardware resources in sequence.

Unfortunately, "Plug and Play" sometimes becomes "Plug and Pray". When a PCI card won't work in your system, you don't have any options to reconfigure it. You might end up wishing your card had switches and jumpers after all. Don't abandon hope. Most newer motherboards (we like the Intel manufactured boards) have PCI configuration options in CMOS setup to help you. Try changing the "PCI Bus Mastering" option for network or SCSI controller card problems. Switch the PCI system interrupt number if your card works but the software drivers won't load.

CHOOSING A HARD DRIVE & CONTROLLER

CHOOSING A HARD DRIVE AND CONTROLLER

With so many different drives and controllers on the market, where do you start? Begin with software requirements. Narrow your choices by eliminating drive interfaces or controllers that are not compatible with your application. For example, an IDE drive might not offer sufficient performance for your network software, or an older machine might not be compatible with Enhanced IDE. In general PC applications, IDE drives are the most compatible since nearly all operating systems will run an IDE drive without additional software drivers.

In terms of performance and flexibility, SCSI is always the best choice. Unfortunately, almost all advanced operating systems like Win 95, OS/2 and Windows NT require software drivers for full performance and support of SCSI controllers. Determine the availability of software drivers for your applications before choosing SCSI.

Consider future expandability and upgradability. SCSI controllers offer the most flexibility and expandability in the long run. With a SCSI controller, you can daisy-chain 7 to 15 different devices, including SCSI hard drives, CD-ROMs, erasable optical drives, DAT and other SCSI peripherals from the same controller.

Most interfaces other than SCSI and IDE are now obsolete. Use them only if you are upgrading an older system that already has them installed. ESDI, RLL, and MFM drives are still available. They may not be the fastest or most economical choice, but they may be a good choice for upgrading an older system.

If you are building a new IBM compatible system, you also have a choice of motherboard bus/controller card configurations. The most popular choices are ISA and PCI. Each bus has it advantages and limitations.

ISA refers to the original 16-bit bus that IBM designed into the first 80286 based AT computers. The IBM ISA specifications strictly limited bus speed to 8MHZ and set firm rules about bus timing. Newer clone motherboards violate this specification and permit operation up to 16MHz. The ISA bus design is capable of accommodating most hard drives and I/O cards without a bottleneck. Its main limitation is video. With the advent of programs like Microsoft Windows, large amounts of data must be transferred quickly to the video card as windows are opened, closed, and scrolled. The original AT bus lacks the band width for acceptable video performance.

To solve the AT-Bus performance problem, a committee called the Video Electronics Standards Association was formed. The VESA local bus standard was established to improve video performance while maintaining compatibility with ISA bus peripherals. VESA bus motherboards have two or three local bus slots that are connected directly to the 32 bit bus of the Intel compatible CPU chips. This permits up to three VESA peripherals to operate at any speed up to the full speed of the processor. The main problem with the VESA bus design is bus loading. As VL-bus speed is increased (VESA bus speed is linked directly to processor speed), the number of adapter cards that can be used decreases. For example, most 50MHz VESA motherboards will support only one or (maybe) two cards. Due to these limitiations, the VESA VL-BUS standard has lost popularity and is now found only in older systems.

A new standard, the Peripheral Connection Interface (or PCI) bus has now taken front stage. The PCI bus offers high performance (up to 133MB/sec in burst mode) and easy installation. PCI doesn't suffer from a limited number of supported slots as VESA does. PCI boards are also autoconfiguring (an advantage over VESA and ISA). As more PCI peripherals become available and prices drop, the price/performance ratio of PCI will make it the only practical bus for SCSI drive interface cards. Insist on both PCI and ISA if you are building up a new system.

Once you've selected a motherboard, it's time to make sure the controller board is really compatible. The EISA bus is so strictly defined that we have seen very few compatibility issues arise. ISA compatibility problems usually occur only when the bus speed is increased over 10MHz or the bus timing is irregular. The VESA bus is famous for compatibility problems between video and controller cards. PCI cards are generally all compatible, but inserting one low performance PCI card in your system will lower the performance of all the other cards.

With standard IDE controllers, bus speed is normally not an issue. With memory or I/O mapped SCSI controllers, you will need an available interrupt and rsufficient address space in the base 640K memory to support the footprint of the controller BIOS. ISA bus mastering controllers of any type can be a nightmare. Bus on/off times and refresh release rates often need to be adjusted to get things working. With a negligible performance difference between bus mastering and memory mapped controllers, you are best off steering clear of bus mastering controllers. ISA bus mastering controllers may also have compatibility problems or performance limitations in machines with more than 16MB of memory.

Our overall recommendations: A fast PCI SCSI controller for new systems. Couple this controller with the largest SCSI drive you can afford. If you are interested in a small capacity drive and controller, an EIDE drive will offer the most for the money. Weigh your storage and speed requirements. For Network server applications, go with the fastest wide SCSI drive you can afford. For workstations or light database applications, a larger capacity drive with a slower access time and lower cost may be preferable. In notebook and portable applications insist on a drive with good shock tolerance. When selecting a drive capacity, be sure to think to the future. It's better to start with a large capacity drive now than to replace the entire drive in the near future.

In summary, for most low capacity applications we recommend a small, inexpensive EIDE drive with an imbedded controller. For maximum software compatibility in sizes below 2GB standard EIDE drives are a good choice. For top performance and upward compatibility with the ability to daisy-chain additional peripherals, choose a SCSI drive and controller.

CONTROLLER SETUP & JUMPERING

In PC applications, controller jumpering is often the first step in installing a new drive and controller. You will need the controller board manual, to correctly jumper the controller, as well as documentation on the other boards installed in the system. Settings for some common controllers are provided in the Controller Information section of this manual.

You may need to jumper the controller board for one or more of the following settings:

ISA Bus Base I/O Address

The base I/O address of your controller can normally be left at the factory default setting unless you are installing two controller boards in the same system. If you are installing two boards, the first board must be set at the primary I/O address, and the second board can use any available I/O address. Be sure to check for conflicts with network boards, tape drive controllers, and video boards before selecting your secondary address.

If you are installing an IDE disk drive, the primary port addresses used are 1F0-1F7H and 3F6-3F7H. At the time of this printing, MS-DOS 6.4 did not support the use of more than one IDE controller at an alternate (secondary) address. Windows '95 and IBM's OS/2, however, do support a secondary IDE controller.

If you are designing an I/O mapped controller card that must coexist with an IDE or similar board, I recommend using a base address of 180H or 320H. These areas are almost never used by other peripherals.

NOTE:
Not all motherboard BIOS ROMs will support controller card BIOS addresses over E000H. If you experience problems, try choosing a BIOS address between A000H and DFFFH

ISA Bus Base BIOS Address

If your controller card has a ROM BIOS, you will need to select a starting address. When selecting a starting BIOS address, add the starting address of the card and the length of the required I/O space. Make sure that the address you select will not cause ROM address conflicts with any other boards (particularly VGA and network boards). If you are unsure of the length of the BIOS ROM on the controller, use DEBUG to dump the third byte of the ROM. This corresponds to the length of the BIOS in 512 byte blocks. Every system configuration is different, but most IBM compatibles have room for a 16K or 32K BIOS starting at C800H or D000H.

ISA Bus DMA Channel

Most controller cards do not use third party DMA. Exceptions to this are some high performance SCSI and ESDI controllers. You can share a DMA channel with another device only in the rare case that your software and hardware support it. Make sure to set both DREQ and DACK jumpers identically.

ISA Bus Controller Interrupt

Most controller boards do not use interrupts in DOS applications, but a hardware interrupt is required for all Novell and most UNIX applications. Select any available interrupt, but be sure to define it correctly when running NETGEN. Interrupts 14 and 15 are generally available on most PC's. IRQ 14 is normally used by the primary IDE controller. Lower interrupt numbers have higher CPU priority.

Floppy Address

A secondary floppy address must be selected for two floppy controllers to peacefully coexist in the same system. OS/2 users will find support for two floppy controllers built into the operating system. If you are running DOS, you will not be able to use the second floppy controller without a device driver installed in your CONFIG.SYS file. If your floppy controller is compatible with the original IBM-XT architecture (copied in all clones from 8088's to P5's), you can use DOS DRIVER.SYS to control your extended floppies.

DOS DRIVER.SYS parameters are listed below. Enter all necessary parameters on the DEVICE = DRIVER.SYS line in your CONFIG.SYS file. For example, if you have one hard disk installed and wish to use a 1.44MB floppy as your third (i.e. D:) drive, add the following line to your CONFIG.SYS:

DEVICE=DRIVER.SYS /F:7 /C

The following switches are supported by MS DOS 5.0:

/T:x   x = number of tracks

/C   indicates that disk change is supported by the drive

/F:x   x = drive form factor code

0 = 360K

2 = 720K

1 = 1.2MB

7 = 1.44MB

9 = 2.88 MB

/H:x   x = number of heads

/S:xx = number of sectors per track

More detailed information on CONFIG.SYS can be found in your DOS manual.

Controller cards with well written BIOS codes (like the CSC FastCache™ series) will operate extended floppy drives without software drivers. If you have one of these cards, modifications to your CONFIG.SYS will not be needed in most cases.

2.88MB drives are now supported as primary (boot) drives by most new motherboard BIOS ROM's, including AMI, and M.R. BIOS.

A Tip for ISA Motherboards With "Extended Chipset" Setup

If you are using a motherboard based on the Chips & Technology 3 chip LSI chips, the newer OPTI chips or other programmable chipset, congratulations! The speed of your RAM and I/O channel can be altered to increase overall system performance by "fine tuning" your motherboard. You can select I/O clock speed and wait states by running the extended setup program that came with your motherboard and using the information in Table A. Be careful when setting I/O channel wait states on these motherboards. It is easy to outrun many controller boards by selecting SYSCLOCK/2 without wait states.

Once your controller is jumpered correctly, proceed to CMOS setup and then low-level format. See the following section that corresponds to your drive type for set-up and low-level formatting instructions.

Recommended C & T, OPTI, Intel, and ETQ Wait States.

SYSCLOCK N	I/O Channel Read/Write Wait States	16-Bit Bus Wait States
Over 8 MHz	1 wait state	2 wait states
8 MHz or less	0 wait states	1 to 2 wait states

NOTE: SYSCLOCK is the CPU clock frequency of your motherboard. Use extended setup to chose betweembetween

SYSCLOCK, SYSCLOCK or SYSCLOCK

3   4

5,6 etc.

to adjust your bus clock frequency.

For example, a system clock of 50MHz and an extended setting of:

SYSCLOCK

5

will provide a bus clock speed of

$$\frac{50}{5} = 10 \ MHz.$$

Most Floppy Controllers will work at bus speeds up to about 10MHz. Many Hard Drive Controllers do not operate reliably much over 10 MHz. These estimates include 2 wait states. Note that I/O operations on the PC bus have one extra wait state when compared to memory operations. This is why memory mapped cards generally transfer data faster than I/O mapped cards.

Your C&T or OPTI motherboard extended setup may also permit disabling the ISA bus REFRESH line. REFRESH is a signal necessary for proper operation if your system contains any expansion cards that use dynamic memory. Cards that require this signal include: EMS cards, laser printer direct video boards, caching controller cards, and several other peripherals. Disabling this line will improve bus throughput by between 1% and 3%. Go ahead and disable it if you need this small performance increase, but be warned of compatibility problems down the road.

DRIVE SETUP & JUMPERING

Typical IDE Drive Installation

CSC's technical support department is constantly asked: "What drive parameters should I use to install my IDE drive?" All modern IDE drives use what is called "automatic translation". This translation helps the drive to match itself to the parameters you choose. For example, a 80-megabyte drive might have 6 heads, 17 sectors per track, and 1230 cylinders. This same drive could be installed using a CMOS configuration of 12 heads, 17 sectors per track and 615 cylinders. Doubling the number of heads and halving the number of cylinders has no effect on the formatted capacity of the drive. The drive automatically translates the "logical parameter" of cylinder 0 head 6, sector 17 into the "physical" parameter of cylinder 1, head 3, sector 17. In fact, for DOS to access the full capacity of a drive, it should be set-up with a configuration of 1024 cylinders or less.

The system BIOS informs the imbedded drive controller of the CMOS settings on power up, and the drive then mimics this logical configuration. This means you can choose any parameters for an IDE drive as long as the CMOS settings do not exceed the physical capacity of the drive. There are also a few other practical limitations to the logical parameters you choose. For reasons described in the next few chapters, the maximum number of cylinders you should use is 1024. The maximum number of sectors per track is limited to 63, and the number of heads should not exceed 64.

To select drive parameters for any IDE drive in the drive list, simply choose a CMOS type with a formatted capacity less than or equal to the drive you are using. If you are using a system with a "user definable" drive type, enter the physical parameters of the drive from the drive list. If the physical parameters exceed 1024 cylinders, double the number of heads and halve the number of cylinders.

If you have a copy of CSC's IDSCAN software, ignore the drive tables and just boot from floppy. Run IDSCAN and we'll take care of setting

HOT TIP

CMOS for you.

Some newer system board BIOS ROM's have ID Scan programs built in! Selecting the correct CMOS configuration parameters may be as easy as running the "automatic configuration" utility in your ROM BIOS setup program!

Once you CMOS is set correctly, proceed to the DOS partitioning and high-level format instructions in the following chapters. If you are using the drive for Novell, a Compsurf may be necessary. Low-level formatting is not required or recommended for any IDE drive.

IDE Drive Jumpering

Most IDE drives have one or more of the following jumpers:

HOST SLV/ACT, C/D, DSP, and ACT.

HSP, when jumpered, grounds the HOST/SLAVE/ACTIVE signal on the IDE interface. This signals the system that a slave drive is present in a two drive system. You need to add this jumper only if you have two IDE drives installed.

C/D is also sometimes labeled DS and is the drive select jumper. This jumper is set on the master (i.e. C:) drive and removed on the slave (i.e. D:) drive.

DSP should only be jumpered on the first drive (i.e. C:) if two IDE drives are installed in the same system. This jumper tells the master (i.e. C:) drive that there is another drive present on the IDE cable.

The ACT jumper connects the -ACTIVE signal to the -HOST SLV/ACT signal on the interface. This signal is used to drive an external LED that indicates drive activity. If the hard drive activity LED doesn't work on your system, chances are you need to add an ACT jumper.

DS0 or DS1 Confusion

Drive select jumpers are often a source of confusion and frustration. It seems that some manufacturers label their four drive-select jumpers DS0, DS1, DS2, and DS3. Others label them DS1, DS2, DS3, and DS4. We will use the more common convention DS0, DS1, DS2, and DS3 throughout this manual.

MFM, RLL, and ESDI Drive Jumpering

If you are installing a single MFM, RLL, or ESDI drive in your system, choose DS0 if your jumpers start with DS0 or choose DS1 if your jumpers start with DS1. These are actually the same jumpers, just numbered differently by the drive manufacturer. What you need in a single drive MFM/RLL installation is the first available drive-select jumper.

If you are installing a second MFM or RLL drive in your system with a twisted cable, choose DS1 if your jumpers start with DS0 or choose DS2 if your jumpers start with DS1. What you really want in this case is the second drive select jumper.

Always connect drive C: to the last connector (after the twist). Connect D: to the middle connector (before the twist).

If your drives have select pins numbered:	And you are installing:		
	1 Drive with a flat cable	2 Drives with a twisted cable	2 Drives with a flat cable
DS0 to DS3	Set C: to DS0	Set C: to DS1 Set D: to DS1	Set C: to DS0 Set D: to DS1
DS1 to DS4	Set C: to DS1	Set C: to DS2 Set D: to DS2	Set C: to DS1 Set D: to DS2

MFM, RLL, and ESDI Drive Jumpering

SCSI Drive Jumpering

SCSI drive jumpering is an altogether different story. SCSI drives usually use three jumpers for addressing. The eight possible on/off configurations of these jumpers represent eight SCSI addresses. Normally these jumpers follow a straight-forward binary sequence with the lowest numbered jumper being the LSB. Check your drive manual or the Connector Pinout section to be sure before jumpering your SCSI drive.

SCSI drives usually have a jumper that selects the source of terminator power. This jumper is important if your controller or system does not supply terminator power. In this case, you will need to jumper the drive so that terminator power is supplied from the drive.

Many SCSI drives also have a jumper for power up spin. This jumper is changed to permit the system to control spin-up of the drive. Many Seagate and Maxtor drives also have jumpers that permit spin up delays based on the SCSI ID jumper. Since each drive has a different SCSI ID, this means that each drive will spin up at a different time. This option is provided because the power requirements are much higher during spin-up than when the drive is running. Many disk arrays and large systems with multiple drives are set up to take advantage of this option. Longer power supply life is the result.

If you have an Adaptec™ controller, you will need to set your boot drive to ID 0. Your second drive should be set to ID 1. If you want to use more than two drives under DOS, you will need to load ASPI4DOS.SYS and ASPIDISK in your CONFIG.SYS file. ASPIDISK will also be necessary if you are running any protected mode software. The driver installation process with these cards can become quite involved.

If you are using a CSC FastCache™, you will need to run FCSETUP when you first install your hard drive or when you make any changes to your SCSI hardware configuration. Once you have run the setup program, NO DRIVERS will be necessary for running up to 7 SCSI hard drives under DOS. Erasable optical drives can also be run without drivers. No changes to your CONFIG.SYS are necessary, and you can set the card to boot from any ID. Also, no drivers are needed for protected mode programs (like Windows™ in 386 Enhanced Mode). Just add an exclude statement to your memory manager so that the memory range of the FastCache is left unchanged. Nice, huh?

Most other SCSI controllers such as the CSC PCI SCSI-III board will scan the SCSI bus each time the system is powered up, adding support for the extended drives at that time.

DRIVE CABLING

IDE Drive Cabling

IDE (Imbedded Drive Electronics) interface disk drives use a 40-pin interface cable. This cable connects the drive logic board (with imbedded controller) to a bus adapter card or to a motherboard IDE connector. IDE adapters are usually called "paddle boards". The paddle board buffers (amplifies) the signals from the drive and provides enough power to drive the PC bus.

Cabling an IDE drive is simple. Connect a 40-pin flat cable from the drive to the controller, being careful to observe pin 1 orientation. If the drive supports it, a second IDE drive can usually be connected to the same cable. To do so, jumper the boot drive in "master" mode, and jumper the second drive as a "slave" as described in the Drive Setup & Jumpering section. Since the IDE interface transfers data and control signals at full bus speed, IDE cable lengths are critical. As a rule of thumb, try to avoid using a cable longer than 18" in any IDE drive installation.

What Are These Twisted Cables?

Why do many drive installations use twisted cables? Simply because IBM used them in the first PC's. In an effort to simplify installation, IBM decided to jumper all of their hard and floppy drives on the second drive select. This eliminated the need for technicians to jumper the drives. The first floppy drive (A:) was connected to the end of the cable (after the twist). The second floppy drive (B:) was connected before the twist. The twist in the cable simply flipped the first and second drive select lines so that all drives could be jumpered identically.

The floppy and hard drive cables in a standard AT look suspiciously similar. Be careful not to interchange them. A significant number of installation problems are a result of interchanged hard and floppy cables. Each cable has a different twist, and they are often not marked. If you are using twisted cables, make sure the floppy drive cable has seven conductors twisted. A twisted cable used with older MFM or RLL hard drives must have only five conductors in the twist. See the cable chart at the end of this section.

Single Drives (MFM, RLL or ESDI) Cables

Cabling a single drive MFM, RLL, or ESDI system is easy. Use a standard 20-pin flat data cable and a 34-pin control cable with no twist. A word of caution: watch out for pin one. Pin one is identified by a red stripe on one side of the cable. This side of the cable must be connected closest to pin one of both the drive and controller. Check the controller card for a small number 1 or a square dot on the silk screen near one edge of the connector. Pin 1 on the drive is nearest a notch in the edge connector. Reversing the data cable can cause damage to the drive, controller, or both. The differential line drivers on the drive and controller are easily damaged by reversed cables. If you are not sure which is pin 1, check the manual, don't try to guess!

Multi Drive MFM and RLL Cabling

Three cables are required when installing two MFM or RLL drives using one controller. Two flat 20-pin data cables and one twisted 34-pin cable will be necessary. The 34-pin control cable should have only the drive select and ground pins twisted (5 conductors twisted). Set both drives to the second drive select position (this position is marked DS1 or DS2 as described in the Drive Setup & Jumpering section). Terminate the control cable on the last drive only.

Termination

In MFM, RLL, and ESDI installations, terminating resistors for the control signals should be installed only in the drive located at the physical end of the control cable. Terminating resistors should be installed at the end of every data cable in these installations. Since most drives come from the factory with terminators installed, you will need to remove terminators in a dual drive installation. See the SCSI installation section for more information on SCSI termination.

Multi Drive ESDI Cabling

Three cables are required when installing two ESDI drives using one controller. Two flat 20-pin data cables and one flat 34-pin cable with two drive connectors are necessary. Set the first ESDI drive jumpers to drive select 0. Set the second drive to drive select 1. Terminate the control cable on the last drive only.

A flat cable is required for applications with more than two ESDI drives. If only two drives will be installed, ESDI drives may also be cabled with a twisted 34-pin cable in a manner identical to MFM cabling.

Although most ESDI controllers support only two drives, the ESDI interface provides the ability to daisy-chain up to 8 drives. If you are installing more than two ESDI drives, use a flat 34-pin cable and set the select jumpers sequentially. A separate 20-pin data cable is required for each drive.

SCSI Drive Cabling

Internal SCSI drives are connected to the controller with a 50-pin ribbon cable. Be extremely careful to observe the pin 1 location when connecting cables to SCSI drives. Reversing SCSI cables on drives often causes a loss of termination power which can result in marginal data transfer or no transfer at all. Some external SCSI drives are connected to the controller with a 25-pin D-type connector, others use a 50-pin Amphenol connector.

The SCSI bus must have a total of 2 terminators - no more and no less. If you are using the controller with one internal hard disk, for example, termination will be installed on the internal hard drive and on the controller card. If you are installing one internal and one external drive, the terminators must be removed from the controller card and installed on the internal and external drives. Check the manual included with your SCSI drives and controller board for terminator installation and removal.

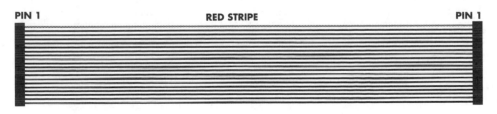

20-Pin Data Cable. 1 used for each MFM, RLL or ESDI Hard Drive.

*34-Pin Control Cable.
Used for single drive
MFM, RLL or ESDI
systems.*

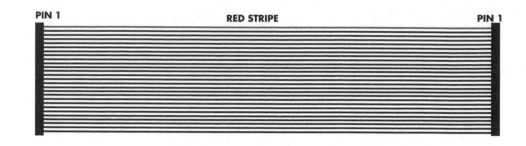

C:DRIVE

*Dual Drive straight
34-Pin Control Cable.
Used for MFM, RLL,
and ESDI drives.*

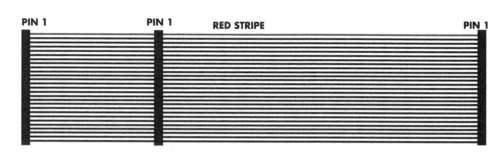

*Note: When using this cable with 2 drives, one must be set to Drive Select 0
and the other for Drive Select 1 (see Table B in previous chapter).*

*Dual Hard Drive
twisted (5 wires) 34-
Pin Control Cable.
Used for MFM, RLL,
and ESDI drives*

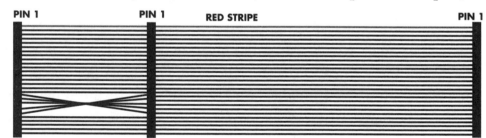

DRIVE C   DRIVE D

*Note: When using this cable with 2 drives, both drives must be set to Drive
Select 1.*

*Dual Floppy Drive
twisted (7 wires) 34-
Pin Cable. Used for
one or two Floppy
Drives*

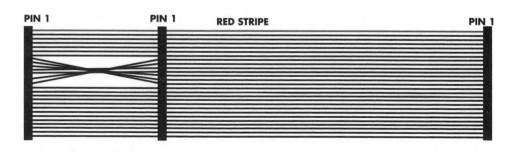

DRIVE A   DRIVE B

Note: Both floppy drives should be set to Drive Select 1.

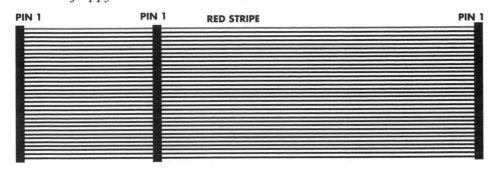

PIN 1   **PIN 1**   **RED STRIPE**   **PIN 1**

40-Pin IDE cable for one or two hard drives

DRIVE C   DRIVE D

SCSI CABLE IDENTIFICATION

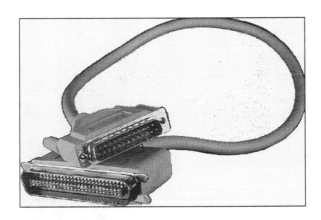

MAC Style DB-25 to Centronics Cable

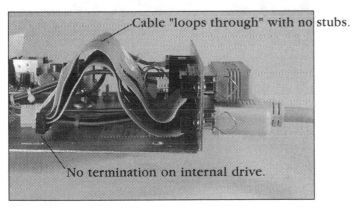

Cable "loops through" with no stubs.

No termination on internal drive.

Correct Enclosure Cabling for External Drives

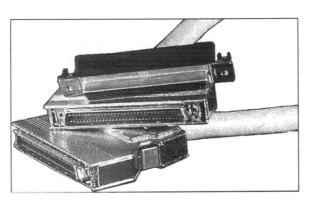

Wide SCSI Cable and Mating Connector

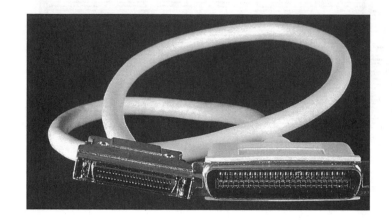

*SCSI-II Amp Style to
Centronics Cable*

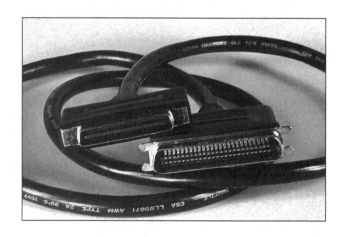

*PS/2 to Centronics
SCSI Cable*

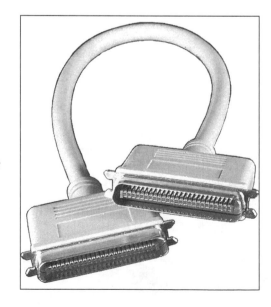

*Centronics to
Centronics SCSI Cable*

LOW-LEVEL FORMATTING

Unlike floppy disks that are low-level formatted at the same time as they are high-level formatted, all hard disks are low-level formatted separately, that is because of the differences in the various types and styles of controller cards, the encoding format, and the interleave that can be used with a hard drive.

If you decide to use a different controller card, or to use a different interleave on the hard disk, it may have to be low-level formatted again. Once the low-level format is completed properly, it will not have to be done again unless the controller card is replaced, the interleave is changed, bad sectors appear, or there is a hard disk failure. Low-level formatting destroys all the data written on the hard disk. Be sure to back-up all data before a hard disk is low-level or high-level formatted.

What is DEBUG?

DEBUG is a program provided on the DOS disks (DEBUG.COM) that is primarily used by programmers and service technicians. The operation of DEBUG is described in detail in the DOS manual. In order to use DEBUG for low-level formatting, only two commands are generally necessary: the G (GO) command, and the Q (QUIT) command. In the following paragraphs, commands such as G=C800:5 will be used to start the ROM based low-level formatting program stored on the hard drive controller.

To start the program, insert a disk containing the DEBUG.COM program into the floppy drive and type DEBUG at the DOS prompt. When the DEBUG prompt (-) is displayed type G= followed by the starting address of the ROM based program (G=C800:5) for example. This means go to ROM address C800:5 and run the program contained in the ROM. After the program is finished, it will usually return you to the DOS prompt (>). If the program returns you to the DEBUG prompt (-) type Q to quit DEBUG and return to the DOS prompt.

What is CSCFMT?

WARNING!
As with any low-level format, CSCFMT will destroy all existing data. Don't use CSCFMT unless you have a verified back-up of all data.

CSCFMT is a low-level format utility supplied on the Hard Drive Bible companion CD-ROM. CSCFMT works with most MFM,RLL, ESDI, IDE and EIDE drives. Low-level formatting is the only way of changing the interleave of a hard drive. CSCFMT is useful if you are installing a hard drive for the first time, or if you need to change the interleave of an installed drive to optimize its performance. For most common DOS installations, CSCFMT is the only program you'll need in addition to DOS FDISK and FORMAT.

To low-level format, just type CSCFMT at the DOS prompt. CSCFMT will ask for the interleave you wish to use. Check the interleave information section for the optimum value for your system configuration.

Choosing a Drive Type

Early IBM ATs only provided 14 (MFM) or so drive types to choose from in the CMOS. The Middle-aged AT's usually have up to 46 (based on the original MFM) types. If you are installing an IDE drive and you find a CMOS drive with a matching total drive capacity, go ahead and use it.

Most new machines have a "User Definable" or "Custom" drive type that can be created and saved in the CMOS, thus providing a standard drive type. "User Definable" drive types are used in most IDE drive installations.

IDE Drive Types

This idea of translation schemes bring us to the AT or IDE (Imbedded Drive Electronics) interface. These drives are intelligent in that they will "mimic" other drive geometries that equal or are very close to the same number of logical blocks. If a "custom" drive type option is not available for an AT drive, simply pick one from the list of available choices that has the same number of total megabytes.

MFM Drive Types

Unlike the newer IDE drives, MFM drive configurations must match the drive geometry exactly!! If the CMOS drive type table lists the exact geometry, great. If not, then check to see if a "Custom" or "User Definable" CMOS option is available.

The last resort is to choose a drive type match that is close but does not exceed either the cylinder or head values. This option will not usually provide the full formatted capacity of the drive. An exact match in the head count is definitely preferred when getting a "close" match. When there is no direct match in the internal drive type tables, a partitioning program may be needed to provide a software driven translation solution in order to achieve full capacity. Keep in mind that the drive will format out only to the capacity of the chosen drive type when not using third-party driver software. Also, some AT 16-bit MFM controllers provide an onboard BIOS that will allow the unique geometry of the drive to be dynamically configured.

RLL and ESDI Drive Types

RLL and ESDI drives are usually not represented at all in the internal drive tables, and consequently the controllers for these drives need onboard a ROM BIOS that either contains its own internal list of choices for the geometry or else provides the ability to dynamically configure (define) the controller to the specific geometry of the drive. In the case of the ESDI interface, the controller gets parameters directly from the drive with the equivalent of a SCSI "Mode Sense" command. Most RLL and ESDI controllers require that CMOS be set to "Type 1". This setting is then overwritten by the controller BIOS after power-up.

A special note on ESDI and other drives that have more than 1024 cylinders. Since DOS cannot access cylinders above this limit, a translation scheme may be elected in the controller's BIOS. As the total number of Logical Blocks Available (LBA's) is defined as CYLINDERS*HEADS*SECTORS PER TRACK, translations that equal the same number of logical blocks with the cylinder count below the 1024 limit will be devised. The controller BIOS will need to be ENABLED in order to utilize translation schemes.

Note: Translated LBA's are always less than or equal to Native LBA's.

SCSI Drive Types

Almost all SCSI drives use DRIVE TYPE 0 or NONE, as the host adapter BIOS and the drive communicate together to establish the drive geometry. The SCSI controller "Scans" the SCSI bus shortly after power-up and installs BIOS support for any attached SCSI devices.

Formatting MFM Drives

The first step in a low-level format of an MFM drive is correct CMOS setup. Check the drive geometry list for the heads and cylinders configuration of your drive. Then check your motherboard manual (or ROM based setup program) for a CMOS drive type that matches your drive geometry. If you find an exact match, set the CMOS to that drive type number and skip the next paragraph.

Table Overrides

If your drive geometry does not match a CMOS drive type, you will need to perform a CMOS type table override. Use Speedstor or Disk Manager software to do this. These programs add a software device driver to the drive that overrides the CMOS drive type settings on power-up, enabling you to use a drive not listed in your setup program.

Check the Tune-Up section for the correct default interleave for your system, then low-level format the drive. If you have a late AMI BIOS, you may have low-level formatting routines built in ROM. If not, use either the setup disk that came with your computer, CSCFMT, IBM Diagnostics, Speedstor, or Disk Manager to low-level format.

Once the drive is low-level formatted, proceed to the partitioning and high level formatting instructions in the following sections.

Formatting RLL Drives

Most of the 16-bit and all of the 8-bit RLL controllers that we have found have low-level formatting routines in ROM firmware on the board. The default address segment for XT controller boards is C800 hex. To find the starting address, enter DEBUG and type U C800:3. The jump instruction is usually found at C800:5 or C800:6. The first two bytes of the ROM are a 55 and AA hex which identify the BIOS ROM. The third byte represents the length of the BIOS ROM in 512 byte blocks.

To format the drive, first select the correct CMOS setup. Consult the manual that came with your RLL controller for the correct setup value.

After setting CMOS, proceed to the low-level format. If you have a ROM based low-level formatting routine available, use it. Otherwise, use CSCFMT, Speedstor, or Disk Manager. Be sure to use the /SECS:26 option if you are using Speedstor.

When formatting lower capacity (i.e. 30MB) RLL drives, be sure to enter the write precompensation cylinder correctly. Write precomp is important to these drives, since RLL encoding leaves less margin for error. Write precomp is handled automatically on almost all newer drives.

Once the drive is low-level formatted, proceed to the partitioning and high-level formatting procedures described in the following sections.

Formatting ESDI Drives

All of the PC-bus ESDI controllers we have come across have low-level formatting routines in ROM firmware. The formatting procedures for these drives vary from controller to controller, so the best advice we can give you here is follow the instructions that came with the card.

In addition to the interleave, you may be asked if you want to use sector sparing when you format. Sector sparing reduces the number of available sectors per track from 36 to 35 or from 54 to 53. This will reduce the available formatted capacity of your drive. Choose sector sparing only if your drive has a large defect map. Sector sparing will allow the controller to remap defective sectors to the spare sector on each track. This means that your application will "see" less defects. Sparing will reduce the capacity of your drive by 1/36th. If your drive has a small error map, sector sparing won't gain you much. If you are running an application that requires a "Defect Free" drive, enable sector sparing to "Hide" the drive's defects.

Many ESDI controllers may also ask you for head and track sector skewing values. These values offset the position of sectors relative to the index so that as the drive steps from track to track and changes from head to head, the next sequential sector is immediately available. To calculate the optimum track skewing value, divide the track-to-track seek time of your drive by 16.6ms. Then multiply this number by the number of sectors per track (rounding up). This will give you the optimum track skewing value. Select 0 when asked for head skew.

You may notice that your large capacity ESDI drive contains a large number of factory defects. Don't sweat it. These defects are mapped by a factory analog tester that is extremely sensitive compared to your controller. Most of these defects could never be detected using your controller. They are usually just small analog spikes or dropouts that are corrected by the ECC on your controller. The factory maps these defects because they are the most likely areas to cause problems as the drive wears over time.

Once your ESDI drive is low-level formatted, proceed to the partitioning and high-level formatting procedures in the following sections.

Note:
Several SCSI drives including some made by Quantum will return almost immediately from a SCSI low-level FORMAT command. These drives report that they have successfully completed a low-level format but don't actually format the disk. A SCSI FORMAT (04h) command does not erase data on all drives. In many cases, data written to the disk is not erased until it's overwritten with a WRITE command.

Formatting SCSI Drives

Most SCSI controllers require that the CMOS setup on X86 machines be set for "no drive installed". On power up, the SCSI BIOS on the adapter card scans the SCSI bus to detect attached devices. Once detected, these devices are added to the list of available drives. Most SCSI controllers support up to seven SCSI devices. More than two drives usually require a third party device driver for use with DOS versions before 5.0.

Almost every SCSI controller includes a low-level format program that is specific to that particular board. The low-level format routines in programs like Speedstor and Disk Manager don't usually work well with SCSI controllers. This is because the controller card BIOS does not translate an interrupt-13 format command into a SCSI format command. In this case, you'll most likely need to use the low-level format program that came with the card.

Once the low-level format is completed, FDISK, Speedstor, or Disk Manager can be used for partitioning and high-level formatting.

Low Level Formatting IDE Drives

Most IDE drives operate in two modes, "native" and "translation". To use an IDE drive in native mode, set CMOS to the actual number of heads and cylinders on the drive, then proceed to partitioning and high-level format.

If the IDE drive you are using has physical characteristics (i.e. heads, cylinders, and sectors/track) that are not listed in your ROM BIOS, and you do not have a BIOS that offers a user defined drive type, you will need to use translation mode. Translation mode remaps the drive's physical characteristics into characteristics that match a common drive type. For example, most 40MB IDE drives offer a translation mode that matches the physical characteristics of the early Seagate 251. Since this type is included in almost all ROM BIOS drive type tables, compatibility is improved.

Most new IDE drives automatically enable translation mode based on CMOS settings. Select a drive type that is close to but does not exceed the megabyte capacity of the drive. The drive will translate to the megabyte capacity you have selected. Some older type IDE drives require a jumper. Like SCSI drives, all IDE drives are low-level formatted at the factory.

Once CMOS and translation mode is set correctly, FDISK, Speedstor, or Disk Manager may be used for partitioning and high-level formatting.

WARNING!
All IDE drives are already low-level formatted at the factory. Low-level formatting an IDE drive could erase the factory recorded defect tables. Defects on these drives are usually mapped out using a burn-in process, not through the interface.

CAUTION!
Unless you need to change interleaves, we don't recommend reformatting older IDE drives. Imbedded factory defect maps on older drives could be accidentally erased by low-level formatting.

DOS PARTITIONING

DOS partitioning and high-level formatting can be tricky. This may be done using DOS FORMAT and FDISK or using a third-party program such as SpeedStor or Disk Manager. Although these menu driven programs are convenient, DOS and its included utilities are all that's necessary. It's important to understand the following DOS partition constraints before beginning.

Old DOS Limitations

Versions of MS DOS and PC DOS before 3.30 have a 32MB storage limitation. There is no way to access over 32MB per physical drive without a device driver, if you are using an old version of DOS. If you are stuck with DOS 3.2 or earlier, you will need SpeedStor or Disk Manager to fully utilize a drive larger than 32MB. The best solution is to upgrade to 3.30 or later version.

The 32MB Barrier

Versions of MS DOS and PC DOS after 3.30 but before 4.0 have a 32MB per partition barrier. Using these DOS versions, you cannot access more than 32MB per logical partition without using a third-party device driver. Both Speedstor and Disk Manager provide a device driver that can be installed in your CONFIG.SYS to bypass this limitation. We recommend use of DOS 4.01 or later if you desire more than 32MB per partition.

The 1024 Cylinder Barrier

All versions of DOS have a 1024 cylinder limitation. This is becoming more and more of a problem as larger capacity drives are introduced with more cylinders. To access more than 1024 cylinders, you will need a device driver or a controller card that offers a "translate mode". Some ESDI and most SCSI controllers (like the CSC FlashCache™64) offer translation mode.

Controllers that feature a translation mode will logically remap a drive's physical parameters so that the system "sees " less cylinders and more heads or sectors per track. For example, an ESDI drive with 1224 cylinders, 15 heads, and 36 sectors per track might be mapped into a configuration of 612 cylinders, 30 heads, and 36 sectors per track. The physical configuration of the drive will remain the same, but the controller card will remap the drive so that DOS will recognize the entire disk.

Translation mode is usually enabled during the low-level format procedure. If your controller does not support translation mode, the only way to bypass the 1024 cylinder limitation is with a device driver.

Once you have decided how you want to partition the drive, use either Speedstor, Disk Manager, or FDISK to do the work for you. Divide the disk into as many partitions as you desire. After you have set the partitions, you will have to reboot the system before any partition changes are recognized. Be sure to mark the partition you want to boot from as the ACTIVE partition. Then proceed to the high-level format procedure described in this section.

Partition Compatibility

All versions of DOS 6.x and later have the ability to access partitions created under older versions of DOS. Most, but not all, older versions of DOS will access partitions created under newer DOS versions. For example, a system booted under DOS 3.3 will recognize a hard drive partition created under DOS 3.2, but not an extended partition created under DOS 4.0. If you're partitioning a drive with a later versions of DOS and using partitions larger than 32MB in size, be aware that you are limiting your compatibility with earlier versions of DOS. If you plan to reformat a drive originally formatted with a late version of DOS, you must use the later version of DOS FDISK to erase the existing partition.

The 2000MB Partition Limit

DOS 6.X is currently limited to 2000MB per partition. In most cases, this is an adequate partition size. Although software is available to bypass this limitation, I don't recommend using it. If you can't partition your data to fit in 2GB partitions, the best solution is another

operating system with a high performance file system like OS/2™ or Windows NT™. As partition sizes increase, the efficiency of DOS decreases. DOS cluster sizes are typically 8K or more in large partitions. Since the minimum allocation size for each file is one cluster, even small files (i.e. 1K) will require 8K of disk space per file. If you have many small files, switching to a smaller partition that decreases your cluster size will improve efficiency.

DOS Format

DOS format (or high-level format) is simple. Use the DOS format program with the /S option or use FORMAT and SYS C: to initialize your bootable partition. If you are using a device driver, install it next and reboot the system before formatting any remaining partitions. You may also use Speedstor or Disk Manager for high-level formatting. Be sure to copy COMMAND.COM and invoke SYS C: to copy the DOS system to the active partition after using these programs.

Congratulations! You are now ready to run. Proceed to the tune-up section for tips on optimizing your software setup.

MACINTOSH DRIVE INSTALLATION

No hard drive technical manual would be complete without instructions for drive installation on the Apple Macintosh™. The Mac is the computer which popularized the SCSI standard. Every Mac since the Plus, introduced in 1984, has a built-in SCSI controller on the motherboard. This makes installing internal and external SCSI devices relatively easy, providing that you pay proper attention to cabling, termination, SCSI ID, and driver software installation.

As stated in the previous chapters, the SCSI bus utilizes "Daisy Chain" cabling with dual-ended termination. This means that each device must be connected in series with either a continuous ribbon cable or a series of external SCSI cables, with proper termination at both ends of the chain.

All Macintoshes use a standard DB-25 connector as the external SCSI port. Most computer stores carry a variety of cables which will connect your Mac to Centronics 50-pin or other industry standard SCSI connectors. If you are unable to locate the cable or terminators you need, CSC carries a comprehensive line of SCSI accessories at reasonable prices. We recommend that you do not use "T" type cables, as they can cause line noise and ringing which result in unreliable operation.

Correct termination is critical for any SCSI device installation. Every SCSI "Daisy Chain" must have a total of two terminating resistors, no more and no less. The first terminator is on the internal drive inside the Mac case. Do not remove the internal terminator for any reason. When upgrading the internal drive always make sure that the replacement device is terminated. If you are adding extra internal devices, you will need to remove all terminators from them, except from the last physical device. If you are adding extra external devices, only the internal drive and final device should be terminated.

The Macintosh CPU is always at SCSI ID number 7 and the internal boot drive should always be set to ID number 0 for reliable operation. Any other external or internal SCSI devices can be set to any other ID numbers, 1 through 6, as long as the number is not duplicated anywhere else on the SCSI chain. Duplicate SCSI ID numbers will cause a Mac to hang on startup. External devices should have a SCSI ID switch somewhere on the outside of the case to set the ID number. Internal devices will have their SCSI ID number set by removing or moving the ID jumpers on the device itself. The jumper settings for most SCSI devices are given in following chapters.

All external SCSI devices attached to the Mac must be powered up before your Macintosh is switched on. Allow the external hard drives enough time to spin-up, and then turn on the Mac. External devices which are attached but not powered up or are started after the Mac can cause the SCSI bus to hang, preventing drive operation, causing unreliable data transfers and "Bombs" to occur.

If you intend to boot from a new hard drive, it is imperative that you install your personal version of the system folder to maintain compatibility and functionality with your existing software. It is vitally important that ONE and only ONE version of the System File is installed on the boot drive. It is possible to have different System Folder on different drives, and then boot from them by choosing which drive is the Start Up Drive in the Startup Disk Control Panel, if you so desire. However, DO NOT have more than one System Folder on any Start Up Drive. It will cause erratic computer behavior, random crashes, "System Bombs" and other problems, if you can get it to start up at all.

There are several ways to replace the internal Start Up drive on the Macintosh. The best way we have found is the following, which assumes that you have had your Mac apart in the past. If you are not familiar with or are uncomfortable with putting hardware into your Mac, there are many comprehensive and more specific books you can refer to, or you can have an authorized technician install the device.

You will need: the appropriate hand tools to open your specific Mac case, a Phillips screwdriver, a "Y" power connector, and a three connector SCSI ribbon cable, in addition to the new drive.

1. Clean up the existing drive. Put all those loose documents in folders, like you always meant to do, toss those games you haven't played in 5 years, and take a look at all those files labeled "stuff".

2. Optimize the drive. There are several good defragmenting and optimizing utilities available on the market. You should also get

third party formatting software with the package. Find one and use it. You'll be amazed at how fast your old drive just became.

3. Shut everything off, but do not unplug the Mac.

4. Open the case and touch the power supply case. This grounds any static electricity.

5. Replace the power connector and the SCSI ribbon on the drive with the "Y" power connector and the three connector SCSI ribbon cable.

6. Set the replacement drive to any SCSI ID except 0 or 7, using the SCSI ID jumpers. Make sure that the drive is terminated as well. Then connect it to the power and ribbon cables.

7. Place it somewhere where the PCB cannot ground out. We prefer a suitably sized piece of cardboard on top of the existing drive. In any case, make sure that it will not short anything out or fall.

8. Restart.

9. Format, initialize, and partition the new drive using the third party driver software you installed earlier.

10. The new partition(s) will now be on the desktop.

11. Open the old internal drive. Press "Command-A" to select all of its contents.

12. Drag to the new drive to copy all, then close all when done.

13. Using the Startup Disk Control Panel on the existing drive, change it to the new drive and restart to check that the installation went as planned.

14. After everything is confirmed, shutdown. Remove the old drive. Set the SCSI ID of the new drive to 0, and install it in the internal bay using the original power connector and SCSI ribbon cable.

15. Reassemble your Mac, and you're done.

Note:

If you make the partitions under 500MB each, the drive will run faster and the minimum file sizes will be smaller.

Installing an external SCSI device is much simpler. You will need to obtain the correct external SCSI cable, usually a DB-25 to Centronics 50-pin, a terminator and some version of the aforementioned third party formatting software. The Apple Hard Drive Toolkit included on the Apple Macintosh System Disks may not work on hard disk drives without Apple firmware.

1. Once again, shut everything off. NEVER install or remove any device while power is on!

2. Connect the external device(s) with the appropriate SCSI cable(s).

3. Check that there are no duplicate SCSI IDs.

4. Confirm that the last device and only the last device has been terminated.
5. Power-up all external SCSI devices and allow them time to spin-up.
6. Switch on your Mac, and launch the third party formatting soft ware.
7. Format, initialize, and partition the new drive using the third party driver software you installed earlier. See note to left.
8. The new partition(s) will now be on the desktop. See note.

It is very important that all of the SCSI hard drives in your Mac SCSI chain have been formatted with the same third party software and are running the same SCSI driver. We often see a multiple hard drive Mac system suddenly report "THIS DISK IS UNREADABLE, WOULD YOU LIKE TO INITIALIZE?". This is most often caused by a SCSI driver conflict, in which two or more drives were formatted with different software. While most of the better third party software packages do offer "work arounds" for this situation, it is preferable that all of the devices be formatted with identical software. Even different versions of the same formatting software can and will cause conflicts.

Virtually all of the SCSI device installation problems which we encounter in Mac systems stem from cabling, termination, or SCSI ID errors. First of all, make absolutely sure of all cables and their orientation. Cables should fit tightly, but never be forced, and all securing clips should snap in to place. There must be two and only two terminators, one on the internal drive and one on the last physical device on the SCSI chain. No SCSI ID number can ever be duplicated on the chain. Please note that the physical placement of a device and its SCSI ID are NOT the same. It is very likely that a device can be set to the SCSI ID of 2, for example, and be the final physical device of four external SCSI devices on the SCSI chain.

WINDOWS DRIVE FORMATTING

Windows '95 Disk Format

Windows '95 uses a standard DOS compatible File Allocation Table (FAT) type disk format. Windows '95 also keeps a reserved area of the disk available for long file name support. The first character of the DOS file name is changed in the directory to indicate that a long file name exists for each file.

Windows '95 should install easily on any preformatted BIOS supported drive. DOS FDISK and FORMAT will still work. Some work will be necessary to save the long file name attributes should you decide to repartition your drive. It's a good idea to back things up before upgrading to '95.

Windows '95 Enhanced IDE Support

Windows '95 supports IDE drives over 540MB (and 1024 cylinders) using one of four methods:

1. ROM BIOS support using 28 bit LBA addressing

This is the most common means of support. Things will work "transparently" if your motherboard BIOS supports LBA addressing and is properly configured. Newer Intel built PCI motherboards are an example.

2. Hard Disk BIOS support

If you have an "Enhanced IDE" controller *with* a BIOS, Windows '95 will support large drives through Int-13h.

3. Truncation

This is a last resort. The capacity of your drive will be limited to 540MB, and only the first 1024 cylinders will work. In upgrading some older machines without EIDE support, truncation may be your only choice.

4. Real-Mode Geometry Support

This mode adds compatibility but sacrifices speed. You won't get true 32-bit driver support, and the Windows '95 protected mode disk driver (called ESDI_503.PDR) won't work. A slower choice, but if options #1 and #2 don't work, it's the only way to get the full capacity of a drive over 540MB.

Windows '95 SCSI Support through Int-13

Yes, your Windows '95 system can use SCSI hard drives and removable drives *without* 32 bit drivers. Things will work properly using Real-Mode Geometry support. Depending on the performance of your controller, you may still get acceptable performance levels. This is the trick to making older non-ASPI SCSI cards run under '95.

Windows '95 SCSI Support through ASPI

Many earlier SCSI cards include ASPI drivers but not Miniport drivers. For these cards, Microsoft provides a "DOS Compatibility Mode". Since CD-ROM's aren't normally supported through interrupt-13, Windows '95 switches into "real" mode and passes commands to these devices through a DOS ASPI manager. The frequent switches between "real" and "protected" modes tend to slow the system down.

This is the second level of compatibility and performance. It's faster than the Int-13 interface described above, but slower than the Miniport driver explained below. If you own an early model controller which doesn't have Windows '95 32 bit miniport driver support, consider upgrading to a newer PCI controller which does. An example is the CSC Universal PCI Wide/Narrow Card.

Windows '95 and NT SCSI Miniport Drivers

For top SCSI performance, your controller needs a Windows '95 "Miniport" driver. This driver passes packets of commands and data between the Windows '95 operating system and your SCSI controller hardware. Using a miniport driver provides true 32 bit performance. Using a miniport driver also helps free the system to "disconnect", "multitask", and complete other operations during the time that SCSI devices are accessed.

In some ways, a miniport driver is simpler than an ASPI driver. When a miniport driver is installed, the operating system becomes responsible for composing SCSI command packets. These packets are standardized and easy to create for devices for hard drives. But devices like CD-ROM changers, jukeboxes, and SCSI tape drives use "vendor unique" commands which vary from one device to another. This shifts the burden of compatibility from the driver to the operating system. So even if your miniport based system won't work with one SCSI application, it may work with others. Take Microsoft Backup as an example. Backup has limited compatibility with SCSI devices. Other tape backup programs such as FastCache backup work fine with devices like Digital Linear Tape (DLT) drives. Both programs pass commands through the same miniport driver "socket". But Backup has a limited number of supported devices.

Windows '95 and Windows NT miniport sockets are very similar in nature. Unfortunately, due to operating system differences, most '95 and NT SCSI software isn't compatible. Don't assume that a SCSI program written to work under '95 will operate when you upgrade to NT.

Disk Manager and Windows '95

Using both Disk Manager and Windows '95 can be opening a can of worms. Make sure you have the latest version (7.0 or later) of Disk Manager before you even attempt it. Disk Manager modifies the MBR (Master Boot Record) of your hard disk. It uses a small program located in the MBR to trap disk calls made through Interrupt 13h. Virus detection programs have been known to mistakenly identify the Disk Manager code stored in the MBR as a virus. If the Disk Manager code is accidentally removed by a virus checker, you'll need to reinstall it.

Windows '95 is smart enough to recognize Disk Manager, and will work with it. Make sure the Disk Manager file "XBIOS.OVL" is located in the root directory of your boot drive before loading Windows '95. The file "DMDRVR.BIN" should be loaded before any other files in your CONFIG.SYS that access the disk.

Getting 32 bit Disk Access from Win 3.1

Windows 3.1 has a 32 bit disk access driver called WDCTRL. It offers a small performance improvement in systems that have AT compatible disks. As the name implies, it works only with devices that are compatible with the Wester Digital Controller used in the original IBM AT. Fortunately, compatible devices include most IDE and EIDE drives, as well as MFM, RLL, and ESDI devices. If WDCTRL won't work in your system, you'll know right away. If the drive and controller you're using doesn't fully comply to the IBM task file specifications, WDCTRL simply won't load. If the drive and controller are *partially* compatible, the system will lock up hard when the driver loads. WDCTRL is not compatible with SCSI controllers, of course.

To enable the 32 bit driver under Win 3.1, add the following lines under the [386Enh] section of your Windows SYSTEM.INI file:

device=*int13
device=*wdctrl

You can turn 32 bit access of in the system control panel or by placing a semicolon ";" before each of these lines to "comment them out".

SMARTDrive 32 bit Disk Access

Windows '95 contains it's own internal software disk cache architecture. The Windows '95 cache is also automatically configured, so you can skip this section if you're using Windows '95.

SMARTDrive is a 32 bit cache program that runs under Windows 386 enhanced mode. It has the ability to "double buffer" data stores frequently used data in system memory for faster access. SMARTDrive integrates well with Windows, and dynamically allocates memory as it is needed. This feature lets Windows use your EMS memory when the cache doesn't need it.

SMARTDrive Write Caching

Earlier versions of SMARTDrive (before version 4.0) only cached read data. Versions 4.0 and later can cache both reads and writes. Caching write data is commonly called "write-behind caching" or "lazy writes". Caching write data definitely improves performance and reduces the overall number of seeks, but it can be dangerous. Since data is written first to memory, not to disk, your data could be lost if a system interruption were to occur.

Enabling write cache will cause loss of data should a system crash or power interruption occur. SMARTDrive has built-in safety features that check for CTRL-ALT-DEL resets and "old" data in cache. Another safety feature flushes the SMARTDrive cache after five seconds. If the system doesn't crash hard enough to interrupt SMARTDrive's internal timer interrupt, these safety features will save your data.

To enable SMARTDrive Write caching, put a plus sign after the drive letter you wish to cache. For example,

SMARTDRV D+ /E:2048

will enable write cache on drive E: with an element size of 2048. The element size specifies the number of bytes to be moved at one time. For more options, type SMARTDRV /?.

NOVELL COMPSURF

Novell's COMPSURF program is a tricky beast. It is one of the most rigorous and intensive test programs available. It's also a necessary prerequisite to installing some versions of Novell Netware on a hard drive. Compsurf was first written in 1984 when large capacity drives were not as reliable as they are today. It uses an intensive random and sequential read/write test to certify the drive. Compsurf takes around one hour per 20MB of disk space to run. After testing, Compsurf partitions the drive for use with Novell, and writes a defect table to the drive.

Before running COMPSURF, make sure you have all the necessary software drivers. ELS level I or level II Netware is designed to support IDE compatible drives only. ELS Compsurf will only work with IDE, MFM, RLL, or ESDI controllers that bear a close resemblance to the original IBM-AT MFM controller. If you are running Netware Lite, Advanced 286, SFT 286, or Netware 386, you have more options. Drivers for SCSI, ESDI, and SMD controllers are available for these versions of Netware. To use a Netware driver, you must follow the Netware installation instructions to the letter, and link the device driver with Compsurf. This will create a custom formatting and testing program that will operate with your controller.

If you are running a SCSI drive with Compsurf, be sure to answer NO when Compsurf asks if you wish to format the drive. Use the low-level formatting program provided with the controller card instead. Compsurf can't format SCSI drives because the SCSI interface only supports a 'FORMAT DRIVE' command, and the 'FORMAT TRACK' command is normally ignored by SCSI controllers.

Many newer controllers offer a "watered down" version of Compsurf in ROM BIOS. We have yet to find a controller card BIOS

Note:
When running Compsurf on SCSI drives, be sure to low-level format the drive first, then answer NO to the following prompts:

FORMAT THE DRIVE:
NO (enter)
MAINTAIN DEFECT LIST:
NO (enter)

that tests as well as the real Compsurf. Our feelings are that the reliability demands of most network users justify the time it takes to run the real Compsurf.

To save time and effort, it's a good idea to ask your drive dealer if he can Compsurf your drive for you. If he's reputable and confident in his product, this service should be available at no extra charge.

Whatever you do, choose a well built, heavy duty hard drive for your fileserver. Novell applications are extremely disk intensive and demand a reliable disk.

HARDWARE COMPATABILITY PROBLEMS

Unfortunately, not all controller cards are compatible with all computers and not all disk drives work with all controller cards.

Some of the major hardware compatibility problems we have come across are listed below.

SCSI Arbitration on Bus Scan

On power-up, a SCSI controller communicates with the attached devices to determine if the device is operating in synchronous or asynchronous mode. Many SCSI controllers do not perform this arbitration process correctly. This failure usually causes the system to hang. The solution is an upgraded controller BIOS or a different controller/drive combination.

SCSI Command Set Issues

SCSI command set problems occur because SCSI commands differ among device manufacturers. These problems can usually be resolved with a firmware upgrade on the SCSI device or controller. Be sure to check for command set compatibility before purchasing any SCSI devices.

In some cases, after market products are available to relieve SCSI compatibility problems. My personal favorites for the Apple Macintosh include FWB's Silverlining and Spot On. Corel makes an excellent set of SCSI disk drivers for ASPI compliant PC controllers. Storage Dimension's Speedstor is a great integration program for Sun platforms.

ISA Bus I/O Channel Ready Timing

Slow devices connected to the AT bus must assert a signal called I/O CHANNEL READY to force the motherboard to wait for data. Many faster motherboards do not conform to the original IBM AT bus timing specs. Because they don't, a controller card requesting a wait state delay using this line may not operate correctly. If you have a Chips & Technology based motherboard, this can be corrected by adding a bus wait state using extended setup. Otherwise the only solution is a new controller card.

ISA Bus 16-Bit Memory Transfers

This problem often occurs in older motherboards that use discrete chip sets. On the AT bus, a signal called MEM16 must be asserted by the bus devices in order to initiate a 16-bit data transfer. This signal must be available almost immediately, or the system may default to 8-bit transfer. Many of the cheaper clone motherboards do not provide valid address signals in time to decode this signal. If the address signals are not presented in time, it is impossible to perform a 16-bit transfer. This causes problems with many 16-bit cards that use memory mapped I/O, such as the WD7000 and DTC3280 SCSI controllers. Older DTK motherboards are notorious in this regard. The solution is to switch to an 8-bit card and suffer a slight loss of performance. If this is not acceptable, the only solution is upgrading to a higher quality motherboard.

ESDI Defect Tables

Many older style controller cards have problems reading the defect tables from some ESDI drives. This is due to the way the defect table is recorded on the drive. The solution is upgrading to a newer style card or rewriting the defect table using a factory analog type drive tester.

VESA VL-Bus Loading Problems

The VESA VL-Bus specification supports two cards at a 33MHz bus speed, and only one card at 40MHz or 50MHz bus speeds. Depending on the quality of their design and construction, some motherboards may exceed these specifications. There's really no way to correct a VESA bus loading problem other than lowering the bus speed or removing one card. A clock doubling CPU (i.e. the Intel 486DX2-66) may be the solution in some cases.

IDE Drive Master/Slave Compatibility

When mixing different manufacturers of IDE drives on the same cable, compatibility problems may occur. This is caused by timing incompatibilities and because some drives use IDE pins for different purposes (i.e. spindle sync). If you encounter a dual drive IDE situation where only one drive works, try reversing the Master/Slave jumpers on both drives to switch their positions in the system.

COMMON INSTALLATION PROBLEMS

The common installation problems below account for 90% of the technical support calls at CSC. Steer clear of trouble by learning about these issues.

Handle Hard Drives Like Eggs!

Hard drives are extremely fragile. Dropping, bumping, or jarring a hard drive can cause permanent damage. Always use a manufacturer approved shipping carton if you need to transport the drive outside of the system. Never transport an optical drive with the media inserted. Rough handling accounts for more drive failures than all other factors combined.

Reversed Cables!

Most drive cables are not keyed - they can easily be installed backwards. Reversed cables account for a large number of hard drive electronic failures.

Reversing a SCSI cable will cause the terminator power line to be grounded. This usually blows a fuse or fusable link on either the drive or controller. Without terminator power, SCSI data transfer will be unreliable. Make certain all cables are oriented correctly before applying power. If you reverse a SCSI cable, you may need to replace the fuse, or return the drive for service. Line drivers on either the controller, drive, or both can easily be damaged if cables are reversed. If you are unsure, don't guess - check the documentation or call the manufacturer!

INSTALLATION CAUTION!

Twisted Cables

Refer to the Drive Cabling section to ensure the proper twisted cable is used when installing multiple Floppy, MFM, RLL, or ESDI drives.

CMOS Setup

Be sure to read the chapter that describes the differences between physical and translated IDE parameters. You must to set CMOS to the translated parameters.

Most ESDI drives use an IBM standard type 1 CMOS setup. This corresponds to a standard 10MB drive. Upon power-up, the BIOS on the ESDI card overrides this drive type. Most SCSI controllers operate with CMOS set to 0 (no drive installed). Double check your controller manual for the correct CMOS setup value. Programs that use drive table overrides for MFM and RLL drives normally use the closest match in the ROM type table with an identical number of heads.

Hardware Conflicts

Hardware conflicts can occur if the controller card conflicts with the interrupt, DMA, I/O address or ROM address of other cards in the system. These conflicts are often difficult to debug. To be sure, check the manuals for ALL of the other boards installed in the system before jumpering the controller card.

Defect Locking

It's important to enter and lock the defect table on all MFM, RLL, and ESDI drives. If these defects are not entered, long term reliability will suffer. IDE and SCSI drives automatically lock out drive defects.

ISA Bus Extended Setup

Be sure to set the following extended setup parameters per your controller card manufacturer's recommendation:

BUS CLOCK SPEED
- Usually 8-12 MHz.
16-BIT BUS WAIT STATES
- Usually 1 or 2 wait states.
AT CLOCK STRETCH
- Usually enabled.

Improper extended setup settings may cause erratic controller operation.

Keep Optical Drives Clean and Cool

Optical drives must be kept clean, cool and dust free for reliable long term operation. If an optical drive is installed without a proper flow of cool, clean air, long term reliability will suffer. When internal optics become contaminated by dust, error rates rise significantly. When temperatures increase, M/O drives will not operate reliably. Most "clone" cases do not provide a proper environment for optical drives. Most optical drives work best installed in external enclosures with proper fans and filters. Clean fan filters regularly. Use cleaning disks regularly on CD-ROM drives. Purchase a cleaning kit for your erasable media.

SCSI Parity Jumpers

Most SCSI drives are shipped from the factory with parity enabled. PC applications sometimes require that parity be disabled by moving a jumper.

SCSI ID and Termination

95% or the problems we have seen with SCSI installations are due to improper ID settings and termination errors. Please read the section on SCSI cabling instructions and the termination and ID warnings before installing your SCSI peripherals. All SCSI installations require a total of two terminators - no more and no less. This includes the terminators that may be installed on the controller card or host adapter.

TROUBLESHOOTING

The following paragraphs list some of the more common problems encountered in drive installation. They are intended for quick troubleshooting reference. If you are receiving an unfamiliar error message, check the Common Error Messages listings later in this chapter.

Bus Mastering Compatibility

Bus Mastering cards usually have jumpers for DMA channels, hardware interrupt levels, and bus on/off time. Check these jumpers first when installing a bus mastering controller. As described in the installation section, each controller must have its own interrupt level and DMA channel. If you intend to use DOS programs like Windows '95 that use the protected mode of the 386/486/Pentium processor with a bus mastering card, you will need a software driver.

Even when they are correctly installed, bus mastering controllers sometimes experience motherboard hardware compatibility problems. If you have trouble getting a bus mastering controller to run with your motherboard, ask the controller manufacturer if your motherboard has been approved for compatibility.

CMOS Drive Type Tables

Matching CMOS tables for IDE Drives

If you are having problems installing a drive that is not listed in your CMOS drive type table, remember that the CMOS type does not need to exactly match the physical parameters of the drive. Modern IDE drives automatically 'translate' to match the physical parameters of the drive to match the logical parameters you select in CMOS. That's why there are two sets of parameters listed in the drive parameters section. Selecting any CMOS drive type that has an identical or lesser formatted capacity than the capacity of the drive will work. IDE translation modes are also used to bypass the DOS 1024 cylinder limitation (see the IDE installation section for more information). If you are installing a high capacity IDE drive in an older system that doesn't have any high capacity drives listed in the CMOS type table, programs like SpeedStor or Disk Manager can be used to override the CMOS table.

ESDI and SCSI Controller Drive Types

All PC SCSI controllers require that CMOS be set to NO DRIVES installed. The only exception to this rule is if an IDE, MFM, or ESDI drive is installed and coexists in the same system as the SCSI controller. If this is the case, set CMOS to the drive type used by the IDE, MFM, or ESDI drive only. Leave additional drive types set to "not installed". SCSI controllers interrogate the SCSI bus and add drive types when the system is first powered up.

Nearly all ESDI controllers require that CMOS be set to 'type 1'. These ESDI cards use an on board BIOS which automatically overrides the CMOS setting on power-up. The few ESDI controllers that don't use a BIOS ROM require that the CMOS type exactly match the physical parameters of the drive. These cards can only be used in systems that have a 'type 47' or user-definable CMOS table or in conjunction with a program like SpeedStor or DiskManager.

Compsurf Failure

Early versions of Novell Netware build the file server operating system during installation by linking a series of object files together to form the Netware 'kernel'. Most installation problems with Netware result from incorrectly installed drivers. The Netware installation process is detailed and complicated. Follow the installation instructions exactly to avoid link problems.

If you are running IDE drives with early versions of Netware, be sure to enable translation to keep the logical number of cylinders below 1024. Early versions of Novell will truncate any additional cylinders.

Watch for potential conflicts between interrupts. Most SCSI cards use IRQ14 or IRQ15, and several network cards use them as well. Under Novell, each card must have its own interrupt level. DOS does not require interrupts, and many SCSI cards do not provide them in the default configurations. If your SCSI controller works under DOS, but not Netware, check the interrupts.

In Netware 386, the drivers are composed of 'NLM's' or Netware Loadable Modules. NLM's are loaded after the file server is up and running. If a driver is not properly configured for Netware 386, the file server will often 'lock up' when the driver is loaded. If this happens, check the software installation and make sure the driver configuration matches your hardware.

DOS Partitioning

The 1024 cylinder barrier is the most common cause of DOS partitioning problems. Most versions of DOS only support 1024 cylinders. To keep the number of cylinders seen by DOS under 1024, do one of the following:

If you are using an IDE drive, enable translation and increase the number of heads of sectors per track to reduce the cylinder count.

If you are using an ESDI drive, enable the "63 sector" or "head mapping" mode to enable controller translation.

If you don't have translation available, the only way to access cylinders above 1024 is by making a boot partition within the first 1024 cylinders, and loading an extended partition driver from within the boot partition.

The 32 Megabyte partition barrier can also be a problem with old versions of DOS. Versions of MS-DOS earlier than 3.3 and Compaq DOS earlier than 3.21 lack the ability to access partitions larger than 32 megabytes. Upgrade to a later version of DOS if you encounter this.

DOS and Windows '95 2.0GB Limit

Yes, there is a partition size limit under DOS and indow '95W. It is 2048MB per partition. If this becomes an issue, consider a different operating system like Windows NT™ or OS/2's high performance file system. Although DOS could theoretically be made to work on larger drives, it's not a great idea. The efficiency of DOS and Windows '95 when storing small files on large drives is poor because the DOS cluster size increases as drive's capacity increases.

Drive Selects

Many manufacturers label the drive select jumpers on drives like this: 0,1,2,3. Others label the same select jumpers 1,2,3,4. The correct jumper depends on the position of the drive in the system, the type of cable you are using, and the way the jumpers are labeled. See the Installation section for more details.

Drive Won't Spin

This is frequently caused by reversed cables in SCSI and IDE installations. Check pin 1 orientation and don't forget to plug a system power cable into the drive! "No-spins" are also often caused by a power problem (see below).

ED Floppy Support

Most existing PC controllers do not yet support the new IBM standard 2.88MB floppy drives. Although many manufacturers advertise the floppy controller section of their boards as "supports 1MHz data rate", the new 2.88 drives use perpendicular recording that requires special write gate timing. Many controllers that support 1MHz data transfer rates only operate at the higher rate with "floppy tape" drives. If you are having problems with an ED drive with a "1MHz" floppy controller, consult the controller manufacturer to make sure the board you have is 2.88 compatible.

ESDI Sector Sparing

Many ESDI controllers offer optional "sector sparing". Sector sparing should be enabled if the drive has any significant number of defects or if the operating system you are using can not tolerate defects. Sector sparing reduces the formatted capacity of the drive slightly but increases the overall reliability significantly. When sector sparing is enabled, the controller can reallocate defects "on the fly". Use sector sparing when ever possible.

IDE Cabling

Since IDE cables carry data at full motherboard bus bandwidth, they must be kept as short as possible. Cables over 18" can cause problems in most installations. The shorter the better.

IDE Master/Slave

Unfortunately, not all IDE drives are created equally. Many IDE drives will not peacefully coexist in the Master/Slave configuration with drives from other manufacturers. See the hardware compatibility section for advice.

Incorrect Drive Parameters

If you are having problems with an IDE, EIDE, SCSI or ESDI drive installation, make sure that the CMOS settings exactly match your drive's physical or logical parameters. Some ESDI controllers reserve one cylinder of the drive for storing configuration information.

Interrupts and DMA Channels

Most controllers running under DOS do not require interrupts. All UNIX and Novell applications require controller interrupts for acceptable performance. If you suspect an interrupt or DMA channel conflict, check the hardware reference manuals for your installed hardware. The most common controller conflicts seem to be with network cards and scanner interface boards.

Long Boot Time

Most SCSI controllers must scan the bus and "interrogate" each SCSI device before booting. This process is long and tedious but occurs only on initial power-up or hardware reset. There is really no way around this with most controllers.

Long Format Time

Depending on the drive and system, a high level format may take up to 15 seconds per cylinder. When the drive steps between cylinders, an audible "click" can usually be heard. If the drive is stepping, be patient and wait for the format to complete. If you are attempting to format an MFM, RLL, or ESDI drive and the drive isn't stepping, check for a reversed 20 pin cable.

Multiple Drive Support Under DOS

Most controllers support only 2 hard drives under DOS. To support additional drives, a software driver is required. If a driver for more drives exists, it is normally only available from the controller manufacturer. An exception to this are CSC's AK-47 and FC-64 boards that support 7 SCSI and 4 floppy drives without any drivers.

No BIOS Sign-On Banner

This is one of the most common installation problems. Check to see that your controller card BIOS does not overlap the memory areas used by other cards. In particular, watch for VGA and network cards. If you still don't get a banner, check extended setup and make sure that the shadow RAM is disabled in the address range occupied by the controller BIOS.

Partition Can't Be Removed

If a drive is formatted with a 'non-dos' partition, FDISK will not delete it. The only solution is to erase the partition sector with a sector editor or low-level format. Older versions of DOS (i.e. 3.3) will not delete the larger partitions used by newer versions of DOS (i.e. 6.0). Later versions of DOS (i.e. DOS 6.0) will delete partitions created in earlier (i.e. DOS 3.3) versions of DOS. If a low level format is not in order, a program called "Zapdisk" is available from the CSC BBS at (408)541-8455 or www.corpsys.com to correct this. Zapdisk will remove all partition information without reformatting the entire drive.

Power Supply

Power supply problems frequently crop up in new drive installations. Most hard disk drives require 5 volts + 5% and 12 volts + 5% at the drive connector. The power supplied to the drive must be clean and well regulated. All modern hard drives include circuitry which monitors the power supply voltages and shuts down the write circuitry if the input power is too far out of range. Many drives won't even spin up if the power supply is too far off. If you suspect a power supply problem, check the voltages at the drive power supply connector while the drive spins up to speed and seeks.

SCSI Cabling

SCSI cables MUST be shielded for reliable operation. Many newer SCSI cables have individually twisted pairs for each signal line. If you can afford it, buy the better quality twisted pair variety. Avoid completely unshielded SCSI cables at any cost.

SCSI ID's

Each device installed on the SCSI bus must have a unique and separate ID number. Most SCSI controllers use ID #7, leaving the ID numbers between 0 and 6 available for disk drives. For reasons unknown, some PC based tape drive software requires ID#7. If you have multiple DASD drives installed, most PC controllers will scan and boot from the lowest SCSI ID number. Exceptions to this are the Adaptec 1540 series which only boots from ID#0 and the CSC FlashCache™64 which can be programmed to boot from any device.

SCSI Termination

A SCSI bus must be terminated at each physical end of the SCSI chain. Only two terminators per bus can be used. The devices at the physical ends of the cable must have terminators. All other devices on the SCSI chain (including the controller if it is not at the end of the chain) must have their terminators removed. If you are using external and internal SCSI devices on a PC controller, remove the terminators from the controller card.

Shadow RAM

System memory should not be used to shadow controllers that are memory mapped. Controllers twhich are I/O mapped (i.e. ESDI cards) should be shadowed. System ROM should always be shadowed for performance.

System Hangs On Power Up

The following are common installation errors which cause the system to hang on power up:

Improper BIOS base address (see above)

Interrupt conflicts (see above)

Bus compatibility jumper (try it both ways)

Reversed SCSI Cable (causes termination power short circuit)

Thermal Problems

Thermal problems are common in multiple hard drive installations and in situations where a hard or optical drive is not adequately cooled. Drives are mechanical devices and heat is their worst enemy. As temperatures increase in a drive, the motor and bearings are subject to increased wear. Always make sure a hard drive has a continuous flow of cooling air and adequate ventilation around it.

Twisted Data Cables

Twisted floppy and hard drive ribbon cables look suspiciously similar. Floppy cables have seven twisted conductors, and hard drive cables have five. Check the diagram in the previous chapter for a quick identification.

Won't Boot (DOS)

If your system has been formatted and won't boot DOS, check to see that the boot partition has been marked active in FDISK. Also make sure that the system (hidden) files have been correctly transferred and that COMMAND.COM is present and matches the version of the hidden files. If your system was booting correctly but suddenly stopped, scan the boot sector for a virus.

Won't Boot (ESDI)

For new ESDI installations, make sure that translation and sparing modes have been set correctly. Also make sure that the system (hidden) files have been correctly transferred and that COMMAND.COM is present and matches the version of the hidden files. If your system was booting correctly but suddenly stopped, scan the boot sector for a virus. Check FDISK and make sure the boot partition is marked active.

Won't Boot (IDE)

If you can use your IDE drive when booting from floppy but are unable to boot directly from the hard drive, check to see if your IDE drive requires "buffered interrupts". If it does, you may need to change a jumper on the controller card. Also make sure that the system (hidden) files have been correctly transferred and that COM-

MAND.COM is present and matches the version of the hidden files. If your system was booting correctly but suddenly stopped, scan the boot sector for a virus. Check FDISK and make sure the boot partition is marked active. Verify that the Master/Slave jumpers are correct. If your drive was booting on an older motherboard, but won't boot on a new one, check to see that the CMOS settings are identical.

Won't Boot (SCSI)

Check for unshielded cables and termination (described above). If you are using a hard drive that has a SCSI mode jumper, try it set both ways. Also make sure that the system (hidden) files have been correctly transferred and that COMMAND.COM is present and matches the version of the hidden files. If your system was booting correctly but suddenly stopped, scan the boot sector for a virus. Check FDISK and make sure the boot partition is marked active.

COMMON ERROR MESSAGES

1790/1791 Errors

1790 is the most common error message encountered in drive installations. A 1790 error will result when a controller has been installed, but the attached drive is not formatted. 1791 is the same message but refers to the second hard drive.

Attempting To Recover Allocation Unit XXX

This message appears in high level format when DOS detects a data verification error. If you are using an IDE or SCSI drive, you shouldn't see this message since the drive's embedded controller should mask out most errors before DOS is aware of them. If you see this message in an IDE or SCSI installation, check for a hardware installation problem. If you see this message in an ESDI installation, make sure the controller is able to read the drive's defect map, and be sure you have enabled sector sparing.

C: Drive Failure or Drive C: Error

This is a generic error message produced by the motherboard BIOS on power-up. It is usually caused by a "not-ready" error from the disk subsystem or an unformatted drive. Check cabling and master/slave jumpers on new installations.

Error Reading Fixed Disk

If you have successfully low-level formatted your drive and you encounter this message from FDISK, the system is unable to verify the partition sector. This is usually caused by a hardware problem, typically cabling or termination.

HDD Controller Failure

This message is usually caused by incorrect hardware installation. Check cabling, jumpers and termination. This message will appear if you install a SCSI controller without setting CMOS to "no drive installed". You will also get this message if you have an IDE drive set for slave operation and there is no master drive in the system.

Insert Disk For Drive C:

This message is caused by incorrect software driver installation. This can happen when DRIVER.SYS is used to add extended floppy drives and the command line switches are incorrect. It also appears when extended partition driver software is incorrectly installed.

Invalid Media Type

You have probably seen this message when formatting floppy disks of the wrong density. It is also generated on hard disks when newer versions of DOS utilities are used on older DOS partitions. For example, a DOS 6.0 CHKDSK of a DOS 3.2 disk causes it. Avoid mixing DOS versions.

No Fixed Disk Present

This message is produced by FDISK when it is unable to locate a drive through BIOS. Check hardware installation, particularly cabling, termination, and BIOS base address.

No Partitions Defined

This FDISK message is normal for a disk which has just been formatted. Be sure to set the bootable partition to "active" after creating it with FDISK.

No ROM Basic

The motherboard BIOS displays this message when it is unable to locate a boot device. In IDE or ESDI installations, this message is usually caused by an incorrect CMOS drive type setting. Most SCSI controllers require CMOS be set to "No drive Installed" or type 0. If this error appears in a SCSI isntallation, check cabling, termination, and the partition sector using FDISK. Most ESDI controllers require that CMOS be set to type 1 for each drive installed. If this message occurs in an ESDI installation, CMOS may be accidentally set to zero. Also make sure that the system (hidden) files have been correctly transferred and that COMMAND.COM is present and matches the version of the hidden files. If your system was booting correctly but suddenly stopped, scan the boot sector for a virus. Check FDISK and make sure the boot partition is marked active.

Non System Disk or Disk Error

Make sure that the system (hidden) files have been correctly transferred and that COMMAND.COM is present and matches the version of the hidden files. Check termination in SCSI installations.

No SCSI Devices Found

If no SCSI devices appear in the bus scan, check SCSI cabling, termination, and make sure that no two SCSI devices are sharing the same ID number. Make sure that no devices are using ID #7. ID#7 is generally reserved for the SCSI controller card.

Track 0 Bad, Disk Unusable

This fatal data error often indicates a bad drive, although it can also be caused by improper termination.

Unable to Access Fixed Disk

This FDISK message is caused by an error reported by BIOS during an attempt to read the drive. Check termination and cabling. When booting from floppy but are unable to boot directly from the hard drive, check to see if your IDE drive requires "buffered interrupts". If it does, you may need to change a jumper on the controller card.

UNIVERSAL IDE PARAMETERS

All newer IDE drives will accept any CMOS parameters that result in a total number of Logical Blocks (LBA's) that are equal to or less than the capacity of the drive. You can calculate any IDE drive's maximum LBA's by taking the total capacity of the drive and dividing it by 512. As long as the product of heads, cylinders, and sectors per track are less than the number LBA's, and within the range of the BIOS, your parameters will work. If you don't know what the manufacturers recommended parameters are, or if you don't have the time or inclination to calculate them, feel free to use the table below.

Note that the location of the DOS partition sector on a drive is determined by the sectors per track used to format the drive. If you are moving a drive from one system to another, you will need to match the number of sectors per track originally used to format the drive in order for DOS to recognize all the partitions on the drive.

FORMATTED CAPACITY	NUMBER OF HEADS	NUMBER OF CYLINDERS	NUMBER OF SECTORS/TRACK
10	4	306	17
15	4	430	17
20	4	614	17
30	4	862	17
40	6	766	17
42	6	804	17
60	8	862	17
80	10	919	17
84	10	965	17
100	16	718	17
105	16	754	17
120	16	862	17
170	16	329	63
200	16	388	63
210	16	407	63
213	16	413	63
240	16	465	63
252	16	488	63
300	16	581	63
320	16	620	63
330	16	639	63
340	16	659	63
380	16	736	63
400	16	775	63
420	16	814	63
450	16	872	63
528	16	1024	63
635	16	1234	63
810	16	1572	63
850	16	1652	63
1050	16	2045	63
1060	16	2064	63
1080	16	2097	63
1260	16	2448	63
1280	16	2484	63
1626	16	3158	63
2161	16	4095	63

HARD DRIVE LIST

L isted in the following chapter are many common hard drives and their parameters. The capacities listed are in formatted megabytes (1,000,000 bytes), with 512 bytes per sector. Formatted capacities may vary slightly depending on how the drive is formatted (i.e., using sector sparing or 35/36 sectors per track). As you would expect, all older MFM drives have 17 sectors per track, and all RLL drives that use the ST-506 interface have 26 sectors per track. ESDI drives have 35, 36, 48, or 63 sectors per track.

Access times listed are those published by the manufacturer. These advertised access times are often slightly lower than the average tested times. Drive information that was unavailable at the time of printing is entered as dashes (-).

Landing Zone

The landing zone, or "park cylinder" of a hard drive is a location to which the drive head carriage should be moved before the drive is transported. Older hard drives that use stepper motor actuators had to be manually parked before they were transported. This parking procedure moved the heads away from the data area of the disk and reduced the chance of data loss if the drive was bumped or jarred with the power off.

All newer hard disk drives with voice coil actuators incorporate automatic parking mechanisms. These mechanisms are as simple as a spring and a small latch that move and lock the heads away from the data areas of the disk when power is removed. Because the manual landing zone is no longer used in modern drives, we have omitted it from the tables. If you have an older stepper motor type drive which does require manual parking, step the heads to the maximum cylinder

+ 1 before removing power from the drive. For example, if you have a ST-225 which has 615 cylinders, step to the 616th cylinder before power down if you intend to transport the drive.

Write Precomp

Write precompensation is a technique that alters the timing of data written to a hard drive on particular cylinders. Since the track length of cylinders that are close to the center of the disk is shorter than the outer cylinders, the timing of data read changes.

To compensate for the difference in read data timing between inner and outer tracks, several drives use "write precompensation" that alters the timing of data written to inner cylinders on the drive. All newer drives automatically generate "write precompensation" using internal logic that senses the position of the head and adjusts the timing of write data accordingly. Older drives depend on the controller card to generate write precompensation. Since write precompensation is either handled internally or not used at all on newer hard drives the starting write precompensation cylinder is not as important as it once was. We have omitted write precomp information in the hard drive list to keep things simple. A valid write precompensation start cylinder for most older drives can be calculated by dividing the maximum cylinder number by two.

CDC, Imprimis or Seagate?

Control Data Corporation (CDC) was one of the first manufacturers of high performance 5.25" hard disk drives. CDC has over the years developed an excellent reputation for reliability. In 1987, Control Data Corporation named its disk drive division Imprimis. Recently, the CDC's Imprimis division was purchased by Seagate.

If you are trying to locate an Imprimis drive, please check both the Seagate and CDC sections.

Miniscribe or Maxtor Colorado?

Due to financial difficulties, Maxtor Corporation aquired Miniscribe in 1990. Miniscribe is now called Maxtor Colorado. Maxtor's management and expertise in high capacity drives has helped improve the Miniscribe product.

If you are trying to locate an older Maxtor Colorado drive, also check in the Miniscribe section.

CONVERTING IMPRIMIS TO SEAGATE NUMBERS					
IMPRIS	SEAGATE	IMPRIMIS	SEAGATE	IMPRIS	SEAGATE
94155-85	ST4085	94205-51	ST253	94351-00S	ST1201NS
94155-86	ST4086	94205-77	ST279R	94351-230S	ST1239NS
94155-96	ST4097	94211-106	ST2106N	94354-090	ST1090A
94155-135	ST4135R	94216-106	ST2106E	94354-111	ST1111A
94161-182	ST4182N	94221-125	ST2125N	94354-126	ST1126A
94166-182	ST4182E	94241-502	ST2502N	94354-133	ST1133A
94171-350	ST4350N	94244-274	ST2074A	94354-155	ST1156A
94171-376	ST4376N	94244-383	ST2383A	94354-160	ST1162A
94181-385H	ST4385N	94246-182	ST2182E	94354-186	ST1186A
94181-702	ST4702N	94246-383	ST2383E	94354-200	ST1201A
94186-383	ST43836E	94351-090	ST1090N	94354-239	ST1239A
94186-383H	ST4384E	94351-111	ST1111N	94355-100	ST1100
94186-442	ST4442E	94351-126	ST1126N	94355-150	ST1150R
94191-766	ST4766N	94351-133S	ST1133NS	94356-155	ST1156E
94196-766	ST4766E	94351-155	ST1156N	94356-200	ST1201E
94204-65	ST274A	94351-155S	ST1156NS	94536-111	ST1111E
94204-71	ST280A	94351-160	ST1162N	94601-12G/M	ST41200N
94204-74	ST274A	94351-186S	ST1186NS	94601-767H	ST4767N
94204-81	ST280A	94351-200	ST1201N		

FINE TUNING

This section contains a few hints on how to get the most out of your hard disk subsystem. There are several ways of measuring disk performance. In the PC world, the most common utility program for comparing hard disks is CORETEST from Core International. Running CORETEST on your drive yields a crude performance rating based on the average seek time and data transfer rate of the drive reported by the system BIOS.

CORETEST is included on the HDB companion CD-ROM.

If you do not specify any command line options when running CORETEST, the program defaults to a block size of 64KB. The performance rating you get based on a 64K block size is only part of the picture. Many common operating systems (including DOS) often transfer data in blocks smaller than 64KB. To get an idea of how your system performs with these smaller block sizes, use the command CORETEST/B:xx where xx is the size of the block you would like to test. Making a graph of the performance ratings you get for different block sizes gives a more complete picture.

CSC Test

HOT TIP

CSC offers its own performance test program called CSCTEST that is supplied on the CD-ROM that is enclosed with the Hard Drive Bible. Since this program is larger than will fit on the disk in uncompressed format, it is supplied in a self extracting compressed archive format. To uncompress it, first change to the directory on your hard drive where you would like to install the test program. Once you are in that directory, type A:CSCTEST, and the program will automatically unpack and transfer itself to your hard disk. To view the results, you will need an EGA, VGA, or Hercules compatible monitor.

CSCTEST gives an evaluation of system performance by accurately measuring the number of seeks per second and 512 byte blocks transferred per second. These ratings are combined to give an overall performance rating. This rating can then be compared with the rankings of other popular systems.

There are several ways of increasing your system performance by optimizing software setups and not changing hardware.

The two most important steps to a tuneup are optimizing interleave and defragmenting files. The optimum interleave for your hard disk system is a function of both the hardware and software in your system. Contrary to popular opinion, 1:1 is not the optimum interleave for ALL applications. If the controller you are using does not feature a full track read-ahead cache (most older MFM, RLL, and some imbedded controllers don't), selecting the optimum interleave will make a significant difference in data transfer rate.

After extensive testing, we have come up with the following rules-of-thumb regarding interleaves for older MFM and RLL controllers:

Use 4:1 Sector Interleave With:
Older 4.77MHz XT class machines.

Use 3:1 Sector Interleave With:
Older XT class machines with DOS applications.
Older 6MHz and 8MHz AT class machines running DOS.

Use 2:1 Sector Interleave With:
Older 10MHz to 16MHz 286/386 machines running DOS.

Use 1:1 Sector Interleave With:
All 20MHz or faster 386 machines running Netware.
All 20MHz or faster 386 machines running DOS.
All newer 486 and Pentium machines.

It's interesting to note that a 20MHz 386 machine running DOS can operate faster with a 2:1 interleave controller than a 1:1. This is because many DOS applications can't operate fast enough to take advantage of the 1:1 interleave. By the time the DOS application requests the next sequential sector of disk data, the 1:1 formatted disk has already spun past that sector, and DOS must wait for the disk to spin another revolution. Fortunately, if you are building up a new system with a clock speed of 20MHz or faster, the choice is clear. Most modern clone boards with 8MHz I/O channels and fast CPU's work best with 1:1 interleave. If you are tuning up an older system with a clock speed of 20MHz or less, 2:1 interleave may be the optimum choice.

There is really only one way of exactly determining the actual optimum interleave for your system. Test it. Popular programs like OPTUNE or SPINRITE let you determine the optimum interleave based on hardware considerations only. Unfortunately, these programs do not take into account the software overhead that DOS and other operating systems create. Format the drive with an interleave value one sector larger than suggested by SPINRITE or OPTUNE. Then load your applications and make your own performance tests. Record the results and then reformat with the interleave recommended by the test program. If performance increases, you have chosen the optimum interleave. If not, the software overhead of your applications is causing the system to operate better at the higher interleave.

Defragmenting files is the next step in increasing system performance. As a disk is used over time, files become fragmented. The simplest way to defragment files is with a program like Central Point Software's COMPRESS. Alternately, the files can be copied to another drive and then restored. Defragmenting files will significantly increase your system performance.

Buffers and FASTOPEN

Appropriate use of the DOS Buffers and FASTOPEN commands will also improve system throughput.

The DOS Buffers command allocates a fixed amount of memory that DOS uses to cache data while reading and writing. As many buffers as possible should be installed in your CONFIG.SYS file. Each buffer will take a total of 548 bytes of memory (512 bytes for data and 36 for pointers). If you have extended memory available, use the /X option to store buffers in extended RAM and keep your basc 640k free and clear. If you are using a caching controller, set the DOS Buffers command as low as possible for best performance.

The DOS FASTOPEN program tracks the locations of files on a disk for fast access. Access to files in a complex directory structure can be time consuming. If you run applications that use several files (such as dBASE, Paradox, or other database programs), FASTOPEN records the name and physical location on the drive. When the file is reopened, access time is significantly reduced. If you are using disk intensive programs without FASTOPEN, your disk performance is suffering.

One of the nicest features of FASTOPEN is its ability to use extended memory. For example adding the line FASTOPEN C:100,10/X to your AUTOEXEC.BAT file would automatically make FASTOPEN load using extended memory to track up to 100 files with a 10 entry extent cache. Unfortunately, once FASTOPEN is loaded, its setup cannot be changed. To change FASTOPEN settings, reboot the computer. FASTOPEN is not needed under Windows '95.

Cache Programs

Caching programs such as DOS SMARTDRV.SYS dramatically improve disk system performance. Another benefit of using a good caching program is extended drive life. Drive life is based not only on the number of power on hours (POH), but also on the number of seek operations. Adding even a small RAM cache will prolong drive life significantly by reducing the number of seeks necessary. If you are using DOS 5.0 or later, we recommend you try the SMARTDRV.SYS program included with DOS. It offers good performance, particularly with expanded memory. You can improve drive performance dramatically without buying extra software by adding SMARTDRV to your CONFIG.SYS file.

 **HOT TIP**

For a few dollars more, many excellent third-party caching programs are available that offer improved performance over SMARTDRV. Two of the best cache programs we have found are PC-Cache from Central Point Software and Speed Cache from Storage Dimensions. Both of these programs enable disk caching using extended or expanded system memory. If you purchased IBM DOS 6.1 or later, you received PC-Cache and a defragmenting program free with DOS - smart buy. PC-Cache has an adjustable read-ahead feature which improves sequential access on large files.

If you are running Unix, Database programs, or other extremely disk intensive programs, the ultimate solution (if you can afford it) is a caching controller card. A caching controller can provide reduced data access times, improve throughputs, and improve your hard drive's life span. A quick Windows performance boost can be had by moving the swap file. If this swap file is located near frequently used data, performance will be increased. If the swap file is moved to a separate drive, performance is even better. For DOS and Microsoft Windows users, a caching controller frees system memory for applications. Due to the large number of requests for an inexpensive, high performance caching controllers, CSC has designed the CSC FastCache™ 64 ISA SCSI controller. We are now designing both caching and non caching VESA VL-Bus and PCMCIA versions. A number of other Fast SCSI caching and non-caching controllers are available, and if disk I/O is a bottleneck, they are all worth considering.

To sum up the fine tuning of your DOS hard drive, perform the following five steps for better disk performance:

1. Find the optimum interleave (Reformat if necessary).

2. Compress and defragment.

3. Set buffers correctly.

4. Install FASTOPEN.

5. Use SMARTDRV, PC-CACHE, or another cache program if you do not have a caching controller.

6. Move swap files to a physical area near data files, or to another drive.

HOT TIP

HARD DRIVE PARAMETERS

MODEL NUMBER	FORMATTED CAPACITY	NO. OF HEADS	NO. OF CYLINDERS	SECTORS PER TRACK	AVERAGE IN MS	INTERFACE	FORM FACTOR	CMOS SETTINGS
ALPS AMERICA								
DRND-10A	10	2	615	17	60	MFM	3.5 x 1"	
DRND-20A	20	4	615	17	60	MFM	3.5 x 1"	
DRPO-20D	20	2	615	26	60	MFM	3.5 x 1"	
DR311C	106	2	2109	63	13	IDE	3.5"	13x954x63
DR311D	106	2	2109	63	13	SCSI	3.5"	
DR312C	212	4	2109	63	13	IDE	3.5"	13x965x33
DR312D	212	4	2109	63	13	SCSI	3.5"	
RPO-20A	20	2	615	26	60	RLL	3.5 x 1"	
AMPEX								
PYXIS-7	5	2	320	17	90	MFM	5.25" FH	
PYXIS-13	10	4	320	17	90	MFM	5.25" FH	
PYSIX-20	15	6	320	17	90	MFM	5.25" FH	
PYXIS-27	20	8	320	17	90	MFM	5.25" FH	
AREAL TECHNOLOGY								
A 120	136	4	1024	60	15	IDE	2.5"	8x548x61
A 180	81	4	1488	60	15	IDE	2.5"	10x715x50
MD-2060	62	2	1024	60	19	IDE	2.5"	2x1024x60
ND-2080	80	2	1323	60	19	IDE	2.5"	9x1021x17
2085	85	2	1410	59	19	IDE	2.5"	10x976x17
2100	100	2	1632	63	19	IDE	2.5"	12x957x17
ATASI TECHNOLOGY, INC.								
AT-676	765	15	1632	54	16	ESDI	5.25" FH	
AT-3020	17	3	645	17	38	MFM	5.25" FH	
AT-3033	28	5	645	17	33	MFM	5.25" FH	
AT-3046	39	7	645	17	33	MFM	5.25" FH	

MODEL NUMBER	FORMATTED CAPACITY	NO. OF HEADS	NO. OF CYLINDERS	SECTORS PER TRACK	AVERAGE IN MS	INTERFACE	FORM FACTOR	CMOS SETTINGS
AT-3051	43	7	704	17	33	MFM	5.25" FH	
AT-3051+	44	7	733	17	33	MFM	5.25" FH	
AT-3075	44	7	733	17	33	MFM	5.25" FH	
AT-3075	67	8	1024	17	33	MFM	5.25" FH	
AT-3085	71	8	1024	26	28	RLL	5.25" FH	
AT-3128	109	8	1024	26	28	RLL	5.25" FH	
AT-6120	1051	15	1925	71	13	ESDI	5.25" FH	

AURA ASSOCIATES

AU63	63	2	1330	43	17	PCMCIA	1.8"	
AU126	125	4	1330	43	17	PCMCIA	1.8"	

BASF

6185	23	6	440	17	99	MFM	5.25" FH	
6186	15	4	440	17	70	MFM	5.25" FH	
6187	8	2	440	17	70	MFM	5.25" FH	
6188-R1	10	2	612	17	70	MFM	5.25" FH	
6188-R3	21	4	612	17	70	MFM	5.25" FH	

BRAND TECHNOLOGIES

BT 3400	400	6	1800	72	12	IDE/SCSI	3.5 x 1"	15x1021x51
BT 3650	650	10	1800	36	12	IDE/SCSI	3.5 x 1"	16x1017x78
BT 8085	71	8	1024	17	25	MFM	5.25" FH	
BT 8128	109	8	1024	26	25	RLL	5.25" FH	
BT 8170	142	8	1024	36	36	ESDI	5.25" FH	
BT 9170A	150	7	1165	36	16	IDE	3.5 x 1"	9x968x33
BT 9170E	150	7	1166	36	16	ESDI	3.5 x 1"	
BT 9170S	150	7	1166	36	16	SCSI	3.5 x 1"	
BT 9220A	200	9	1209	36	16	IDE	3.5 x 1"	12x968x33
BT 9220E	200	9	1210	36	16	ESDI	3.5 x 1"	
BT 9220S	200	9	1210	36	16	SCSI	3.5 x 1"	

BULL

D-530	25	3	987	17	65	MFM	5.25" FH	
D-550	43	5	987	17	65	MFM	5.25" FH	
D-570	60	7	987	17	65	MFM	5.25" FH	
D-585	71	7	1166	17	65	MFM/RLL	5.25" FH	

C. ITOH ELECTRONICS (also see Ye-Data)

YD-3042	44	4	788	26	26	RLL	5.25" FH	
YD-3082	87	8	788	26	26	RLL	5.25" FH	

MODEL NUMBER	FORMATTED CAPACITY	NO. OF HEADS	NO. OF CYLINDERS	SECTORS PER TRACK	AVERAGE IN MS	INTERFACE	FORM FACTOR	CMOS SETTINGS
YD-3530	32	5	731	17	26	MFM	5.25" FH	
YD-3540	45	7	731	17	26	MFM	5.25" FH	

CARDIFF

MODEL NUMBER	FORMATTED CAPACITY	NO. OF HEADS	NO. OF CYLINDERS	SECTORS PER TRACK	AVERAGE IN MS	INTERFACE	FORM FACTOR	CMOS SETTINGS
F-3053	44	5	1024	17	20	MFM	3.5 x 1"	
F-3080E	68	5	1024	26	20	ESDI	3.5 x 1"	
F-3080S	68	5	1024	26	20	SCSI	3.5 x 1"	
F-3127E	109	5	1024	35	20	ESDI	3.5 x 1"	
F-3127S	109	5	1024	35	20	SCSI	3.5 x 1"	

CDC (see also Seagate)

MODEL NUMBER	FORMATTED CAPACITY	NO. OF HEADS	NO. OF CYLINDERS	SECTORS PER TRACK	AVERAGE IN MS	INTERFACE	FORM FACTOR	CMOS SETTINGS
94155-19	18	3	697	17	28	MFM	5.25" FH	
94155-21	21	3	697	17	28	MFM	5.25" FH	
94155-25 Wren I	24	4	697	17	28	MFM	5.25" FH	
94155-28	24	4	697	17	28	MFM	5.25" FH	
94155-36 Wren I	36	5	697	17	28	MFM	5.25" FH	
94155-38	31	5	733	17	28	MFM	5.25" FH	
94155-48 Wren II	40	5	925	17	28	MFM	5.25" FH	
94155-51 Wren II	43	5	989	17	28	MFM	5.25" FH	
94155-57 Wren II	48	6	926	17	28	MFM	5.25" FH	
94155-67 Wren II	56	7	926	17	28	MFM	5.25" FH	
94155-77 Wren II	64	8	926	17	28	MFM	5.25" FH	
94155-85 Wren II	71	8	1024	17	28	MFM	5.25" FH	
94155-86 Wren II	72	9	925	17	28	MFM	5.25" FH	
94155-96 Wren II	80	9	1024	17	28	MFM	5.25" FH	
94155-120 Wren II	102	8	960	26	28	RLL	5.25" FH	
94155-135 Wren II	115	9	960	26	28	RLL	5.25" FH	
94156-48 Wren II	40	5	925	17	28	ESDI	5.25" FH	
94156-67 Wren II	56	7	925	17	28	ESDI	5.25" FH	
94161-86 Wren II	72	9	925	17	28	ESDI	5.25" FH	
94161-86 Wren III	86	9	969	26	17	SCSI	5.25" FH	
94161-101 Wren III	86	9	969	26	16	SCSI	5.25" FH	
94161-121 Wren III	120	7	969	26	17	SCSI	5.25" FH	
94161-141 Wren III	140	7	969	26	16	SCSI	5.25" FH	
94161-155	150	9	969	36	16	SCSI	5.25" FH	
94161-182 Wren III	155	9	969	36	16	SCSI	5.25" FH	
94166-101 Wren III	84	5	969	34	18	ESDI	5.25" FH	
94166-141 Wren III	118	7	969	34	18	ESDI	5.25" FH	
94166-182 Wren III	152	9	969	34	16	ESDI	5.25" FH	
94171-300	288	9	1365	36	18	SCSI	5.25" FH	
94171-344	335	9	1549	36	18	SCSI	5.25" FH	

MODEL NUMBER	FORMATTED CAPACITY	NO. OF HEADS	NO. OF CYLINDERS	SECTORS PER TRACK	AVERAGE IN MS	INTERFACE	FORM FACTOR	CMOS SETTINGS
94171-350 Wren IV	300	9	1412	46	17	SCSI	5.25" FH	
94171-375 Wren IV	375	9	1549	35	16	SCSI	5.25" FH	
94171-376 Wren IV	330	9	1546	45	18	SCSI	5.25" FH	
94181-385D	337	15	791	36	11	SCSI	5.25" FH	
94181-385H	330	15	791	55	11	SCSI	5.25" FH	
94181-574 Wren V	574	15	1549	36	16	SCSI	5.25" FH	
94181-702 Wren V	601	15	1546	54	16	SCSI	5.25" FH	
94181-702M Wren V	613	15	1549	54	16	SCSI	5.25" FH	
94186-265 Wren V	221	9	1412	34	18	ESDI	5.25" FH	
94186-324 Wren V	270	11	1412	34	18	ESDI	5.25" FH	
94186-383 Wren V	319	13	1412	34	18	ESDI	5.25" FH	
94186-383H	319	15	1224	34	15	ESDI	5.25" FH	
94186-383S Wren V	338	13	1412	34	19	ESDI	5.25" FH	
94186-442 Wren V	368	15	1412	34	16	ESDI	5.25" FH	
94186-442H Wren V	368	15	1412	34	16	ESDI	5.25" FH	
94191-766 Wren VI	676	15	1632	54	16	SCSI	5.25" FH	
94191-766M	676	15	1632	54	16	SCSI	5.25" FH	
94196-383 Wren VI	338	13	1412	34	16	ESDI	5.25" FH	
94196-766 Wren VI	664	15	1632	54	16	ESDI	5.25" FH	
94204-65	65	5	948	26	29	IDE	5.25" HH	
94204-71	71	5	1032	26	29	IDE	5.25" HH	5x989x27
94204-74 Wren II	71	5	948	26	29	IDE	5.25" HH	8x933x17
94204-81 Wren II	71	5	1032	26	28	IDE	5.25" HH	8x1024x27
94205-30 Wren II	25	3	989	26	28	RLL	5.25" HH	
94205-41 Wren II	38	3	989	26	28	RLL	5.25" HH	
94205-51 Wren II	43	5	989	26	28	RLL	5.25" HH	
94205-77	65	5	989	26	28	RLL	5.25" HH	
94205-75 Wren II	60	5	989	26	30	IDE	5.25" HH	5x989x26
94211-91 Wren II	91	5	969	36	16	SCSI	5.25" FH	
94211-106 Wren III	91	5	1022	26	18	SCSI	5.25" FH	
94211-209 Wren V	142	5	1547	36	18	SCSI	5.25" FH	
94216-106 Wren III	89	5	1024	34	18	ESDI	5.25" HH	
94221-125 Wren V	107	3	1544	36	18	SCSI	5.25" HH	
94221-190 Wren V	190	5	1547	36	18	SCSI	5.25" HH	
94221-209 Wren V	183	5	1544	36	18	SCSI	5.25" HH	
94241-383 Wren VI	338	7	1261	36	14	SCSI	5.25" HH	
94241-502 Wren VI	435	7	1755	69	16	SCSI	5.25" HH	
94244-219	191	4	1747	54	16	IDE	5.25" HH	16x536x44
94244-274 Wren VI	191	4	1747	54	16	IDE	5.25" HH	14x983x33
94244-383 Wren VI	338	7	1747	54	16	IDE	5.25" HH	11x952x63
94246-182 Wren VI	160	4	1453	54	15	ESDI	5.25" HH	

MODEL NUMBER	FORMATTED CAPACITY	NO. OF HEADS	NO. OF CYLINDERS	SECTORS PER TRACK	AVERAGE IN MS	INTERFACE	FORM FACTOR	CMOS SETTINGS
94246-383 Wren VI	338	7	1747	54	15	ESDI	5.25" HH	
94295-51	43	5	989	17	28	MFM	5.25" FH	
94311-136S	120	5	1068	36	15	SCSI-2	3.5" 3H	
94314-136	120	5	1068	36	15	IDE	3.5" 3H	11x917x17
94316-111 Swift	98	5	1072	36	23	ESDI	3.5 x1"	
94316-136	120	5	1268	36	15	ESDI	3.5 x 1"	
94316-155	138	7	1072	36	15	ESDI	3.5 x 1"	
94316-200 Swift	177	9	1072	36	15	ESDI	3.5 x 1"	
94335-55	46	5	1268	17	25	MFM	3.5 x 1"	
94335-100	83	9	1268	17	25	MFM	3.5 x 1"	
94351-90	79	5	1068	29	15	SCSI	3.5 x 1"	
94351-111	98	5	1068	36	15	SCSI	3.5 x 1"	
94351-126	111	7	1068	29	15	SCSI	3.5 x 1"	
94351-128	111	7	1068	36	15	SCSI	3.5 x 1"	
94351-133 Swift	116	7	1268	36	15	SCSI	3.5 x 1"	
94351-133S Swift	116	5	1268	36	15	SCSI-2	3.5 x 1"	
94351-134	117	7	1068	36	15	SCSI	3.5 x 1"	
94351-155 Swift	138	7	1068	36	15	SCSI	3.5 x 1"	
94351-155S Swift	138	7	1068	36	15	SCSI-2	3.5 x 1"	
94351-160 Swift	142	9	1068	29	15	SCSI	3.5 x 1"	
94351-172	150	9	1068	36	15	SCSI	3.5 x 1"	
94351-186S	163	7	1268	36	15	SCSI-2	3.5 x 1"	
94351-200	177	9	1068	36	15	SCSI	3.5 x 1"	
94351-200S	177	9	1068	36	15	SCSI-2	3.5 x 1"	
94351-230 Swift	210	9	1272	36	15	SCSI	3.5 x 1"	
94351-230S Swift	210	9	1268	36	15	SCSI-2	3.5 x 1"	
94354-90 Swift	79	5	1072	29	15	IDE	3.5 x 1"	10x536x29
94354-111 Swift	98	5	1072	36	15	IDE	3.5 x 1"	10x1024x17
94354-126 Swift	111	7	1072	29	15	IDE	3.5 x 1"	13x984x17
94354-133 Swift	117	5	1272	36	15	IDE	3.5 x 1"	14x961x17
94354-155 Swift	138	7	1072	36	15	IDE	3.5 x 1"	16x993x17
94354-160 Swift	143	9	1072	29	15	IDE	3.5 x 1"	9x942x33
94354-186 Swift	164	7	1272	36	15	IDE	3.5 x 1"	10x971x33
94354-200 Swift	177	9	1072	36	15	IDE	3.5 x 1"	11x956x33
94354-230 Swift	211	9	1272	36	15	IDE	3.5 x 1"	12x989x3
94355-55 Swift	46	5	1072	17	16	MFM	3.5 x 1"	
94355-100 Swift	83	9	1072	17	15	MFM	3.5 x 1"	
94355-150 Swift	128	9	1072	25	15	RLL	3.5 x 1"	
94356-111 Swift	98	5	1072	36	15	ESDI	3.5 x 1"	
94356-155 Swift	138	7	1072	36	15	ESDI	3.5 x 1"	
94356-200 Swift	171	9	1072	36	15	ESDI	3.5 x 1"	

MODEL NUMBER	FORMATTED CAPACITY	NO. OF HEADS	NO. OF CYLINDERS	SECTORS PER TRACK	AVERAGE IN MS	INTERFACE	FORM FACTOR	CMOS SETTINGS
94601-12G/M	1037	15	1931	VAR	15	SCSI	5.25" FH	
94601-767H	665	15	1356	64	12	SCSI-2	5.25" FH	
94601-767M	676	15	1508	54	12	SCSI	5.25" FH	
97155-36	30	5	733	17	28	MFM	8"	
9720-1123 SABRE	964	19	1610	VAR	15	SMD	8"	
9720-1230 SABRE	1236	15	1635	VAR	15	SMD/SCSI	8"	
9720-2270 SABRE	1948	19	2551	VAR	12	SMD	8"	
9720-2500 SABRE	2145	19	2220	VAR	12	SMD	8"	
9720-368 SABRE	368	10	1635	VAR	18	SMD/SCSI	8"	
9720-500 SABRE	500	10	1217	VAR	18	SMD/SCSI	8"	
9720-736 SABRE	741	15	1217	VAR	15	SMD/SCSI	8"	
9720-850 SABRE	851	15	1635	VAR	15	SMD/SCSI	8"	
97229-1150	990	19	1784	VAR	15	IPI-2	8"	
97500-12G	1050	17	1884	VAR	15	IPI-2	5.25" FH	
97500-15G Elite	1285	17	1991	VAR	16	SCSI-2	5.25" FH	
BJ7D5A /77731608	29	5	670	17	28	MFM	5.25" FH	
BJ7D5A/77731613	33	5	733	17	28	MFM	5.25" FH	
BJ7D5A/77731614	23	4	670	17	28	MFM	5.25" FH	

CENTURY DATA

MODEL NUMBER	FORMATTED CAPACITY	NO. OF HEADS	NO. OF CYLINDERS	SECTORS PER TRACK	AVERAGE IN MS	INTERFACE	FORM FACTOR	CMOS SETTINGS
CAST 10203E	55	3	1050	35	28	ESDI	5.25" FH	
CAST 10203S	55	3	1050	35	28	SCSI	5.25" FH	
CAST 10304E	75	4	1050	35	28	ESDI	5.25" FH	
CAST 10304S	75	4	1050	35	28	SCSI	5.25" FH	
CAST 10305E	94	5	1050	35	28	ESDI	5.25" FH	
CAST 10305S	94	5	1050	35	28	SCSI	5.25" FH	
CAST 14404E	114	4	1590	35	25	ESDI	5.25" FH	
CAST 14404S	114	4	1590	35	25	SCSI	5.25" FH	
CAST 14405E	140	5	1590	35	25	ESDI	5.25" FH	
CAST 14405S	140	5	1590	35	25	SCSI	5.25" FH	
CAST 14406E	170	6	1590	35	25	ESDI	5.25" FH	
CAST 14406S	170	6	1590	35	25	SCSI	5.25" FH	
CAST 24509E	258	9	1599	35	18	ESDI	5.25" FH	
CAST 24509S	258	9	1599	35	18	SCSI	5.25" FH	
CAST 24611E	315	11	1599	35	18	ESDI	5.25" FH	
CAST 24611S	315	11	1599	35	18	SCSI	5.25" FH	
CAST 24713E	372	13	1599	35	18	ESDI	5.25" FH	
CAST 24713S	372	13	1599	35	18	SCSI	5.25" FH	

CMI

MODEL NUMBER	FORMATTED CAPACITY	NO. OF HEADS	NO. OF CYLINDERS	SECTORS PER TRACK	AVERAGE IN MS	INTERFACE	FORM FACTOR	CMOS SETTINGS
CM 3206	10	4	306	17	99	MFM	5.25" FH	

MODEL NUMBER	FORMATTED CAPACITY	NO. OF HEADS	NO. OF CYLINDERS	SECTORS PER TRACK	AVERAGE IN MS	INTERFACE	FORM FACTOR	CMOS SETTINGS
CM 3426	20	4	615	17	85	MFM	5.25" FH	
CM 5018H	4	2	256	17	105	MFM	5.25" FH	
CM 5206	5	2	306	17	99	MFM	5.25" FH	
CM 5410	8	4	256	17	105	MFM	5.25" FH	
CM 5412	10	4	306	17	99	MFM	5.25" FH	
CM 5616	13	6	256	17	105	MFM	5.25" FH	
CM 5619	15	6	306	17	105	MFM	5.25" FH	
CN 5826	21	8	306	17	99	MFM	5.25" FH	
CM 6213	11	2	640	17	105	MFM	5.25" FH	
CM 6426	21	4	615	17	40	MFM	5.25" FH	
CM 6426S	22	4	640	17	40	MFM	5.25" FH	
CM 6640	33	6	640	17	40	MFM	5.25" FH	
CM 7660	50	6	960	17	40	MFM	5.25" FH	
CM 7880	67	8	960	17	40	MFM	5.25" FH	

CMS ENHANCEMENTS, INC.

F115ESDI-T	114	7	915	35	30	ESDI	5.25" FH	
F150AT-CA	150	9	969	34	17	IDE	5.25" FH	9x986x33
F150AT-WCA	150	7	1224	36	17	IDE	5.25" FH	9x986x33
F150EQ-WCA	150	7	1224	36	17	ESDI	5.25" FH	
F320AT-CA	320	15	1224	36	15	ESDI	5.25" FH	
F70ESDI-T	73	2	1224	36	30	ESDI	5.25" FH	
H330E1	330	7	1780	54	14	ESDI	5.25" FH	
H340E1	340	7	1780	54	14	ESDI	5.25" FH	
PS Express/150	150	7	1224	36	17	ESDI	5.25" FH	
PS Express/320	320	15	1224	36	15	ESDI	5.25" FH	

COGITO

CG-906	5	2	306	17	85	MFM	5.25" FH	
CG-912	11	4	306	17	65	MFM	5.25" FH	
CG-925	21	4	612	17	65	MFM	5.25" FH	
PT-912	11	2	612	17	40	MFM	5.25" FH	
PT-925	21	4	612	17	40	MFM	5.25" FH	

COMPORT

2040	44	4	820	26	35	MFM	5.25" HH	
2041	44	4	820	26	29	IDE	5.25" HH	
2082	86	6	820	34	29	SCSI	5.25" HH	

CONNER PERIPHERALS, INC.

CP-340	42	4	788	26	29	SCSI	3.5 x 1"	

MODEL NUMBER	FORMATTED CAPACITY	NO. OF HEADS	NO. OF CYLINDERS	SECTORS PER TRACK	AVERAGE IN MS	INTERFACE	FORM FACTOR	CMOS SETTINGS
CP-342	40	4	805	26	29	IDE	3.5 x 1"	4x805x26
CP-344	43	4	788	26	29	IDE	3.5 x 1"	4x788x26
CP-2020	21	2	642	32	23	SCSI	3.5 x 1"	
CP-2024 KATO	21	2	653	32	40	IDE	2.5 HH	2x653x32
CP-2034 PANCHO	32	2	823	38	119	IDE	2.5 HH	2x823x38
CP-2064 PANCHO	64	4	823	38	19	IDE	2.5 HH	4x823x38
CP-2084 PANCHO	85	8	548	38	19	IDE	2.5 HH	8x548x38
CP-2304	215	8	1348	39	19	IDE	3.5 x 1"	12x989x35
CP-3000	43	5	976	17	27	IDE	3.5 x 1"	5x988x17
CP-3020	21	2	622	33	27	SCSI	3.5 x 1"	
CP-3022	21	2	622	33	27	IDE	3.5 x 1"	2x622x33
CP-3024	22	2	636	33	27	IDE	3.5 x 1"	2x636x33
CP-3040	42	2	1026	40	25	SCSI	3.5 x 1"	
CP-3044	43	2	1047	40	25	IDE	3.5 x 1"	5x988x17
CP-3100	105	8	776	33	25	SCSI	3.5 x 1"	
CP-3102	104	8	776	33	25	IDE	3.5 x 1"	8x776x33
CP-3104	105	8	776	33	25	IDE	3.5 x 1"	8x776x33
CP-3111	112	8	832	33	25	IDE	3.5 x 1"	8x832x33
CP-3114	112	8	832	33	25	IDE	3.5 x 1"	8x832x33
CP-3180	84	6	832	33	25	SCSI	3.5 x 1"	
CP-3184	84	6	832	33	25	IDE	3.5 x 1"	6x832x33
CP-3200F	213	8	1366	38	19/16	SCSI	3.5 x 1"	
CP-3204F	213	16	683	38	19/16	IDE	3.5 x 1"	6x683x33
CP-3209F	213	4	1366	38	16	MCA	3.5 x 1"	6x683x38
CP-3304	340	8	1806	46	16	IDE	3.5 x 1"	16x659x63
CP-3360	360	8	1806	49	12	SCSI-2	3.5 x 1"	
CP-3364	360	8	1806	6349	12	IDE	3.5 x 1"	11x702x63
CP-3500	510	12	1695	49	12	SCSI	3.5 x 1"	
CP-3504	509	12	1695	49	12	IDE	3.5 x 1"	16x987x63
CP-3540	540	12	1806	49	12	SCSI-2	3.5 x 1"	
CP-3544	540	12	1806	49	12	IDE	3.5 x 1"	16x987x38
CP-4024 STUBBY	22	2	627	34	29	IDE	3.5 x 1"	
CP-4044 STUBBY	43	2	1104	38	29	IDE	3.5 x 1"	7x699x17
CP-30060	60	2	1524	39	19	SCSI	3.5 x 1"	
CP-30064	61	2	1522	39	-	IDE	3.5 x 1"	4x762x39
CP-3544	540	12	1806	49	12	IDE	3.5 x 1"	16x987x38
CP-3554	544	16	1054	63	12	IDE	3.5 x 1"	CMOS
CP-4024 STUBBY	22	2	627	34	29	IDE	3.5 x 1"	2x627x34
CP-4044 STUBBY	43	2	1104	38	50	IDE	3.5 x 1"	7x699x17
CP-30060	60	2	1524	39	19	SCSI	3.5 x 1"	
CP-30064	61	2	1522	39	14	IDE	3.5 x 1"	4x762x39

MODEL NUMBER	FORMATTED CAPACITY	NO. OF HEADS	NO. OF CYLINDERS	SECTORS PER TRACK	AVERAGE IN MS	INTERFACE	FORM FACTOR	CMOS SETTINGS
CP-30080E	85	2	1806	47	17	IDE/SCSI	3.5 x 1"	
CP-30080	84	4	1053	39	17	SCSI	3.5 x 1"	8x529x39
CP-30084	84	4	1058	39	19	IDE	3.5 x 1"	8x529x39
CP-30084E	85	4	903	46	19	IDE	3.5 x 1"	8x529x39
CP-30100 HOPI	120	4	1522	39	19	SCSI	3.5 x 1"	
CP-30104H Allegh.	120	4	1522	39	19	IDE	3.5 x 1"	8x762x39
CP-30104 HOPI	120	4	1522	39	19	IDE	3.5 x 1"	8x762x39
CP-30109 HOPI	120	4	1522	39	19	MCA	3.5 x 1"	
CP-30170E	170	4	1806	46	17	IDE	3.5 x 1"	11x941x33
CP-30200	212	4	2119	49	12	SCSI-2	3.5 x 1"	
CP-30204	213	4	2119	49	12	IDE	3.5 x 1"	16x683x38
CP-30254	251	4	1984	62	12	IDE	3.5 x 1"	4x990x33
CP-30344	343	4	1121	60	13	IDE	3.5 x 1"	11x966x63
CP-30540	545	6	1984	62	10	FSCSI-2	3.5 x 1"	
CP-31370	1371.80	14	2694	63	10	FSCSI-2	3.5 x 1"	

CORE INTERNATIONAL

MODEL NUMBER	FORMATTED CAPACITY	NO. OF HEADS	NO. OF CYLINDERS	SECTORS PER TRACK	AVERAGE IN MS	INTERFACE	FORM FACTOR	CMOS SETTINGS
AT 30	31	5	733	17	26	MFM	5.25" FH	
AT 30R	48	5	733	26	26	RLL	5.25" FH	
AT 32	31	5	733	17	21	MFM	5.25" HH	
AT 32R	48	5	733	26	21	RLL	5.25" HH	
AT 40	40	5	924	17	26	MFM	5.25" FH	
AT 40R	61	5	924	26	26	RLL	5.25" FH	
AT 63	42	5	988	17	26	MFM	5.25" FH	
AT 63R	65	5	988	26	26	RLL	5.25" FH	
AT 72	72	9	924	17	26	MFM	5.25" FH	
AT 72R	107	9	924	26	26	RLL	5.25" FH	
AT 150	150	8	1024	36	18	ESDI	5.25" FH	
HC 40	40	4	564	35	10	RLL	5.25" FH	
HC 90	91	5	969	35	16	RLL	5.25" HH	
HC 150	156	9	969	35	16	RLL	5.25" FH	
HC 175	177	9	1072	35	16	ESDI	5.25" FH	
HC 260	260	12	1212	35	25	RLL	5.25" FH	
HC 310	311	12	1582	35	16	RLL	5.25" FH	
HC 315	340	8	1447	57	16	ESDI	5.25" FH	
HC 380	383	15	1412	35	16	ESDI	5.25" FH	
HC 650	658	15	1661	53	16	ESDI	5.25" FH	
HC 650S	663	14	1661	56	18	SCSI	5.25" FH	
HC 655	680	16	1447	57	16	ESDI	5.25" FH	
HC 1000S	1200	16	1918	64	18	SCSI	5.25" FH	
OPTIMA 30	31	5	733	17	21	MFM	5.25" HH	

MODEL NUMBER	FORMATTED CAPACITY	NO. OF HEADS	NO. OF CYLINDERS	SECTORS PER TRACK	AVERAGE IN MS	INTERFACE	FORM FACTOR	CMOS SETTINGS
OPTIMA 30R	48	5	733	26	21	RLL	5.25" HH	
OPTIMA 40	41	5	963	17	26	MFM	5.25" HH	
OPTIMA 40R	64	5	963	26	26	RLL	5.25" HH	
OPTIMA 70	72	9	918	17	26	MFM	5.25" FH	
OPTIMA 70R	109	9	918	26	26	RLL	5.25" FH	

CORPORATE SYSTEMS CENTER

MODEL NUMBER	FORMATTED CAPACITY	NO. OF HEADS	NO. OF CYLINDERS	SECTORS PER TRACK	AVERAGE IN MS	INTERFACE	FORM FACTOR	CMOS SETTINGS
GD 2024	21	2	653	32	23	IDE	2.5" HH	4x615x17
GD 2044	40	4	552	38	19	IDE	2.5" HH	5x980x17
GD 2061	60	4	823	38	19	IDE	2.5" HH	4x823x38
GD 2064	60	4	823	38	19	IDE	2.5" HH	4x823x38
GD 2081	85	4	1097	38	19	IDE	2.5" HH	10x976x17
GD 2084	85	4	1097	38	19	IDE	2.5" HH	10x976x17
GD 2088	121	4	1097	38	19	IDE	2.5" HH	10x976x17
GD 2121	120	4	1123	53	17	IDE	2.5" HH	14x992x17
GD 2124	120	4	1123	53	19	IDE	2.5" HH	14x99x17
GD 2254	252	6	1339	47	12	IDE	2.5" HH	16x489x63
GD 30001A	42	2	1045	40	19	IDE	3.5 x 1"	5x980x17
GD 30080E	80	4	1053	39	15	SCSI	3.5 x 1"	
GD 30084E	85	4	1053	39	19	IDE	3.5 x 1"	8x526x39
GD 30085E	80	2	1806	46	19	IDE	3.5 x 1"	4x903x46
GD 30087	80	2	1806	46	19	IDE	3.5 x 1"	4x903x46
GD 30100	121	4	1522	39	19	SCSI-2	3.5 x 1"	
GD 30100D	121	4	1524	39	19	IDE	3.5 x 1"	8x762x39
GD 30174E	170	4	1806	46	15	IDE	3.5 x 1"	8x903x46
GD 30175E	170	2	2116	63	19	IDE	3.5 x 1"	8x904x46
GD 30200	212	4	2119	49	12	SCSI-2	3.5 x 1"	
GD 30204	212	4	2119	49	12	IDE	3.5 x 1"	12x989x35
GD 30214	213	4	2119	49	14	IDE	3.5 x 1"	16x685x38
GD 30254	251	4	1895	62	15	IDE	3.5 x 1"	10x895x55
GD 30270	270	16	524	63	10	SCSI-2	3.5 x 1"	
GD 30344	330	4	2116	63	12	IDE	3.5 x 1"	16x904x46
GD 3040A	42	2	1026	40	25	SCSI	3.5 x 1"	
GD 3044	42	2	1047	40	25	IDE	3.5 x 1"	5x988x17
GD 3045	42	2	1047	40	25	IDE	3.5 x 1"	5x977x17
GD 30540	545	6	2243	60	10	SCSI-2	3.5 x 1"	
GD 30544	540	6	2249	59	12	IDE	3.5 x 1"	16x1023x63
GD 30544	540	6	2242	47	10	SCSI-2	3.5 x 1"	
GD 31050	1037	8	2756	47	10	SCSI-2	3.5 x 1"	
GD 3114	112	8	832	33	15	IDE	3.5 x 1"	8x832x33
GD 31370	1300	14	2387	37	10	SCSI-2	3.5 x 1"	

MODEL NUMBER	FORMATTED CAPACITY	NO. OF HEADS	NO. OF CYLINDERS	SECTORS PER TRACK	AVERAGE IN MS	INTERFACE	FORM FACTOR	CMOS SETTINGS
GD 3200D	212	8	1366	38	15	SCSI	3.5 x 1"	
GD 3200F	212	8	1366	38	15	SCSI	3.5 x 1"	
GD 3300	340	8	1807	46	12	SCSI-2	3.5 x 1"	
GD 3301	85	8	1806	46	12	IDE	3.5 x 1"	16x659x63
GD 3500	510	12	1695	49	12	SCSI-2	3.5 x 1"	
GD 3504	510	12	1806	46	12	IDE	3.5 x 1"	16x987x63
GD 3544	524	6	1053	63	12	IDE	3.5 x 1"	16x1023x63
GD 5500	510	16	1441	62	12	IDE	3.5 x 1"	
PI - 16E	1340	19	1772	77	15	ESDI	5.25" FH	
McHuge	334	20	1020	36	18	SCSI	EXT	
McHuge II	641	15	1224	48	16	SCSI	EXT	

DATA TECH MEMORIES

MODEL NUMBER	FORMATTED CAPACITY	NO. OF HEADS	NO. OF CYLINDERS	SECTORS PER TRACK	AVERAGE IN MS	INTERFACE	FORM FACTOR	CMOS SETTINGS
DTM-553	44	5	1024	17	65	MFM	5.25" FH	
TM-853	44	8	640	17	65	MFM	5.25" FH	
DTM-885	71	8	1024	17	36	MFM	5.25" FH	

DIGITAL EQUIPMENT CORPORATION

MODEL NUMBER	FORMATTED CAPACITY	NO. OF HEADS	NO. OF CYLINDERS	SECTORS PER TRACK	AVERAGE IN MS	INTERFACE	FORM FACTOR	CMOS SETTINGS
DSP2022A	220	5	-	-	-	IDE	2.5" 4H	
DSP2022S	220	5	-	-	-	FSCSI-2	2.5" 4H	
DSP3053L	535	4	-	-	9.5	FSCSI-2	3.5" 3H	
DSP3085	852	14	-	-	9	FSCSI-2	3.5 x 1"	
DSP3105	1050	14	-	-	9	FSCSI-2	3.5 x 1"	
DSP3107L	1070	8	-	-	9.5	FSCSI-2	3.5 3H	
DSP3133L	1337	10	-	-	9.5	FSCSI-2	3.5 3H	
DSP3160	1600	16	-	-	9.7	FSCSI-2	3.5 x 1"	
DSP3210	2148	16	-	-	9.5	FSCSI-2	3.5 x 1"	
DSP5200	2000	21	-	-	12	FSCSI-2	5.25" FH	
DSP5300	3000	21	-	-	12	FSCSI-2	5.25" FH	
DSP5350	3572	25	-	-	12	FSCSI-2	5.25" FH	
DSP5400	4000	26	-	-	12	FSCSI-2	5.25" FH	
DSP34300	4300	20	-	-	9	FSCSI-2	3.5 x 1"	
VP3107	1075	5	-	-	9	FSCSI-2	3.5" 3H	
VP3215	2150	10	-	-	9	FSCSI-2	3.5" 3H	

DISC TEC

MODEL NUMBER	FORMATTED CAPACITY	NO. OF HEADS	NO. OF CYLINDERS	SECTORS PER TRACK	AVERAGE IN MS	INTERFACE	FORM FACTOR	CMOS SETTINGS
RHD-20	21	2	615	34	23	IDE	3.5 x 1"	
RHD-60	63	2	1024	60	22	IDE	3.5 x 1"	

DISCTRON (ALSO SEE OTARI)

MODEL NUMBER	FORMATTED CAPACITY	NO. OF HEADS	NO. OF CYLINDERS	SECTORS PER TRACK	AVERAGE IN MS	INTERFACE	FORM FACTOR	CMOS SETTINGS
D-503	3	2	153	17	85	MFM	5.25" FH	

MODEL NUMBER	FORMATTED CAPACITY	NO. OF HEADS	NO. OF CYLINDERS	SECTORS PER TRACK	AVERAGE IN MS	INTERFACE	FORM FACTOR	CMOS SETTINGS
D-504	4	2	215	17	85	MFM	5.25" FH	
D-506	5	4	153	17	85	MFM	5.25" FH	
D-507	5	2	306	17	85	MFM	5.25" FH	
D-509	8	4	215	17	85	MFM	5.25" FH	
D-512	11	8	153	17	85	MFM	5.25" FH	
D-513	11	6	215	17	85	MFM	5.25" FH	
D-514	11	4	306	17	85	MFM	5.25" FH	
D-518	15	8	215	17	85	MFM	5.25" FH	
D-519	16	6	306	17	85	MFM	5.25" FH	
D-526	21	8	306	17	85	MFM	5.25" FH	

DMA

306	11	2	612	17	85	MFM	5.25" FH	

DTC

HF12	10	2	301	78	65	SCSI	5.25" HH	
HF24	20	2	506	78	60	SCSI	5.25" HH	

ECOL. 2

EC-50	50	1	1720	60	40	IDE	3.5 x 1"	2x860x60
EC-100	100	2	1720	60	40	IDE	3.5 x 1"	2x1005x17
EC3-100	100	1	2300	85	20	IDE	3.5 x 1"	2x957x17
EC3-200	200	2	2300	85	20	IDE	3.5 x 1"	2x986x33

ELCOH

DISCACHE 10	10	4	320	17	65	MFM	5.25" FH	
DISCACHE 20	20	8	320	17	65	MFM	5.25" FH	

EMULEX

EMS/760	663	-	-	-	18	ESDI	5.25"	
ER2E/760	663	-	-	-	17	ESDI	5.25"	
ES36/760-1	663	-	-	-	17	ESDI	5.25"	

EPSON

HD 850	11	4	306	17	99	MFM	5.25" HH	
HD 860	21	4	612	17	99	MFM	5.25" HH	

ESPERT

EP-340A	42	4	1040	27	25	IDE	3.5 x 1"	5x919x17

MODEL NUMBER	FORMATTED CAPACITY	NO. OF HEADS	NO. OF CYLINDERS	SECTORS PER TRACK	AVERAGE IN MS	INTERFACE	FORM FACTOR	CMOS SETTINGS
FUJI								
FK301-13	10	4	306	17	65	MFM	3.5 x 1"	
FK302-13	10	2	612	17	65	MFM	3.5 x 1"	
FK302-26	21	4	612	17	65	MFM	3.5 x 1"	
FK302-39	32	6	612	17	65	MFM	3.5 x 1"	
FK303-52	40	8	615	17	65	MFM	3.5 x 1"	
FK305-26	21	4	615	17	65	MFM	3.5 x 1"	
FK305-39	32	6	615	17	65	MFM	3.5 x 1"	
FK305-39R	32	4	615	26	65	RLL	3.5 x 1"	
FK305-58R	49	6	615	26	65	RLL	3.50 HH	
FK308S-39R	31	4	615	26	65	SCSI	3.50 HH	
FK308S-58R	45	6	615	26	65	SCSI	3.50 HH	
FK309-26	20	4	615	17	65	MFM	3.50 HH	
FK309-39	32	6	615	17	65	MFM	3.50 HH	
FK309-39R	30	4	615	26	65	RLL	3.50 HH	
FK309S-50R	41	4	615	26	47	SCSI	3.50 HH	
FUJITSU AMERICA, INC.								
M 2225D/D2	21	4	615	32	40/35	MFM	3.5 x 1"	
M 2225DR	32	4	615	26	35	RLL	3.5 x 1"	
M 2226D/D2	30	6	615	32	40/35	MFM	3.5 x 1"	
M 2225DR	49	6	615	26	35	RLL	3.5 x 1"	
M 2227D/D2	40	8	615	32	40/35	MFM	3.5 x 1"	
M 2227D/D2	65	8	615	26	35	RLL	3.5 x 1"	
M 2230AS	5	2	320	17	65	MFM	5.25" FH	
M 2230AT	5	2	320	17	65	MFM	5.25" FH	
M 2231	5	2	306	17	80	MFM	5.25" FH	
M 2233AS	11	4	320	17	80	MFM	5.25" FH	
M 2233AT	11	4	320	17	95	MFM	5.25" HH	
M 2234AS	16	6	320	17	80	MFM	5.25" FH	
M 2235AS	22	8	320	17	80	MFM	5.25" FH	
M 2241AS/AS2	25	4	754	32	33/30	MFM	5.25" FH	
M 2242AS/AS2	43	7	754	17	33/30	MFM	5.25" FH	
M 2243AS/AS2	68	11	754	17	33/30	MFM	5.25" FH	
M 2243R	110	7	1186	26	25	RLL	5.25" FH	
M 2243T	68	7	1186	17	25	MFM	5.25" HH	
M 2245SA	120	7	823	35	25	SCSI	5.25" HH	
M 2246E	172	10	823	35	25	ESDI	5.25" FH	
M 2246SA	148	10	823	35	25	SCSI	5.25" FH	
M 2247E	143	7	1243	64	18	ESDI	5.25" FH	

MODEL NUMBER	FORMATTED CAPACITY	NO. OF HEADS	NO. OF CYLINDERS	SECTORS PER TRACK	AVERAGE IN MS	INTERFACE	FORM FACTOR	CMOS SETTINGS
M 2247S	138	7	1243	65	18	SCSI	5.25" FH	
M 2247SA	149	7	1243	36	18	SCSI	5.25" FH	
M 2247SB	160	7	1243	19	18	SCSI	5.25" FH	
M 2248E	224	11	1243	64	18	ESDI	5.25" FH	
M 2248S	221	11	1243	65	18	SCSI	5.25" FH	
M 2248SA	238	11	1243	36	18	SCSI	5.25" FH	
M 2248SB	252	11	1243	19	18	SCSI	5.25" FH	
M 2249E	305	15	1243	64	18	ESDI	5.25" FH	
M 2249S	303	15	1243	65	18	SCSI	5.25" FH	
M 2249SA	324	15	1243	36	18	SCSI	5.25" FH	
M 2249SB	343	15	1243	19	18	SCSI	5.25" FH	
M 2261E	326	8	1658	53	16	ESDI	5.25" FH	
M 2262E	448	11	1658	48	16	ESDI	5.25" FH	
M 2614T	180	8	1334	33	20	IDE	3.5 x 1"	
M 26/22SA	330	8	1435	56	12	SCSI	3.5 x 1"	
M 2622T	330	8	1435	56	12	IDE	3.5 x 1"	
M 2623SA	425	10	1435	56	12	SCSI	3.5 x 1"	
M 2623T	425	10	1435	56	12	IDE	3.5 x 1"	
M 2624SA	520	12	1435	56	12	SCSI	3.5 x 1"	
M 2624T	520	12	1435	56	12	IDE	3.5 x 1"	
M 2635FA	425	9	1435	64	12	SCSI-1&2	3.5 x 1"	
M 2651S	1313	16	1944	64	11	SCSI-2	5.25" FH	
M 2652S	1752	20	1944	84	11	SCSI-2	5.25" FH	
M 2652P	1586	20	1893	84	11	IPI-2	5.25" FH	
M 2653	1400	15	2078	88	12	SCSI	5.25" FH	
M 2654	2100	21	2179	88	12	SCSI	5.25" FH	
M 2671P	2640	15	2671	88	12	IPI-2	5 x8.5 x15"	

HEWLETT-PACKARD

MODEL NUMBER	FORMATTED CAPACITY	NO. OF HEADS	NO. OF CYLINDERS	SECTORS PER TRACK	AVERAGE IN MS	INTERFACE	FORM FACTOR	CMOS SETTINGS
HP-97500	20	-	-	-	-	SCSI	3.5x 1"	
HP-97530E	136	4	-	-	18	SCSI	5.25" FH	
HP-97530S	204	6	-	-	18	SCSI	5.25" FH	
HP-97532E	103	-	-	-	17	ESDI	5.25" FH	
HP-97500	20	4	615	17	28	SCSI	3.5 x 1"	
HP-97530E	136	4	1229	36	18	ESDI	5.25" FH	
HP-97530S	204	6	1643	64	18	SCSI	5.25" FH	
HP-97532E	103	4	1643	64	17	ESDI	5.25" FH	
HP-97533E	155	6	1643	64	17	ESDI	5.25" FH	
HP-97536E	311	12	1643	64	17	ESDI	5.25" FH	
HP-97544E	340	8	1457	57	17	ESDI	5.25" FH	
HP-97544S/D	331	8	1447	56	17	SCSI	5.25" FH	

MODEL NUMBER	FORMATTED CAPACITY	NO. OF HEADS	NO. OF CYLINDERS	SECTORS PER TRACK	AVERAGE IN MS	INTERFACE	FORM FACTOR	CMOS SETTINGS
HP-97544T/P	331	8	1447	56	17	SCSI-2	5.25" FH	
HP-97548E	680	16	1457	57	17	ESDI	5.25" FH	
HP-97548S/F	663	16	1447	56	17	SCSI	5.25" FH	
HP-97548T/P	663	16	1447	56	17	SCSI-2	5.25" FH	
HP-97549T/P	1000	16	1911	64	18	SCSI-2	5.25" FH	
HP-97556E	681	11	1680	72	14	ESDI	5.25" FH	
HO-97556	677	11	1670	72	13.5	SCSI-2	5.25" FH	
HP-97556T/P	673	11	1670	72	14	SCSI-2	5.25" FH	
HP-97558E	1084	15	1962	72	14	ESDI	5.25" FH	
HP-97558	1069	15	1935	72	13.5	SCSI-2	5.25" FH	
HP-97558T/P	1075	15	1952	72	14	SCSI-2	5.25" FH	
HP-97560	1355	19	1935	72	13.5	SCSI-2	5.25" FH	
HP-97560E	1374	19	1962	72	14	ESDI	5.25" FH	
HP-97560T/P	1363	19	1952	72	14	SCSI-2	5.25" FH	
HP-C2233	234	5	1546	72	12.6	IDE/SCSI	3.5 x 1"	
HP-C2233S	238	5	1511	49	13	SCSI-2	3.5 x 1"	
HP-C2234	328	7	1546	61	12.6	IDE	3.5 x 1"	10x1016x63
HP-C2234S	334	7	1511	61	13	SCSI-2	3.5 x 1"	
HP-C2235	422	9	1546	61	12.6	IDE/SCSI	3.5 x 1"	13x1006x63
HP-C2235S	429	9	1511	73	13	SCSI-2	3.5 x 1"	
HP-C3007	1370	13	2255	73	11.5	SCSI-2	5.25" FH	
HP-C3009	1792	17	2255	73	11.5	SCSI-2	5.25" FH	
HP-C3010	2003	19	2255	73	11.5	SCSI-2	5.25" FH	
HP-C3010	1027	19	1100	73	9	SCSI-2	5.25" FH	
HP-D1660A	333	8	1457	57	16	ESDI	5.25" FH	
HP-D1661A	667	16	1457	57	16	ESDI	5.25" FH	

HITACHI AMERICA

MODEL NUMBER	FORMATTED CAPACITY	NO. OF HEADS	NO. OF CYLINDERS	SECTORS PER TRACK	AVERAGE IN MS	INTERFACE	FORM FACTOR	CMOS SETTINGS
DK 301-1	10	4	306	17	85	MFM	3.5 x 1"	
DK 301-2	15	6	306	17	85	MFM	3.5 x 1"	
DK 312C-25	209	10	1076	38	16	SCSI	3.5 x 1"	
DK 312C-25	251	12	1076	38	16	SCSI	3.5 x 1"	
DK 314C-41	419	14	1076	38	17	SCSI	3.5 x 1"	
DK 315C-11	1100	15	1457	63	11.8	FSCSI-2	3.5 x 1"	
DK 315C-14	1400	15	1457	63	11.8	FSCSI-2	3.5 x 1"	
DK 502-2	21	4	615	17	85	MFM	5.25" HH	
DK 511-5	30	5	699	17	30	MFM	5.25" FH	
DK 511-5	42	7	699	17	30	MFM	5.25" FH	
DK 511-8	67	10	823	17	23	MFM	5.25" FH	
DK 512-8	67	5	823	34	23	ESDI	5.25" FH	
DK 512C-8	67	5	823	34	23	SCSI	5.25" FH	

MODEL NUMBER	FORMATTED CAPACITY	NO. OF HEADS	NO. OF CYLINDERS	SECTORS PER TRACK	AVERAGE IN MS	INTERFACE	FORM FACTOR	CMOS SETTINGS
DK 512-12	94	7	823	34	23	ESDI	5.25" FH	
DK 512C-12	94	7	823	34	23	SCSI	5.25" FH	
DK 512-17	134	10	823	34	23	ESDI	5.25" FH	
DK 512C-17	134	10	819	34	23	SCSI	5.25" FH	
DK 514-38	330	14	903	51	16	ESDI	5.25" FH	
DK 514C-38	321	14	903	51	16	SCSI	5.25" FH	
DK 514S-38	330	14	903	51	14	SMD	5.25" FH	
DK 515-12	1229	15	1224	69	14	ESDI	5.25" FH	
DK 515-78	673	14	1361	69	16	ESDI	5.25" FH	
DK 515C-78	370.5	14	1261	69	16	ESDI	5.25" FH	
DK 515C-78	670.5	14	1261	69	16	ESDI	5.25" FH	
DK 516-12	1230	15	1778	77	16	ESDI	5.25" FH	
DK 516-15	1320	15	2235	77	14	ESDI	5.25" FH	
DK 516C-16	1500	15	2172	81	14	SCSI-2	5.25" FH	
DK 517C	2900	21	2381	81	12.8	FSCSI-2	5.25" FH	
DK 517C-26	2000	14	2381	81	12	SCSI-2	5.25" FH	
DK 517C-37	2000	21	2381	81	12	SCSI-2	5.25" FH	
DK 521-5	42	6	823	17	25	MFM	5.25" HH	
DK 522-10	103	6	823	36	25	ESDI	5.25" HH	
DK 522C-10	88	6	819	35	25	SCSI	5.25" HH	

HYOSUNG

MODEL NUMBER	FORMATTED CAPACITY	NO. OF HEADS	NO. OF CYLINDERS	SECTORS PER TRACK	AVERAGE IN MS	INTERFACE	FORM FACTOR	CMOS SETTINGS
HC 8085	71	8	1024	17	25	MFM	5.25" FH	
HC 8128	109	8	1024	26	25	MFM	5.25" FH	
HC 8170E	150	8	1024	36	25	ESDI	5.25" FH	

IBM CORPORATION

MODEL NUMBER	FORMATTED CAPACITY	NO. OF HEADS	NO. OF CYLINDERS	SECTORS PER TRACK	AVERAGE IN MS	INTERFACE	FORM FACTOR	CMOS SETTINGS
20MB(2)	21	4	615	17	40	MFM	5.25" FH	
20MB(13)	21	8	306	17	40	MFM	5.25" FH	
30MB(22)	31	5	733	17	40	MFM	5.25" FH	
0660-371	320	14	949	48	12	SCSI-2	3.5 x 1"	
0661-467	400	14	1199	48	11	SCSI-2	3.5 x 1"	
0663-H11/L11	868	13	2051	66	10	SCSI	3.5 x 1"	
0663-H12/L12	1004	15	2051	66	10	SCSI	3.5 x 1"	
0671E	319	15	1224	34	20	ESDI	5.25" HH	
0671S	319	15	1224	34	20	SCSI	5.25" HH	
0681	476	11	1458	58	13	SCSI-2	5.25" HH	
WDS-L40	41	2	1038	39	17	SCSI-2	3.5 x 1"	
WDA-L42	42	2	1067	39	17	IDE	3.5 x 1"	
WDS-L42	42	2	1066	39	17	SCSI	3.5 x 1"	
WS-240	43	2	1120	38	19	PS/2	2.5"	

MODEL NUMBER	FORMATTED CAPACITY	NO. OF HEADS	NO. OF CYLINDERS	SECTORS PER TRACK	AVERAGE IN MS	INTERFACE	FORM FACTOR	CMOS SETTINGS
WDA-240	43	2	1122	38	19	IDE	2.5"	14x10214x33
WDS-240	43	2	1120	38	19	SCSI	2.5"	
WD-380	80	4	1021	39	16	PS/2	3.5 x 1"	
WDA-380	80	4	1021	39	16	IDE	3.5 x 1"	9x1021x17
WDS-380	80	4	1021	39	16	SCSI-2	3.5 x 1"	
WD-387	61	4	928	32	23	PS/2	3.5 x 1"	
WD-3100	105	2	1990	44	12	SCSI-2	3.5 x 1"	
WD-3158	120	8	920	32	23	PS/2	3.5 x 1"	
WD-3160	160	8	1021	39	16	PS/2	3.5 x 1"	
WDA-3160	160	8	1021	39	16	IDE	3.5 x 1"	8x1021x39
WDS-3160	160	8	1021	39	16	SCSI-2	3.5 x 1"	
WDS-2200	210	4	1990	44	12	SCSI	3.5 x 1"	

IMI

MODEL NUMBER	FORMATTED CAPACITY	NO. OF HEADS	NO. OF CYLINDERS	SECTORS PER TRACK	AVERAGE IN MS	INTERFACE	FORM FACTOR	CMOS SETTINGS
5006	5	2	306	17	85	MFM	5.25" FH	
5007	5	2	312	17	85	MFM	5.25" FH	
5012	10	4	306	17	85	MFM	5.25" FH	
5018	15	6	306	17	85	MFM	5.25" FH	
5021H	15	4	306	17	85	MFM	5.25" FH	
7720	21	4	310	17	85	MFM	8"	
7740	43	8	315	17	85	MFM	8"	

INTERGRAL PERIPHERALS

MODEL NUMBER	FORMATTED CAPACITY	NO. OF HEADS	NO. OF CYLINDERS	SECTORS PER TRACK	AVERAGE IN MS	INTERFACE	FORM FACTOR	CMOS SETTINGS
1862	64	3	-	17	18	IDE	-	

IOMEGA

MODEL NUMBER	FORMATTED CAPACITY	NO. OF HEADS	NO. OF CYLINDERS	SECTORS PER TRACK	AVERAGE IN MS	INTERFACE	FORM FACTOR	CMOS SETTINGS
MultiDisk 150	150	2	1380	36	18	SCSI-2	Remov 5.25"	

JCT

MODEL NUMBER	FORMATTED CAPACITY	NO. OF HEADS	NO. OF CYLINDERS	SECTORS PER TRACK	AVERAGE IN MS	INTERFACE	FORM FACTOR	CMOS SETTINGS
100	5	2	226	17	110	MFM	5.25" HH	
105	7	4	306	17	110	MFM	5.25" HH	
110	14	8	306	17	130	MFM	5.25" HH	
120	20	4	615	17	100	MFM	5.25" HH	
1000	5	2	226	17	110	Comm.	5.25" HH	
1005	7	4	306	17	110	Comm.	5.25" HH	
1010	14	8	306	-	130	Comm.	5.25" HH	

JVC COMPANIES OF AMERICA

MODEL NUMBER	FORMATTED CAPACITY	NO. OF HEADS	NO. OF CYLINDERS	SECTORS PER TRACK	AVERAGE IN MS	INTERFACE	FORM FACTOR	CMOS SETTINGS
JD-E2042M	42	2	973	43	16	IDE	2.5" 4H	
JD-E2085M	85	4	973	43	16	IDE	2.5" 4H	
JD-E2825P(A)	21	2	581	36	25	IDE	3.5" 4H	

MODEL NUMBER	FORMATTED CAPACITY	NO. OF HEADS	NO. OF CYLINDERS	SECTORS PER TRACK	AVERAGE IN MS	INTERFACE	FORM FACTOR	CMOS SETTINGS
JD-E2825P(S)	21	2	581	36	25	SCSI	3.5" 4H	
JD-E2825P(X)	21	2	581	36	25	IDE	3.5" 4H	
JD-E2850P(A)	42	3	791	35	25	IDE	3.5" 4H	
JD-E2850P(S)	42	3	791	35	25	SCSI	3.5" 4H	
JD-E2850P(X)	42	3	791	35	25	XT-IDE	3.5" 4H	
JD-E3824TA	21	2	436	48	28	-	3.5" 3H	
JD-E3848HA	42	4	436	48	29	-	3.5" 3H	
JD-E3848P(A)	42	2	862	48	25	IDE	3.5" 4H	
JD-E3848P(S)	42	2	862	48	25	SCSI	3.5" 4H	
JD-E3848P(X)	42	2	862	48	25	XT-IDE	3.5" 4H	
JD-E3896P(A)	84	4	862	48	25	IDE	3.5" 4H	
JD-E3896P(S)	84	4	862	48	25	SCSI	3.5" 4H	
JD-E3896P(X)	84	4	862	48	25	XT-IDE	3.5" 4H	
JD-E3896V(A)	84	4	862	48	25	IDE	3.5" 3H	
JD-E3896V(S)	84	4	862	48	25	SCSI	3.5" 3H	
JD-E3896V(X)	84	4	862	48	25	XT-IDE	3.5" 3H	
JD-F2042M	42	2	973	43	16	IDE	2.5" 4H	
JD3842HA	21	2	436	48	28	-	3.5" 3H	
JD3848HA	43	4	436	48	29	-	3.5" 3H	

KALOK CORPORATION

MODEL NUMBER	FORMATTED CAPACITY	NO. OF HEADS	NO. OF CYLINDERS	SECTORS PER TRACK	AVERAGE IN MS	INTERFACE	FORM FACTOR	CMOS SETTINGS
KL 320 Octagon I	21	4	615	17	48	MFM	3.5 x 1"	
KL 330 Octagon I	32	4	615	26	40	RLL	3.5 x 1"	
KL 341 Octagon I	40	4	644	26	25	SCSI	3.5 x 1"	
KL 343 Octagon I	42	4	676	31	25	IDE	3.5 x 1"	
KL 3100 Octagon II	105	6	820	35	19	IDE	3.5 x 1"	
KL 3120 Octagon II	120	6	820	40	19	IDE	3.5 x 1"	
P5-125	125	2	2048	80	17	IDE	3.50 x .5"	
P5-250	251	4	2048	80	17	IDE	3.50 x .5"	

KYOCERA ELECTRONICS, INC.

MODEL NUMBER	FORMATTED CAPACITY	NO. OF HEADS	NO. OF CYLINDERS	SECTORS PER TRACK	AVERAGE IN MS	INTERFACE	FORM FACTOR	CMOS SETTINGS
KC 20A/B	21	4	615	17	65/62	MFM	3.5 x 1"	
KC 30A/B	32	4	615	26	65/62	RLL	3.5 x 1"	
KC 40GA	41	2	1075	26	28	IDE	3.5 x 1"	
KC 80C	87	8	787	28	28	SCSI	3.5 x 1"	

LANSTOR

MODEL NUMBER	FORMATTED CAPACITY	NO. OF HEADS	NO. OF CYLINDERS	SECTORS PER TRACK	AVERAGE IN MS	INTERFACE	FORM FACTOR	CMOS SETTINGS
LAN-64	71	8	1024	17	-	MFM	5.25" FH	
LAN-115	119	15	918	17	-	MFM	5.25" FH	
LAN-140	142	8	1024	34	-	ESDI	5.25" FH	
LAN-180	180	8	1024	26	-	RLL	5.25" FH	

MODEL NUMBER	FORMATTED CAPACITY	NO. OF HEADS	NO. OF CYLINDERS	SECTORS PER TRACK	AVERAGE IN MS	INTERFACE	FORM FACTOR	CMOS SETTINGS
LAPINE								
3522	10	4	306	17	65	MFM	3.5 x 1"	
LT 10	10	2	615	17	65	MFM	3.5 x 1"	
LT 20	20	4	615	17	65	MFM	3.5 x 1"	
LT 200	20	4	614	17	65	MFM	3.5 x 1"	
LT 300	32	4	614	26	65	RLL	3.5 x 1"	
LT 2000	20	4	614	17	65	MFM	3.5 x 1"	
TITAN 20	21	4	615	17	65	MFM	3.5 x 1"	
TITAN 30	33	4	615	26	65	RLL	3.5 x 1"	
TITAN 3532	32	4	615	26	65	RLL	3.5 x 1"	
MAXTOR CORPORATION								
2585	85	4	1092	36	15	IDE	2.5" HH	10x976x17
25128A	128.2	4	1092	48	15	IDE	2.5" HH	15x980x17
25252A, S	251	6	1320	63	12	IDE/SCSI	17 mm high	15x990x33
7080A, S	80	4	1170	36	17	IDE/SCSI	1" high	9x1021x17
7120A, S	120	4	1516	42	15	IDE/SCSI	1" high	14x984x17
7213A, S	213	4	1690	48	15	IDE/SCSI	1" high	13x969x33
7245A, S	244	4	1881	48	15	IDE/SCSI	1" high	15x962x33
LXT-50S	48	4	733	32	27	SCSI	3.5 x 1"	
LXT-100S	96	8	733	32	27	SCSI	3.5 x 1"	
LXT-200A	207	7	1320	45	15	IDE	3.5 x 1"	12x1020x33
LXT-200S	191	7	1320	33	15	SCSI	3.5 x 1"	
LXT-213A	213	7	1320	55	15	IDE	3.5 x 1"	13x969x33
LXT-213S	200	7	1320	55	15	SCSI	3.5 x 1"	
LXT-340A	320	7	1560	47	13	IDE	3.5 x 1"	10x992x63
LXT-340S	320	7	1560	47	15	SCSI	3.5 x 1"	
LXT-4/37A	437	9	1560	63	13	IDE	3.5 x 1"	14x967x63
LXT-437S	437	9	1560	63	13	SCSI	3.5 x 1"	
LXT-535A	535	11	1560	63	12	IDE	3.5 x 1"	
LXT-535S	535	11	1560	63	12	SCSI	3.5 x 1"	
P0-12S Panther	1224	15	1224	63	13	SCSI-2	5.25" FH	
P1-08E Panther	696	9	1778	72	12	ESDI	5.25" FH	
P1-08S Panther	696	9	1778	72	12	SCSI	5.25" FH	
P1-12E Panther	1051	15	1778	72	13	ESDI	5.25" FH	
P1-12S Panther	1005	19	1216	72	10	SCSI	5.25" FH	
P1-13E Panther	1160	15	1778	72	13	ESDI	5.25" FH	
P1-16E Panther	1331	19	1778	72	13	ESDI	5.25" FH	
P1-17E Panther	1470	19	1778	72	13	ESDI	5.25" FH	
P1-17S Panther	1759	19	1778	85	13	SCSI-2	5.25" FH	

MODEL NUMBER	FORMATTED CAPACITY	NO. OF HEADS	NO. OF CYLINDERS	SECTORS PER TRACK	AVERAGE IN MS	INTERFACE	FORM FACTOR	CMOS SETTINGS
MXT 540SL/AL	540	7	2367	41	7.5/8.5	IDE	3.5 x 1"	16x1024x63
MXT 1240S	1.24GB	15	2367	41	8.5/9	SCSI-2	3.5"	
RXT-800HS	786	1	2410	88	108	SCSI	5.25" FH	
TAHITI (M/O)	650	1	2870	104	35	SCSI	5.25" FH	
XT 1050	38	5	902	17	30	MFM	5.25" FH	
XT 1065	52	7	918	17	30	MFM	5.25" FH	
XT 1085	69	8	1024	17	27	MFM	5.25" FH	
XT 1105	82	11	918	17	30	MFM	5.25" FH	
XT 1120R	104	8	1024	26	27	RLL	5.25" FH	
XT 1140	116	15	918	17	26	MFM	5.25" FH	
XT 1140E	140	15	1141	17	28	ESDI	5.25" FH	
XT 1240R	196	15	1024	26	27	RLL	5.25" FH	
XT 2085	72	7	1224	17	30	MFM	5.25" FH	
XT 2140	113	11	1224	17	30	MFM	5.25" FH	
XT 2190	159	15	1224	17	28	MFM	5.25" FH	
XT 3170	129	9	1224	26	30	SCSI	5.25" FH	
XT 3280	216	15	1224	26	30	SCSI	5.25" FH	
XT 3380	277	15	1224	26	27	SCSI	5.25" FH	
XT 4170E	157	7	1224	35	14	ESDI	5.25" FH	
XT 4170S	157	7	1224	36	14	SCSI	5.25" FH	
XT 4175E	149	7	1224	34	27	ESDI	5.25" FH	
XT4179E	158	7	1224	36	14	ESDI	5.25" FH	
XT 4230E	203	9	1224	35	15	ESDI	5.25" FH	
XT 4280E	234	11	1224	34	27	ESDI	5.25" FH	
XT 4280S	241	11	1224	36	27	SCSI	5.25" FH	
XT 4380E	338	15	1224	35	16	ESDI	5.25" FH	
XT 4380S	337	15	1224	36	16	SCSI	5.25" FH	
XT 8380E	360	8	1632	54	14	ESDI	5.25" FH	
XT 8380EH	361	8	1632	54	13.5	ESDI	5.25" FH	
XT 8380S	360	8	1632	54	14	SCSI	5.25" FH	
XT 8380SH	361	8	1632	54	13.5	SCSI	5.25" FH	
XT 8610E	541	12	1632	54	16	ESDI	5.25" FH	
XT 8702S	616	15	1490	54	16	SCSI	5.25" FH	
XT 8760E	676	15	1632	54	16	ESDI	5.25" FH	
XT 8760EH	677	15	1632	54	13.5	ESDI	5.25" FH	
XT 8760SH	670	15	1632	54	14.5	SCSI	5.25" FH	
XT 8800E	694	15	1274	71	16	ESDI	5.25" FH	
XT 81000E	889	15	1632	54	16	ESDI	5.25" FH	

MAXTOR COLORADO (also see Miniscribe)

7040A Cheyene	42	2	1170	36	17	IDE	3.5 x 1"	5x977x17

MODEL NUMBER	FORMATTED CAPACITY	NO. OF HEADS	NO. OF CYLINDERS	SECTORS PER TRACK	AVERAGE IN MS	INTERFACE	FORM FACTOR	CMOS SETTINGS
7040S Cheyene	40	2	1155	36	17	SCSI	3.5 x 1"	
7060A Cheyene	65	2	1516	42	15	IDE	3.5 x 1"	7x984x17
7060S Cheyene	65	2	1516	42	15	SCSI	3.5 x 1"	
7080A Cheyene	81	4	1170	36	17	IDE	3.5 x 1"	9x1021x17
7080S Cheyene	65	4	1155	36	15	IDE	3.5 x 1"	
7120A Cheyene	65	4	1516	42	15	IDE	3.5 x 1"	14x984x17
7120S Cheyene	130	4	1516	42	15	SCSI	3.5 x 1"	
8051A	43	4	745	28	28	IDE	3.5 x 1"	5x977x17

MEGA DRIVE SYSTEMS

MODEL NUMBER	FORMATTED CAPACITY	NO. OF HEADS	NO. OF CYLINDERS	SECTORS PER TRACK	AVERAGE IN MS	INTERFACE	FORM FACTOR	CMOS SETTINGS
P-42	42	3	834	33	19	SCSI	3.5 x 1"	
P-84	84	6	834	33	19	SCSI	3.5 x 1"	
P-105	105	6	1019	33	19	SCSI	3.5 x 1"	
P-120	120	5	1123	33	14	SCSI	3.5 x 1"	
P-170	170	7	1123	33	14	SCSI	3.5 x 1"	
P-210	210	7	1156	33	14	SCSI	3.5 x 1"	
P-425	425	9	1512	63	12	SCSI	3.5 x 1"	

MEMOREX

MODEL NUMBER	FORMATTED CAPACITY	NO. OF HEADS	NO. OF CYLINDERS	SECTORS PER TRACK	AVERAGE IN MS	INTERFACE	FORM FACTOR	CMOS SETTINGS
310	2	2	118	17	80	MFM	5.25" FH	
321	5	2	320	17	90	MFM	5.25" FH	
322	10	4	320	17	90	MFM	5.25" FH	
323	15	6	320	17	90	MFM	5.25" FH	
324	20	8	320	17	90	MFM	5.25" FH	
450	10	2	612	17	90	MFM	5.25" FH	
512	25	3	961	17	90	MFM	5.25" FH	
513	41	5	961	17	90	MFM	5.25" FH	
514	58	7	961	17	90	MFM	5.25" FH	

MICROPOLIS CORPORATION

MODEL NUMBER	FORMATTED CAPACITY	NO. OF HEADS	NO. OF CYLINDERS	SECTORS PER TRACK	AVERAGE IN MS	INTERFACE	FORM FACTOR	CMOS SETTINGS
1202	45	7	977	17	-	MFM	8"	
1223	45	7	977	17	-	MFM	8"	
1302	20	3	830	17	30	MFM	5.25" FH	
1303	34	5	830	17	30	MFM	5.25" FH	
1304	41	6	830	17	30	MFM	5.25" FH	
1323	35	4	1024	17	28	MFM	5.25" FH	
1323A	44	5	1024	17	28	MFM	5.25" FH	
1324	53	6	1024	17	28	MFM	5.25" FH	
1324A	62	7	1024	17	28	MFM	5.25" FH	
1325	71	8	1024	17	28	MFM	5.25" FH	
1333	35	4	1024	17	28	MFM	5.25" FH	

MODEL NUMBER	FORMATTED CAPACITY	NO. OF HEADS	NO. OF CYLINDERS	SECTORS PER TRACK	AVERAGE IN MS	INTERFACE	FORM FACTOR	CMOS SETTINGS
1333A	44	5	1024	17	28	MFM	5.25" FH	
1334	53	6	1024	17	28	MFM	5.25" FH	
1334A	62	7	1024	17	28	MFM	5.25" FH	
1335	71	8	1024	17	28	MFM	5.25" FH	
1352	30	2	1024	36	23	ESDI	5.25" FH	
1352A	41	3	1024	36	23	ESDI	5.25" FH	
1353	75	4	1024	36	23	ESDI	5.25" FH	
1353A	94	5	1024	36	23	ESDI	5.25" FH	
1354	113	6	1024	36	23	ESDI	5.24" FH	
1354A	132	7	1024	36	23	ESDI	5.25" FH	
1355	151	8	1024	36	23	ESDI	5.25" FH	
1373	73	4	1024	36	23	SCSI	5.25" FH	
1373A	91	5	1024	36	23	SCSI	5.25" FH	
1374	109	6	1024	36	23	SCSI	5.25" FH	
1374A	127	7	1024	36	23	SCSI	5.25" FH	
1375	146	8	1024	36	23	SCSI	5.25" FH	
1488-15	675	15	1628	54	16	SCSI	5.25 "FH	
1516-10S	678	10	1840	72	13	ESDI	5.25" FH	
1517-13	922	13	1925	72	14	ESDI	5.25" FH	
1518	1419	15	2100	72	14.5	ESDI	5.25" FH	
1518-14	993	14	1925	72	14	ESDI	5.25" FH	
1518-15	1064	15	1925	72	14	ESDI	5.25" FH	
1528	1341	15	2094	72	14.5	SCSI-2	5.25" FH	
1528-15	1354	15	2106	84	14	SCSI-2	5.25" FH	
1538-15	872	15	1925	71	15	ESDI	5.25" FH	
1548	1748	15	2096	72	14	FSCSI-2	5.25" FH	
1551	149	7	1224	34	18	ESDI	5.25" FH	
1554-7	158	7	1224	36	18	ESDI	5.25" FH	
1554-11	234	11	1224	34	18	ESDI	5.25" FH	
1555-8	180	8	1224	36	18	ESDI	5.25" FH	
1555-9	203	9	1224	36	18	ESDI	5.25" FH	
1555-12	255	12	1224	34	18	ESDI	5.25" FH	
1556-10	226	10	1224	36	18	ESDI	5.25" FH	
1556-11	248	11	1224	36	18	ESDI	5.25" FH	
1556-13	276	13	1224	34	18	ESDI	5.25" FH	
1557-12	270	12	1224	36	18	ESDI	5.25" FH	
1557-13	293	13	1224	36	18	ESDI	5.25" FH	
1557-14	315	14	1224	36	18	ESDI	5.25" FH	
1557-15	338	15	1224	36	18	ESDI	5.25" FH	
1558-14	315	14	1224	36	18	ESDI	5.25' FH	
1558-15	338	15	1224	36	18	ESDI	5.25" FH	

MODEL NUMBER	FORMATTED CAPACITY	NO. OF HEADS	NO. OF CYLINDERS	SECTORS PER TRACK	AVERAGE IN MS	INTERFACE	FORM FACTOR	CMOS SETTINGS
1566-11	496	11	1632	54	16	ESDI	5.25" FH	
1567-12	541	12	1632	54	16	ESDI	5.25" FH	
1567-13	586	13	1632	54	16	ESDI	5.25" FH	
1568-14	631	14	1632	54	16	ESDI	5.25" FH	
1568-15	676	15	1632	54	16	ESDI	5.25" FH	
1576-11	243	11	1224	36	18	SCSI	5.25" FH	
1577-12	266	12	1224	36	18	SCSI	5.25" FH	
1577-13	287	13	1224	36	18	SCSI	5.25" FH	
1578-14	310	14	1224	36	18	SCSI	5.25" FH	
1578-15	332	15	1224	36	18	SCSI	5.25" FH	
1586-11	490	11	1632	54	16	SCSI	5.25" FH	
1578-12	535	12	1632	54	16	SCSI	5.25" FH	
1587-13	279	13	1632	54	16	SCSI	5.25" FH	
1588	667	15	1626	54	16	SCSI	5.25" FH	
1588-14	624	14	1632	54	16	SCSI	5.25" FH	
1588-15	668	15	1632	54	16	SCSI	5.25" FH	
1596-10S	668	10	1834	72	35	SCSI	5.25" FH	
1597-13	909	13	1919	72	14	SCSI	5.25" FH	
1598	1034	15	1922	72	14.5	SCSI-2	5.25" FH	
1598-14	979	14	1919	72	14	SCSI	5.25" FH	
1598-15	1098	15	1928	71	14.5	SCSI-2	5.25" FH	
1624	667	7	2099	72	15	FSCSI-2	5.25" HH	
1653-4	92	4	1249	36	16	ESDI	5.25" HH	
1653-5	115	5	1249	36	16	ESDI	5.25" HH	
1654-6	138	6	1249	36	16	ESDI	5.25" HH	
1654-7	161	7	1249	36	16	ESDI	5.25" HH	
1663-4	197	4	1780	36	14	ESDI	5.25" HH	
1663-5	246	5	1780	36	14	ESDI	5.25" HH	
1664-7	345	7	1780	54	14	ESDI	5.25" HH	
1673-4	90	4	1249	36	16	SCSI	5.25" HH	
1673-5	112	5	1249	36	16	SCSI	5.25" HH	
1674-6	135	6	1249	36	16	SCSI	5.25" HH	
1674-7	158	7	1249	36	16	SCSI	5.25" HH	
1683-4	193	4	1776	54	14	SCSI	5.25" HH	
1683-5	242	5	1776	54	14	SCSI	5.25" HH	
1684-6	201	6	1776	54	14	SCSI	5.25" HH	
1684-7	340	7	1776	54	14	SCSI	5.25" HH	
1743-5	112	5	1140	28	15	IDE	3.5 x 1"	
1744-6	135	6	1140	28	15	IDE	3.5 x 1"	
1744-7	157	7	1140	28	15	IDE	3.5 x 1"	10X929X33
1745-8	180	8	1140	28	15	IDE	3.5 x 1"	11X968X33

MODEL NUMBER	FORMATTED CAPACITY	NO. OF HEADS	NO. OF CYLINDERS	SECTORS PER TRACK	AVERAGE IN MS	INTERFACE	FORM FACTOR	CMOS SETTINGS
1745-9	202	9	1140	28	15	IDE	3.5 x 1"	12X986X33
1773-5	115	5	1140	28	15	SCSI	3.5 x 1"	
1774-6	135	6	1140	28	15	SCSI	3.5 x 1"	
1774-7	157	7	1140	28	15	SCSI	3.5 x 1"	
1775-8	180	8	1140	28	15	SCSI	3.5 x 1"	
1775-9	202	9	1140	28	15	SCSI	3.5 x 1"	

MICROSCIENCE INTERNATIONAL CORPORATION

MODEL NUMBER	FORMATTED CAPACITY	NO. OF HEADS	NO. OF CYLINDERS	SECTORS PER TRACK	AVERAGE IN MS	INTERFACE	FORM FACTOR	CMOS SETTINGS
4050	45	5	1024	17	18	MFM	3.5 x 1"	
4060	68	5	1024	26	18	RLL	3.5 x 1"	
4070	62	7	1024	17	18	MFM	3.5 x 1"	
4090	95	7	1024	26	18	RLL	3.5 x 1"	
5040	46	3	855	35	18	ESDI	3.5 x 1"	
5070	77	5	855	35	18	ESDI	3.5 x 1"	
5070-20	86	5	960	35	18	ESDI	3.5 x 1"	
5100	107	7	855	35	18	ESDI	3.5 x 1"	
5100-20	120	7	960	35	18	ESDI	3.5 x 1"	
5160	159	7	1271	35	18	ESDI	3.5 x 1"	
6100	110	7	855	36	18	SCSI	3.5 x 1"	
7040	47	3	855	36	18	IDE	3.5 x 1"	6x890x17
7070-20	86	5	960	35	18	IDE	3.5 x 1"	9x919x17
7100	107	7	855	35	18	IDE	3.5 x 1"	12x1024x17
7100-20	120	7	960	35	18	IDE	3.5 x 1"	14x984x17
7100-21	121	5	1077	44	18	IDE	3.5 x 1"	14x984x17
7200	201	7	1277	44	18	IDE	3.5 x 1"	12x964x33
7400	420	8	1904	39	15	IDE	3.5 x 1"	13x1001x63
8040	43	2	1047	40	25	IDE	3.5 x 1"	5x977x17
8040/MLC	42	2	1024	40	25	IDE	3.5 x 1"	5x977x17
8080	85	2	1768	47	17	IDE	3.5 x 1"	10x976x17
8200	210	4	1904	39	16	IDE	3.5 x 1"	12x986x33
FH 2414	367	8	1658	54	14	ESDI	5.25" FH	
FH 2777	688	15	1658	54	14	ESDI	5.25" FH	
FH 3414	367	8	1658	54	14	SCSI	5.25" FH	
FH 3777	688	15	1658	54	14	SCSI	5.25" FH	
FH 21200	1062	15	1921	72	13	ESDI	5.25" FH	
FH 21600	1418	15	2147	86	14	ESDI	5.25" FH	
FH 31200	1062	15	1921	72	13	SCSI	5.25" FH	
FH 31600	1418	15	2147	86	14	SCSI	5.25" FH	
HH 312	10	4	306	17	65	MFM	5.25" HH	
HH 315	10	4	306	17	65	MFM	5.25" HH	
HH 325	21	4	612	17	80	MFM	5.25" HH	

MODEL NUMBER	FORMATTED CAPACITY	NO. OF HEADS	NO. OF CYLINDERS	SECTORS PER TRACK	AVERAGE IN MS	INTERFACE	FORM FACTOR	CMOS SETTINGS
HH 330	33	4	612	26	105	RLL	5.25" HH	
HH 612	11	4	306	17	85	MFM	5.25" HH	
HH 625	21	4	612	17	65	MFM	5.25" HH	
HH 712	11	2	612	17	105	MFM	5.25" HH	
HH 712A	11	2	612	17	75	MFM	5.25" HH	
HH 725	21	4	612	17	105	MFM	5.25" HH	
HH 738	33	4	612	26	105	RLL	5.25" HH	
HH 825	21	4	615	17	65	MFM	5.25" HH	
HH 830	33	4	615	26	65	RLL	5.25" HH	
HH 1050	45	5	1024	17	28	MFM	5.25" HH	
HH 1060	66	5	1024	25	28	RLL	5.25" HH	
HH 1075	62	7	1024	17	28	MFM	5.25" HH	
HH 1080	68	7	1024	26	28	RLL	5.25" HH	
HH 1090	80	7	1314	17	28	MFM	5.25" HH	
HH 1095	95	7	1024	26	28	RLL	5.25" HH	
HH 1120	122	7	1314	26	28	RLL	5.25" HH	
HH 2012	10	4	306	17	80	MFM	5.25" HH	
HH 2120	128	7	1024	35	28	ESDI	5.25" HH	
HH 2160	160	7	1276	35	28	ESDI	5.25" HH	
HH 3120	121	5	1314	36	28	SCSI	5.25" HH	
HH 3160	169	7	1314	36	28	SCSI	5.25" HH	

MINISCRIBE CORPORATION

MODEL NUMBER	FORMATTED CAPACITY	NO. OF HEADS	NO. OF CYLINDERS	SECTORS PER TRACK	AVERAGE IN MS	INTERFACE	FORM FACTOR	CMOS SETTINGS
1006	5	2	306	17	179	MFM	5.25" FH	
1012	10	4	306	17	179	MFM	5.25" FH	
2006	5	2	306	17	93	MFM	5.25" FH	
2012	11	4	306	17	85	MFM	5.25" HH	
3006	5	2	306	17	-	MFM	5.25" HH	
3012	10	2	612	17	155	MFM	5.25" HH	
3053	44	5	1024	17	25	MFM	5.25" HH	
3085	71	7	1170	17	28	MFM	5.25" FH	
3085E	72	3	1270	36	17	ESDI	5.25" HH	
3085S	72	3	1255	36	17	SCSI	5.25" HH	
3130E	112	5	1250	36	17	ESDI	5.25" HH	
3130S	115	5	1255	36	17	SCSI	5.25" HH	
3180E	157	7	1250	36	17	ESDI	5.25" HH	
3180S	153	7	1255	36	17	SCSI	5.25" HH	
3180SM	160	7	1250	36	17	SCSI	5.25" HH	
3212/3212 PLUS	11	2	612	17	85/53	MFM	5.25" HH	
3412	21	4	615	17	60	MFM	5.25" HH	
3425/3425 PLUS	21	4	615	17	85/53	MFM	5.25" HH	

MODEL NUMBER	FORMATTED CAPACITY	NO. OF HEADS	NO. OF CYLINDERS	SECTORS PER TRACK	AVERAGE IN MS	INTERFACE	FORM FACTOR	CMOS SETTINGS
3438/3438 PLUS	32	4	615	26	85/53	RLL	5.25" HH	
3650/3650F	42	6	809	17	61/46	MFM	5.25" HH	
3675	63	6	809	26	61	RLL	5.25" HH	
4010	8	2	480	17	133	MFM	5.25" FH	
4020	17	4	480	17	133	MFM	5.25" FH	
5330	25	6	480	17	80	MFM	5.25" FH	
5338	32	6	612	17	65	MFM	5.25" FH	
5440	32	8	480	17	65	MFM	5.25" FH	
5451	43	8	612	17	65	MFM	5.25" FH	
6032	26	3	1024	17	28	MFM	5.25" FH	
6053/6053 II	44	5	1024	17	28	MFM	5.25" FH	
6074	62	7	1024	17	28	MFM	5.25" FH	
6085	71	8	1024	17	28	MFM	5.25" FH	
6128	110	8	1024	26	28	RLL	5.25" FH	
6170E	130	8	1024	36	28	ESDI	5.25" FH	
6212	10	2	612	17	90	MFM	5.25" FH	
7040A	40	4	980	36	19	IDE	3.5 x 1"	
7040S	40	2	1156	36	19	SCSI	3.5 x 1"	
7080A	80	4	980	36	19	IDE	3.5 x 1"	
7080S	81	4	1155	36	19	SCSI	3.5 x 1"	
7426	21	4	612	17	65	MFM	3.5"	
8048	40	4	1024	36	65	SCSI	3.5 x 1"	
8051A	43	4	745	28	28	IDE	3.5 x 1"	
8051AT	42	4	745	28	28	IDE	3.5 x 1"	
8051	45	4	793	28	28	SCSI	3.5 x 1"	
8212	11	2	612	17	68	MFM	3.5 x 1"	
8225	20	2	771	26	68	RLL	3.5 x 1"	
8225AT	21	2	745	28	28	IDE	3.5 x 1"	
8225C	21	2	798	26	68	RLL	3.5 x 1"	
8225S	21	2	804	26	68	SCSI	3.5 x 1"	
8225XT	21	2	805	26	68	XT-IDE	3.5 x 1"	
8412	10	4	306	17	50	MFM	3.5 x 1"	
8425/8425F	21	4	615	17	68/40	MFM	3.5 x 1"	
8425S	21	4	612	17	68	SCSI	3.5 x 1"	
8425XT	21	4	615	17	68	XT-IDE	3.5 x 1"	
8434F	32	4	615	26	40	RLL	3.5 x 1"	
8438/8438F	32	4	615	26	68/40	RLL	3.5 x 1"	
8438XT	31	4	615	26	68	XT-IDE	3.5 x 1"	
8450	40	4	771	26	45	RLL	3.5 x 1"	
8450AT	42	4	745	28	40	IDE	3.5 x 1"	
8450C	42	4	748	26	45	RLL	3.5 x 1"	
8450XT	42	4	805	26	45	XT-IDE	3.5 x 1"	
9000E	338	15	1224	36	16	ESDI	5.25" FH	

MODEL NUMBER	FORMATTED CAPACITY	NO. OF HEADS	NO. OF CYLINDERS	SECTORS PER TRACK	AVERAGE IN MS	INTERFACE	FORM FACTOR	CMOS SETTINGS
9000S	347	15	1220	36	16	SCSI	5.25" FH	
9230E	203	9	1224	36	36	ESDI	5.25" FH	
9230S	203	9	1224	36	36	SCSI	5.25" FH	
9380E	338	15	1224	36	16	ESDI	5.25" FH	
9380S	347	15	1224	36	16	SCSI	5.25" FH	
9380SM	319	15	1218	36	16	SCSI	5.25" FH	
9424E	360	8	1661	54	17	ESDI	5.25" FH	
9424S	355	8	1661	54	17	SCSI	5.25" FH	
9780E	676	15	1661	54	17	ESDI	5.25" FH	
9780S	668	15	1661	54	17	SCSI	5.25" FH	

MITSUBISHI ELECTRONICS

MODEL NUMBER	FORMATTED CAPACITY	NO. OF HEADS	NO. OF CYLINDERS	SECTORS PER TRACK	AVERAGE IN MS	INTERFACE	FORM FACTOR	CMOS SETTINGS
M2860-1	21	4	620	17	120	MFM	8"	
M2860-2	50	6	681	17	120	MFM	8"	
M2860-3	85	8	681	17	120	MFM	8"	
MR 521	10	2	612	17	85	MFM	5.25" HH	
MR 522	20	4	612	17	85	MFM	5.25" HH	
MR 533	25	3	971	17	85	MFM	5.25" HH	
MR 535	42	5	977	17	28	MFM	5.25" HH	
MR 535R	65	5	977	26	28	RLL	5.25" HH	
MR 535S	50	5	977	26	28	SCSI	5.25" HH	
MR 537S	76	5	977	26	28	SCSI	5.25" HH	
MR 5310E	101	5	977	26	28	ESDI	5.25" HH	

MITSUMI ELECTRONICS CORPORATION

MODEL NUMBER	FORMATTED CAPACITY	NO. OF HEADS	NO. OF CYLINDERS	SECTORS PER TRACK	AVERAGE IN MS	INTERFACE	FORM FACTOR	CMOS SETTINGS
HD2509AA	92	4	-	52	16	IDE	2.5" x 4H	
HD 2513AA	130	4	-	52	16	ide	2.5" X 4H	

MMI

MODEL NUMBER	FORMATTED CAPACITY	NO. OF HEADS	NO. OF CYLINDERS	SECTORS PER TRACK	AVERAGE IN MS	INTERFACE	FORM FACTOR	CMOS SETTINGS
M 106	5	2	306	17	75	MFM	3.5 x 1"	
M 112	10	4	306	17	75	MFM	3.5 x 1"	
M 125	20	8	306	17	75	MFM	3.5 x 1"	
M 212	10	4	306	17	75	MFM	5.25" HH	
M 225	20	8	306	17	75	MFM	5.25" HH	
M 306	5	2	306	17	75	MFM	3.5 x 1"	
M 312	10	4	306	17	75	MFM	5.25" HH	
M 325	20	8	306	17	75	MFM	5.25" HH	
M 5012	10	4	306	17	75	MFM	3.5 x 1"	

NCR CORPORATION

MODEL NUMBER	FORMATTED CAPACITY	NO. OF HEADS	NO. OF CYLINDERS	SECTORS PER TRACK	AVERAGE IN MS	INTERFACE	FORM FACTOR	CMOS SETTINGS
6091-5101	323	9	1350	26	27	SCSI	5.25"	
6091-5301	675	15	1350	26	25	SCSI	5.25"	

MODEL NUMBER	FORMATTED CAPACITY	NO. OF HEADS	NO. OF CYLINDERS	SECTORS PER TRACK	AVERAGE IN MS	INTERFACE	FORM FACTOR	CMOS SETTINGS
NEC TECHNOLOGIES INC.								
2247	87	6	841	VAR	80	SMD	8"	
D 3126	20	4	615	17	85	MFM	3.5 x 1"	
D 3142	42	8	642	17	28	MFM	3.5 x 1"	
D 3146H	40	8	615	17	35	MFM	3.5 x 1"	
D 3661	118	7	915	36	40	ESDI	3.5 x 1"	
D 3735	56	2	1084	41	20	AT-IDE	3.5 x 1"	
D 3755	105	4	1250	41	20	AT-IDE	3.5 x 1"	
D 3756	105	4	1251	41	19	PC/AT	3.5"	
D 3761	114	7	915	35	20	AT-IDE	3.5 x 1"	
D 3765	176	4	1486	58	16.5	PC/AT	3.5"	
D 3772	331	7	1468	63	14	PC/AT	3.5"	
D 3781	425	9	1464	63	15	PC/AT	3.5"	
D 3835	45	2	1084	41	20	SCSI	3.5 x 1"	
D 3855	105	4	1250	41	20	SCSI	3.5 x 1"	
D 3856	105	4	1251	41	19	SCSI	3.5"	
D 3861	114	7	915	35	20	SCSI	3.5 x 1"	
D 3865	176	4	1486	58	16.5	SCSI	3.5"	
D 3872	331	7	1468	63	14	SCSI	3.5"	
D 3881	425	9	1464	63	15	SCSI-2	3.5 "	
D 5114	5	2	305	17	-	MFM	5.25"	
D 5124	10	4	309	17	85	MFM	5.25" HH	
D 5126/D 5216H	20	4	612	17	85/40	MFM	5.25" HH	
D 5127H	32	4	615	26	85	RLL	5.25" HH	
D 5146/D 5146H	40	8	615	17	85/40	MFM	5.25" HH	
D 5147H	65	8	615	26	85	RLL	5.25" HH	
D 5392	22	8	615	26	14	IPI-2	5.25" FH	
D 5452	71	10	823	17	65	MFM	5.25" HH	
D 5652	143	10	823	17	23	ESDI	5.25" HH	
D 5655	153	7	1224	35	18	ESDI	5.25" HH	
D 5662	319	15	1224	34	16	ESDI	5.25" FH	
D 5682	664	15	1633	53	16	ESDI	5.25" FH	
D 5862	385	8	1633	65	18	SCSI	5.25" FH	
D 5882	665	15	1633	53	16	SCSI	5.25" FH	
D 5892	1404	19	1678	86	14	SCSI	5.25" FH	
SD040S	40	-	-	-	<.35	SCSI	5.25 "	
SD1205	120	-	-	-	<.35	SCSI	5.25 "	
NEI								
RD 3127	10	2	612	17	150	MFM	5.25"	
RD 3255	21	4	612	17	150	MFM	5.25"	

MODEL NUMBER	FORMATTED CAPACITY	NO. OF HEADS	NO. OF CYLINDERS	SECTORS PER TRACK	AVERAGE IN MS	INTERFACE	FORM FACTOR	CMOS SETTINGS
RD 4127	10	4	3066	17	150	MFM	5.25"	
RD 4255	21	8	306	17	150	MFM	5.25"	

NEWBERRY DATA

NDR 320	21	4	615	17	150	MFM	5.25"	
NDR 340	42	8	615	17	40	MFM	3.5 x 1"	
NDR 360	65	8	615	26	150	RLL	-	
NDR 1065	55	7	918	17	25	MFM	5.25" FH	
NDR 1085	71	8	1025	17	26	MFM	5.25" FH	
NDR 1105	87	11	918	17	25	MFM	5.25" FH	
NDR 1140	119	15	918	17	25	MFM	5.25" FH	
NDR 2085	74	7	1224	17	28	MFM	5.25" FH	
NDR 2140	117	11	1224	17	28	MFM	5.25" FH	
NDR 2190	191	15	918	17	28	MFM	5.25" FH	
NDR 3170S	146	9	1224	26	28	SCSI	5.25" FH	
NDR 3280S	244	15	1224	26	28	SCSI	5.25" FH	
NDR 4170	149	7	1224	34	28	ESDI	5.25" FH	
NDR 4175	179	7	1224	36	28	ESDI	5.25" FH	
NDR 4380	384	15	1224	36	28	ESDI	5.25" FH	
NDR 4380S	319	15	1224	34	28	SCSI	5.25" FH	
PENNY 340	42	8	615	17	28	MFM	5.25"	

NPL

4064	5	2	306	17	-	MFM	5.25" FH	
4127	10	4	306	17	-	MFM	5.25" FH	
4191S	15	6	306	17	-	MFM	5.25" FH	
4255	20	4	615	17	-	MFM	5.25" FH	
NP 02-26S	22	4	640	17	-	MFM	5.25"	
NP 03-13	10	4	306	17	-	MFM	5.25"	
NP 03-6	5	2	306	17	-	MFM	5.25"	

OKIDATA

OD 526	31	4	612	26	65	RLL	3.5 x 1"	
OD 540	47	6	612	26	65	RLL	3.5 x 1"	

OLIVETTI

HD662/11	10	2	612	17	65	MFM	5.25" HH	
HD662/12	20	4	612	17	65	MFM	5.25" HH	
XM 5210	10	4	612	17	65	MFM	5.25" HH	
XM 5220/2	20	4	612	17	85	MFM	5.25" HH	

MODEL NUMBER	FORMATTED CAPACITY	NO. OF HEADS	NO. OF CYLINDERS	SECTORS PER TRACK	AVERAGE IN MS	INTERFACE	FORM FACTOR	CMOS SETTINGS
ORCA TECHNOLOGY CORPORATION								
OT5H 53M	45	5	1024	17	28	MFM	5.25" HH	
OT5H 80R	65	5	1024	26	28	RLL	5.25" HH	
OT5H 138E	115	4	1600	35	25	ESDI	5.25" HH	
OT5H 138S	115	4	1600	35	25	SCSI	5.25" HH	
OT5H 172E	140	5	1600	35	25	ESDI	5.25" HH	
OT5H 172S	140	5	1600	35	25	SCSI	5.25" HH	
OT5H 207E	170	6	1600	35	25	ESDI	5.25" HH	
OT5H 207S	170	6	1600	35	25	SCSI	5.25" HH	
OT5H 760S	702	15	1024	28	14	SCSI	5.25" FH	
OTARI (also see Disctron)								
C 214	10	4	306	17	79	MFM	5.25" FH	
C 507	5	2	306	17	79	MFM	5.25" FH	
C 514	10	4	306	17	79	MFM	5.25" FH	
C 519	15	6	306	17	79	MFM	5.25" FH	
C 526	21	8	306	17	65	MFM	5.25" FH	
PACIFIC MAGTRON								
MT-4115E	115	4	1600	35	16	ESDI	5.25" HH	
MT-4115S	115	4	1600	35	16	SCSI	5.25" HH	
MT-4140E	140	5	1600	35	16	ESDI	5.25" HH	
MT-4140S	140	5	1600	35	16	SCSI	5.25" HH	
MT-4170E	170	6	1600	35	16	ESDI	5.25" HH	
MT-4170S	170	6	1600	35	16	SCSI	5.25" HH	
MT-5400E	360	8	1632	54	14	ESDI	5.25" HH	
MT-5400S	359	8	1623	54	14	SCSI	5.25" HH	
MT-5760E	677	15	1632	54	14	ESDI	5.25" HH	
MT-5760S	673	15	1623	54	14	SCSI	5.25" HH	
PANASONIC								
JU-116	20	4	615	17	85	MFM	3.5 x 1"	
JU-128	42	7	733	17	35	MFM	3.5 x 1"	
PLUS DEVELOPMENT								
HARDCARD 20	21	47	615	17	40	IDE	3.5" 3H	
HARDCARD 40	42	8	612	17	40	IDE	3.5" 3H	
HARDCARD II-40	40	5	925	17	25	IDE	-	
HARDCARD II-80	80	10	925	17	25	IDE	3.5" 3H	
HARDCARD II-XL	105	105	15	806	17	17	IDE	
HARDCARD II-XL	50	52	10	601	17	17	IDE	

MODEL NUMBER	FORMATTED CAPACITY	NO. OF HEADS	NO. OF CYLINDERS	SECTORS PER TRACK	AVERAGE IN MS	INTERFACE	FORM FACTOR	CMOS SETTINGS
IMPULSE 105AT/LP	105	16	755	17	17	IDE	3.5" 3H	16x755x17
IMPULSE 105S	105	6	1019	-	19	SCSI-2	3.5 x 1"	
IMPULSE 1005S/LP	105	4	1056	-	17	SCSI-2	3.5" 3H	
IMPULSE 120AT	120	5	1123	42	15	IDE	3.5 x 1"	9x814x32
IMPULSE 120S	120	5	1123	42	15	SCSI-2	3.5 x 1"	
IMPULSE 170AT	169	7	1123	42	15	IDE	3.5 x 1"	10x966x34
IMPULSE 170S	169	7	1123	42	15	SCSI-2	3.5 x 1"	
IMPULSE 210AT	174	7	1156	42	15	IDE	3.5 x 1"	13x873x36
IMPULSE 210S	174	7	1156	42	15	SCSI-2	3.5 x 1"	
IMPULSE 330AT	331	-	-	-	14	IDE	3.5 x 1"	
IMPULSE 330S	331	-	-	-	14	SCSI-2	3.5 x 1"	
IMPULSE 40AT	41	5	965	17	19	IDE	3.5 x 1"	5x968x17
IMPULSE 40S	42	3	834	-	19	SCSI-2	3.5 x 1"	
IMPULSE 425AT	425	-	-	-	14	IDE	3.5 x 1"	
IMPULSE 52AT/LP	52	8	751	17	17	IDE	3.5" 3H	8x751x17
IMPULSE 52S/LP	52	2	-	-	17	SCSI-2	3.5" 3H	
IMPULSE 80AT	83	10	965	17	19	IDE	3.5 x 1"	6x611x17
IMPULSE 80AT/LP	85	16	616	17	17	IDE	3.5" 3H	6x611x17
IMPULSE 80S	84	6	918	-	19	SCSI-2	3.5 x 1"	
IMPULSE 80S/LP	85	4	-	-	17	SCSI-2	3.5" 3H	

PRAIRIETEK CORPORATION

Prairie 120	21	2	615	34	23	IDE	2.5"	
Prairie 140	40	2	615	34	23	IDE	2.5"	8x615x17
Prairie 220A	20	2	612	34	28	IDE	2.5"	4x615x17
Prairie 220B	20	4	612	34	28	SCSI	2.5"	
Prairie 240	43	4	615	34	28	IDE	2.5"	8x615x17
Prairie 242A	41	4	6615	34	28	IDE	2.5"	8x615x17
Prairie 242S	41	4	1820	34	28	IDE	2.5"	5x942x17
Prairie 282A	82	4	1031	34	28	IDE	2.5"	99x1021x17
Prairie 282S	82	4	1031	34	28	SCSI	2.5"	

PRIAM CORPORATION (also see Vertex)

502	46	7	755	17	65	MFM	5.25" FH	
504	46	7	755	17	65	MFM	5.25" FH	
514	117	11	1224	17	22	MFM	5.25" FH	
519	160	15	1224	17	22	MFM	5.25" FH	
617	153	7	1225	36	20	ESDI	5.25" FH	
623	196	15	752	34	65	ESDI	5.25" FH	
628	241	11	1225	36	20	ESDI	5.25" FH	
630	319	15	1224	34	15	ESDI	5.25" FH	

MODEL NUMBER	FORMATTED CAPACITY	NO. OF HEADS	NO. OF CYLINDERS	SECTORS PER TRACK	AVERAGE IN MS	INTERFACE	FORM FACTOR	CMOS SETTINGS
638	329	15	1225	36	20	ESDI	5.25" FH	
717	153	7	1225	36	20	SCSI	5.25" FH	
728	241	11	1225	36	20	SCSI	5.25" FH	
738	329	15	1225	36	20	SCSI	5.25" FH	
3504	44	5	771	17	65	MFM	3.5 x 1"	
ID20	26	3	987	17	23	MFM	5.25" FH	
ID45H	44	5	1024	17	23	MFM	5.25" FH	
ID330	338	15	1225	36	18	ESDI	5.25" FH	
ID/ED40	43	5	987	17	23	MFM	5.25" FH	
ID/ED45	44	5	1166	17	23	MFM	5.25" FH	
ID/ED60	59	7	1018	17	30	MFM	5.25" FH	
ID/ED62	62	7	1166	17	23	MFM	5.25" FH	
ID/ED75	73	5	1166	25	23	RLL	5.25" FH	
ID/ED100	103	7	1166	25	15	RLL	5.25" FH	
ID/ED120	121	7	1024	33	28	ESDI	5.25" FH	
ID/ED130	132	15	1224	17	13	MFM	5.25" FH	
ID/ED150	159	7	1276	35	28	ESDI	5.25" HH	
ID/ED160	158	7	1225	36	18	ESDI	5.25" FH	
ID160E-PS2	152	7	1195	36	18	PS2	5.25" FH	
ID200L-1	200	15	1195	25	15	IDE	5.25" FH	15x1024x28
ID/ED230	233	15	1224	25	11	RLL	5.25" FH	
ID/ED250	248	11	1225	36	18	ESDI	5.25" FH	
ID330E	336	15	128	36	18	ESDI	5.25" FH	
ID330-PS2	330	15	1195	36	18	PS2	5.25" FH	
ID330S	338	15	1218	36	18	SCSI	5.25" FH	
ID340H-U	340	7	1776	54	14	ESDI	525" FH	
ID660-U	660	15	1628	54	16	ESDI	5.25" FH	
ID700E	701	15	1774	54	16	ESDI	5.25" FH	
ID700S	68	15	1774	54	16	SCSI	5.25" FH	
V 130R	39	3	987	26	28	RLL	5.25" FH	
V 150	42	5	987	17	28	MFM	5.25" FH	
V 160	50	5	1166	17	28	MFM	5.25" FH	
V 170	60	7	987	17	28	MFM	5.25" FH	
V 170R	91	7	987	26	28	RLL	5.25" FH	
V 185	71	7	1166	17	28	MFM	5.25" FH	
V 519	159	15	1224	17	28	MFM	5.25" FH	
V 519-x	62	7	1024	17	28	MFM	5.25" FH	

PROCOM TECHNOLOGY

Propaq 185-15	189	5	1224	36	15	IDE	3.5 x 1"	11x1016x33
HiPer 380	388	8	1224	63	17	ESDI	5.25"	

MODEL NUMBER	FORMATTED CAPACITY	NO. OF HEADS	NO. OF CYLINDERS	SECTORS PER TRACK	AVERAGE IN MS	INTERFACE	FORM FACTOR	CMOS SETTINGS
Si 200/PS3	209	4	1224	63	18	SCSI	3.5 x 1"	
Si 585/S5	601	8	1224	54	17	SCSI	5.25"	
Si 1000/S5	1037	8	1731	77	15	SCSI	5.25"	

PTI (PERIPHERAL TECHNOLOGY)

MODEL NUMBER	FORMATTED CAPACITY	NO. OF HEADS	NO. OF CYLINDERS	SECTORS PER TRACK	AVERAGE IN MS	INTERFACE	FORM FACTOR	CMOS SETTINGS
PT-225	21	4	615	17	35	MFM	3.5 x 1"	
PT-234	28	4	820	17	35	MFM	3.5 x 1"	
PT-238A	32	4	615	26	35	IDE	3.5 x 1"	4x615x26
PT-238R	32	4	615	26	35	RLL	3.5 x 1"	
PT-238S	32	4	615	26	35	SCSI	3.5 x 1"	
PT-251A	43	4	820	26	33	IDE	3.5 x 1"	4x820x26
PT-251R	43	4	820	26	35	RLL	3.5 x 1"	
PT-251S	43	4	820	26	35	SCSI	3.5 x 1"	
PT-325R	21	4	615	26	65	RLL	3.5 x 1"	
PT-338	32	6	615	17	35	MFM	3.5 x 1"	
PT-338R	32	4	615	26	65	RLL	3.5 x 1"	
PT-351	42	6	820	17	35	MFM	3.5 x 1"	
PT-351R	60	6	820	26	35	RLL	3.5 x 1"	
PT-357A	49	6	615	26	35	IDE	3.5 x 1"	6x820x26
PT-357R	49	6	615	26	35	RLL	3.5 x 1"	
PT-357S	49	6	615	26	35	SCSI	3.5 x 1"	
PT-376A	65	6	820	26	35	IDE	3.5 x 1"	
PT-376R	65	6	820	26	35	RLL	3.5 x 1"	
PT-376S	65	6	820	26	35	SCSI	3.5 x 1"	
PT-468	57	8	820	17	35	MFM	3.5 x 1"	
PT-4102A	54	5	820	26	35	IDE	3.5 x 1"	8x820x26
PT-4102R	87	8	820	26	28	RLL	3.5 x 1"	

QUANTUM CORPORATION

MODEL NUMBER	FORMATTED CAPACITY	NO. OF HEADS	NO. OF CYLINDERS	SECTORS PER TRACK	AVERAGE IN MS	INTERFACE	FORM FACTOR	CMOS SETTINGS
2010	10	-	-	17	-	MFM	8"	
2020	20	-	-	17	-	MFM	8"	
2030	30	-	-	17	-	MFM	8"	
2040	40	-	-	17	-	MFM	8"	
2080	80	-	-	17	-	MFM	8"	
GoDrive 40	43	2	957	48	16	IDE/SCSI2	2.5"	5x977x17
GoDrive 80	86	4	957	48	16	IDE/SCSI2	2.5"	10x977x17
GoDrive120	127	4	1097	19	<17	IDE/SCSI2	2.5"	15x965x17
GRS 160	169	4	966	38	<17	IDE/SCSI2	2.5"	4x839x19
Hardcard EZ42	42	5	977	17	19	PC ISA-Slot		
Hardcard EZ85	85	10	977	17	19	PC ISA-Slot		
Hardcard EZ127	127	16	919	17	19	PC ISA-Slot		

MODEL NUMBER	FORMATTED CAPACITY	NO. OF HEADS	NO. OF CYLINDERS	SECTORS PER TRACK	AVERAGE IN MS	INTERFACE	FORM FACTOR	CMOS SETTINGS
Hardcard EZ240	245	15	966	33	16	PC ISA-Slot		
Passport XL42	42	5	965	17	19	SCSI-2	Remov	
Passport XL42	85	10	976	17	17	SCSI-2	Remov	
Passport XL127	127	15	973	17	17	SCSI-2	Remov	
Passport XL170	170	10	1005	33	17	SCSI-2	Remov	
Passport XL240	245	14	1014	33	16	SCSI-2	Remov	
Passport XL525	525	16	1015	63	10	SCSI-2	Remov	
Plus Hardcard XL	50	52	6	957	17	ISA-slot	Slot	
Plus Hardcard XL	105	105	12	1005	17	ISA-Slot	Slot	
XL 231 Plus HC	231	14	976	33	9	ISA-Slot	Slot	
XL 311 Plus HC	311	10	955	63	9	ISA-Slot	Slot	
XL 360 Plus HC	360	11	958	63	9	ISA-Slot	Slot	
ProDrive 40AT	42	3	834	52	19	IDE	3.5 x 1"	5x900x17
ProDrive 40S	42	3	834	52	19	SCSI	3.5 x 1"	
ProDrive 80AT	84	6	834	63	19	IDE	3.5 x 1"	10x960x17
ProDrive 80S	84	6	834	63	19	SCSI	3.5 x 1"	
ProDrive 105S	105	6	1019	63	19	SCSI	3.5 x 1"	
ProDrive 120AT	120	5	1123	63	19	IDE	3.5 x 1"	14x984x17
ProDrive 120S	120	5	1123	63	15	SCSI	3.5 x 1"	
ProDrive 170AT	168	4	1536	65	19	IDE	3.5 x 1"	
ProDrive 170S	168	4	1536	65	15	SCSI	3.5 x 1"	
ProDrive 210AT	210	7	1156	63	15	IDE	3.5 x 1"	13x950x33
ProDrive 210S	210	7	1156	63	15	SCSI	3.5 x 1"	
ProDrive 330AT	330	7	1536	63	14	IDE	3.5 x 1"	10x1023x63
ProDrive 330S	330	7	1536	63	14	SCSI	3.5 x 1"	
ProDrive 425AT	425	7	1800	63	14	IDE	3.5 x 1"	13x1013x63
ProDrive 425S	425	7	1800	63	14	SCSI	3.5 x 1"	
ProDrive 700S	700	8	1921	63	12	SCSI-2	3.5 x 1"	
ProDrive 1050	1050	12	2224	63	12	SCSI-2	3.5 x 1"	
ProDrive 1225	1225	14	2224	63	12	SCSI-2	3.5 x 1"	
ProDrive ELS 42	42	1	977	63	19	SCSI-2	3.5 x 1"	
ProDrive ELS 127	85	2	977	63	17	SCSI-2	3.5 x 1"	
ProDrive ELS 170	170	4	1011	63	17	SCSI-2	3.5 x 1"	
ProDrive LPS 80	85	4	611	63	15	SCSI	3.5 x 1"	
ProDrive LPS 105	105	4	1219	63	17	SCSI	3.5 x 1"	
ProDrive LPS 105AT	105	4	1219	63	17	IDE	3.5 x 1"	12x1000x17
ProDrive LPS 105S	105	4	1219	63	17	SCSI	3.5 x 1"	
ProDrive LPS 120	122	2	-	44	16	IDE/SCSI	3.5 x 1"	14x980x17
ProDrive LPS 240	245	4	1530	44	16	IDE	3.5 x 1"	14x1014x33
ProDrive LPS 525	525	6	1800	81	10	SCSI2/IDE	3.5 x 1"	16x1017x63
Q-160	200	12	971	36	16	SCSI	5.25" HH	

MODEL NUMBER	FORMATTED CAPACITY	NO. OF HEADS	NO. OF CYLINDERS	SECTORS PER TRACK	AVERAGE IN MS	INTERFACE	FORM FACTOR	CMOS SETTINGS
Q-250	53	4	823	36	28	SCSI	5.25" HH	
Q-280	80	6	823	36	28	SCSI	5.25" HH	
Q-510	8	2	512	17	85	MFM	5.25" HH	
Q-520	18	4	512	17	85	MFM	5.25" HH	
Q-530	27	6	512	17	47	MFM	5.25" FH	
Q-540	36	8	512	17	40	MFM	5.25" FH	

RICOH

MODEL NUMBER	FORMATTED CAPACITY	NO. OF HEADS	NO. OF CYLINDERS	SECTORS PER TRACK	AVERAGE IN MS	INTERFACE	FORM FACTOR	CMOS SETTINGS
RH-5130	10	2	612	17	85	MFM	-	
RH-5260	10	2	615	17	85	MFM	-	
RH-5261	10	2	612	-	85	SCSI	-	
RH-5500	50	2	1285	76	25	SCSI	5.25" HH	
RH-9150AR	49	2	1285	76	25	SCSI	5.25" HH	

RMS

MODEL NUMBER	FORMATTED CAPACITY	NO. OF HEADS	NO. OF CYLINDERS	SECTORS PER TRACK	AVERAGE IN MS	INTERFACE	FORM FACTOR	CMOS SETTINGS
RMS 506	5	4	153	17	130	MFM	5.25"	
RMS 509	7.5	6	153	17	130	MFM	5.25"	
RMS 512	10	8	153	17	130	MFM	5.25"	

RODIME SYSTEMS, INC.

MODEL NUMBER	FORMATTED CAPACITY	NO. OF HEADS	NO. OF CYLINDERS	SECTORS PER TRACK	AVERAGE IN MS	INTERFACE	FORM FACTOR	CMOS SETTINGS
Cobra 40AT	44	8	640	17	20	IDE	3.5 x 1"	8x640x17
Cobra 80AT	80	4	1030	28	20	IDE	3.5 x 1"	4x1024x17
Cobra 110AT	105	7	1053	28	20	ESDI	3.5 x 1"	13x972x17
Cobra 110E	1105	7	1053	28	18	SCSI-2	3.5 x 1"	
Cobra 210AT	210	7	1156	62	20	IDE	3.5 x 1"	13x956x33
Cobra 210E	210	7	1156	62	18	SCSI-2	3.5 x 1"	
Cobra 650E	650	15	1224	63	17	SCSI-2	5.25"	

RODIME, INC.

MODEL NUMBER	FORMATTED CAPACITY	NO. OF HEADS	NO. OF CYLINDERS	SECTORS PER TRACK	AVERAGE IN MS	INTERFACE	FORM FACTOR	CMOS SETTINGS
RO 101	3	2	192	17	85	MFM	5.25" FH	
RO 102	6	4	192	17	85	MFM	5.25" FH	
RO 103	9	6	192	17	85	MFM	5.25" FH	
RO 104	12	8	192	17	85	MFM	5.25" FH	
RO 201	5	2	321	17	90	MFM	5.25" FH	
RO 201E	11	2	640	17	55	MFM	5.25" FH	
RO 202	11	4	321	17	90	MFM	5.25" FH	
RO 202E	22	4	640	17	55	MFM	5.25" FH	
RO 203	16	6	321	17	90	MFM	5.25" FH	
RO 203E	33	6	640	17	55	MFM	5.25" FH	
RO 204	22	8	320	17	90	MFM	5.25" FH	
RO 204E	44	8	640	17	55	MFM	5.25" FH	

MODEL NUMBER	FORMATTED CAPACITY	NO. OF HEADS	NO. OF CYLINDERS	SECTORS PER TRACK	AVERAGE IN MS	INTERFACE	FORM FACTOR	CMOS SETTINGS
RO 251	5	2	306	17	85	MFM	5.25" HH	
RO 252	11	4	306	17	85	MFM	5.25" HH	
RO 351	5	2	306	17	85	MFM	3.5 x 1"	
RO 352	11	4	306	17	85	MFM	3.5 x 1"	
RO 652A	20	4	306	33	85	SCSI	3.5 x 1"	
RO 652B	20	4	306	33	85	SCSI	3.5 x 1"	
RO 752A	20	4	306	33	85	SCSI	3.5 x 1"	
RO 3045	37	5	872	17	28	MFM	3.5 x 1"	
RO 3055	45	6	872	17	28	MFM	3.5 x 1"	
RO 3055T	45	3	1053	28	24	SCSI	3.5 x 1"	
RO 3057S	45	5	680	26	28	SCSI	3.5 x 1"	
RO 3058A	45	3	868	34	18	IDE	3.5 x 1"	3x868x34
RO 3058T	45	3	868	34	18	SCSI	3.5 x 1"	
RO 3060R	49	5	750	26	28	RLL	3.5 x 1"	
RO 3065	53	7	872	17	28	MFM	3.5 x 1"	
RO 3075R	59	6	750	26	28	RLL	3.5 x 1"	
RO 3085R	69	7	750	26	28	RLL	3.5 x 1"	
RO 3085S	70	7	750	26	28	SCSI	3.5 x 1"	
RO 3088A	75	5	868	34	18	IDE	3.5 x 1"	5x868x34
RO 3088T	76	5	868	34	18	SCSI	3.5 x 1"	
RO 3090T	75	5	1053	28	24	SCSI	3.5 x 1"	
RO 3095A	80	5	923	34	19	IDE	3.5 x 1"	5x923x34
RO 3099AP	80	4	1030	28	18	IDE	3.5 x 1"	4x1024X29
RO 3121A	122	4	1207	53	14	IDE	3.5 x 1"	14x1001x17
RO 3128A	105	7	868	34	18	IDE	3.5 x 1"	14x868x17
RO 3128T	105	7	868	34	18	SCSI	3.5 x 1"	
RO 3129TS	105	5	1091	41	18	SCSI	3.5 x 1"	
RO 3130T	105	7	1053	28	24	SCSI	5.25" HH	
RO 3135A	112	7	923	34	19	IDE	3.5 x 1"	14x923x17
RO 3139A	112	7	923	28	18	IDE	3.5 x 1"	14x923x17
RO 3139TP	112	5	1148	42	18	SCSI	3.5 x 1"	
RO 3199AP	112	5	1168	28	18	IDE	3.5 x 1"	13x989X17
RI 3199TS	163	7	1216	41	18	SCSI	3.5 x 1"	
RO 3209A	163	15	759	28	18	IDE	3.5 x 1"	10x964x33
RO 3259A	213	15	990	28	18	IDE	3.5 x 1"	13x990x33
RO 3259AP	213	9	1235	28	18	IDE	3.5 x 1"	13x969x33
RO 3259T	210	9	1216	41	18	SCSI	3.5 x 1"	
RO 3259TP	210	9	1189	42	18	SCSI	3.5 x 1"	
RO 3259TS	210	9	1216	41	18	SCSI	3.5 x 1"	
RO 5065	53	5	1224	17	28	MFM	5.25" HH	
RO 5075E	65	3	1224	35	22	ESDI	5.25" HH	

MODEL NUMBER	FORMATTED CAPACITY	NO. OF HEADS	NO. OF CYLINDERS	SECTORS PER TRACK	AVERAGE IN MS	INTERFACE	FORM FACTOR	CMOS SETTINGS
RO 5075S	61	3	1219	33	28	SCSI	5.25" HH	
RO 5078S	61	5	1219	33	18	SCSI	5.25" HH	
RO 5090	74	7	1224	17	28	MFM	5.25" HH	
RO 5125E	109	5	1224	35	22	ESDI	5.25" HH	
RO 5125S	103	5	1219	33	24	SCSI	5.25" HH	
RO 5128S	103	7	1219	33	19	SCSI	5.25" HH	
RO 54130R	114	7	1224	26	28	RLL	5.25" HH	
RP 5178S	144	7	1219	33	19	SCSI	5.25" HH	
RO 5180E	153	7	1224	35	22	ESDI	5.25" HH	
RO 5180S	144	7	1219	33	24	SCSI	5.25" HH	

SAMSUNG

MODEL NUMBER	FORMATTED CAPACITY	NO. OF HEADS	NO. OF CYLINDERS	SECTORS PER TRACK	AVERAGE IN MS	INTERFACE	FORM FACTOR	CMOS SETTINGS
SHD-3101A	105	4	1282	40	19	IDE	3.5 x 1"	
SHD-3201S	211	7	1376	43	16	SCSI	3.5 x 1"	

SEAGATE TECHNOLOGIES

This table shows how to identify Seagate drive model numbers

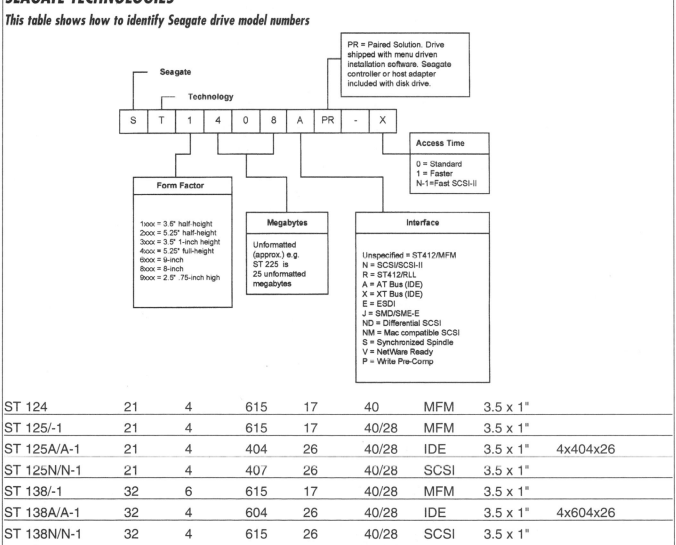

MODEL NUMBER	FORMATTED CAPACITY	NO. OF HEADS	NO. OF CYLINDERS	SECTORS PER TRACK	AVERAGE IN MS	INTERFACE	FORM FACTOR	CMOS SETTINGS
ST 124	21	4	615	17	40	MFM	3.5 x 1"	
ST 125/-1	21	4	615	17	40/28	MFM	3.5 x 1"	
ST 125A/A-1	21	4	404	26	40/28	IDE	3.5 x 1"	4x404x26
ST 125N/N-1	21	4	407	26	40/28	SCSI	3.5 x 1"	
ST 138/-1	32	6	615	17	40/28	MFM	3.5 x 1"	
ST 138A/A-1	32	4	604	26	40/28	IDE	3.5 x 1"	4x604x26
ST 138N/N-1	32	4	615	26	40/28	SCSI	3.5 x 1"	

MODEL NUMBER	FORMATTED CAPACITY	NO. OF HEADS	NO. OF CYLINDERS	SECTORS PER TRACK	AVERAGE IN MS	INTERFACE	FORM FACTOR	CMOS SETTINGS
ST 138R/R-1	33	4	615	26	40/28	RLL	3.5 x 1"	
ST 151	43	5	977	17	24	MFM	3.5 x 1"	
ST 157A/A-1	45	6	560	26	40/28	IDE	3.5 x 1"	6x560x26
ST 157N/N-1	49	6	615	26	40/28	SCSI	3.5 x 1"	
ST 157R/R-1	49	6	615	26	40/28	RLL	3.5 x 1"	
ST 177N	61	5	921	26	24	SCSI	3.5 x 1"	
ST 206	5	2	306	17	-	MFM	5.25" HH	
ST 212	10	4	306	17	65	MFM	5.25" HH	
ST 213	10	2	615	17	65	MFM	5.25" HH	
ST 225	21	4	615	17	65	MFM	5.25" HH	
ST 225N	21	4	615	17	65	SCSI	5.25" HH	
ST 225R	21	2	667	31	70	RLL	5.25" HH	
ST 238R	32	4	615	26	65	RLL	5.25" HH	
ST 250R	42	4	667	31	70	RLL	5.25" HH	
ST 251/-1	43	6	820	17	40/28	MFM	5.25" HH	
ST 251N	43	4	820	26	40	SCSI	5.25" HH	
ST 251N-1	43	4	630	34	28	SCSI	5.25" HH	
ST 252	43	6	820	17	40	MFM	5.25" HH	
ST 253	43	5	989	17	28	MFM	5.25" HH	
ST 274A	65	5	948	26	29	IDE	5.25" HH	5x948x26
ST 277N	65	6	820	26	40	SCSI	5.25" HH	
ST 277N-1	65	6	628	34	28	SCSI	5.25" HH	
ST 277R/R-1	66	6	820	26	40/28	RLL	5.25" HH	
ST 278R/R-1	66	6	820	26	40/28	RLL	5.25" HH	
ST 279R	65	5	989	26	28	RLL	5.25" HH	
ST 280A	71	5	1032	27	29	IDE	5.25" HH	5x1024x27
ST 296N	80	6	820	34	28	SCSI	5.25" HH	
ST 325A/X	21	4	615	17	28	IDE	3.5 x 1"	4x615x17
ST 351 A/X	42.8	6	820	17	28	IDE	3.5 x 1"	6x820x17
ST 406	5	2	306	17	85	MFM	5.25" FH	
ST 412	10	4	306	17	85	MFM	5.25" FH	
ST 419	15	6	306	17	85	MFM	5.25" FH	
ST 506	5	4	153	17	85	MFM	5.25" FH	
ST 1057A	53	6	1024	17	18	IDE	3.5 x 1"	6x1024x17
ST 1090A	79	5	1072	29	15	IDE	3.5 x 1"	5x1024x33
ST 1090N	79	5	1068	29	15	SCSI	3.5 x 1"	
ST 1096N	80	7	906	26	20	SCSI	3.5 x 1"	
ST 1100	83	9	1072	17	15	MFM	3.5 x 1"	
ST 1102A	89	10	1024	17	18	IDE	3.5 x 1"	10x1024x17
ST 1106R	91	7	977	26	24	RLL	3.5 x 1"	
ST 1111A	98	5	1072	36	15	IDE	3.5 x 1"	5x1024x37

MODEL NUMBER	FORMATTED CAPACITY	NO. OF HEADS	NO. OF CYLINDERS	SECTORS PER TRACK	AVERAGE IN MS	INTERFACE	FORM FACTOR	CMOS SETTINGS
ST 1111E	98	5	1072	36	15	ESDI	3.5 x 1"	
ST 1111N	98	5	1068	36	15	SCSI	3.5 x 1"	
ST 1126A	111	7	1072	29	15	IDE	3.5 x 1"	13x980x17
ST 1126N	111	7	1068	29	15	SCSI	3.5 x 1"	
ST 1133A	117	5	1272	36	15	IDE	3.5 x 1"	14x960x17
ST 1133NS	116	5	1268	36	15	SCSI-2	3.5 x 1"	
ST 1144A	130	15	1385	36	18	IDE	3.5 x 1"	15x1001x17
ST 1150R	128	9	1072	26	15	RLL	3.5 x 1"	
ST 1156A	138	7	1072	36	15	IDE	3.5 x 1"	16x990x17
ST 1156E	138	7	1072	36	15	ESDI	3.5 x 1"	
ST 1156N/NS	138	7	1068	36	15	SCSI 1&2	3.5 x 1"	
ST 1162A	143	9	1072	29	15	IDE	3.5 x 1"	9x1024x30
ST 1162N	142	9	1068	29	15	SCSI	3.5 x 1"	
ST 1186A	164	7	1272	36	15	IDE	3.5 x 1"	10x970x33
ST 1186NS	163	7	1268	36	15	SCSI-2	3.5 x 1"	
ST 1201A	177	9	1072	36	15	IDE	3.5 x 1"	9x804x48
ST 1201E	177	9	1072	36	15	ESDI	3.5 x 1"	
ST 1201N/NS	177	9	1068	36	15	SCSI 1&2	3.5 x 1"	
ST 1239A	211	9	1272	36	15	IDE	3.5 x 1"	12x954x36
ST 1239NS	210	9	1268	36	15	SCSI-2	3.5 x 1"	
ST 1400A	331	7	1475	62	14	IDE	3.5 x 1"	15x736x62
ST 1400N	331	7	1476	62	14	SCSI-2	3.5 x 1"	
ST 1401A	340	9	1121	62	12	IDE	3.5 x 1"	15x736x62
ST 1401N	338	9	1121	62	12	SCSI-2	3.5 x 1"	
ST 1480A	426	9	1474	-	14	IDE	3.5 x 1"	15x895x62
ST 1480N/ND	426	9	1476	62	14	SCSI-2	3.5 x 1"	
ST 1480N/NV	426	9	1476	62	14	SCSI-2	3.5 x 1"	
ST 1481N	426	9	1476	62	14	F SCSI	3.5 x 1"	
ST 1581N	525	9	1476	77	14	F SCSI	3.5 x 1"	
ST 1980N/ND	860	13	1730	77	9.9/11.4	F SCSI	3.5 x 1"	
ST 2106E	92	5	1024	36	18	ESDI	5.25" HH	
ST 2106N/NM	91	5	1022	36	18	SCSI	5.25" HH	
ST 2125 N/NM/NV	107	3	1544	45	18	SCSI	5.25" HH	
ST 2182E	160	4	1453	54	16	ESDI	5.25" HH	
ST 2209 N/NM/NV	179	5	1544	45	18	SCSI	5.25" HH	
ST 2274A	241	5	1747	54	16	IDE	5.25" HH	16x465x63
ST 2383A	338	7	1747	54	16	IDE	5.25" HH	16x737x56
ST 2383A	338	7	1747	54	16	ESDI	5.25" HH	
ST 2383 ALL	332	7	1261	74	14	SCSI 1&2	5.25" HH	
ST 2502 ALL	435	7	1755	69	16	SCSI 1&2	5.25" HH	
ST 3051A	43.1	7	706	17	16	IDE	3.5 x 1"	6x820x17

MODEL NUMBER	FORMATTED CAPACITY	NO. OF HEADS	NO. OF CYLINDERS	SECTORS PER TRACK	AVERAGE IN MS	INTERFACE	FORM FACTOR	CMOS SETTINGS
ST 3096A	89.1	16	590	17	14	IDE	3.5 x 1"	10x1024x17
ST 3120A	106.9	16	754	17	15	IDE	3.5 x 1"	12x1024x17
ST 3144A	130.7	16	953	17	16	IDE	3.5 x 1"	15x1001x17
ST 3243S	214	16	413	63	16	IDE	3.5 x 1"	12x1024x36
ST 3283A	245.3	16	470	63	12	IDE	3.5 x 1"	16x470x63
ST 3283N	248.6	N/A	N/A	-	12	FSCSI	3.5 x 1"	
ST 3385A	340	14	767	63	12	IDE	3.5 x 1"	16x659x63
ST 3500A	426	8	1820	36	10	IDE	3.5 x 1"	16x825x63
ST 3500N/ND	426	16	825	63	10	SCSI-2	3.5 x 1"	
ST 3550A	452.4	7	1810	63	12	IDE	3.5 x 1"	16x876x63
ST 3550N	456.5	7	1810	63	12	FSCSI	3.5 x 1"	
ST 3600A	540	7	1874	-	10.5/12	IDE	3.5 x 1"	16x1024x63
ST 3600N/ND	525	7	1872	-	10.2/12	FSCSI-2	3.5 x 1"	
ST 3601N/ND	535	7	1872	-	10.2/12	FSCSI	3.5 x 1"	
ST 4026	21	4	615	17	40	MFM	5.25" FH	
ST 4038	31	5	733	17	40	MFM	5.25" FH	
ST 4051	42	5	977	17	40	MFM	5.25" FH	
ST 4053	45	5	1024	17	28	MFM	5.25" FH	
ST 4085	71	8	1024	17	28	MFM	5.25" FH	
ST 4086	72	9	925	17	28	MFM	5.25" FH	
ST 4096	80.2	9	1024	17	28	RLL	5.25" FH	
ST 4097	80	9	1024	17	28	MFM	5.25" FH	
ST 4135R	115	9	960	26	28	RLL	5.25" FH	
ST 4144R	122.7	9	1024	26	28	MFM	5.25" FH	
ST 4182E	160	9	969	36	16	ESDI	5.25" FH	
ST 4182N/NM	155	9	969	35	16	SCSI	5.25" FH	
ST 4350N/NM	300	9	1412	46	17	SCSI	5.25" FH	
ST 4376N/NM/NV	330	9	1546	45	18	SCSI	5.25" FH	
ST 4383E	338	13	1412	36	18	ESDI	5.25" FH	
ST 4384E	338	15	1224	36	14.5	ESDI	5.25" FH	
ST 4385N/NM/NV	330	15	1412	55	10.7	SCSI	5.25" FH	
ST 4442E	380	15	1412	36	16	ESDI	5.25" FH	
ST 4702N/NM	601	15	1546	50	16.5	SCSI	5.25" FH	
ST 4766E	676	15	1632	54	15.5	SCSI	5.25" FH	
ST 9095A	85.3	16	1024	63	16	IDE	2.5"	
ST 9096A	85.3	16	1024	63	16	IDE	2.5"	
ST 9096N	85	-	-	-	16	SCSI-2	2.5 x .75"	
ST 9100AG	85.3	16	1024	-	16	IDE	2.5"	
ST 9144	42.6	16	1024	63	16	IDE	2.5"	
ST 9144A	127.9	16	1024	63	16	IDE	2.5 x.75"	
ST 9144N	128	-	-	-	16	SCSI-2	2.5 x.75"	

MODEL NUMBER	FORMATTED CAPACITY	NO. OF HEADS	NO. OF CYLINDERS	SECTORS PER TRACK	AVERAGE IN MS	INTERFACE	FORM FACTOR	CMOS SETTINGS
ST 9235N	209	N/A	N/A	-	16	SCSI	2.5"	
ST 9295AG	261	16	1024	-	16	IDE	2.5"	
ST 11200N/ND	1050	15	1877	-	10.5/	FSCSI2	3.5 x 1"	
ST 11200N/ND	1050	15	1877	-	10.512/	FWSCSI2	3.5 x 1"	
ST 11700N/ND	1430	13	2626	-	9/10.5	FSCSI2	3.5 x 1"	
ST 11701N/ND	1430	13	2626	63	9/10.5	FWSCSI2	3.5 x 1"	
ST 11750N/ND	1437	12	2756	63	8/9	FSCSI2	3.5 x 1"	
ST 11751N/ND	1437	12	2756	63	8/9	FWSCSI2	3.5 x 1"	
ST 12400N/ND	2100	19	2626	63	9/10.5	FSCSI2	3.5 x 1"	
ST 12401N/ND	2100	19	2626	63	9/10.5	FWSCSI2	3.5 x 1"	
ST 12550N/ND	2100	19	2756	63	8/9	FSCSI2	3.5 x 1"	
ST 12551N/ND	2100	19	2756	63	8/9	FSCSI2	3.5 x 1"	
ST 31200N/ND	1050	9	2626	63	9/10.5	FSCSI2	3.5 x 1"	
ST 41097J	1097	17	2101	71	12	SMD	5.25" FH	
ST 41200N/NM/NV	1037	15	1931	71	15	SCSI	5.25" FH	
ST 41201J/K	1200	15	2101	71	11.5	SMD	5.25" FH	
ST 41291K	1200	15	2101	71	11.5	DP-IPI	5.25" FH	
ST 41520K	1370	18	2101	71	11.5	DP-SCSI2	5.25" FH	
ST 41600N/ND	1370	18	2101	75	11.5	SCSI2	5.25" FH	
ST 41601N/ND	1370	18	2101	75	11.5	FSCSI2	5.25" FH	
ST 41650N/ND	1415	15	2107	87	15	SCSI-2	5.25" FH	
ST 41651N/ND	1415	15	2107	77	15	FSCSI2	5.25" FH	
ST 41800K	1624	15	2627	81	11	DP IPI-2	5.25" FH	
ST 42000N/ND	1792	15	2627	84	11	FSCSI2	5.25" FH	
ST 42100N	1900	15	2574	84	12.9	FSCSI2	5.25" FH	
ST 42100NM/ND/NV	1037	15	1931	84	15	SCSI-2	5.25" FH	
ST 42101N/ND	1900	15	2574	84	13	FWSCSI2	5.25" FH	
ST 42400N	2100	19	2653	84	11	SCSI-2	5.25" FH	
ST 43200K	3385*	19	2738	91	10/11	FWSCSI2	5.25" FH	
ST 43400N/ND	2912	19	2738	88	11	FSCSI2	5.25" FH	
ST 43401N/ND	2912	19	2738	88	10/11	FWSCSI2	5.25" FH	
ST 43402ND	2912	19	2738	88	10/11	FWSCSI2	5.25" FH	
ST 81236J/K/N	1056	17	1635	64	15	IPI-2/SCSI	8"	
ST 81123J	1123*	17	1635	64	15	SMD	8"	
ST 81154K	1154*	17	1635	64	15	IPI-2	8"	
ST 82030J/K	2030*	21	2120	64	11	IPI-2	8"	

SHUGART

MODEL NUMBER	FORMATTED CAPACITY	NO. OF HEADS	NO. OF CYLINDERS	SECTORS PER TRACK	AVERAGE IN MS	INTERFACE	FORM FACTOR	CMOS SETTINGS
SA 604	5	4	160	17	140	MFM	5.25" FH	
SA 606	7	6	160	17	140	MFM	5.25" FH	
SA 607	5	2	306	17	80	MFM	5.25" FH	

MODEL NUMBER	FORMATTED CAPACITY	NO. OF HEADS	NO. OF CYLINDERS	SECTORS PER TRACK	AVERAGE IN MS	INTERFACE	FORM FACTOR	CMOS SETTINGS
SA 612	11	4	306	17	100	MFM	5.25" FH	
SA 706	6	2	320	17	120	MFM	5.25" FH	
SA 712	11	4	320	17	80	MFM	5.25" FH	
SA 724	20	8	320	17	80	MFM	5.25" FH	
SA 1002	5	8	320	17	120	MFM	8"	
SA 1004	10	-	-	17	-	MFM	8"	
SA 1106	30	-	-	17	-	MFM	8"	
SA 4004	14	-	-	17	-	MFM	14"	
SA 4008	29	-	-	17	-	MFM	14"	
SA 4100	56	-	-	17	-	MFM	14"	

SIEMENS

1200	174	8	1216	35	25	ESDI	5.25" FH	
1300	261	12	1216	35	25	ESDI	5.25" FH	
2200	174	8	1216	35	25	SCSI	5.25" FH	
2300	261	12	1216	35	25	SCSI	5.25" FH	
4410	322	11	1100	52	16	ESDI	5.25" FH	
4420	334	11	1100	54	17	SCSI	5.25" FH	
5710	655	15	1224	48	16	ESDI	5.25" FH	
5720	655	15	1224	48	16	SCSI	5.25" FH	
5810	688	15	1658	54	14	ESDI	5.25" FH	
5820	688	15	1658	54	14	SCSI	5.25" FH	
6200	1062	15	1921	72	14	SCSI	5.25" FH	

STORAGE DIMENSIONS

AT-40	44	5	1024	17	28	MFM	5.25" HH	
AT-70	71	8	1024	17	28	MFM	5.25" HH	
AT-100R	109	8	1024	26	28	RLL	5.25" FH	
AT-100S	105	3	1224	54	19	SCSI	3.5 x 1"	
AT-120	119	15	918	17	27	MFM	5.25" FH	
AT-133	133	15	1024	17	28	MFM	5.25" FH	
AT-140	142	8	1024	34	28	ESDI	5.25" FH	
AT-155E	157	7	1224	52	14	ESDI	5.25" FH	
AT-155S	156	9	1224	36	36	SCSI	5.25" FH	
AT-160	159	15	1224	17	28	MFM	5.25" FH	
AT-200	204	15	1024	26	28	RLL	5.25" FH	
AT-200S	204	7	1021	26	15	SCSI	3.5 x 1"	
AT-320E	329	15	1224	35	16	ESDI	5.25" FH	
AT-320S	320	15	1224	36	16	SCSI	5.25" FH	
AT-335E	338	15	1224	36	16	ESDI	5.25" FH	
AT-650E	651	15	1632	52	16	ESDI	5.25" FH	

MODEL NUMBER	FORMATTED CAPACITY	NO. OF HEADS	NO. OF CYLINDERS	SECTORS PER TRACK	AVERAGE IN MS	INTERFACE	FORM FACTOR	CMOS SETTINGS
AT-650S	651	15	1632	54	16	SCSI	5.25" FH	
AT-1000S	1000	15	1632	63	15	SCSI	5.25" FH	
MAC-195	195	7	-	-	15	SCSI	3.5 x 1"	
PS-155E	156	9	1224	36	14	ESDI	5.25" FH	
PS-155S	156	9	1224	36	14	SCSI	5.25" FH	
PS-320S	320	15	1224	36	16	SCSI	5.25" FH	
PS-335E	338	15	1224	36	16	ESDI	5.25" FH	
PS-650S	651	15	1632	54	16	SCSI	5.25" FH	

SYQUEST TECHNOLOGY

MODEL NUMBER	FORMATTED CAPACITY	NO. OF HEADS	NO. OF CYLINDERS	SECTORS PER TRACK	AVERAGE IN MS	INTERFACE	FORM FACTOR	CMOS SETTINGS
SQ 225F	20	4	615	17	85	MFM	5.25" HH	
SQ 306F	5	4	306	17	85	MFM	5.25" HH	
SQ 306R	5	2	306	17	85	MFM	5.25" HH	
SQ 306RD	5	2	306	17	85	MFM	5.25" HH	
SQ 312	10	2	615	17	85	MFM	4" HH	
SQ 312RD	10	2	615	17	85	MFM	4" HH	
SQ 315F	21	4	612	17	65	MFM	4" HH	
SQ 319	10	2	612	17	85	MFM	4" HH	
SQ 325	21	4	612	17	85	MFM	4" HH	
SQ 325F	20	4	615	17	65	MFM	4" HH	
SQ 338F	30	6	615	17	65	MFM	4" HH	
SQ 340AF	38	6	640	17	65	MFM	4" HH	
SQ 555	44	2	1021	42	20	SCSI	5.25" HH	5x1011x17
SQ 2542A	43	2	1481	41	15	IDE	2.5"	5x988x17
SQ 5110	89	2	1720	82	20	SCSI	5.25" HH	13x972x17

TANDON COMPUTER CORPORATION

MODEL NUMBER	FORMATTED CAPACITY	NO. OF HEADS	NO. OF CYLINDERS	SECTORS PER TRACK	AVERAGE IN MS	INTERFACE	FORM FACTOR	CMOS SETTINGS
TM 244	41	4	782	26	37	RLL	5.25" HH	
TM 246	62	6	782	26	37	RLL	5.25" HH	
TM 251	5	2	306	17	85	MFM	5.25" HH	
TM 252	10	4	306	17	85	MFM	5.25" HH	
TM 261	10	2	615	17	85	MFM	3.5 x 1"	
TM 262	21	4	615	17	65	MFM	3.5 x 1"	
TM 262R	20	2	782	26	85	RLL	3.5 x 1"	
TM 264	41	4	782	26	85	RLL	3.5 x 1"	
TM 344	41	4	782	26	37	RLL	3.5 x 1"	
TM 346	62	6	782	26	37	RLL	3.5 x 1"	
TM 361	10	2	615	17	65	MFM	3.5 x 1"	
TM 362	21	4	615	17	65	MFM	3.5 x 1"	
TM 362R	20	2	782	26	85	RLL	3.5 x 1"	
TM 364	41	4	782	26	85	RLL	3.5 x 1"	

MODEL NUMBER	FORMATTED CAPACITY	NO. OF HEADS	NO. OF CYLINDERS	SECTORS PER TRACK	AVERAGE IN MS	INTERFACE	FORM FACTOR	CMOS SETTINGS
TM 501	5	2	306	17	85	MFM	5.25" FH	
TM 502	10	4	306	17	85	MFM	5.25" FH	
TM 503	15	6	306	17	85	MFM	5.25" FH	
TM 602S	5	4	153	17	85	MFM	5.25" FH	
TM 603S	10	6	153	17	85	MFM	5.25" FH	
TM 603SE	21	6	230	17	85	MFM	5.25" FH	
TM 702	20	4	615	26	40	RLL	5.25" FH	
TM 702AT	8	4	615	17	35	MFM	5.25" FH	
TM 703	10	5	733	17	40	MFM	5.25" FH	
TM 703C	25	5	733	17	40	MFM	5.25" FH	
TM 703AT	31	5	733	17	35	MFM	5.25" FH	
TM 705	41	5	962	17	40	MFM	5.25" FH	
TM 755	43	5	981	17	33	MFM	5.25" HH	
TM 2085	74	9	1004	36	25	SCSI	5.25" FH	
TM 2128	115	9	1004	36	25	SCSI	5.25"	
TM 2170	154	9	1344	36	25	SCSI	5.25"	
TM 3085	71	8	1024	17	37	MFM	3.5 x 1"	
TM 3085R	71	8	1024	17	37	MFM	3.5 x 1"	
TM 3085R	104	8	1024	26	37	RLL	3.5 x 1"	

TANDY CORPORATION

25-1045	20	4	615	17	35	IDE	5.25" HH	4x615x17
25-1046	43	4	782	27	28	IDE	5.25" HH	
25-1047	20	4	615	17	35	IDE	-	4x615x17

TEAC AMERICA, INC.

SD 150	10	4	306	17	80	MFM	5.25" FH	
SD 340A	43	2	1050	40	23	IDE	3.5 x 1"	
SD 340S	43	2	1050	40	23	SCSI	3.5 x 1"	
SD 380	86	4	1050	40	20	IDE	3.5 x 1"	
SD 380S	86	4	1050	40	20	SCSI	3.5 x 1"	
SD 510	10	4	306	17	65	MFM	5.25" FH	
SD 520	20	4	615	17	65	MFM	5.25" FH	
SD 540	40	8	615	17	65	MFM	5.25" FH	
SD 3105H	105	4	1381	48	-20	IDE	3.5 x 1"	12x1005x17

TEXAS INSTRUMENTS

TI-5	5	4	153	17	65	MFM	5.25" FH	

TOKICO

DK 503-2	10	4	306	17	105	MFM	5.25" FH	

MODEL NUMBER	FORMATTED CAPACITY	NO. OF HEADS	NO. OF CYLINDERS	SECTORS PER TRACK	AVERAGE IN MS	INTERFACE	FORM FACTOR	CMOS SETTINGS
TOSHIBA AMERICA, INC.								
MK 53FA (M)	43	5	830	17	30	MFM	5.25" FH	
MK 53FA (R)	64	5	830	26	30	RLL	5.25" FH	
MK 53FB (M)	43	5	830	17	25	MFM	5.25" FH	
MK 53FB (R)	64	5	830	26	25	RLL	5.25" FH	
MK 54FA (M)	60	7	831	17	30	MFM	5.25" FH	
MK 54FA (R)	90	7	830	26	25	RLL	5.25" FH	
MK 54FB (M)	60	7	830	17	25	MFM	5.25" FH	
MK 54FB (R)	90	7	830	26	25	RLL	5.25" FH	
MK 56FA (M)	86	10	830	17	30	MFM	5.25" FH	
MK 56FA (R)	129	10	830	26	30	RLL	5.25" FH	
MK 56FB(M)	72	10	830	17	25	MFM	5.25" FH	
MK 56FB (R)	105	10	830	26	25	RLL	5.25" FH	
MK 72	72	10	830	17	25	MFM	3.5 x 1"	
MK 72PCR	105	10	830	26	25	RLL	3.5 x 1"	
MK 130	53	9	733	17	25	MFM	3.5 x 1"	
MK 134FA (M)	44	7	733	17	25	MFM	3.5 x 1"	
MK 134FA (R)	65	7	733	26	23	RLL	3.5 x 1"	
MK 153FA	74	5	830	35	23	ESDI	5.25" FH	
MK 153FB	74	5	830	35	23	SCSI	5.25" FH	
MK 154FA	104	7	830	35	23	ESDI	5.25" FH	
MK 154FB	104	7	830	35	23	SCSI	5.25" FH	
MK 156FA	145	10	830	35	23	ESDI	5.25" FH	
MK 156FB	145	10	830	35	23	SCSI	5.25" FH	
MK 232FB	45	3	845	35	25	SCSI	3.5 x 1"	
MK 233FB	76	5	845	35	25	SCSI	3.5 x 1"	
MK 234FB	101	7	845	35	25	IDE	3.5 x 1"	12x945x17
MK 234FC	101	7	845	35	25	IDE	3.5 x 1"	12x945x17
MK 250FA	382	10	1224	35	18	ESDI	5.25" FH	
MK 250FB	382	10	1224	35	18	SCSI	5.25" FH	
MK 355FA	459	9	1632	53	16	ESDI	5.25" FH	
MK 355FB	459	9	1632	53	16	SCSI	5.25" FH	
MK 358FA	676	15	1661	53	16	ESDI	5.25" FH	
MK 358FB	676	15	1661	53	16	SCSI	5.25" FH	
MK 556FA	152	10	830	36	23	ESDI	5.25" FH	
MK 1034FC	107	4	1339	39	16	IDE	3.5"	8x664x39
MK 1122FC	43	5	988	17	23	IDE	2.5"	
MK 2024FC	86	2	988	17	19	IDE	2.5"	16x615x17
MK 2124FC	130	6	1820	48	17	IDE	2.5"	16x1155x17

MODEL NUMBER	FORMATTED CAPACITY	NO. OF HEADS	NO. OF CYLINDERS	SECTORS PER TRACK	AVERAGE IN MS	INTERFACE	FORM FACTOR	CMOS SETTINGS
TULIN								
TL 213	10	2	640	17	105	MFM	5.25" HH	
TL 226	22	4	640	17	85	MFM	5.25" HH	
TL 238	22	4	640	17	85	MFM	5.25" HH	
TL 240	33	6	640	17	65	MFM	5.25" HH	
TL 258	33	6	640	17	65	MFM	5.25" HH	
TL 326	22	4	640	17	65	MFM	5.25" HH	
TL 340	33	6	640	17	65	MFM	5.25" HH	
VERTEX (also see Priam)								
V 130	26	3	987	17	40	MFM	5.25" FH	
V 150	43	5	987	17	40	MFM	5.25" FH	
V 170	60	7	987	17	28	MFM	5.25" FH	
WESTERN DIGITAL								
WS 262	20	4	615	17	80	MFM	3.5 x 1"	
WD 344R	40	4	782	26	40	RLL	3.5 x 1"	
WD 362	20	4	615	17	80	MFM	3.5 x 1"	
WD 382R	20	2	782	26	85	RLL	3.5 x 1"	
WD 383R	30	4	615	26	85	RLL	3.5 x 1"	
WD 384R	40	4	782	26	85	RLL	3.5 x 1"	
WD 544R	40	4	782	26	40	RLL	3.5 x 1"	
WD 582R	20	2	782	26	85	RLL	3.5 x 1"	
WD 383R	30	4	615	26	85	RLL	3.5 x 1"	
WD 384R	40	4	782	26	85	RLL	3.5 x 1"	
WD 93024A	20	2	782	27	28	IDE	3.5 x 1"	
WD 93024X	20	2	782	27	39	IDE	3.5 x 1"	
WD 93028A/AD	20	2	782	27	69	IDE	3.5 x 1"	
WD 93028X	20	2	782	27	80	IDE	3.5 x 1"	
WD 93034X	30	3	782	27	39	IDE	3.5 x 1"	
WD 93038X	30	3	782	27	80	IDE	3.5 x 1"	
WD 93044A	40	4	782	27	28	IDE	3.5 x 1"	
WD 93044X	40	4	782	27	39	IDE	3.5 x 1"	
WD 93048AD	40	4	782	27	69	IDE	3.5 x 1"	
WD 93048A	40	4	782	27	69	IDE	3.5 x 1"	
WD 93048X	40	4	782	27	80	IDE	3.5 x 1"	
WD 95024A	20	2	782	27	28	IDE	5.25" HH	
WD 95024X	20	2	782	27	39	IDE	5.25" HH	
WD 95028Z	20	2	782	27	39	IDE	5.25" HH	
WD 95028AD	20	2	782	27	69	IDE	3.5 x 1"	
WD 95028X	20	2	782	27	80	IDE	5.25" HH	

MODEL NUMBER	FORMATTED CAPACITY	NO. OF HEADS	NO. OF CYLINDERS	SECTORS PER TRACK	AVERAGE IN MS	INTERFACE	FORM FACTOR	CMOS SETTINGS
WD 95034X	30	3	782	27	39	IDE	3.5 x 1"	
WD 95044A	40	4	782	27	28	IDE	3.5 x 1"	
WD 95044X	40	4	782	27	39	IDE	3.5 x 1"	
WD 95048A	40	4	782	27	69	IDE	3.5 x 1"	
WD 95048AD	40	4	782	27	69	IDE	3.5 X 1"	
WD 95048X	40	4	782	27	80	IDE	5.25" HH	
WD AB130	32	5	733	17	19	IDE	2.5"	
WD AH260	63	7	1024	17	19	IDE	2.5"	
WD AC140	42	5	980	17	18	IDE	3.5"	
WD AC160	62	7	1024	17	17	IDE	3.5 x 1"	
WD AC280	85	10	980	17	18	IDE	3.5 x 1"	
WD AC2120	125	8	872	35	17	IDE	3.5 x 1"	
WD AP4200	212	12	987	35	15	IDE	3.5 x 1"	
WD M1130-44	41	2	1104	33	19	MCA	3.5 x 1"	
WD M1130-72	68	4	1104	32	19	MCA	3.5 x 1"	
WD SC8320	320	6	2105	35	12	SCSI-2	3.5 x 1"	
WD SC8400	400	8	1900	35	12	SCSI-2	3.5 x 1"	
WD SP4200	209	4	1900	35	14	SCSI-2	3.5 x 1"	
Condor	320	6	2105	35	13	SCSI	3.5 x 1"	
Piranha 105A	105	2	1917	35	15	IDE	3.5 x 1"	13x1000x16
Piranha 105S	105	2	1917	35	15	SCSI	3.5 x 1"	
Piranha 210A	210	4	1917	35	15	IDE	3.5 x 1"	13x950x33
Piranha 210S	210	4	1917	35	15	SCSI	3.5 x 1"	

XEBEX

OWL I	10	4	306	17/32	65	MFM	5.25" HH	
OWL II	20	4	612	17/32	65	MFM	5.25" HH	
OWL III	40	4	888	27	38	MFM	5.25" HH	

YE-DATA AMERICA, INC. (also see C. Itoh)

YD-3042	44	4	788	42	28	SCSI	3.5 x 1"	
YD-3081B	45	2	1057	42	28	SCSI	3.5 x 1"	
YD-3082	87	8	788	42	28	SCSI	3.5 x 1"	
YD-3082B	90	4	1057	42	28	SCSI	3.5 x 1"	
YD-3083B	136	6	1057	42	28	SCSI	3.5 x 1"	
YD-3084B	181	8	1057	42	28	SCSI	3.5 x 1"	
YD-3161B	45	2	1057	42	19	IDE	3.5 x 1"	
YD-3162B	90	4	1057	42	19	IDE	3.5 x 1"	
YD-3181B	45	2	1057	42	19	SCSI	3.5 x 1"	
YD-3182B	90	4	1057	42	19	SCSI	3.5 x 1"	
YD-3530	32	5	731	17	-	MFM	5.25" HH	

MODEL NUMBER	FORMATTED CAPACITY	NO. OF HEADS	NO. OF CYLINDERS	SECTORS PER TRACK	AVERAGE IN MS	INTERFACE	FORM FACTOR	CMOS SETTINGS
YD-3540	45	7	731	17	-	MFM	5.25" HH	

ZENTEC

MODEL NUMBER	FORMATTED CAPACITY	NO. OF HEADS	NO. OF CYLINDERS	SECTORS PER TRACK	AVERAGE IN MS	INTERFACE	FORM FACTOR	CMOS SETTINGS
ZH 3100	86	-	-	-	20	IDE/SCSI	3.5 x 1"	
ZH 3140	121	-	-	-	20	IDE/SCSI	3.5 x 1"	
ZH 3240	237	-	-	-	12	IDE/SCSI	3.5 x 1"	
ZH 3380	332	-	-	-	12	IDE/SCSI	3.5 x 1"	
ZH 3490	427	-	-	-	12	IDE/SCSI	3.5 x 1"	

CONTROLLER INFORMATION

Listed on the following pages are descriptions of common controller cards with performance ratings and jumper settings. The jumper setting listed are the default or most common configuration we've seen.

The jumper settings needed to make the card work in your system may be different. Use the settings shown a reference guide only. Be sure to consult the controller card manual for detailed information.

ADAPTEC CONTROLLERS

Adaptec 1520
Adaptec 1522

A 16-bit controller that also supports SCSI-II. The 1520 is a hard drive only controller. The 1522 also supports 2 floppy drives.

Default Jumpers:

In: J5-2, J5-5, J5-6,
        J6-1, J6-2, J6-3, J6-5,
        J7-1*, J7-2*, J7-4*, J7-6*,
        J8-4,
        J9-2, J9-6, J9-7, J9-8

Notes: * Used only on 1522 (floppy jumpers).

Adaptec 1540A
Adapted 1542A

A 16-bit SCSI controller. The 1540A is a hard drive only controller. The 1542A also supports 2 floppy drives.

Default Jumpers:

In: J1-10, J6-1, J7-1, J14-2, J15-2, J17-1 & 2*,
     J18-1& 2*, J19-1 & 2*

Notes: * Used only on 1542 (floppy jumpers).

Adaptec AHA 1542CF

A 16-bit SCSI host adapter. Supports a total of 7 internal and external devices. Also supports floppy drives.

Default Jumpers:
All switches off.

Adaptec 2070A

An 8-bit controller that controls 2 hard drives only.

Default Jumpers:
None installed.

To format, use: G=C800:CCC

Notes: Jumper E-F for removable cartridge 0.
        Jumper G-H for removable cartridge drive 1.
        Jumper K-L for controller internal diagnostics.
        Boards with P/N 401400 Rev. C or later are required for use in AT class machines.

Adaptec 2320A
Adaptec 2322A
Adaptec 2322A-8

A 16-bit ESDI controller that controls 2 hard drives at 10MHz and supports 1:1 interleave. The 2322A also supports two floppy drives. The 2322A-8 supports data rates up to 15 MHz.

Default Jumpers:

In: J13-1 & 2, J18-1 & 2, J19-1 & 2*, J20-1 & 2*, J21-2 &3*

To format, use: G=C800:5

Notes: *2322A only for floppy control.

CCAT CONTROLLERS

CCAT 200A IDE Card p/n 6620000440

A 16-bit IDE controller that controls 2 IDE drives and 2 floppy drives.

Default Jumpers:
    None installed.

To format, use: G=C800:5

CONNER PERIPHERALS CONTROLLERS

Conner IDE Card p/n 02090-002

A 16-bit IDE paddle board that controlls 2 IDE drives.

Default Jumpers:
    E1, E2, and E4 installed.

CORPORATE SYSTEM CENTER CONTROLLERS

CSC AK-47 VESA SCSI-II

A 16-bit high speed SCSI-II controller. Controls up to 7 total internal or external hard, optical, and tape drives. Also supports up to 4 floppy drives.

Memory Base Address Setting:

SW7	SW8	Address Range
Off	On	D000-D7FF**
On	Off	D800-DFFF
On	On	C800-CFFF
Off	Off	E000-E7FF

I/O Base Address Setting:

SW6	I/O Address Range
On	180H-19FH
Off	320H-33FH**

Floppy Drive Enable/Disable:

SW1	Floppy Control
On	Disable Floppy
Off	Enable Floppy

Interrupt Select Options:

I/O Address	Valid IRQ
180-19FH	IRQ14
320-33FH	IRQ15

CSC Caching ESDI Card

A 16-bit caching controller which supports up to a total of 7 ESDI hard drive devices, and up to 4 floppy drives. Up to 32MB on board cache.

Jumper Functions and Defaults

Jumper	Function	Default	Jumper
W1	BIOS Address	On	On
W2	BIOS Address	On	On

Jumper	Function	Default	Jumper
W3	Hard Disk Enable	On	On
W4	Fixed Disk Address	Off	Off
W5	Floppy Enable	On	On
W6	Cache Enable	Off	On
W7	DACK2 Enable	On	On
W9	Floppy Address	3FX	1/2

IRQ Settings on SIP Switch SW1:

IRQ Level	1	2	3	4	5	6	7	8
11	On	On	Off	Off	Off	Off	Off	Off
12	Off	Off	On	On	Off	Off	Off	Off
14	Off	Off	Off	Off	On	On	Off	Off
15	Off	Off	Off	Off	Off	Off	On	On

Notes: To disable the hard drive controller: remove the jumper from W# and turn ALL switches on SW1 to OFF.
To disable the floppy controller: remove the jumpers from W5 and W7.
To disable the Caching Algorithm: install the jumper at W6.

CSC FastCache 32

Supports up to 7 SCSI devices and 4 floppy drives. Up to 32MB on board cache. A single 8-bit position dipswitch is used for hardware configurationsa and are shown below.

Base Address			Floppy Drive	
SW0	SW1		SW5	
On	On	D000	On	Enabled
On	Off	C800	Off	Disabled
Off	On	E000		
Off	Off	D800		

Bus Speed		Module Type		
SW4		SW2	SW3	
On	Fast	On	On	256K
Off	Faster	On	Off	1MB
		Off	On	4MB

Notes: Switches 6 & 7 controll the floppy disk density and should be left ON for standard floppy drives. Switch 8 is not in use.

CSC FastCache 64

Supports up to 7 SCSI devices and 4 floppy drives. Up to 64MB onboard cache. A single 8-bit position dipswitch is used for hardware configurations and are shown below.

Interrupt				Floppy Drive	
SW1	SW2			SW3	
Off	Off	None		On	Enabled
On	Off	IRQ14		Off	Disabled
Off	On	IRQ15			

Bus Speed				Module Type		
SW4				SW%	SW6	
On	Non-Std.			On	On	256K
Off	Standard			Off	On	1MB
				On	Off	4MB
				Off	Off	16MB

Base Address		
SW7	SW8	Address
Off	On	C800
On	Pn	D000
Off	Off	D800
On	Off	E000

CSC IDE FastCache 64

The IDE FastCache 64 controls up to 2 IDE drives and 4 floppy drives and can have up to 64MB of onboard cache memory.

Base Address				SIMM Type		
SW1	SW2	Address		SW3	SW4	Module
On	Off	C800*		On	On	256KB
On	On	D000		On	Off	1MB
Off	Off	D800		Off	On	4MB
Off	On	E000		Off	Off	16MB

Bus Compatibility				Floppy Drives	
SW5				SW6	
Off	Primary*			On	Enabled*
On	Non-Standard			Off	Disabled

IDE Address		Drive Interrupt	
SW7		SW8	
On	Primary*	On	Buffered*
Off	Secondary	Off	Unbuffered

DTC CONTROLLERS

DTC 3250

An 8-bit SCSI controller that also controls 2 floppy drives.

Default Jumpers:
In: W1

On: SW2-1, SW2-8, SW2-9

To format, use: GSDIAG

DTC 3180
DTC 3280

A 16-bit SCSI controller. 3280 also controls floppy drives.

Default Jumpers:
In: W1-2 &3, W2-1 & 2*, SW1-8*, SW1-10*

To format, use: GSDIAG program

Notes: * 3280 only for floppy drives.

DTC 3290

An EISA bus SCSI controller with up to 4MB cache RAM. Controls up to 7 SCSI devices and two floppy drives.

Default Jumpers:
None installed

To format, use: GSDIAG program

DTC 5150

An XT (8-bit) MFM controller for 2 hard drives. 2:1 interleave.

Default Jumpers:
    In: W1-1 & 2, W2, W3-2 & 3

    On: SW4-4

    To format, use: G=C800:5

DTC 5180C Rev. C
DTC 5180C Rev. G
DTC 5180CR
DTC 5180 CRH
DTC 5180I

These are 16-bit MFM hard drives, 2:1 interleave controllers.

Default Jumpers:
    C Rev. c: W1
    C Rev. G: W2, W3, W6
    CR: W4-2 & 3, W5-2 & 3
    CRH: W5-1 & 2, W6, W7
    I: W4-2 & 3

To format, use: G=C800:5

DTC 5187
DTC 5187-1
DTC 5187CR
DTC 5187CRH
DTC 5187I

These are 16-bit RLL hard drives, 2:1 interleave controllers.

Default Jumpers:
    87 & 87-1: W1, W2, W4, W7-7 & 8
    CR: W1, W4-2 & 3, W5-1 & 2, W6, W7, W8
    CRH: W1, W4-1 & 2, W5-2 & 3, W6, W7, W8
    I: W4-2 & 3, W6, W7, W8

To format, use: G=C800:5

DTC 5280CA-1
DTC 5280CZ-1
DTC 5280CRA
DTC 5280CRZ
DTC 5280I

These are 16-bit MFM hard drives, 2:1 interleave controllers that also controll 2 floppy drives.

Default Jumpers:
    All Models: W5, W6

To format, use: G=C800:5

DTC 5387
DTC 5287CR
DTC 5287IO

These are 16-bit RLL hard drive, 2:1 interleave controllers that also control 2 floppy drives.

Default Jumpers:
    87: W3, W5, W6, W7
    CR: W5, W6-2 & 3, W8, W10
    I: W5, W6, W8, W10

To format, use: G=C800:5

DTC 6180A
DTC 6280A

A 16-bit ESDI, 1:1 interleave controller for 2 hard drives at 10MHz. Model 6280 also controls 2 floppy drives.

Default Jumpers:
    6180: W3, SW1-4
    6280: W2

To format, use: G=C800:5

DTC 6180-15T
DTC 6280-15T

A 16-bit ESDI, 1:1 interleave controller for 2 hard drives at 10MHz. Model 6280-15T also controlls 2 floppy drives.

Default Jumpers:
    6180-15T: W4-2 &3, SW1-1, SW1--4, SW1-7, SW1-8
    6280-15T: SW1-2, SW1-6, SW1-9, SW1-10

To format, use: G=C800:5

DTC 6180-15TX
DTC 6280-15TX
DTC 6282-24

These are 16-bit ESDI, 1:1 interleave controllers that control 2 hard drives. Models 6280-15TX and 6282-24 also control 2 floppy drives. These controllers can operate at data rates up to 15 MHz.

Default Jumpers:
    6180-15TX: W4-1 & 2, W5-1 & 2, SW1-1, SW1-4, SW1-7, SW1-8
    6280-15TX: W4-1 & 2, W5-1 & 2, SW1-2, SW1-6, SW1-9, SW1-10
    6282-24: W1-5 & 6, W1-7 & 8, W1-9 & 10, W2-21 & 22, W2-25 &26

To format, use: G=C800

DTC 6290-24
DTC 6290E

EISA, ESDI, 1:1 interleave controllers with up to 4MB cache. Controls up to 4 ESDI drives and 2 floppy drives.

Default Jumpers:
    6290-24: SW1-4, SW1-5
    6290E: SW1-4

To format, use: G=c800:5

Notes: Supports translation mode for large capacity drives.

DTC 6195
DTC 6295

EISA, ESDI, 1:1 interleave hard drive controllers. Model 6295 also controls 2 floppy drives.

Default Jumpers:
    6195: SW1-4
    6295: SW1-4, SW1-8

To format, use: G=C800:5

Notes: Supports translation mode for large capacity drives.

DTC 7180
DTC 7280

An MFM, 1:1 interleave hard drive controller. Model 7280 also supports 2 floppy drives.

Default Jumpers:
    7180: W4-2 & 3, W6
    7280: W5, W6

To format, usc: G=C800:5

DTC 7187
DTC 7287

An RLL, 1:1 interleave hard drive controller. Model 7287 also supports 2 floppy drives.

Default Jumpers:
    7187: W4-2 & 3, W6, W7, W8
    7287: W5, W6, W8

To format, use: G=C800:5

DTK CONTROLLERS (Data Enterprises)

PTI-215

A 16-bit IDE controller for 2 hard drives and 2 floppy drives.

Default Jumpers:
W1-1 & 2, W2-1 & 2, W3-2 & 3

To format, use: DOS

EVEREX CONTROLLERS

EVEREX EV-346

A 16-Bit, 1:1 interleave, MFM hard drive and floppy controller.

Default Jumpers:
None installed.

To format, use: Speedstor or Disk Manager.

Future Domain CONTROLLERS

Future Domain TMC-885

An 8-bit SCSI host adapter, also controls 2 floppy drives.

Default Jumpers:
W1 & W2

To format, use: Future Domain software.

Future Domain TMC-1670SVP

A 16-bit SCSI-2 host adapter, also controlls 2 floppy drives.

Default Jumpers: None

To format, use: Future Domain software.

Future Domain TMC-1660DNK
Future Domain TMC-1680DNK

A 16-bit SCSI-II host adapter. The 1680 also controls 2 floppy drives.

Default Jumpers: None.

To format, use: Future Domain software.

LONGSHINE CONTROLLERS

Longshine LCS-6210D

A 8-bit MFM controller for 2 hard drives.

Default Jumpers:
1-8 hcads: JPI 1 & 2
9-16 heads: JPI 2 & 3

G=C800:5

NCL CONTROLLERS

NDC 5125

A 16-bit MFM controller for 2 hard drives and 2 floppy drives.

Default Jumpers:
JP5, lower two pins jumpered.

To format, use: DIAGS, Speedstor, or Disk Manager.

SEAGATE CONTROLLERS

Seagate ST-01
Seagate ST-02

An 8-bit SCSI controller for up to 7 devices. ST-02 also supports 2 floppy drives.

Default Jumpers:
  JP6-N & O, JP6-Q & R

To format, use: G=C800:5

Notes: * For ST-02 only.

Seagate ST-05X

An 8-bit XT-IDE controller for up to 2 hard drives.

Default Jumpers:
  None installed

To format, use: DOS

Seagate ST-07A
Seagate ST08A

A 16-bit AT-ide controller for up to 2 hard drives. Model ST-08A also controls up to 2 floppy drives.

Default Jumpers:
  JP4-1 & 1*, JP5-1 & 2

To format, use: DOS

Notes: * For ST-08A

Seagate ST-11M
Seagate ST-11R

ST-11M is an 8-bit MFM drive controller. ST-11R is an 8-bit RLL hard drive controller.

Default Jumpers:
    None installed.

To format, use: G=C800:5

Seagate SR21-M
Seagate SR21-R
Seagate SR22-M
Seagate SR21-R

ST-21M and ST-22M are 16-bit MFM hard drive ontrollers. ST-21R and ST-22R are 16-bit RLL controllers. ST-22M and ST-22R also control 2 floppy drives.

Default Jumpers:
    JP4*

To format, use: G=C800:5

Notes: * ST-22M & ST-22R only.

SMS/OMTI CONTROLLERS

SMS/OMTI 510

An 8-bit SCSI controller for 2 hard drives only.

Default Jumpers:
    W1-2 & 3, W2-2 & 3, W3-1 & 2, W4-2 & 3

To format, use: G=C800:5 pr OMT/DISK

Notes: HA7 BIOS may cause partitioning problems with DOS
             4.0 or later.

SMS/OMTI 822

A 16-bit SCSI controller for 2 hard drives and 2 floppy drives.

Default Jumpers:
W5, W7, W17, W21, W24, W28, W32, W33-1 & 2, W35, W38-2 & 3

To format, use: G=C800:6

Notes: Drivers for Novell and more than 2 SCSI drives are available. May not operated in machines with 8MHz bus speed and no wait states.

SMS/OMTI 5520

An 8-bit MFM controller for 2 hard drives only.

Default Jumpers:
None installed.

To format, use: G=C800:6

SMS.OMTI 5527

An 8-bit RLL controller for 2 hard drives only.

Default Jumpers:
None installed

To format, use: G=C800:6

SMS/OMTI 8120

A 16-bit MFM controller for 2 hard drives only.

Default Jumpers:
None installed

To format, use: G=C800:6

SMS/OMTI 8140
SMS/OMTI 8240

A 16-bit MFM controller for 2 hard drives. Supports 1:1 interleave and fast (average 700Kb/sec transfer). The 8240 also supports 2 floppy drives.

Default Jumpers:
   None installed.

To format, use: OMPI/DISK software.

Notes: Incompatible with some motherboards due to timing problem., but runs solid as a rock in boards with the original AT-IBM bus timing specifications.

SMS/OMTI 8630

A 16-bit ESDI controller for 2 hard drives and 2 floppy drives. Operates with drive rates up to 10MHz. Supports 1:1 interleave, and has 32K look-ahead cache.

Default Jumpers:
   W17, W20-2 &3, W23, W24, W25

To format, use: G=CA00:6

SMS/OMTI 8640

A 16-bit ESDI controller for 2 hard drives and 2 floppy drives. Operates with drive rates up to 15MHZ. Supports 1:1 interleave, and has 32K look-ahead cache.

Default Jumpers:
   W17, W20-2 &3, W23, W24, W25

To format, usc: G=CA00:6

Storage Dimension Controllers

Storage Dimension SDC-801
Storage Dimension SDC-802

An 8-bit SCSI host adapter. SDC-802 also controlls 2 floppy drives.

Default Jumpers:
SDC-801: JP1-3
SDC-802: W3

To format, use: SpeedStor or Disk Manager.

Ultrastor Controllers

Ultrastor 12C

A 1:1 interleave caching controller for 2 ESDI drives at up to 24MHz. Also controls up to 3 floppy drives. Up to 16MB of caching memory can be installed.

Default Jumpers:
None installed.

To format, use: G=C800:5

Ultrastor 12F
Ultrastor 12F-24

A 1:1 interleave controller for 2 ESDI drives at up to 22MHz. Also controls up to 3 floppy drives. The 12F-24 supports 24MHz drives.

Default Jumpers:
None installed.

To format, use: G=C800:5

Ultrastor 15C
Ultrastor 15CM

A caching controller for 2 IDE drives and 3 floppy drives. Up to 8 MB of cache memory can be installed. The 15CM also provides 2 serial ports, 2 parallel ports, and a game port.

Default Jumpers:
    None installed.

To format, use: G=C800:5

Ultrastor 22C
Ultrastor 22F

An ESDI bus ESDI controller for 2 hard drives only. Supports 24MHz drives. The 22C caching controller supports up to 16MB of cache memory.

Default Jumpers:
    None installed.

To format, use: G=C800:5

Ultrastor 24C
Ultrastor 24F

An EISA bus SCSI controller for up to 7 devices and 3 floppy drives. The 24C supports up to 16MB of cache memory.

Default Jumpers:
    None installed.

To format, use: G=C800:5

Wangtec Controllers

Wangtec EV-831

Controls QIC-36 tape drives.

Default Jumpers:
E 3 & 4, E 8 & 9, E 11 & 12, W1, W2, W3

Notes: See manual for switch settings, DMA settings and inter rupt jumpers. Most reported problems with this card are a result of DMA interrupt problems.

Western Digital Controllers

Western Digital WD AT140

A 16-bit adapter board for 2 AT type IDE drives and 2 floppy drives.

Default Jumpers:
W1- 3 & 4

To format, use: DOS

Western Digital WD AT240

A 16-bit adapter board for 2 AT type IDE drives and 2 floppy drives.

Default Jumpers:
W1-3 & 4, W2-1 & 2

To format, use: DOS

Western Digital WD AT440

A 16-bit adapter board for 2 AT type IDE drives and 2 floppy drives. This board also has 2 serial ports and 1 parallel port.

Default jumpers:
W3-3 & 4, W4-1 & 2, W7-3 & 4, W7-5 & 6, W7-7 & 8, W8-1 & 2, W8-5 & 6, W8-9 & 10, W9-1 & 2, W9-3 & 4

To format, use: DOS

WesternDigital WD XT140

An 8-bit adapter board for 2 XT type IDE drives.

Default jumpers:
No jumpers on board.

To format, use: G=C800:5

Notes: Does not support daisy-chain cables. A separate cable must be used for each drive.

Western Digital WD XT150R

An 8-bit adapter board for 1 XT type IDE drive.

Default jumpers:
W1- 2 & 3, W2-1 & 2, W3-1 & 2

To format, use: G=C800:5

Notes: Does not support daisy-chain cables.

Western Digital WD SCS-XTAT

An 8-bit SCSI host adapter for AT and XT type computers.

Default jumpers: See Manual.

To format, use: See Manual.

Western Digital WD XTGEN
Western Digital WD XTGEN2
Western Digital WD XTGENR

XT-GEN and XT-GEN2 are 8-bit MFM controllers for 2 hard drives only. XT-GENR is an 8-bit RLL controller.

Default jumpers:
    GEN: No jumpers on board.
    GEN2: None.
    GEN2R: None.

To format, use: G=C800:5

Western Digital WD 1002A-FOX F001/003

The F001 controls 2 floppy drives only (No BIOS on card). The F003 includes a ROM BIOS.

Default jumpers:
    W4-2 & 3

Western Digital WD 1002A-FOX F002/004

F002 controls 4 floppy drives only. F004 has a BIOS on card which permits installation of 1.2 and 1.44 MB drives in XT machines that normally only support 360K or 720K drives.

Default jumpers:

    W1-2 & 3, W2-2 & 3, W3-1 & 2, W5-2 & 3, W6-2 & 3

To format, use: DOS

Notes: Uses WS-37C65 chip, works well in 286/386 machines.

Western Digital WD 1002-27X
Western Digital WD 1002A-27X

An 8-bit RLL controller for 2 hard drives only.

Default jumpers:

    1002-27X: W3, W4-2 & 3, W6-2 & 3, W8-2 & 3, S1-5, S1-6, W9
    1002A-27X: W1, W2

To format, use: G=C800:5

Western Digital WD 1002A-WX1

An 8-bit MFM controller for 2 hard drives only.

Default jumpers:

    W3, W4-2 & 3, W6-2 & 3, W8-2 & 3, S1-8 (AT Mode)

To format, use: G=C800:5

Western Digital WD 1003-WAH

A 16-bit MFM, 3:1 interleave controller that supports 2 hard drives only.

Default jumpers:

    W6-2 & 3, W4-2 & 3, W5-1 & 2

To format, use: DIAGS, SpeedStor, or Disk Manager.

Western Digital WD 1003-WA2

Controls 2 hard drives at 3:1 interleave and 2 floppy drives.

Default jumpers:
E 2 & 3, E 4 & 5, E 7 & 8

To format, use: DIAGS, SpeedStor, or Disk Manager.

Western Digital WD 1003V-MM1
Western Digital WD 1003V-MM2

MM1 is a 16-bit MFM controller for 2 hard drives at 2:1 interleave. MM2 also controls 2 floppy drives.

Default jumpers:
None installed.

To format, use: DIAGS, SpeedStor, or Disk Manager.

Western Digital WD 1003V-SR1
Western Digital WD 1003V-SR2

SR1 is a 16-bit controller for 2 hard drives at 2:1 interleave. SR2 also controls 2 floppy drives.

Default jumpers:
None installed

To format, use: DIAGS, SpeedStor, or Disk Manager.

Western Digital WD 1004-27X
Western Digital WD 1004A-27X

An 8-bit controller for 2 hard drives only.

Default jumpers:

W25

To format, use: G=C800:5

Western Digital WD 1004A-WX1

An 8-bit MFM controller for 2 hard drives only.

Default jumpers:

See manual.

To format, use: G=C800:5

Western Digital WD 10045A-WAH

An ESDI controller for 2 hard drives only.

Default jumpers:

See manual.

To format, use: G=C800:5

Western Digital WD 1006V-MC1
Western Digital WD 1006V-MCR

MC1 is an MFM micro channel controller, and MCR is an RLL micro channel controller.

Default jumpers:

No jumpers on board.

To format, use: System supplied software.

Western Digital WD 1006V-MM1
Western Digital WD 1006V-MM2

MM1 is a 16-bit MFM controller for 2 hard drives at 1:1 inteleave. MM2 also controls 2 floppy drives.

Default jumpers:
No jumpers installed.

To format, use: DIAGS, SpeedStorm or Disk Manager.

Western Digital WD 1006V-SR1
Western Digital WD 1006V-SR2

SR1 is a 16-bit RLL controller for 2 hard drives at 1:1 inteleave. SR2 also controls 2 floppy drives.

Default jumpers:
None installed.

To format, use: C800:5

Western Digital WD 1007A-WA2
A 16-bit ESDI controller for 2 hard drives and 2 floppy drives. Supports 1:1 interleave, and 10MBits/sec transfer.

Default jumpers:
See manual.

To format, use: C800:5

Western Digital WD 1007A-WAH

A 16-bit ESDI controller for 2 hard drives. 10 Mb/ps at 1:1 interleave.

Default jumpers:
    W1-2 & 3, W2-2 & 3, W3

To format, use: C800:5

Western Digital WD 1007V-MC1

A micro channel controller for 2 ESDI drives.

Default jumpers:
    No jumpers on board.

To format, use: System supplies software.

Western Digital WD 1007V-SE1
Western Digital WD 1007V-SE2

A 16-bit ESDI controller for 2 hard drives at 1:1 interleave with 32K look-ahead cache. Model SE2 also controls 2 floppy drives.

Default jumpers:
W7-1 & 2, W8-2 & 3

To format, use: G=C00:5 or C800:5 is W8 jumpered to 1 & 2.

Western Digital WD 1009V-SE1
Western Digital WD 1009V-SE2

A high-speed 16-bit ESDI controller with 64K cache, 1:1 interleave, and up to 24Mbit/sec transfer. Available in ISA or EISA bus models. Model SE2 also supports up to 3 floppy drives.

Default jumpers:
    W2-2 & 3 (floppy), W3-1 & 2, W7 (EISA only).

To format, use: C800:5

Western Digital WD 7000 FASST

A 16-bit SCSI controller that supports up to 7 SCSI devices and 2 floppy drives.

Default jumpers:
SA3, SA4, SA6, SA7, SA13, SA14, SA15, SA16, W1-1 & 2, W2-3 & 4, W2-9 & 10. W5

To format, use: Supplied software.

Notes: Negotiates for synchronous SCSI transfer. Driver s available for Novell and Xenix.

CONNECTOR PINOUTS

The following pages contain pinout information on various interfaces.

Table A - Pinout for Apple's External HDI-30 Connector

Pin	Internal Connector	External Connector
1	DISK.+5	-LINK.SEL
2	DISK.+5	-DB(0)
3	GROUND	GROUND
4	GROUND	-DB(1)
5	GROUND	TERMPWR*
6	-DB(0)	-DB(2)
7	-DB(1)	-DB(3)
8	-DB(2)	GROUND
9	-DB(3)	-ACK
10	-DB(4)	GROUND
11	-DB(5)	-DB(4)
12	-DB(6)	GROUND
13	-DB(7)	GROUND
14	-DB(P)	-DB(5)
15	DISK.+5	GROUND
16	-BSY	-DB(6)
17	-ATN	GROUND
18	-ACK	-DB(7)
19	GROUND	-DB(P)
20	-MSG	GROUND
21	-RST	-REQ
22	-SEL	GROUND
23	-C/D	-BSY
24	-I/O	GROUND
25	-REQ	-ATN
26	GROUND	-C/D
27	GROUND	-RST
28	GROUND	-MSG
29	DISK.+5	-SEL
30	DISK.+5	-I/O

Figure B - Apple and Future Domain 25-Pin D-Sub

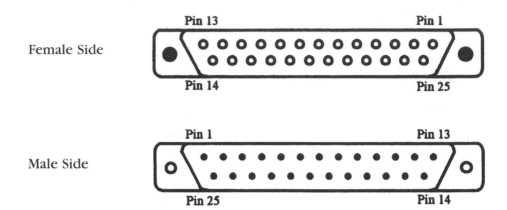

Table B - Pinout for Apple and Future Domain Single-Ended SCSI Connectors Shown Above

Apple Single-ended SCSI Pinout

Pin	Signal	Pin	Signal
1	-REQ	14	RES/GND
2	-MSG	15	-C/D
3	-I/O	16	RES/GND
4	-RST	17	-ATN
5	-ACK	18	GND
6	-BSY	19	-SEL
7	GND	20	-DBP
8	-DB0	21	-DB1
9	GND	22	-DB2
10	-DB3	23	-DB4
11	-DB5	24	GND
12	-DB6	25	TermPwr*
13	-DB7		

Future Domain Single-ended SCSI Pinout

Pin	Signal	Pin	Signal
1	GND	14	-DB(0)
2	-DB(1)	15	-DB(2)
3	-DB(3)	16	-DB(4)
4	-DB(5)	17	-DB(6)
5	-DB(7)	18	-DB(P)
6	GND	19	GND
7	-SEL	20	-ATN
8	GND	21	-MSG
9	Spare	22	-ACK
10	-RST	23	-BSY
11	-C/D	24	-REQ
12	-I/O	25	-GND
13	GND		

Pin 25 - Termination Power is not connected in the Mac Plus connector.

Non-Official Standard SCSI Connectors

For whatever reasons, some companies decided to introduce non-standard SCSI connectors. The most common are Future Domain's 25-pin D-sub connector, used on their early SCSI host adapters, Apple's 25-pin D-sub connector with a different and totally incompatible pinout scheme, and IBM's proprietary PS/2 SCSIL connector. See above figures and tables.

ALERT

When looking at Table B, keep in mind that the connector numbers shown in the table and in Figure B are the ones that connector manufacturers, like AMP, use on the connectors. These are not the numbers used by SUN. For whatever reason, SUN used an unusual numbering scheme, which differs from the counting scheme the connector manufacturers use and print on the connector bodies. So, if you use an older SUN device, be extremely careful when using factory cables.

Table C - Pinout for Single-Ended and Differential B-Cables

Single-ended SCSI Pinout, B-Cable				**Differential SCSI Pinout, B-Cable**			
Pin	Signal	Pin	Signal	Pin	Signal	Pin	Signal
1	GND	35	GND		GND		GND
2	GND	36	-DB(8)		+DB(8)		-DB(8)
3	GND	37	-DB(9)		+DB(9)		-DB(9)
4	GND	38	-DB(10)		+DB(10)		-DB(10)
5	GND	39	-DB(11)		+DB(11)		-DB(11)
6	GND	40	-DB(12)		+DB(12)		-DB(12)
7	GND	41	-DB(13)		+DB(13)		-DB(13)
8	GND	42	-DB(14)		+DB(14)		-DB(14)
9	GND	43	-DB(15)		+DB(15)		-DB(15)
10	GND	44	-DB(P1)		+DB(P1)		-DB(P1)
11	GND	45	-ACKB		+ACKB		-ACKB
12	GND	46	GND		GND		DIFFSENS
13	GND	47	-REQB		+REQB		-REQB
14	GND	48	-DB(16)		+DB(16)		-DB(16)
15	GND	49	-DB(17)		+DB(17)		-DB(17)
16	GND	50	-DB(18)		+DB(18)		-DB(18)
17	TermPwrB	51	TermPwrB		TermPwrB		TermPwrB
18	TermPwrB	52	TermPwrB		TermPwrB		TermPwrB
19	GND	53	-DB(19)		+DB(19)		-DB(19)
20	GND	54	-DB(20)		+DB(20)		-DB(20)
21	GND	55	-DB(21)		+DB(21)		-DB(21)
22	GND	56	-DB(22)		+DB(22)		-DB(22)
23	GND	57	-DB(23)		+DB(23)		-DB(23)
24	GND	58	-DB(P2)		+DB(P2)		-DB(P2)
25	GND	59	-DB(24)		+DB(24)		-DB(24)
26	GND	60	-DB(25)		+DB(25)		-DB(25)
27	GND	61	-DB(26)		+DB(26)		-DB(26)
28	GND	62	-DB(27)		+DB(27)		-DB(27)
29	GND	63	-DB(28)		+DB(28)		-DB(28)
30	GND	64	-DB(29)		+DB(29)		-DB(29)
31	GND	65	-DB(30)		+DB(30)		-DB(30)
32	GND	66	-DB(31)		+DB(31)		-DB(31)
33	GND	67	-DB(P3)		+DB(P3)		-DB(P3)
34	GND	68	GND		GND		GND

68-Pin Wide SCSI B-, P-, and Q-Cables

The pinout for single-ended and differential B-cables is shown in Table C.

The P-cable use a much smaller high-density connector because the smaller 3½-inch devices don't have enough mounting space to fit an IDC connector with 68 pins. The connector is the same for internal and external cables, but the internal version is unshielded with a plastic body and without locking mechanisms. The male connector is the cable connector, and the device has the female connector.

In 1992, there was a proposed cable standardization for Wide SCSI devices but the Q-cable did not gain industry acceptance.

Table D - Pinout for Single-Ended and Differential P-Cables

Single-ended SCSI Pinout, P-Cable				Differential SCSI Pinout, P-Cable			
Pin	Signal	Pin	Signal	Pin	Signal	Pin	Signal
1	GND	35	-DB(12)		+DB(12)		-DB(12)
2	GND	36	-DB(13)		+DB(13)		-DB(13)
3	GND	37	-DB(14)		+DB(14)		-DB(14)
4	GND	38	-DB(15)		+DB(15)		-DB(15)
5	GND	39	-DB(P1)		+DB(P1)		-DB(P1)
6	GND	40	-DB(0)		GND		GND
7	GND	41	-DB(1)		+DB(0)		-DB(0)
8	GND	42	-DB(2)		+DB(1)		-DB(1)
9	GND	43	-DB(3)		+DB(2)		-DB(2)
10	GND	44	-DB(4)		+DB(3)		-DB(3)
11	GND	45	-DB(5)		+DB(4)		-DB(4)
12	GND	46	-DB(6)		+DB(5)		-DB(5)
13	GND	47	-DB(7)		+DB(6)		-DB(6)
14	GND	48	-DB(P)		+DB(7)		-DB(7)
15	GND	49	GND		+DB(P)		-DB(P)
16	GND	50	GND		DIFFSENS		GND
17	TermPwr	51	TermPwr		TermPwr		TermPwr
18	TermPwr	52	TermPwr		TermPwr		TermPwr
19	Reserved	53	Reserved		Reserved		Reserved
20	GND	54	GND		+ATN		-ATN
21	GND	55	-ATN		GND		GND
22	GND	56	GND		+BSY		-BSY
23	GND	57	-BSY		+ACK		-ACK
24	GND	58	-ACK		+RST		-RST
25	GND	59	-RST		+MSG		-MSG
26	GND	60	-MSG		+SEL		-SEL
27	GND	61	-SEL		+C/D		-C/D
28	GND	62	-C/D		+REQ		-REQ
29	GND	63	-REQ		+I/O		-I/O
30	GND	64	-I/O		GND		GND
31	GND	65	-DB(8)		+DB(8)		-DB(8)
32	GND	66	-DB(9)		+DB(9)		-DB(9)
33	GND	67	-DB(10)		+DB(10)		-DB(10)
34	GND	68	-DB(11)		+DB(11)		-DB(11)

Table E - Pinout for 50-Pin, Single-Ended and Differential Centronics-Syyle Connector (A Cable)

Single-ended SCSI Pinout

Pin	Signal	Pin	Signal
1	GND	26	-DB(0)
2	GND	27	-DB(1)
3	GND	28	-DB(2)
4	GND	29	-DB(3)
5	GND	30	-DB(4)
6	GND	31	-DB(5)
7	GND	32	-DB(6)
8	GND	33	-DB(7)
9	GND	34	-DB(P)
10	GND	35	GND
11	GND	36	GND
12	Reserved	37	Reserved
13	Not Connected	38	TERMPWR
14	Reserved	39	Reserved
15	GND	40	GND
16	GND	41	-ATN
17	GND	42	GND
18	GND	43	-BSY
19	GND	44	-ACK
20	GND	45	-RST
21	GND	46	-MSG
22	GND	47	-SEL
23	GND	48	-C/D
24	GND	49	-REQ
25	GND	50	-I/O

Differential SCSI Pinout

Pin	Signal	Pin	Signal
1	GND	26	GND
2	+DB(0)	27	-DB(0)
3	+DB(1)	28	-DB(1)
4	+DB(2)	29	-DB(2)
5	+DB(3)	30	-DB(3)
6	+DB(4)	31	-DB(4)
7	+DB(5)	32	-DB(5)
8	+DB(6)	33	-DB(6)
9	+DB(7)	34	-DB(7)
10	+DB(P)	35	-DB(P)
11	DIFFSENS	36	GND
12	Reserved	37	Reserved
13	TERMPWR	38	TERMPWR
14	Reserved	39	Reserved
15	+ATN	40	-ATN
16	GND	41	GND
17	+BSY	42	-BSY
18	+ACK	43	-ACK
19	+RST	44	-RST
20	+MSG	45	-MSG
21	+SEL	46	-SEL
22	+C/D	47	-C/D
23	+REQ	48	-REQ
24	+I/O	49	-I/O
25	GND	50	GND

Table F - ESDI Control Signals (J1/P1)

Control Signal Name	Ground	Signal Pin	Transmission
-Head Select 3	1	2	To Drive
-Head Select 2	3	4	To Drive
-Write Gate	5	6	To Drive
-Config/-Status Data	7	8	To Controller
-Transfer Ack	9	10	To Controller
-Attention	11	12	To Controller
-Head Select 0	13	14	To Drive
-Sector/-Address Mark Found	15	16	To Controller
	17	18	To Drive
-Head Select 1	19	20	To Controller
-Index	21	22	To Controller
-Ready	23	24	To Drive
-Transfer Request	25	26	To Drive
-Drive Select 1	27	28	To Drive
-Drive Select 2	29	30	To Drive
-Drive Select 3	31	32	To Drive
-Read Gate	33	34	To Drive

Table G - ESDI Control Signals Continued (J2/P2)

Control Signal Name	Ground	Signal Pin	Transmission
-Drive Selected		1	To Controller
-Sector Address Mark		2	To Controller
Found		3	To Controller
-Seek Complete		4	To Drive
-Address Mark Enable	6	5	To Controller
-Reserved for Step Mode		7	To Drive
+Write Clock		8	To Drive
-Write Clock		9	To Controller
-Cartridge Changed		10	To Controller
+Read Reference Clock	12	11	To Controller
-Read Reference Clock		13	To Drive
+NRZ Write Data	15,16	14	To Drive
-NRZ Write Data		17	To Controller
+NRZ Read Data	19	18	To Controller
-NRZ Read Data		20	To Controller

Table H - IBM I/O Channel Pinout (Sides A & B)

Pin	Signal Name	Pin	Signal Name
A1	/IOCHCK	B1	GND
A2	SD7	B2	RESETDRV
A3	SD6	B3	+5VCC
A4	SD5	B4	IRQ9
A5	SD4	B5	-5VCC
A6	SD3	B6	DRQ2
A7	SD2	B7	-12VCC
A8	SD1	B8	OWS
A9	SD0	B9	+12VCC
A10	/IOCHRDY	B10	GND
A11	AEN	B11	/SMEMW
A12	SA19	B12	/SMEMR
A13	SA18	B13	/IOW
A14	SA17	B14	//IOR
A15	SA16	B15	/DACK3
A16	SA15	B16	DRQ3
A17	SA14	B17	/DACK1
A18	SA13	B18	DRQ1
A19	SA12	B19	/REFRESH
A20	SA11	B20	CLK
A21	SA10	B21	IRQ7
A22	SA9	B22	IRQ6
A23	SA8	B23	IRQ5
A24	SA7	B24	IRQ4
A25	SA6	B25	IRQ3
A26	SA5	B26	/DACK2
A27	SA4	B27	T/C
A28	SA3	B28	ALE
A29	SA2	B29	+5VCC
A30	SA1	B30	OSC
A31	SA0	B31	GND

Table I - IBM I/O Channel Pinout Continued (Sides C & D)

Pin	Signal Name	Pin	Signal Name
C1	SBHE	D1	/MEMCS16
C2	LA23	D2	/IOCS16
C3	LA22	D3	IRQ10
C4	LA21	D4	IRQ11
C5	LA20	D5	IRQ12
C6	LA19	D6	IRQ15
C7	LA18	D7	IRQ14
C8	LA17	D8	/DACK0
C9	/MEMR	D9	DRQ0
C10	/MEMW	D10	/DACK5
C11	SD08	D11	DRQ5
C12	SD09	D12	/DACK6
C13	SD10	D13	DRQ6
C14	SD11	D14	/DACK7
C15	SD12	D15	DRQ7
C16	SD13	D16	+5VCC
C17	SD14	D17	/MASTER
C18	SD15	D18	GND

Table J - Pinout Table for IBM High-Density PS/2 Connector

Pin	Signal Name	Pin	Signal Name
1	GND	31	GND
2	-DB(0)	32	-ATN
3	GND	33	GND
4	-DB(1)	34	GND
5	GND	35	GND
6	-DB(2)	36	-BSY
7	GND	37	GND
8	-DB(3)	38	-ACK
9	GND	39	GND
10	-DB(4)	40	-RST
11	GND	41	GND
12	-DB(5)	42	-MSG
13	GND	43	GND
14	-DB(6)	44	-SEL
15	GND	45	GND
16	-DB(7)	46	-C/D
17	GND	47	GND
18	-DB(P)	48	-REQ
19	GND	49	GND
20	GND	50	-I/O
21	GND	51	GND
22	GND	52	Reserved
23	Reserved/GND	53	Reserved
24	Reserved/GND	54	Reserved
25	Not Connected	55	Reserved
26	TERMPWR	56	Reserved
27	Reserved	57	Reserved
28	Reserved	58	Reserved
29	GND	59	Reserved
30	GND	60	Reserved

Table K - IDE Interface Pinout

Pin	Signal Name	Pin	Signal Name
01	-Host Reset	02	Ground
03	+ Host Data 7	04	+ Host Data 8
05	+ Host Data 6	06	+ Host Data 9
07	+ Host Data 5	08	+ Host Data 10
09	+ Host Data 4	10	+ Host Data 11
11	+ Host Data 3	12	+ Host Data 12
13	+ Host Data 2	14	+ Host Data 13
15	+ Host Data 1	16	+ Host Data 14
17	+ Host Data 0	18	+ Host Data 15
19	Ground	20	Key
21	Reserved	22	Ground
23	-Host IOW	24	Ground
25	-Host IOR	26	Ground
27	Reserved	28	+ Host ALE
29	Reserved	30	Ground
31	+Host IRQ 14	32	+ Host IO16
33	+Host ADDR 1	34	- Host PDIAG
35	+Host ADDR 0	36	+ Host ADDR 2
37	-Host CS0	38	- Host CS1
39	-Host SLV/ACT	40	Ground

Table L - QIC-36 Connector Pin Assignments

The QIC-36 interface is implemented through a 50-pin dual inline header. The suggested mating connector is a 3M P/N 3425-60XX, 3425-70XX or equivalent. Maximum cable length is 10 feet (3 meters).

Description	Signal	Source	Pin	Return
Tape Motion Enable	GO-	C	2	1
Tape Direction Control	REV-	C	4	3
Track Select 2/3	TR3-	C	6	5
Track Select 2/2	TR2-	C	8	7
Track Select 2/1	TR1-	C	10	9
Track Select 2/0	TR0-	C	12	11
Reset (Initialize Drive)	RST-	C	14	13
Reserved (Not Used)	DS3-	C	16	15
Reserved (Not Used)	DS2-	C	18	17
Reserved (Not Used)	DS1-	C	20	19
Drive Select 0	DS0-	C	22	21
High Write Current	HC-	C	24	23
Read Data (Pulse Output)	RDP-	D	26	25
Upper Tape Position Code	UTH-	D	28	27
Lower Tape Position Code	LTH-	D	30	29
Drive Select Response	SLD-	D	32	31
Cartridge In Place	CIN-	D	34	33
Unsafe (No Write Protect)	USF-	D	36	35
Capstan Tachometer Pulse	TCH-	D	38	37
Write Data Signal -	WDA-	C	40	39
Write Data Signal +	WDA-	C	42	41
Threshold (35% Read Margin)	TDH-	C	44	43
High Speed Slew Select	HSD-	C	46	45
Write Enable	WEN-	C	48	47
Erase Enable	EEN-	C	50	49

Table M - SCSI Pinout - Centronics, Mac, and Differential

IDC Pin Number	Centronics Pin Number	Mac DB-25 Pin Number	Signal-Ended Signal Name	Differential Signal Name
1	1		Ground	Shield Gnd
2	26	8	-Data Bus Bit 0	Ground
3	2		Ground	+DB(0)
4	27	21	-Data Bus Bit 1	–DB(0)
5	3		Ground	+DB(1)
6	28	22	-Data Bus Bit 2	–DB(1)
7	4		Ground	+DB(2)
8	29	10	-Data Bus Bit 3	–DB(2)
9	5		Ground	+DB(3)
10	30	23	-Data Bus Bit 4	–DB(3)
11	6		Ground	+DB(4)
12	31	11	-Data Bus Bit 5	–DB(4)
13	7		Ground	+DB(5)
14	32	12	-Data Bus Bit 6	–DB(5)
15	8		Ground	+DB(6)
16	33	13	-Data Bus Bit 7	–DB(6)
17	9		Ground	+DB(7)
18	34	20	-Data Bus Parity	–DB(7)
19	10		Ground	+DB(P)
20	35	7	Ground	–DB(P)
21	11		Ground	DIFFSENS
22	36	9	Ground	Ground
23	12		Ground	Ground
24	37	24	Ground	Ground
25	13	25	Not Connected	TERMPWR
26	38		TERMPWR	TERMPWR
27	14		Ground	Ground
28	39	14	Ground	Ground
29	15		Ground	+ATN
30	40	16	Ground	–ATN
31	16		Ground	Ground
32	41	17	-ATN	Ground
33	17		Ground	+BSY
34	42	18	Ground	–BSY
35	18		Ground	+ACK
36	43	6	-BSY	–ACK
37	19		Ground	+RST
38	44	5	-ACK	–RST
39	20		Ground	+MSG
40	45	4	-RST	–MSG
41	21		Ground	+SEL
42	46	2	-MSG	–SEL
43	22		Ground	+C/D
44	47	19	-SEL	–C/D
45	23		Ground	+REQ
46	48	15	-C/D	–REQ
47	24		Ground	+I/O
48	49	1	-REQ	–I/O
49	25		Ground	Ground
50	50	3	-I/O	Ground

Table N - SA-400 Interface Signals and Pin Designations

Signal Name	Direction	Signal Pin	Return Pin
HD (High Density)/LSP (Speed)	Out/In	2	1
In Use/Head Load	Input	4	3
-Drive Select 3	Input	6	5
-Index Pulse	Output	8	7
-Drive Select 0	Input	10	9
-Drive Select 1	Input	12	11
-Drive Select 2	Input	14	13
-Motor On	Input	16	15
-Direction Select	Input	18	17
-Step	Input	20	19
-Write Data	Input	22	21
-Write Gate	Input	24	23
-Track 00	Output	26	25
-Write Protect	Output	28	27
-Read Data	Output	30	29
-Side One Select	Input	32	31
-Ready/Disk Change	Output	34	33

Table O - ST-506 Data Signals - J2/P2

Control Signal Name	Ground	Signal Pin	Transmission
-Drive Selected	2	1	To Controller
Reserved	4	3	- - - - - -
Reserved	6	5	- - - - - -
Reserved (to J1 pin 16)	8	7	- - - - - -
Reserved		9	- - - - - -
Reserved		10	- - - - - -
Ground	11,12		- - - - - -
+MFM Write Data		13	To Drive
-MFM Write Data		14	To Drive
Ground	15,16		- - - - - -
+MFM Read Data		17	To Controller
-MFM Read Data		18	To Controller
Ground	19,20		- - - - - -

Figure P - Sun Microsystems' 50-Pin D-Sub Connector

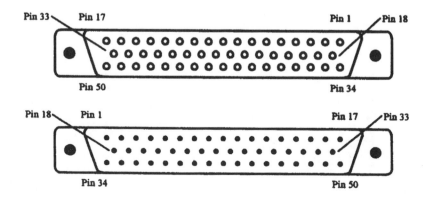

Table P - Sun Single-Ended SCSI Cable

Pin	Signal	Pin	Signal
1	Ground	26	Reserved
2	-DB(1)	27	Ground
3	Ground	28	Ground
4	-DB(4)	29	-BSY
5	Ground	30	Ground
6	-DB(7)	31	-MSG
7	Ground	32	Ground
8	Ground	33	-REQ
9	Not Connected	34	-DB(0)
10	Reserved	35	Ground
11	Ground	36	-DB(3)
12	Ground	37	Ground
13	Ground	38	-DB(6)
14	-RST	39	Ground
15	Ground	40	Ground
16	-C/D	41	Reserved
17	Ground	42	TERMPWR
18	Ground	43	Ground
19	-DB(2)	44	-ATN
20	Ground	45	Ground
21	-DB(5)	46	-ACK
22	Ground	47	Ground
23	-DB(P)	48	-SEL
24	Ground	49	Ground
25	Reserved	50	-I/O

DRIVE JUMPERS

The following pages contain information on jumper settings for common hard drives. This information has been complied from numerous sources, including the manufacturers of the drives. When compiling a chapter of this length, the chances for typing and resource error is great. The authors and publisher would greatly appreciate being notified of any inaccurate or missing information. Some of the older   drives (especially those from companies who have gone out of business) are very difficult to obtain accurate and verifiable specifications for. If you have access to non-copyrighted specification sheets, etc. please send us a copy so that we may add the information to future editions.

For more complete information on your particular drive(s), refer to the OEM manual available from your supplier.

Copyrighted specifications from Maxtor, Seagate, Quantum and Conner Peripherals are reprinted with written permission of their technical support departments.

ATASI 3085

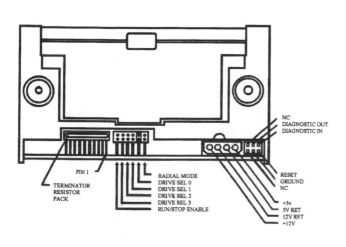

CDC WREN III SERIES

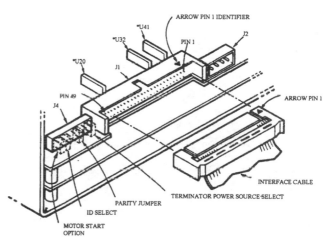

CDC WREN III SERIES ESDI

CDC WREN III SERIES (SCSI JUMPER LOCATION)

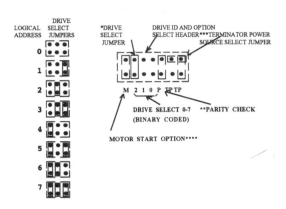

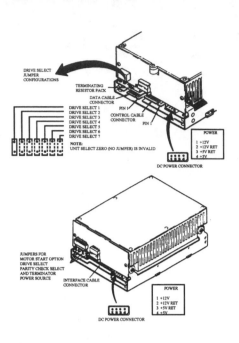

DRIVE SELECT 0-7
(BINARY CODED)

**PARITY CHECK

MOTOR START OPTION****

NOTE:
UNIT SELECT ZERO (NO JUMPER) IS INVALID

* Drive ID is binary coded jumper position (most significant bit on left). i.e., jumper in position 2 would be Drive ID 4, no jumpers mean ID 0.

** Jumper plug installed means parity checking by the WREN III is enabled.

*** Jumper in vertical position means terminator power (+5V) is from WREN III power connector. Jumper in horizontal position means terminator power is taken from interface cable. If unit is not terminated, TP jumper is to be left off.

**** Jumper plug installed enables Motor Start Option. In this mode of operation, the drive will wait for a Start Unit command from the Host before starting the motor. If the jumper plug is not installed, the motor will start as soon as DC power is applied to the unit.

CDC WREN III SERIES (SCSI JUMPER LOCATION)

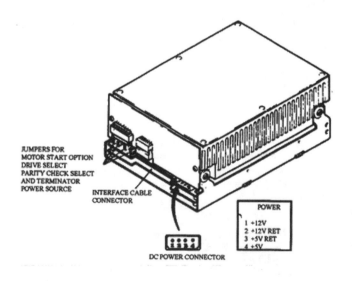

CDC WREN V SERIES

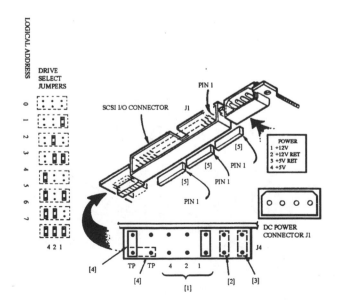

© CSC 1996

CONNER CFA1080A

The C/D jumper is used to determine whether the drive is a master (drive C) or a slave (drive D). The drive is configured as a master, when jumpered, and a slave when not jumpered. The ATA/ISA jumper is used when when daisy-chaining two drives. This jumper may have to be removed when this drive is used together with older (Pre-ATA) drives.

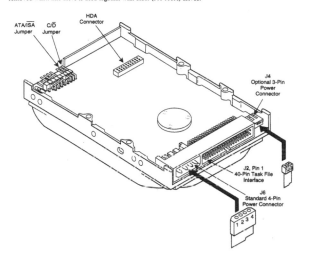

CONNER CFA1275A

The C/D jumper is used to determine whether the drive is a master (drive C) or a slave (drive D). The drive is configured as a master, when jumpered, and a slave when not jumpered. The ATA/ISA jumper is used when when daisy-chaining two drives. This jumper may have to be removed when this drive is used together with older (Pre-ATA) drives.

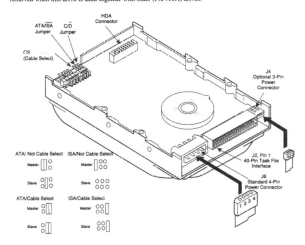

CONNER CFA170A (CP3017)

The C/D jumper is used to determine whether the drive is a master (drive C) or a slave (drive D). The drive is configured as a master, when jumpered, and a slave when not jumpered. The ATA/ISA jumper is used when when daisy-chaining two drives. This jumper may have to be removed when this drive is used together with older (Pre-ATA) drives.

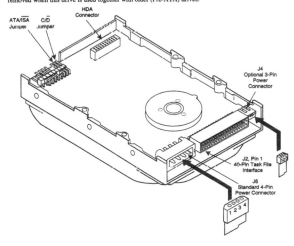

CONNER CFA340A (CP3034)

The C/D jumper is used to determine whether the drive is a master (drive C) or a slave (drive D). The drive is configured as a master, when jumpered, and a slave when not jumpered. The ATA/ISA jumper is used when daisy-chaining two drives. This jumper may have to be removed when this drive is used together with older (Pre-ATA) drives.

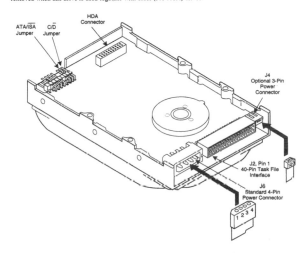

CONNER CFA340S/CFA170S

SCSI Bus Address
There are three jumpers available for configuration of SCSI ID: ADDR1, ADDR 2, and ADDR 3. The following table defines the settings:

SCSI Bus	Addresses		
ADDR 1	ADDR 2	ADDR 3	SCSI ID
OUT	OUT	OUT	O
IN	OUT	OUT	1
OUT	IN	OUT	2
IN	IN	OUT	3
OUT	OUT	IN	4
IN	OUT	IN	5
OUT	IN	IN	6
IN	IN	IN	7

Disable Spin: A jumper in the DSPN location, disables spin up on power-on. Disabling spin up on application of power can also be enabled by settting the DSPN bit in MODE SELECT page 0.

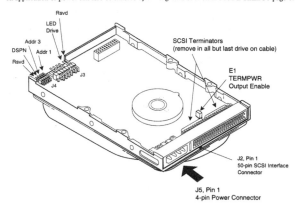

CONNER CFA540A

The C/D jumper is used to determine whether the drive is a master (drive C) or a slave (drive D). The drive is configured as a master, when jumpered, and a slave when not jumpered. The ATA/ISA jumper is used when when daisy-chaining two drives. This jumper may have to be removed when this drive is used together with older (Pre-ATA) drives.

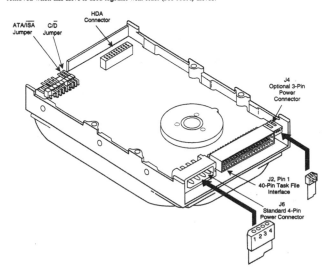

CONNER CFA540S

SCSI Bus Address
There are three jumpers available for configuration of SCSI ID: ID1, ID2, and ID3. The following
table defines the settings:

SCSI Bus	Addresses*		
ID1	ID2	ID3	SCSI ID
OUT	OUT	OUT	O
IN	OUT	OUT	1
OUT	IN	OUT	2
IN	IN	OUT	3
OUT	OUT	IN	4
IN	OUT	IN	5
OUT	IN	IN	6
IN	IN	IN	7

Disable spin: A jumper in the 0E4 location, disables spin up on power-on. Disabling spin up on application of power can also be enabled by settting the DSPN bit in MODE SELECT page 0.

0E4	Disable Spin on Power on
E1	Term Power In/Out enable

CONNER CFA810A

The C/D jumper is used to determine whether the drive is a master (drive C) or a slave (drive D). The drive is configured as a master, when jumpered, and a slave when not jumpered. The ATA/ISA jumper is used when when daisy-chaining two drives. This jumper may have to be removed when this drive is used together with older (Pre-ATA) drives.

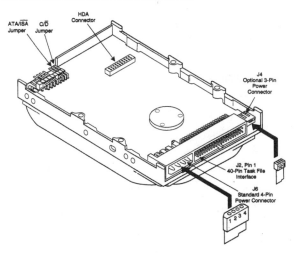

CONNER CFA850A

The C/D jumper is used to determine whether the drive is a master (drive C) or a slave (drive D). The drive is configured as a master, when jumpered, and a slave when not jumpered. The ATA/ISA jumper is used when when daisy-chaining two drives. This jumper may have to be removed when this drive is used together with older (Pre-ATA) drives.

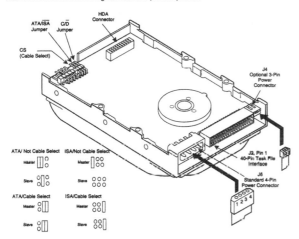

CONNER CFL350A

The CFL350A drive is designed to operate either as a Master drive (C Drive) or a Slave Drive (D Drive). Commands from the host are written in parallel to both drives. When the C/D jumper on the drive is closed, the drive will assume the role of a master. When C/D is open, the drive will act as a slave. In Single-drive configurations, C/D must remain in the closed (master) position.

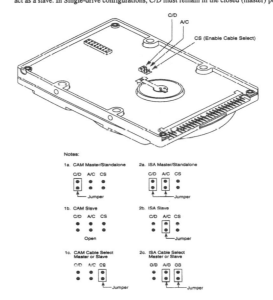

CONNER CFL420A

The CFL420A drive is designed to operate either as a Master drive (C Drive) or a Slave Drive (D Drive). Commands from the host are written in parallel to both drives. When the C/D jumper on the drive is closed, the drive will assume the role of a master. When C/D is open, the drive will act as a slave. In Single-drive configurations, C/D must remain in the closed (master) position.

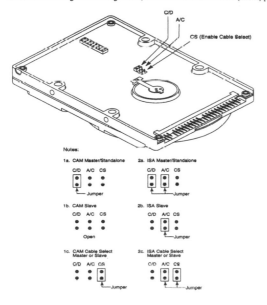

CONNER CFN170A

The CFN170A drive is designed to operate either as a Master drive (C Drive) or a Slave Drive (D Drive). Commands from the host are written in parallel to both drives. When the C/D jumper on the drive is closed, the drive will assume the role of a master. When C/D is open, the drive will act as a slave. In Single-drive configurations, C/D must remain in the closed (master) position.

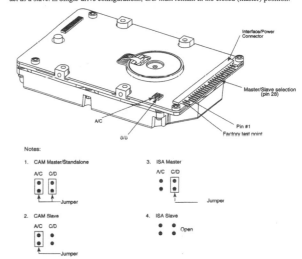

CONNER CFN170S

The following table defines the settings:

J3, Pin	5	6	7
SCSI ID	E1	E2	E3
0	high	high	high
1	low	high	high
2	high	low	high
3	low	low	high
4	high	high	low
5	low	high	low
6	high	low	low
7	low	low	low

CONNER CFN250A

The CFN250A drive is designed to operate either as a Master drive (C Drive) or a Slave Drive (D Drive). Commands from the host are written in parallel to both drives. When the C/D jumper on the drive is closed, the drive will assume the role of a master. When C/D is open, the drive will act as a slave. In Single-drive configurations, C/D must remain in the closed (master) position.

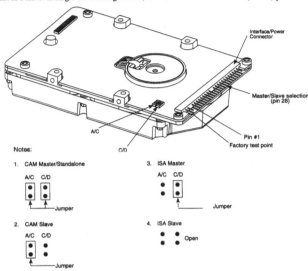

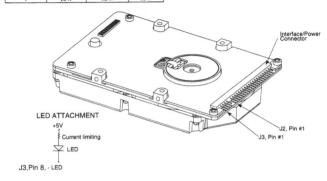

CONNER CFN250S

The following table defines the settings:

J3, Pin	5	6	7
SCSI ID	E1	E2	E3
0	high	high	high
1	low	high	high
2	high	low	high
3	low	low	high
4	high	high	low
5	low	high	low
6	high	low	low
7	low	low	low

CONNER CFN340A

The CFN340A drive is designed to operate either as a Master drive (C Drive) or a Slave Drive (D Drive). Commands from the host are written in parallel to both drives. When the C/D jumper on the drive is closed, the drive will assume the role of a master. When C/D is open, the drive will act as a slave. In Single-drive configurations, C/D must remain in the closed (master) position.

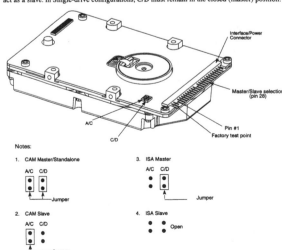

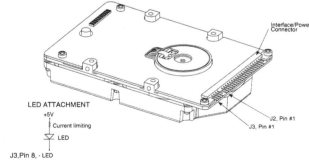

CONNER CFP1060S

SCSI Bus Address
There are three jumpers available for configuration of SCSI ID: E1, E2, and E3. The following table defines the settings:

SCSI Bus	Addresses*		
E1/0E1	E2/0E2	E3/0E3	SCSI ID
OUT	OUT	OUT	0
IN	OUT	OUT	1
OUT	IN	OUT	2
IN	IN	OUT	3
OUT	OUT	IN	4
IN	OUT	IN	5
OUT	IN	IN	6
IN	IN	IN	7

*Use either but not both : E1 to E3 or 0E1 to 0E3. The 0E header is not installed on drive configurations with a LED on the PCBA.
Disable Spin: A jumper in the E5 or 0E5 location, disables spin up on power-on. Disabling spin up on application of power can also be enabled by setting the DSPN bit in MODE SELECT page 0.

E4	Reserved
E5/0E5	Disable Spin on Power-on
E6	Spin delay by SCSI ID
E7	Disable SCSI Bus Parity

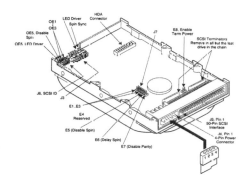

CONNER CFP1060W

SCSI Bus Address
There are four jumpers available for configuration of SCSI ID: E1, E2, E3, and E4 or alternatively pins 1,3,5, and 7 or J5. The following table defines the the relationship between the jumpers or the pins on J5 and the SCSI ID:

SCSI ID	E1/Pin 1	E2/Pin 3	E3/Pin 5	E4/Pin 7
0	Out/open	Out/open	Out/open	Out/open
1	In/Ground	Out/open	Out/open	Out/open
2	Out/open	In/Ground	Out/open	Out/open
3	In/Ground	In/Ground	Out/open	Out/open
4	Out/open	Out/open	In/Ground	Out/open
5	In/Ground	Out/open	In/Ground	Out/open
6	Out/open	In/Ground	In/Ground	Out/open
7	In/Ground	In/Ground	In/Ground	Out/open
8	Out/open	Out/open	Out/open	In/Ground
9	In/Ground	Out/open	Out/open	In/Ground
10	Out/open	In/Ground	Out/open	In/Ground
11	In/Ground	In/Ground	Out/open	In/Ground
12	Out/open	Out/open	In/Ground	In/Ground
13	In/Ground	Out/open	In/Ground	In/Ground
14	Out/open	In/Ground	In/Ground	In/Ground
15	In/Ground	In/Ground	In/Ground	In/Ground

Disable Spin: A jumper in the E5 location, disables spin up on power-on. Disabling spin up on application of power can also be enabled by setting the DSPN bit in MODE SELECT page 00H.

E5	DSPN	Result
In	0	Spin Disabled
In	1	Spin Disabled
Out	0	Spin up on Power On
Out	1	Spin Disabled

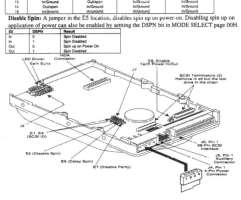

CONNER CFP1080S

SCSI Bus Address
There are three jumpers available for configuration of SCSI ID: E1, E2, and E3. The following table defines the settings:

SCSI Bus	Addresses*		
E1/0E1	E2/0E2	E3/0E3	SCSI ID
OUT	OUT	OUT	0
IN	OUT	OUT	1
OUT	IN	OUT	2
IN	IN	OUT	3
OUT	OUT	IN	4
IN	OUT	IN	5
OUT	IN	IN	6
IN	IN	IN	7

*Use either but not both : E1 to E3 or 0E1 to 0E3. The 0E header is not installed on drive configurations with a LED on the PCBA.
Disable Spin: A jumper in the E4 location, disables spin up on power-on. Disabling spin up on application of power can also be enabled by setting the DSPN bit in MODE SELECT page 0.

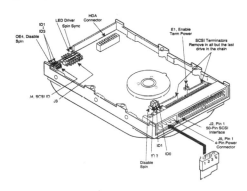

CONNER CFP2105S

SCSI Bus Address
There are three jumpers available for configuration of SCSI ID: E1, E2, and E3. The following table defines the settings:

SCSI Bus	Addresses*		
E1/0E1	E2/0E2	E3/0E3	SCSI ID
OUT	OUT	OUT	0
IN	OUT	OUT	1
OUT	IN	OUT	2
IN	IN	OUT	3
OUT	OUT	IN	4
IN	OUT	IN	5
OUT	IN	IN	6
IN	IN	IN	7

*Use either but not both : E1 to E3 or 0E1 to 0E3. The 0E header is not installed on drive configurations with a LED on the PCBA.
Disable Spin: A jumper in the E5 location, disables spin up on power-on. Disabling spin up on application of power can also be enabled by setting the DSPN bit in MODE SELECT page 00H.

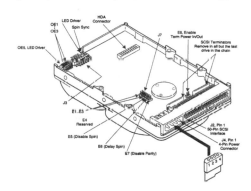

CONNER CFP2107S

SCSI Bus Address

There are three jumpers available for configuration of SCSI ID: E1, E2, and E3. The following table defines the settings:

SCSI Bus	Addresses*		
E1/OE1	E2/OE2	E3/OE3	SCSI ID
OUT	OUT	OUT	0
IN	OUT	OUT	1
OUT	IN	OUT	2
IN	IN	OUT	3
OUT	OUT	IN	4
IN	OUT	IN	5
OUT	IN	IN	6
IN	IN	IN	7

*Use either but not both : E1 to E3 or 0E1 to 0E3. The 0E header is not installed on drive configurations with a LED on the PCBA.

Disable Spin: A jumper in the E5 location, disables spin up on power-on. Disabling spin up on application of power can also be enabled by settting the DSPN bit in MODE SELECT page 00H.

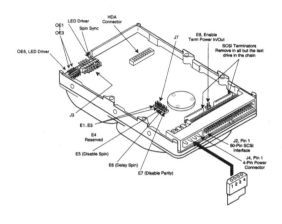

CONNER CFP2107W

SCSI Bus Address

There are four jumpers available for configuration of SCSI ID: E1, E2, and E3, and E4. The following table defines the settings:

SCSI Bus	Addresses*			
E1/Pin 1	E2/Pin 3	E3/Pin 5	E4/pin 7	SCSI ID
OUT/OPEN	OUT/OPEN	OUT/OPEN	OUT/OPEN	0
IN/GROUND	OUT/OPEN	OUT/OPEN	OUT/OPEN	1
OUT/OPEN	IN/GROUND	OUT/OPEN	OUT/OPEN	2
IN/GROUND	IN/GROUND	OUT/OPEN	OUT/OPEN	3
OUT/OPEN	OUT/OPEN	IN/GROUND	OUT/OPEN	4
IN/GROUND	OUT/OPEN	IN/GROUND	OUT/OPEN	5
OUT/OPEN	IN/GROUND	IN/GROUND	OUT/OPEN	6
IN/GROUND	IN/GROUND	IN/GROUND	OUT/OPEN	7
OUT/OPEN	OUT/OPEN	OUT/OPEN	IN/GROUND	8
IN/GROUND	OUT/OPEN	OUT/OPEN	IN/GROUND	9
OUT/OPEN	IN/GROUND	OUT/OPEN	IN/GROUND	10
IN/GROUND	IN/GROUND	OUT/OPEN	IN/GROUND	11
OUT/OPEN	OUT/OPEN	IN/GROUND	IN/GROUND	12
IN/GROUND	OUT/OPEN	IN/GROUND	IN/GROUND	13
OUT/OPEN	IN/GROUND	IN/GROUND	IN/GROUND	14
IN/GROUND	IN/GROUND	IN/GROUND	IN/GROUND	15

Disable Spin: A jumper in the E5 location, disables spin up on power-on. Disabling spin up on application of power can also be enabled by settting the DSPN bit in MODE SELECT page 00H.

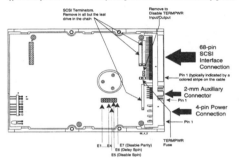

CONNER CFP4207S

SCSI Bus Address

There are three jumpers available for configuration of SCSI ID: E1, E2, and E3. The following table defines the settings:

SCSI Bus	Addresses*		
E1/OE1	E2/OE2	E3/OE3	SCSI ID
OUT	OUT	OUT	0
IN	OUT	OUT	1
OUT	IN	OUT	2
IN	IN	OUT	3
OUT	OUT	IN	4
IN	OUT	IN	5
OUT	IN	IN	6
IN	IN	IN	7

*Use either but not both : E1 to E3 or 0E1 to 0E3. The 0E header is not installed on drive configurations with a LED on the PCBA.

Disable Spin: A jumper in the E5 location, disables spin up on power-on. Disabling spin up on application of power can also be enabled by settting the DSPN bit in MODE SELECT page 00H.

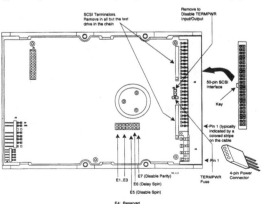

CONNER CFP4207W

SCSI Bus Address

There are four jumpers available for configuration of SCSI ID: E1, E2, and E3, and E4. The following table defines the settings:

SCSI Bus	Addresses*			
E1/Pin 1	E2/Pin 3	E3/Pin 5	E4/pin 7	SCSI ID
OUT/OPEN	OUT/OPEN	OUT/OPEN	OUT/OPEN	0
IN/GROUND	OUT/OPEN	OUT/OPEN	OUT/OPEN	1
OUT/OPEN	IN/GROUND	OUT/OPEN	OUT/OPEN	2
IN/GROUND	IN/GROUND	OUT/OPEN	OUT/OPEN	3
OUT/OPEN	OUT/OPEN	IN/GROUND	OUT/OPEN	4
IN/GROUND	OUT/OPEN	IN/GROUND	OUT/OPEN	5
OUT/OPEN	IN/GROUND	IN/GROUND	OUT/OPEN	6
IN/GROUND	IN/GROUND	IN/GROUND	OUT/OPEN	7
OUT/OPEN	OUT/OPEN	OUT/OPEN	IN/GROUND	8
IN/GROUND	OUT/OPEN	OUT/OPEN	IN/GROUND	9
OUT/OPEN	IN/GROUND	OUT/OPEN	IN/GROUND	10
IN/GROUND	IN/GROUND	OUT/OPEN	IN/GROUND	11
OUT/OPEN	OUT/OPEN	IN/GROUND	IN/GROUND	12
IN/GROUND	OUT/OPEN	IN/GROUND	IN/GROUND	13
OUT/OPEN	IN/GROUND	IN/GROUND	IN/GROUND	14
IN/GROUND	IN/GROUND	IN/GROUND	IN/GROUND	15

Disable Spin: A jumper in the E5 location, disables spin up on power-on. Disabling spin up on application of power can also be enabled by settting the DSPN bit in MODE SELECT page 00H.

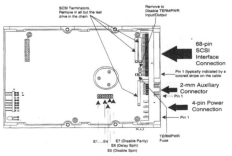

CONNER CFS1275A

The C/D jumper is used to determine whether the drive is a master (drive C) or a slave (drive D). The drive is configured as a master, when jumpered, and a slave when not jumpered. The ATA/ISA jumper is used when when daisy-chaining two drives. This jumper may have to be removed when this drive is used together with older (Pre-ATA) drives.

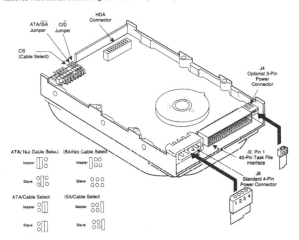

CONNER CFS210A

The C/D jumper is used to determine whether the drive is a master (drive C) or a slave (drive D). The drive is configured as a master, when jumpered, and a slave when not jumpered. The ATA/ISA jumper is used when when daisy-chaining two drives. This jumper may have to be removed when this drive is used together with older (Pre-ATA) drives.

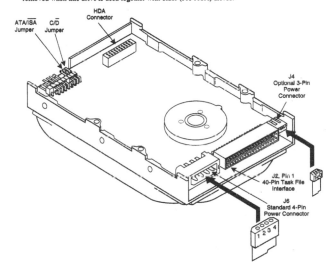

CONNER CFS270A

The C/D jumper is used to determine whether the drive is a master (drive C) or a slave (drive D). The drive is configured as a master, when jumpered, and a slave when not jumpered.

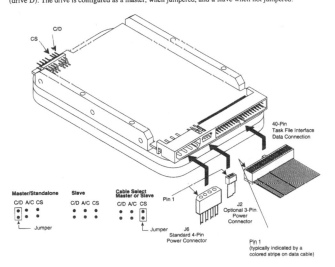

CONNER CFS420A

The C/D jumper is used to determine whether the drive is a master (drive C) or a slave (drive D). The drive is configured as a master, when jumpered, and a slave when not jumpered. The ATA/ISA jumper is used when when daisy-chaining two drives. This jumper may have to be removed when this drive is used together with older (Pre-ATA) drives.

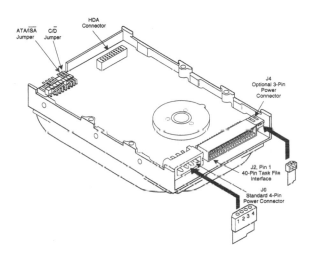

CONNER CFS425A

The C/D jumper is used to determine whether the drive is a master (drive C) or a slave (drive D). The drive is configured as a master, when jumpered, and a slave when not jumpered.

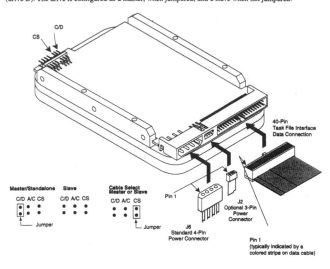

CONNER CFS540A

The C/D jumper is used to determine whether the drive is a master (drive C) or a slave (drive D). The drive is configured as a master, when jumpered, and a slave when not jumpered. The ATA/ISA jumper is used when when daisy-chaining two drives. This jumper may have to be removed when this drive is used together with older (Pre-ATA) drives.

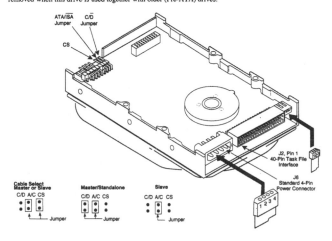

CONNER CP2034

The CP2034 is designed to operate as a master (Drive C) or as a Slave (Drive D). This feature is dependent on two settings; Jumper E1 and the firmware setting of a feature bit. E1 closed and the feature bit is set, the drive will be the Master. E1 open the drive will be the Slave. As a single drive, E1 should be closed.

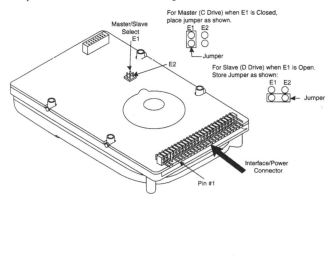

CONNER CFS850A

The C/D jumper is used to determine whether the drive is a master (drive C) or a slave (drive D). The drive is configured as a master, when jumpered, and a slave when not jumpered.

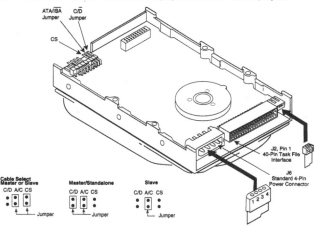

CONNER CP2044/CP2044P

The CP2124 drive is designed to operate either as a Master drive (C Drive) or a Slave Drive (D Drive). This feature is dependent on two drive settings; the status of hardware Jumper M/S and the firmware setting of a feature bit. When (M/S) is closed, and the feature bit is set, the drive will assume the role of a Master Drive. When (M/S) is open, and the feature bit reset, the drive will act as the Slave. In single drive configurations M/S must remain in the closed position.

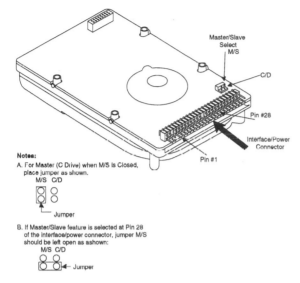

Notes:
A. For Master (C Drive) when M/S is Closed, place jumper as shown.

B. If Master/Slave feature is selected at Pin 28 of the interface/power connector, jumper M/S should be left open as ashown:

CONNER CP2064

The CP2064 is designed to operate as a master (Drive C) or as a Slave (Drive D). This feature is dependent on two settings; Jumper E1 and the firmware setting of a feature bit. E1 closed and the feature bit is set, the drive will be the Master. E1 open the drive will be the Slave. As a single drive, E1 should be closed.

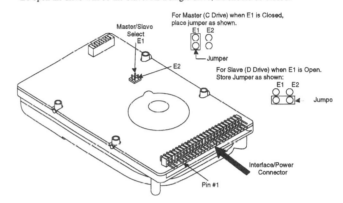

CONNER CP2084

The CP2084 drive is designed to operate either as a Master drive (C Drive) or a Slave Drive (D Drive). This feature is dependent on two drive settings; the status of hardware Jumper M/S and the firmware setting of a feature bit. When (M/S) is closed, and the feature bit is set, the drive will assume the role of a Master Drive. When (M/S) is open, and the feature bit reset, the drive will act as the Slave. In single drive configurations M/S must remain in the closed position.

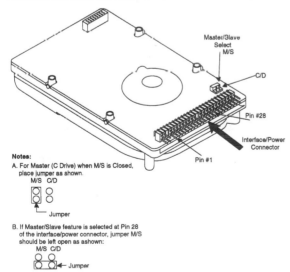

Notes:
A. For Master (C Drive) when M/S is Closed, place jumper as shown.

B. If Master/Slave feature is selected at Pin 28 of the interface/power connector, jumper M/S should be left open as ashown:

CONNER CP2088

The CP2088 is designed to operate as a master (Drive C) or as a Slave (Drive D). This feature is dependent on two settings; Jumper E1 and the firmware setting of a feature bit. E1 closed and the feature bit is set, the drive will be the Master. E1 open the drive will be the Slave. As a single drive, E1 should be closed.

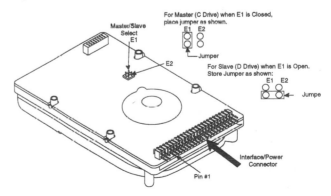

CONNER CP2124

The CP2124 drive is designed to operate either as a Master drive (C Drive) or a Slave Drive (D Drive). This feature is dependent on two drive settings; the status of hardware Jumper M/S and the firmware setting of a feature bit. When (M/S) is closed, and the feature bit is set, the drive will assume the role of a Master Drive. When (M/S) is open, and the feature bit reset, the drive will act as the Slave. In single drive configurations M/S must remain in the closed position.

CONNER CP3000

There are four jumper options available for configuration: *HSP, C/D, DSP, and ACT.
The following table shows what the jumper settings should be for various system configurations.

Single Drive = ACT and C/D Jumpered
Master Drive = C/D and DSP Jumpered
Slave Drive = No Jumpers installed

* Note: HSP is not used.

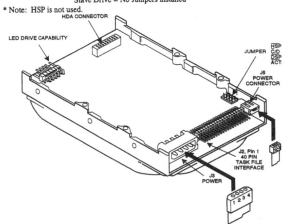

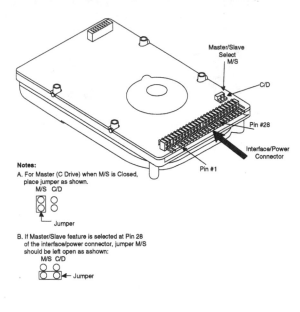

Notes:
A. For Master (C Drive) when M/S is Closed, place jumper as shown.

B. If Master/Slave feature is selected at Pin 28 of the interface/power connector, jumper M/S should be left open as ashown:

CONNER CP 30060 SCSI

There are three jumpers available for configuration: E1, E2, and E3. These jumpers are used to select the drive's SCSI ID. The following table defines the settings:

SCSI ID	Jumper
0	None
1	E1
2	E2
3	E1 & E2
4	E3
5	E1 & E3
6	E2 & E3

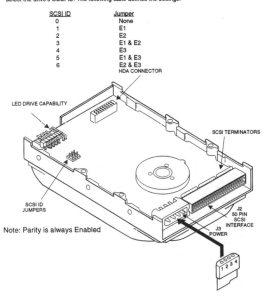

Note: Parity is always Enabled

CONNER 30064

The drive has one set of jumpers labeled C/D, DSP, E1.

Single Drive = C/D Jumpered
Master = C/D and DSP Jumpered
Slave = No Jumpers Installed
E1 = Not used.

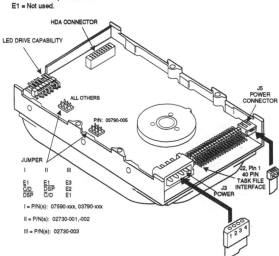

I	II	III
E1	E1	E3
C/D	DSP	E2
DSP	C/D	E1

I = P/N(s): 07590-xxx, 03790-xxx

II = P/N(s): 02730-001,-002

III = P/N(s): 02730-003

CONNER CP30064H

The drive has one set of jumpers labeled C/D, DSP, E1.

Single Drive = C/D Jumpered
Master = C/D and DSP Jumpered
Slave = No Jumpers Installed
E1 = Not used.

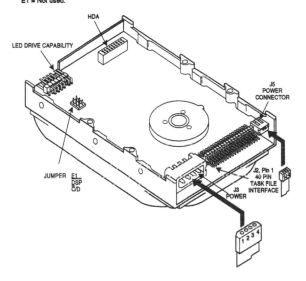

CONNER CP30080

There are three jumpers available for configuration: E1, E2, and E3. These jumpers are used to select the drive's SCSI ID. The following table defines the settings:

SCSI ID	Jumper
0	None
1	E1
2	E2
3	E1 & E2
4	E3
5	E1 & E3
6	E2 & E3

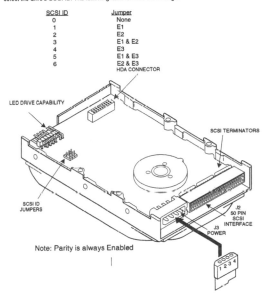

Note: Parity is always Enabled

CONNER CP30080E

E1, E2 and E3 are used to select the SCSI ID. The drive is shipped as ID 7, with all three jumpers installed.
The following table describes the SCSI ID:

SCSI ID	Jumpers installed
0	None
1	E1
2	E2
3	E1,E2
4	E3
5	E1, E3
6	E2,E3

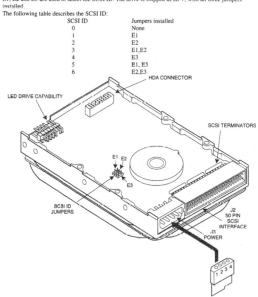

CONNER CP30084

The drive has one set of jumpers labeled C/D, DSP, E1.

Single Drive = C/D Jumpered
Master = C/D and DSP Jumpered
Slave = No Jumpers Installed
E1 = Not used.

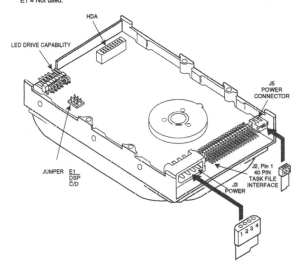

CONNER CP30084E

The C/D jumper is used to determine whether the drive is a master (drive C) or slave (drive D). The drive is configured as a master (drive C) when jumpered and as a slave drive (D drive) when not jumpered.

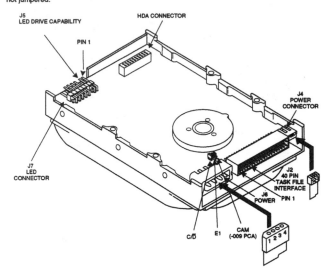

CONNER CP30100 SCSI

There are three jumpers available for configuration: E1, E2, and E3. These jumpers are used to select the drive's SCSI ID. The following table defines the settings:

SCSI ID	Jumper
0	None
1	E1
2	E2
3	E1 & E2
4	E3
5	E1 & E3
6	E2 & E3

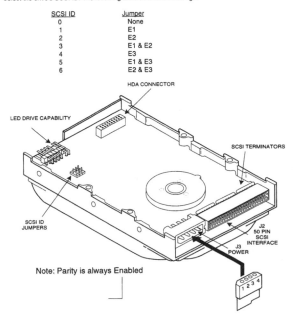

Note: Parity is always Enabled

CONNER CP30104

The drive has one set of jumpers labeled C/D, DSP, E1.

Single Drive = C/D Jumpered
Master = C/D and DSP Jumpered
Slave = No Jumpers Installed
E1 = Not used.

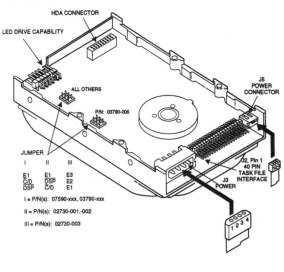

JUMPER		
I	II	III
E1	E1	E3
C/D	DSP	E2
DSP	C/D	E1

I = P/N(s): 07590-xxx, 03790-xxx

II = P/N(s): 02730-001, -002

III = P/N(s): 02730-003

CONNER CP30104H

The drive has one set of jumpers labeled C/D, DSP, E1.

Single Drive = C/D Jumpered
Master = C/D and DSP Jumpered
Slave = No Jumpers Installed
E1 = Not used.

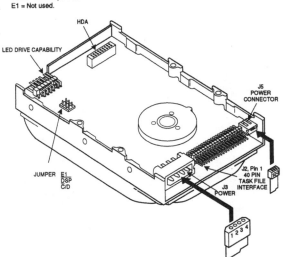

CONNER CP30124

The C/D jumper is used to determine whether the drive is a master (drive C) or a slave
(drive D). The drive is configured as a master, when jumpered, and a slave when not jumpered.
The ATA/ISA jumper is used when when daisy-chaining two drives. If another manufacturers
drive is being connected to the conner drive, you may need to install this jumper.

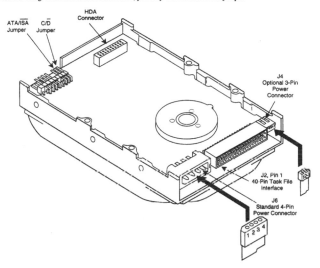

CONNER CP30170E

E1, E2 and E3 are used to select the SCSI ID. The drive is shipped as ID 7, with all three jumpers
installed.
The following table describes the SCSI ID:

SCSI ID	Jumpers installed
0	None
1	E1
2	E2
3	E1,E2
4	E3
5	E1, E3
6	E2,E3

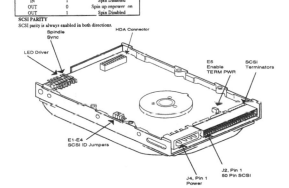

CONNER CP30174E

The C/D jumper is used to determine whether the drive is a master (drive C) or slave (drive D).
The drive is configured as a master (drive C) when jumpered and as a slave drive (D drive) when
not jumpered.

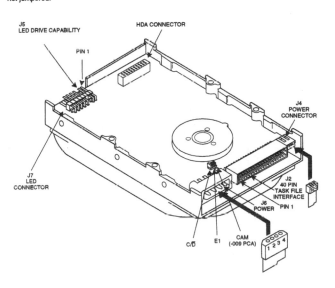

CONNER CP30200

There are three jumpers availabel for configuration; E1,E2, and E3 are used to select
the drive SCSI ID. The following table defines the settings. Note: SCSI parity is always
enabled.
The following table defines the settings for jumpers E1, E2, and E3:

Jumper Options			
E1	E2	E3	SCSI ID
OUT	OUT	OUT	O
IN	OUT	OUT	1
OUT	IN	OUT	2
IN	IN	OUT	3
OUT	OUT	IN	4
IN	OUT	IN	5
OUT	IN	IN	6
IN	IN	IN	7

Delay Spin: A jumper in the E4 location, disables spin up on power-on. Disabling spin up on
application of power can also be enabled by settting the DSPN bit in MODE SELECT page 0.

E4	DSPN	Result
IN	0	Spin Disabled
IN	1	Spin Disabled
OUT	0	Spin up onpower on
OUT	1	Spin Disabled

SCSI PARITY
SCSI parity is always enabled in both directions.

CONNER CP30204

The C/D jumper is used to determine whether the drive is a master (drive C) or slave (drive D). The drive is configured as a master (drive C) when jumpered and as a slave drive (D drive) when not jumpered.

DSP & SS: This pair of jumpers determines the signals on pin 39 of the interface connector.

Jumper		Action
DSP	SS	
X		- spindle synchronization signal disabled on pin 39. - activity LED signal available on pin 39. - Must be in place for CAM /ATA drives.
	X	- spindle synchronization signal enabled on pin 39. - activity LED signal disabled from pin 39.
		- pin 39 floating.

Jumper	
E1	Disable Spin Up until command received
E2	Not used
E3	Not used

CONNER CP3024

There are four jumper options available for configuration: *HSP, C/D, DSP, and ACT.
The following table shows what the jumper settings should be for various system configurations.

Single Drive = ACT and C/D Jumpered
Master Drive = C/D and DSP Jumpered
Slave Drive = No Jumpers installed
* Note: HSP is not used.
DOS Drive Type= 2

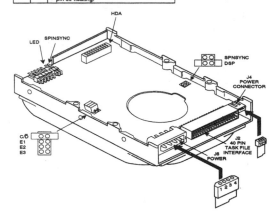

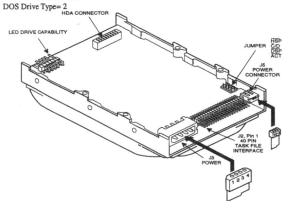

CONNER CP30254

The C/D jumper is used to determine whether the drive is a master (drive C) or a slave (drive D). The drive is configured as a master, when jumpered, and a slave when not jumpered. The ATA/ISA jumper is used when daisy-chaining two drives. This jumper may have to be removed when this drive is used together with older (Pre-ATA) drives.

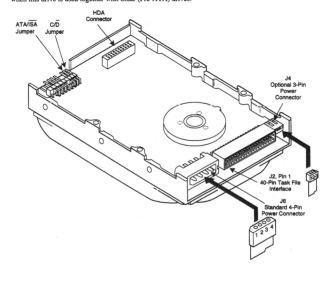

CONNER CP3040

There are four jumpers available for configuration. Three of these jumpers, E1, E2, and E3 are used to select the drive's SCSI ID, installing E4 disables parity. The following table defines the settings for jumpers E1, E2, and E3:

E1	E2	E3	SCSI ID
OUT	OUT	OUT	0
IN	OUT	OUT	1
OUT	IN	OUT	2
IN	IN	OUT	3
OUT	OUT	IN	4
IN	OUT	IN	5
OUT	IN	IN	6
IN	IN	IN	7

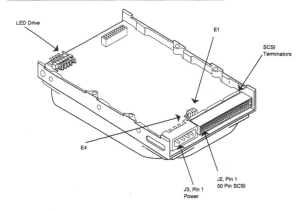

CONNER CP3044

There are four jumper options available for configuration: *HSP, C/D, DSP, and ACT.
The following table shows what the jumper settings should be for various system configurations.

Single Drive = ACT and C/D Jumpered
Master Drive = C/D and DSP Jumpered
Slave Drive = No Jumpers installed

* Note: HSP is not used.

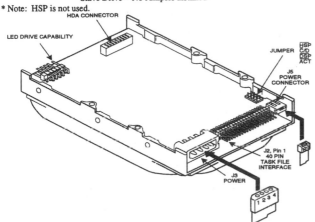

CONNER CP30540

SCSI Bus Address
There are three jumpers available for configuration of SCSI ID: E1, E2, and E3. The following table defines the settings:

SCSI Bus	Addresses*		
E1/0E1	E2/0E2	E3/0E3	SCSI ID
OUT	OUT	OUT	0
IN	OUT	OUT	1
OUT	IN	OUT	2
IN	IN	OUT	3
OUT	OUT	IN	4
IN	OUT	IN	5
OUT	IN	IN	6
IN	IN	IN	7

*Use either but not both : E1 to E3 or 0E1 to 0E3. The 0E header is not installed on drive configurations with a LED on the PCBA.
Disable Spin: A jumper in the E4 location, disables spin up on power-on. Disabling spin up on application of power can also be enabled by setting the DSPN bit in MODE SELECT page 0.

E4	Disable Spin on Power on	
E5	Terminators on	0E5

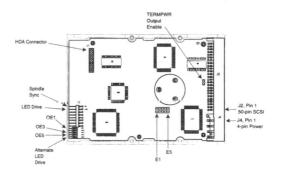

CONNER CP30544

C/D
Up to two drives may be daisy chained together utilizing the 40 pin Task File connector. The maximum cable length is 18 inches. In order to install more than one drive, it is necessary to set a jumper option. The C/D jumper is used to determine whether the drive is master (drive C) or slave (drive D). The drive is configured as a master (drive C) when jumpered and as a slave drive (D drive) when not jumpered.

DSP & SS This pair of jumpers determines the signals on pin 39 of the interface connector.

Jumper		Action
DSP	SS	
X		-Spindle synchronization signal disable on pin 39.
		-Activity LED signal available on pin 39.
	X	-Spindle synchronization signal enable on pin 39
		-Activity LED signal disabled from pin 39.
		-Pin 39 floating.

Jumper	Function	
	ATA/CAM	Non-CAM
Block A E2	OUT	IN
Block A E3	OUT	IN
Block A E4	OUT	IN
Block A E5	IN	OUT
Block A E6	IN	OUT
Block A E7	IN	OUT
Block A E8	IN	OUT
Block B ATA/ISA	IN	OUT

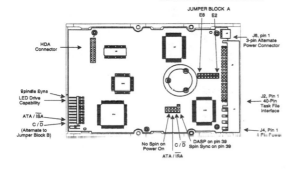

CONNER CP3100

There are six jumpers available for configuration. Three of these jumpers, E1, E2, and E3 are used to select the drive's SCSI ID, while E4 (installed) disables parity. Jumpers E5 and E6 are used to enable either the spindle synchronization signal, or LED, respectively.
The following table defines the settings for jumpers E1, E2, and E3

E1	E2	E3	SCSI ID
OUT	OUT	OUT	0
IN	OUT	OUT	1
OUT	IN	OUT	2
IN	IN	OUT	3
OUT	OUT	IN	4
IN	OUT	IN	5
OUT	IN	IN	6
IN	IN	IN	7

J3 POWER PIN ASSIGNMENTS	
SIGNAL	PIN NO.
+ 12V	1
GND	2
GND	3
+5V	4

J4 FACTORY TEST PORT	
SIGNAL	PIN NO.
+ 5V	1
LED/SYNC	2
UNUSED	3-14

CONNER CP31370 BAJA SCSI

SCSI Bus Address

There are three jumpers available for configuration of SCSI ID: E1, E2, and E3. The following table defines the settings:

SCSI Bus	Addresses*		
E1/0E1	E2/0E2	E3/0E3	SCSI ID
OUT	OUT	OUT	0
IN	OUT	OUT	1
OUT	IN	OUT	2
IN	IN	OUT	3
OUT	OUT	IN	4
IN	OUT	IN	5
OUT	IN	IN	6
IN	IN	IN	7

*Use either but not both : E1 to E3 or 0E1 to 0E3. The 0E header is not installed on drive configurations with a LED on the PCBA.

Disable Spin: A jumper in the E4 location, disables spin up on power-on. Disabling spin up on application of power can also be enabled by settting the DSPN bit in MODE SELECT page 0.

E4	Disable Spin on Power on	
E5	Terminators on	0E5

CONNER CP3104

The jumper options available are:

    Single Drive = ACT and C/D are Jumpered
    Master Drive = C/D and DSP are Jumpered
    Slave Drive = No Jumpers Installed
    -HSP, is not used.

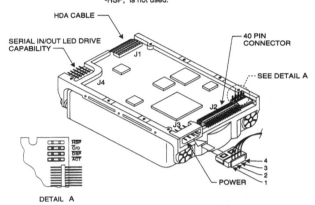

DETAIL A

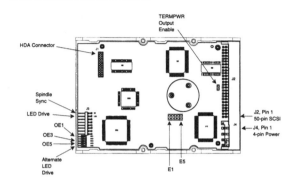

CONNER CP3200F

There are three jumpers availabel for configuration; E1,E2, and E3 are used to select the drive SCSI ID. The following table defines the settings. Note: SCSI parity is always enabled

The following table defines the settings for jumpers E1, E2, and E3:

Jumper	Options		
E1	E2	E3	SCSI ID
OUT	OUT	OUT	0
IN	OUT	OUT	1
OUT	IN	OUT	2
IN	IN	OUT	3
OUT	OUT	IN	4
IN	OUT	IN	5
OUT	IN	IN	6
IN	IN	IN	7

PIN	SIGNAL
1	+12V
2	GND
3	GND
4	+5V

CONNER CP3184

The jumper options available are:

    Single Drive = ACT and C/D are Jumpered
    Master Drive = C/D and DSP are Jumpered
    Slave Drive = No Jumpers Installed
    -HSP, is not used.

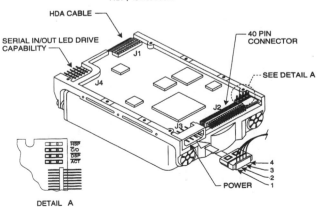

DETAIL A

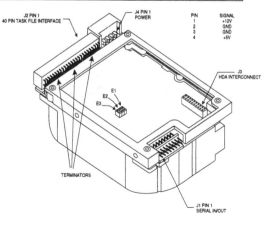

CONNER CP3204F

The CP3204F has two jumper options, DSP and C/D The jumper configuration is as follows.

Single Drive=Jumper C/D only
Master Drive=Jumper C/D and DSP jumpered
Slave Drive=No Jumpers installed.

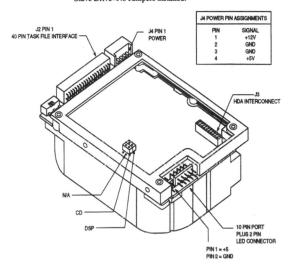

J4 POWER PIN ASSIGNMENTS	
PIN	SIGNAL
1	+12V
2	GND
3	GND
4	+5V

CONNER CP3304

C/D
The C/D jumper is used to determine whether the drive is a master (drive C) or slave (drive D). The drive is configured as a master (drive C) when jumpered and as a slave drive (D drive) when not jumpered.

DSP & SS This pair of jumpers determines the signals on pin 39 of the interface connector.

Jumper		Action
DSP	SS	
X		- spindle synchronization signal disabled on pin 39.
		- activity LED signal available on pin 39.
		- Must be in place for CAM /ATA drives.
	X	- spindle synchronization signal enabled on pin 39.
		- activity LED signal disabled from pin 39.
		- pin 39 floating.

Jumper	
E1	Disable Spin Up until command received
E2	Not used
E3	Not used

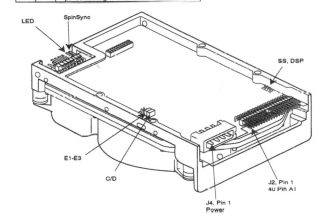

CONNER CP3360/CP3540

There are three jumpers available for configuration of SCSI ID: E1, E2, and E3. The following table defines the settings:

ID	Jumper
0	None
1	E1
2	E2
3	E1 & E2
4	E3
5	E1 & E3
6	E2 & E3

Delay Spin A jumper in the E4 location, disables spin up on power-on. Disabling spin up on application of power can also be enabled by setting the DSPN bit in MODE SELECT page 0.

E4	DSPN	Result
In	0	Spin Disabled
In	1	Spin Disabled
Out	0	Spin up on Power On
Out	1	Spin Disabled

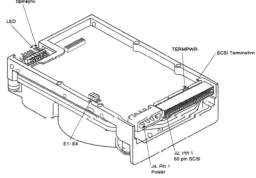

CONNER CP3364

C/D
The C/D jumper is used to determine whether the drive is a master (drive C) or slave (drive D). The drive is configured as a master (drive C) when jumpered and as a slave drive (D drive) when not jumpered.

DSP & SS This pair of jumpers determines the signals on pin 39 of the interface connector.

Jumper		Action
DSP	SS	
X		- spindle synchronization signal disabled on pin 39.
		- activity LED signal available on pin 39.
		- Must be in place for CAM /ATA drives.
	X	- spindle synchronization signal enabled on pin 39.
		- activity LED signal disabled from pin 39.
		- pin 39 floating.

Jumper	
E1	Disable Spin Up until command received
E2	Not used
E3	Not used

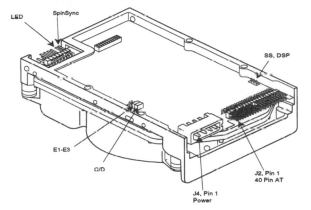

CONNER CP3504

C/D

The C/D jumper is used to determine whether the drive is a master (drive C) or slave (drive D). The drive is configured as a master (drive C) when jumpered and as a slave drive (D drive) when not jumpered.

DSP & SS This pair of jumpers determines the signals on pin 39 of the interface connector.

Jumper DSP	SS	Action
X		- spindle synchronization signal disabled on pin 39.
		- activity LED signal available on pin 39.
		- Must be in place for CAM /ATA drives.
	X	- spindle synchronization signal enabled on pin 39.
		- activity LED signal disabled from pin 39.
		- pin 39 floating.

Jumper	
E1	Disable Spin Up until command received
E2	Not used
E3	Not used

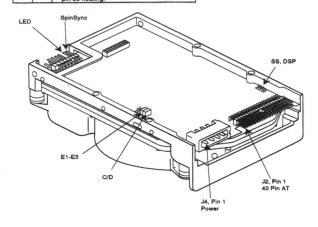

CONNER CP340

There are four jumpers available for configuration; three of the jumpers, E2, E3, and E4 are used to select the drive's SCSI ID, while E1 (installed) disables parity. The following table defines the settings for these jumpers.

E2	E3	E4	Device
OUT	OUT	OUT	0
IN	OUT	OUT	1
OUT	IN	OUT	2
IN	IN	OUT	3
OUT	OUT	IN	4
IN	OUT	IN	5
OUT	IN	IN	6
IN	IN	IN	7

J4 FACTORY TEST PORT	
SIGNAL	PIN NO.
+ 5V	1
LED/SYNC	2
UNUSED	3-14

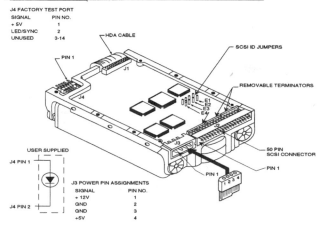

J3 POWER PIN ASSIGNMENTS	
SIGNAL	PIN NO.
+ 12V	1
GND	2
GND	3
+5V	4

DIGITAL DSP3000 SERIES

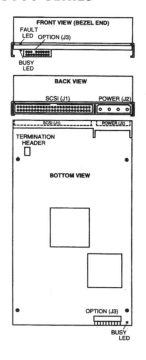

CONNER CP3544

C/D

The C/D jumper is used to determine whether the drive is a master (drive C) or slave (drive D). The drive is configured as a master (drive C) when jumpered and as a slave drive (D drive) when not jumpered.

DSP & SS This pair of jumpers determines the signals on pin 39 of the interface connector.

Jumper DSP	SS	Action on pin 39
X		- DASP signal available
		- activity LED available
	X	- spindle synchronization output
		- activity LED disabled
		- open

Jumper	
E1	Disable spin-up until command received
E2	Not used
E3	Not used (spare jumper retainer)

These jumpers only apply to PCB P/N 09400-001

Jumper	
E6	ISA - DMAEN on J2, pin 21
E7	ISA - DMARQ on J2, pin 29
E8	ISA - DMACK on J2, pin 27
E9	ATA - IORDY on J2, pin 27
E10	ATA - Spin Sync on J2, pin 28 (remove unless spin sync is used)
E11	ATA - DMACK on J2, pin 29
E12	ATA - DMARQ on J2, pin 21

DIGITAL DSP5000 SERIES

SCSI ID – DSP5300W/5350W/5400W

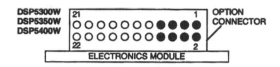

DSP5300W
DSP5350W
DSP5400W

OPTION CONNECTOR

ELECTRONICS MODULE

SCSI ID	JUMPER LOCATION			
	PINS 7-8	PINS 5-6	PINS 3-4	PINS 1-2
0	0	0	0	0
1	0	0	0	1
2	0	0	1	0
3	0	0	1	1
4	0	1	0	0
5	0	1	0	1
6	0	1	1	0
7	0	1	1	1
8	1	0	0	0
9	1	0	0	1
10	1	0	1	0
11	1	0	1	1
12	1	1	0	0
13	1	1	0	1
14	1	1	1	0
15	1	1	1	1

0 = JUMPER NOT INSTALLED
1 = JUMPER INSTALLED

DIGITAL DSP5200

REAR VIEW

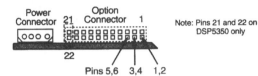

Power Connector

Option Connector

Note: Pins 21 and 22 on DSP5350 only

Pins 5,6   3,4   1,2

ID JUMPER SETTINGS		
SCSI ID Pins 5,6	3,4	1,2
0		
1		
2		
3		
4		
5		
6		
7		

DIGITAL DSP5350

REAR VIEW

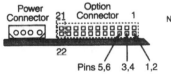

Power Connector

Option Connector

Note: Pins 21 and 22 on DSP5350 only

Pins 5,6   3,4   1,2

ID JUMPER SETTINGS		
SCSI ID Pins 5,6	3,4	1,2
0		
1		
2		
3		
4		
5		
6		
7		

FUJITSU M2246SA

On the M2246SA model, parameter settings are made with jumpers between pairs of pins on terminal strip CN105. The figure below shows the location of CN105 as you see it when you flip over the drive, identifies the purpose of each pin pair, and shows whether a shorting plug is installed at the factory. Read the descriptions to determine whether the factory settings are correct for your system.

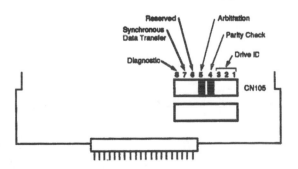

Terminal strip CN105-M2246SA

FUJITSU M2249SA

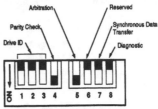

DIP switch-M2249SA

Drive ID
This setting determines the ID by which the host adaptor identifies the drive. You make the setting with the first three pin pairs on terminal strip CN105 (M2246SA) or with the first three toggles on the DIP switch (M2249SA). The table shows the settings and the corresponding IDs.

Drive ID	Pin pair/toggle 1	2	3
0	OPEN	OPEN	OPEN
1	SHORT	OPEN	OPEN
2	OPEN	SHORT	OPEN
3	SHORT	SHORT	OPEN
4	OPEN	OPEN	SHORT
5	SHORT	OPEN	SHORT
6	OPEN	SHORT	SHORT
7	SHORT	SHORT	SHORT

FUJITSU M2247/M2248/M2249SA

Short plugs are inserted as follows when shipped from the factory.

CN3:   Between 11 and 12, 13 and 14
CNH104: Between 3 and 4
CNH105: Between 15 and 16

The following settings are model specific.

CNH105: Between 13 and 14 : M2249
             Between 11 and 12 : M2248
             No short plugs between 11 and 12 or 13 and 14 : M2247

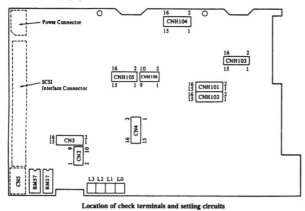

Location of check terminals and setting circuits

FUJITSU M226xS

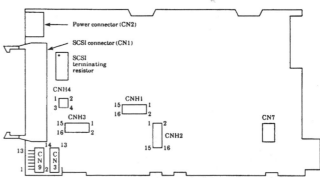

The Setting Terminals and Terminating Resistor (M226xS)

FUJITSU M226xH

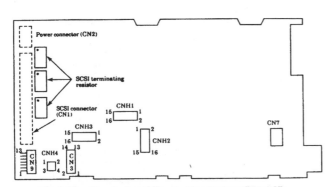

The Setting Terminals and Terminating Resistor (M226xH)

FUJITSU M226xS/H

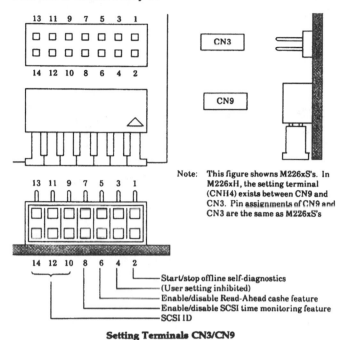

Note: This figure showns M226xS's. In M226xH, the setting terminal (CNH4) exists between CN9 and CN3. Pin assignments of CN9 and CN3 are the same as M226xS's

Setting Terminals CN3/CN9

FUJITSU M226xS/H

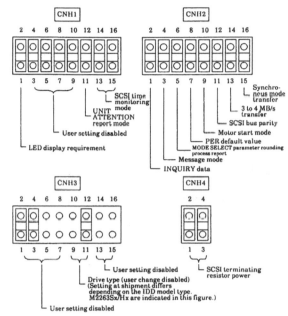

Setting Terminals CNH1, CNH2, CNH3, and CNH4

FUJITSU M2611T/M2612T

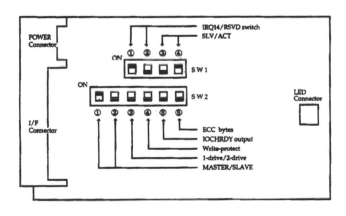

FUJITSU M265xH (REV. 02)

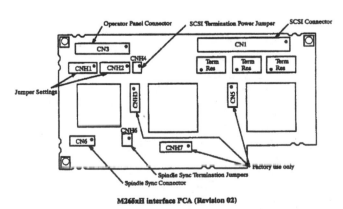

M265xH interface PCA (Revision 02)

FUJITSU M265xHD

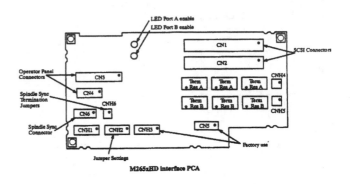

M265xHD interface PCA

FUJITSU M265xH (REV. 03)

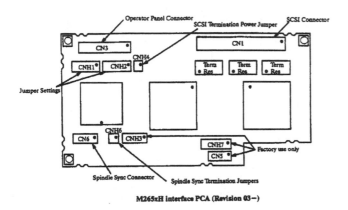

M265xH interface PCA (Revision 03—)

HITACHI DK514C

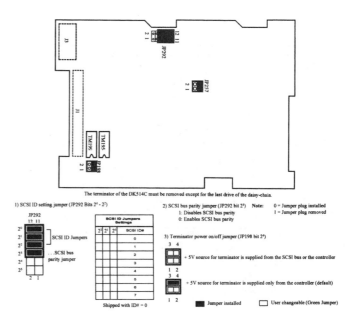

FUJITSU M265xS (REV. 03)

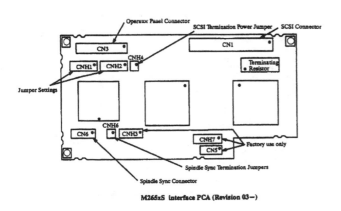

M265xS interface PCA (Revision 03—)

HITACHI DK515 (PCB REV.0)

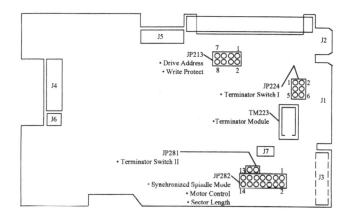

HITACHI DK515 (PCB REV.1+)

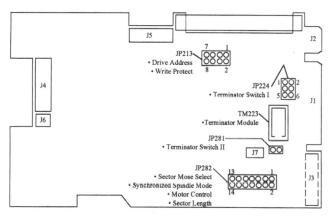

HITACHI DK515C

Spindle Synchronization
J7 – Pin 1 ~ 4   (Signal connector)
JP266   (Signal termination)
JP223 – 2¹~2²   (Mode Setting Jumper)

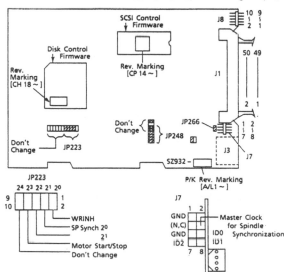

HITACHI DK516C

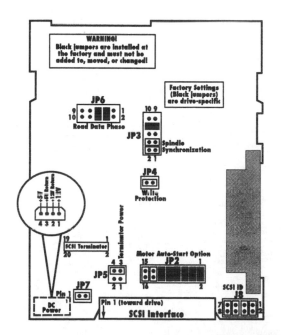

HEWLETT PACKARD 9753xE ESDI

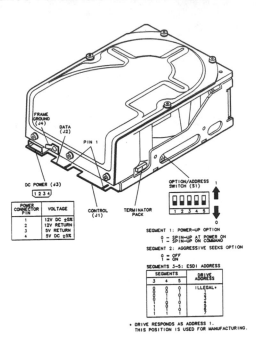

SEGMENT 1: POWER-UP OPTION

0 = SPIN-UP AT POWER ON
1 = SPIN-UP ON COMMAND

SEGMENT 2: AGGRESSIVE SEEKS OPTION

0 = OFF
1 = ON

SEGMENTS 3-5: ESDI ADDRESS

SEGMENTS			DRIVE ADDRESS
3	4	5	
0	0	0	ILLEGAL*
0	0	1	1
0	1	0	2
0	1	1	3
1	0	0	4
1	0	1	5
1	1	0	6
1	1	1	7

* DRIVE RESPONDS AS ADDRESS 1.
THIS POSITION IS USED FOR MANUFACTURING.

POWER CONNECTOR PIN	VOLTAGE
1	12V DC ±5%
2	12V RETURN
3	5V RETURN
4	5V DC ±5%

HITACHI DK517C-37

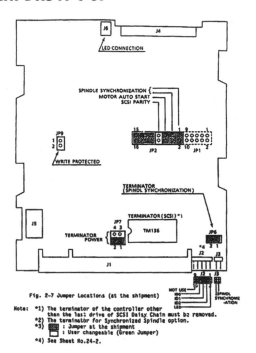

Fig. 2-7 Jumper Locations (at the shipment)

Note: *1) The terminator of the controller other
than the last drive of SCSI Daisy Chain must be removed.
*2) The terminator for Synchronized Spindle option.
*3) ▨ : Jumper at the shipment
□ : User changeable (Green Jumper)
*4) See Sheet No.24-2.

HEWLETT PACKARD 97556/97558/97560

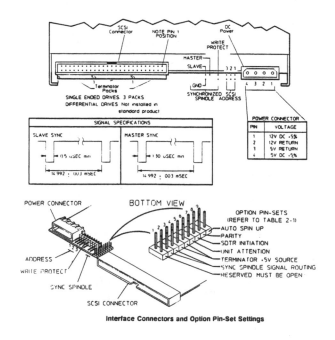

SINGLE ENDED DRIVES. 3 PACKS
DIFFERENTIAL DRIVES Not installed in
standard product

SIGNAL SPECIFICATIONS

POWER CONNECTOR	
PIN	VOLTAGE
1	12V DC +5%
2	12V RETURN
3	5V RETURN
4	5V DC +5%

OPTION PIN-SETS
(REFER TO TABLE 2-1)
- AUTO SPIN UP
- PARITY
- SDTR INITIATION
- UNIT ATTENTION
- TERMINATOR +5V SOURCE
- SYNC SPINDLE SIGNAL ROUTING
- RESERVED MUST BE OPEN

Interface Connectors and Option Pin-Set Settings

HEWLETT PACKARD 9753xS/T/D

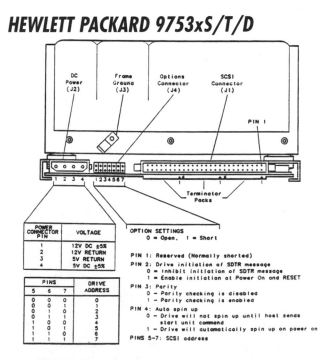

POWER CONNECTOR PIN	VOLTAGE
1	12V DC ±5%
2	12V RETURN
3	5V RETURN
4	5V DC ±5%

PINS			DRIVE ADDRESS
5	6	7	
0	0	0	0
0	0	1	1
0	1	0	2
0	1	1	3
1	0	0	4
1	0	1	5
1	1	0	6
1	1	1	7

OPTION SETTINGS
0 = Open, 1 = Short

PIN 1: Reserved (Normally shorted)
PIN 2: Drive initiation of SDTR message
0 = Inhibit initiation of SDTR message
1 = Enable initiation at Power On and RESET
PIN 3: Parity
0 = Parity checking is disabled
1 = Parity checking is enabled
PIN 4: Auto spin up
0 = Drive will not spin up until host sends
start unit command
1 = Drive will automatically spin up on power on
PINS 5-7: SCSI address

HEWLETT PACKARD C2244/45/46/47 NARROW DIFFERENTIAL

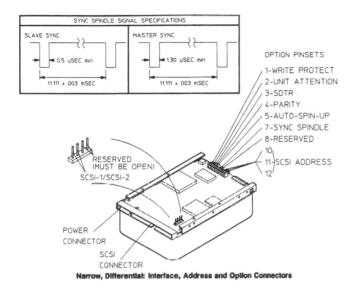

Narrow, Differential: Interface, Address and Option Connectors

HEWLETT PACKARD C2244/45/46/47 NARROW SINGLE ENDED

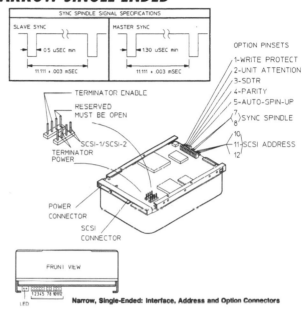

Narrow, Single-Ended: Interface, Address and Option Connectors

HEWLETT PACKARD C2244/45/46/47 WIDE DIFFERENTIAL

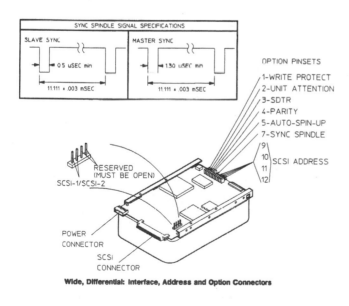

Wide, Differential: Interface, Address and Option Connectors

HEWLETT PACKARD C2490A NARROW DIFFERENTIAL

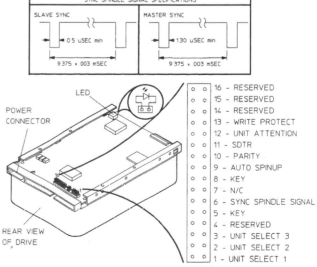

Narrow, Differential: Interface, Address and Option Configurations

HEWLETT PACKARD C2490A
WIDE DIFFERENTIAL

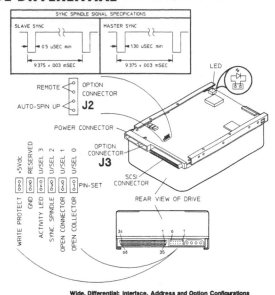

Wide, Differential: Interface, Address and Option Configurations

HEWLETT PACKARD C2490A
NARROW SINGLE ENDED

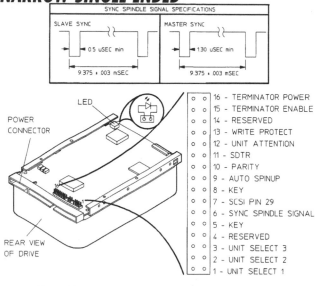

16 - TERMINATOR POWER
15 - TERMINATOR ENABLE
14 - RESERVED
13 - WRITE PROTECT
12 - UNIT ATTENTION
11 - SDTR
10 - PARITY
9 - AUTO SPINUP
8 - KEY
7 - SCSI PIN 29
6 - SYNC SPINDLE SIGNAL
5 - KEY
4 - RESERVED
3 - UNIT SELECT 3
2 - UNIT SELECT 2
1 - UNIT SELECT 1

Narrow, Single-Ended: Interface, Address and Option Configurations

HEWLETT PACKARD C3010 12-Pin Version

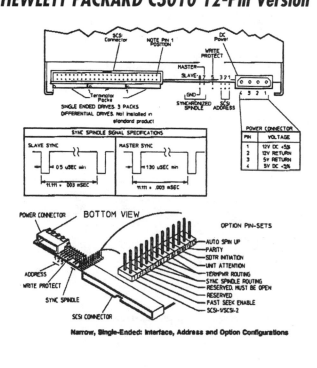

Narrow, Single-Ended: Interface, Address and Option Configurations

HEWLETT PACKARD 9-Pin Version

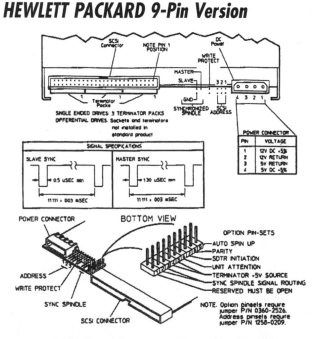

Narrow, Single-Ended, Interface, Address, and Option Connectors (9-Pin-set Version)

IBM 0632

Subsystem Interface Connector (J3)
The subsystem interface connector (J3)⁴ allows direct communications between a library autochanger and the drive subassembly. The subsystem interface connector (J3) also allows setting of various options through a remotely mounted switch cabled to the connector. The pin assignments are shown below.

Pin	Signal Name	Definition
1	LIB Interface Eject	Instructs the drive to eject the media. Driven active low by the subsystem and pulled up to 5 volts by the drive.
2	LED Pipe	Represents the drive front panel activity indicator LED. Active low signal.
3	PWRDNREQ	Instructs the drive to synchronous the cache immediately (transfer data from the write cache to the media). Driven active low by the subsystem and pulled up to 5 volts by the drive.
4	LIB Interface Busy	Indicates drive activity during cartridge insertion, spin-down, and removal. Driven active low by the drive and pulled up to 5 volts by the sussystem (220-ohm resistor).
5	SCSI TERMPWR	Connects to the same pin as the SCSI connector TERMPWR signal.
6	SCSI TERMPWR SRC	Supplies +5V AC source voltage throught isolation diode for TERMPWR. Connecting Pin 6 to Pin 5 enables the SCSI TERMPWR signal.
7	Not Connected	Not connected to the drive electronics
8	Reserved for Mfg.	Reserved for manufacturer's use. Should not be connected
9	Reserved for Mfg.	Reserved for manufacturer's use. Should not be connected.
10	CART_IN_DRIVE	Indicates a cartridge has been inserted into the drive. Driven by active low by the drive and pulled up to 5 volts by the subsystem (220 ohm resistor).
11	Sub Reset	Instructs the drive to perform a hard reset.
12	Reserved for Mfg.	Reserved for manufacturer's use. Should not be connected.
13	SCSI Parity Disabled	Disables SCSI parity on the drive. Driven by active low by the subsystem and pulled up to 5 volts by the drive.
14	LIB Interface Spin-down	Instructs the drive to spin-down the media. Driven active low by the subsystem and pulled up to 5 volts by the drive.
15	SCSI ID2	SCSI ID select bit 2. Driven active low by the subsystem and pulled up to 5 volts by the drive.
16	Reserved for Mfg.	Reserved for manufacturer's use. Should not be connected.
17	SCSI ID1	SCSI ID select bit 1. Driven active low by the subsystem and pulled up to 5 volts by the drive.
18	SCSI Termination Disable	Disables SCSI termination.
19	SCSI ID0	SCSI ID select bit 0. Driven active low by the subsystem and pulled up to 5 volts by the drive.
20	Ground	Ground.

IBM 0632 (Continued)

SCSI Address Switch (J4)
The SCSI address of the drive can be selected using the 4-position address switch (J4) or the subsystem interface connector (J3). The address is read at power up and when the drive is reset. See the figure below for location and switch positions.

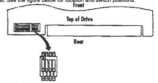

SCSI Adress Switch Settings

SCSI Drive Address	Switch 1 (ID0)	Switch 2 (ID1)	Switch 3 (ID2)	Switch 4
0	Off (inactive)	Off (inactive)	Off (inactive)	Not connected
1	On (active)	Off (inactive)	Off (inactive)	Not connected
2	Off (inactive)	On (active)	Off (inactive)	Not connected
3	On (active)	On (active)	Off (inactive)	Not connected
4	Off (inactive)	Off (inactive)	On (active)	Not connected
5	On (active)	Off (inactive)	On (active)	Not connected
6	Off (inactive)	On (active)	On (active)	Not connected
7	On (active)	On (active)	On (active)	Not connected

The correct SCSI address must be applied to the SCSI address switch or subsystem interface connector while the address is read by the drive. The SCSI address is read by the drive approximately 1.75 seconds after the power is applied to the drive or after a SCSI reset condition is initiated. The address setting must be applied to the switch or connector at least 1.5 seconds after applying drive power until the drive is powered off.
The user should only use one SCSI address source, either the SCSI address switch OR the subsystem interface connector. The other (unused) source must be set to an address of 0.
The SCSI address switch is preset in the factory to SCSI address 1.

Feature Switches (J5 and J6)
J5

Switch	Setting	Description
A1	Off	Enable Unit Attention on POR/SCSI Reset.
	On*	Feature Switch 2 Off: Disable Unit Attention on POR/SCSI Reset for Apple-attach. Feature Switch 2 On: Support Mode Sense/Select pages for DEC-attach.
A2	Off*	Peripheral Device Type in Inquiry data is X'07', Optical Memory Device.
	On	Peripheral Device Type in Inquiry data is X'00', Direct Address Device.
A3	Off*	Spin automatically on power-up or cartridge insert.
	On	No spin-up on power-up but spin-up on cartridge insert.
A4	Off*	Force verify on Write command is default mode.
	On	Inhibit verify on Write command is default mode.
A5	Off*	Enable SCSI termination.
	On	Disable SCSI termination.

Bold* = Default

IBM 0632 (Continued)

Feature Switches (J5 and J6)

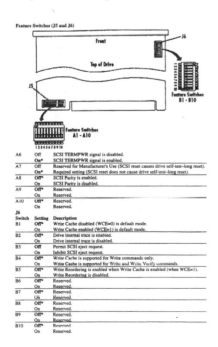

	Off	SCSI TERMPWR signal is disabled.
A6	On*	SCSI TERMPWR signal is enabled.
A7	Off	Reserved for Manufacturer's Use (SCSI reset causes drive self-test–long reset).
	On*	Required setting (SCSI reset does not cause drive self-test–long reset).
A8	Off*	SCSI Parity is enabled.
	On	SCSI Parity is disabled.
A9	Off*	Reserved.
	On	Reserved.
A10	Off*	Reserved.
	On	Reserved.

J6

Switch	Setting	Description
B1	Off*	Write Cache disabled (WCE=0) is default mode.
	On	Write Cache enabled (WCE=1) is default mode.
B2	Off*	Drive internal trace is enabled.
	On	Drive internal trace is disabled.
B3	Off	Permit SCSI eject request.
	On	Inhibit SCSI eject request.
B4	Off*	Write Cache is supported for Write commands only.
	On	Write Cache is supported for Write and Write Verify commands.
B5	Off*	Write Reordering is enabled when Write Cache is enabled (when WCE=1).
	On	Write Reordering is disabled.
B6	Off*	Reserved.
	On	Reserved.
B7	Off*	Reserved.
	On	Reserved.
B8	Off*	Reserved.
	On	Reserved.
B9	Off*	Reserved.
	On	Reserved.
B10	Off*	Reserved.
	On	Reserved.

IBM 0662

Electrical Connector Locations - The electrical connectors are shown below, consisting of an option block, a SCSI connector and a power connector.

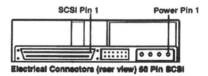

Electrical Connectors (rear view) 68 Pin SCSI

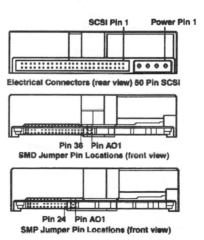

Electrical Connectors (rear view) 50 Pin SCSI

SMD Jumper Pin Locations (front view)

SMP Jumper Pin Locations (front view)

IBM 0662 (Continued)

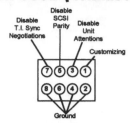

Bottom Options Jumper Block for SMP Versions

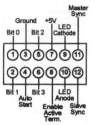

Rear Options Jumper Block for 68 pin models

IBM 0662 (Continued)

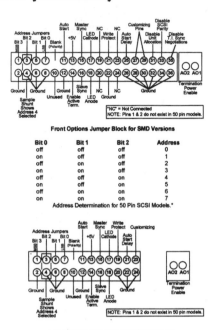

Front Options Jumper Block for SMD Versions

Bit 0	Bit 1	Bit 2	Address
off	off	off	0
on	off	off	1
off	on	off	2
on	on	off	3
off	off	on	4
on	off	on	5
off	on	on	6
on	on	on	7

Address Determination for 50 Pin SCSI Models.*

Front Options Jumper Block for SMP Versions

Bit 0	Bit 1	Bit 2	Bit 3	Address
off	off	off	off	0
on	off	off	off	1
off	on	off	off	2
on	on	off	off	3
off	off	on	off	4
on	off	on	off	5
off	on	on	off	6
on	on	on	off	7
off	off	off	on	8
on	off	off	on	9
off	on	off	on	10
on	on	off	on	11
off	off	on	on	12
on	off	on	on	13
off	on	on	on	14
on	on	on	on	15

Address Determination for 50 Pin SCSI Models.*

IBM DBOA 2360

Drive Address
A jumper cable is available at the interface connector to determine the drive address.
Using Cable Selection, the drive address depends on the condition of pin 28 of the AT interface cable. In the case when pin 28 is ground or low, the drive is a Master. If pin 28 is open or high level, the drive is a Slave.

Cabling
The maximum cable length from the host system to the HDD plus circuit pattern length in the host system shall not exceed 18 inches.
AT Signal Connector
The AT signal connector is designed to mate with Dupont part number 69764-044 or equivalent.

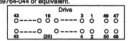

NOTES: Pin position 20 is left blank for secure connector insertion.
Pin position 47 through 50 are used for drive address setting.

IBM 31080

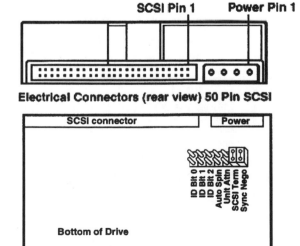

IBM DBOA 2528

Drive Address
A jumper cable is available at the interface connector to determine
the drive address.
Using Cable Selection, the drive address depends on the
condition of pin 28 of the AT interface cable. In the case when pin
28 is ground or low, the drive is a Master. If pin 28 is open or high
level, the drive is a Slave.

Cabling
The maximum cable length from the host system to the HDD plus
circuit pattern length in the host system shall not exceed 18 inches.
AT Signal Connector
The AT signal connector is designed to mate with Dupont part
number 69764-044 or equivalent.

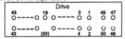

NOTES: Pin position 20 is left blank for secure connector insertion.
Pin position 47 through 50 are used for drive address setting.

IBM DBOA 2540

Drive Address
A jumper cable is available at the interface connector to determine
the drive address.
Using Cable Selection, the drive address depends on the
condition of pin 28 of the AT interface cable. In the case when pin
28 is ground or low, the drive is a Master. If pin 28 is open or high
level, the drive is a Slave.

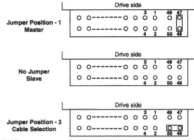

Cabling
The maximum cable length from the host system to the HDD plus
circuit pattern length in the host system shall not exceed 18 inches.
AT Signal Connector
The AT signal connector is designed to mate with Dupont part
number 69764-044 or equivalent.

NOTES: Pin position 20 is left blank for secure connector insertion.
Pin position 47 through 50 are used for drive address setting.

IBM DBOA 2720

Drive Address
A jumper cable is available at the interface connector to determine
the drive address.
Using Cable Selection, the drive address depends on the
condition of pin 28 of the AT interface cable. In the case when pin
28 is ground or low, the drive is a Master. If pin 28 is open or high
level, the drive is a Slave.

Cabling
The maximum cable length from the host system to the HDD plus
circuit pattern length in the host system shall not exceed 18 inches.
AT Signal Connector
The AT signal connector is designed to mate with Dupont part
number 69764-044 or equivalent.

NOTES: Pin position 20 is left blank for secure connector insertion.
Pin position 47 through 50 are used for drive address setting.

IBM DHAS 2270

Driver/Receiver
The drives support single ended drivers and receivers.

Connector
The SCSI signal connectors is designed to mate with AMP part number
6-176135 or equivalent. Size and location of the mounting holes
compkly with MCC.

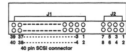

J2 Pin No.	-ID1 5	-ID2 6	-ID4 7	Device Address
	open	open	open	0
	gnd	open	open	1
	open	gnd	open	2
	gnd	gnd	open	3
	open	open	gnd	4
	gnd	open	gnd	5
	open	gnd	gnd	6
	gnd	gnd	gnd	7

Cabling
The maximum cable length from the host system to the drive is limited
to 6 inches with external 1K-ohm pull up resistors.
In case that appropriate termination resistors are externally equipped to
the interface lines, the cable length can be extended. The maximum
cable length depends on the condition of the various electrical
parameters of the interface.

Device Address
The drive recognizes its device address, namely SCSI ID, with the
condition of -ID1, -ID2, and -ID4. The signal condition and the device
address are shown above.

Signal Termination
The drive does not ahve termination nor pull up resistors for SCSI
interface.

IBM DHAS 2540

Connector

The SCSI signal connectors is designed to mate with AMP part number 6-176135 or equivalent. Size and location of the mounting holes compkly with MCC.

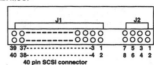

40 pin SCSI connector

J2 Pin No.	-ID1 5	-ID2 6	-ID4 7	Device Address
	open	open	open	0
	gnd	open	open	1
	open	gnd	open	2
	gnd	gnd	open	3
	open	open	gnd	4
	gnd	open	gnd	5
	open	gnd	gnd	6
	gnd	gnd	gnd	7

Cabling

The maximum cable length from the host system to the drive is limited to 6 inches with external 1K-ohm pull up resistors.
In case that appropriate termination resistors are externally equipped to the interface lines, the cable length can be extended. The maximum cable length depends on the condition of the various electrical parameters of the interface.

Device Address

The drive recognizes its device address, namely SCSI ID, with the condition of -ID1, -ID2, and -ID4. The signal condition and the device address are shown above.

IBM DHAS 2405

Connector

The SCSI signal connectors is designed to mate with AMP part number 6-176135 or equivalent. Size and location of the mounting holes compkly with MCC.

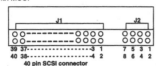

40 pin SCSI connector

J2 Pin No.	-ID1 5	-ID2 6	-ID4 7	Device Address
	open	open	open	0
	gnd	open	open	1
	open	gnd	open	2
	gnd	gnd	open	3
	open	open	gnd	4
	gnd	open	gnd	5
	open	gnd	gnd	6
	gnd	gnd	gnd	7

Cabling

The maximum cable length from the host system to the drive is limited to 6 inches with external 1K-ohm pull up resistors.
In case that appropriate termination resistors are externally equipped to the interface lines, the cable length can be extended. The maximum cable length depends on the condition of the various electrical parameters of the interface.

Device Address

The drive recognizes its device address, namely SCSI ID, with the condition of -ID1, -ID2, and -ID4. The signal condition and the device address are shown above.

IBM DSAS 3270

Connectors

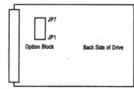

The DC power connector is designed to mate with AMP part 1-480424 (using AMP pins P/N 350078-4). Equivalent connectors may be used. Pin assignments are shown above as viewed from the end of the drive.

SCSI Signal Connector

The SCSI Signal Connector is a 50 pin connector meeting the ANSI SCSI specification.
NOTE: It is intended that the hard disk drive should only be in electrical contact with the chassis of the PC at a designated set of mounting holes. Other electrical contact may degrade error rate performance. As a result of this it is recommended that there should be no metal contact to the hard disk drive except at the mounting holes or the side rails into which holes are taped.

Option Block

Jumper position and function are as shown below. Pin pitch is 2mm.
The jumpers control SCSI Device ID, Auto Spin-Up, Unit Attention, SCSI Terminator Connection and Target Initiated Synchronous Negotiation.

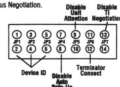

IBM DPRA 21215

Drive Address

A jumper cable is available at the interface connector to determine the drive address.

Using Cable Selection, the drive address depends on the condition of pin 28 of the AT interface cable. In the case when pin 28 is ground or low, the drive is a Master. If pin 28 is open or high level, the drive is a Slave.

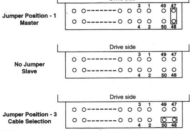

Cabling

The maximum cable length from the host system to the HDD plus circuit pattern length in the host system shall not exceed 18 inches.

AT Signal Connector

The AT signal connector is designed to mate with Dupont part number 69764-044 or equivalent.

NOTES: Pin position 20 is left blank for secure connector insertion.
Pin position 47 through 50 are used for drive address setting.

IBM DSAS 3270 (Continued)

NOTE:

1. The jumper of JP1, 2, and 3, define SCSI ID of the drive.

   If JP1, JP2, JP3 are Off, Off, Off, the SCSI ID is 0 - default

   If JP1, JP2, JP3 are On, Off, Off, the SCSI ID is 1

   If JP1, JP2, JP3 are Off, On, Off, the SCSI ID is 2

   If JP1, JP2, JP3 are On, On, Off, the SCSI ID is 3

   If JP1, JP2, JP3 are Off, Off, On, the SCSI ID is 4

   If JP1, JP2, JP3 are On, Off, On, the SCSI ID is 5

   If JP1, JP2, JP3 are Off, On, On, the SCSI ID is 6

   If JP1, JP2, JP3 are On, On, On, the SCSI ID is 7

2. If JP4 is Off, the drive will spin up automatically after power on reset.

   If JP4 is On, the drive will not spin up unless the host system issues a start command to the drive.

3. If JP5 is On, Unit Attention after power on reset or SCSI bus reset is disabled.

4. If JP6 is On, the internal SCSI terminator works.

5. If JP7 is On, Target Initiated Synchronous Negotiation is disabled, and then the Initiator is required to start a negotiation handshake if Synchronous SCSI transfers are desired.

Default Setting

JP1	JP2	JP3	JP4	JP5	JP6	JP7	Position
1-2	3-4	5-6	7-8	9-10	11-12	13-14	Pin
OFF	OFF	OFF	OFF	OFF	ON	OFF	Jumper

TI Sync Nego Enabled
SCSI Terminator ON
Unit Attention Enabled
Auto Spin-Up Enabled
SCSI Device ID = 0

IBM DSAS 3360

Connectors

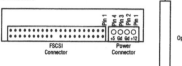

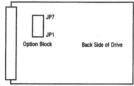

The DC power connector is designed to mate with AMP part 1-480424 (using AMP pins P/N 350078-4). Equivalent connectors may be used. Pin assignments are shown above as viewed from the end of the drive.

SCSI Signal Connector

The SCSI Signal Connector is a 50 pin connector meeting the ANSI SCSI specification.

NOTE: It is intended that the hard disk drive should only be in electrical contact with the chassis of the PC at a designated set of mounting holes. Other electrical contact may degrade error rate performance. As a result of this it is recommended that there should be no metal contact to the hard disk drive except at the mounting holes or the side rails into which holes are taped.

Option Block

Jumper position and function are as shown below. Pin pitch is 2mm.

The jumpers control SCSI Device ID, Auto Spin-Up, Unit Attention, SCSI Terminator Connection and Target Initiated Synchronous Negotiation.

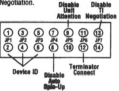

IBM DSAS 3360 (Continued)

NOTE:

1. The jumper of JP1, 2, and 3, define SCSI ID of the drive.

   If JP1, JP2, JP3 are Off, Off, Off, the SCSI ID is 0 - default

   If JP1, JP2, JP3 are On, Off, Off, the SCSI ID is 1

   If JP1, JP2, JP3 are Off, On, Off, the SCSI ID is 2

   If JP1, JP2, JP3 are On, On, Off, the SCSI ID is 3

   If JP1, JP2, JP3 are Off, Off, On, the SCSI ID is 4

   If JP1, JP2, JP3 are On, Off, On, the SCSI ID is 5

   If JP1, JP2, JP3 are Off, On, On, the SCSI ID is 6

   If JP1, JP2, JP3 are On, On, On, the SCSI ID is 7

2. If JP4 is Off, the drive will spin up automatically after power on reset.

   If JP4 is On, the drive will not spin up unless the host system issues a start command to the drive.

3. If JP5 is On, Unit Attention after power on reset or SCSI bus reset is disabled.

4. If JP6 is On, the internal SCSI terminator works.

5. If JP7 is On, Target Initiated Synchronous Negotiation is disabled, and then the Initiator is required to start a negotiation handshake if Synchronous SCSI transfers are desired.

Default Setting

JP1	JP2	JP3	JP4	JP5	JP6	JP7	Position
1-2	3-4	5-6	7-8	9-10	11-12	13-14	Pin
OFF	OFF	OFF	OFF	OFF	ON	OFF	Jumper

TI Sync Nego Enabled
SCSI Terminator ON
Unit Attention Enabled
Auto Spin-Up Enabled
SCSI Device ID = 0

IBM DSAS 3540

Connectors

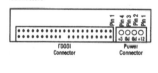

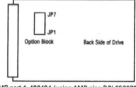

The DC power connector is designed to mate with AMP part 1-480424 (using AMP pins P/N 350078-4). Equivalent connectors may be used. Pin assignments are shown above as viewed from the end of the drive.

SCSI Signal Connector

The SCSI Signal Connector is a 50 pin connector meeting the ANSI SCSI specification.

NOTE: It is intended that the hard disk drive should only be in electrical contact with the chassis of the PC at a designated set of mounting holes. Other electrical contact may degrade error rate performance. As a result of this it is recommended that there should be no metal contact to the hard disk drive except at the mounting holes or the side rails into which holes are taped.

Option Block

Jumper position and function are as shown below. Pin pitch is 2mm.

The jumpers control SCSI Device ID, Auto Spin-Up, Unit Attention, SCSI Terminator Connection and Target Initiated Synchronous Negotiation.

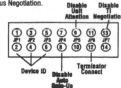

IBM DSAS 3720

Connectors

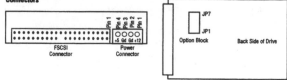

FSCSI Connector   Power Connector   Back Side of Drive

The DC power connector is designed to mate with AMP part 1-480424 (using AMP pins P/N 350078-4). Equivalent connectors may be used. Pin assignments are shown above as viewed from the end of the drive.

SCSI Signal Connector

The SCSI Signal Connector is a 50 pin connector meeting the ANSI SCSI specification.

NOTE: It is intended that the hard disk drive should only be in electrical contact with the chassis of the PC at a designated set of mounting holes. Other electrical contact may degrade error rate performance. As a result of this it is recommended that there should be no metal contact to the hard disk drive except at the mounting holes or the side rails into which holes are taped.

Option Block

Jumper position and function are as shown below. Pin pitch is 2mm.

The jumpers control SCSI Device ID, Auto Spin-Up, Unit Attention, SCSI Terminator Connection and Target Initiated Synchronous Negotiation.

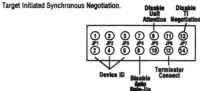

IBM DSAS 3540 (Continued)

If JP1, JP2, JP3 are Off, Off, Off, the SCSI ID is 0 - default
If JP1, JP2, JP3 are On, Off, Off, the SCSI ID is 1
If JP1, JP2, JP3 are Off, On, Off, the SCSI ID is 2
If JP1, JP2, JP3 are On, On, Off, the SCSI ID is 3
If JP1, JP2, JP3 are Off, Off, On, the SCSI ID is 4
If JP1, JP2, JP3 are On, Off, On, the SCSI ID is 5
If JP1, JP2, JP3 are Off, On, On, the SCSI ID is 6
If JP1, JP2, JP3 are On, On, On, the SCSI ID is 7

2. If JP4 is Off, the drive will spin up automatically after power on reset.
   If JP4 is On, the drive will not spin up unless the host system issues a start command to the drive.
3. If JP5 is On, Unit Attention after power on reset or SCSI bus reset is disabled.
4. If JP6 is On, the internal SCSI terminator works.
5. If JP7 is On, Target Initiated Synchronous Negotiation is disabled, and then the Initiator is required to start a negotiation handshake if Synchronous SCSI transfers are desired.

Default Setting

JP1	JP2	JP3	JP4	JP5	JP6	JP7	Position
1-2	3-4	5-6	7-8	9-10	11-12	13-14	Pin
OFF	OFF	OFF	OFF	OFF	ON	OFF	Jumper

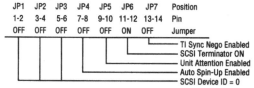

- TI Sync Nego Enabled
- SCSI Terminator ON
- Unit Attention Enabled
- Auto Spin-Up Enabled
- SCSI Device ID = 0

IBM DVAA 2810

Drive Address

A jumper cable is available at the interface connector to determine the drive address.

Using Cable Selection, the drive address depends on the condition of pin 28 of the AT interface cable. In the case when pin 28 is ground or low, the drive is a Master. If pin 28 is open or high level, the drive is a Slave.

Cabling

The maximum cable length from the host system to the HDD plus circuit pattern length in the host system shall not exceed 18 inches.

AT Signal Connector

The AT signal connector is designed to mate with Dupont part number 69764-044 or equivalent.

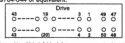

NOTES: Pin position 20 is left blank for secure connector insertion.
Pin position 47 through 50 are used for drive address setting.

IBM DSAS 3720 (Continued)

NOTE:

1. The jumper of JP1, 2, and 3, define SCSI ID of the drive.
   If JP1, JP2, JP3 are Off, Off, Off, the SCSI ID is 0 - default
   If JP1, JP2, JP3 are On, Off, Off, the SCSI ID is 1
   If JP1, JP2, JP3 are Off, On, Off, the SCSI ID is 2
   If JP1, JP2, JP3 are On, On, Off, the SCSI ID is 3
   If JP1, JP2, JP3 are Off, Off, On, the SCSI ID is 4
   If JP1, JP2, JP3 are On, Off, On, the SCSI ID is 5
   If JP1, JP2, JP3 are Off, On, On, the SCSI ID is 6
   If JP1, JP2, JP3 are On, On, On, the SCSI ID is 7

2. If JP4 is Off, the drive will spin up automatically after power on reset.
   If JP4 is On, the drive will not spin up unless the host system issues a start command to the drive.
3. If JP5 is On, Unit Attention after power on reset or SCSI bus reset is disabled.
4. If JP6 is On, the internal SCSI terminator works.
5. If JP7 is On, Target Initiated Synchronous Negotiation is disabled, and then the Initiator is required to start a negotiation handshake if Synchronous SCSI transfers are desired.

Default Setting

JP1	JP2	JP3	JP4	JP5	JP6	JP7	Position
1-2	3-4	5-6	7-8	9-10	11-12	13-14	Pin
OFF	OFF	OFF	OFF	OFF	ON	OFF	Jumper

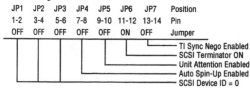

- TI Sync Nego Enabled
- SCSI Terminator ON
- Unit Attention Enabled
- Auto Spin-Up Enabled
- SCSI Device ID = 0

IBM H2172-A2

Drive Address

A jumper cable is available at the interface connector to determine the drive address.

Using Cable Selection, the drive address depends on the condition of pin 28 of the AT interface cable. In the case when pin 28 is ground or low, the drive is a Master. If pin 28 is open or high level, the drive is a Slave.

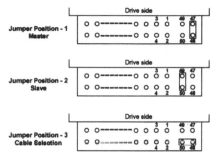

Cabling

The maximum cable length from the host system to the HDD plus circuit pattern length in the host system shall not exceed 18 inches.

AT Signal Connector

The AT signal connector is designed to mate with Dupont part number 69764-044 or equivalent.

NOTES: Pin position 20 is left blank for secure connector insertion.
Pin position 47 through 50 are used for drive address setting.

IBM H2172-S2

Connector

The SCSI signal connectors is designed to mate with AMP part number 6-176135 or equivalent. Size and location of the mounting holes comply with MCC.

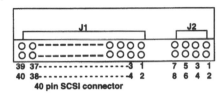

40 pin SCSI connector

J2 Pin No.	-ID1 5	-ID2 6	-ID4 7	Device Address
	open	open	open	0
	gnd	open	open	1
	open	gnd	open	2
	gnd	gnd	open	3
	open	open	gnd	4
	gnd	open	gnd	5
	open	gnd	gnd	6
	gnd	gnd	gnd	7

IBM 2258-A3

Drive Address

A jumper cable is available at the interface connector to determine the drive address.

Using Cable Selection, the drive address depends on the condition of pin 28 of the AT interface cable. In the case when pin 28 is ground or low, the drive is a Master. If pin 28 is open or high level, the drive is a Slave.

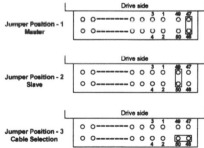

Cabling

The maximum cable length from the host system to the HDD plus circuit pattern length in the host system shall not exceed 18 inches.

AT Signal Connector

The AT signal connector is designed to mate with Dupont part number 69764-044 or equivalent.

NOTES: Pin position 20 is left blank for secure connector insertion.
Pin position 47 through 50 are used for drive address setting.

IBM H2258-S3

Connector

The SCSI signal connectors is designed to mate with AMP part number 6-176135 or equivalent. Size and location of the mounting holes comply with MCC.

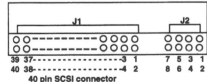

40 pin SCSI connector

J2 Pin No.	-ID1 5	-ID2 6	-ID4 7	Device Address
	open	open	open	0
	gnd	open	open	1
	open	gnd	open	2
	gnd	gnd	open	3
	open	open	gnd	4
	gnd	open	gnd	5
	open	gnd	gnd	6
	gnd	gnd	gnd	7

IBM H2344-S4

IBM H2344-A4

Drive Address

A jumper cable is available at the interface connector to determine the drive address.

Using Cable Selection, the drive address depends on the condition of pin 28 of the AT interface cable. In the case when pin 28 is ground or low, the drive is a Master. If pin 28 is open or high level, the drive is a Slave.

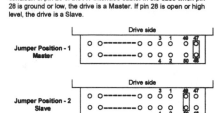

Cabling
The maximum cable length from the host system to the HDD plus circuit pattern length in the host system shall not exceed 18 inches.

AT Signal Connector
The AT signal connector is designed to mate with Dupont part number 69764-044 or equivalent.

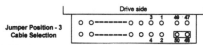

NOTES: Pin position 20 is left blank for secure connector insertion.
Pin position 47 through 50 are used for drive address setting.

Connector
The SCSI signal connectors is designed to mate with AMP part number 6-176135 or equivalent. Size and location of the mounting holes comply with MCC.

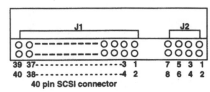

40 pin SCSI connector

J2 Pin No.	-ID1 5	-ID2 6	-ID4 7	Device Address
	open	open	open	0
	gnd	open	open	1
	open	gnd	open	2
	gnd	gnd	open	3
	open	open	gnd	4
	gnd	open	gnd	5
	open	gnd	gnd	6
	gnd	gnd	gnd	7

IBM H3171-A2

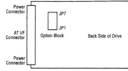

Shipping Default Settings
MASTER is set to on (i.e. jumper on pins 1 and 2). No other jumpers are fitted.
NOTE: LED connections, pin 13 can source up to 18mA. Pin 14 can sink up to 100mA.
The jumper positions JP1, JP2, and JP3 must not be selected concurrently.

Connectors
There is a choice of 2 power connections to this drive. One DC power connector is designed to mate with AMP part 1-480424 (using AMP pins P/N 350078-4). The other (3 pin) DC power connector is designed to mate with MOLEX 5480-03 (using MOLEX pins 5479). Equivalent connectors may be used. Pin assignments are shown below, as viewed from the end of the drive.

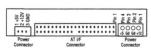

AT Signal Connector
The drive uses single-ended drivers and receivers. The connector is designed to mate with 3M part 3417-7000 or equivalent.
NOTE: It is intended that the hard disk drive should only be in electrical contact with the chassis of the PC at a disignated set of mounting holes. Other electrical contact may degrade error rate performance. As a result of this it is recommended that there should be no metal contact to the hard disk drive except at the mounting holes or the side rails into which the mounting holes are tapped.

Option Block
Jumper Settings - Jumpers may be fitted to select the following options:

MASTER active	Pin Numbers 1 and 2
SLAVE activbe	Pin Numbers 3 and 4
Cable Select	Pin Numbers 5 and 6
LED drive lines	Pin Numbers 13 and 14

IBM H3133-A2

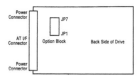

Shipping Default Settings
MASTER is set to on (i.e. jumper on pins 1 and 2). No other jumpers are fitted.
NOTE: LED connections, pin 13 can source up to 18mA. Pin 14 can sink up to 100mA.
The jumper positions JP1, JP2, and JP3 must not be selected concurrently.

Connectors
There is a choice of 2 power connections to this drive. One DC power connector is designed to mate with AMP part 1-480424 (using AMP pins P/N 350078-4). The other (3 pin) DC power connector is designed to mate with MOLEX 5480-03 (using MOLEX pins 5479). Equivalent connectors may be used. Pin assignments are shown below, as viewed from the end of the drive.

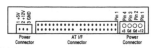

AT Signal Connector
The drive uses single-ended drivers and receivers. The connector is designed to mate with 3M part 3417-7000 or equivalent.
NOTE: It is intended that the hard disk drive should only be in electrical contact with the chassis of the PC at a disignated set of mounting holes. Other electrical contact may degrade error rate performance. As a result of this it is recommended that there should be no metal contact to the hard disk drive except at the mounting holes or the side rails into which the mounting holes are tapped.

Option Block
Jumper Settings - Jumpers may be fitted to select the following options:

MASTER active	Pin Numbers 1 and 2
SLAVE activbe	Pin Numbers 3 and 4
Cable Select	Pin Numbers 5 and 6
LED drive lines	Pin Numbers 13 and 14

IBM H3256-A3

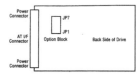

Shipping Default Settings

MASTER is set to on (i.e. jumper on pins 1 and 2). No other jumpers are fitted.

NOTE: LED connections, pin 13 can source up to 18mA. Pin 14 can sink up to 100mA.

The jumper positions JP1, JP2, and JP3 must not be selected concurrently.

Connectors

There is a choice of 2 power connections to this drive. One DC power connector is designed to mate with AMP part 1-480424 (using AMP pins P/N 350078-4). The other (3 pin) DC power connector is designed to mate with MOLEX 5480-03 (using MOLEX pins 5479). Equivalent connectors may be used. Pin assignments are shown below, as viewed from the end of the drive.

AT Signal Connector

The drive uses single-ended drivers and receivers. The connector is designed to mate with 3M part 3417-7000 or equivalent.

NOTE: It is intended that the hard disk drive should only be in electrical contact with the chassis of the PC at a disignated set of mounting holes. Other electrical contact may degrade error rate performance. As a result of this it is recommended that there should be no metal contact to the hard disk drive except at the mounting holes or the side rails into which the mounting holes are tapped.

Option Block

Jumper Settings - Jumpers may be fitted to select the following options:

MASTER active	Pin Numbers 1 and 2
SLAVE activbe	Pin Numbers 3 and 4
Cable Select	Pin Numbers 5 and 6
LED drive lines	Pin Numbers 13 and 14

IBM H3342-A4

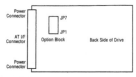

Shipping Default Settings

MASTER is set to on (i.e. jumper on pins 1 and 2). No other jumpers are fitted.

NOTE: LED connections, pin 13 can source up to 18mA. Pin 14 can sink up to 100mA.

The jumper positions JP1, JP2, and JP3 must not be selected concurrently.

Connectors

There is a choice of 2 power connections to this drive. One DC power connector is designed to mate with AMP part 1-480424 (using AMP pins P/N 350078-4). The other (3 pin) DC power connector is designed to mate with MOLEX 5480-03 (using MOLEX pins 5479). Equivalent connectors may be used. Pin assignments are shown below, as viewed from the end of the drive.

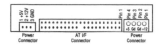

AT Signal Connector

The drive uses single-ended drivers and receivers. The connector is designed to mate with 3M part 3417-7000 or equivalent.

NOTE: It is intended that the hard disk drive should only be in electrical contact with the chassis of the PC at a disignated set of mounting holes. Other electrical contact may degrade error rate performance. As a result of this it is recommended that there should be no metal contact to the hard disk drive except at the mounting holes or the side rails into which the mounting holes are tapped.

Option Block

Jumper Settings - Jumpers may be fitted to select the following options:

MASTER active	Pin Numbers 1 and 2
SLAVE activbe	Pin Numbers 3 and 4
Cable Select	Pin Numbers 5 and 6
LED drive lines	Pin Numbers 13 and 14

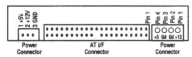

IBM WDA-L160

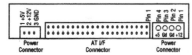

AT Signal Connector

The drive uses single-ended drivers and receivers. The connector is designed to mate with 3M part 3417-7000 or equivalent.

NOTE: It is intended that the hard disk drive should only be in electrical contact with the chassis of the PC at a disignated set of mounting holes. Other electrical contact may degrade error rate performance. As a result of this it is recommended that there should be no metal contact to the hard disk drive except at the mounting holes or the side rails into which the mounting holes are tapped.

Option Block

Jumper Settings - Jumpers may be fitted to select the following options:

IOCHRDY active	Pin Numbers 1 and 2
MASTER active	Pin Numbers 3 and 4
LED drive lines	Pin Numbers 13 and 14

IBM WDA-L80

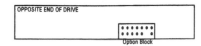

AT Signal Connector

The drive uses single-ended drivers and receivers. The connector is designed to mate with 3M part 3417-7000 or equivalent.

NOTE: It is intended that the hard disk drive should only be in electrical contact with the chassis of the PC at a disignated set of mounting holes. Other electrical contact may degrade error rate performance. As a result of this it is recommended that there should be no metal contact to the hard disk drive except at the mounting holes or the side rails into which the mounting holes are tapped.

Option Block

Jumper Settings - Jumpers may be fitted to select the following options:

IOCHRDY active	Pin Numbers 1 and 2
MASTER active	Pin Numbers 3 and 4
LED drive lines	Pin Numbers 13 and 14

IBM WDA-280

44 Pin AT connector and Jumper pin

Electrical Interface

Drive Address - A jumper fitted to position JP1 will select drive address 0 (Master). If no jumper is installed the drive address is 1 (Slave).

Interface Connector - The drive connector is 2mm pitch. AMP, DuPont and Hirose all make suitable mating connector.

Cabling - Maximum cable length from host system to HDD shall not exceed 18 inches (45.7 cm).

Operating Modes
Description

Spin-Up - The time taken for the motor to reach full speed from a stopped or power down condition.

Seek, Read, Write - Seek, read or write operating modes.

Idle - Spindle motor and servo system working, all modules (except servo control and interface) are 'sleeping'. Commands can be received and processed immediately.

Standby - Spindle motor is stopped, all modules (except interface) are 'sleeping'. The drive is waiting for an interrupt and commands can be processed immediately. This is the lowest power dissipation mode.

Command Description
The following Commands are supported by the Drive:

Commands	(Hex)	Commands	(Hex)
Check Power Mode	(E5)	Recalibrate	(1X)
Execute Drive Diagnostics	(90)	Seek	(7X)
Format Track	(50)	Set Features	(EF)
Identify Drive	(EC)	Set Multiple	(C6)
Idle	(E3)	Sleep	(E6)
Idle Immediate	(E1)	Standby	(E2)
Initialize Drive Parameters	(91)	Standby Immediate	(E0)
Read Buffer	(E4)	Write Buffer	(E8)
Read Long (retry)	(22)	Write Long (retry)	(32)
Read Long (no retry)	(23)	Write Long (no retry)	(33)
Read Multiple	(C4)	Write Multiple	(C5)
Read Sectors (retry)	(20)	Write Sectors (retry)	(30)
Read Sectors (no retry)	(21)	Write Sectors (no retry)	(31)
Read Verify Sectors (retry)	(40)	Write Verify	(3C)
Read Verify Sectors (no retry)	(41)		

IBM WDA-240

44 Pin AT connector and Jumper pin

Electrical Interface

Drive Address - A jumper fitted to position JP1 will select drive address 0 (Master). If no jumper is installed the drive address is 1 (Slave).

Interface Connector - The drive connector is 2mm pitch. AMP, DuPont and Hirose all make suitable mating connector.

Cabling - Maximum cable length from host system to HDD shall not exceed 18 inches (45.7 cm).

Operating Modes
Description

Spin-Up - The time taken for the motor to reach full speed from a stopped or power down condition.

Seek, Read, Write - Seek, read or write operating modes.

Idle - Spindle motor and servo system working, all modules (except servo control and interface) are 'sleeping'. Commands can be received and processed immediately.

Standby - Spindle motor is stopped, all modules (except interface) are 'sleeping'. The drive is waiting for an interrupt and commands can be processed immediately. This is the lowest power dissipation mode.

Command Description
The following Commands are supported by the Drive:

Commands	(Hex)	Commands	(Hex)
Check Power Mode	(E5)	Recalibrate	(1X)
Execute Drive Diagnostics	(90)	Seek	(7X)
Format Track	(50)	Set Features	(EF)
Identify Drive	(EC)	Set Multiple	(C6)
Idle	(E3)	Sleep	(E6)
Idle Immediate	(E1)	Standby	(E2)
Initialize Drive Parameters	(91)	Standby Immediate	(E0)
Read Buffer	(E4)	Write Buffer	(E8)
Read Long (retry)	(22)	Write Long (retry)	(32)
Read Long (no retry)	(23)	Write Long (no retry)	(33)
Read Multiple	(C4)	Write Multiple	(C5)
Read Sectors (retry)	(20)	Write Sectors (retry)	(30)
Read Sectors (no retry)	(21)	Write Sectors (no retry)	(31)
Read Verify Sectors (retry)	(40)	Write Verify	(3C)
Read Verify Sectors (no retry)	(41)		

IBM WDS-2120

Interface Connectors

The drive connector is 2mm pitch. AMP, DuPont and Hirose all make suitable mating connectors.

To select an address, the appropriate pin(s) must be connected to ground. The illustration below shows which pins to ground to select a particular drive address.

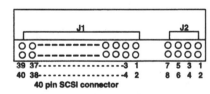

40 pin SCSI connector

J2

Pin:	
1	unused
2	unused
3	INDEX
4	unused
5	Addr 0
6	Addr 1
7	Addr 2
8	LED

J2 Pin No.	Addr2	Addr1	Addr0	Device Address
	open	open	open	0
	gnd	open	open	1
	open	gnd	open	2
	gnd	gnd	open	3
	open	open	gnd	4
	gnd	open	gnd	5
	open	gnd	gnd	6
	gnd	gnd	gnd	7

IBM WDS-380

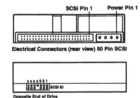

SCSI Pin 1   Power Pin 1

Electrical Connectors (rear view) 50 Pin SCSI

xxxx321

SCSI ID

Opposite End of Drive

Jumper Settings

This section describes jumper settings.
A 14 pin connector is populated on the card as illustrated below. These pins are used to select SCSI ID or for other optional features.
Pin pitch is 2mm.

① ③ ⑤ ⑦ ⑨ ⑪ ⑬
② ④ ⑥ ⑧ ⑩ ⑫ ⑭

Device ID and LED portion pin assignment.

Pin #	Status	Description	Signal Name
1	In	–Device Address Select Line #0	–DAS0
2	–	Ground	GND
3	In	–Device Address Select Line #1	–DAS1
4	–	Ground	GND
5	In	–Device Address Select Line #2	–DAS2
6	–	Ground	GND
7	–	Polarity KEY	KEY
8	Out	–LED (might be used as SPN READY)	–LED
9	In	–Motor Start	–M_START
10	–	Ground	GND
11	In	–Hard Reset Input	–H_RESET
12	–	Ground	GND
13	Out	+LED	+LED
14	Out	–LED	–LED

MAXTOR 25252A

25252A Jumper Designation

	S301	S302	S303	S304
Master/Slave				
Only drive in single drive system*	J			
Master in dual drive system	J			
Slave in dual drive system	O			
Reserved for Factory				
Normal operation*			O	O
Factory operatin			J	J
Idle Mode Latch				
Option Disabled		O		
Option Enabled*		J		

* = Default J = Jumpered O = Open

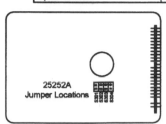

25252A
Jumper Locations

25252A
Physical Specifications

Height = 0.678" (17 mm)
Length = 4.00" (101.6 mm)
Width = 2.75" (69.84 mm)
Weight = 0.419 lbs. (190 gm)

MAXTOR 2585A/25128A

2585A and 25128A Jumper Designation

	J306	J307	J308	J309
Master/Slave				
Only drive in single drive system*			J	
Master in dual drive system			J	
Slave in dual drive system			O	
Reserved for Factory				
Normal operation*		O		O
Factory operatin		J		J
Idle Mode Latch				
Option Disabled*		O		
Option Enabled		J		

* = Default J = Jumpered O = Open
J304 and J305 reserved for future use.

2585A and 25128A
Jumper Locations

2585A and 25128A
Physical Specifications

Height = 0.69" (17.5 mm)
Length = 4.00" (101.6 mm)
Width = 2.75" (69.84 mm)
Weight = 0.374 lbs. (170 gm)

MAXTOR 7040A

7080A/7040A Jumper Designation

	J20	J18	J17	J11
Master/Slave				
Only drive in single drive system / Master in dual drive system*	J			
Slave in dual drive system	O			
ECC Bytes				
4 Bytes*		J		
7 Bytes		O		
Drive Model Number				
7080A			J	
7040A			O	
I/O Channel Ready				
Disabled*				O
Enabled				J

J = Jumpered O = Open * = Default

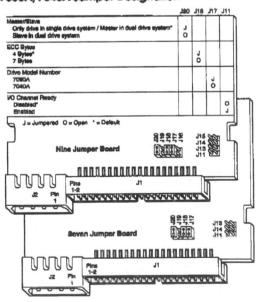

Nine Jumper Board

Seven Jumper Board

MAXTOR 7040S

7080S/7040S Jumper Functions (PCBA Rev ≥ 43)

Jumper	Function
J001	Terminator Power
J003	Diagnostic Mode (factory use only)
J005	Disable Parity
J004	reserved
J002	Power-up Option
J009	reserved
J008	Target ID Address (most significant bytes - MSB)
J007	Target ID Address
J006	Target ID Address (least significant bytes - LSB)

7080S/7040S Jumper Designation (PCBA Rev ≥ 43)

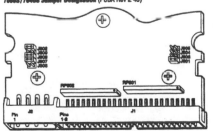

MAXTOR 7060A PCB>48

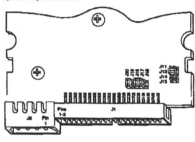

	J20	J18	J17	J14	J13	J11
Master/Slave						
Master in dual drive system	J					
Slave in dual drive system	O					
ECC Bytes						
4 Bytes *		J				
7 Bytes		O				
Drive Model Number						
7120A			J			
7060A			O			
Power-up Configuration						
7120A Cyl Hds Sec MB						
939 16 17 130.9 *						
1024 14 17 124.8			J			
7060A 925 8 17 64.4 *				O		
1024 7 17 62.4						
I/O Channel Ready						
Disabled *					O	
Enabled					J	

J = Jumpered   O = Open   * = Default
Note: J14, J15, J16, and J19 are reserved. Abnormal operation may occur if altered.

Jumper Locations: PCBA ≥ 48

MAXTOR 7060A PCB<38

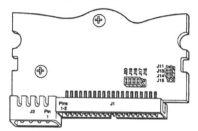

	J20	J19	J18	J17	J14	J13	J11
Master/Slave							
Only drive in single drive system	J	J					
Master in dual drive system	J	O					
Slave in dual drive system	O	J					
ECC Bytes							
4 Bytes *			J				
7 Bytes			O				
Drive Model Number							
7120A				J			
7060A				O			
Power-up Configuration							
7120A Cyl Hds Sec MB							
939 16 17 130.9 *					J	J	
1024 14 17 124.8					O	O	
762 8 39 121.7					J	O	
900 15 17 117.5					O	J	
7060A 467 16 17 65.0 *					J	J	
1024 7 17 62.4					O	O	
762 4 39 60.9					J	O	
925 8 17 64.4					O	J	
I/O Channel Ready							
Disabled *							O
Enabled							J

J = Jumpered   O = Open   * = Default
Note: J15 and J16 are reserved. Abnormal operation may occur if altered.

Jumper Locations: PCBA ≤ 38

MAXTOR 7080A

7080A/7040A Jumper Designation

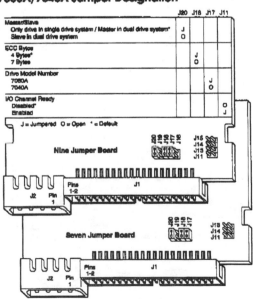

	J20	J18	J17	J11
Master/Slave				
Only drive in single drive system / Master in dual drive system*	J			
Slave in dual drive system	O			
ECC Bytes				
4 Bytes*		J		
7 Bytes		O		
Drive Model Number				
7080A			J	
7040A			O	
I/O Channel Ready				
Disabled*				O
Enabled				J

J = Jumpered   O = Open   * = Default

Nine Jumper Board

Seven Jumper Board

MAXTOR 7060S

7120S/7060S Jumper Functions (All PCBA Revisions)

Jumper Block	Pin Location	Function
J801	1 - 2	Terminator Power
J801	3 - 4	Diagnostic Mode (factory use only)
J801	5 - 6	Disable Parity
J801	7 - 8	reserved
J802	1 - 2	Power-up Option
J802	3 - 4	reserved
J802	5 - 6	Target ID Address (most significant bytes - MSB)
J802	7 - 8	Target ID Address
J802	9 - 10	Target ID Address (least significant bytes - LSB)

7120S/7060S Jumper Designation (All PCBA Revisions)

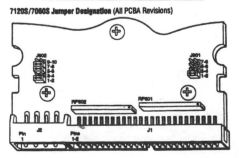

MAXTOR 7080S

7080S/7040S Jumper Functions (PCBA Rev ≥ 43)

Jumper	Function
J801	Terminator Power
J803	Diagnostic Mode (factory use only)
J805	Disable Parity
J804	reserved
J802	Power-up Option
J809	reserved
J808	Target ID Address (most significant bytes - MSB)
J807	Target ID Address
J806	Target ID Address (least significant bytes - LSB)

7080S/7040S Jumper Designation (PCBA Rev ≥ 43)

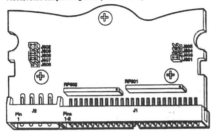

MAXTOR 7120A PCB<38

	J20	J19	J18	J17	J14	J13	J11
Master/Slave							
Only drive in single drive system	J						
Master in dual drive system	O	J					
Slave in dual drive system		O					
ECC Bytes							
4 Bytes *			J				
7 Bytes			O				
Drive Model Number							
7120A					J		
7060A					O		
Power-up Configuration							
7120A Cyl Hds Sec MB							
936 16 17 130.3 *						J	J
1024 14 17 124.8						O	O
762 8 39 121.7						J	J
900 15 17 117.5						O	O
7060A 487 16 17 65.0 *						J	O
1024 7 17 62.4						O	J
782 4 39 60.9						J	O
925 8 17 64.4						O	J
I/O Channel Ready							
Disabled *							
Enabled							O

J = Jumpered   O = Open   * = Default
Note: J15 and J16 are reserved. Abnormal operation may occur if altered.

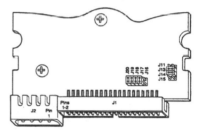

Jumper Locations: PCBA ≤ 38

MAXTOR 7120A PCB>48

	J20	J18	J17	J13	J11
Master/Slave					
Only drive in single drive system	J				
Master in dual drive system	J				
Slave in dual drive system	O				
ECC Bytes					
4 Bytes *		J			
7 Bytes		O			
Drive Model Number					
7120A			J		
7060A			O		
Power-up Configuration					
7120A Cyl Hds Sec MB					
936 16 17 130.3 *				J	
1024 14 17 124.8				O	
7060A 925 8 17 64.4 *				J	
1024 7 17 62.4				O	
I/O Channel Ready					
Disabled *					O
Enabled					J

J = Jumpered   O = Open   * = Default
Note: J14, J15, J16, and J19 are reserved. Abnormal operation may occur if altered.

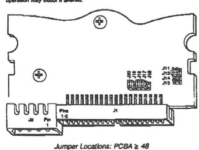

Jumper Locations: PCBA ≥ 48

MAXTOR 7120S

7120S/7060S Jumper Functions (All PCBA Revisions)

Jumper Block	Pin Location	Function
J801	1 - 2	Terminator Power
J801	3 - 4	Diagnostic Mode (factory use only)
J801	5 - 6	Disable Parity
J801	7 - 8	reserved
J802	1 - 2	Power-up Option
J802	3 - 4	reserved
J802	5 - 6	Target ID Address (most significant bytes - MSB)
J802	7 - 8	Target ID Address
J802	9 - 10	Target ID Address (least significant bytes - LSB)

7120S/7060S Jumper Designation (All PCBA Revisions)

MAXTOR 7245A

SYNC Spindle Control	J23	J22	J20	J16
Sync Spindle Disabled*	O			
Sync Spindle Enabled	J			
Sync Slave		O		
Sync Master		J		
Master/Slave				
Only drive in single drive system*			J	
Master in dual drive system			J	
Slave in dual drive system			O	
I/O Channel Ready				
Option Disabled*				O
Option Enabled				J

J = Jumpered   O = Open   * = Default

MAXTOR 7213S

JUMPER LOCATIONS and FUNCTIONS

Jumper Functions		
Jumper	Function	Factory Default
J301/J26	Terminator Power	Installed
J302/J25	Power-up Option	Installed
J303/J24	Disable Parity	Removed
J304/J23	Reserved	Removed
J305/J22	Reserved	Removed
J306/J20	Reserved	Removed
J307/J19	Target ID Address (MSB)	Installed
J308/J18	Target ID Address	Installed
J309/J17	Target ID Address (LSB)	Removed

Jumper locations may have a 2-digit or 3-digit designator dependent on PCBA revision.

PHYSICAL SPECS	SCSI ID	PRIORITY	J307	J308	J309
Height - 1.00" (2.54 cm)	0	Lowest	O	O	O
Length - 5.75" (14.61 cm)	1		O	O	J
	2		O	J	O
	3		O	J	J
Width - 4.00" (10.16 cm)	4		J	O	O
	5		J	O	J
Weight - 1.2 lbs. (.57 kg)	6		J	J	O
	7	Highest	J	J	J

Jumper Locations

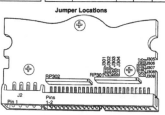

MAXTOR 7245S

JUMPER LOCATIONS and FUNCTIONS

Jumper Functions		
Jumper	Function	Factory Default
J301/J26	Terminator Power	Installed
J302/J25	Power-up Option	Installed
J303/J24	Disable Parity	Removed
J304/J23	Reserved	Removed
J305/J22	Reserved	Removed
J306/J20	Reserved	Removed
J307/J19	Target ID Address (MSB)	Installed
J308/J18	Target ID Address	Installed
J309/J17	Target ID Address (LSB)	Removed

Jumper locations may have a 2-digit or 3-digit designator dependent on PCBA revision.

PHYSICAL SPECS	SCSI ID	PRIORITY	J307	J308	J309
Height - 1.00" (2.54 cm)	0	Lowest	O	O	O
Length - 5.75" (14.61 cm)	1		O	O	J
	2		O	J	O
	3		O	J	J
Width - 4.00" (10.16 cm)	4		J	O	O
	5		J	O	J
Weight - 1.2 lbs. (.57 kg)	6		J	J	O
	7	Highest	J	J	J

Jumper Locations

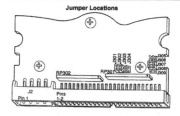

MAXTOR 7290S

JUMPER LOCATIONS and FUNCTIONS

7290S Jumper Functions

Jumper	Function	As shipped
J301	Terminator Power	Installed
J302	Power-up Option	Installed
J303	Disable Parity	Removed
J304	Reserved	Removed
J305	Reserved	Removed
J306	Reserved	Removed
J307	Target ID Address (MSB)	Installed
J308	Target ID Address	Installed
J309	Target ID Address (LSB)	Removed

Drive Addressing

SCSI ID	Priority	J307	J308	J309
0	Lowest	O	O	O
1		O	O	J
2		O	J	O
3		O	J	J
4		J	O	O
5		J	O	J
6		J	J	O
7	Highest	J	J	J

MAXTOR 7345A

7345A Jumper Designation

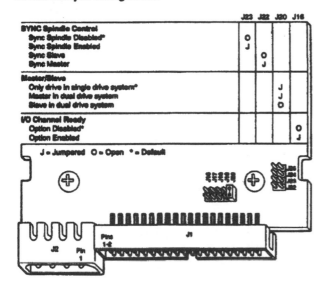

MAXTOR 7345S

JUMPER LOCATIONS and FUNCTIONS

Jumper	Function	Factory Default
J301/J26	Terminator Power	Installed
J302/J25	Power-up Option	Installed
J303/J24	Disable Parity	Removed
J304/J23	Reserved	Removed
J305/J22	Reserved	Removed
J306/J20	Reserved	Removed
J307/J19	Target ID Address (MSB)	Installed
J308/J18	Target ID Address	Installed
J309/J17	Target ID Address (LSB)	Removed

Jumper locations may have a 2-digit or 3-digit designator dependent on PCBA revision.

PHYSICAL SPECS		SCSI ID	PRIORITY	J307	J308	J309
Height - 1.00" (2.54 cm)		0	Lowest	O	O	O
Length - 5.75" (14.61 cm)		1		O	O	J
Width - 4.00" (10.16 cm)		2		O	J	O
Weight - 1.2 lbs. (.57 kg)		3		O	J	J
		4		J	O	O
		5		J	O	J
		6		J	J	O
		7	Highest	J	J	J

Jumper Locations

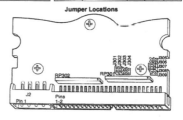

MAXTOR LXT DRIVES

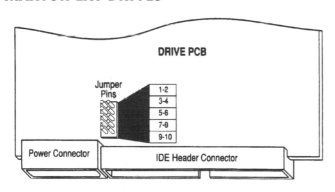

PIN NUMBERS		JUMPER	SINGLE DRIVE SYSTEM	DUAL DRIVE SYSTEM	
				MASTER	SLAVE
1	2	Slave Drive	Removed	Removed	Installed
3	4	Drive Active LED	Optional	Optional	Optional
5	6	Slave Present	Removed	Removed	Optional
7	8	Master Drive	Removed	Installed	Removed
9	10	Synchronous Spindle	Removed (N/A)	Optional*	Removed

* Only one drive (the master) in an array should have this jumper installed.

MAXTOR LXT-213SY

SCSI ID	PRIORITY	PINS 5 & 6 (MSB)	PINS 3 & 4	PINS 1 & 2 (LSB)
0	Lowest	Out	Out	Out
1		Out	Out	In
2		Out	In	Out
3		Out	In	In
4		In	Out	Out
5		In	Out	In
6		In	In	Out
7	Highest	In	In	In

In = Installed, Shorted
Out = Not Installed, Open

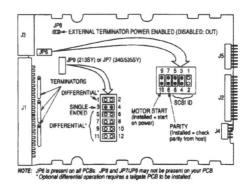

NOTE: JP6 is present on all PCBs. JP8 and JP7/JP9 may not be present on your PCB.
* Optional differential operation requires a tailgate PCB to be installed.

MAXTOR LXT-340SY

SCSI ID	PRIORITY	PINS 5 & 6 (MSB)	PINS 3 & 4	PINS 1 & 2 (LSB)
0	Lowest	Out	Out	Out
1	↑	Out	Out	In
2		Out	In	Out
3		Out	In	In
4		In	Out	Out
5	↓	In	Out	In
6		In	In	Out
7	Highest	In	In	In

In = Installed, Shorted
Out = Not Installed, Open

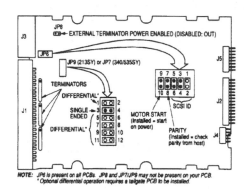

NOTE: JP6 is present on all PCBs. JP8 and JP7/JP9 may not be present on your PCB.
* Optional differential operation requires a tailgate PCB to be installed.

MAXTOR LXT-340A

Jumper Locations

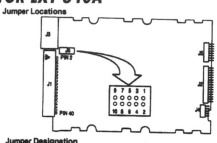

Jumper Designation

Pins	1, 2	3, 4	5, 6	7, 8	9, 10
Master/Slave					
Only drive in single system*	R				
Master in dual drive system	R				
Slave in dual drive system	J				
Drive Active					
One drive in a single drive sys		O			
Master in dual drive system		O			
Slave in dual drive system		O			
Slave Present					
One drive in a single drive sys			R		
Master in dual drive system			R		
Slave in dual drive system			O		
Two Drive System					
One drive in a single drive sys				R	
Master in a dual drive system				J	
Slave in a dual drive system				R	
Sync Spindle Pulse Source					
If receiving the pulse					R
If transmitting a pulse*					J

J = Jumpered   R = Removed   O = Optional
* This jumper may be installed in only one drive in an array!

MAXTOR LXT-535SY

SCSI ID	PRIORITY	PINS 5 & 6 (MSB)	PINS 3 & 4	PINS 1 & 2 (LSB)
0	Lowest	Out	Out	Out
1	↑	Out	Out	In
2		Out	In	Out
3		Out	In	In
4		In	Out	Out
5	↓	In	Out	In
6		In	In	Out
7	Highest	In	In	In

In = Installed, Shorted
Out = Not Installed, Open

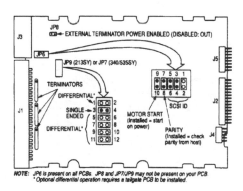

NOTE: JP6 is present on all PCBs. JP8 and JP7/JP9 may not be present on your PCB.
* Optional differential operation requires a tailgate PCB to be installed.

MAXTOR LXT-437SY

SCSI ID	PRIORITY	PINS 5 & 6 (MSB)	PINS 3 & 4	PINS 1 & 2 (LSB)
0	Lowest	Out	Out	Out
1		Out	Out	In
2		Out	In	Out
3		Out	In	In
4		In	Out	Out
5		In	Out	In
6		In	In	Out
7	Highest	In	In	In

In = Installed, Shorted
Out = Not Installed, Open

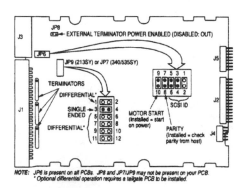

NOTE: JP6 is present on all PCBs. JP8 and JP7/JP9 may not be present on your PCB.
* Optional differential operation requires a tailgate PCB to be installed.

MAXTOR MXT-540SL

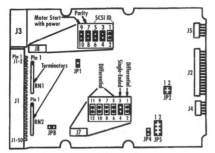

*SCSI ID 6 is shown in this figure.
**Requires a tailgate differential PCB to be installed.
All solid jumper blocks indicate that the drive is shipped with those jumpers installed.

SCSI ID SELECTION

SCSI ID jumpers (pins one through six on JP6) are provided to configure each disk drive with a SCSI device ID for use in multiple SCSI device configurations.

The table below is a reference table for the SCSI ID jumper configuration, the ID, and the priority on the SCSI bus. An ID of seven is the highest priority in a multiple device configuration, and is usually used by the initiator.

SCSI ID	PRIORITY	PINS 5&6	PINS 3&4	PINS 1&2
0	LOWEST	OUT	OUT	OUT
1		OUT	OUT	IN
2		OUT	IN	OUT
3		OUT	IN	IN
4		IN	OUT	OUT
5		IN	OUT	IN
6		IN	IN	OUT
7	HIGHEST	IN	IN	IN

MAXTOR MXT-1240A

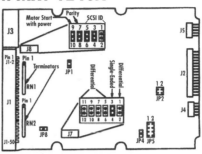

*SCSI ID 6 is shown in this figure.
**Requires a tailgate differential PCB to be installed.
All solid jumper blocks indicate that the drive is shipped with those jumpers installed.

SCSI ID SELECTION

SCSI ID jumpers (pins one through six on JP6) are provided to configure each disk drive with a SCSI device ID for use in multiple SCSI device configurations.

The table below is a reference table for the SCSI ID jumper configuration, the ID, and the priority on the SCSI bus. An ID of seven is the highest priority in a multiple device configuration, and is usually used by the initiator.

SCSI ID	PRIORITY	PINS 5&6	PINS 3&4	PINS 1&2
0	LOWEST	OUT	OUT	OUT
1		OUT	OUT	IN
2		OUT	IN	OUT
3		OUT	IN	IN
4		IN	OUT	OUT
5		IN	OUT	IN
6		IN	IN	OUT
7	HIGHEST	IN	IN	IN

MAXTOR MXT-7345A

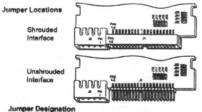

Jumper Designation

	J24	J23	J22	J20	J18	J17	J16
Cable Select							
Disabled*	O						
Enabled	J						
Write Cache							
Enabled*		O					
Disabled		J					
Drive Compatibility							
Disabled*			O				
Enabled			J				
Master/Slave							
Only drive in single system*				J			
Master in dual drive system				J			
Slave in dual drive system				O			
Low Power Spin Mode							
Disabled*					O		
Enabled					J		
ECC							
11-Byte*						O	
4-Byte emulation						J	
I/O Channel Ready							
Option Disabled*							O
Option Enabled							J

* = Default   J = Jumpered   O = Open
NOTE: Jumper J25 factory reserved.   Jumper J19 is a spare shunt

MAXTOR MXT-7546A

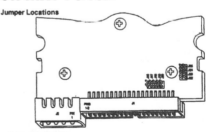

Jumper Designation

	J24	J23	J20	J19	J18	J16
Cable Select						
Disabled*	O					
Enabled	J					
Write Cache						
Enabled*		O				
Disabled		J				
Master/Slave						
Only drive in single system*			J			
Master in dual drive system			J			
Slave in dual drive system			O			
Deferred Spin Up						
Disabled*				O		
Enabled				J		
Automatic Idle Mode						
Disabled*					O	
Enabled					J	
I/O Channel Ready						
Option Disabled*						O
Option Enabled						J

* = Default   J = Jumpered   O = Open
NOTE: Jumpers J25, J22 and J17 factory reserved. Do not use.

MICROPOLIS 1598-15

Jumper Addressing and Interface Termination
ID0, ID1, ID2 - SCSI Address Jumpers
The SCSI ID (drive address) jumpers are identified as ID0, ID1, and ID2. ID selection is binary as shown in the table below.
For multiple drive installations, on one Host Adapter, each drive must have a unique address. Drives are configured as SCSI ID 7 at the factory.
RN9 Interface - Terminator
The interface Terminator factory installed at RN9 provides proper termination for the interface lines. When daisy-chaining multiple drives, leave the terminator installed only in the last physical drive on the daisy chain cable; remove the terminator from each of the other drives.
W1, W2 - Terminator Option
W1 and W2 select the source of terminator power (+5V) for the interface terminator. If a jumper is installed at W1 (the factory default configuration), and no jumper is installed at W2 the drive provides terminator power. This configuration is used for PC/AT applications. If a jumper is on W2 the host adapter will supply terminator power. If a jumper is installed at W2 and W11, and no jumper is installed at W1 the drive provides terminator power to it's on-board terminators and also to the SCSI bus via interface connector J1, pin 26.
W11 - Bus Option
W11 allows the drive to supply interface terminator power to the SCSI bus. If W11 is not installed and W1 is jumpered (the factory default configuration), the drive does supply SCSI bus interface terminator power. W11 should not be installed for PC/AT application.   (Continued on reverse)

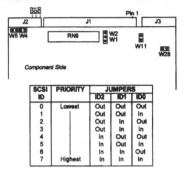

Component Side

SCSI ID	PRIORITY	JUMPERS		
		ID2	ID1	ID0
0	Lowest	Out	Out	Out
1		Out	Out	In
2		Out	In	Out
3		Out	In	In
4		In	Out	Out
5		In	Out	In
6		In	In	Out
7	Highest	In	In	In

MAXTOR 7213A

		J23	J22	J20	J16
SYNC Spindle Control					
Sync Spindle Disabled*		O			
Sync Spindle Enabled		J			
Sync Slave			O		
Sync Master			J		
Master/Slave					
Only drive in single drive system*				J	
Master in dual drive system				J	
Slave in dual drive system				O	
I/O Channel Ready					
Option Disabled*					O
Option Enabled					J

J = Jumpered   O = Open   * = Default

J1

J2   Pins 1-2   Pin 1

MICROPOLIS 1664-7

Drive Addressing and Interface Termination

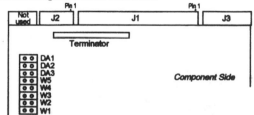

Component Side

RN1 - Interface Terminator.
The interface terminator factory installed at RN1 will provide proper termination for the interface lines. When daisy-chaining multiple drives, leave the terminator installed only in the last physical drive on the daisy chain. In most PC/AT installations, the C: drive is actually at the end of the cable and should retain the terminator.
DA1, DA2, DA3 - Drive Address Jumpers.
The drive address jumpers are identified as DA1, DA2, and DA3. Address selection is binary, as shown in the table below. The ESDI controller's documentation will specify the drive address to use.

Drive Address	Select Jumpers		
	DA3	DA2	DA1
1	Out	Out	In
2	Out	In	Out
3	Out	In	In
4	In	Out	Out
5	In	Out	In
6	In	In	Out
7	In	In	In

MICROPOLIS 1664-7 (Continued)

"Drive Address 0" (no jumper at DA1, DA2, or DA3) is a "deselect" (i.e., no drive selected). Drives are factory configured as Drive Address 1. For many multiple drive installations, each drive must have a unique address. An exception is that for every drive in a PC/AT installation, verify that the only Drive Address is at DA2; move the jumper if necessary (the special twisted interface cable that is generally used takes care of assigning a unique address to each drive). PC/AT controller can typically support a maximum of two drives.
W5 - Selects the Spindle Control Option.
W5 selects the spindle control option. If W5 is installed, the drive waits for a Start Spindle command (after power is applied) to start the spindle motor. If W5 is not installed (the factory default configuration), the drive automatically starts the spindle motor at power-on. W5 is not installed for PC/AT applications.
W1 - Selects the Sectoring Mode.
If W1 is installed, the drive operates in the soft-sectored mode. If W1 is not installed (the factory default configuration), the drive operates in the hard-sector mode. S1 is not installed for most PC/AT in applications.

W2, W3, and W4 - Sector Size and Number Options
The number of bytes per sector may be specified using the Set Bytes Per Sector command or by selecting a default sector configuration with jumpers W2, W3, and W4 as follows:

Jumpers			Sectors per track	Bytes/Sector	
W4	W3	W2		Formatted	Unformatted
Out	Out	Out	53	512	588
*Out	Out	In	54	512	576
Out	In	Out	28	1024	1116
Out	In	In	14	2048	2232
In	Out	Out	7	4096	4464
			—Reserved—		
In	In	Out	97	256	321
In	In	In	1	31,248	31,248

* This is the default (factory installed) configuration and is recommended for PC/AT applications.

MICROPOLIS 1924

Device Addressing and Interface Termination
Up to eight devices (the host and seven targets) cn be attached to the SCSI bus.
The 1924 drive has three id jumpers - ID0, ID1, and ID2. These jumpers are used
to assign one of the eight SCSI ID bits (0 through 7) to the drive. *(see table)*
In multiple-device systems, each drive must have it own unique ID.

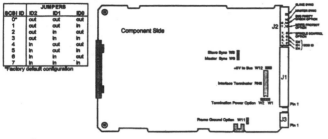

SCSI ID	JUMPERS		
	ID2	ID1	ID0
0*	out	out	out
1	out	out	in
2	out	in	out
3	out	in	in
4	in	out	out
5	in	out	in
6	in	in	out
7	in	in	in

*Factory default configuration

The electrical interface between the 1924 drive and the host system is accomplished via five connectors: J1, J2, J3, J4, and J5.
Signal Connector J1 is a 50-pin connector. The signals on J1 include the 8-bit SCSI
bus and various control and handshaking lines.
J2 is a 24-pin, multi-function connector/jumper block.
J3 is a 4-pin, keyed, AMP MATE-N-LOCK connector. Both +5V and +12V are
supplied to the drive via this connector.
J4 and J5 are provided for grounding; J4 is located on the HDA, and J5 is located
on the frame.

Drive Option Selection
Interface Terminator pack RN6 provides proper termination for the interface lines.
For a multiple-drive system, the terminator pack is installed in the last drive on the
cable.

MICROPOLIS 1991

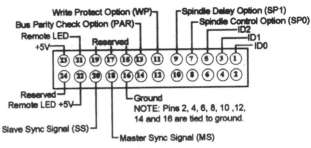

J2 Multi-Function Connector

MICROPOLIS 1991 (Continued)

Configuration/Options
• **SCSI Address.** Jumpers at ID0, ID1, and ID2 select the SCSI address. Each
SCSI device on one Host Adapter must have a unique address.

SCSI ID	PRIORITY	JUMPERS		
		ID2	ID1	ID0
0	Lowest	Out	Out	Out
1		Out	Out	In
2		Out	In	Out
3		Out	In	In
4		In	Out	Out
5		In	Out	In
6		In	In	Out
7	Highest	In	In	In

• **Interface Termination.** If terminators are installed at RN1 and RN2 (default), the
drive provides termination for the SCSI interface. If the terminators are not
installed, the drive does not provide interface termination.
SCSI terminators are installed only in the end devices on the SCSI cable; remove
the terminators from each of the other devices. The SCSI Host Adapter card and
the last drive in the chain should have terminators.
• **Terminator Power.** W1 and W2 select the source of terminator power (+5V) for
interface terminators RN1 and RN2; W3 controls the drive supplying +5V to the
bus.

W1	W2	W3	
Y	N	-	Drive provides terminator power. (Default)
N	Y	-	Host provides terminator pwr via J1 pin 26 to RN1 and RN2.
-	-	Y	Drive supplies +5V to the bus via J1 pin 26. (Default)

• **Frame Ground Option.** A jumper at W9 selects the frame ground option.

Jumper	Frame ground connected to logic ground.
No jumper	Frame ground not connected to logic ground.

• **Spindle Options.** Jumpers at SP0 (J2 pins 7 and 8) and SP1 (J2 pins 9 and 10)
control the spindle options.

SP0	SP1	
N	N	The drive starts the spindle motor at power-on. (Default)
Y	N	The drive waits for a Start Unit SCSI command to start the spindle motor.
N	Y	Spindle start-up is delayed based on SCSI ID address.
		(12 seconds per ID)

(Continued on reverse)

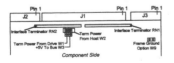

Component Side

MICROPOLIS 1991 (Continued)

• **Write Protect.** A jumper at WP (J2 pins 11 and 12) selects the write protect option..

Jumper	The drive is write protected.
No jumper	The drive is not write protected. (Default)

• **Parity.** A jumper at PAR (J2 pins 13 and 14) selects the bus parity chech option.
The drive **always generates** parity regardless of this option.

Jumper	SCSI interface parity checking disabled.
No jumper	SCSI interface parity checking on. (Default)

• **Spindle Sync Termination.** Jumpers at MS (Master Sync, J2 pin 18) and SS
(Slave Sync, J2 pin 20) control spindle sync termination. This depends on system
configuration; i.e. Master Mode or Master Controller Mode.

MS	SS	
Y	Y	Spindle sync is terminated. (Default)
N	N	Spindle sync not terminated.

• **Remote LED.** A user-supplied LED may be connected to Remote LED (J2 pin 21).

MICROPOLIS 2217

Drive Addressing and Interface Termination
ID0, ID1, ID2 - SCSI Address Jumpers
The SCSI ID (drive address) jumpers are identified as ID0, ID1, and ID2.
ID selection is binary as shown in the table below.
For multiple drive installations, on one Host Adapter, each drive must have a unique address. Drives are configured as SCSI ID 7 at the factory.
RN1, RN2, (RN3) Interface Terminator
The Interface Terminator factory installed at RN1, RN2, and RN3 provides proper termination for the interface lines. When daisy-chaining multiple drives, leave the terminators installed only in the last physical drive on the daisy chain cable; remove all three terminators from each of the other drives (or host computer). Note that there is no RN3 on the revision 2 board.
Bus Termination Power Option
A jumper is installed at W1, at W2, or at W2 and W3 to select the source of terminator power (+5V) for the SCSI Bus terminator packs on the device electronics board.
When a jumper is installed at W1 (the factory default configuration), the drive provides terminator power to it's on-board terminators.
When a jumper is installed at W2, terminator power is provided by the host lsystem via the interface cable J1, pin 26 (TERMPWR).
When a jumper is installed at both W2 and W3, the drive provides terminator power to its on-board terminators and also to the SCSI bus via interface cable J1, pin 26 (TERMPWR).

SCSI ID	PRIORITY	JUMPERS		
		ID2	ID1	ID0
0	Lowest	Out	Out	Out
1		Out	Out	In
2		Out	In	Out
3		Out	In	In
4		In	Out	Out
5		In	Out	In
6		In	In	Out
7	Highest	In	In	In

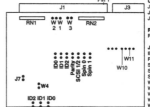

Connectors
J1 = 50 Pin Ribbon Cable
J3 = 4 Pin Power Cable
J7 = External LED Light

Resistors
RN (1-2) = Terminators (x2)

Jumpers
ID (0-2) = SCSI ID
Parity = Parity enable/disable
SCSI 1/2 = Write Protect
Spin 0 = Spindle Control
Spin 1 = Spindle Delay
W1/W2 = Termination Power
W3 = +5V to Bus
W4 = Bezel LED Option
W10 = Slave Sync Term
W11 = Master Sync Term

MICROPOLIS 2112A

Drive emulates both Master and Slave: Specifies that one 2112A drive can emulate both the Master drive (Drive 0) and the Slave drive (Drive 1). This option allows for existing host systems to utilize the full capacity of the drive.
When the drive is configured as both the Master and the Slave, the Master's (Drive 0) capacity is set to 1024 logical cylinders, 16 logical heads, and 63 logical sectors. This setting yields 528,482,304 bytes. The Slave's (Drive 1) capacity is set to the remaining storage on the disk drive.
For this configuration, the recommended drive type setting in the computer's CMOS memory is as follows:
Drive 0: 1024 logical cylinders, 16 logical heads, 63 logical sectors
Drive 1: 1010 logical cylinders, 16 logical heads, 63 logical sectors

NOTE
The capacity of the 2112A drive may exceed the capacity that the host can access. This limitation stems from the communication link between the DOS and the BIOS. A typical limit is 1024 cylinders, 16 heads, and 63 sectors. For optimum use of the following options, the BIOS may need to be modified.

Drive is Master, Slave is present: Specifies the Master drive (Drive 0) when two 2112A drives are used in a system. The other drive is Slave.

Drive is Slave: Specifies the Slave drive (Drive 1) when two 2112A drives are used in a system. The other drive is Master.

Drive is Master: Specifies the Master drive (Drive 0) when one 2112A drive is used in a system.

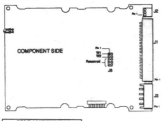

COMPONENT SIDE

DRIVE CONFIGURATION		
W1	W2	Description
In	In	Drive emulates *both* Master and Slave*
In	Out	Drive is Master, Slave is present
Out	In	Drive is Slave
Out	Out	Drive is Master

*The factory default configuration

QUANTUM 8 and 10 JUMPER LOCATIONS

Eight- and Ten-Jumper Location and Settings

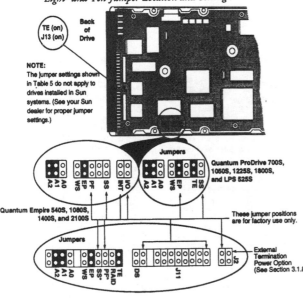

NOTE:
The jumper settings shown in Table 5 do not apply to drives installed in Sun systems. (See your Sun dealer for proper jumper settings.)

Quantum Empire 540S, 1080S, 1400S, and 2100S

Quantum ProDrive 700S, 1050S, 1225S, 1800S, and LPS 525S

These jumper positions are for factory use only.

External Termination Power Option (See Section 3.1.8)

Quantum Grand Prix XP32151S and XP34301S

QUANTUM 3.5" 5-JUMPER

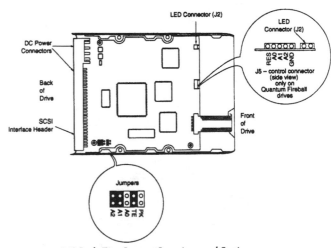

3.5-Inch Five-Jumper Locations and Settings

CAUTION: Verify that no two drives on the SCSI bus have the same address (see Table 4 for drive address information).

QUANTUM 3.5" 6-JUMPER

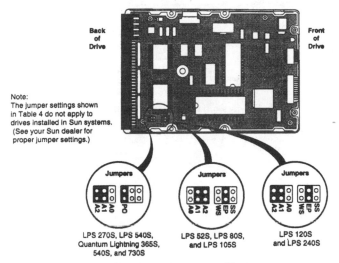

Note:
The jumper settings shown in Table 4 do not apply to drives installed in Sun systems. (See your Sun dealer for proper jumper settings.)

Back of Drive — **Front of Drive**

Jumpers
LPS 270S, LPS 540S, Quantum Lightning 365S, 540S, and 730S

Jumpers
LPS 52S, LPS 80S, and LPS 105S

Jumpers
LPS 120S and LPS 240S

3.5-Inch Six-Jumper Locations and Settings

QUANTUM 3.5" PC-AT

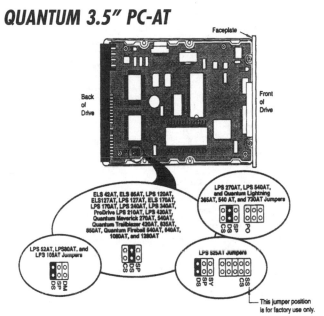

Faceplate

Back of Drive — **Front of Drive**

ELS 42AT, ELS 85AT, LPS 120AT, ELS127AT, LPS 127AT, ELS 170AT, LPS 170AT, LPS 240AT, LPS 340AT, ProDrive LPS 210AT, LPS 420AT, Quantum Maverick 270AT, 540AT, Quantum Trailblazer 420AT, 635AT, 850AT, Quantum Fireball 540AT, 640AT, 1080AT, and 1280AT

LPS 270AT, LPS 540AT, and Quantum Lightning 365AT, 540 AT, and 730AT Jumpers

LPS 52AT, LPS80AT, and LPS 105AT Jumpers

LPS 525AT Jumpers

This jumper position is for factory use only.

3.5-Inch PC-AT Drive Jumper Block Locations

QUANTUM DSP SERIES 16-BIT

Quantum DSP 3210S, DSP 3133L S, DSP 3107L S, and DSP 3053L S

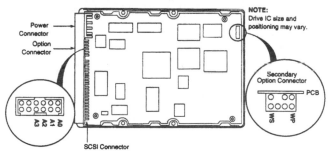

Power Connector

Option Connector

NOTE:
Drive IC size and positioning may vary.

Secondary Option Connector

PCB

SCSI Connector

Quantum DSP Series (16-bit) Jumper Locations and Settings

QUANTUM DSP SERIES 8-BIT

Quantum DSP 3210S, DSP 3133L S, DSP 3107L S, and DSP 3053L S

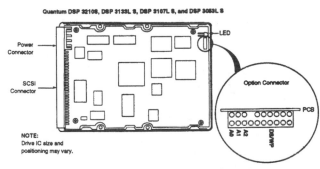

Power Connector

SCSI Connector

LED

Option Connector

PCB

NOTE:
Drive IC size and positioning may vary.

DSP Series (8-bit) Jumper Location and Settings

QUANTUM ELS 127AT

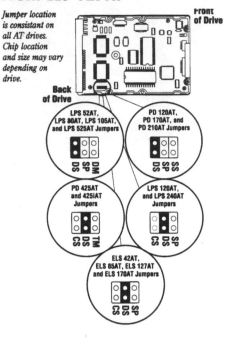

Jumper location is consistant on all AT drives. Chip location and size may vary depending on drive.

QUANTUM ELS 127

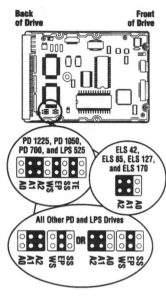

Jumper and Terminator location is constant on all SCSI drives. Chip location and size may vary depending on drive.

ProDrive Address Jumpers			SCSI ID
A2	A1	A0	
OFF	OFF	OFF	0
OFF	OFF	ON	1
OFF	ON	OFF	2
OFF	ON	ON	3
ON	OFF	OFF	4
ON	OFF	ON	5
ON*	ON*	OFF*	6*
ON	ON	ON	7

* Indicates the factory default jumper setting.
ON indicates that the jumper is connected.
OFF indicates that the jumper is not installed.

QUANTUM ELS 170AT

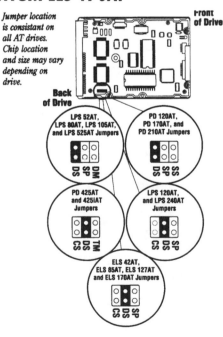

Jumper location is consistant on all AT drives. Chip location and size may vary depending on drive.

QUANTUM ELS 170

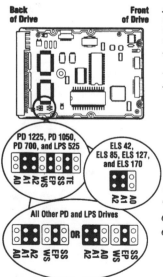

Jumper and Terminator location is constant on all SCSI drives. Chip location and size may vary depending on drive.

ProDrive Address Jumpers			SCSI ID
A2	A1	A0	
OFF	OFF	OFF	0
OFF	OFF	ON	1
OFF	ON	OFF	2
OFF	ON	ON	3
ON	OFF	OFF	4
ON	OFF	ON	5
ON*	ON*	OFF*	6*
ON	ON	ON	7

* Indicates the factory default jumper setting.
ON indicates that the jumper is connected.
OFF indicates that the jumper is not installed.

QUANTUM ELS 42

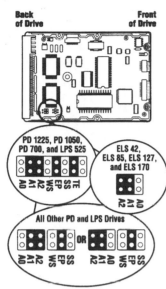

Back of Drive   **Front of Drive**

Jumper and Terminator location is constant on all SCSI drives. Chip location and size may vary depending on drive.

ProDrive Address Jumpers			SCSI ID
A2	A1	A0	
OFF	OFF	OFF	0
OFF	OFF	ON	1
OFF	ON	OFF	2
OFF	ON	ON	3
ON	OFF	OFF	4
ON	OFF	ON	5
ON*	ON*	OFF*	6*
ON	ON	ON	7

* Indicates the factory default jumper setting.
ON indicates that the jumper is connected.
OFF indicates that the jumper is not installed.

QUANTUM ELS 42AT

Jumper location is consistant on all AT drives. Chip location and size may vary depending on drive.

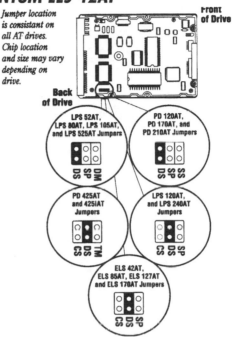

QUANTUM ELS 85

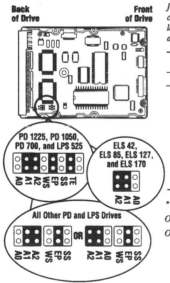

Back of Drive   **Front of Drive**

Jumper and Terminator location is constant on all SCSI drives. Chip location and size may vary depending on drive.

ProDrive Address Jumpers			SCSI ID
A2	A1	A0	
OFF	OFF	OFF	0
OFF	OFF	ON	1
OFF	ON	OFF	2
OFF	ON	ON	3
ON	OFF	OFF	4
ON	OFF	ON	5
ON*	ON*	OFF*	6*
ON	ON	ON	7

* Indicates the factory default jumper setting.
ON indicates that the jumper is connected.
OFF indicates that the jumper is not installed.

QUANTUM ELS 85AT

Jumper location is consistant on all AT drives. Chip location and size may vary depending on drive.

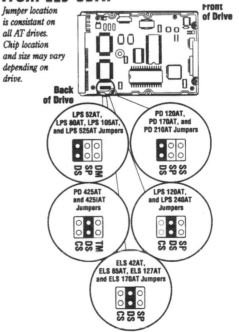

QUANTUM GO DRIVE AT

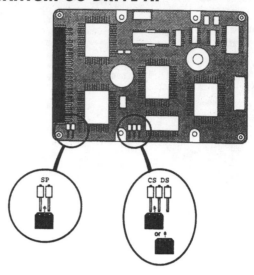

Quantum Go•Drive AT Jumper Block Locations

QUANTUM EUROPA SERIES

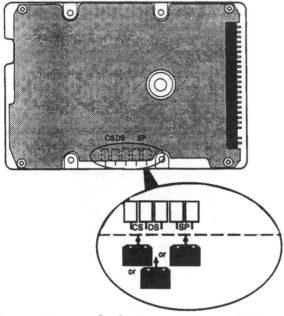

Jumper Locations for the Quantum Europa Series

QUANTUM LPS/MAVERICK

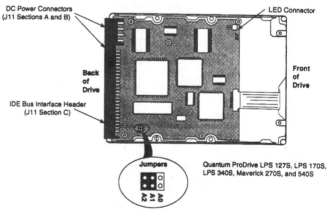

Quantum ProDrive LPS 127S, LPS 170S, LPS 340S, Quantum Maverick 270S, and 540S Jumper Location and Settings

The black jumper body indicates that a jumper is installed (the setting is ON).

QUANTUM GO DRIVE GLS/DAYTONA

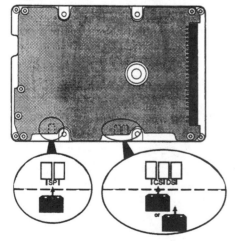

Quantum Go•Drive GLS and Quantum Daytona AT Jumper Locations

QUANTUM LPS 105AT

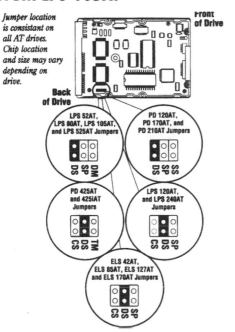

Jumper location is consistant on all AT drives. Chip location and size may vary depending on drive.

QUANTUM LPS 120AT

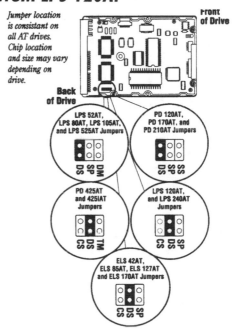

Jumper location is consistant on all AT drives. Chip location and size may vary depending on drive.

QUANTUM LPS 240AT

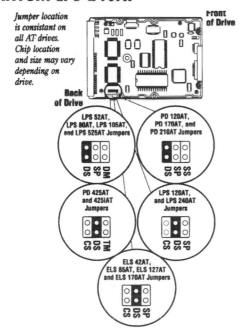

Jumper location is consistant on all AT drives. Chip location and size may vary depending on drive.

QUANTUM LPS 525

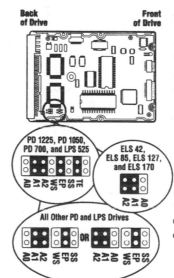

Jumper and Terminator location is constant on all SCSI drives. Chip location and size may vary depending on drive.

ProDrive Address Jumpers			SCSI ID
A2	A1	A0	
OFF	OFF	OFF	0
OFF	OFF	ON	1
OFF	ON	OFF	2
OFF	ON	ON	3
ON	OFF	OFF	4
ON	OFF	ON	5
ON*	ON*	OFF*	6*
ON	ON	ON	7

* Indicates the factory default jumper setting.
ON indicates that the jumper is connected.
OFF indicates that the jumper is not installed.

QUANTUM LPS 52AT

Jumper location is consistant on all AT drives. Chip location and size may vary depending on drive.

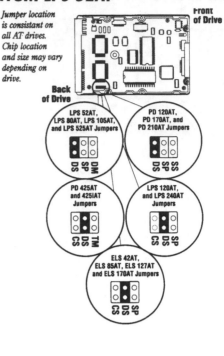

QUANTUM LPS 525AT

all AT drives. Chip location and size may vary depending on drive.

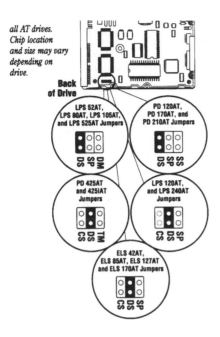

QUANTUM LPS 80AT

Jumper location is consistant on all AT drives. Chip location and size may vary depending on drive.

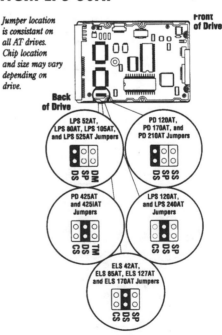

QUANTUM PD 1050

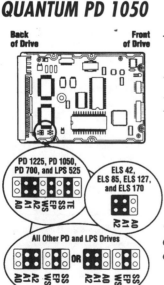

Jumper and Terminator location is constant on all SCSI drives. Chip location and size may vary depending on drive.

ProDrive Address Jumpers			SCSI ID
A2	A1	A0	
OFF	OFF	OFF	0
OFF	OFF	ON	1
OFF	ON	OFF	2
OFF	ON	ON	3
ON	OFF	OFF	4
ON	OFF	ON	5
ON*	ON*	OFF*	6*
ON	ON	ON	7

* Indicates the factory default jumper setting.
ON indicates that the jumper is connected.
OFF indicates that the jumper is not installed.

© CSC 1996

QUANTUM PD 120AT

Jumper location is consistant on all AT drives. Chip location and size may vary depending on drive.

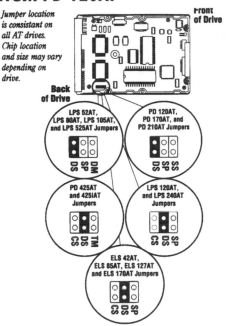

QUANTUM PD 1225

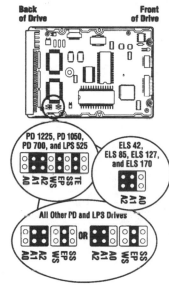

Jumper and Terminator location is constant on all SCSI drives. Chip location and size may vary depending on drive.

ProDrive Address Jumpers			SCSI ID
A2	A1	A0	
OFF	OFF	OFF	0
OFF	OFF	ON	1
OFF	ON	OFF	2
OFF	ON	ON	3
ON	OFF	OFF	4
ON	OFF	ON	5
ON*	ON*	OFF*	6*
ON	ON	ON	7

* Indicates the factory default jumper setting.
ON indicates that the jumper is connected.
OFF indicates that the jumper is not installed.

QUANTUM PD 170AT

Jumper location is consistant on all AT drives. Chip location and size may vary depending on drive.

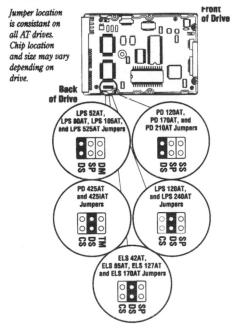

QUANTUM PD 210AT

Jumper location is consistant on all AT drives. Chip location and size may vary depending on drive.

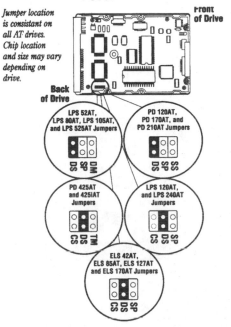

QUANTUM PD 700

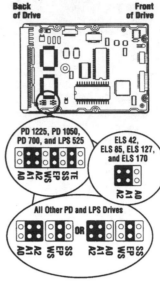

Back of Drive ... **Front of Drive**

Jumper and Terminator location is constant on all SCSI drives. Chip location and size may vary depending on drive.

ProDrive Address Jumpers			SCSI ID
A2	A1	A0	
OFF	OFF	OFF	0
OFF	OFF	ON	1
OFF	ON	OFF	2
OFF	ON	ON	3
ON	OFF	OFF	4
ON	OFF	ON	5
ON*	ON*	OFF*	6*
ON	ON	ON	7

* Indicates the factory default jumper setting.
ON indicates that the jumper is connected.
OFF indicates that the jumper is not installed.

PD 1225, PD 1050, PD 700, and LPS 525

ELS 42, ELS 85, ELS 127, and ELS 170

All Other PD and LPS Drives

QUANTUM PD 425AT/425iAT

Jumper location is consistant on all AT drives. Chip location and size may vary depending on drive.

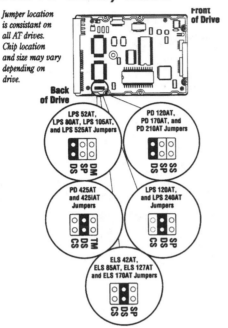

Front of Drive

Back of Drive

LPS 52AT, LPS 80AT, LPS 105AT, and LPS 525AT Jumpers

PD 120AT, PD 170AT, and PD 210AT Jumpers

PD 425AT and 425iAT Jumpers

LPS 120AT, and LPS 240AT Jumpers

ELS 42AT, ELS 85AT, ELS 127AT and ELS 170AT Jumpers

QUANTUM PRODRIVE ELS

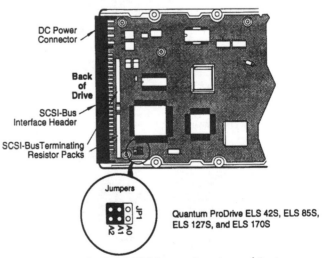

DC Power Connector

Back of Drive

SCSI-Bus Interface Header

SCSI-Bus Terminating Resistor Packs

Jumpers

Quantum ProDrive ELS 42S, ELS 85S, ELS 127S, and ELS 170S

Quantum ProDrive ELS Jumper Location and Settings

QUANTUM PRODRIVE

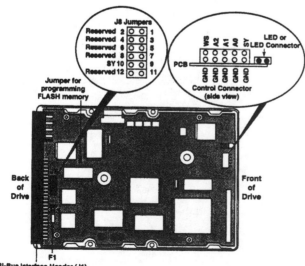

J8 Jumpers
Reserved 2 — 1
Reserved 4 — 3
Reserved 6 — 5
Reserved 8 — 7
SY 10 — 9
Reserved 12 — 11

Jumper for programming FLASH memory

WS A2 A1 A0 SY   LED or LED Connector
PCB
GND GND GND GND GND
Control Connector (side view)

Back of Drive

Front of Drive

F1
SCSI-Bus Interface Header (J1)

Quantum ProDrive LPS 525S, 700S, 1050S, 1225S, and 1800S Options

QUANTUM PRODRIVE/LIGHTNING

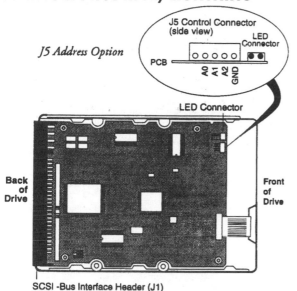

J5 Address Option

J5 Control Connector
(side view)

LED Connector

PCB

A0 A1 A2 GND

LED Connector

Back of Drive

Front of Drive

SCSI -Bus Interface Header (J1)

The PCB address jumpers (A0, A1, and A2) must be removed if the J5 remote address connector is used.

SEAGATE 31230W/WC/WD

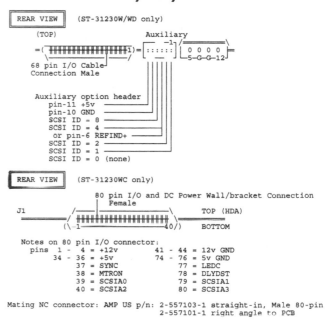

REAR VIEW (ST-31230W/WD only)

(TOP)   Auxiliary

68 pin I/O Cable
Connection Male

Auxiliary option header
pin-11 +5v
pin-10 GND
SCSI ID = 8
SCSI ID = 4
  or pin-6 REFIND+
SCSI ID = 2
SCSI ID = 1
SCSI ID = 0 (none)

REAR VIEW (ST-31230WC only)

80 pin I/O and DC Power Wall/bracket Connection
Female

J1   TOP (HDA)

                                        BOTTOM

Notes on 80 pin I/O connector:
pins 1 - 4 = +12v   41 - 44 = 12v GND
     34 - 36 = +5v   74 - 76 = 5v GND
          37 = SYNC   77 = LEDC
          38 = MTRON   78 = DLYDST
          39 = SCSIA0   79 = SCSIA1
          40 = SCSIA2   80 = SCSIA3

Mating NC connector: AMP US p/n: 2-557103-1 straight-in, Male 80-pin
                                 2-557101-1 right angle to PCB

SEAGATE 3491A

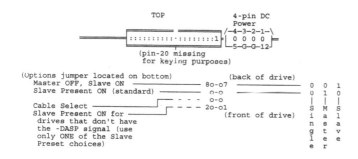

TOP   4-pin DC
                       Power
                     /-4-3-2-1-\
:::::::::::::::::1   0 0 0 0
                     5-G-G-12
(pin-20 missing
for keying purposes)

(Options jumper located on bottom)   (back of drive)
Master OFF, Slave ON ————————— 8o-o7   0 0 1
Slave Present ON (standard) —— o-o   0 1 0   S
                               - - - o-o   1 0 0   i
Cable Select ——————————   - - - | | | n
Slave Present ON for ————————— 2o-o1 | | | g
drives that don't have   (front of drive)   l
the -DASP signal (use   S M S e
only ONE of the Slave   i a l
Preset choices)   n s a
                                             g t v
                                             l e e
                                             e r

SEAGATE ST11200N

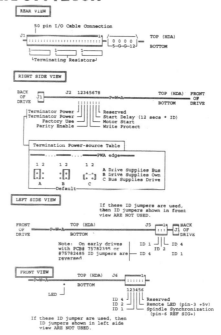

REAR VIEW

50 pin I/O Cable Connection

J1   TOP (HDA)
                                BOTTOM
└Terminating Resistors┘

RIGHT SIDE VIEW

BACK   J2 12345678   P=W=A   TOP (HDA) FRONT
OF   J1   OF
DRIVE   :::::::: BOTTOM   DRIVE

Terminator Power———┘||||||┘┌——Reserved
Terminator Power————┘||||└———Start Delay (12 secs * ID)
Factory Use—————————┘||└————Motor Start
Parity Enable———————┘└—————Write Protect

Termination Power-source Table

——.....———————PWA edge——————

1 2   1 2   1 2
                        A Drive Supplies Bus
                        B Drive Supplies Own
 A   B   C   C Bus Supplies Drive
└——Default——┘

LEFT SIDE VIEW

If these ID jumpers are used,
then ID jumpers shown in front
view ARE NOT USED.

FRONT   TOP (HDA)   J5   BACK
OF   P=W=A   :::   J1 OF
DRIVE   BOTTOM   DRIVE

Note: On early drives   ID 1   ID 4
with PCB# 75782395 or   ID 2   ID 2
#75782485 ID jumpers are ID 4   ID 1
reversed

FRONT VIEW

             TOP (HDA) J6
     P=W=A   :::::::
             BOTTOM

LED   123456

ID 4   Reserved
ID 2   Remote LED (pin-3 +5v)
ID 1   Spindle Synchronization
                         (pin-6 REF SIG+)

If these ID jumper are used, then
ID jumpers shown in left side
view ARE NOT USED.

SEAGATE ST1144A

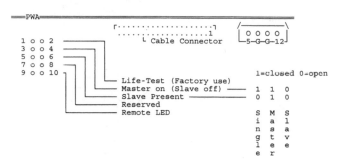

SEAGATE ST1144A-32

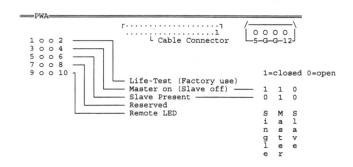

SEAGATE ST11910ND (Continued)

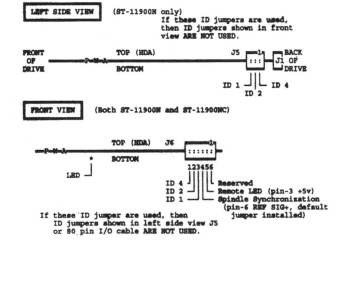

SEAGATE ST11910ND

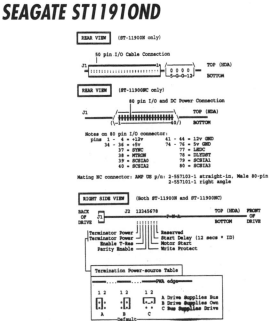

SEAGATE ST12450W

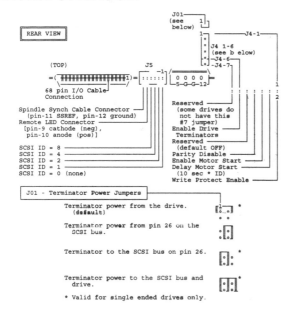

REAR VIEW

(TOP)   J5
=([████████████████] 1) = [::::::] = [0 0 0 0]
68 pin I/O Cable   5-G-G-12
Connection

J01
(see below) 1

J4-1
J4 1-6 (see b elow)
J4-6
J4-7

Spindle Synch Cable Connector
(pin-11 SSREF, pin-12 ground)
Remote LED Connector
[pin-9 cathode (neg),
pin-10 anode (pos)]

SCSI ID = 8
SCSI ID = 4
SCSI ID = 2
SCSI ID = 1
SCSI ID = 0 (none)

Reserved
(some drives do
not have this
#7 jumper)
Enable Drive
Terminators
Reserved
(default OFF)
Parity Disable
Enable Motor Start
Delay Motor Start
(10 sec * ID)
Write Protect Enable

J01 - Terminator Power Jumpers

Terminator power from the drive.
(default)

Terminator power from pin 26 on the
SCSI bus.

Terminator to the SCSI bus on pin 26.

Terminator power to the SCSI bus and
drive.

* Valid for single ended drives only.

SEAGATE ST12550N

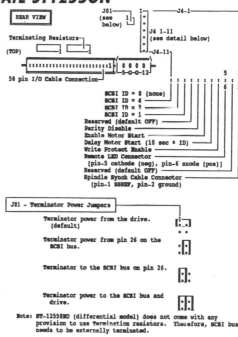

REAR VIEW

Terminating Resistors

(TOP)
[||||||||||||||||||||||] 1 [0 0 0 0]
50 pin I/O Cable Connection   5-G-G-12

J01
(see below) 1

J4-1
J4 1-11
(see detail below)
J4-11

5 1
6 2

SCSI ID = 0 (none)
SCSI ID = 4
SCSI ID = 2
SCSI ID = 1
Reserved (default OFF)
Parity Disable
Enable Motor Start
Delay Motor Start (10 sec * ID)
Write Protect Enable
Remote LED Connector
[pin-5 cathode (neg), pin-6 anode (pos)]
Reserved (default OFF)
Spindle Synch Cable Connector
(pin-1 SSREF, pin-2 ground)

J01 - Terminator Power Jumpers

Terminator power from the drive.
(default)

Terminator power from pin 26 on the
SCSI bus.

Terminator to the SCSI bus on pin 26.

Terminator power to the SCSI bus and
drive.

Note: ST-12550ND (differential model) does not come with any
provision to use Termination resistors. Therefore, SCSI bus
needs to be externally terminated.

SEAGATE ST12550N/ND/W/WD

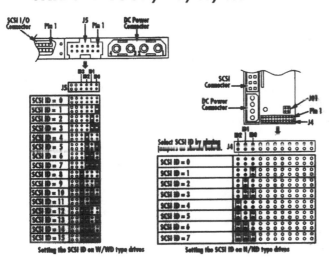

SCSI I/O Connector   Pin 1   J5   Pin 1   DC Power Connector

SCSI Connector
DC Power Connector
J01
Pin 1
J4

SCSI ID = 0
SCSI ID = 1
SCSI ID = 2
SCSI ID = 3
SCSI ID = 4
SCSI ID = 5
SCSI ID = 6
SCSI ID = 7
SCSI ID = 8
SCSI ID = 9
SCSI ID = 10
SCSI ID = 11
SCSI ID = 12
SCSI ID = 13
SCSI ID = 14
SCSI ID = 15

Setting the SCSI ID on W/WD type drives

Select SCSI ID by placing
jumpers on shaded field.   J4

SCSI ID = 0
SCSI ID = 1
SCSI ID = 2
SCSI ID = 3
SCSI ID = 4
SCSI ID = 5
SCSI ID = 6
SCSI ID = 7

Setting the SCSI ID on N/ND type drives

SEAGATE ST12550N/ND/W/WD (Continued)

The ST12550W drives are equipped with permanently mounted IC terminators.
This means you can either enable or disable termination using jumpers as
described below.

To terminate ST12550W drives (enable termination), install a jumper on J4 pins
11 and 12
To remove termination (disable termination), remove the jumper from J4 pins 11
and 12.

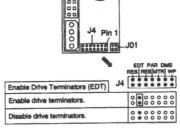

J4   Pin 1
J01

EDT PAR DMS
RES RES MTR WP
J4

Enable Drive Terminators (EDT)
Enable drive terminators.
Disable drive terminators.

ST12550ND/WD drives have no provisions for internal termination. To terminate
these drives, you must provide external termination.

SEAGATE ST1255ON/ND/W/WD (Continued)

Changing other applicable jumper options for ST12550N/ND

Barracuda 1 and 2 drives are designed to be used in a variety of systems. Unique instllations may require you to change one or more of the other jumpers to meet specific system requirements; however, in most cases, you will not need to change any of these jumpers for normal drive operation. These figures provide the information necessary to configure all N and ND drive jumpers not discussed elsewhere in this manual.

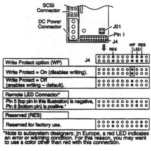

SEAGATE ST1255ON/ND/W/WD (Continued)

Termination power

Single-ended (N and W) drives have four valid configurations for terminator power (see below). Differential (ND and WD drives) must be configured with a jumper on J01 pins 1 and 3 only.

SEAGATE ST1255ON/ND/W/WD (Continued)

Additional jumper options for 12550W/WD

These figures provide the information necessary to configure all W and WD drive jumpers not discussed elsewhere in this manual.

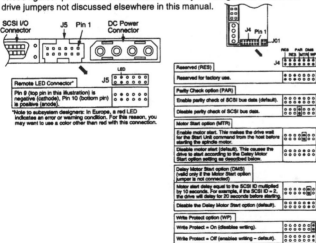

SEAGATE ST1255ON/ND/W/WD (Continued)

Synchronizing spindles

If you are installing two or more Barracuda drives, you may (optionally) want to synchronize their spindles to reduce the latency associated with switching from one drive to another. Spindle sync cables are used to connect the drives.

For N- and ND-type drives, use pins 1 and 2 on the J4 connector to attach the spindle sync cable. Pin 1 provides the reference index signal (REFSIG+) and pin 2 provides ground (GND). *see below*

For W- and WD-type drives, use pins 11 and 12 on the J5 connector to attach the spindle sync cable. Pin 11 provides the reference index signal (REFSIG+) and pin 12 provides ground (GND). *see below*

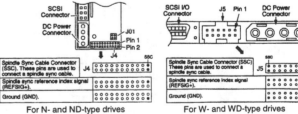

For N- and ND-type drives   For W- and WD-type drives

SEAGATE ST1401N

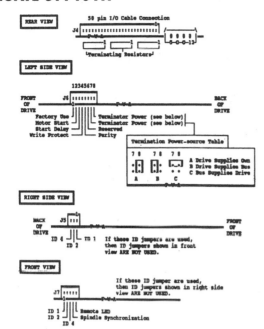

SEAGATE ST1480A

NOTE: This figure and the following description of each jumper position is only valid on drives that have J6 with 4 pins (2x2).-->

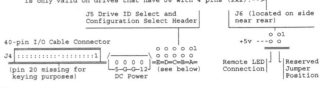

J5
JUMPER | FUNCTION:

A   REFSIG. This location provides a port for external connection of the synchronized spindle reference signal (pin-1) and ground (pin-2). The reference signal is bi-directional, single-ended, and terminated without an external resistor. It is also available on J4 pin-28 if the factory jumper is installed. The drive will self-determine if it is a master of slave for spindle synchronization.

B   HOST SLV/ACT: When this shunt is installed, -SLAVE PRESENT (provided by the output of a 74HCT14) is applied to J4 pin-39 for systems that require this signal from the Master drive. If jumper "B" is installed, then jumper "E" must not be installed.

C   MASTER: When this shunt is installed, the drive is configured as the Master. When not installed, the drive is a Slave.

D   SLAVE PRESENT: When installed, this shunt indicates to the Master drive that a Slave is present. This shunt must be installed on the Master drive in a two-drive system.

E   ACTIVE: When this shunt is installed, DASP- is made present on J4 pin-39. If "E" is installed, then "B" must not be installed.

SEAGATE ST1480A (Continued)

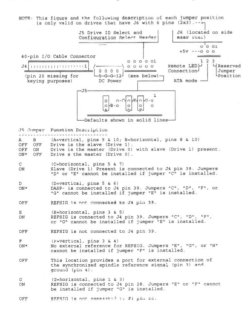

NOTE: This figure and the following description of each jumper position is only valid on drives that have J6 with 6 pins (2x3).-->

J5 Jumper Function Description

A   B
OFF OFF   (A=vertical, pins 9 & 10; B=horizontal, pins 8 & 10)
OFF OFF   Drive is the slave (Drive 1).
OFF ON   Drive is the master (Drive 0) with slave (Drive 1) present.
ON* OFF   Drive s the master (Drive 0).

C
ON   (C=horizontal, pins 5 & 7)
      Slave (Drive 1) Present is connected to J4 pin 39. Jumpers "D" or "E" cannot be installed if jumper "C" is installed.

D
ON*   (D=vertical, pins 5 & 6)
      DASP- is connected to J4 pin 39. Jumpers "C", "D", "F", or "G" cannot be installed if jumper "E" is installed.
OFF   REFSIG is not connected to J4 pin 39.

E
ON   (E=horizontal, pins 3 & 5)
      REFSIG is connected to J4 pin 39. Jumpers "C", "D", "F", or "G" cannot be installed if jumper "E" is installed.
OFF   REFSIG is not connected to J4 pin 39.

F
ON*   (F=vertical, pins 3 & 4)
      No external reference for REFSIG. Jumpers "E", "G", or "H" cannot be installed if jumper "F" is installed.
OFF   This location provides a port for external connection of the synchronized spindle reference signal (pin 3) and ground (pin 4).

G
ON   (G=horizontal, pins 1 & 3)
      REFSIG is connected to J4 pin 28. Jumpers "E" or "F" cannot be installed if jumper "G" is installed.
OFF   REFSIG is not connected to J4 pin 28.

SEAGATE ST1480N

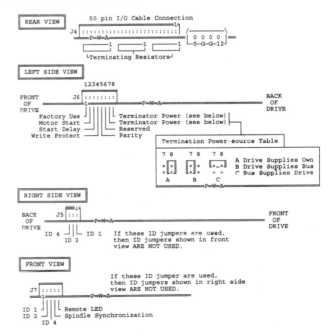

SEAGATE ST15150W

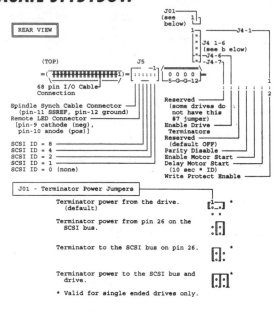

SEAGATE ST15150N

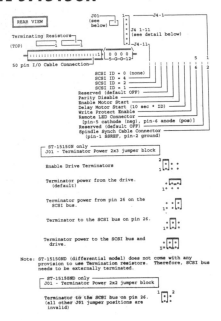

SEAGATE ST157N

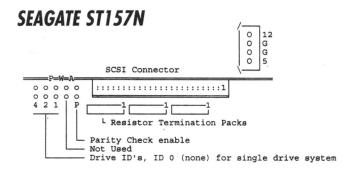

SEAGATE ST15230N

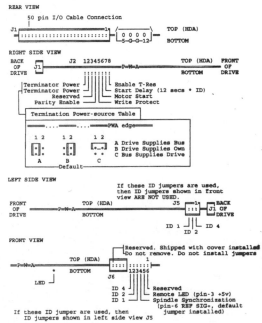

SEAGATE ST31230N

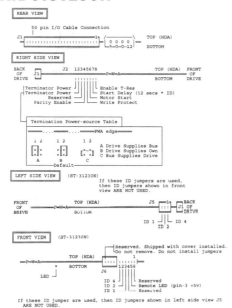

SEAGATE ST31230W/WD/WC

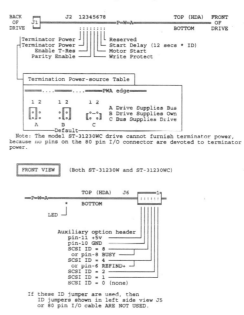

SEAGATE ST32550N

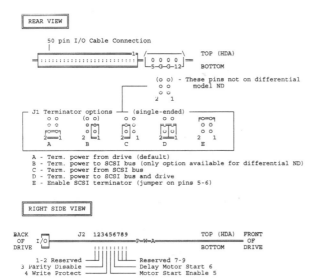

SEAGATE ST32550N (Continued)

pins	1 - 4 = +12v	41 - 44 = 12v GND
	34 - 36 = +5v	74 - 76 = 5v GND
	37 = SYNC	77 = LEDC
	38 = MTRON	78 = DLYDST
	39 = SCSIA0	79 = SCSIA1
	40 = SCSIA2	80 = SCSIA3

Mating WC connector: AMP US p/n: 2-557103-1 straight-in, Male 80-pin
2-557101-1 right angle to PCB

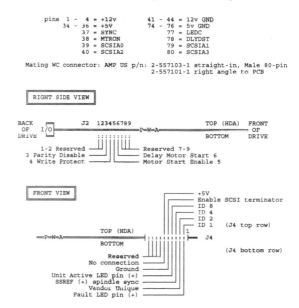

SEAGATE ST32550W/WD (Continued)

```
pins 1 - 4 = +12v        41 - 44 = 12v GND
     34 - 36 = +5v        74 - 76 = 5v GND
          37 = SYNC            77 = LEDC
          38 = MTRON           78 = DLYDST
          39 = SCSIA0          79 = SCSIA1
          40 = SCSIA2          80 = SCSIA3
```

Mating WC connector: AMP US p/n: 2-557103-1 straight-in, Male 80-pin
                                 2-557101-1 right angle to PCB

SEAGATE ST32550W/WD

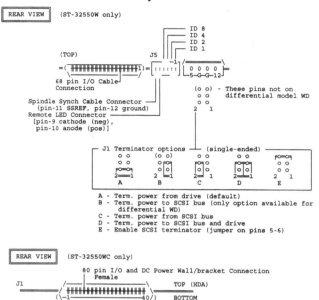

```
REAR VIEW   (ST-32550W only)
```

A - Term. power from drive (default)
B - Term. power to SCSI bus (only option available for
    differential WD)
C - Term. power from SCSI bus
D - Term. power to SCSI bus and drive
E - Enable SCSI terminator (jumper on pins 5-6)

```
REAR VIEW   (ST-32550WC only)
```

80 pin I/O and DC Power Wall/bracket Connection
Female

Notes on 80 pin I/O connector:

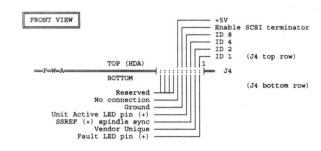

```
RIGHT SIDE VIEW
```

```
BACK                                        TOP (HDA)  FRONT
OF    I/O    J2  123456789        P=W=A                 OF
DRIVE                                        BOTTOM    DRIVE

1-2 Reserved        Reserved 7-9
3 Parity Disable    Delay Motor Start 6
4 Write Protect     Motor Start Enable 5
```

```
FRONT VIEW
```

```
                                          +5V
                                          Enable SCSI terminator
                                          ID 8
                                          ID 4
                                          ID 2
                                          ID 1   (J4 top row)
=P=W=A=    TOP (HDA)              1    J4
           BOTTOM

           Reserved                       (J4 bottom row)
           No connection
           Ground
Unit Active LED pin (+)
SSREF (+) spindle sync
Vendor Unique
Fault LED pin (+)
```

SEAGATYE ST3390N

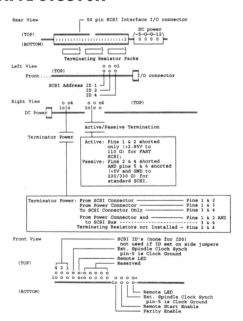

SEAGATE ST3295A

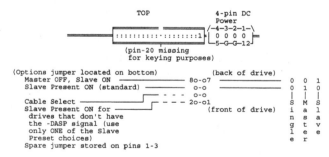

```
                TOP        4-pin DC
                           Power
                           -4-3-2-1-
                           0 0 0 0
:::::::::::::::::::::::1    5-G-G-12
                (pin-20 missing
                for keying purposes)
```

(Options jumper located on bottom)   (back of drive)
Master OFF, Slave ON ———————— 8o-o7 ———————————— 0 0 1
Slave Present ON (standard) ——— o-o ——————————————— 0 1 0
                             - - - o-o ——————————————— 1 0 0
Cable Select ——————————— - - - 2o-o1
Slave Present ON for   (front of drive)   S M S
  drives that don't have   i a l
  the -DASP signal (use   n s a
  only ONE of the Slave   g t v
  Preset choices)   l e e
Spare jumper stored on pins 1-3   e r

SEAGATE ST3391A

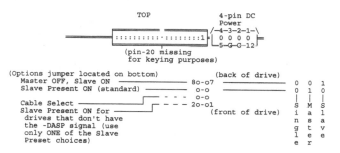

```
                    TOP              4-pin DC
                                      Power
                                   /-4-3-2-1-\
         ::::::::::::::::::::::1     0 0 0 0
                                   |_5-G-G-12_|
                 (pin-20 missing
                  for keying purposes)
```

```
(Options jumper located on bottom)                          (back of drive)   0  0  1
  Master OFF, Slave ON ──────────────── 8o-o7 ──────────     0  1  0
  Slave Present ON (standard) ─────────── o-o                 |S |M |S
                                      - - - o-o               |i |a |l
  Cable Select ──────────────┐         - - 2o-o1              |n |s |a
  Slave Present ON for ───────┘                (front of drive)|g |t |v
   drives that don't have                                     |l |e |e
   the -DASP signal (use                                      |e |r |
   only ONE of the Slave
   Preset choices)
```

SEAGATE ST3660A

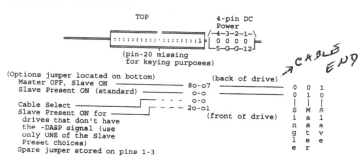

```
                    TOP              4-pin DC
                                      Power
                                   /-4-3-2-1-\
         ::::::::::::::::::::::1     0 0 0 0
                                   |_5-G-G-12_|
                 (pin-20 missing              →CABLE
                  for keying purposes)            END
```

```
(Options jumper located on bottom)                          (back of drive)   0  0  1
  Master OFF, Slave ON ──────────────── 8o-o7 ──────────     0  1  0
  Slave Present ON (standard) ─────────── o-o                 |S |M |S
                                      - - - o-o               |i |a |l
  Cable Select ──────────────┐         - - 2o-o1              |n |s |a
  Slave Present ON for ───────┘                (front of drive)|g |t |v
   drives that don't have                                     |l |e |e
   the -DASP signal (use                                      |e |r |
   only ONE of the Slave
   Preset choices)
  Spare jumper stored on pins 1-3
```

SEAGATE ST41800W

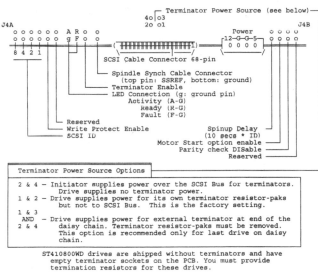

```
                          ┌─ Terminator Power Source (see below)─┐
                         4o│o3
 J4A                     2o│o1              Power           J4B
 o o o o o o A R o o  (::::::::::::::1)   ┌12-G-G-5┐   o o o o
 o o o o o o g F o o  (::::::::::::::1)    0 0 0 0
 8 4 2 1                  SCSI Cable Connector 68-pin
 │ │ │ │      │ │ │
 │ │ │ │      │ │ └── Spindle Synch Cable Connector
 │ │ │ │      │ │       (top pin: SSREF, bottom: ground)
 │ │ │ │      │ └──── Terminator Enable
 │ │ │ │      └────── LED Connection (g: ground pin)
 │ │ │ │                Activity (A-G)
 │ │ │ │                Ready (R-G)
 │ │ │ │                Fault (F-G)
 │ │ │ └─ Reserved
 │ │ └─── Write Protect Enable          Spinup Delay
 │ └───── SCSI ID                       (10 secs * ID)
 │                            Motor Start option enable ─┘
 │                            Parity check DISable ──────┘
 │                            Reserved ──────────────────┘
```

```
┌─Terminator Power Source Options────────────────────────────────┐
│  2 & 4 ─ Initiator supplies power over the SCSI Bus for terminators.│
│           Drive supplies no terminator power.                   │
│  1 & 2 ─ Drive supplies power for its own terminator resistor-paks│
│           but not to SCSI Bus. This is the factory setting.     │
│  1 & 3                                                          │
│   AND  ─ Drive supplies power for external terminator at end of the│
│  2 & 4   daisy chain. Terminator resistor-paks must be removed. │
│          This option is recommended only for last drive on daisy│
│          chain.                                                 │
└────────────────────────────────────────────────────────────────┘
```

ST410800WD drives are shipped without terminators and have empty terminator sockets on the PCB. You must provide termination resistors for these drives.

SEAGATE ST41080N

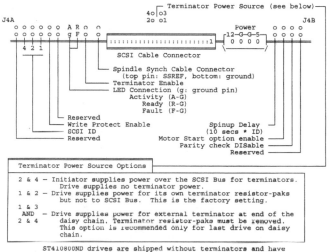

```
                          ┌─ Terminator Power Source (see below)─┐
                         4o│o3
 J4A                     2o│o1              Power           J4B
 o o o o o o A R o o  :::::::::::::::::::::::::1   ┌12-G-G-5┐   o o o o
 o o o o o o g F o o     SCSI Cable Connector      0 0 0 0
   4 2 1      │ │ │
 │ │ │        │ │ └── Spindle Synch Cable Connector
 │ │ │        │ │       (top pin: SSREF, bottom: ground)
 │ │ │        │ └──── Terminator Enable
 │ │ │        └────── LED Connection (g: ground pin)
 │ │ │                Activity (A-G)
 │ │ │                Ready (R-G)
 │ │ │                Fault (F-G)
 │ │ └─ Reserved
 │ └─── Write Protect Enable            Spinup Delay
 │      SCSI ID                         (10 secs * ID)
 └───── Reserved              Motor Start option enable ─┘
                              Parity check DISable ──────┘
                              Reserved ──────────────────┘
```

```
┌─Terminator Power Source Options────────────────────────────────┐
│  2 & 4 ─ Initiator supplies power over the SCSI Bus for terminators.│
│           Drive supplies no terminator power.                   │
│  1 & 2 ─ Drive supplies power for its own terminator resistor-paks│
│           but not to SCSI Bus. This is the factory setting.     │
│  1 & 3                                                          │
│   AND  ─ Drive supplies power for external terminator at end of the│
│  2 & 4   daisy chain. Terminator resistor-paks must be removed. │
│          This option is recommended only for last drive on daisy│
│          chain.                                                 │
└────────────────────────────────────────────────────────────────┘
```

ST410800ND drives are shipped without terminators and have empty terminator sockets on the PCB. You must provide termination resistors for these drives.

SEAGATE ST41600N

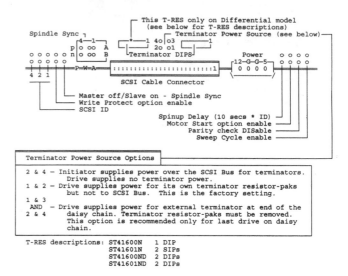

Spindle Sync

```
          This T-RES only on Differential model
          (see below for T-RES descriptions)
              Terminator Power Source (see below)
        1 4o o3
        2o o1
     Terminator DIPS
```

```
4 1
p o oo A
n o oo B
```

P=W=A ::::::::::::::::::::::1 SCSI Cable Connector 12-G-G-5 Power

Master off/Slave on - Spindle Sync
Write Protect option enable
SCSI ID

Spinup Delay (10 secs * ID)
Motor Start option enable
Parity check DISable
Sweep Cycle enable

Terminator Power Source Options

2 & 4 — Initiator supplies power over the SCSI Bus for terminators.
         Drive supplies no terminator power.
1 & 2 — Drive supplies power for its own terminator resistor-paks
         but not to SCSI Bus. This is the factory setting.
1 & 3
AND   — Drive supplies power for external terminator at end of the
2 & 4   daisy chain. Terminator resistor-paks must be removed.
         This option is recommended only for last drive on daisy
         chain.

T-RES descriptions: ST41600N   1 DIP
                     ST41601N   2 SIPs
                     ST41600ND 2 DIPs
                     ST41601ND 2 DIPs

SEAGATE ST41200N

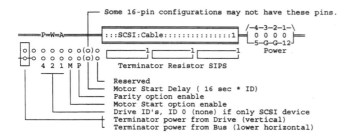

Some 16-pin configurations may not have these pins.

```
P=W=A    :::SCSI:Cable::::::::::::::::1    /-4-3-2-1-\
                                           0 0 0 0
   o o o o o o o(o)o        1      1      1  5-G-G-12-/   Power
   o o o o o o o(o)o
   4 2 1 M P         Terminator Resistor SIPS
```

Reserved
Motor Start Delay (16 sec * ID)
Parity option enable
Motor Start option enable
Drive ID's, ID 0 (none) if only SCSI device
Terminator power from Drive (vertical)
Terminator power from Bus (lower horizontal)

SEAGATE ST43400N

```
          This T-RES only on Differential model
          (see below for T-RES descriptions)
              Terminator Power Source (see below)
        1 4o o3
        2o o1
     Terminator DIPS
```

Spindle Sync

```
4 1
p o oo A
n o oo B
```

P=W=A ::::::::::::::::::::::1 SCSI Cable Connector 12-G-G-5 Power

Master off/Slave on - Spindle Sync
Write Protect option enable
SCSI ID

Spinup Delay (10 secs * ID)
Motor Start option enable
Parity check DISable
Sweep Cycle enable

Terminator Power Source Options

2 & 4 — Initiator supplies power over the SCSI Bus for terminators.
         Drive supplies no terminator power.
1 & 2 — Drive supplies power for its own terminator resistor-paks
         but not to SCSI Bus. This is the factory setting.
1 & 3
AND   — Drive supplies power for external terminator at end of the
2 & 4   daisy chain. Terminator resistor-paks must be removed.
         This option is recommended only for last drive on daisy
         chain.

T-RES descriptions: ST43400N   2 SIPs
                     ST43400ND 2 DIPs

SEAGATE ST42000N

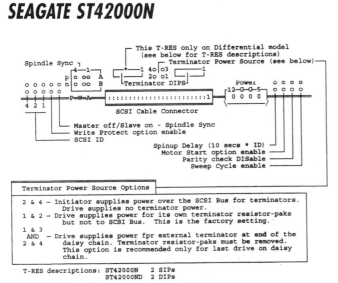

```
          This T-RES only on Differential model
          (see below for T-RES descriptions)
              Terminator Power Source (see below)
        1 4o o3
        2o o1
     Terminator DIPS
```

Spindle Sync

```
4 1
p o oo A
n o oo B
```

P=W=A :::::::::::::::::::::::1 SCSI Cable Connector 12-G-G-5 Power

Master off/Slave on - Spindle Sync
Write Protect option enable
SCSI ID

Spinup Delay (10 secs * ID)
Motor Start option enable
Parity check DISable
Sweep Cycle enable

Terminator Power Source Options

2 & 4 — Initiator supplies power over the SCSI Bus for terminators.
         Drive supplies no terminator power.
1 & 2 — Drive supplies power for its own terminator resistor-paks
         but not to SCSI Bus. This is the factory setting.
1 & 3
AND   — Drive supplies power fpr external terminator at end of the
2 & 4   daisy chain. Terminator resistor-paks must be removed.
         This option is recommended only for last drive on daisy
         chain.

T-RES descriptions: ST42000N   2 SIPs
                     ST42000ND 2 DIPs

SEAGATE ST43401N/ND

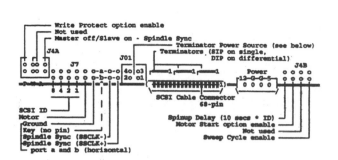

SEAGATE ST4766N

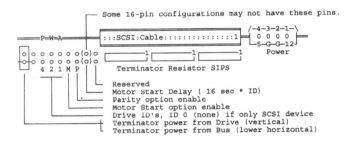

SEAGATE ST9145AG

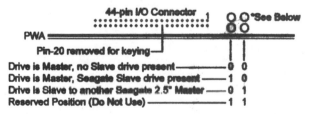

Drive is Master, no Slave drive present ———— 0 0
Drive is Master, Seagate Slave drive present —— 1 0
Drive is Slave to another Seagate 2.5" Master — 0 1
Reserved Position (Do Not Use) ——————— 1 1

*Drive uses +5VDC power supplied to the drive via the interface connector. The drive does NOT make use of a +12VDC power line.
Pin-41 +5VDC - Logic
Pin-42 +5VDC - Motor
Pin-43 - Ground
Pin-44 - Reserved

WESTERN DIGITAL WDAC 1210

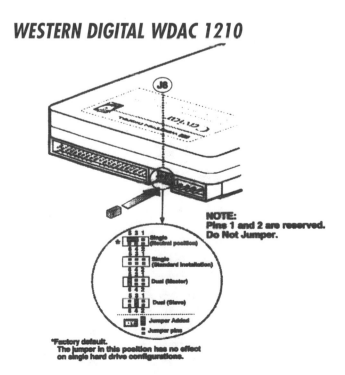

NOTE:
Pins 1 and 2 are reserved.
Do Not Jumper.

*Factory default.
The jumper in this position has no effect on single hard drive configurations.

WESTERN DIGITAL WDAC 1270

WESTERN DIGITAL WDAC 1365

WESTERN DIGITAL WDAC 2200

WESTERN DIGITAL WDAC 2420

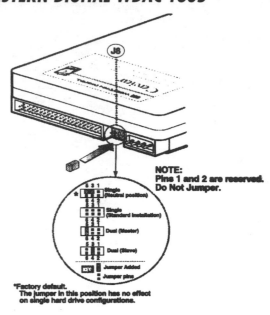
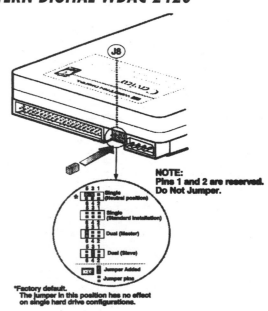
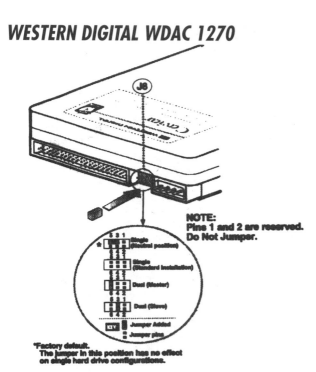
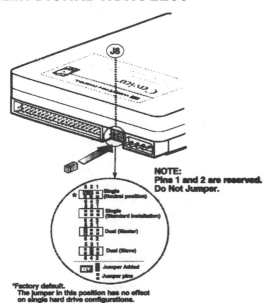

CD-ROM

CD-ROM

Compact Disk Read Only Memory is the future of software distribution. Programs which were once shipped on dozens of floppy disks can now be reproduced inexpensively on a single CD-ROM disk. With over 600 Megabytes of capacity, CD-ROM technology provides a medium for full motion multimedia games, movies, and educational software. This new technology will replace the floppy disk for information distribution in the near future, and may eventually replace some magnetic tape technologies, such as video tape. Well established standards insure media interchange between different CD-ROM drives, platforms, and operating systems.

At the time of this writing, the cost of mass producing a CD-ROM in Hong Kong had dropped to around 50 cents per disk. On a per megabyte basis, CD-ROM is the most inexpensive way to distribute data.

CD MEDIA

CD-ROM disks are built on a transparent polycarbonate plastic substrate. This substrate is coated with a thin aluminum layer. Recordable, write once CD media is identical to mass produced disks, except that the aluminum layer is replaced with a thinner gold metallic layer. CD's store information using microscopic pits in the metal layer that are detected by a minute laser beam. Each pit is approximately 5 by 3 micrometers in size, and there are over a billion pits per disk. Since these pits are much smaller than dust particles, CD's must be manufactured in a clean room environment. To provide an immunity from smaller dust particles and unavoidable scratches, the optical recording layer is placed away from the surface of the plastic disk.

To mass produce CD-ROM's, etched glass CD masters are first made using a photo lithography process. These glass masters are then used to press thousands of disks. Smaller quantities of disks can also be produced on a desktop using a CD-R drive. A CD-R drive uses write-once media and is similar in operation to a WORM drive.

CD-ROM DRIVE OPERATION

Unlike hard disk drives, CD-ROM's are not segmented into multiple tracks of data. Technically, a CD-ROM disk has only one track! The CD-ROM uses a single track of data over three miles long that is wound 50,000 times in a spiral, similar to an LP record. On a CD, data is recorded from the inside of the spiral outwards. A single speed CD-ROM drive spins the disk at varying speeds, starting at 550RPM and working down to about 220RPM. It takes about 75 minutes to read the entire disk at this "single" speed.

Data is encoded using an "EFM" modulation scheme that isn't the ideal way to pack data on an optical disk, but it was chosen to keep the complexity and cost of the CD-ROM and audio player drives down. As the disk spins, a tiny low power laser is focused through a lens onto the surface of the disk. The reflected light from this laser is detected using a photo diode, and the EFM encoded data is detected and sent to the drive electronics. Because a scratch or dust particle can cover thousands of bits of data, a special error correcting system called CIRC (for Cross Interleaved Reed Soloman Code) is used to correct any errors detected by the drive electronics.

Two closed loop servo systems are used in CD-ROM drives. The first system moves the small focusing lens located above the laser to focus it on the disk. The second system moves the entire laser, lens, and photo diode assembly to place it correctly on the spiral.

CD ROM STANDARDS

ISO 9660

ISO-9660 is the current International Standards Organization technical specification which defines the physical format of CD-ROM data. The major contributors to this specification were DEC, Phillips and Sony. This specification evolved from the "High Sierra" format, and is now used in almost all mass produced CD-ROM disks to insure compatibility in the wide range of available drives and systems. The ISO 9660 specification defines file and directory formats, interchange levels, and recording formats. A copy of the ISO 9660 specification can be ordered from ANSI by calling (212)642-4900.

MODE 1

Two "modes" or formats are used to record data on CD-ROM disks. Mode 1 uses more error correction and is the most popular format used today. Each sector recorded in Mode 1 is 2048 bytes, with an additional 280 bytes of error correction data stored at the end of the sector. This error correcting code is in addition to the CIRC codes mentioned above. By adding multiple layers of error correction, MODE 1 significantly increases the reliability of the CD media.

MODE 2

The Mode 2 format is identical to Mode 1, but the error correcting codes are removed. Removing the ECC's yields about 15% more data storage area on the CD by increasing the sector size to 2,336 bytes. Mode 2 disks are also more susceptible to errors. A new Mode 2 disk will typically have three or four errors when played in an average drive. In most audio applications, the Mode 2 format is fine, since the human ear is usually unable to detect these errors. Mode 2 is also often used with graphic files and imaging applications.

CD-ROM XA

The XA format was developed by Microsoft, Sony and Phillips. The XA format has two modes, called FORM 1 and FORM 2. XA FORM 1 is almost identical to MODE 1 format. XA FORM 2 is a new format used for recording compressed audio, video, or graphics. XA FORM 2 is designed so that errors will cause only minute clicks in sound or a tiny dot (pixel) change in a photograph.

CD-I

MPEG is a data compression technique developed by the Motion Pictures Experts Group. CD-I uses MPEG to compress full motion video down to CD-ROM compatible data rates. With CD-I, a complete

74 minutes of video can be recorded on a CD. CD-I players may someday compete with video recorders, since the CD media is less expensive and easier to produce than video tape. At the time of this writing, Phillips was the only manufacturer commercially mass producing a CD-I player for home use. Experts estimate that the cost of a CD-I player will soon be lower than the cost of an equivalent video cassette player. When this happens, CD-I will challenge video tape for commercial distribution of movies.

PHOTO CD

Photo CD is a standardized recording system developed by Kodak for storing high resolution images on CD-ROM disks. Photo CD "service bureaus" are now available across the country. These service bureaus will take your 35mm or professional format film, scan it, and translate it into images on CD. Each image is scanned at high resolution, color corrected, and stored in a proprietary compressed format called YCC, then placed on CD-R disks. The recorded images can be reconstructed in several image resolutions, ranging from 128x192 pixels to 2048 by 3072 pixels in 24 bit color. For fast access, three image formats are stored in uncompressed formats at resolutions up to 512x768 pixels. Kodak's photo CD software converts their 24 bit YCC chroma and luminance data into a 3 by 8 bit RGB format usable in your machine. To save costs, you can use your photo CD disk more than once. If your disk isn't completely full, you may return it to Kodak for additional "multisession" images. The term "multisession" refers to more than one photo CD recordings on a single disk. To use a multisession disk, you will need a CD-ROM drive with multisession compatible firmware.

QUICK TIME

Apple Computer developed Quick Time as a multi platform multimedia format standard. Quick time uses a program called the Movie Manager to combine sound, animation, and video from compressed files. Quick Time movies are low resolution (160x120), but their low data rate is ideal for CD-ROM storage. Quick Time offers a choice of software and hardware compression through a program called Image Compression Manager.

CHOOSING A CD-ROM DRIVE

Insist on the following before purchasing a CD-ROM drive:

- ☞ You must have full MPC level-II compliance.
- ☞ You must have full XA compliance.
- ☞ You must have MODE-1 and MODE-2 compatibility.
- ☞ You may want Multisession Photo CD compatibility.
- ☞ You may want 4X, 6X or faster spin speeds.
- ☞ You will want sub 200ms access times.
- ☞ You may want a SCSI interface.
- ☞ You may want a "caddyless" drive mechanism.

Here's why: You need MPC, XA, MODE 1, and MODE 2 to play the wide range of available CD-ROM disks. You need Multisession if you plan to use Kodak Photo CD's. You'll want quad speed or faster if you are running multimedia games. A faster access time will help if you're transferring a volume of small files from CD-ROM. A SCSI interface is essential for your Mac, and gives more upgradability for your PC. A "caddyless" drive saves you money, by storing disks in jewel cases instead of caddies.

THE MPC STANDARDS

A committee of manufacturers including Microsoft, Intel, and others has developed two standards called MPC level 1 and MPC level 2. These standards the minimum hardware required to run multimedia programs. These standards are significantly less than we recommend below.

MPC level 1 standard requires:
- ☞ A CD-ROM with access time less than 1000ms.
- ☞ A 386SX CPU with 2MB RAM.
- ☞ VGA, 1.33MB Floppy, and an 8 or 16 bit sound card.

MPC level 2 requires:
- ☞ A 486SX CPU with 20MHz or better clock speed.

As you can see, almost any modern PC or CD ROM drive exceeds the MPC level 2 compliance recommendations. So when a drive is touted as "Fully MPC Compliant!", they really aren't saying much.

BUILDING A REAL MULTIMEDIA PC

To build a multimedia PC, or to upgrade your existing PC, you'll need the following:

- ☛ A fast Pentium processor.
- ☛ A PCI video card.
- ☛ A Sound Blaster 2.0 compatible sound board.
- ☛ A quad speed or faster CD drive (SCSI is preferred)
- ☛ A large hard disk if you plan to manipulate images.

Stay within your budget, but the faster the processor the better. If you're manipulating images in a program like Adobe PhotoShop, you may need 32MB or more memory. Full resolution Kodak Photo CD images are 4.5MB each! A PCI 32 bit video board with a Windows accelerator is recommended. A quad speed or faster CD-ROM will help give you smooth video motion. Most multimedia programs require a Sound Blaster 2.0 compatible sound card.

CD-R and CD-WO

CD-R is the new desktop technology that enables you to write a CD-ROM disk. A CD-R drive plugs right into your PC, Mac, or SparcStation, and allows you to burn your own CD's.

CD-R drives use the gold media described above and a high power laser to burn pits into the metallic layer and write disks. These disks are available in all formats and lengths, up to 74 minutes. The blank disks are inexpensive (around $20 in volume). Of course, these disks can be written only once.

Depending on the mastering software you use, you may be able to create disks one track at a time, or you may need to create a complete mastered image on your hard disk (650MB or more of space is required) and then copy this image to the CD-R disk. CD-R writers are available in speeds up to 6X, and they are surprisingly affordable. CD-R drives are available from CSC and other suppliers.

MASTERING YOUR OWN CD-ROM

Yes! The technology is here today to master your own CD-ROM. At the time of this printing, publishing about 100 disks cost less than $1000. To master your own CD, first read about the available formats. You will need to understand them and organize your data to be compatible with them.

Next, shop for CD mastering software. This software is available in all costs and qualities, from free public domain programs to professional programs costing several thousands of dollars. Using this CD mastering software, you can organize your data in the correct file and directory formats required for CD-ROM. Once your data is ready for mastering, you will need to make a "One Off" to test your programs. A "One Off" is made using a CD-R machine as described above. If you plan to mass produce your disk, it would be better to have the same company which will mass produce your disk manufacture the "one off". Your data may be transported to this manufacturing company on Erasable Optical disks, DAT, on 8MM tape, or by actually shipping them a hard drive (not recommended). The following companies are excellent CD-ROM manufacturers:

3M Optical Recording Department
3M Center Building 223
St. Paul, MN 55144-1000
(612)733-2142

Disk Manufacturing, Inc.
1409 Foulk Road, Suite 202
Wilmington, DE 19803
(416)298-8190

Sony Electronic Publishing Company
Recorded Media Division
1800 N. Fruitridge Ave.
Terra Haute, IN 47804
(812)462-8260

US Optical Disk, Inc.
Eagle Drive
Sanford, NE 04073
(207)324-1124

CD HANDLING HAZARDS

Contrary to popular opinion, CD disks are not as rugged as they look. While small scratches on the data side of the disk may not damage data, you can destroy a disk completely by bending it, writing on the top of the disk with a ball point pen, or deeply scratching either side of the disk.

Some data errors can be caused by dust, dirt, or greasy material on the surface of the disk. A spray bottle of lens cleaner and a soft lint free rag can be used to correct this. Treat your CD's with care and they will last a lifetime. Consider buying a caddy for each of your disks, or at bare minimum, store your disks in plastic jewel boxes.

CD drives are also susceptible to contamination with microscopic dust particles. When installing an internal drive, choose the location furthest away from the fan in your computer to prevent the flow of dust into the drive.

FLOPPY DRIVES

FLOPPY DRIVES

At present, the computer industry has standardized the five floppy drive types listed below. 1.44MB drives are the most popular, although a large number of 5.25 and low density 3.5 diskettes still exist in field installations.

INDUSTRY STANDARD FLOPPY DRIVES

Capacity	Tracks	Transfer Rate	Form Factor
360K	40	250KHz	5.25"
1.2MB*	40/80	250/500KHz	5.25"
720K	40	250KHz	3.50"
1.44MB	40/80	250/500KHz	3.50"
2.88MB	80	1000KHz	3.50"
100MB	~700	1000khz+	External Zip Drive

*Note:
Some early 1.2MB drives used a data transfer rate of 300KHz when reading 360K disks.*

FLOPTICAL DRIVES

The original floptical drive standard stored 20MB on a disk. This disk used optical tracking to ìclose the loopî and increase track density. This standard is now obsolete.

ZIP DRIVES

The Bornoullei Zip drive uses high coercivity flexible disk media coupled with imbedded servo to achieve higher densities than standard diskettes. Zip drives store 100MB per cartridge. Zip cartridges donít interchange with standard floppy diskettes. Data transfer rates are slightly faster than 2.88MB drives.

ACCELERATED FLOPPY DRIVES

CSC manufactures accelerated floppy drive/controller kits for workstations and diskette duplication. These drives combine an intelligent controller with 1.5MB cache memory and a special drive mechanism. The drive mechanism uses faster spindle speeds and simultaneous double sided (SDS) data transfer to achieve performance which is typically 10 times that of standard, uncached drives. Call (408) 734-DISK for more information on X10 floppy drives.

FLOPPY DRIVE LIST

The floppy drive list below is designed to aid in identifying some of the more common floppy drives.

Manufacturer	Model No.	Drive Type
CannonMD	5501	1.2MB
Chinnon	F2506	1.2MB
Fujitsu	2532	720K
Fujitsu	2537	1.44MB
Fujitsu	2551	360K
Fujitsu	2553	1.2MB
Mitsubishi	MB4853	360K
Tandon	75-8	1.2MB
Toshiba	FDD4603	720K
Toshiba	FDD6471	360K
Toshiba	FDD6784	1.2MB
Toshiba	FDD6882	1.2MB
Teac	55BV	360K
Teac	55GFV	1.2MB
Teac	FD-235A	1.44MB
Teac	FD-235HG	1.44MB
YE-Data	646	720K

OPTICAL DISK DRIVE TECHNOLOGY

OPTICAL DISK DRIVE TECHNOLOGY

There is a constant struggle between optical and magnetic disk drive manufacturers. Respected industry analysts have predicted that optical drives may replace magnetics in the near future. But hard drive designs keep improving and optical drive manufacturers constantly struggle to approach the capacity and performance of magnetic drives.

In theory, the density of optical media can exceed that of magnetic media. In practice, an optical disk drive engineer faces the same problems encountered in hard drive design.

Recording density is limited by the ability to design a manufacturable system with precise mechanical alignment. Most hard drives employ only one closed loop servo system. Most optical drive employ two or three servo systems. These servo systems interact, making it more difficult to design optical drives for high performance.

The main advantage of today's optical storage devices is removability. Nearly all optical drives feature rugged removable media. This optical media is generally much less expensive than an equivalent hard disk. At the time of this printing, a good 1GB magnetic hard disk drive costs around $200. The equivalent optical drive costs about $1000. The performance of the magnetic drive is roughly twice that of the optical drive. But adding an additional 1GB by purchasing an extra optical cartridge costs only $60. The total cost of 20GB of storage with the optical drive is $2200, but the total cost of a magnetic system is $4000!

Optical removability only makes sense in applications where large amounts of data can be stored without immediate access. Optical drives are popular in applications like online network backup and graphic image storage.

Optical disk drives can be divided into three basic categories: CD-ROM, WORM, and Erasable. CD-ROM drives are read-only devices. CD-ROM disks are mass produced from a glass master using expensive equipment. The cost of producing a CD-ROM disk using this equipment is low in volume. CD-ROMs produced one at a time are called one-off disks. One-offs are produced using a CD compatible WORM disk, called a CD-R drive. See the CD-R chapter for more information on how this is done.

CD-ROM Drives

CD-ROM disks are the future of software distribution. Instead of distributing programs on floppy diskettes, software manufacturers have switched to CD-Rom. In quantity, a 650MB CD-ROM costs around 50 cents to produce. This compares with a cost of 25 cents each for six 1.44MB floppy diskettes. The immense storage capacity, low production cost, and inherent difficulties in making unauthorized copies, make CD-ROM attractive to software manufacturers. When this article was written, the cost of a CD-ROM drive in large quantity had dropped below $30.

WORM Drives

The acronym W.O.R.M. stands for Write Once, Read Many. WORM drives use a laser to ablate (burn) tiny pits in optical media. Once these pits are burned, they cannot be erased. The WORM compensates for this limitation by offering immense storage capacity and removable media. WORM drives are available with capacities of up to 15GB per disk. WORM media is also usually much cheaper than erasable optical media.

Driver software is often used with WORM drives so that the inability to erase becomes invisible to the operating system. When previously recorded files are erased or changed, the old files are mapped out and the available capacity of the WORM disk decreases.

Though the present trend is moving away from WORM drives toward erasable optical drives, the low cost and good performance of

WORM drives still offers an economical solution for data storage where fast access is required.

Erasable Optical Drives

Modern erasable optical drives offer an alternative to large capacity magnetic drives. Although the performance and reliability of erasable optical drives has not yet matched magnetic drives, removability makes them attractive in many applications.

Erasable optical drives do not require driver software for most operating systems since they are functionally identical to hard disk drives. Drive software is needed only for hot cartridge changing of the media while the operating system is running.

Newer erasable opticals record on both sides of the media and store 2600MB or more (unformatted) per cartridge. Erasable optical media is constantly coming down in price, and is now cost-effective for on-line backup.

The newer Hewlett Packard erasable drives offer access times approaching hard disks. These drives are among the highest performance optical drives available.

DVD AND HDCD

The future of WORM disks will lie in one of two competing technologies. The Digital Video Disk (DVD) standard is currently being developed by a consortium of 10 consumer electronics companies, and will likely become an industry standard. DVD disks are double sided and hold 5GB of data per side. This is enough for both computer applications and home video.

DVD's competitor is High Density Compact Disk (HDCD)

IIDCDisks hold 3.7GB per layer. Current standards proposed by Phillips (the original creator of CD-ROM), support 2 layers for a total capacity of 7.4GB per single sided disk. HDCD drives will also be able to read exsisting CD-ROM and CD-audio disks. Although the HDCD standard appears technically more robust than DVD, it won't necessarily become the industry standard. The first manufacturer with volume availability of products will likely determine the market.

OPTICAL DISK CAPACITY

Erasable Drive Capacities

Form Factor	Generation	Capacity	Typical Access
3.5"	1	128MB	65ms
3.5"	2	230MB	35ms
3.5"	3	650MB	30ms
5.25"	1	650MB	65ms
5.25"	2	1.3GB	30ms
5.25"	3	2.6GB	25ms
12"Nikon	1	8GB	40ms

WORM Drive Capacities

Form Factor	Generation	Capacity	Typical Access
CD-R	1	650MB	100ms
DVD	1	5GB	60ms
HDCD	1	3.7GB	60ms
HDCD (2 layer)	2	7.4GB	60ms
12" Sony	1	15GB	40ms

OPTICAL JUKEBOXES

New erasable optical drives offer removability, reliability, and performance approaching hard drive speeds. The catch is that it's tough to find a reliable optical drive that stores more than 2.6GB per cartridge. The simple solution is to add more cartridges. Optical cartridges are cheap, removable, easy to ship, and reliable. Here's where optical jukeboxes fit in. They work just like the old Wurlitzer jukebox at the pool hall.

An optical jukebox is a computer controlled robotics mechanism designed to insert and remove cartridges quickly. Larger jukeboxes (like the HP unit pictured below) may have several drives fed from a library of cartridges. These drives are connected to an array controller that can "stripe" data between cartridges to increase performance. Additional drives can be added to form a RAID style array which can be configured to offer redundancy.

This HP jukebox uses a feed tray to insert cartridges, storing them in the magazine located in the center of the drive. A system of DC servo motors move a "pick arm" which shuttles up and down the stack of cartridges. The pick are also moves horizontally

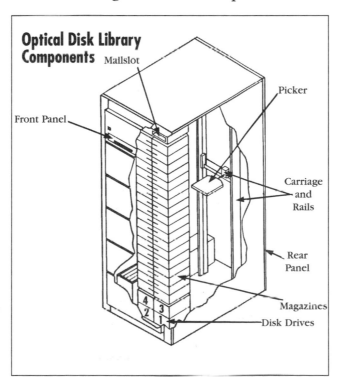

HP Jukebox

to select different stacks and drives. This particular jukebox can "feel" the cartridges by sensing differences in the pressure required to move the pick arm.

The performance of a jukebox is rated in changing time and reliability. Typical changing times range from 5 to 60 seconds per cartridge switch. This makes jukeboxes useful primarily for "near on line" storage applications.

OPTICAL DRIVE SPECIFICATIONS

MODEL NUMBER	FORM FACTOR	TYPE	CAPACITY	ACCESS TIME	INTERFACE	MEDIA	AUDIO
A.D.I.C							
Data Optic 600	5.25"	WMRM	594MB	67ms	SCSI	-	-
A.D.S.I							
MQO-151	5.25"	WMRM	594MB	95ms	SCSI	-	-
MVO-151	5.25"	WMRM	594MB	95ms	SCSI	-	-
MZO-151	5.25"	WMRM	594MB	95ms	SCSI	-	-
Optical/HSC	5.25"	WMRM	594MB	95ms	SCSI	-	-
Accel							
AEO650	5.25"	WMRM	650MB	95ms	SCSI	-	-
Allegro							
PVCD650S	5.25"	RO	650MB	340ms	Prop.	-	-
Alphatronix							
IDQ10-M	5.25"	WMRM	650MB	83ms	Q-BUS	-	-
IDQ20-D,T,S,R	5.25"	WMRM	1300MB	83ms	Q-BUS	-	-
IDU10-M	5.25"	WMRM	650MB	83ms	UNIBUS	-	-
IDU20-D,T,S,R	5.25"	WMRM	1300MB	83ms	UNIBUS	-	-
IMC10-M	5.25"	WMRM	616MB	83ms	SCSI(M)	-	-
IMC20-D,T,S,R	5.25"	WMRM	1232MB	83ms	SCSI(M)	-	-
IPA10-M	5.25"	WMRM	650MB	83ms	XT/AT	-	-
IPA20-D,T,S,R	5.25"	WMRM	1300MB	83ms	XT/AT	-	-
IPN10-M	5.25"	WMRM	650MB	83ms	XT/AT	-	-
IPN20-D,T,S,R	5.25"	WMRM	1300MB	83ms	XT/AT	-	-
IPS10-M	5.25"	WMRM	650MB	83ms	MCA	-	-
IPS20-D,T,S,R	5.25"	WMRM	1300MB	83ms	MCA	-	-
ISS10-M	5.25"	WMRM	592MB	83ms	SCSI(S)	-	-
ISS20-D,T,S,R	5.25"	WMRM	1184MB	83ms	SCSI(S)	-	-
APT Odessa							
ROS-3250EIS	5.25"	WMRM	560MB	107ms	SCSI	-	-

MODEL NUMBER	FORM FACTOR	TYPE	CAPACITY	ACCESS TIME	INTERFACE	MEDIA	AUDIO
Apple Computer							
CD SC	5.25" FH	-	550MB	600ms	SCSI-M	Disk	Yes
Axis Computer							
RO-5030E	5.25"	WMRM	652MB	67ms	SCSI	-	-
ASC							
MO-55	5.25"	WMRM	596MB	49ms	SCSI	-	-
CD Technology							
T3201Portadrive	5.25" FH	-	-	350ms	SCSI-M	Disk	Yes
Chinon							
CDA-431	5.25" HH	-	550MB	350ms	SCSI-M	-	Yes
CDS-431	5.25" HH	-	550MB	350ms	SCSI	-	Yes
CDX-431	5.25" HH	-	550MB	350ms	SCSI	-	Yes
Concurrent							
R/W Optical	5.25"	WMRM	1000MB	49ms	SCSI	-	-
Consan, Inc.							
RS600/N	5.25"	WMRM	596MB	67ms	SCSI	-	-
Corel Systems							
650-MO	5.25"	WMRM	650MB	95ms	SCSI	Cart	-
Deltaic System							
OptiServer 600	5.25"	WMRM	595MB	67ms	SCSI	-	-
OptiServer 650	5.25"	WMRM	595MB	67ms	SCSI	-	-
Denon							
DRD-253	5.25" HH	RO	-	400ms	SCSI	-	Yes
Dophin Systems							
Sonar-600S	5.25"	WMRM	600MB	95ms	SCSI	-	-
Dynatek Systems							
DROS600	5.25"	WMRM	1200MB	50ms	SCSI	-	-
MOS1600	5.25"	WMRM	600MB	50ms	SCSI	-	-
MOS2600	5.25"	WMRM	600MB	50ms	SCSI	-	-
MOS3600	5.25"	WMRM	600MB	50ms	SCSI	-	-
ROS600	5.25"	WMRM	600MB	50ms	SCSI	-	-
Exsys Storage							
Laser RA-2M	5.25"	WMRM	934MB	35ms	SDI	-	-

MODEL NUMBER	FORM FACTOR	TYPE	CAPACITY	ACCESS TIME	INTERFACE	MEDIA	AUDIO
Exsys Storage	**(continued...)**						
Laser RA-2S	5.25"	WMRM	674MB	95ms	SDI	-	-
Laser RA-4M	5.25"	WMRM	1868MB	35ms	SDI	-	-
Laser RA-4S	5.25"	WMRM	1188MB	95ms	SDI	-	-
Laser RA-7M	5.25"	WMRM	3269MB	35ms	SDI	-	-
Laser RA-7S	5.25"	WMRM	2079MB	95ms	SDI	-	-
FWB							
Hammerdisk 1000	5.25"	WMRM	1000MB	35ms	SCSI	-	-
Hammerdisk 600S	5.25"	WMRM	574MB	107ms	SCSI	-	-
General Micro							
MO/D 220	5.25"	WMRM	924MB	35ms	SCSI(S)	-	-
Genstar							
2000	5.25"	RO	650MB	450ms	Prop.	-	-
Herstal							
50652A	5.25"	WMRM	652MB	44ms	SCSI	-	-
51000A	5.25"	WMRM	1000MB	35ms	SCSI	-	-
Hewlett-Packard							
50720A	5.25" HH	RO	-	500ms	PRO	-	-
C1711A	5.25"	WMRM	650MB	107ms	SCSI	-	-
Hitachi							
CDR-1700S	5.25"	RO	600MB	350ms	SCSI	Disk	-
CDR-1750S	5.25"	RO	600MB	320ms	SCSI	-	-
OD-112-1	5.25"	WMRM	644MB	75ms	SCSI	-	-
IBM							
3510-001	5.25"	RO	600MB	380ms	SCSI	-	Yes
0162	3.5"	WMRM	-	-	SCSI	-	-
Laser Magnetics							
CM-201	5.25" HH	RO	600MB	400ms	IDE	Cart	Digital
CM-212	5.25" HH	RO	600MB	400ms	SCSI	Cart	Digital
CM-221	5.25" HH	RO	600MB	500ms	IDE	Cart	Analog
CM-231	5.25" HH	RO	600MB	400ms	SCSI	Cart	Analog
LM-510	5.25" FH	WORM	654MB	61ms	SCSI	Cart	-
LM-520	5.25" FH	WMRM	654MB	70ms	SCSI	Cart	-
D-4100	Rack	WMRM	5.6GB	80ms	SCSI	Cart	-
LF-4500	Rack	WMRM	28.0GB	80ms	SCSI	Cart	-

MODEL NUMBER	FORM FACTOR	TYPE	CAPACITY	ACCESS TIME	INTERFACE	MEDIA	AUDIO
M.O.S.T.							
RMD-5100-S	3.5" HH	WMRM	128MB	35ms	SCSI	-	-
Macsetra							
Genesis 6000	5.25"	WMRM	600MB	95ms	SCSI	-	-
Maxcess							
M-600L	5.25"	WMRM	600MB	95ms	SCSI	-	-
Maxoptix							
RXT-800HS	5.25" HH	WORM	786MB	35ms	SCSI	Cart	-
Tahiti	5.25" FH	WMRM	1GB	35ms	SCSI	Cart	-
Meridian							
100T Network	5.25" HH	RO	-	250ms	-	Disk	N/A
Micro Design							
Laserbank 600CD	5.25" HH	RO	600MB	350ms	SCSI	Disk	Yes
Laserbank 600R	5.25" HH	RO	600MB	350ms	SCSI	Disk	-
Micronet							
SB-SMO/DOS	5.25"	WMRM	586MB	107ms	SCSI	-	-
Mirror Technology							
CDR-10	5.25"	RO	600MB	350ms	SCSI	Disk	Yes
RM600	5.25"	WMRM	594MB	61ms	SCSI	-	-
Mitsubishi							
MW-5D1	5.25" FH	-	300MB	63ms	ESDI	-	-
MW-5U1	5.25" FH	WORM	300MB	68ms	SCSI	-	-
NEC							
CDR-73	5.25" HH	RO	600MB	300ms	SCSI	-	Yes
N/Hance							
R6501mce-DOS,LAN,OS/2	5.25"	WMRM	650MB	95ms	SCSI	-	-
R6501sce-DOS,LAN,MAC	5.25"	WMRM	650MB	95ms	SCSI	-	-
R6501sci-DOS	5.25"	WMRM	650MB	95ms	SCSI	-	-
W6501	5.25"	WMRM	594MB	107ms	SCSI	-	-

MODEL NUMBER	FORM FACTOR	TYPE	CAPACITY	ACCESS TIME	INTERFACE	MEDIA	AUDIO
Ocean							
Tidalwave 650	5.25"	WMRM	564MB	107ms	SCSI	-	-
Online Products							
OPC-OSU-202	5.25" HH	RO	600MB	350ms	SCSI,P	Disk	N/A
Optima							
Concorde	5.25"	WMRM	564MB	107ms	SCSI	-	-
Panasonic							
LF-5010	5.25" FH	WORM	940MB	90ms	SCSI-2	Cart	-
LF-7010	5.25" HH	WMRM	1000MB	90ms	SCSI-2	Cart	-
Pinnacle Microsystems							
REO-130	5.25" HH	RO	128MB	28ms	SCSI,M	Disk	Opt
REO-1300	5.25" HH	WMRM	1300MB	65ms	SCSI,M	Disk	Opt
REO-650	5.25" FH	WMRM	650MB	65ms	SCSI,M	Disk	Opt
REO-6500	5.25" FH	RO	6500MB	65ms	SCSI,M	Disk	Opt
REO-36000	5.25" FH	RO	36000MB	65ms	SCSI,M	Disk	Opt
Pioneer							
DD-U5001	5.25" FH	-	654MB	60ms	SCSI	Cart	-
DE-S7001	5.25"	WMRM	654MB	53m	SCSI	Cart	-
DE-U7001	5.25" FH	WMRM	654MB	53ms	SCSI	Cart	-
DRM-600	5.25" FH	RO	6x540MB	600ms	SCSI	Disk	Yes
DD-8001	8.00" FH	WMRM	1500MB	250ms	SCSI	Cart	-
DJ-1	8.00"	WMRM	1500MB	250ms	SCSI	Cart	-
PLI Peripherals							
Infinity Optical	5.25" FH	WMRM	562MB	107ms	SCSI	Cart	-
CD-ROM	5.25"	RO	600MB	380ms	SCSI	-	-
Procom Technology							
MCDRom-650	5.25"HH	RO	-	350ms	SCSI,M	Disk	Yes
MEOD650/E	5.25"	WMRM	568MB	107ms	SCSI	-	-
Reference Technology							
500AT Dual	5.25" HH	RO	-	500ms	SCSI	Disk	Optical
500AT External	5.25" HH	RO	-	500ms	PRO	Disk	Optical
500AT Ext. SCSI	5.25" HH	RO	-	500ms	SCSI	Disk	Optical
500AT Internal	5.25" HH	RO	-	500ms	PRO	Disk	Optical

MODEL NUMBER	FORM FACTOR	TYPE	CAPACITY	ACCESS TIME	INTERFACE	MEDIA	AUDIO
Reference Technology (continued...)							
500AT Int. SCSI	5.25" HH	RO	-	500ms	SCSI	Disk	Optical
500PS2 External	5.25" HH	RO	-	500ms	PRO	Disk	Optical
500PS2 Ext SCSI	5.25" HH	RO	-	500ms	SCSI	Disk	Optical
Relax Technology							
500AT Dual SCSI	5.25" HH	RO	-	500ms	SCSI	Disk	Optical
Ricoh							
RO-5030E II	5.25" HH	WMRM	652MB	67ms	SCSI	Cart	-
RA-9100H	5.25" HH	WORM	800MB	168ms	SCSI	Cart	-
RS-9200E II	5.25" FH	WMRM	652MB	67ms	SCSI	Cart	-
SONY							
CDU-7205	5.25"	RO	600MB	340ms	IDE	-	-
CDU-7211	5.25"	RO	600MB	380ms	SCSI	-	-
SMO-D501/C501	5.25"	WMRM	650MB	95ms	SCSI	-	-
SMO-S501	5.25"	WMRM	650MB	95ms	SCSI	-	-
SST Storage							
STAK II	5.25"	WMRM	650MB	67ms	SCSI	-	-
Storage Dimensions							
Erasable Optical	5.25"	WMRM	562MB	107ms	SCSI	-	-
LNE1-1000AT	5.25"	WMRM	900MB	49ms	SCSI	-	-
LSE1-1000AT	5.25"	WMRM	900MB	49ms	SCSI	-	-
MCE880-HC1	5.25"	WMRM	900MB	49ms	SCSI	-	-
Summus Company							
SO-600	5.25"	WMRM	594MB	900ms	SCSI	-	-
Sumo System							
RSSM600-C	5.25"	WMRM	594MB	50ms	SCSI	Cart	-
RSSM600 DEC	5.25"	WMRM	594MB	50ms	SCSI	Cart	-
RSSM600S(Sun)	5.25"	WMRM	594MB	50ms	SCSI(S)	Cart	-
Tandy							
CDR-1000	5.25"	RO	600MB	1000ms	Prop	-	-
Techmar							
Laservault	5.25"	WMRM	1000MB	107ms	SCSI	-	-

MODEL NUMBER	FORM FACTOR	TYPE	CAPACITY	ACCESS TIME	INTERFACE	MEDIA	AUDIO
Texel							
DM-5021	5.25"	RO	600MB	340ms	SCSI	-	-
Todd							
TCDR-6000	5.25"	RO	600MB	340ms	Prop	-	-
Toshiba							
TXM-3301-E1	5.25"	RO	600MB	325ms	SCSI	-	-
WM-070	5.25"	WORM	900MB	90ms	SCSI	-	-
XM-3301-A1 MAC	5.25" HH	RO	600MB	350ms	SCSI(M)	-	Yes
XM-3201-A1 PC	5.25" HH	RO	600MB	350ms	SCSI	-	Yes
XM-3201-PS/2	5.25" HH	RO	600MB	350ms	SCSI	-	Yes
XM-3201B	5.25" HH	RO	683MB	350ms	SCSI	Cart	Yes
XM-5100A	5.25" HH	RO	683MB	380ms	SCSI(M)	Cart	Yes
XM-5100A PCF	5.25" HH	RO	683MB	380ms	SCSI	Cart	Yes
XM-5100A PS2	5.25" HH	RO	683MB	380ms	SCSI	Cart	Yes
WM-500	-	WORM	5000MB	160ms	SCSI	Cart	Yes
Trimarchi							
LaserAce	5.25"	WMRM	600MB	45ms	SCSI	-	-
Tristar							
PE3600-1D	5.25"	WMRM	600MB	61ms	SCSI	-	-
PE3660-1DQ	5.25"	WMRM	600MB	61ms	Q-Bus	-	-
PE3660-1R	5.25"	WMRM	600MB	61ms	SCSI	-	-
PE3660-2R	5.25"	WMRM	1200MB	61ms	SCSI	-	-
U.S. Design							
QD1000-Q	5.25"	WMRM	1000MB	35ms	Q-Bus	-	-
QD1000-S	5.25"	WMRM	1000MB	35ms	SCSI	-	-
QD1000-U	5.25"	WMRM	1000MB	35ms	Unibus	-	-
QT1000-Q	5.25"	WMRM	1000MB	35ms	Q-Bus	-	-
QT1000-S	5.25"	WMRM	1000MB	35ms	SCSI(S)	-	-
QT-1000-U	5.25"	WMRM	1000MB	35ms	Unibus	-	-
Xyxis							
XY600RW	5.25"	WMRM	574MB	61ms	SCSI	-	-
Zetaco							
SKR-600	5.25"	WMRM	650MB	95ms	SCSI	-	-

TAPE DRIVES

TAPE DRIVES

Tape Drive Interfaces

L isted below are the most common tape drive interfaces.

FLOPPY TAPE

The Floppy Tape interface is simply an SA-400 floppy drive pinout. Floppy tape drives can be connected just like a floppy drive and usually do not require a separate interface card. There is a performance penalty paid for this convenience though: most floppy tape drives can not transfer data faster than 500Kbits/sec. Some newer floppy controller chips, like the Intel 82078SL and National Semiconductor 8477 can support 1Mbit/sec transfer rates with newer drives. National Semiconductor integrated motherboard floppy and PCI I/O controllers also support 1Mbit/sec transfer rates. Some new chips will support 2Mbit/sec transfer rates, although we aren't aware of any tape drives that can run that fast.

PERTEC

The Pertec standard interface dates back to the mainframe tape drives of the early 70's. Nearly all 9 track reel to reel tape drives use the Pertec interface. Pertec and Fujitsu 9 track drives are still commonly used for information interchange between minicomputers, mainframes, and PC's.

QIC02

QIC-02 is a hardware interface and software command set standard. QIC-02 drives have an imbedded microprocessor which controls them and uses standard commands to read and write blocks of data and control the tape (similar to the SCSI interface). A QIC-02 style command set is also used by most QIC-36 controllers.

QIC-36

QIC-36 is a low level hardware interface used by most all DC600 style tape drives. This interface offers no "intelligence"; it connects directly to the drive motors and heads. An intelligent controller is required to use the QIC-36 interface.

SCSI

The SCSI interface is now used on all of the newer DAT and most 1/4 tape drives. Many companies offer "bridge controllers" that connect QIC-02 and QIC-36 drives to the SCSI bus. Faster high end tape drives are also available with Fast & Wide SCSI-II interfaces.

ESCON

Escon is IBM's standardized high performance mainframe optical fiber interface. Escon is used only on high end tape and disk storage arrays.

FIRE WIRE

The Fire Wire interface has recently been standardized by the IEEE. Fire Wire interfaces are now available on high end tape drives.

Data Compression and Honest Capacity

Since digital tape drives have inherently slow access times, they are used primarily for backup and archival storage and large capacity information transfer. Since most backup and archival processes benefit greatly from data compression, many manufacturers include data compression software with their tape drives. Many also advertise the capacity of the tape drive AFTER DATA COMPRESSION. This advertising is deceptive because the actual storage capacity of the tape will vary depending on how much the incoming data can be compressed before it is recorded. Most data compression schemes will compress typical data to a maximum 2:1 ratio. The actual compression ratio you get will depend on the type of files you are compressing. Most graphics and text files can be easily compressed, while programs generally do not compress well. Some tape drives include data compression algorithms on the drive. Examples of these are the Exabyte 8505CS and Archive DDS-2 autoloaders.

Choosing a Tape Drive

To choose a tape drive, first determine the maximum capacity you need. Beware of deceptive advertising when selecting a drive based on capacity. While certain manufacturers may advertise floppy tape drives with capacities of 800MB or more, many of these drives store less than 300MB of data (not including compression). As we mentioned earlier, many types of data will not compress at all!

Another main consideration in selecting a tape drive is data transfer rate. In PC applications, floppy tape drives are generally the slowest and SCSI drives are generally the fastest available. Using data compression can slow data transfer significantly. The table below lists the backup times and transfer rates of some typical drives tested at CSC. These real world tests were made with a CSC Wide/Narrow SCSI card connected to an Intel 120mhz Pentium motherboard. The actual transfer rate and backup time you achieve will depend on several factors including: processor speed, bus speed, hard drive speed, and controller setup. So the performance you get may differ, but this chart does provide a relative reference.

TAPE DRIVE RELATIVE PERFORMANCE TESTS

Tape Drive:	Archive/Conner 2750 1/4"
Interface :	Fast SCSI-II
Controller:	CSC PCI Wide/Narrow
Rated Capacity:	1350MB
Honest Capacity:	1388MB to end of Tape
Entire tape transfer Rate:	17.5MB/minute
Time to write 100MB:	6 minutes
Average Price (May, 1996):	$195

Tape Drive:	Exabyte 8500CS 8mm
Interface :	Fast SCSI-II
Controller:	CSC PCI Wide/Narrow
Rated Capacity:	5000MB
Honest Capacity:	4870MB to end of Tape
Entire tape transfer Rate:	9.1MB/minute
Time to write 100MB:	10 minutes
Average Price (May, 1996)	$1595

Tape Drive:	Archive/ConnerDDS-2 Autloader P/N 4586NP
Interface :	Fast SCSI-II
Controller:	CSC PCI Wide/Narrow
Rated Capacity:	4000MB per tape, 48GB per 12 tape cartridge
Honest Capacity:	4000MB to end of Tape
Entire tape transfer Rate:	14.6MB/minute
Time to write 100MB:	6 minutes
Average Price (May, 1996)	$895

Tape Drive:	DEC/Quantum DLT 10
Interface :	Fast SCSI-II
Controller:	CSC PCI Wide/Narrow
Rated Capacity:	10GB per tape
Honest Capacity:	10540MB to end of Tape
Entire tape transfer Rate:	14.6MB/minute
Time to write 100MB:	6 minutes
Average Price (May, 1996):	$1795

Tape Drive:	Archive/Conner Travan
Interface :	Floppy Controller
Rated Capacity:	800MB per tape
Honest Capacity:	425MB to end of Tape
Entire tape transfer Rate:	4.5MB/minute
Time to write 100MB:	20 minutes
Average Price (May, 1996):	$149

Tape Drive:	PerSci 9 Track 6250BPI reel-reel
Interface:	Pertec
Controller:	MicroTech
Capacity with 9" tape:	165MB
Transfer Rate:	5MB/minute
Time to write 40MB:	8 minutes
Average Price (May, 1996):	$2195

It's interesting to note that the 8mm drives offer a transfer rate similar to the DAT drives, although advertising purports that 8mm is much faster. The speed of the floppy tape drive was slower than most CD-Writers.

Extended Length Tapes

The maximum capacity of a tape drive can also be increased using an extended length tape. To increase the length of a tape cartridge, the tape material must be made thinner than normal. Some thin tapes tend to tear under heavy use. If you don't need the extra capacity that extended length tapes provide, or if you use your tapes frequently, a standard length tape will prove more reliable. Thinner tapes often have an XL added to the tape part number. The chart below lists the standard capacities of most common standard and extra length tape cartridges.

STANDARD TAPE CAPACITY

Cartridge Type	Length (feet)	Tracks	Capacity (no compression)
DC 100	10MB	16	10MB
DC 1000	100	16	10MB
DC 1000 Alphamat	100	24	20MB
DC 2000	200	24	40MB
DC 2000XL	200	24	60MB
DC 2120	220	30	120MB
DC 2120XL	220	30	170MB
QW5122F	222	30	208MB
.315"Travan TR1	350	30	400MB
DC 615	150	9	15MB
DC 600	600	9	60MB
DC 600A	600	9	60MB

STANDARD TAPE CAPACITY
(continued....)

Cartridge Type	Length (feet)	Tracks	Capacity (no compression)
DC 600A	600	9	60MB
DC 600XTD	600	15	125MB
DC 600XL	960	15	200MB
DC 6135	1000	41	1350MB
.315" 3M Travan TR2	800	24	600MB
.315" 3M Travan TR3	1200	24	1600MB
1/2" IBM 3480 Cart	200	18	200MB
1/2" IBM 3490 Cart	400	36	800MB
1/2" IBM 3490E Cart	400	36	800MB
4MM DAT (DDS-1)	275	Helical Scan	1300MB
4MM DAT (DDS-1)	275	Helical Scan	2000MB
4MM DAT (DDS-2)	275	Helical Scan	4000MB
4MM DAT (DDS-2)	360	Helical Scan	6000MB
8MM Exabyte 8200	175	Helical Scan	2200MB
8MM Exabyte 8500	175	Helical Scan	5000MB
DLT 2.6	200	Serpentine	2600MB
DLT 6.0	200	Serpentine	6000MB
DLT 10.0	200	Serpentine	10GB
Sony ID2	1500	Helical Scan	175GB
Ampex DST	2000	Helical Scan	165GB

Reel to Reel Tapes

9 TRACK 800BPI	2400'	9	20.7MB
9 TRACK 1600BPI	2400'	9	41.5MB
9 TRACK 6250BPI	2400'	9	162MB

Tape Technology Improvements

1/4 Improvements

Minnesota Mining and Manufacturing (The 3M Company) continues to push the capacities of its 1/4 and Travan tapes. In an attempt to enter the midrange market, capacities of 100GB per 1/4 cartridge are planned for late 1998. Tape widths have been increased to .315" per cartridge, and an attempt is being made to make the newer drives downward compatible with older 1/4 cartridges.

Travan

Travan is a 3M trademark for data minicartridges used mainly in PC applications. Travan tapes are up to 750 feet long and are slightly wider (.065") than previous generations of floppy tape minicartridges.

Most manufacturers (including Colorado, Mountain and Conner/Archive) have modified their drives to handle the slightly larger Travan cartridge. Most of these drives can read and write smaller capacity cartridges from the same QIC family. This makes the following tapes generally compatible in newer QIC-80 drives:

DC2120	120MB
DC2120XL	170MB
QW5122F	208MB
TR1(Travan)	400MB

The newer TR3 series of cartridges are available in the following capacities:

DC3010XL	346MB
QW3010XLF	425MB
DC3020XL	692MB
QW3020XLF	850MB
TR3	1600MB

4mm Improvements

Current 4mm DAT drives store between 1.3GB per 90M tape in DDS-1format to 6GB per 120 meter tape in DDS-2 format. Attempts are being made to increase tape lengths to 200 meters while maintaining acceptable reliability. DAT drives already use sophisticated tape tensioning controls to avoid stretching and damaging tapes. New standards should increase DAT capacity to 10GB per cartridge in the near future.

8mm Future Improvements

One manufacturer, Exabyte Corporation, appears to hold a lock on

8mm tape drive production. All their products use the SCSI interface, and have evolved from the original 220KB/sec EXB 8200 2.2GB model that offered good reliability but slow seek times, to the current EXB 8500 series which holds 5GB per tape and transfers at 500 KB/sec. Their new product is called Mammoth and holds 20GB uncompressed per cartridge, at sustained transfer rates of 1.1MB/s. As of May, 1996, the Mammoth had not reached the market in volume. DLT drives are significant competitors to 8mm products, and may overtake Exabyte drives in the future.

DLT Future Improvements

DLT was originally developed by DEC in the late 1980's, and stands for Digital Linear tape. DEC grew the technology to hold over 10GB per tape. Quantum purchased this production line from DEC in 1995. Development continues on tapes that will hold over 50GB in the near future. DLT drives hold the best reputation for reliability and have fast transfer rates (1.265MB/sec sustained for DLT20 drives). Prices on DLT drives are significantly higher than 8mm drives, but in mission critical applications, the extra reliability may be worth it. DLT drives have a good reputation for downward compatibility, so you can expect the newer drives to read DLT tapes you may already have. DEC also builds autoloaders for these drives.

ID1 and ID2 Tape drives

4mm and 8mm tape drives were originally intended for consumer applications like Digital Audio Tape and video camcorders. Two types of video tape (D1 and D2) have now been adapted for computer data storage. These 3/4 helical scan drives are produced by Sony Corporation, and are highly modified versions of professional video recorders. These drives pump data at up to 40MB/sec an store up to 175GB per tape. These high end drives are extremely expensive (around $125K), but transfer rates are impressive, and they provide good competition for tape drive arrays in fast applications. Sony continues to improve the reliability and tape wear characteristics of these drives. Capacities over 250GB per tape are expected soon.

CSC BENCHMARK TESTS

CSC Benchmark Tests

CSC has selected several high performance drives for review. The average seek times are those advertised by the manufacturer, along with actual test results. Seek times were tested on Flexstar factory testers of the type used for factory final test.

Our PCI test computer was an Intel PCI motherboard with a 120MHz Pentium Processor. We used the CSC PCI wide/narrow controller to connect SCSI drives, and the on-board IDE connector for testing IDE drives.

Model:	Maxtor 71626AP E-IDE
Formatted Capacity:	1620MB
Rated Average Seek:	14
Tested Average Seek:	13.7
Rated MTBF:	300,000 hours
Average Data Transfer Rate:	3,105KB/sec

Model:	Conner CFP31200A E-IDE
Formatted Capacity:	1200MB
Rated Average Seek:	15ms
Tested Average Seek:	15.3ms
Rated MTBF:	350,000 hours
Average Data Transfer Rate:	2,630KB/sec

Model:	Western Digital WDAP200 IDE
Formatted Capacity:	212MB
Rated Average Seek:	12ms
Tested Average Seek:	14.7ms

Rated MTBF:	150,000 hours
Average Data Transfer Rate:	1,420KB/sec

Model:	Seagate ST15150WC SCA
Formatted Capacity:	4200MB
Rated Average Seek:	8ms
Tested Average Seek:	8.2ms
Rated MTBF:	300,000 hours
Average Data Transfer Rate:	5,240KB/sec

Model:	Seagate ST32550W WIDE
Formatted Capacity:	2100MB
Rated Average Seek:	8ms
Tested Average Seek:	8.6ms
Rated MTBF:	300,000 hours
Average Data Transfer Rate:	4,130KB/sec

Model:	Micropolis 2217AV
Formatted Capacity:	2044MB
Rated Average Seek:	10ms
Tested Average Seek:	9.2ms
Rated MTBF:	300,000 hours
Average Data Transfer Rate:	3,110KB/sec

SOFTWARE

SOFTWARE

The software included with the Hard Drive Bible is a collection of disk utilities that you will find useful. This software is copyrighted by the various authors of the programs and provided through the courtesy and with the written permission from manufacturers including Maxtor Corporation and Seagate Technologies. Some of the programs are referred to as "shareware", which is a means of distributing software for evaluation before paying for it.

All of the programs have their own documentation and indicate whether a fee is required after an evaluation period. A software utility called PKUNZIP is provided by PKWare, Inc., and is used by typing:

PKUNZIP<filename>

If you need a manual for a difficult to find drive (including those not listed in the jumpers section), try our automatic document printer. To install the document printer, type:

HDBDOC<return>

or select it from the Windows file manager. The document printer includes manuals for CSC products, including the disk drives sold by CSC.

DISCLAIMER

CSC, DTC, Maxtor Corporation, and Seagate Technology expressly disclaim any liability which may arise from the use of the software included with the Hard Drive Bible. To the best of our knowledge, this software is workable and free of any major bugs, but no guarantee of performance of fitness for any particular application is made. This software is provided free of charge, but may not be duplicated without consent as listed below.

COPYRIGHT NOTICE

These programs are copyrighted by their respective authors and may not be reproduced in any form without proper written consent. The software enclosed is protected by US copyright law. Additional copyright and disclaimer notices may be contained in the files.

This list of the most commonly used CD-ROM files is provided by Maxtor Corporation:

1ADAY10.ZIP   MAIN
>	116K 09/92 Run files daily, weekly, monthly
>	Runs files once a day, weekly, or on a certain day of the month.

2SOCKET.DOC   PCMCIA
>	2.7K 11/94 Socket App for >=10MB flashcards
>	2-Socket application for 10MB or greater Flashcards. This docu ment is in WS for Windows 2.0 Format.

3DRVS260.ZIP   MAIN
>	73K 11/93 Driver for 3 drives in one system
>	Device driver to add a 2nd 16bit HDD interface to your DOS AT (286+) system. Windows compatible.
>	Shareware, version 2.60 by Dustbowl Designs

4DRVU100.ZIP   MAIN
>	32K 11/93 Inquiry utility for up to 4 drives
>	Inquiry for drives on both primary and secondary drive ports.
>	Shareware, V1.0 by Dustbowl Designs.

4SPD100.ZIP   MAIN
>	64K 11/93 Graphical HDD data transfer rate test utility
>	Graphical Hard Drive Test utility.
>	Shareware, V1.0 by Dustbowl Designs

7000LLF.EXE   MAIN
>	47K 03/96 7000 A series Low Level Format program
>	Self-extracting zip file.

7000LLF.EXE   MAIN

    47K 03/96 7000A series Low Level format program.
    Self-extracting zip file.

ACCULOG.TXT   3RDPARTY

    5.9 10/93 Acculogic IDE controller card documentation.

AMIGA.ZIP   MAIN

    3.5K 12/93 Notes on installing IDE & SCSI's on Amiga
    Amiga computer installation notes and tips.

AN001HP.DOC   PCMCIA

    15K 1MB Flashcard install into HP 95LX PC
    1MB Flashcard installation procedure for HP 95LX Palmtop PC.
    This document is in MS Word for Windows 2.0 format.

AN002HP.DOC   PCMCIA

    12K 11/94 2MB+ Flashcard install into PP 95LS PC
    2MB thru 20MB Flashcard installation procedure for HP 95LX
    Palmtop PC. This document is in MS Word for Windows 2.0 format.

AN003HP.DOC   PCMCIA

    12K 11/94 1MB Flashcard install into HP x00LX PC
    1MB Flashcard installation procedure for HP 100LX/200LX
    Palmtop. This document is in MS Word for Windows 2.0 format

AN004HP.DOC   PCMCIA

    10K 11/94 2MB+ Flashcard install into HP x00LX PC
    2MB thru 20MB Flashcard installation procedure for HP 100
    LX/200LX Palmtop PC. This document is in MS Word for Windows
    2.0 format.

ASPITOOL.ZIP   MAIN

    2.4K 06/92 Tahiti Temp (TX-TEMP) /Scan
    (SCANS The To Files (TX-TEMP/SCANSCSI) are to little tools to
    check the temperature of a MaxOptix Tahiti Sub-System
    (TX-TEMP) and Scanning all Host Adapters for SCSI-Devices
    (SCANSCSI). All you need is an ASPI-DOS Driver installed for
    each Host Adapter.
    Christoph Kummer/datacomp ag/Switzerland

AT_V1.ZIP   MAIN
11K 09/92 ASPI-TOOLS
ASPI-Tool contains some programs such as SCSISCAN,
UNITATTN.EXE, TX-TEMP.EX, FMT-512, FMT-1024. Please
put this file on the Banyon for Michael Davis, Maxtor UK.

AUTOCORE.EXE   MAIN
101K 02/95 Runs CORETEST in "automatic" mode. That is,
it executes Coretest several times changing bl size each time.
CORETEST TEST UTILITY

BEEPCODE.DOC   MAIN
652 11/93 Beep error codes for AMI BIOS's
List of what errors the Beep codes stand for in the American
Megatrends International BIOS.

BIOSBNC.ZIP   MAIN
159K 08/93 BIOS Bench Mark
Maxtor's BIOS Benchmark Program.   Sorry, no documents,
how to use it and interpretation of results is up to you.

OTT140.ZIP   MAIN
81K 10/93 Boot Mgt Pgm
Manages boot up environments, ie: different CONFIG.SYS and
AUTOEXEC.BAT

CACHE.EXE   MAIN
3.6K 08/93 Turn 7000A CACHE on or off.

CARD112.EXE   PCMCIA
49K 06/94 Cardlock - Lock access to MobileMax Drvs
Cardlock V1.12 Limits acccss to your MobileMax card with
single or multiple passwords.

CARDTALK.EXE   PCMCIA
618K 11/94 Cardtalk V2.20.15 drivers for deskrunner
Cardtalk V2.20.15 drivers for Maxtor's Deskrunner PC/AT
PCMCIA adapter.
Self-extracting ZIP file.

CLEAN112.ZIP   MAIN
271K 03/94 McAffee Virus Clean V112.

COMPORT.DOC   PCMCIA
    4.2K 11/94 Deskrunner COM Port problem tips
    Some solutions for COM port problems encountered while
    installing Deskrunner. This document is in MS Word for
    Windows 2.0 format.

CORETEST.EXE   MAIN
    64K 05/88 CORETEST - Hard disk benchmark utility.

CT-303.EXE   PCMCIA
    944K 07/94 Cardtalk V3.03 for Maxtor Deskrunner
    Self-extracting ZIP file.

DBK310.ZIP   PCMCIA
    1.1 05/95 Latest release of Desk Runner Drivers.
    5/11/95

DESKRUNR.TXT   PCMCIA
    4.7K 01/94 PC/AT Adapter for desktop computers.

DISABLE   MAIN
    23K 10/93 MAC pgm. Make MXT drives MAC Compat.
    Makes MXT-1240s & mxt-540Sl Macintosh compatible by
    disabling Unit Attention. MAC Pgm should have Extent of NIT!

DISK.ID   PCMCIA
    63 07/94 Correct ID file for DRUNR303.EXE.

DMOS2INS.TXT   MAIN
    4.4K 04/95 Installation procedure for Disk Manager and OS
    Written by: David Meisner.
    For reference only. Contact IBM for support.

DO-ONC14.ZIP   MAIN
    10K 10/92 Run a file once a day or week
    Runs a file once a day or once a week on bootup, for instance;
    CHKDSK 1st thing in the morning or a Virus Check every
    Monday.

DQWIK211.ZIP   MAIN
    129K 08/94 DiskQwik v2.11 - D.Driver activates IDE block
    mode transfer.

DRS120.ZIP   MAIN

114K 02/92 Data Recovery Software. Reads BAD disks.

DRVSYS.TXT   PCMCIA

2.0K 11/94 Adjusting CardTalk Drv Letter Assignment
How to use DRIVER.SYS to reassign the drive letter for your
PCMCIA Hardrive in a DESKRUNNER PCMCIA Adapter.

DSKPDR.EXE   MAIN

69K 10/93 HDD Diagnostic Pgm V1.6 Self-extracting
Tests IDE drives, either destructive or non-destructive.
By Larry Clanton
Self-extracting Zip file.

DSK_APP.DOC   PCMCIA

5.2K 11/94 Deskrunner installation tips
Troubleshooting tips for installing MobileMax 1.8" hard drive
disks into Deskrunner PC/AT to PCMCIA adapter. This
document is in MS Word for Windows 2.0 format.

DUGIDE10.ZIP   MAIN

12K 01/93 Show the IDE disk info. Includes C source code.

DYNABOOT.ZIP   MAIN

32K 10/93 Boot Mgr Pgm
Boot up management, ie: different AUTOEXEC.BAT and
CONFIG.SYS files.

ESDI.ZIP   MAIN

13K 08/93 Spec & Jumpers for ESDI drives
Specifications & jumpers for all ESDI drives.

ESDIDISK.EXE   MAIN

63K 08/93 Compsurf Novell 2.15C w/WD1007-9 Ctlr
A version of "Compsurf" to initialize Maxtor ESDI drives for
Novell Versions 2.15 to 2.2 (use this instead of the Novell
supplied version of Compsurf). ESDI controllers ONLY!

ESTIM11.ZIP   MAIN

22K 11/94 Estimate storage needs for back-up of files on
hard disk.

FAQ20A.ZIP   MAIN
        22K 07/92 Frequently Asked Questions about OS/2 v2.0

FBECCS.ZIP   MAIN
        11K 10/93 FBE Config Control Sys V1.5
        Boot manager program.

FIPS12.ZIP   MAIN
        104K 11/94 FIPS: Nondestructive partition split utility.

FLEXP300.ZIP   MAIN
        217K 07/93 Flexiback Plus:
        Hard disk backup with compression.

FRE561.ZIP   MAIN
        20K 01/94 Multi-drive disk space check info with graphic
        display.

GEOCLOCK.ZIP   MAIN
        103K 10/93 Colorful world clock/map
        Shows world map with daylite/night time shadow.

GREENDRV.ZIP   MAIN
        11K 04/94 To place 7000A drives in "sleep mode".
        Programmable standby mode. Cause drive to spin down and
        park after X amount of time with no activity. X = 20 sec. to
        21.2 minutes. Energy Star compiant, AKA Green PC. (Replaces
        SPINDOWN.EXE).
         Version 2.2 by Sean Dykstra

HIDDIR.ZIP   MAIN
        45K 08/93 Creates and manipulates hidden Dir's.
        Creates and manipulates Hidden directories under the MS/PC
        DOS environment. Great for parents with curious kids, and
        vice versa. Doesn't show up in DOS nor in Windows, but are
        nonetheless still accessible.   Source code included, Quick
        Pascal 1.0

IDE.DOC   IDE
        2.7K 01/94 Generic "How To" IDE installation
        IDE Installation example.

IDE.EXE   MAIN

    59K 02/94 Self-Extracting ZIP of all IDE drives
    Same as the IDE.ZIP file. All IDE drive specifications, jumpers,
    and parameters.

IDE.ZIP   IDE

    69K 09/94 Data on all Maxtor IDE drives
    Specifications, parameters and jumper settings for Maxtor IDE
    drives.

IDE.ZIP   MAIN

    56K 02/94 Specs & Jumpers for all IDE Drives
    Specifications & jumper settings for all IDE Drives.

IDEID150.ZIP   MAIN

    25K 08/93 Displays info on IDE drives.

IDEINF10.ZIP   MAIN

    30K 08/94 Displays info on IDE drives, including ATA-2.

IDEINFO.ZIP   MAIN

    3.8K 01/93 Excellent utility reads IDE firmware.

IDENTIFY.EXE   MAIN

    27K 03/94 To identify IDE drives, Cyl, Hds, Sect.
    Identify IDE drives, finds cylinders, heads, sectors per track
    etc., also shows serial number.

IDE_CMOS.TXT   IDE

    6.7K 09/94 Parameter listing for IDE drives
    List of CMOS parameter settings for all IDE drives.

IDE_CMOS.TXT   MAIN

    6.7K 09/94 CMOS Parameters for all IDE Drives
    CMOS setup parameters for all Maxtor IDE drives.

IDE_CTLR.TXT   IDE

    1.9K 09/93 Maxtor IDE adapter card
    Jumper settings, ANSII drawing for Maxtor IDE adapter card.

LXTLLF.EXE   MAIN

    37K 03/96 Low Level format program for LXT-xxxA drives.
    Self-extracting file.

LXTLLF.EXE   IDE

    37K 03/96 Low Level format program for LXT-xxxA drives.
Self-extracting file.

MAX-AT.ZIP   MAIN

    85K 10/93 Maxtor IDE test program
Maxtor IDE drive test program.

MAXBLAST.EXE   MAIN

    354K 05/95 Ontrack's Disk Manager v6.03.05
Max-Blast software is required to install drives larger than 528
megabytes on a standard IDE interface or on an older BIOS.
NOTE: *If you are using an EIDE interface this file is NOT
required, use the drivers provided with your interface for
correct installation.
* Providing your BIOS or interface support LBA.
USEAGE: MAXBLAST -d
This creates the sub-directory for OS/2

MAXOPTIC.ZIP   MAIN

    815 05/93 Diagnostic Utility for Maxoptic Products
Read, write, compare, low-level format any Maxoptics products -
Tahiti, RXT, etc.

MAXTEST.ZIP   MAIN

    131K 10/93 Test/Modify SCSI Drives
This is a test program for MAXTOR SCSI drives. This program
must be used with the Adaptec 154XX Or Bustek 54XX. For
more information on this program call Tech Support at
1-800-2MAXTOR. (If you don't have PKZIP, DI, MAXTESTS.EXE)

MAXTESTS.EXE   MAIN

    134K 10/93 MAXTEST (Self-extracting ZIP)
To modify SCSI drive data table (capacity, bytes per sector, etc).
Must be used with and Adaptec 154X controller (or compatible).
Self-extracting Zip file.

MINISCRB.ZIP   MAIN

    56K 04/94 Text file on all MiniScribe drives
Covers all MiniScribe drives. May not cover all jumpers tho!
Call 800-262-9867, Option 3 for FAX info Miniscribe jumper
setting info.

MXLINIT.EXT   PCMCIA
　　　21K 03/94 Initialize MobileMAX 105MB Drive
　　　To initialize the MobileMAX (MXL-105) PCMCIA drive.

MXTA_53.EXE   MAIN
　　　41K 03/94 MXT540A/AL Firmware Rev 5.3
　　　MXT540A/AL Firmware Rev 5.3 code.

MXTA_54.EXE   MAIN
　　　40K 03/94 MXT540A/AL Firmware Rev 5.3
　　　Firmware Upgrade for MXT_540AT Drive. Use only if you
　　　have a problem, or it is recommended by a technician.
　　　Self-extracting ZIP file.

MXTA_55.EXE   MAIN
　　　40K 03/94 MXT 540A/AL Firmware Rev 5.5
　　　Firmware Upgrade for MXT-540AT Drive. Use only if you
　　　have a problem, should be recommended by a technician.
　　　Self-extracting ZIP file.

MXTA_60.EXE   MAIN
　　　41K 03/94 MXT 540A/AL Firmware Rev 6.0
　　　Firmware Upgrade for MXT-540AT Drive. Use only if you have a
　　　problem, or it is recommended by a technician.
　　　Self-extracting ZIP file.

MXTLLF.EXE   MAIN
　　　30K 04/96 Low Level Format FOR MXT6540A/AL ONLY^M
　　　Self-extracting zip file.

MXTLLF.EXE   IDE
　　　30K 04/96 Low Level Format FOR MXT6540A/AL ONLY
　　　Self-extracting zip file

MXT_1-5.ZIP   MAIN
　　　205K 01/94 MXT-540/1240S Firmware Upgrade to V1.5
　　　MXT-540S/SL MXT-1240S Firmware upgrade Version 1.5.

MXT_SPIN.ZIP   MAIN
　　　175 04/94 MXTxxxxS Spinup delay program
　　　Spinup delay modification for MXT1240S & MXT540S/SL
　　　drives. For use if you don't have a big enough power supply
　　　to power more than one SCSI drive up at a time. Inserts a 11-13
　　　second spinup delay between drives.

OMNIBK.DOC   PCMCIA

    4.0K 11/94 MXL install tips for HP OmniBook300/430 into

    HP OmniBook 300/430 laptop systems.

    This document is in MS Word for Windows 2.0 format.

ONBOOT.ZIP   MAIN

    5.4K 10/93 Control autoexec program executions

    Have AUTOEXEC programs run daily, on Warmboot only, or on

    Coldboot only.

OS2IBM75.DOC   PCMCIA

    6.6K 11/94 MXL install for IBM Thinkpad 750 - OS/2

    Tips for MXL drive install into IBM Thinkpad 750 using

    OS/2. This document is in MS Word for Windows 2.0 format.

OS2TOSH.DOC   PCMCIA

    7.1K 11/94 MXL install tips for Toshiba - OS/2

    Configuration of MXL hard drive in Toshiba T4500, T4600,

    T4700 systems running OS/2 ver 2.1. This document is in

    MS Word for Windows 2.0 format

PARKIT.ZIP   MAIN

    9.4K 09/92 HDD Head park pgm

    Hard Disk Head parking utility V1.0 by Andrew Appel.

PART.ZIP   MAIN

    23K 01/94 Provides HD partition table & controller info.

PC-PARK.ZIP   MAIN

    1.1K 09/92 Head Parking Pgm from PC Mag

    PC Magazine HDD head parking program.

PCMATA.SYS   MAIN

    18K 04/95

PCMCIA.EXE PCMCIA

    9.0K 01/94 Self-Extract file of all PCMCI devices

    Self-extracting ZIP file of all PCMCIA devices (MobileMax,

    MobileMax Flash, DeskRunner)

PCMCIA.ZIP   PCMCIA

    6.0K 01/94 ZIP file of all PCMCIA devices.

PKUNZIP.EXE   MAIN
28K 03/93 PKUNZIP.EXE V2.04G
PKUNZIP V2.04G 2.1.93.

PKZ204G.EXE   MAIN
197K 03/93 Self-extracting PKZIP V2.04G 2/1/93
PKZIP V2.04G 2/1/93 self-extracting file. Contains PKZIP,
PKUNZIP, etc.

PLUGNGO.TXT   3RDPARTY
1.2K 05/94 Plug N Go External Parallel IDE Adapter
Adapter to allow use of a 1" high 3.5" IDE drive in an external
cabinet w/power supply, IDE to Parallel adapter and software to
install.

PRESZ110.ZIP   MAIN
58K 12/94 The Partition Resizer.
Safe HD repartitioning.

QDPMI101.ZIP   MAIN
70K 03/93 QuarterDeck DOS Protected Mode Interface
DOS Protected Mode Interface V0.9 by QuarterDeck. A
companion to QEMM386. Allows PKZIP/UNZIP to use EMS/UMB
memory and speed up execution dramaticly! ZIP'd w/V2.04G.

QINFO42.ZIP   MAIN
55K 10/93 Quick Info, on Drives, CPU, Speed, etc
Nice display of Drives with usage and space left, CPU type,
speed, etc.

RDP391.LHA   MAIN
98K 05/93 Amiga IDE read multiple fix V3.91
Latest version of RDPREP for Amiga. Fixes read multiple
problems by informing the Amiga to only use 255 sector
blocks instead of 256. This keeps the data intact.

REBOOTER.ZIP   MAIN
3.6K 10/93 How to build an auto-builder for a BBS.
How-to-text file. If your BBS hangs while no one is around,
build this device to automatically reboot the system.

RIPTM153.ZIP   MAIN
584K 01/94 Ripterm v1.53
RIP graphics communication package. Try it on this BBS!

R_UTILS.ZIP   3RDPARTY
>110K 10/93 Reynolds Data Recovery Utility Demo.

SALES.ZIP   MAIN
>1.5K 10/93 Maxtor Nat'l sales office listing
>Maxtor Sales Office Information.

SCABV112.ZIP   MAIN
>252K 03/94 McAfee virus scanner (Feb 1994).

SCN-216E.ZIP   MAIN
>364K 02/95 VirusScan for DOS new version 2.1.5
>(216)02/23/95 by McAfee, Inc.
>Scans and cleans PC's/LAN's for known and new viruses.
>Requires DOS 3.0+

SCOPE140.EXE   MAIN
>99K 10/93 RS232 Data Analyzer Scope SelfExtracting
>View RS232 data streams to analyze modem/comm problems.
>V1.40

SCSI.DOC   MAIN
>1.7K 01/94 Generic "How To" SCSI Installation.

SCSI.DOC   SCSI
>1.7K 01/94 Generic "How To" SCSI Installation.
>SCSI installation example.

SCSI.ZIP   MAIN
>205K 05/93 Specs & Jumpers for all SCSI Drives
>Specifications & jumper settings for all SCSI Drives.

SCSI.ZIP   SCSI
>205K 11/93 Specs & jumpers for all SCSI Drives.

SCSI2GO.DOC   PCMCIA
>3.2K 11/94 MXL install for FD SCSI2GO w/Deskrunner
>Configuration of Future Domain SCSI2GO PCMCIA
>Controller Kit with the Mobilemax Deskrunner. This document
>is in MS Word for Windows 2.0 format

SEEKTIME.TXT   MAIN
>3.5K 08/93 How drive seek times are determined
>Document explaining seektime measurment.

SIDE3.TXT   IDE

1.8K 12/93 Acculogic sIDE-3 IDE Adapter card
IDE-3 Adapter. ANSII Drawing, jumpers, etc.

SMRTDTXT.ZIP   MAIN

9.4K 09/92 Text File:MS SMARTDRIVE.SYS & DblBuffer
Text file from MicroSoft about using Smartdrive & Double
Buffering

SPINUP.EXE   MAIN

42K 05/93 For Panther drives to set Spinup option
For Panther PO-12S or P1-17S drives with "Origional"PCBs.
This program sets the Spinup Option to spin when power is
applied, or spin up by SCSI ID sequence, or spin up each
drive in 13 second intervals. Panther drives with "Common"
PCBs use jumpers and don't need this program.

STACK.ZIP   PCMCIA

177K 05/95 Stacker files, preloaded on flashcards.

TCAL   MAIN

24K 07/94 MXT-S Thermal Calib. on/off for MAC
For MXT-1240S & MXT-540SL Drives. For Macintosh computers
Turn TCAL on or off for data streaming. Caution! Let drive
"warm up" for about 1 hour before using. Do NOT leave TCAL
disable for too long, or drive crash will result.

TCAL.EXE   MAIN

24K 07/94 Turn MXT-S Thermal Calibration on/off
For MXT-1240S & MXT-540SL drives. Turn T-Cal on or off from
this program. Use with caution, let drive "warm up" for
leastone hour befor using. Leaving TCAL off too long (>1 hr)
could crash the drive!!! Self-extracting zip file.

TFFS325.ZIP   PCMCIA

533K 04/95 True Flash Driver v3.2.05
USEAGE: PKUNZIP TFFS325.ZIP

TIMEPARK.ZIP   MAIN

8.9K 09/92 HDD timed head parking pgm
HDD head parking program, moves heads to parking zone after
selectable period of HDD inactivity.

UNITATTN.EXE   MAIN

     2.3K 0892 Checking UNIT-ATTENTION on SCSI Device
     This program is for checking the Unit-Attention (enabled or
     disabled) on every connected SCSI device supported by the
     Adaptec-ASPI-Driver.

USABBS.ZIP   MAIN

     72K 01/95 An extensive listing of USA BBS's!

USAFAX.ZIP   MAIN

     48K 01/95 Over 100,000 FAX numbers! A must have!

UU520.ZIP   MAIN

     32K 06/94 YYENCODE/UUDECODE for DOS V5.20
     For ASCII encoding and decoding of binary files. Useful
     for exchanging files through Internet EMail attachments when
     binary attachments won't work.

V10N04.ZIP   MAIN

     61K 10/93 PCMag 2/26/92 Incl. MBOOT Boot Manager Program
     PC Magazine Vol 10, Number 4. Includes MBOOT boot manager
     program.

VIRSIM2C.ZIP   MAIN

     65K 11/94 Virus Simulator Ver 2C<ASAD><ASP>
     Audit and demonstrate anti-virus protection.
     Rosenthal Engineering's absolute neccessity for anyone serious
     about virus defense, security and training. "Unreservedly
     recommended!" by Computer Virus Developments Quarterly.
     Used in tests conducted by National Software Testing Labs for
     Software Digest and PC Digest. Written about in Computerworld,
     Virus Bulletin, Virus News Int., Telecomputing, etc.

WASTED10.ZIP   MAIN

     28K 12/94 Reports disk space WASTED due to cluster size.

WFWG_FIX.TXT   MAIN

     789 01/94 Win for WkGrps Fast File Access "Fix"
     If you're having problems with Windows for Workgroups,
     "Fast File Access" not working or working slowly, try these
     changes.....

WFWIN5.ZIP   MAIN

     952K 03/95 IBM Driver for OS/2 for drives larger than 528

WPAPERS.ZIP   PCMCIA
                33K 04/94 PCMCIA White Papers (about PCMCIA)
                PCMCIA Whitepapers

SYSTEM NOTES

Use the following pages to enter data pertaining to your system. This information may be required if you need to call a dealer for technical assistance or if you have a system failure.

Computer

Make: _____

Model: _____

Serial Number: _____

Monitor

Make: _____

Model: _____

Serial Number: _____

System BIOS

Make: _____

Version: _____

Motherboard

Make: _____

Model: _____

Serial Number: _____

Bus Speed: _____

Wait States: _____

Memory Installed: _____

Floppy Drive A

Make: _____

Model: _____

Capacity: _____

Serial Number: _____

Floppy Drive B

Make: _____

Capacity: _____

Serial Number: _____

Extended Floppy #1

Make: _____

Model: _____

Capacity: _____

Serial Number: _____

Extended Floppy #2

Make: _____

Model: _____

Capacity: _____

Serial Number: _____

Hard Drive #1

Make: _____

Model: _____

Capacity: _____

Serial Number: _____

Heads: _____

Cylinders: _____

Sectors per Track: _____

Hard Drive #2

Make: _____

Model: _____

Capacity: _____

Serial Number: _____

Heads: _____

Cylinders: _____

Sectors per Track: _____

Tape Backup

Make: _____

Model: _____

Capacity: _____

Serial Number: _____

You may use the spaces below to paste a printout of your AUTOEXEC.BAT and CONFIG.SYS files.

AUTOEXEC.BAT

CONFIG.SYS

Software

Program: _____

Version: _____

Serial Number: _____

Program: _____

Version: _____

Serial Number: _____

Program: _____

Version: _____

Serial Number: _____

Program: _____

Version: _____

Serial Number: _____

Program: _____

Version: _____

Serial Number: _____

Program: _____

Version: _____

Serial Number: _____

Program: _____

Version: _____

Serial Number: _____

Program: _____

Version: _____

Serial Number: _____

Program: _____

Version: _____

Serial Number: _____

INDUSTRY PHONE NUMBERS

To the best of our knowledge these numbers are correct; but CSC cannot assume liability for their use.

#1 Components, Inc......,,(800)424-6780
1776 Inc........................(310)215-1776
   Tech Support............(310)215-1776
3COM Corporation...... ..(800)876-3266
3D Visions-Stanford........(800)729-4723
3E Corporation.............(800)682-5175
3G Graphics..................(800)456-0234
   Tech Support...........(206)774-3518
3M Company..................(512)984-3897
3M Corporation.............(800)362-3456
   Tech Support...........(800)362-3455
3M Data Products-CA......(800)328-9438
3M Data Products-MN.....(612)736-1866
3M Electrical Prods-TX ...(800)225-5373
3PM Planet, Inc.............(319)393-7932
7-Sigma........................(612)721-4280
A Bit Better Sftwr Publ..(206)627-6111
A C Technology.............(714)228-1633
A Cad-Group.................(404)315-8901
A J Computer Supplies..(714)895-5802
A-Comm Electronics......(201)334-3017
A-Matic International.....(818)855-8888
A.C. Powerline.............(716)288-6870
A.J. Post.....................(508)393-7192
A4Tech Corporation......(714)468-0071
AA Computech...............(800)360-6801
   Tech Support............(805)257-6804
AAA International Co....(714)951-0747
Aadtech Micro Sys........(415)659-0756
Aamazing Technologies.(714)255-1688
ABA Systems/USA, Inc..(801)561-8681
Abacus Accounting Sys .(403)489-5994
Abacus Concepts...........(800)666-7828
   Tech Support...........(510)540-1949
Abacus Concepts...........(800)666-7828
Abacus Software............(800)451-4319
Abaton-Everex Systems .(800)821-0806
   Tech Support...........(800)821-0806
Abbott Systems.............(800)552-9157
   Tech Support...........(914)747-4171
ABC Computer Corp.....(310)325-4005
ABC Products.................(714)373-9898

ABC Systems & Devel....(508)463-8602
Abekas Video Systems....(415)369-5111
Aberdeen.......................(800)552-6868
   Tech Support............(213)725-3360
ABL Electronics Corp....(410)584-2700
Able Soft......................(800)545-9009
Above Dariana Sftwr ......(800)892-9950
Above Software..............(714)851-2283
   Tech Support.............(714)851-2283
Abra MacDabra Sftwr....(408)737-9454
Abaracadata....................(800)451-4871
   Tech Support............(503)342-3030
Abrams Creative Serv......(818)343-6365
ABS Cmptr Technology..(800)876-8088
   Tech Support............(800)876-8088
AC & DC.......................(818)336-1388
ACC-Alamo City Cmptr.(512)545-1010
ACC Microelectronics...(408)980-0622
Access Cmptr Compont.(800)332-3778
   Tech Support............(214)380-8010
Access Technology, Inc..(508)655-9191
Acco USA, Inc...............(708)541-9500
Accolade.......................(800)245-7744
   Tech Support............(408)296-8400
Accts Microsystems.......(206)643-2050
AcctonTechnology.........(408)452-4900
   Tech Support............(800)926-9288
Accufast Products...........(800)447-9990
Acculogic.....................(714)454-2441
Accurite Technologies...(408)433-1980
Ace Software Corp........(408)232-0300
   Tech Support............(408)232-0303
Ace Technologoes, Inc...(408)734-0100
.....................................(800)825-9977
Acecad Inc....................(800)676-4223
   Tech Support...........(408)655-9911
Acer America..................(800)848-2237
Acer Peripherals............(609)924-1153
Acer Technologies Corp .(800)833-8241
Achieva Computer.........(800)388-2918
   Tech Support...........(408)894-0200
Aci Us, Inc....................(408)252-4444
   Tech Support............(408)252-4444
ACL Inc.......................(800)782-8420
ACM, Inc.....................(800)342-6626
Acme Electric Corp.......(800)325-5848

Accoustic Research.......(800)225-9847
AcrossTheOcean Import .(415)660-7804
Action Communications..(612)636-3559
Action Electronics Co...(818)813-1500
Action Multimedia.........(800)322-3132
Action Plus Software.....(801)255-0600
   Tech Support............(801)255-0600
Activisilin.......................(310)207-4500
.....................................(310)479-5644
   Tech Support...........(310)479-5644
Actix Systems, Inc..........(800)820-1276
Acucobol, Inc................(800)262-6585
Acumos,Inc...................(415)570-0535
Acxiom Corporation.....(501)329-6836
AD Costas Projects....... (415)462-3111
   Tech Support...........(415)426-5040
Ad Lib, Inc....................(800)463-2686
   Tech Support...........(418)529-6252
Ad Lib Multimedia, Inc..(418)529-9676
Ad Research...................(800)926-7365
   Tech Support...........(800)873-7365
Adaptec........................(408)945-8600
Adaptive Software..........(714)729-3180
Adaptive Technologies...(805)448-8832
ADDA Technologies.......(510)770-9899
Addison-Wesley Publ.......(800)447-2226
ADDS...........................(800)645-6504
AddTech Group..............(510)623-7583
AdtronTechnologyCo....(510)770-0120
Allegro MicroSystems...(508)853-5000
ADI Systems, Inc............(800)228-0530
ADI/Execufold...............(209)683-2126
ADIC............................(800)336-1233
Adisoft, Inc...................(510)483-5605
AdjileSystems................(800)347-7621
Adobe Systems, Inc........(800)447-3577
   Tech Support - MAC.(408)986-6500
   Tech Support - PC....(408)986-6530
AdRem Technologies.....(416)886-7899
Adtran/PTT...................(205)971-8000
Adv. Instit'l Mgmt. Sftwr.,(516)496-7700
Advanced Cmptr Cable.(800)626-3608
AdvancedCmptrInnov....(716)383-1939
AdvancedCmptrTech......(212)679-4040
Advanced Digital Info....(800)336-1233
Advanced Digital Sys......(800)888-5244

INDUSTRY PHONE NUMBERS

Tech Support...........(800)888-5244	Alf Products, Inc............(800)321-4668	Amcom Corporation......(800)320-4723
Advanced Electr. Supp....(800)446-2377	ALfa Power, Inc.............(818)937-6529	Amdahl Corp.................(800)538-8460
Advanced Gravis BC......(800)663-8558	Alias Research................(800)267-8697	Amdek Corporation......(800)800-9973
Tech Support...........(604)431-1807	Tech Support...........(800)267-8697	Tech Support...........(800)800-9973
Advanced Hrdwr Arch....(208)883-8000	Aiisa Systems...............(800)992-5472	AME, Inc....................(408)955-9666
Tech Support...........(208)883-8001	Alki Software Corp........(206)286-2600	AMEC Cmptr Eronom...(800)759-5060
Advance Input Devises .(208)765-8000	All Computers...............(800)387-2744	American Grp. Cmptr....(800)288-8025
Adv. Integration Rsrch..(408)428-0800	Tech Support...........(416)960-0111	Tech Support...........(818)765-3887
Advanced Logic Rsrch...(800)444-4257	All Electronics..............(818)904-0524	American Business Sys..(508)250-9600
Tech Support...........(714)458-1952	Allegro Microsystems....(508)853-5000	American Cmptr Engnrs..(619)587-9002
Advanced Matrix Tech...(800)637-7878	Allen Communication...(801)537-7800	American Cmptr Exprss..(800)533-4604
Adv. Micro Cmptr Sys....(800)866-0829	Allied Cmptr Services....(319)378-1383	American Cmptr Hrdwr...(800)447-1237
Tech Support...........(302)368-9300	Allied Telesis (ATI)........(800)424-4284	American Cmptr Repair..(211)539-1010
Adv. Micro Devices........(408)732-2400	Tech Support...........(206)821-2056	American Cmptr Rsrces...(203)380-4600
Adv. Micro Technology...(714)598-6124	AllMicro.....................(800)653-4933	American Covers, Inc....(800)228-8967
Adv. Microcmptr Sys......(305)784-0900	Alloy Cmptr Products....(508)486-0900	Tech Support...........(800)228-8987
Advanced Network.......(408)779-2209	Tech Support...........(508)486-0900	American Cybernetics...(800)221-9280
Advanced Software........(800)346-5392	Allsop, Inc...................(206)734-9090	American Databankers......(800)323-7767
Tech Support...........(408)733-0745	Allstate Office Supply....(714)692-9100	American Digicom Corp..(408)245-1580
Adv. Tech & Sevices.......(310)676-0487	Alltech Electronics.........(714)543-5011	American Digital............(617)449-9292
Tech Support...........(310)676-0487	Alltel Corporation..........(216)650-7000	American Ed. Service.....(703)256-5315
Advanced Technology....(408)942-1780	Almo Distributing..........(303)595-7000	American Elect. Heater....(313)875-2502
Advanced Vision Rsrch..(800)544-6243	Tech Support...........(617)272-3680	American Enhance, Inc...(510)438-9180
Tech Support...........(800)544-6243	Alpha Systems Lab, Inc..(714)252-0117	Amer. Financial Equip..(513)436-0110
Adweeks Mktg Cmptrs..(800)722-6658	Alpha Technologies........(206)647-2360	American Fundware......(800)551-4458
AEC Management.........(800)346-9413	Alphatronix..................(800)849-2611	Amer. Healthware Sys....(718)435-6300
Tech Support...........(703)450-2318	Alpha Wire Corp............(906)925-8000	American Ink Jet Corp. .(508)667-0600
AEC Software................(800)346-9413	Alps America.................(800)950-2577	Amer. Laubscher Corp...(516)694-5900
Tech Support...........(703)450-2318	Tech Support...........(800)950-2577	Amer. Magnetics Corp...(213)775-8651
AER Energy Resources..(404)433-2127	ALR............................(714)581-6770	American Mngmt Sys....(800)826-4395
Aeronics.....................(512)258-2303	Alsoft..........................(800)257-6381	American Microsys........(800)648-4452
AESP, Inc....................(305)944-7710	Tech Support...........(713)353-1510	Amer. Nat. Standard Inst..(212)642-4900
Aetech........................(619)755-1277	Alsys...........................(617)270-0030	American On-Line..........(919)942-0220
Affinity.......................(800)367-6771	Altec Lansing.................(800)648-6663	Tech Support...........(919)942-0220
Tech Support...........(303)442-4840	Tech Support...........(800)648-6663	Amer. Power Conversion.(800)800-4272
After Hours Sftwr-Aldus ...(619)558-6000	Altec Lansing Consumer...(800)648-6663	Tech Support...........(800)800-4272
Tech Support...........(619)558-6000	Tech Support...........(800)648-6663	American ProImage.......(310)949-9797
AgData.......................(209)784-5500	Altech, Inc...................(314)576-5100	American Reliance, Inc..(800)654-9838
AGELogic,Inc...............(619)455-8600	Alternative Cmptr Prod....(805)522-4984	American Rsrch. Corp....(800)423-3877
Agfa Compugraphics.....(800)424-8973	Altex Electronics-Austin....(512)832-9131	American Ribbon............(800)327-1013
Tech Support...........(800)937-7787	Altex Electronics-Corp.....(512)655-8882	American Serv. Resource..(800)333-1157
Agfa Division................(914)365-0190	Altex Electronics-Dallas....(214)386-8882	Amer. Small Bus. Cmptr...(918)825-4844
Agfa Division................(800)424-8973	Altex Electronics-San Ant..(800)531-5369	Tech Support...........(918)825-4844
Ags Computers.............(908)654-4321	Altima Systems, Inc........(800)356-9990	American Software, Inc....(404)261-4381
Agsadivision.................(508)658-5600	Altos Computer Sys.......(800)258-6787	Tech Support...........(404)261-4381
Ahead Systems, Inc........(510)623-0900	Altron, Inc...................(800)678-8802	Amer. Suntek Int'l Corp....(800)888-7813
A1 Today......................(304)965-5548	Altsys.........................(214)680-2060	American Systec Corp...(714)993-0882
Aicom Corporation........(408)453-8251	Tech Support...........(214)680-2093	American Trader's Post..(301)695-8438
Aim Motherboard Corp .(800)786-2566	Altus Systems.................(800)522-5887	Ameritech....................(312)750-5000
Aim Tech......................(603)883-0220	Tech Support...........(909)598-7769	Ames Supply Company.(800)323-3856
Tech Support...........(603)883-0200	Aluminum Filter Co.......(805)684-7651	Aemteck, Inc.................(212)935-8640
AIQ Systems.................(800)332-2999	Alumni Computer Grp..(800)387-9785	Amherst Intl Corp........(800)547-5600
Tech Support...........(702)831-2999	Always Technologies.....(818)597-1400	Amita Corporation.........(512)218-8857
Aitech International.......(800)882-8184	Tech Support...........(818)597-9595	Amkty Systems, Inc........(714)727-0788
AJM, Inc......................(408)980-8631	Alysis.........................(800)825-9747	AMP...........................(717)564-0100
AJS Publishing..............(310)215-9145	Tech Support...........(800)825-9747	...................................(800)522-6752
Al Expert Magazine.......(415)905-2200	Alywa Computer Corp..(713)440-1393	Ampex ....(800)262-6739
Alacrity Systems, Inc......(908)813-2400	AM Electronics (AME)....(408)955-9666	Amphenol Corporation.(203)281-3200
Aladdin Sftwr Security...(516)424-5100	Ama Inc.......................(416)897-2153	Amplicom.....................(619)693-9127
Aladdin Systems.............(408)761-6200	Amatix, Inc...................(800)869-0744	Ampro Computers, Inc...(800)966-5200
Tech Support...........(408)761-6200	Amax Applied Tech........(818)300-8828	Amprobe Instrument.....(516)593-5600
Alamo Components......(800)890-8900	Amax Engineering Corp..(800)888-2629	Amptron International..(818)912-5789
Aldridge Company,The..(800)548-5019	AMAZE!-Delrina Sftwr....(800)367-4802	AMR............................(408)732-2400
Aldus Corp. (Adobe)......(800)628-2320	Tech Support...........(416)441-4628	...................................(800)538-8450
Tech Support...........(800)628-2320	AMBI Circuit Board Elec..(800)879-2624	AmRam........................(408)559-0603
Alexander Batteries.......(515)423-8955	Ambra Computer Corp...(800)252-6272	Amrel Technology, Inc...(818)575-5110

INDUSTRY PHONE NUMBERS

AMRIS Training Systems.(800)842-3693	Applied Data Comm......(714)731-9000	Arthur Anderson & Co..(800)458-8851
AMS.................................(305)784-0900	Tech Support............(800)422-3635	Arthur Dent Associates..(508)858-3742
................................(800)886-3536	Applied Design Co......(612)378-0094	Articulate Systems.........(800)443-7077
Amstrad Inc.................(800)999-0174	Applied Instruments......(510)490-7117	Tech Support............(617)935-2220
Amtec Cmptr Services...(515)270-2480	Applied Magnetics Corp.(800)328-5640	Artisoft...........................(800)846-9726
AmTech Organization....(617)344-1550	Applied Microsystems...(800)426-3925	Tech Support............(602)670-7000
Amtron Inc...................(213)721-1717	Applied Optical Media..(800)321-7259	Artist Graphics...............(800)627-8478
Anacapa Micro Prods. ...(805)339-0305	Tech Support............(800)321-7259	Artnet International.......(203)348-1141
Anacom General Corp. .(714)774-8080	Applix, Inc....................(508)870-0300	Asante Technologies......(800)662-9686
Anacomp, Inc................(317)844-9666	Tech Support............(800)827-7549	Tech Support............(800)662-7464
Analog & Digital Periph.(513)339-2241	Appoint.......................(800)448-1184	ASCII Group, Inc.,The..(301)718-2600
Analog Devices, Inc.......(800)426-2564	Tech Support............(800)448-1184	Ascom Timeplex, Inc.....(800)669-2298
Analog Technology Ctr..(603)673-0404	APPRO International.....(408)985-5359	ASD Software, Inc..........(900)624-2594
Analog Technology Corp.(818)357-0098	Tech Support............(408)448-6093	Tech Support............(900)624-2594
Analogic Corporation....(800)343-8333	Approach Software-Lotus..(800)277-7622	Asean Cmptr Techn ....(909)598-2828
Analysts Int'l. Corp.........(800)328-9929	Tech Support............(508)988-2500	Tech Support............(909)598-5498
Analytical Software........(206)362-2855	Apricom.........................(619)271-4880	Ashby Industries, Inc.....(405)722-1705
AnaTek Corporation......(800)999-0304	APS Packaging Systems..(201)575-1040	Ashton-Tate (Borland)....(408)431-1000
Ancot Corporation.........(415)322-5322	APS Technologies...........(800)235-2753	Asia Communications....(514)434-9373
Anderson Bell................(303)940-0595	Aptech Systems..............(800)443-3732	Asia Source.....................(510)226-8000
Andgate Systems Corp...(714)468-3084	Aquidneck Sys. Int'l......(401)295-2691	Tech Support............(510)226-8878
Ando Corporation.........(301)294-3365	AR Industries (CP+).......(800)274-4277	Asian Computer Corp...(818)575-5271
Andor Systems, Inc........(408)996-9010	Tech Support............(800)274-4277	Asian Micro Sources......(510)376-9111
Andrew Corporation.....(310)320-7126	Arabesque Software.......(800)457-4243	AsianSource Cmptr Prod.(708)475-1900
Andromeda Research....(513)831-9708	Tech Support............(206)885-0559	Asiatek Inc.....................(818)333-3802
Tech Support............(513)831-7562	Arbor Image Corp..........(313)741-8700	ASJ Support Services.....(800)262-0089
Andromeda Systems......(818)709-7600	Arche Technologies........(510)623-8100	Ask Computer Systems .(415)969-4442
Angelica Uniform Grp...(800)222-3112	Tech Support............(800)322-2724	Ask-Me Information Ctr.(612)531-0603
Angia Communications.(801)371-0488	Archive Corporation......(714)890-8602	AskSam Systems.............(800)800-1997
ANGOSS Software.........(416)593-1122	Archive Sftwr-Conner....(800)821-8782	ASP Cmptr Products......(800)445-6190
Anix Tech Corporation..(408)737-9935	Tech Support............(800)227-6296	Tech Support............(408)746-2965
Anixter Brothers, Inc.....(708)677-2600	Archive Technology........(800)537-2724	Aspect Telecomm...........(800)541-7799
Anjene International......(908)704-0304	Archtek America Corp...(818)912-9800	Aspen Imaging Int'l........(800)955-5555
Ann Arbor Software.......(800)345-6777	Arco Electronics, Inc.....(305)925-2688	Assoc. For Cmpt'g Mach..(212)869-7440
Annabooks.....................(800)462-1042	Arcom Electronics, Inc..(408)452-0678	Assoc. Data Services.......(800)772-9812
Answer Computer.........(800)677-2679	Area TV & Computers...(814)453-3918	Assoc. Distr. Logistics......(800)443-3443
AnswerSet Corporation..(408)996-8683	Areal Technology, Inc.....(408)436-6800	Associated Research.......(800)858-8378
Antec, Inc.....................(510)770-9590	Tech Support............(408)436-6843	Associates Cmptr Supply ..(718)543-3364
Tech Support............(510)770-1200	ARES Microdevelpmnt...(800)322-3200	Assoc. of Shareware Prof.(317)322-2000
Antex Electronics Corp..(310)532-3092	Ares Software................(800)783-2737	AST Computer...............(800)876-4278
Anthem Technology Sys.(800)359-3580	Tech Support............(415)578-9090	AST Research, Inc..........(800)876-4278
Anthes Universal, Inc.....(800)828-0308	Arion Technologies, Inc..(203)775-6939	Astea International.........(617)275-5440
Anthro Co.....................(800)325-3841	Aris Entertainment.........(310)821-0234	Astec Co........................(201)595-7001
Anvil Cases...................(800)359-2684	Arista Enterprises...........(800)274-7824	Astec Standard Power....(619)757-1880
AOC Int'l (USA)Ltd........(800)433-7516	Tech Support............(800)274-7824	Astra Computer Prods....(619)278-2682
Aox Inc.........................(800)232-1269	Aristo Computers, Inc...(800)327-4786	Astro Memory Prods......(800)652-7876
Tech Support............(800)726-0269	Aristosoft, Inc................(800)338-2629	Astrocom Corporation..(612)227-8651
Apex Computer............(800)654-8222	Arity.............................(800)722-7489	Astrotech Int'l Corp.......(412)391-1896
Apex Data....................(800)841-2739	Arix Corporation...........(408)432-1200	Asymetrix.....................(206)637-1500
Tech Support............(800)841-2739	ARK Multimedia Publ....(804)220-4722	AT & T Paradyne...........(800)482-3333
Apex Software..............(800)858-2739	Arkay Technologies, Inc. .(800)786-2419	At&T.............................(201)331-4134
Tech Support............(412)681-4343	Arkenstone Inc.............(408)752-2200	AT&T Capital Corp........(800)874-7123
Apian Software.............(800)237-4565	Arkwright Inc...............(800)548-5105	AT&T Computer Sys......(800)247-1212
Aplus Computer............(800)886-2671	Arlington Cmptr Prods..(800)548-5105	AT&T Lang. Line Serv.......(800)752-6096
Tech Support............(800)886-3536	Tech Support............(708)228-1470	AT&T Microelectronics.(800)372-2447
APM Technologies.........(404)476-3596	Arlington Elect.Whlsale..(703)524-2412	AT&T Natl Parts Sales Ctr..(800)222-7278
Appian...........................(800)422-7369	Arnet Corporation..........(800)377-6686	AT&T/NCR Crisis Mgmt..(800)626-3495
Appian Technology, Inc.(408)730-5400	Tech Support............(800)366-8844	Atari Corporation...........(800)443-8020
Apple Computer, Inc.....(800)776-2333	Aropa Corporation.........(408)734-2001	Atech Software...............(818)765-5311
Tech Support............(800)767-2775	Array Analysis................(800)451-8514	Aten Research, Inc..........(800)755-0561
Applications Techniques.(800)433-5201	Arrow Electronics, Inc...(800)932-7769	ATG Cygnet...................(800)729-4638
Tech Support............(506)433-8464	Arrowfield Int'l, Inc.......(714)669-0101	Athana Inc.....................(800)421-1591
Applied Bus.Technology.(212)219-8945	Ars Nova Software.........(800)445-4866	ATI Technologies............(416)882-2600
Applied Cmptr Servs.....(800)525-2400	Tech Support............(206)889-0927	ATI Technologies, Inc....(800)955-5284
Applied Cmptr Tech......(214)271-6550	Artek Cmptr Systems.....(510)490-8402	ATI Technologies, Inc.....(416)882-2600
Applied Concepts, Inc..(800)393-2277	Artful Applications.........(416)920-7395	Atkins/Jones Cmptr Serv.(714)953-4351

INDUSTRY PHONE NUMBERS

Atlantic Cmptr Prods.....(800)245-2284
Atlantic Inc................(310)273-3163
Atlantic Scientific Corp.(800)544-4737
Atlantis Laser Center......(800)733-9155
Atlas Business Solutions..(708)208-1373
Atlas Micro Distributing..(310)530-6300
Atmel Corporation.........(408)441-0311
Atrix International Inc...(800)222-6154
Attachmate Corporation.(800)426-6283
Attain....................(617)776-1110
Attitash Software...........(800)736-4198
Attitude Inc..............(714)680-8112
ATTO Technology, Inc...(716)688-4259
Audio Digital Imaging...(708)439-1335
Aurora Cmptr & Access..(800)852-3344
Aurum Software, Inc......(408)562-6370
Austek Microsystems.....(408)968-8556
Austin Direct, Inc..........(800)752-4171
Austin Marsh Comm......(416)840-7840
Auto Trol Technology.....(303)452-4919
AutoDesk Inc..............(800)228-3601
   Tech Support...........(800)873-3375
Autodesk Retail Prods...(800)228-3601
   Tech Support...........(206)487-2934
Automap..................(800)440-6277
   Tech Support...........(800)441-6277
Automated Crtrdge Lib..(800)536-2251
Automated Design Sys...(800)366-2552
Automated Tech. System..(516)231-7777
Automatic Data Process'g.(201)994-5000
Automatic Tool/Connect.(800)524-2857
Automation Technology...(800)777-6368
Automatrix Inc.............(508)667-7900
Automecha Ltd..............(800)447-9990
AutoSoft, Inc...................(404)594-8855
Autrec, Inc..................(919)759-9493
Autumn Hill Software....(303)494-8865
Auva Computer, Inc.......(714)562-6999
Ava Instrumentation......(408)336-2281
Avalan Technology.........(800)441-2281
Avalon Hill Game Co.....(410)254-9200
Avance Logic Inc...........(510)226-9555
Avanpro...................(213)454-3866
Avant Industries, Inc......(818)330-0166
Avant-Garde Computing.(609)778-7000
Avantek Security............(408)727-0700
Avantos Performance Sys..(510)654-4600
   Tech Support...........(510)654-4727
Avatar/DCA.................(800)348-3221
   Tech Support...........(404)740-0300
Avery Dennison.............(818)858-8214
Avery International........(800)252-8379
   Tech Support...........(214)888-2699
Avery Label...............(800)252-8379
   Tech Support...........(214)888-2699
Avex Electronics Corp..(800)877-7623
AVI Systems Inc...........(510)535-1020
Avnet, Inc.................(516)466-7000
Avocet.....................(800)448-8500
   Tech Support...........(207)236-6010
AVR Technology Inc......(408)434-1115
Award Software, Ltd......(415)968-4433
   Tech Support...........(408)370-7979
AXA Corporation.........(714)757-1500
Axelen Inc..................(206)643-2781
Axik Computer.............(408)735-1234

   Tech Support............(408)735-1437
Axion....................(800)829-4664
Axis Communications...(508)777-7957
Axonix Corporation......(800)866-9797
Axxion Group Corp......(800)828-6475
Axxis Software.............(800)394-3549
Aydin Corporation.........(215)657-7510
Az-Tech Software..........(816)776-2700
Azerty Inc..................(800)888-8080
   Tech Support...........(716)662-7616
Azure Technologies........(800)233-3800
B&B Electronics Mfg......(815)434-0846
B&K Precision.............(312)889-1448
B & C Microsytems........(408)730-5511
Babbages Inc................(800)288-9020
Back Thru Future Micro..(201)644-9587
Baggerty & Assoc., Inc...(808)875-2510
Baker & Taylor Aff. Label..(800)775-4200
.........................(415)721-3333
.........................(415)392-4357
   Tech Support...........(415)721-3333
.........................(415)392-4357
Baler Software.............(800)327-6108
   Tech Support...........(708)506-1770
Ball Aerospace............(505)298-5445
Balt, Inc...................(817)697-4953
Banctec Inc.................(800)527-5918
Banctec Service Corp....(800)435-7832
Bandy Inc..................(214)272-5455
Banner Band..............(800)333-0549
Banner Blue Software....(510)794-6850
   Tech Support...........(510)794-6850
Bantam Electronic Publ..(212)765-6500
Banyan Systems Inc.......(508)898-1000
Bar-Tec Inc..................(800)433-1409
   Tech Support...........(800)356-1695
Barbados Ind. Devel......(212)867-6420
Barbey Electronics.........(215)376-7451
Barcode Industries, Inc...(301)498-5400
   Tech Support...........(301)498-6498
Barouh Easton Ltd.........(800)268-9955
Barrister Info. System.....(716)845-5010
Barrons Educational Serv.(800)645-3476
Baseline Publishing........(901)527-2501
   Tech Support...........(901)527-2501
BASF.....................(800)669-2273
   Tech Support...........(800)225-4350
Basic + Micro Products.(510)887-8186
Basic Computer.............(216)873-1000
Basic Needs.................(800)633-3703
   Tech Support...........(800)633-3703
Basic Systems, Inc..........(305)584-5422
Basmark...................(216)621-7650
Battelle Memorial Inst...(614)424-6424
Battery Biz.................(800)848-6782
Battery Power Inc..........(800)949-1000
Battery Specialties..........(800)854-5759
Battery Technology Inc...(800)982-8284
Bay Technical Assoc.......(800)523-2702
Baysoft....................(415)527-3300
Bayware Inc.................(415)312-0980
BCC Advanced Research.(714)752-0526
BCTOP Inc..................(213)383-0791
Beacon Software, Inc.....(800)753-2322
Beacon Technology........(719)594-4884
   Tech Support...........(719)594-4884

Beame & Whiteside Sftwr..(416)765-0822
Bear Rock Technology....(916)622-4640
Beaver Computer Corp.(800)827-4222
BEC......................(714)731-6116
BEC Computer............(408)954-8828
BEC Inc. Cert. Calib. Labs.(800)523-3808
BEC Lynkers..............(714)731-6117
Backman Industrial........(800)854-2708
Bedford Cmptr Systems..(714)586-3700
Bel Merit Corporation...(714)586-3700
Belden Wire and Cable...(800)235-3361
Belgian For. Trade Office.(213)857-1244
Belkin Components.......(800)223-5546
   Tech Support...........(310)898-1100
Bell & Howell Prods Co..(708)933-3125
Bell Atlantic Bus. System..(800)634-9827
   Tech Support...........(215)296-6180
Bell Atlantic Corp..........(215)963-6000
Bell Atlantic CTS-MA......(800)688-1492
Bell Atlantic CTS-CA......(800)345-7950
Bell Atlantic CTS-CA.......(500)350-3475
Bell Atlantic CTS-PA......(800)888-2622
Bell Atlantic CTS-ESS-WI..(800)888-2622
Bell Industries, Inc.........(310)826-2355
Bell of Pennsylvania.......(215)466-7978
Bendata Mgt Systems.....(719)731-5007
Benedict Computers......(800)346-5186
Benefit Concept Sys.......(401)438-7100
Bentley Company...........(617)221-8590
Berkeley Systems Design.(800)877-5535
   Tech Support...........(510)540-5535
Berkshire Products, Inc..(404)271-0088
Berg Electronics.............(717)938-7620
.........................(800)237-2374
Best Cmptr Supplies......(800)544-3470
   Tech Support...........(702)826-4393
Best Data Products, Inc..(818)773-9600
   Tech Support...........(818)773-9600
Best PC Supply, Inc........(415)875-6888
Best Power Technology..(800)356-5794
   Tech Support...........(800)356-5737
Best Programs, Inc.........(703)820-9300
Beta Automation Inc......(800)421-8462
Bethesda Softworks.......(301)926-8300
   Tech Support...........(301)963-2002
Better Business Systems..(800)829-9991
   Tech Support...........(818)373-7525
BGS Systems.................(617)891-0000
BGW Systems Inc..........(310)973-8090
Bi-Link Computer, Inc....(800)888-5369
   Tech Support...........(310)695-5166
Biblesoft...................(800)877-0778
Big Blue Products Inc....(516)261-1000
Binary Research............(215)233-3200
Biomation.................(800)934-2466
Birmingham Data Sys...(313)362-0860
Bis Technology Inc.........(818)856-5888
Bit 3 Computer Corp....(612)881-6955
BIT Computer Inc..(800)935-0209
Bit Software Inc...........(510)490-2928
   Tech Support...........(510)490-9470
Bits Technical Corp........(713)981-1166
Bitstream Inc................(800)223-3176
   Tech Support...........(617)497-7514
Bitwise Designs, Inc.......(800)367-5906
Biz Base-Santa Fe Sftwr..(800)833-8892

INDUSTRY PHONE NUMBERS

Tech Support............(619)673-7355	Brown-Wagh................(408)378-3838	Cable Connection..........(408)395-6700
BJS Electronics, Inc.......(408)456-8989	Tech Support............(408)378-3838	Cable Systems, Inc.........(617)389-7080
Black & White Int'l.........(800)932-9202	Brown-Wagh Publ.........(408)378-3838	Cable-Tech.....................(817)477-5013
Black Box Corporation..(800)321-0746	Tech Support............(408)378-3838	Cables To Go..................(800)225-8646
Tech Support............(412)746-5565	Bruce Krobusek............(716)258-8722	Cabletron Systems........(603)332-9400
BlackCurrant Technology..(714)432-6514	BSE Company................(714)258-8722	CableWorks...................(619)450-1929
Blackship Cmptr Sys......(800)877-6249	BSI (Broadax Sys.)..........(800)872-4547	CablExpress...................(315)476-3000
Blaise Computing..........(800)333-8087	Tech Support............(818)442-7038	Cache Computers Inc...(510)226-9922
Bleuel Associates Inc.....(818)907-7162	BSM Computers.............(800)888-3475	CACI International Inc..(703)841-7800
BLOC Publishing Corp..(305)445-0903	BTECH Inc....................(201)428-1779	CAD & Graphic Cmptrs.(800)288-1611
Blue Fin Technologies....(603)433-2223	Budget Computer..........(800)370-1212	Tech Support............(415)647-9671
Blue Line Comm............(800)258-7810	Tech Support............(800)370-1313	CAD Warehouse.............(800)487-0485
Blue Rose Computer......(800)685-3035	Buerg Software..............(707)778-1811	Tech Support............(216)487-0631
Bluebird Systems.........(619)438-2220	Buffalo Creek Software..(515)255-9552	Cadec Systems, Inc........(800)223-3220
Bluelynx......................(800)832-4526	Buffalo Products Inc......(800)345-2356	Cadence Design Sys.......(408)943-1234
Tech Support............(800)642-5888	Tech Support............(800)345-2027	CADRE Technology........(800)548-7645
Bluesky Software...........(800)677-4946	Bull HN Info. System......(800)999-2181	Cacrc Corporation.........(800)535-7226
Blythe Software.............(800)346-6647	Tech Support............(800)226-4357	Tech Support............(800)462-2373
BMI Inc........................(415)570-5355	Bull Information Sys.......(800)233-2855	CAF Technology Inc......(800)289-8299
Board Exchange Inc......(407)678-2269	Bulldog Cmptr Prods.....(800)438-6039	Cahners Publishing Co..(617)694-3030
Boardwatch Magazine...(303)973-6038	Bullseye Software..........(702)831-2523	Caig Laboratories..........(619)451-1799
Boca Research..............(407)997-6227	Bureau Development.....(201)808-2700	Cal-Abco......................(800)669-2226
Tech Support............(407)241-8088	Tech Support............(201)808-2700	Calan, Inc....................(800)544-3392
BodyCello.....................(619)578-6969	Bureau of Elect. Publ..(800)828-4766	Calcomp.......................(800)541-7877
Bogen Communication.(201)935-8500	Tech Support............(201)808-2700	Tech Support............(800)225-2667
Bolt Beranek & Newman..(617)873-2000	Burndy Corporation......(203)838-4444	Calculus.......................(305)481-2334
Bolt Systems..................(301)656-7133	Burr-Brown Corp...........(800)227-3947	Calculus Inc...................(305)481-2334
Bondhus Corporation....(800)328-8310	Burroughs Corp.............(800)247-5617	Calera Recognition Sys..(800)422-5372
Bondwell Industrial Co.(800)627-6888	Bus Cmptr Systems........(212)627-4485	Tech Support............(408)702-0999
Tech Support............(800)288-4388	Buse Communications...(800)521-1117	Caliper Computer Corp..(213)727-8530
Book Tech Distributing..(303)329-0300	Business Cmptr Sys........(800)333-2955	California Peripherals.....(213)538-1030
Boole And Babbage, Inc..(800)222-6653	Tech Support............(804)420-6658	California Sftwr Prods....(714)973-0440
Boonton Elect. Corp......(201)584-1077	Business Credit Leasing.(800)328-5371	Calif. Switch & Signal.....(310)538-9830
Borland........................(800)841-8180	Business Develop. Int'l...(201)891-1040	Calluna Technology........(408)453-4753
Tech Support............(408)461-9155	Business Logistics Serv...(901)395-7112	CalSOFT Technology......(805)497-8054
Bostek.........................(800)926-7835	Business Sense Inc.........(801)963-1384	Caltex Software...........(214)522-9840
Boston Bus. Computing.(508)470-0444	Business Sys. Direct........(800)777-4068	Caltronex......................(716)359-9780
Boston Cmptr Exchange.(800)262-6399	Business Vision Mgt Sys.(414)629-3233	Calyx Corporation..........(800)558-2208
Botton Line Industries...(818)700-1922	BusinessWare Inc...........(714)492-8958	Tech Support............(800)866-1008
Bourbaki......................(208)342-5849	BusinessWise, Inc...........(408)866-5960	Calzone Case Co.............(203)367-5766
Bowers Development....(508)369-8175	BusLogic Inc..................(408)492-9090	Cambria Corporation....(609)665-3600
Bracking, Jim.................(408)725-0628	Button Ware Inc.............(214)713-6370	Cambridge Elect. Labs...(617)629-2805
Brand Technologies........(818)407-4040	Tech Support............(900)555-8800	Cameo Communication..(603)465-2940
Tech Support............(818)407-4040	Bux Tek Corporation.....(408)492-9090	Camintonn Corporation..(800)843-8336
Bravo Communication...(800)366-0297	Buzzwords, Int'l.............(314)334-6317	Campbell Services Inc...(800)345-6747
Bravo Technology..........(510)841-8552	Byte Brothers.................(206)271-9567	Tech Support............(810)559-5955
Tech Support............(510)841-8552	Byte Info. Exch (BIX).....(603)924-7681	Canada, External Affairs.(613)993-6576
BRC Electronics............(800)255-3027	BYTE Magazine..............(603)924-9281	Canon..........................(516)488-6700
Bretford Manufacturing.(708)678-2545	Bytel Corporation..........(415)527-1157	Canon (Printers)............(800)848-4123
Brian Instruments, Inc...(714)992-5540	Bytronix Corporation....(714)879-0810	Tech Support............(800)423-2366
Brian R. White Co...........(707)462-9795	C C Steven & Associates..(805)658-0207	Cannon-Still Video/East..(714)753-7002
Brier Technology............(408)435-8463	C H Products.................(619)598-2518	Cannon-Still Video/West..(714)753-4002
Tech Support............(404)564-5550	C Hoelzie Associates......(714)251-9000	Tech Support............(714)753-4323
Bright Star Technology...(206)451-3697	C J Carrigan Ent............(714)598-1276	Canon Cmptr Systems...(800)423-2366
Brightbill Roberts.........(800)444-3490	C Source......................(816)478-1888	Tech Support............(800)423-2366
Brightwork Develpment..(800)552-9876	C&D Charter Pwr. Sys....(215)828-9000	Canon USA(East)............(800)221-3333
Tech Support............(908)530-9650	C&F Associates..............(800)688-9112	Tech Support............(908)521-7000
Brim Electronics Inc......(201)796-2886	C&S Sales Inc................(800)292-7711	Canon USA(Mid West)...(708)250-6200
Broadtech Int'l..............(714)773-1820	C-88 International Corp..(408)956-8345	Tech Support............(705)250-6200
Broadview Associates....(201)461-7929	C-Tech Associates Inc...(201)726-9000	Canon USA(South East)..(404)448-1430
Brock Control Systems..(800)221-0775	C-Tech Electronics, Inc..(800)347-4017	Tech Support............(404)448-1430
Broderbund Software....(800)521-6263	C Itoh Electronics, Inc..(213)327-9100	Canon USA(South West).(214)830-9600
Tech Support............(415)382-4700	C2 Micro Systems Inc....(510)683-8888	Tech Support............(214)830-9600
Brooks Electronics.........(800)052-3010	CA Retail Solutions.........(800)668-3767	Canon USA(West)..........(714)753-4200
Brooks Power Systems...(800)523-1551	CA Technology, Ltd........(212)260-7661	Tech Support............(714)753-4200
Brother International.....(908)356-8880	Cabinets Galore Inc.......(619)586-0555	CanTech.......................(800)255-3999

INDUSTRY PHONE NUMBERS

Capital Data.....................(517)371-3700
Capricorn Systems.........(804)355-9371
Capstone Technology.....(510)438-3500
   Tech Support.............(305)373-7770
Cardiff Software Inc......(800)659-8755
Cardinal Technologies....(717)293-3049
   Tech Support.............(717)293-3124
Caritech Cmptr Corp....(915)584-9817
Carlisle Memory Prods..(800)433-7632
CarNel Enterprises Inc..(800)962-1450
Carroll Touch...............(512)244-3500
Cartridge Technologies..(800)869-8570
Carvey Databook, Inc....(716)889-4204
Casady & Green.............(800)359-4920
   Tech Support.............(408)484-9228
Case Logic Inc...............(303)530-3800
Casecom Inc...................(408)942-5416
Casecom Technology.....(510)490-7122
Caseworks, Inc...............(800)635-1577
Casio.............................(201)361-5400
   Tech Support.............(201)361-5400
Castelle.........................(408)496-0474
   Tech Support.............(408)496-0474
Catalyst Seminconductor..(408)748-7700
Catalytix.......................(617)738-1516
Catspaw.........................(719)539-3884
Cayman Systems.............(800)473-4776
   Tech Support.............(617)932-1100
CBM America Corp........(800)421-6516
   Tech Support.............(310)767-7838
CC:Mail.........................(800)448-2500
   Tech Support.............(800)448-2500
CCI...............................(604)465-1540
CD Systems...................(909)595-5736
CD Technologies.............(408)752-8500
   Tech Support.............(408)752-8499
CD-ROM Direct............(800)332-2404
CDB Systems, Inc...........(303)444-7463
CDC (Imprimis)............(800)852-3475
CDCE Inc......................(714)630-4633
CE Software..................(515)224-1955
Celestica.......................(800)461-2913
Cellular Data Inc............(415)856-9800
Cellular Dig. Packet Data.(206)828-8691
Cellular Product Dist......(310)312-0909
CenTech........................(800)255-3999
Centel Corporation.......(800)323-2174
Centon Electronics Inc..(714)855-9111
Centennial Technology..(508)670-0646
Central Cmptr Prods.....(800)456-4123
   Tech Support.............(805)524-4189
Central Data..................(800)482-0315
Central Point.................(800)445-4208
   Tech Support.............(503)690-8080
Centrepoint S-W Tech....(613)235-7054
Centron Software...........(800)848-2424
   Tech Support.............(800)848-2424
Century Cmptr Mktg.....(310)827-0999
Century Data Systems...(919)821-5696
Century Microelect.......(408)748-7788
Century Software...........(801)268-3088
   Tech Support.............(801)268-3088
CERA Inc......................(800)966-3070
Ceres Software...............(800)877-4292
   Tech Support.............(503)245-9011
Cermetek Microelect.....(408)752-5000

Cerner Corporation.......(816)221-1024
Certified Mgt Software..(801)534-1231
Certus Int'l-Semamtic....(800)441-7234
CH Ellis Company Inc...(317)636-3351
CH Products..................(800)624-5804
   Tech Support.............(619)598-2518
Chain Store Guide.........(800)927-9292
Champion Bus. Sys.........(303)792-3606
Champion Duplicators..(800)752-2145
CHAMPS Inc................(904)795-2362
Chancery Software Ltd..(604)294-1233
Chang Laboratories.......(408)727-8096
   Tech Support.............(408)727-8096
Chaplet Systems.............(408)732-7950
Chapman Corporation..(207)773-4726
Charles Charles & Assoc.(800)348-1354
Chatsworth Prods. Inc...(818)882-8596
CheckFree.....................(614)899-7500
CheckMark Software.....(800)444-9922
   Tech Support.............(303)225-0387
Checkmate Technology.(602)966-5802
CheckSum.....................(206)653-4861
ChemCorp.....................(510)226-6280
Chemimnics Inc.............(800)645-5244
   Tech Support.............(800)424-9300
Chen & Associates.........(504)928-5765
CHEQsys........................(416)475-4121
Cherry Electrical Prods.(708)662-9200
Cheyenne Software.......(800)243-9832
   Tech Support.............(800)243-9832
CHI/COR Info. Mgmt....(312)322-0150
Chic Technology Corp...(206)833-4836
Chicago Case Company...(312)927-1600
Chicony America Inc.....(714)380-0928
Chinon America.............(800)441-0222
   Tech Support.............(800)441-0222
Chips & Technology.......(408)434-0600
Chips For Less................(214)250-0009
   Tech Support.............(214)250-9335
ChipSoft, Inc. (Intuit).....(619)453-4446
   Tech Support.............(619)550-5009
Chisholm......................(800)888-4210
Chloride Power Elect....(800)333-0529
Choice Courier Sys........(212)370-1999
Choice Technical Serv....(714)522-8123
CHRONOS Software.......(415)626-4244
Chrysler 1st Commercial.(215)437-8680
Chuck Atkinson Prog.....(800)826-5009
Ci Design Company, Inc..(714)261-5524
CIBD.............................(510)676-6466
CIE America, Inc.............(714)833-8445
CIM Engineering, Inc.....(415)578-9998
Cimmetry Systems Inc..(514)735-3219
Cincinnati Bell Inc.........(513)397-9900
Cincinnati Milacron Inc.(513)841-8100
Cincom Systems Inc......(513)662-2300
CIO Publishing..............(508)872-8200
Ciprico Inc....................(800)727-4669
Circle Computer Inc......(617)821-4114
Circo Computer Sys......(800)678-1688
Circuit Repair Corp........(508)948-7973
Circuit Test...................(510)463-2432
Cirris Systems Corp......(800)441-9910
Cirrus Logic...................(510)623-8300
.....................................(800)424-7787
Cirvis Inc......................(714)891-2000

Citel America Inc...........(800)248-3548
Citizen America.............(800)556-1234
   Tech Support.............(310)453-0614
Citrix Systems................(800)437-7503
   Tech Support.............(800)437-7503
CJF Enterprises Inc........(305)491-1850
Clarify Inc.....................(408)428-2000
Clarion Software...........(800)354-5444
   Tech Support.............(305)785-4556
Claris Corporation........(800)325-2747
   Tech Support.............(408)727-9054
Clarity..........................(800)235-6736
Clark Development Co..(801)261-1686
Clary Corporation..........(818)359-4486
Clear Software...............(800)338-1759
   Tech Support.............(617)965-5019
Cleo Communications...(800)233-2536
   Tech Support.............(313)662-4194
Cliff Notes....................(800)228-4078
   Tech Support.............(402)421-8324
Clipper Products............(513)528-7011
Clone Technologies.......(314)365-2050
Clovis...........................(508)486-0005
CMD Technology Inc.....(800)426-3832
CMG Computer Prods..(512)329-8220
CMI Communications...(800)825-5150
CMO.............................(800)233-8950
   Tech Support.............(800)221-4283
CMP Publications..........(516)562-5000
CMS Enhancements.......(714)222-6000
.....................................(800)555-1671
   Tech Support.............(714)222-6000
CMX.............................(800)668-6413
   Tech Support.............(800)285-2699
CNet Technology...........(800)486-2638
   Tech Support.............(408)954-8800
CNS.............................(800)843-2978
CNS Inc........................(201)625-4056
Coactive Computing.....(415)802-2882
   Tech Support.............(415)802-2882
Coast Computer Power.(800)822-2587
Coastal Electronics.........(912)352-1444
Cobalt Blue...................(404)518-1116
Coconut Computing......(619)456-2002
Coda Music Software.....(612)854-1288
   Tech Support.............(612)854-9649
Codenoll.......................(914)965-6300
Coefficient Systems.......(800)833-4220
Cognitech-Shopwr Help....(800)487-4275
   Tech Support.............(800)487-4275
Cognitive Systems, Inc..(203)773-0726
Cognitronics Corp.........(800)243-2594
Colad Group Inc...........(716)849-1776
Color Age Incorporated...(800)873-4367
Colorado Memory...........(303)669-8000
   Tech Support.............(303)635-1501
Colorado Tech Designs..(303)449-0963
Colorage.......................(800)437-3336
   Tech Support.............(508)663-8213
Columbia Data Systems.(407)869-6700
Columbia Power/Data..(206)576-5045
   Tech Support.............(800)791-1181
Comarco, Inc.................(714)921-0672
Comb.............................(800)328-0609
Comclok Inc..................(714)991-1580
Comdale Technologies...(416)252-2424

Comdisco Parts..............(800)635-2211	Tech Support.............(800)533-7839	Computer Gate Int'l.......(408)730-0673
Comedge Inc................(818)336-7522	CompuLink Mgt. Ctr.......(310)212-5465	Cmptr Hand Holding.....(415)882-0517
Comlite Systems Inc......(800)354-3821	Tech Support.............(310)212-5465	Cmptr Horizons Corp....(800)847-4092
Command Comm. Inc...(800)288-3491	Compulits Inc............(317)581-7600	Computer Hot Line........(214)233-5131
Tech Support.............(303)752-1422	CompuMedia Techn.......(510)656-9811	Computer Hotline Mag..(800)866-3241
Command Cmptr Corp.(201)288-7000	Compumetrics Inc.........(212)323-8150	Cmptr Identics Corp.....(800)343-0846
Command Sftwr Sys......(407)575-3200	CompuRegister Corp.....(314)365-2050	Computer Ind. Almanac.(800)377-6810
Command Technology...(800)336-3320	CompUSA, Inc..............(800)266-7872	Computer Innovations...(908)542-5930
Commax Technologies..(800)526-6629	CompuServe.................(800)848-8199	Tech Support.............(201)542-5920
Tech Support.............(408)435-8272	Tech Support.............(800)848-8199	Computer Intelligence...(619)450-1667
Commadore Bus. Mach..(614)666-7950	Compusol Inc..............(714)253-9533	Tech Support.............(609)450-0255
Common Cents Sftwr....(719)481-4682	ComputAbility Cons......(800)588-0003	Computer Labs Inc........(315)635-7236
Comnwlth of Puerto Rico.(212)245-1200	Compute Publications...(212)496-6100	Computer Lang. Mag......(800)525-0643
Commstar, Inc.............(612)941-8188	Computeach..............(206)885-0517	Computer Law & Tax.....(212)879-3325
Comm. Automation.......(215)776-6669	Tech Support.............(206)885-0517	Cmptr Law Strategist.....(212)741-8300
Comm. Research Group....(504)923-0888	Cmptr & Control Sol.....(800)782-3525	Computer Law Sys.........(800)328-1913
Comm. Tech Group........(800)626-2715	Cmptr & Monitor Maint..(800)466-4411	Computer Library..........(212)503-4400
Comm. Test Design........(800)223-3910	Computer Aided Mgt.....(707)795-4100	Cmptr Locators Int'l......(407)627-7797
COMP USA.....................(800)541-7638	Computer Analysis.........(808)848-4878	Computer Logic Ltd......(800)359-0599
COMPAC Microelect......(510)656-3333	Computer Assistance.....(503)895-3347	Computer Logistics Ltd.(216)349-8600
Compact Disk Products..(908)290-8087	Computer Associates.....(706)505-6000	Computer Maint. Plus...(303)427-5181
Tech Support.............(212)737-8400	Computer Assoc. Int'l...(800)531-5236	Computer Maint. Serv....(800)333-4267
Compaq.......................(800)888-5858	Tech Support.............(406)432-1764	Cmptr Maint. Training....(800)952-5977
Tech Support.............(800)345-1518	Cmptr Automation.........(714)833-8830	Computer Mgt Service..(510)732-0644
Compatible Systems......(800)356-0283	Cmptr Auxillary Prods...(714)465-0911	Computer Marketplace.(800)858-1144
CompEd Inc.................(800)456-5338	Computer Bay.............(414)357-7705	Computer Media & Serv..(800)798-9078
Compeq USA Ltd...........(800)852-0105	Computer Boards..........(508)261-1123	Computer Modules Inc.(408)496-1881
Tech Support.............(714)404-1619	Computer Book Club....(717)794-2191	Cmptr Mnthly/Reseller..(205)988-9708
Compex Technology......(818)855-7988	Cmptr Bus. Services.......(800)343-8014	Cmptr Music Supply.......(714)594-5051
Compex, Inc................(714)630-7302	Tech Support.............(317)758-9612	Tech Support.............(714)594-6821
Complementary Solutions.(404)454-8033	Cmptr Buyers Guide......(212)807-8220	Cmptr Netwrk Serv-CNS.(303)682-0090
Complete Computer......(415)549-3153	Cmptr Buying World......(617)246-3800	Cmptr Network Tech.....(800)638-8324
Complete PC, The..........(407)997-9683	Cmptr Cable & Conn....(201)993-9285	Computer Parts Outlet...(800)475-1655
Complex, Inc...............(714)630-7302	Computer Care............(703)528-8700	Cmpter Parts Unlimited.(818)879-1100
Tech Support.............(714)630-5451	Computer Care Inc........(800)552-4283	Cmptr Periph. Repair......(407)486-0011
Complus......................(510)623-1000	Computer Channel Inc..(516)921-5170	Computer Place, The......(602)962-1030
Compo Group Inc.........(203)222-1335	Computer Classifieds.....(206)643-2316	Computer Power, Inc.....(800)526-5088
Component Sales Corp.(408)894-1870	Computer Clipboard.....(800)777-4932	Tech Support.............(908)638-8600
Comport......................(408)437-2404	Cmptr Comm Specials...(404)441-3114	Computer Products.......(305)974-5500
Comprehensive Sftwr....(213)318-2561	Cmptr Commodities Int'l.(800)365-3475	Computer Prods Corp...(800)338-4273
Tech Support.............(213)214-1461	Cmptr Comm................(800)421-1178	Cmptr. Prods. Plus (CP+).(800)274-4277
Compro Cmptr Services.(412)255-3616	Cmptr Compnent Source.(800)356-1227	Tech Support.............(800)274-4277
Compsee, Inc...............(407)724-4321	Cmptr Compnents.........(800)356-1227	Computer Publishers.....(708)390-7000
Compteck Research, Inc.(716)842-2700	Computer Connection...(800)552-2331	Computer Publ. & Adv...(914)833-0600
Compton's NewMedia...(619)929-2626	Cmptr Connection Corp.(612)884-0758	Computer Publ. Ent........(619)576-0353
Tech Support.............(619)929-2626	Computer Control Sys...(904)752-0912	Computer Recyclers......(800)466-6449
Comptronics.................(919)779-7268	Cmptr Covers Unltd......(800)722-6837	Cmptr Ref. Products......(206)869-7840
Compu-D International.(818)787-3282	Computer Coverup.......(312)327-9200	Computer Renaissance..(612)942-5062
Compu-Gard Inc...........(508)761-4520	Computer Craftsmen......(414)567-1700	Cmptr Repss Assn..........(407)788-3666
Compu-Tek International.(800)531-0190	Computer Currents.......(415)547-6800	Computer Research.......(800)245-2710
Tech Support.............(214)994-0193	Computer Data Sys........(301)921-7000	Cmptr Reseller News Mag.(516)562-5000
CompuAdd Corp...........(800)925-3000	Computer DataVault.......(714)362-3839	Computer Reset.............(214)276-8072
Tech Support.............(800)925-0995	Computer Design Mag..(800)225-0556	Computer Resources......(800)662-0034
CompuCase................(800)255-9617	Computer Dis. Wrhse....(800)726-4239	Cmptr Retail Week Mag.(516)562-5000
CompuClassics..............(800)733-3888	Tech Support.............(706)291-7575	Computer Sales Prof......(800)950-6660
CompuClean................(800)444-9038	Computer Doctor.........(512)467-9355	Cmptr Sciences Corp.....(213)615-0311
Compucom Systems.....(609)848-2300	Computer Doctors.........(301)474-3095	Cmptr Service & Maint...(619)944-1228
CompuCover.................(800)874-6391	Computer Dynamics......(803)877-8700	Computer Service Ctr....(201)843-6290
Tech Support.............(904)863-2200	Computer Exchange......(404)446-7960	Computer Service Exp..(502)366-3188
CompuD International..(800)929-9333	Computer Expressions..(800)443-8278	Computer Serv. Labs....(800)220-6860
Tech Support.............(818)787-3282	Cmptr Factory Outlct....(800)486-9975	Computer Serv. Supply..(800)255-7815
Compudyne.................(800)486-8810	Tech Support.............(602)829-7751	Computer Serv. Tech......(214)241-2662
Tech Support.............(800)447-3895	Computer Field Serv......(617)246-4090	Computer Serv. Group...(212)819-0122
CompuLan Technology..(800)486-8810	Computer Fixer............(215)568-1100	Cmptr Shopper Mag......(305)269-3211
Tech Support.............(408)954-8864	Computer Friends, Inc...(800)547-3303	Computer Site Tech.......(305)425-0638
Compulaw....................(800)559-4991	Computer Fun..............(619)279-1919	Computer Solutions.......(201)672-6000

INDUSTRY PHONE NUMBERS

Computer Support........(214)661-8960
   Tech Support............(214)661-8960
Cmptr Support Prods....(506)281-6554
Computer Sys.Advisors..(800)537-4262
Computer Sys Assoc......(704)871-8367
Computer Sys. News......(516)365-4600
Computer Sys. Repair.....(310)217-8901
Computer Task Group...(716)882-8000
Cmptr Techn. Review.....(310)208-1335
Computer Techn Serv....(714)855-8667
Cmptr Terminal Serv......(916)368-4300
Cmptr Time of America.(800)456-1159
   Tech Support............(614)759-0100
Computer Trade Exch....(201)226-1528
Computer Trading Int'l..(818)764-0615
Computer Trend Inc......(205)442-6376
ComputerEasy Int'l........(602)829-9614
ComputerGear..............(800)234-3434
Computerland Corp......(510)734-4000
   Tech Support............(800)922-5263
ComputerLand Corp.....(201)575-7110
Cmptrlnd Depot Repair..(800)445-6879
Computers For Less.......(800)634-1415
   Tech Support............(714)975-0542
Computers Inc..............(800)637-4832
Computers Plus.............(401)434-9180
Computervision.............(619)535-1527
Computerwise Inc.........(913)829-0600
Computerworld.............(508)879-0700
Computime Inc.............(800)423-8826
Computone..................(800)541-9915
Computone Corp..........(800)241-3946
   Tech Support............(404)475-2725
Computrac, Inc.............(214)234-4241
CompuTrend Sys. Inc....(818)333-5121
Comshare.....................(313)994-4800
Comtech Publishing......(800)456-7005
Comtrade.....................(800)969-2123
   Tech Support............(800)8994508
Comtrol Corporation.....(800)926-6876
Concentric Data...........(800)325-9035
   Tech Support............(800)325-9035
Concept Omega Corp...(800)524-9035
Conceptual Software......(713)667-4222
Concurrent Computer...(908)758-7000
Concurrent Computer...(908)870-4128
Concurrent Controls......(800)487-2249
Conde Systems..............(800)826-6332
   Tech Support............(205)633-3876
Conductive Containers..(800)327-2329
Conley........................(212)682-0162
Conlux USA Corporation.(800)792-0101
Connect......................(415)435-7446
Connect Software..........(800)234-9497
   Tech Support............(800)234-9497
Connect Tech Inc..........(519)836-1291
Connect-Air Int'l...........(800)247-1978
Connectix Corporation.(800)950-5880
   Tech Support............(800)950-5880
Connector Rsrce. Unltd.(408)942-9077
Conner International.....(408)456-4415
Conner Peripherals........(408)433-3340
...............................(408)456-3200
Conner/Maynard Electr.(800)227-6296
Connexperts.................(800)433-5373
   Tech Support............(214)352-2281

Consmi Development...(310)835-9687
   Tech Support............(800)654-8829
Consolidated Electr........(513)252-5662
Consultex.....................(800)243-3338
Consulting Spectrum.....(214)484-9330
Consultronics................(800)267-7255
Consumer Tech NW.......(800)356-3983
Consumers Software......(604)688-4548
Contact East................(800)225-5334
Contact Software Int'l....(800)365-0606
   Tech Support............(800)365-0606
Contek Int'l Corp..........(203)853-4313
Contemporary Cmptr....(516)563-8880
Continental Info. Sys......(315)437-1900
Continental Resources...(800)937-4688
Contingency Planning...(516)997-1100
Control Cable...............(410)298-4411
Control Concepts Corp.(800)288-6169
Control Data Corp.........(612)853-8100
Control Technology........(405)840-3163
Controlled Power Co.....(313)528-3700
Convergent World..........(800)888-5093
Conversion Systems.......(714)870-1626
Convex Corporation......(800)642-0602
Conway Engineering.....(510)568-4028
Cook's Computer Maint..(805)323-6036
Cooper Industries...........(317)983-5200
Coordinated Service......(508)486-0388
Copam USA, Inc............(800)828-4200
Copia International........(706)682-8898
Copy Technologies........(714)975-1477
Cordata........................(213)603-2901
Core International..........(407)997-6044
   Tech Support............(407)997-6033
Core Software Inc..........(713)292-2177
Corel Systems Corp.......(800)772-6735
   Tech Support............(613)726-1990
Corim Int'l Corp............(212)883-0030
Cornell Computer Sys...(800)886-7200
Cornerstone Data Sys....(714)772-5527
Cornerstone Imaging....(408)435-8900
   Tech Support............(408)435-8900
Cornerstone Technology..(800)562-2552
   Tech Support............(408)435-8900
Corollary Inc.................(714)250-4040
Coromandel Industries..(800)535-3267
   Tech Support............(718)793-7966
Corporate Mgt. & Mktg..(201)989-0229
Corporate Microsystems.(603)448-5193
Corporate Software........(617)821-4500
Corporate Systems Center.(408)734-3475
Cortex Corporation.......(612)894-3354
Corvus Systems, Inc.......(800)426-7887
Cosmi............................(800)292-6967
Cosmic Enterprises.......(800)292-6967
Costa Dist., West...........(800)926-7829
CoStar...........................(800)426-7827
   Tech Support............(203)661-9700
Costas Systems..............(510)443-2332
Costem Inc....................(408)734-9235
Cougar Mountain Sftwr.(800)388-3038
   Tech Support............(800)727-9912
Counter Peripherals.......(800)222-5871
Courseware Technology..(800)736-1936
...............................(619)452-2726
Courtland Group Inc.....(410)730-7668

CPE Inc........................(214)313-1133
CPI..............................(805)499-6021
Cpt Corporation............(612)937-8000
CPU Products................(316)788-3749
Cranel Inc.....................(800)727-2635
Cray Research................(612)452-6650
CRC Systems Ltd...........(800)231-0743
Creative Cmptr Apps.....(818)880-6700
Creative Controllers.......(800)950-6224
Creative Data Products..(800)366-1020
Creative Labs................(405)742-6622
Creative Multimedia......(503)241-4351
   Tech Support............(503)241-1530
Creative Programming...(214)416-6447
Creotec Corporation......(214)717-1272
Crescent Project Mgt.....(415)493-4787
Crescent Software.........(203)438-5300
Cresta Batteries..............(800)638-7120
Crisis Computer Corp..(800)726-0726
   Tech Support............(800)729-0729
CRM Cmptr Parts-ON....(800)284-2865
CRM Cmptr PartsFL.......(800)759-5539
Crosby Creations...........(800)842-8445
Crosfield Dicomed.........(612)895-3000
Crossly Group Inc The..(404)751-3703
Crosstalk Comm...........(404)442-4000
CrossTies......................(214)732-9060
   Tech Support............(214)732-9060
Crown Mats & Matting..(800)628-5463
Crump Electronics.........(303)936-4407
Crutchfield-Hardware....(800)537-4050
Crutchfield-Software......(800)538-4050
Crystal Computer Sys....(310)946-1447
Crystal Semiconductor..(512)445-7222
Crystal Services.............(604)681-3435
   Tech Support............(604)681-3435
CrystalGraphics Inc.......(408)496-6175
CS Electronics................(714)259-9100
CSC CompuSource........(919)460-1234
CSP Inc.........................(617)272-6020
CSR..............................(201)671-7711
CSS Laboratories, Inc.....(714)852-8161
CST Inc.........................(214)241-2662
CTC Corporation...........(510)770-8787
CTI..............................(703)264-8900
CTS Services.................(508)528-7720
CTSI International Inc...(516)467-1281
CTX International..........(800)282-2205
   Tech Support............(800)282-2205
Cubix Corporation........(800)829-0550
CUE Paging Corp..........(800)858-8828
Cuesta Systems Corp....(800)332-3440
CUI...............................(800)458-6686
   Tech Support............(408)988-2703
Cullinet Software..........(617)329-7700
Cumulus.......................(216)464-2211
Curtis Inc......................(612)631-9512
Curtis Mfg. Company.....(800)955-5544
   Tech Support............(603)532-4123
Custom Application.......(508)667-8585
   Tech Support............(508)663-8213
Custom Cmptr Cable....(612)941-5651
Custom Real-Time Soft..(201)228-7623
Cust. Satisfaction Rsrch..(913)894-6166
Customer Serv. Institute.(301)585-0730
Cut Craft Inc.................(817)332-6151

INDUSTRY PHONE NUMBERS

CW Electronics	(303)832-1111	
CWay Software	(215)368-9494	
Tech Support	(215)368-7233	
CXR Digilog	(408)435-8520	
CyberTechnics Corp.	(408)986-9686	
Cybex Corporation	(205)534-0011	
Cyborg Corporation	(617)964-9020	
Cycare Systems	(800)545-2483	
Cyclades Corporation	(510)770-9727	
Cyco International	(800)323-2926	
Cylix Corporation	(805)379-3155	
Cyma Systems Inc	(800)292-2962	
Cypress Research	(408)752-2700	
Tech Support	(408)752-2700	
Cyrix Corporation	(800)462-9749	
Tech Support	(800)462-9749	
D-C-Drives	(800)473-0960	
Tech Support	(713)333-2099	
D-Link Systems, Inc	(714)455-1688	
Da Vinci Systems	(919)781-5924	
DacEasy, Inc	(800)322-3279	
Tech Support	(214)248-0205	
Daewoo Int'l Corp	(201)935-8700	
Dairyland Cmptr Cnsult	(800)323-6987	
Daisy Disc Corporation	(800)537-3475	
Daisycom	(214)881-4700	
Dak Industries, Inc	(800)325-0800	
DakTech Inc	(800)325-3238	
Dalco Electronics	(800)445-5342	
Tech Support	(800)543-2526	
Dallas Digital Corp	(800)842-6333	
Dallas Fax Inc	(214)699-8999	
Dallas Semiconductor	(214)450-0400	
Damark International	(800)729-9000	
Dana Commercial Credit	(313)689-7000	
Danish Consulate Gen	(213)387-4277	
Danpex Corporation	(408)437-7557	
Dantona Industries Inc	(516)596-1515	
Dantz Development	(510)849-0293	
Tech Support	(510)849-0293	
Danwill Industrial Ltd	(818)810-8880	
Dariana Software	(714)236-1380	
Tech Support	(714)236-1380	
Darius Technology Inc	(206)483-8889	
Dash Computer Inc	(408)773-1488	
Dat Entry Inc	(407)339-5062	
Data 3 Systems	(707)528-6560	
Data Access Corp	(800)451-3539	
Tech Support	(305)232-3142	
Data Accessories Cor	(416)292-9963	
Data Base Solutions	(800)336-6060	
Data Code	(516)331-7848	
Data Communications	(212)512-6950	
Data Comm. 2000	(714)255-7090	
Data Connections	(800)225-1855	
Data Depot	(800)767-3424	
Tech Support	(800)775-3825	
Data Engineering	(603)893-3374	
Data Entry Systems, Inc	(205)539-2483	
Data Envelope & Pkg	(800)544-4417	
Data Exchange Corp	(805)388-1711	
Data General Corp	(508)366-8911	
Data I/O	(800)332-8246	
	(206)881-6444	
DataMate North America	(310)316-5161	
Data Pad Corporation	(800)755-8218	

Data Plus, Inc	(713)641-6158	
Data Pro	(908)756-7300	
Data Pro Acctg Software	(800)836-6377	
Tech Support	(813)888-5847	
Data Processing Security	(817)457-9400	
Data Quest Hawaii	(808)545-5482	
Data Race	(210)558-1900	
Tech Support	(210)558-1900	
Data Recording Prods	(310)633-7198	
Data Retrieval Serv-FL	(800)952-7530	
Data Retrieval Serv-CA	(800)942-4472	
Data Services Corp	(404)246-3700	
Data Set Cable Co	(800)344-9684	
Data Shield	(312)329-1601	
Data Solutions	(714)637-5060	
Data Spec	(800)431-8124	
Tech Support	(818)772-9977	
Data Storage Mktg-CO	(800)543-6090	
Tech Support	(800)543-6098	
Data Storage Mktg-NJ	(800)424-2203	
Data Storage Mktg-TX	(800)654-6311	
Data Sys/Micro Connect	(800)445-3282	
Data Technology	(408)942-4000	
Tech Support	(408)942-4000	
Data Transforms	(303)832-1501	
Data Translation	(508)481-3700	
Tech Support	(508)481-3700	
Data Viz	(800)733-0030	
Tech Support	(203)268-4000	
Data Watch	(919)549-0711	
Tech Support	(919)549-0711	
Data-Cal Corporation	(800)223-0123	
Data-Doc Electronics	(512)928-8926	
Tech Support	(512)928-8926	
Data/Ware Devel. Inc	(619)453-7660	
Database Applications	(609)924-2900	
Database Prog. & Design	(415)905-2200	
Dataability Sftwr Sys	(212)807-7800	
Datacap Inc	(914)332-7515	
Datacap Systems, Inc	(215)699-7051	
Datacom Technologies	(800)468-5557	
Datadesk International	(804)477-3473	
Tech Support	(503)692-9601	
DataEase International	(800)243-5123	
Tech Support	(203)374-2825	
DataExpert Corp	(408)737-0880	
Datafix Inc	(501)562-3554	
Datagate Inc	(408)946-6222	
Dataguard Recvry Serv	(800)325-3977	
DataJets International	(714)630-6662	
Datalight	(360)435-8086	
Datalynx Marketing	(604)765-1162	
Datamar Systems	(800)223-9963	
Datamate	(918)664-7276	
Datamation	(617)964-3030	
Datapath Technologies	(510)651-5580	
Datapoint Corporation	(512)593-7000	
Datapro Info. Serv	(609)764-0100	
Datapro Research Grp	(800)328-2776	
Dataproducts (CA)	(818)887-8440	
Dataproducts (NH)	(603)673-9100	
Dataq Instruments Inc	(216)668-1444	
Dataquest/Ledgeway	(506)370-5555	
Datashield/Tripp Lite	(312)329-1777	
Tech Support	(312)329-1602	
Datasouth Cmptr Corp	(800)476-2450	

DataSpec/ORA Electr	(800)431-8124	
Datastor	(714)833-8000	
Datastorm Technologies	(314)443-3282	
Tech Support	(314)875-0530	
Datasure Technologies	(510)935-9899	
DataSym Inc	(519)758-5800	
Datatech Depot Inc	(714)970-1600	
Datatek Periph. Services	(800)829-2099	
Datatran Corporation	(303)778-0870	
DataTrek Corporation	(219)522-8000	
Datatronics Inc.	(713)367-0567	
Dataviz	(800)733-0030	
Tech Support	(203)268-0030	
Dataware	(800)426-4844	
Datawatch	(919)549-0711	
DATEC (WA)	(800)525-9905	
DATEC (OR)	(503)641-6644	
Datel	(508)339-3000	
Dauphin Technology	(708)627-4004	
David Smith Software	(508)249-9056	
David Systems, Inc	(800)762-7848	
Tech Support	(408)541-6884	
Davidson & Associates	(800)545-7677	
Tech Support	(310)793-0600	
Davox Corporation	(508)667-4455	
DayFlo Software	(714)474-1364	
Dayna Communications	(801)269-7200	
Tech Support	(801)269-7200	
DayStar Digital	(800)962-2077	
Tech Support	(800)960-2077	
DBMS	(415)358-9500	
DC Battery Products	(612)616-7478	
DCA	(404)740-0300	
Tech Support	(404)740-0300	
DCA/Crosstalk Comm	(800)348-3221	
Tech Support	(404)442-3210	
DCI Companies	(800)234-2202	
DCM Data Products	(817)870-2202	
DCSI	(703)823-8886	
DD & TT Ent. USA	(213)780-0099	
Tech Support	(213)780-0099	
DDC Publishing	(800)528-3897	
Tech Support	(800)528-3897	
DEVC Professional	(215)957-1500	
Decision Inc	(903)586-0556	
Decision Industries	(215)674-3300	
Dee One Systems	(800)831-8808	
Dee Van Enterprise USA	(800)878-0691	
Deerfield Systems Inc	(800)356-8170	
Dees Comm. Eng	(604)946-8433	
Delkin Services Inc	(619)571-1234	
Dell Computer Corp	(800)426-5150	
Tech Support	(800)624-9896	
DeLorme Mapping	(207)865-1234	
Delphi	(800)695-4005	
Delphi Data	(800)335-7445	
Delrina Technology	(800)268-6082	
Tech Support	(800)268-6082	
Delta Computer Inc	(201)440-8585	
Delta Phase Int'l	(714)768-6842	
Delta Products	(706)487-1037	
Delta Technology Int'l	(715)832-7575	
Delta Warranty	(206)391-2000	
DeltaPoint Inc	(408)648-4000	
Tech Support	(408)375-4700	
Deltec Corporation	(800)854-2658	

INDUSTRY PHONE NUMBERS

Deltron Inc....................(800)523-2332
Demosource..................(800)283-4759
Dempa Publications......(212)752-3003
Deneba Software...........(305)596-5644
　　Tech Support.........(305)596-5644
Departmental Techn......(201)786-5838
Depot America..............(800)648-6833
Desco Industries...........(714)598-2753
DeScribe, Inc...............(800)448-1586
　　Tech Support.........(916)646-1111
Design Creations...........(209)532-8413
Design Science.............(800)827-0685
　　Tech Support.........(213)433-6969
DesignCAD...................(918)825-4844
Desk Top Graphics........(817)346-0556
Deskin Research Grp.....(408)496-5300
Desktop AI..................(203)255-3400
Desktop Sales Inc...........(708)272-9695
Destiny Techn. Corp......(408)262-9400
DEW Int'l Corp.............(800)326-7114
DF Blumberg & Assoc...(215)643-9060
DFM Systems, Inc..........(800)922-4336
DH Serv.......................(800)548-7862
DH Technology..............(619)451-3485
DI/AN Controls.............(800)878-3134
Diagnostic Technology..(416)542-8674
DiagSoft Inc.................(800)342-4763
　　Tech Support.........(408)438-8247
Diamond Cmptr Sys......(408)736-2000
　　Tech Support.........(408)736-2000
Diamond Data Mgt........(800)955-3330
Diamond Flower Inst....(916)568-1234
Diamond Systems..........(904)241-4550
Dianachart Inc.............(201)625-2299
DIC Digital..................(201)224-9344
Dick Berg & Associates..(619)452-2745
Diebold.......................(216)489-4110
Digi-Data Corporation..(800)782-6395
Digi-Key Corporation...(800)344-4539
Digiboard, Inc..............(800)344-4273
　　Tech Support.........(612)943-9020
Digicom Systems Inc.....(800)833-8900
Digit Head Inc..............(703)524-0101
Digital Comm. (DCA)....(800)348-3221
Digital Computer Serv..(215)358-6045
Digital Data Systems......(800)762-7811
Digital Dynamics...........(714)529-6328
Digital Engineering........(713)271-5200
　　Tech Support.........(713)271-5200
Digital Equip. Corp-MA..(800)332-7378
Digital Equip. Corp-MA..(800)332-4636
Digital Equip. Corp-MA..(800)354-9000
Digital Equip. Corp-MA..(508)841-3627
Digital Equip. Corp-NH..(800)354-9000
Digital Data Recovery....(414)353-1219
Digital Mind................(407)354-0045
Digital News & Reviews.(617)964-3030
Digital Processing Sys....(606)371-5533
Digital Products Inc.......(800)243-2337
Digital Products, Inc......(800)243-3333
Digital Research............(800)848-1498
Digital Review..............(617)964-3030
Digital Solutions Inc......(916)773-1551
Digital Storage Inc.........(800)232-3475
Digital Sys. Research......(714)455-1620
Digital Typeface Corp....(612)944-9264

Tech Support............(612)941-8652
Digital Vision.................(617)329-5400
　　Tech Support.........(617)329-5400
Digitalk........................(800)531-2344
　　Tech Support.........(714)513-3000
Digitech Industries Inc..(203)797-2676
Digitronix Inc...............(402)339-5340
Digitz.........................(919)828-5227
DigiVox Corporation.....(415)494-6200
Digix America Corp.......(305)593-8070
Direct Drives................(708)481-1111
DISC..........................(800)669-2333
Disc & Tape Services.....(603)889-5722
Disc Distributing Corp..(800)688-4545
Disc Manufacturing Inc.(302)479-2500
Disc Tec.....................(407)671-5500
Dismimagery................(212)675-8500
Discis Knowledge Rsrch.(800)567-4321
Discount Micro..............(800)574-3325
　　Tech Support.........(714)827-7090
Discoversoft Inc............(510)814-1690
Discus Knowledge Rsrch.(416)250-6537
　　Tech Support.........(416)250-6537
Disk Drive Repair.........(206)575-3181
Disk Software................(800)635-7760
Disk Technologies..........(407)645-0001
....................................(800)553-0337
Disk's & Labels To Go....(800)426-3303
Diskette Connection......(800)654-4058
Diskettes Unlimited.......(800)364-3475
Disks & Labels To Go....(609)265-1500
Disney Cmptr Software.(818)841-3326
　　Tech Support.........(818)841-3326
Display Technologies.....(708)931-2136
Distinct Corporation.....(408)741-0781
Distr. Logic Corp...........(714)476-0303
Distr. Processing Tech....(407)830-5522
Distributed Technology.(206)395-7800
Ditek International........(416)479-1990
DiVA..........................(800)949-2843
Diverse Business Grp....(604)596-6088
Diversified Case Co.......(315)736-3028
Diversified Technology..(800)443-2667
Diesko Associates...........(201)435-8401
DM............................(516)462-0440
DM............................(800)821-3354
DNA Networks, Inc........(800)999-3622
Document Management..(602)224-9777
Document Storage Sys...(303)757-1455
DocuPoint Inc...............(510)770-1189
Dolch Computer Sys.....(800)538-7506
Dominion Blueline Inc..(416)444-6621
DotShop Inc.................(800)487-6025
Dover Electr. Mfg...........(303)772-5933
Dovetail Comm.............(800)432-1414
Dow Jones & Company..(800)922-0358
DP Nemeth Associates...(609)737-1166
DP Tech......................(713)492-1894
DP-Tek, Inc..................(800)727-3130
DPT-Distr. Process Tech..(407)830-5522
　　Tech Support.........(407)830-5522
Dr. Dobb's Journal.........(415)358-9500
Dr.T's Music Software...(617)455-1454
Dragon Systems Inc.......(617)965-5200
Dranetz Technology.......(800)372-6832
Dresselhaus Cmptr Prod.(800)368-7737

Tech Support............(909)945-5600
Drexler Technology.......(415)969-7277
Drive Repair Serv. Co......(510)430-0595
DSA Systems.................(508)477-2540
DSC Communications...(214)519-3000
DSE Inc.......................(808)578-0237
DSG Communications..(306)665-6107
DSK Inc.......................(801)224-4828
DSP Solutions...............(415)494-8086
　　Tech Support.........(415)494-8088
DST Systems.................(816)221-5545
DTK Computer Inc.......(818)810-6880
Dual Group, Inc............(310)542-0788
Duble-Click Software....(800)359-9079
　　Tech Support.........(800)266-9525
Dudley Software............no main number
　　Tech Support.........(615)966-3667
Duffy Consulting Grp....(416)966-4015
Dukane Corporation.....(708)584-2300
Dumont Oscilloscope...(201)575-8666
Duplication Technology.(303)444-6157
Duracell Inc.................(203)796-4000
Durham Off. Mach. Spec..(408)462-4989
Dustin Discount Sftwre.(800)274-6611
DW Smith & Associates.(415)349-7725
Dyatron Corporation.....(800)334-3471
Dyna Micro, Inc............(408)943-0100
Dynamic Electronics Inc.(714)855-0411
Dynamic Pathways........(714)720-8462
Dynamic Power System..(800)422-0708
Dynatech Cmptr Power.(800)638-9098
Dynatech Corporation...(617)272-6100
DynaTek Auto. Systems..(416)636-3000
Dynaware USA..............(415)349-5700
Dytel Inc.....................(708)519-9850
E-Cam Technology Inc...(602)443-1949
E-Comms......................(800)247-1431
E-Machines...................(800)344-7274
　　Tech Support.........(800)344-7274
E-Systems.....................(214)661-1000
E-Tech Research Inc.......(408)988-8108
E-Toor Corporation.......(818)333-5521
E-WARE.......................(714)236-1380
　　Tech Support.........(714)236-1380
Eagle Electronics...........(800)992-3191
Eagle Perform. Software..(214)539-7855
Eagle Technology...........(800)733-2453
　　Tech Support.........(800)726-5267
Easel Corporation..........(617)221-2100
Eastern Time Designs....(603)645-6578
Easterntech Corp...........(800)289-8128
　　Tech Support.........(800)685-5006
Eastman Kodak.............(716)724-4000
Easy Automation Sys......(800)627-3274
　　Tech Support.........(404)840-0475
EAZY..........................(412)746-5500
EBS Consulting.............(215)493-7315
Eclipse Marketing Inc....(800)284-0779
　　Tech Support.........(506)598-9640
Eclipse Systems............(312)541-0260
Ecol 2.........................(408)456-0272
Edgell Enterprises..........(201)895-3300
Edimax Computer Co...(408)496-1105
Edison Technologies......(800)334-7668
Edmark.......................(800)426-0856
　　Tech Support.........(206)556-8400

INDUSTRY PHONE NUMBERS

Edmund Scientific ....(609)573-6250	Eletch Electronics, Inc...(714)385-1707	Equilibrium ....(415)332-4343
EDP Rsrch & Devel........(203)399-5018	Elgar Corporation..........(619)450-0085	Tech Support...........(415)332-4343
EDS Corporation...........(214)661-6000	Elisa Technology Inc......(510)651-5817	Equinox.......................(305)255-3500
Educom USA Inc...........(800)553-2212	Elite...........................(310)370-2762	Equinox Systems Inc.....(800)275-3500
Educational Systems......(800)553-2212	Elite Microelectronics....(408)943-0500	Tech Support...........(305)255-3500
EECO Inc.....................(714)835-6000	Elitegroup Cmptr Sys ....(510)226-7333	ERA...........................(312)649-1333
EF Industries................(310)523-2290	Tech Support...........(510)226-7333	Ergo Computing, Inc....(508)535-7510
EFA Corp. of America ....(301)670-6166	Elographics, Inc............(615)482-4100	Ergo Management Co....(800)348-8633
EFAR Microsystems Inc.(408)452-1888	ELSA America Inc..........(415)615-7799	Ergo Systems Inc..........(203)282-9767
Efficient Field Service....(800)257-4745	ELT Systems of CA.........(510)226-9057	Ergodyne....................(612)642-9889
Effron Sales ....(714)962-1016	Eltrex Industries Inc......(716)454-6100	Ergotron......................(800)888-8458
EFI Electronics.............(800)877-1174	Elvo...........................(914)241-1008	ErgoView Technologies.(212)995-2673
Tech Support...........(800)877-1174	Elxsi Corporation..........(408)994-9301	ERM/Crazy Bob's ....(800)776-5865
Egghead Discount Sftwr.(206)391-0800	EMAC/EVEREX ....(510)498-4411	Tech Support...........(617)662-2046
Eicon Technology ....(514)631-2592	Tech Support...........(510)498-4411	Ero Surge Inc. ....(908)776-4220
EID Center ....(408)733-5501	Emax International Inc..(310)637-6380	ERS Electr. Repair Serv...(210)623-4420
Eight Hundred Sftwr .....(800)888-4880	EMC Corporation..........(800)222-3622	Escaa Corporation........(206)822-6800
EJ Bilingual Inc............(310)320-8139	Emerald Intelligence......(313)663-8757	ESCOD Industries.........(800)533-4736
EKD Cmptr Sales/Supp. (516)736-0500	Emerald Systems...........(800)767-2587	Esico-Triton................(203)526-5361
El Camino Rsrcs Ltd ......(818)226-6600	Tech Support...........(800)366-4349	Esker..........................(415)341-9065
Elan Computer Grp........(415)964-2200	Emerging Techn. Cons...(303)447-9495	Tech Support...........(415)341-9065
Elan Software Corp........(800)654-3526	Emerson Cmptr Corp....(800)222-5877	ESoft Product Support...(303)699-6565
Tech Support...........(310)459-1222	Emerson Cmptr Pwr .....(800)222-5877	ESP Inc.......................(800)338-4353
Elcee Computek, Inc.....(407)750-8061	Tech Support...........(800)222-5877	Etak Inc......................(415)328-3825
Elco...........................(818)284-2181	Emerson Electric ....(314)553-2000	ETC Computer Inc........(510)226-6250
.................................(814)643-0700	Emery World Wide.........(800)443-6379	ETCON Corporation .....(708)325-6100
.................................(818)284-7018	EML Associates..............(617)341-0781	Eteq Microsystems, Inc..(408)432-8147
.................................(800)653-3526	Empac Int'l Corp............(510)683-8800	ETN Corporation...........(800)326-9273
Elecom Computer Prod..(310)802-0077	Empress Software Inc....(301)220-1919	ETS Incorporated........no main number
Electrified Discounters..(800)678-8585	Emulex Corporation......(800)368-5393	Tech Support...........(801)265-2490
Electro Media Publ ....(408)374-9804	Enable Software.............(800)888-0684	European Cmptr Mkt ....(619)929-0955
Electro Products Inc......(800)423-0646	Tech Support...........(518)877-8236	European Cmptr Source.(708)475-1900
Electro Rent Corp..........(818)787-2100	ENCAD.......................(619)578-4070	Evans & Sutherland Co .(801)582-5847
Electro Standards Lab....(401)943-1164	Enclosure Technologies....(313)481-2200	Everest Cmptr Corp.......(408)997-1674
Electro Static Techn ......(207)795-6416	Encore Computer Corp...(508)460-0500	Everex ....(800)821-0806
Electro Tech Industries..(619)745-3575	Endl Publications...........(408)867-6642	Tech Support...........(510)498-4411
Electro-Tech Systems.....(215)887-2196	Enertronics Research......(314)427-7578	Everfit Cmptr Supply....(408)894-9003
Electrodata Inc.............(800)441-6336	Engage Comm................(408)688-1021	Evergreen Technologies...(800)733-0934
Electrografics Int'l..........(215)443-5190	Engineered Data Prods..(800)432-1337	Evolution Computing....(800)874-4028
Tech Support...........(215)443-9564	Eng. Computers & Apps..(800)950-1217	Tech Support...........(800)874-4028
Electrohome Projection..(519)744-7111	Engineering Services.....(800)525-5608	Evtek Corporation.........(216)267-8499
Electromatic.................(708)882-5757	English Knowledge Sys.(408)438-6922	Ex Machina Inc............(718)965-0309
Electronic Arts Distr ......(800)448-8822	Enhance Memory Prods...(800)343-0100	Ex-Cel Solutions............(402)333-6541
Tech Support...........(415)572-2787	Tech Support...........(818)343-3066	Exabyte.......................(800)445-7736
Electronic Assist. Corp...(817)778-7978	Enigma Logic Inc...........(415)827-5707	Tech Support...........(913)492-6002
Electronic Associates.....(908)229-1100	Enlight Corporations......(310)693-8885	Excalibur Comm...........(918)496-7881
Electronic Buyers' Mag..(516)562-5000	Enterprise Sys. Journal...(214)343-3717	Excel, Inc....................(800)624-2001
Electronic City..............(602)622-1173	Entrepreneur.................(714)261-2325	Excelan (Novell)...........(408)434-2300
Electronic Data Assoc....(816)966-0669	Entropy Engineering......(301)770-6886	Tech Support...........(800)638-9273
Electronic Eng. Times.....(516)562-5000	Envelope Manager.........(415)321-2640	Excelta Corporation......(805)686-4686
Electronic Ind. Assoc......(202)457-4500	Environgen....................(714)863-7474	Executive Systems Inc...(805)541-0604
Electronic Mktg. Grp .....(800)955-2688	Tech Support...........(714)863-7474	EXFO Electro-Optical.....(800)663-3936
Electronic News ....(800)883-6397	Envisions Sol. Techn.......(800)365-7226	Exide Electronics Grp....(919)870-3285
Electronic Prods. Mag....(516)227-1300	Tech Support...........(415)692-9067	Exima International.......(408)970-9225
Electronic Prods Serv ....(404)448-0748	EO (AT&T)...................(800)458-0880	ExMachina....................(718)965-0309
Electronic Services ....(313)341-1821	Tech Support...........(800)458-0880	EXP Computer...............(516)496-3703
Electronic Specialists.....(508)655-1532	EOS Distributing...........(913)827-7377	Experience in Software.(800)678-7008
Electronic Speech Sys....(510)783-3100	EOS Technology............(408)727-0111	Experience Software.....(303)796-0790
Electronics of Salina......(913)827-7377	EPE Technologies, Inc....(714)557-1636	Expert Software...........(305)567-9990
Electronics Unlimited....(216)835-0520	EPrinceton Cmptr Supp...(609)921-8889	ExperVision Inc............(800)732-3897
Electroservice Labs........(800)336-4375	Epsilon Data Mgmt........(800)225-3333	Tech Support...........(408)428-9234
Elegant Graphics Corp..(303)879-4334	Epson America, OEM Div.(213)782-0770	Expo Tech....................(800)284-3976
Elek-Tek, Inc.................(800)395-1000	Epson America, Inc........(800)289-3776	Exponent Corporation..(201)808-9423
Elektro Assemblies........(800)533-1558	Tech Support...........(800)922-8911	Tech Support...........(201)808-9423
Elenco Electronics........(708)541-3800	Epson Direct................(800)374-7300	Express Cmptr Supply...(800)342-4542
Elesys........................(800)637-0500	Tech Support...........(800)922-8911	Exsel Inc......................(800)624-2001

INDUSTRY PHONE NUMBERS

Tech Support............(800)624-2001	Flexstar Technology........(510)440-0170	Fujikura America, Inc......(404)956-7200
Exsys.........................(505)256-8356	Flight Form Cases...........(206)435-6688	Fujitsu America ....(800)626-4686
Extech Instruments......(617)890-7440	Flip Track One................(800)424-8668	Tech Support............(408)432-1300
Extended Systems Inc...(800)235-7576	Floating Point Sys Co.....(503)641-3151	Fujitsu Computer Prod..(800)626-4686
Exxus Direct.................(800)557-1000	Tech Support............(503)641-3151	Tech Support............(408)894-3950
Tech Support............(800)557-4000	Fluke, John Mfg.............(800)443-5853	Fujitsu Microelectronics...(800)637-0683
EyeTel Comm. Inc.........(604)984-2522	Flytech Techn. Co. Ltd....(408)727-7373	Tech Support............(800)642-7616
EZI America Corporate..(805)987-5885	Focus Electronics Corp.(714)468-5533	Fujitsu Personal Sys......(408)982-5900
EZX Publishing.............(713)280-9900	Focus Info. Sys..............(510)657-2845	Tech Support............(408)764-9388
F Systems Industries......(800)432-8051	Focus Microsys.............(408)436-2336	Fullmark International...(800)233-3855
Facit, Inc......................(603)647-2700	Folex Film Systems........(800)631-1150	FuncKey Enterprises.....(800)255-4433
Fairchild Defense..........(301)428-6677	Folio Corporation.........(801)375-3700	Funk Software..............no main number
Faircom.......................(314)445-6833	Footprint Software.........(416)860-0477	Tech Support............(617)497-6339
Tech Support............(800)234-8180	Fora Inc.......................(408)944-0393	Futaba Corp of America..(714)455-9888
Fairhaven Software.......(800)582-4747	Forbin Project...............(319)266-0543	Future Graphics Inc. ....(818)341-6314
Tech Support............(617)341-1969	Foresight Resources......(800)231-8574	Future Soft Eng. Inc.......(713)496-9400
Falcon Systems.............(800)326-1002	Tech Support............(816)891-8418	Tech Support............(713)496-9400
Falltech Electronics.......(714)543-5011	FormalSoft....................(800)962-7118	Future Solutions............(800)886-1278
Fam. & Home Off. Comp..(212)505-3580	FormGen Corporation...(416)857-4141	Tech Support............(510)440-1210
Family Scrapbook.........(904)247-0062	Formgen, Inc................(602)443-4109	FutureComm, Inc..........(203)932-4881
Farallon Computing.......(510)814-5000	Tech Support............(602)443-4109	FutureSoft Inc..............(713)496-9400
Tech Support............(510)814-5000	Formax Cmptr Corp......(908)874-7122	Futurmaster USA ....(305)371-4555
Fargo Electronics Inc.....(800)327-4622	Fort's Software...............(913)537-2897	Futurus Corporation .....(800)327-8296
FarPoint Comm.............(805)726-4420	Forte Computer Serv.....(708)985-7222	G & H Ribbons, Inc. ......(215)953-1970
FAST Electronic U..........(508)655-3278	Fortron/Source Corp.....(510)373-1008	G C I.............................(505)522-4600
FAX-Stor Corporation ...(408)287-2700	Forval America Inc.........(408)452-8887	Tech Support............(800)874-2383
Faxback Inc...................(503)645-1114	Forval America, Inc........(801)561-8080	Galacticomm Inc...........(305)583-5990
FDK America, Inc...........(408)432-8331	Fotec Inc......................(800)537-8254	Galaxy Appl. Eng...........(415)347-9953
FDP Corporation...........(305)858-8200	Foundationware.............(216)752-8181	Galaxy Cmptr Serv........(612)688-7454
FEC.............................(714)692-1170	Fountain Technology.....(908)563-4800	Galaxy Computers.........(800)771-4049
Fedco Electronics, Inc...(703)689-7711	Four Seasons Publ.........(212)599-2141	Galizia Inc....................(310)763-2184
Federal Computer Week .(703)876-5100	Fourgen Software, Inc....(800)333-4436	Gallant Intellgnt Cmptrs...(800)848-8088
Fellowes.......................(708)893-1600	Tech Support............(800)444-3398	Tech Support............(818)575-3781
Fessenden Technology...(417)485-2501	Fourth Party Maint.........(416)479-1910	Gama Computers Inc....(602)741-9550
FFE Software.................(510)232-6800	Fox Software.................(419)874-0162	Gamatek........................(800)927-4263
Fiber Instrument Sales...(800)445-2901	Foxconn Int'l, Inc..........(408)749-1228	Tech Support............(800)927-4263
FiberOptic Netwrk Sol...(508)842-4744	Fractal Design Corp.......(408)688-8800	GammaLink...................(408)744-1400
Ficus Systems...............(617)938-7055	Tech Support............(408)688-5300	Tech Support............(408)745-2250
Tech Support............(617)938-7055	Frame Technology..........(408)975-6000	Gandalf.........................(708)517-3615
Fidelity International.....(908)828-7948	Tech Support............(408)975-6466	Gandalf Premier............(310)312-9522
Fidelity Prof Develpmnt...(612)897-3875	Franklin Datacom.........(805)373-8688	Gandalf Technologies ...(613)723-6500
Fieldpiece Instruments..(714)992-1239	Franklin Electr. Publ......(609)261-4800	Gap Development.........(714)496-3774
Fieldtex Products Inc. ...(716)473-5237	Franklin Quest Co..........(804)975-9999	Gartech ....(612)379-7930
Fifth Generation Sys......(800)873-4384	Tech Support............(801)975-9999	Gates Distributing..........(800)332-2222
Tech Support............(800)766-7283	Frederick Engineering...(410)290-9000	Gates FA Distributing ....(800)332-2222
Fifth Generation Sys......(504)291-7221	Free Cmptr Techn..........(408)945-1118	Gateway 2000................(800)846-2000
Tech Support............(504)291-7221	FrecSoft Company........(412)846-2700	..................................(605)232-2000
Filenet Corporation.......(714)966-3400	French Expositions in US.(212)265-5676	Gateway Book Binding...(204)663-9214
Finalsoft Corporation.....(800)232-8228	Fresh Technology Grp...(602)497-4200	Gateway Electronics-MO..(314)427-6116
First Byte.......................(800)545-7677	Tech Support............(602)497-4235	Gateway Electronics-CO...(303)458-5444
Tech Support............(800)556-6141	Fridays Electronics.........(800)488-6575	Gateway Electronics-CA...(619)279-6802
First Financial Mgt.........(404)321-0120	Tech Support............(408)294-5295	Gazelle Systems ....(800)786-3278
First Int'l Computer.......(510)475-7885	Friendly Software Store.(800)848-0486	Tech Support............(801)377-1289
First Source Int'l ....(800)535-5892	Tech Support............(415)593-8275	GBC Technologies ....(800)229-2296
First United Leasing Corp..(708)615-0992	Frontline Network Sys...(508)393-1911	GBM Design/COS..........(310)677-8801
Fischer International......(813)643-1500	Frontline Systems ....(800)451-0303	GC/Thorsen..................(800)435-2931
Fiserv, Inc.....................(800)558-8413	Frontline Test Equip.......(708)653-8570	GCC Technologies ....(800)422-7777
FIT Software.................(408)562-5990	Frost & Sullivan, Inc.......(800)435-1080	Tech Support............(617)275-1795
Tech Support............(408)562-5990	FRS Inc........................(916)928-1107	GDT Softworks..............(800)663-6222
Flagship Accounting......(214)248-0305	Fry's Electronics............(415)496-6100	Tech Support............(604)299-3379
Flagship Group, The......(214)342-2801	Frye Computer..............(800)234-3793	GE Rental/Lease............(800)437-3687
Flagstaff Engineering.....(602)779-3341	FTG Data Systems.........(800)962-3900	GEC Plessey Semicond..(408)438-2900
Flambeaux Software......(800)833-7355	FTP Software Inc...........(508)685-4000	Geller Software Labs .....(201)746-7402
Fleetmasters-Comtech...(310)539-7900	Fuji.............................(510)438-9700	Gemini Inc....................(800)533-3631
Fleming Software..........(703)591-6451	Fuji Photo Film USA ......(914)789-8100	Gemplus Card Int'l........(301)990-8800
Flexistand Inc. ....(908)421-6868	Fujikama USA................(708)832-1166	Gen 2 Ventures............(408)446-2277

Genamation Industries..(416)475-9434	
Genemax Monitor'g Sys..(416)923-9000	
General Cmptr Corp.....(800)521-4548	
Genl Datacomm Ind......(203)574-1118	
Genl Diagnostics Inc.....(310)715-1222	
General Disk Corp.........(408)432-0505	
General Electric.............(800)543-0440	
General Parametrics......(510)524-3950	
General Power Corp.....(800)854-3469	
General Ribbon............(800)423-5400	
General Sales Equip.......(310)828-2577	
General Semicond. Ind..(602)968-3101	
Genl Services Admin.....(202)472-2205	
General Signal Corp......(203)357-8800	
Generic Software, Inc....(800)228-3601	
Genesis Develpmnt Corp..(801)568-1212	
Genesis Integrated Sys..(612)544-4445	
Genesis Technology.......(510)782-4800	
Genesoft.......................(714)394-0010	
Genicom.......................(800)535-4364	
Tech Support............(703)949-1031	
Genigraphics Corp........(800)638-7348	
Tech Support............(203)925-1919	
Genisco Techn. Corp.....(619)661-5100	
Genoa...........................(408)432-9090	
Genovation, Inc.............(714)833-3355	
Genus Microprgram......(800)227-0918	
Tech Support............(713)977-0680	
Geocomp.......................(800)822-2669	
Georgans Industries......(800)255-5350	
GeoSystems...................(717)293-7500	
GeoWorks.....................(510)814-1660	
Tech Support............(510)644-0883	
Gerber Scientific............(203)644-1551	
GETC............................(604)684-3230	
Gibson Research............(800)736-0637	
Tech Support............(714)362-8900	
Giga-Byte Techn. Co......(818)854-9334	
Gigatek Memory Sys.....(619)438-9010	
GigaTrend Inc...............(619)931-9122	
Tech Support............(619)931-9122	
Gilmore Systems...........(805)379-3210	
Gimpel Software............(215)584-4261	
Gizmo Technology.........(510)623-7899	
Glenco Engineering......(800)562-2543	
Tech Support............(708)808-0315	
Glendale Technology.....(708)305-9100	
Glenn A Barber & Assoc...(818)951-4744	
Global Cmptr Supply....(800)845-6225	
Global Eng. Documents...(800)854-7179	
Global Specialties..........(800)345-6251	
Global Village Comms......(800)736-4821	
Tech Support............(415)390-8300	
Globalink, Inc................(800)255-5660	
Globe Manufacturing....(800)227-3258	
Tech Support............(908)232-7301	
GlobeTech Int'l..............(800)654-7314	
GMC Techn. Corp.........(818)401-3743	
GMP.............................(215)357-5500	
GN Navtel.....................(800)262-8835	
GN Navtel Limited........(800)262-8835	
Go Corporation.............(415)345-7400	
GO Technology..............(702)831-3100	
Tech Support............(702)832-7762	
Gold Disk.....................(310)320-5080	
Gold Disk, Inc...............(800)465-3375	

Tech Support............(416)602-4357	
Gold Hill Computers.....(617)621-3300	
GoldDisk (AMI)............(800)465-3375	
Tech Support............(905)602-4357	
GoldDisk (MAC)...........(800)465-3375	
Tech Support............(905)602-0395	
GoldDisk (PC)...............(800)465-3375	
Tech Support............(900)602-5292	
Golden Bow Systems....(800)284-3269	
Golden Coast Electr.......(619)268-8447	
Golden Image Techn.....(800)327-4482	
Golden Power Sys.........(805)582-4400	
Golden Ribbon.............(303)443-6966	
Golden Star Inc.............(800)821-2792	
Golden Triangle............(800)326-1858	
Golden-Lee Book Distr....(718)857-6333	
Goldstar Precision Co...(619)268-8447	
Goldstar Techn. Corp.....(800)777-1192	
Tech Support............(800)777-1192	
Good Software...............(214)713-6370	
Tech Support............(214)713-6370	
Gorrell's Cmptr Serv.....(606)299-8468	
Gotoless Conversion.....(214)625-2323	
Gould Inc......................(216)328-7000	
Governmnt Cmptr News..(301)650-2000	
GRACE Electr. Materials...(617)935-4850	
Gradco Inc.....................(714)770-1223	
GrafPoint......................(800)426-2230	
Graham Magnetics Inc....(817)868-5000	
Granite Corporation......(818)887-5533	
Grapevine LAN Prods...(206)869-2707	
Tech Support............(206)836-8822	
Graphic Ent. of Ohio.....(800)321-9874	
Tech Support............(216)456-5107	
Graphic Software Sys....(503)641-2200	
GRAPHIC TECH.............(413)536-7800	
Graphic Utilities, Inc.....(800)669-4723	
Graphics Development...(800)969-4434	
Graphics Simulations....(214)699-7400	
Tech Support............(214)699-7400	
Graphsoft......................(301)461-9488	
Graybar Electric Co.......(800)825-5517	
Graymark.......................(800)854-7393	
Great Amer. Software......(603)889-5400	
Great Eastern Techn......(800)875-0025	
Great Falls Cmptr..........(703)759-5570	
Great Plain Software......(701)281-0550	
Tech Support............(800)456-0025	
Great Software Ideas.....(800)486-7800	
Tech Support............(714)261-9744	
Great Tek Inc.................(408)943-1005	
Great Wave Software......(408)438-1990	
Tech Support............(408)438-1990	
Greatlink Electr. USA.....(510)683-0655	
Greco Systems...............(800)234-7326	
Greengage Dvlpmnt Corp.(408)243-8960	
Greenleaf Int'l Inc.........(408)734-8888	
Greenleaf Software........(800)524-9830	
.................................(800)523-9830	
Greystone Peripherals....(408)866-4739	
GRID Systems................(800)326-4743	
Grolier Electr. Publ........(800)356-5590	
Tech Support............(800)356-5590	
Group 1 Software...........(301)731-2300	
Tech Support............(301)731-2300	
Group 4 Electronics......(800)229-7189	

Group One Elec. Co......(818)993-4575	
Group Technologies.......(800)476-8781	
Tech Support............(703)841-4357	
Group Three Electronics...(310)781-9191	
Gruber Industries Inc....(602)863-2655	
Gryphon Software.........(619)536-8815	
Tech Support............(619)536-8815	
GST, Inc.......................(714)739-0106	
GTCO Corporation........(301)381-6688	
GTE Corporation...........(203)965-2000	
GTE Electr. Repair Serv...(714)945-2313	
GTE Supply Electr.Repair..(214)615-7599	
GUIS America, Inc..........(714)590-0801	
Gupta Technologies.......(800)876-3267	
Tech Support............(415)321-4484	
GW Computer Sys.........(604)244-7118	
H & H Enterprises.........(702)876-6292	
H&J Electronics Int'l......(800)275-2447	
H.Allen & Company......(708)769-4040	
H. Co. Memory Prods....(714)833-3222	
H. Co. Mem. Upgrades...(800)726-2477	
Tech Support............(714)833-3364	
Ha-Lo Adv. Specialtie......(708)676-5305	
Hadron, Inc..................(703)359-6201	
Hahn & Company.........(503)248-0262	
Halcyon Software..........(408)378-9898	
Haliburton NUS Environ...(301)258-6000	
Haltek Electronics.........(415)969-0510	
Hamilton Dig. Controls....(315)797-2370	
Hamilton Tel.................(800)363-7626	
Hampton Bus. Mach......(800)974-2402	
Hand Held Products......(704)541-1380	
Handok Company, Ltd...(408)736-3191	
Hands On Learning........(617)272-0068	
Handtop Computers......(818)884-4076	
Hanson Data Sys...........(800)879-1371	
Harbor Electronics........(203)438-9625	
Hard Drive Assoc..........(503)233-2821	
Hard Drive Super Source..(800)252-9777	
Tech Support............(408)739-4110	
Hard Drive Whsle..........(408)559-1773	
Hard Drives Int'l...........(800)927-7848	
Hardigg Cases...............(413)665-2163	
HARDISK Technology...(408)374-5157	
Hardware House-AR......(501)225-4477	
Hardware House-IN......(317)842-8244	
Hardware House-KY......(502)425-1402	
Hardware House-NE......(402)498-5677	
Hardware House-OH......(513)489-0668	
Hardware Hse-Memphis...(901)756-6677	
Hardware Hse-Nashville....(615)356-2888	
Harley Systems Inc........(800)237-2885	
Harmony Computers......(718)692-2828	
Tech Support............(800)441-1144	
Harris Adacom Network..(214)386-2000	
Harris Corporation........(407)727-9100	
Harvard Bus. Systems.....(800)288-7750	
Tech Support............(310)207-7750	
Harvard Softworks.........(513)748-0390	
Hauppauge Cmptr Works..(800)443-6284	
Tech Support............(516)434-3197	
HavenTree Software.......(800)267-0668	
Tech Support............(613)544-6035	
Hawaii Sftwr Serv. Ctr....(808)733-2042	
Hawk Computers...........(408)436-8999	
Hawk Data Systems.......(805)371-1764	

INDUSTRY PHONE NUMBERS

Hayes Microcomp. Prod..(800)874-2937	Tech Support............(800)397-9211	PC Tech Supprt Faxback.(800)426-3395
Tech Support............(404)441-1617	Hoppecke Battery Sys...(201)492-0045	PC Direct Mail Order...(800)426-2968
HB Cmptr Techn. Co......(310)644-2602	Horizon Technology......(800)888-9600	Personal Sys Help Line..(800)772-2227
HCI.............................(800)486-0001	Horizon USA Data Supp...(209)848-1001	Product Info Line........(800)426-7699
HCR Corporation..........(416)922-1937	Hornet Technology USA..(818)333-9667	PS/1 BBS.....................(404)835-8230
Tech Support............(800)567-4357	Tech Support............(818)572-3784	PS/1 Dealer Locator....(800)426-3377
HD Computer...............(800)347-0493	Hotronic Inc................(408)378-3888	Software Supp/Serv.....(800)336-5430
Tech Support............(800)676-0164	House of Batteries.........(800)432-3385	Software Supp Line.....(800)237-5511
HDC Computer Corp....(800)321-4606	Houston Cmptr Serv......(713)493-9900	Storage Systems Div....(507)253-1897
Health Care Keybrd Co.(414)253-4131	Houston Data Ctr. Inc....(713)880-0042	Tech Support............(507)253-5005
Health Software, Inc......(216)759-2103	Houston Instruments.....(800)444-3425	Technical Manuals.......(800)426-7282
Healthkit.....................(800)253-0570	Tech Support............(800)444-3425	IBM Corporation (NY)..(914)288-3000
HEI FastPoint Light Pens..(612)443-2500	Howard W. Sams...........(800)428-7267	IBM Desktop Software..(800)426-7699
Helix Software Co..........(800)451-0551	Howe Industries Inc......(800)322-1830	IBM National Distr. Div..(800)426-9397
Tech Support............(718)392-3735	HSC Software...............(310)392-8441	IBM OEM Division......(914)288-3000
Helix Technologies........(800)364-4354	Tech Support............(310)392-8441	IBM Pers. Sys. Card Rpr..(800)759-6995
Tech Support............(200)451-0551	Hubbell Inc..................(203)337-3100	IBM Pers Sys Tech Sol Mag.(800)551-2832
Help Desk Institute.......(800)248-5667	Hughes Lan Systems......(415)966-7300	IBM Technical Directory..(800)426-7282
Hercules Cmptr Techn..(800)532-0600	Humana Cmptr Publ.....(403)245-2194	IC Designs....................(206)821-9202
Tech Support............(510)623-6050	Humancad-Bio Mech.....(516)752-3550	Tech Support............(206)821-8218
Heritage Cmptr Parts....(800)828-8266	Huron Cmptr of PA.......(412)776-6110	Icarus Corporation........(301)881-9350
Hermann Marketing......(800)523-9009	Husky Computers..........(800)486-7774	ICM Int'l Components...(800)748-6232
Hermeneutika..............(206)824-9673	Hutchinson Technology..(612)587-3797	Icom Simulations...........(800)877-4266
Hersey Micro Consult...(313)994-3259	Hy-Tronix Instrument....(800)835-1005	Icon Computer Corp.....(800)966-4266
Hetra Cmptr & Comm..(800)327-0661	Hydra Systems.............(408)253-5800	ICON CS Canada Inc.....(613)722-0115
Hewlett-Packard Co.......(800)544-9976	Hyperception Inc..........(214)343-8525	Icons International.........(800)959-4266
Hewlett-Packard Wldwide..(415)986-5600	HyperGlot Software.......(800)726-5087	Icot Corporation...........(800)227-8068
H-P, Disk Memory...........(208)396-6000	Tech Support............(615)584-4379	ICS Electro-Pac Division.(708)543-6200
Tech Support............(208)323-2551	Hyperkinetic...............(714)935-0823	ICS Inc........................(805)257-6900
Hexacon Electric Co......(908)245-6200	Hyperpress Publishing..(800)633-4252	ID Systems....................(603)924-9631
Hi Tech Expressions......(800)216-1750	Tech Support............(415)345-4620	IDE.............................(612)946-4100
Tech Support............(305)581-4240	Hypro Systems.............(310)473-2937	Idea Courier..................(800)528-1400
Hi-Tech Asset Recovery.(805)966-5454	Hysung.......................(408)733-0810	IDEA Servcom Inc.........(602)894-7000
Hi-Tech Cmptr Prods.....(800)950-6991	Hyundai Electr.America...(800)289-4986	Ideal Industries Inc........(800)435-0705
Hi-TECH Connections...(215)372-1401	Tech Support............(800)289-4986	Ideassociates...............(508)663-6878
Hi-Tech USA................(800)831-2888	I-Data Inc....................(516)351-1333	Idek-Iiyama North Amer..(800)394-4335
Tech Support............(408)956-8285	I/O Design...................(800)241-2122	Identica.......................(408)727-2600
Hi-Techniques Inc..........(800)248-1633	Tech Support............(800)241-2122	Tech Support............(408)727-2600
Hi-TEK Services Inc.......(800)285-3508	IBC.............................(800)654-3790	Identity Sys Technology...(214)235-3330
High Techn. Developmnt..(808)625-5293	IBC/Integrated Bus Cmptr..(818)882-9007	IDER...........................(800)622-4337
Highland Products Inc...(201)366-0156	IBEX Technologies Inc...(916)921-4342	Tech Support............(818)288-4008
Hilgraeve....................(313)243-0576	Ibis Software...............(415)546-1917	IEEE Cmptr Graphics....(714)821-8380
Tech Support............(313)243-0576	Tech Support............(415)546-0405	IEEE Cmptr Soc. Press...(714)821-8380
Hillside Electr. Corp.......(413)238-5566	IBM Corporation (ON)..(416)946-9000	IEEE Service Center.......(201)981-0060
Hirose Electric, Inc.......(805)522-7958	IBM Corporation (GA)...(800)426-9402	IET Labs.....................(800)899-8438
Hitachi (NY)................(800)536-6721	Auth. Dealer Locator....(800)447-4700	IEV Corporation...........(800)438-6161
Tech Support............(800)536-6721	CAD Assistance...........(303)924-7262	Ilcon Corporation.........(408)779-7466
Hitachi (CA)................(510)785-9770	Cust. Relations Dept....(201)930-3443	Iliad Group...................(415)563-2053
Hitachi America (CA).....(800)448-2244	Direct.......................(800)426-2968	Image Club Graphics.....(403)262-8008
Hitachi America (NY).....(914)332-5800	Tech Support............(800)426-7763	Tech Support............(403)262-8008
Tech Support............(800)323-9712	Disabilities/Sp. Need Info.(800)426-2133	Image Research Corp....(602)998-1113
Hitachi Home Electr......(800)369-0422	Educational Dept.........(800)222-7257	Image Smith.................(310)325-1359
Tech Support............(800)241-6558	Employee Sales Dept...(800)426-3675	Tech Support............(310)325-1359
HMC-HUB Material Co...(800)482-4440	General Information....(800)426-3333	Image-In.....................(800)345-3540
Hokkins Systemation.....(408)436-8303	Ind Developer Reg......(800)982-6408	Imageline.....................(804)644-0766
Holmes Microsys..........(801)975-9929	Industrial PC Support..(800)526-6602	ImageSoft Inc...............(800)245-8840
Home Office Cmpting...(212)505-3688	Indust. PC Tech Supp...(800)241-1620	ImageWare Software......(619)457-8600
Honeywell....................(612)870-5431	Lookup & Part # ID.....(303)924-4015	Image Club Graphics.....(403)262-8008
Tech Support............(612)782-7646	Maint.Agreemnts Dept..(800)624-6875	Imagine That...............(408)365-0305
Honeywell, Inc.............(800)445-6939	Mfg. Systems Info........(800)526-6602	Imaging Magazine.........(212)691-8215
Honeywell-IAC.............(602)789-5393	Multi-Media Mktg Line..(800)426-9402	IMC Networks Corp......(800)624-1070
Hong Kong Trade..........(213)622-3194	Multi-Media Tech Supp...(800)241-1620	IMP............................(408)432-9100
Hooleon Corporation....(800)937-1337	NSD Hdwr Serv/PC Rpr..(800)426-7378	Impact.........................(800)777-4323
Hooper Int'l, Inc...........(407)851-3100	OS/2 Prods. Order Ctr.(800)342-6672	Tech Support............(512)966-3621
Tech Support............(407)851-3100	Parts Order Line..........(303)924-4100	Implements..................(508)358-5858
Hopkins......................(800)397-9211	PC Prod Info Faxback.(800)426-4329	Impulse Software..........(800)328-0184

Tech Support.............(612)566-0221	
IMSI Software.................(800)833-8082	
Tech Support...........(415)454-7101	
In Focus Systems Inc.....(800)327-7231	
In Shape Co. Ltd...........(408)432-9025	
In Win Development.....(818)333-1986	
InaCom.........................(402)392-3900	
Inacomp Cmptr Ctrs.....(313)649-5580	
Inbit..............................(415)967-1788	
Incas Corporation..........(818)332-3443	
Incas Corp. USA.............(609)424-7811	
Incider..........................(603)924-9471	
Incomm Data Systems...(708)459-8881	
Incomnet......................(818)887-3400	
Independt Cmptr Supp....(215)687-0900	
Index Applications.........(512)822-4818	
Individual Softwar..........(800)822-3522	
Tech Support...........(800)331-3313	
Inductel, Inc.................(800)367-4497	
Indus International........(608)786-0300	
Indus-Tool....................(800)662-5021	
Ind. Commercial Elect...(800)442-3462	
Industrial CPU Sys. Int'l.(714)957-2815	
Industrious Soft............(310)330-7602	
Inference Corporation...(310)322-0200	
Infinite Solutions............(713)492-1894	
Infiniti Manufacturing....(818)960-4509	
Infodata.........................(703)578-3430	
Infoextend....................(619)587-9140	
Infomatic Power Sys......(310)948-2217	
Infonetics.....................(508)393-8088	
Inforite Corporation......(800)366-4635	
Tech Support............(800)366-4635	
Information Builders.....(800)444-4303	
Information Center........(617)542-0146	
Information Concepts...(202)682-0330	
Information Consultants..(714)859-7123	
Information Machines...(818)884-5779	
Information Pkg. Corp...(800)776-7633	
Information Processing.(407)331-5200	
Information Science......(201)592-0009	
Information Stratagics...(212)971-5000	
Information Sys. Cons....(214)490-1881	
Informationweek...........(516)365-4600	
Informix Software/IBM...(800)274-8184	
Tech Support............(800)274-8184	
Informtech Int'l..............(310)836-8993	
InfoShare.......................(703)791-2910	
Infoworld......................(415)572-7341	
Infralink.........................(703)522-4412	
Ingram Micro.................(714)566-1000	
Ingram/Micro D.............(714)566-1000	
Inland Data Pak.............(313)583-6220	
Inline Design.................(617)935-1515	
Tech Support...........(617)935-1515	
Inline, Inc.....................(800)882-7117	
Inmac...........................(408)435-1700	
Innotech Inc.................(416)492-3838	
Innovative Concepts......(408)436-1777	
Innov. Data Design-IDD.(510)680-6818	
Tech Support............(510)680-6818	
Innovative Mfg.............(305)836-1035	
Innovative Resources....(612)377-5701	
Innovative Techn ....(713)583-1141	
Innovative Techn ....(800)647-8877	
Innovative Techn ....(800)253-4001	

Tech Support............(405)243-0030	
Inovatic..........................(703)522-3053	
Inset Systems ....(800)828-0068	
Tech Support...........(203)740-2400	
Insight Development.....(800)825-4115	
Tech Support............(303)339-7072	
Insight International......(800)927-7848	
Insight Resource...........(914)332-1589	
Insignia Solutions...........(800)848-7677	
Tech Support...........(415)694-7694	
Insite Peripherals..........(408)946-8080	
Instant Replay. ....(801)272-0671	
Instaplan.......................(415)389-1414	
Institute for VAR Devel..(702)656-7611	
Institiute, The.................(212)705-7555	
Instructware Inc...........(800)267-0101	
Instrmt. Repair Labs... ...(800)345-6140	
Instrument Specialties...(717)424-8510	
InstrumentMart.............(516)487-7430	
Instruments & Equip.....(201)579-0009	
Int'l Electr. Research .....(818)848-8872	
Intcomex.......................(305)477-6230	
Intec Computer Serv.....(800)225-1187	
Integral Systems.............(510)939-3900	
Integrated Circuit Sys....(215)666-1900	
Integrtd Cmptr Solution.(201)808-9646	
Integrated Cmptr Serv..(818)960-1921	
Integrated Data Tech... ..(215)726-6124	
Integrated Devel. Corp..(603)329-5522	
Integrated Device Tech..(408)727-6116	
Integrated Electronics ...(303)292-5537	
Integrated Inference Mach.(714)978-6776	
Tech Support............(714)978-6202	
Integrated Info.Techn...(800)832-0770	
Tech Support............(408)727-1676	
Integrated Workstations ...(800)832-6526	
Integrix.........................(800)300-8288	
Intek..............................(206)455-9935	
Intel Corporation...........(800)538-3373	
Tech Support............(503)629-7000	
Intel PCEO....................(800)538-3373	
Tech Support............(503)629-7000	
Intelecsis, Inc................(512)682-0649	
Intelect.........................(310)828-7310	
Intellicom.....................(800)992-2882	
Tech Support...........(818)407-3900	
Intellicorp.....................(415)965-5500	
Intelligence Technology ...(214)250-4277	
Intlligenceware..............(310)417-8896	
Intelligent Controls........(206)771-8107	
Intelligent Electronics....(215)458-5500	
Intell. Instrumentation...(602)624-2434	
Intelligent Sys. Master.....(404)381-2900	
IntelliMedia.....................(800)706-0077	
Tech Support...........(616)925-3675	
IntelliPower Inc............(714)587-0155	
Intellisystems, Inc..........(818)341-7000	
Intelogic Trace Inc.........(800)531-7186	
InterAct.........................(304)258-1611	
Interacter Inc................(203)630-0199	
Interactive Imaging.......(813)996-4316	
InterActive Inc..............(606)363-5117	
Interactive Multimedia..(410)626-1380	
Interactive Sftwr Eng....(805)685-1006	
Interactive Sys. Corp.....(213)453-8649	
Interactive Training........(503)681-0343	

Interchange Standards...(800)423-7823	
InterComp Inc...............(408)928-1588	
Intercon Associates........(716)244-1250	
Interex Cmptr Prods......(316)524-4747	
Interface Electronics......(503)393-2838	
Interface Group, The......(617)449-6600	
Interface Systems...........(800)544-4072	
Interface Technologies...(314)434-0046	
Intergral Peripherals......(303)449-8009	
Intergraph.....................(213)479-3400	
Interleaf, Inc.................(617)290-0710	
Intermatic Inc...............(805)675-2321	
Intermec.......................(206)348-2600	
Intermetrics..................(617)661-1840	
Int'l. Power Machines....(214)272-8000	
Int'l. Business Software..(408)522-8001	
Int'l. Buyers Market........(702)647-3632	
Int'l. Compliance...........(817)491-3696	
Int'l. Computer Center...(818)894-2222	
Int'l. Computer Power....(818)443-7557	
Int'l. Data Corporation...(508)879-0700	
Int'l. Data Engineering...(602)946-4100	
Int'l. Data Sciences..........(800)437-3282	
Int'l. Keytech Corp.........(714)596-6219	
Int'l. Meta Systems.........(213)375-4700	
Int'l. Open Systems........(508)535-2080	
Int'l. Power Machines....(800)527-1208	
Int'l. Software ....(305)823-8088	
Int'l.Technical Systems..(206)486-9031	
Int'l.Transware................(415)903-2300	
Tech Support............(415)903-2300	
Int'l. Cmptr. & Comm....(310)836-7561	
Interphase Corporation.(214)919-9000	
InterPlay Productions.....(800)969-4263	
Tech Support...........(714)553-6676	
Interpos Systems Inc.....(416)513-9209	
Interpreter.....................(800)232-4687	
Intersecting Concepts...(805)373-3900	
Intersolv (Sage Software)..(301)230-3200	
Tech Support............(800)443-1601	
Intersolve (Polytron).......(503)645-1150	
Tech Support............(800)548-4000	
Intex Solutions Inc........(617)449-6222	
Intra Electronics US.......(408)744-1706	
Intuit..............................(800)624-8742	
Tech Support............(415)858-6010	
InView System Inc........(508)428-5688	
Invisible Software..........(415)570-5967	
Invisible Software Inc....(800)982-2962	
IOcomm Int'l.Techn......(213)644-6100	
Ioline.............................(206)821-2140	
IOMEGA.........................(800)456-5522	
Tech Support............(800)456-5522	
Ion Systems..................(800)367-2452	
Iowa America.................(800)920-2673	
IPC Corporation Ltd......(404)594-8281	
IPL Systems, Inc............(800)338-8475	
Tech Support............(617)487-2057	
IPX Infomatic Pwr. Sys ..(310)946-2217	
IQ Engineering..............(800)765-3668	
IQ Software...................(404)446-8880	
IQ Technologies.............(800)752-6526	
Tech Support............(206)823-2273	
IQI Accessories..............(415)567-3500	
IQV Corporation..........(708)253-5196	
Iris Software Products...(617)341-1990	

INDUSTRY PHONE NUMBERS

Irma DCA	(404)740-0300	JMR Electronics, Inc.	(818)993-4801	Key Tronic	(800)262-6006
IronMountain	(800)883-8000	Jo-Dan Int'l Inc.	(313)340-0300	Tech Support	(800)262-6006
Irons Group Inc.,The	(212)645-4737	John Anderson Assoc.	(602)474-9555	Keydata International	(800)486-7010
Irwin Magnetics Sys	(800)421-1879	John Fluke Mfg.	(800)443-5853	Tech Support	(800)486-9100
ISC Systems	(509)927-5600	John Wiley & Sons	(212)850-6000	Keyfile	(603)883-3800
ISC/MSC Ribbons	(718)706-8833	Johnson Controls	(414)274-4000	Tech Support	(603)883-3800
ISI Systems	(800)255-1580		(414)961-6500	Keylogic USA/Europe	(619)242-7722
Tech Support	(508)682-5500	Joindata Systems Inc	(818)330-6553	Keypoint Technology	(310)944-3041
ISICAD, Inc.	(800)634-1223	Jones Business Sys.	(800)225-1923	KFA USA Inc	(714)546-0336
Island Graphics	(800)255-4499	Jordan Industries Corp.	(914)793-0700	Kidasa Software Inc.	(800)765-0167
Tech Support	(415)491-1000	Joseph Electronics	(708)297-4200	Kidde-Fenwal Inc	(508)881-2000
Islandview/MGI	(804)673-5601	Journal of Info. Sys.	(212)971-5000	Kikusui International	(800)545-8784
Ithaca Software	(510)523-5900	Jovian Logic Corp.	(510)651-4823	Killer Tracks	(714)435-2600
ITS	(818)882-7747	Tech Support	(510)651-4823	Kimpsion International	(408)988-8808
ITT Commercial Finance	(800)727-9090	JSB Corporation	(408)438-8300	Kings Electronics	(914)793-5000
ITT Consumer Financial	(612)540-8799	J.S.T. Corporation	(708)803-3300	Kingston Electronics	(800)835-6575
ITT Corporation	(212)258-1000		(800)947-1110	Tech Support	(714)435-2600
ITT Pomona Electronics	(909)623-3463	Julie Associates Inc.	(508)667-1958	Kinzuid, Inc.	(716)665-3087
ITT PowerSystems	(602)889-7600	Jump Microsystems Inc.	(510)440-8006	Kiss Software Corp.	(800)472-5477
ITW Linx	(706)952-8844	Juno Technical Serv.	(510)487-7601	Kiwi Software	(805)685-4031
Iverson Technology	(703)749-1200	JVC Companies/America	(714)965-2610	Klein Tools Inc.	(708)677-9500
Tech Support	(800)677-7881	Tech Support	(714)965-2610	Klever Computers, Inc.	(408)735-7723
J&S Custom Cmptr Serv.	(800)995-5840	JVC Info. Products	(408)988-7506	KLM Services	(805)376-2825
JB Technologies Inc	(805)529-0908	JWP	(408)437-0400	Knowledge Access	(415)969-0606
J Bond Cmptr Systems	(510)490-8290	JWP Info. Systems	(617)821-4100	Knowledge Adventure	(800)542-4240
J Bond Cmptr Systems	(408)946-9622	JYACC	(800)458-3313	Tech Support	(818)542-4200
J P N Corporation	(510)770-3962	K & A Manufacturing	(800)678-3805	Knowledge Dynamics	(800)331-2783
J-Mark Computer Corp.	(818)814-9472	K D I Precision Prods.	(513)943-2000	Knowledge Garden	(516)246-5400
Jabert USA Inc	(214)644-2084	K&R International Inc.	(714)598-8738	KnowledgePoint	(800)727-1133
Jactech Corporation	(714)228-1633	K-N Electronics	(216)724-9953	Knozall Systems Inc.	(800)333-8698
Jade Computer	(800)421-5500	Kaetron Software	(713)298-1547	Koala Acquisitions	(408)776-8181
JAE Electronics	(714)753-2600	Tech Support	(713)296-1547	Kobetron Inc.	(513)298-8244
Jain Tools for Sales	(415)941-9191	Kalglo Electronics Co.	(800)524-0400	Kodak Diconix	(800)255-3434
JAM Enterprises	(619)673-8180	Kalok Corporations-JTS	(408)734-4258	Tech Support	(800)344-0006
Jam Software	(203)630-0055	Tech Support	(408)747-1315	Kodiak Technology	(510)226-7840
Tech Support	(206)630-0055	Kanix Inc.	(714)693-1888	Kofax Image Prods Inc.	(714)727-1733
Jameco Elect Cmptr Prod.	(800)831-0084	Kansai Electric, USA	(800)733-3374	Konami	(708)215-5111
Tech Support	(415)592-8097	Tech Support	(800)388-7062	Konic Electronics	(714)770-3267
James Burn/American	(914)454-8200	Kantek Inc.	(516)593-3212	Konica Bus. Machin.	(203)683-2222
Jameslee Corporation	(312)271-6000	Kao Infosystems	(800)274-5520	Kontrax Software Inc.	(416)451-1610
Jasick Designs	(510)322-1386	Kay Elemetrics Corp.	(201)227-2000	Korea Trade Center	(213)954-9500
Javelin Software Corp.	(617)890-1100	Kazcom Inc.	(800)444-0543	Koss Stereo Phones	(414)964-5000
JAZ Designs	(512)659-8946	KCI Canada	(416)633-0351	Koutech Systems, Inc.	(310)699-5340
JB Saunders	(303)442-1212	KCI Computing, Inc.	(310)478-6100	KPT.	(714)468-5555
JB Technologies	(800)688-0908	KDM Associates	(800)553-5171	Kres Engineering	(818)957-6322
JC Enterprises	(818)773-0296	KEA Systems Ltd.	(604)431-0727	Kris Technologies	(415)875-6728
JDR Microdevices	(800)538-5000	Keane, Inc.	(617)241-9200	Krystaltech International	(212)385-1900
Tech Support	(800)538-5002	Kedwell Software	(415)899-8525	KS Brotherbox Co	(818)814-0516
JDV Engineering Co.	(201)796-1720	Kelly Computer Sys.	(415)960-1010	KTV Inc.	(201)440-9090
Jem Computers	(617)254-5500	Kelly Microsystems	(714)859-3900	Kurta	(800)445-8782
Jems Data Unlimited	(800)838-5367	Kenfil Distribution	(800)487-9889	Tech Support	(602)276-5533
Jenistar Inc.	(508)230-2414	Kennsco	(800)229-1758	Kurzweil	(617)890-2929
Jensen Tools, Inc.	(800)426-1194	Kenosha Cmptr Corp.	(800)255-2989	KW Control Systems	(914)355-5000
Jensen-Jones Inc.	(800)688-7080	Tech Support	(414)697-9595	KYE International Corp.	(714)590-3940
Tech Support	(908)530-7788	Kensington Microware	(800)535-4242	Kye International Corp.	(714)923-3510
JET FAX	(800)753-8329	Tech Support	(800)535-4242	Kyocera	(908)560-3400
JetFill Inc	(713)933-1900	Kent Marsh	(800)325-3587	Kyocera Electronics	(619)576-2669
JetForm Corporation	(617)647-7700	Tech Support	(713)522-8906	L & M Computer Prods.	(800)544-2910
Jetpad Systems	(617)536-7526	Kenwood USA	(310)639-4200	L-Com Inc.	(800)343-1455
JH America Inc.	(310)328-0051	Kepler Company	(612)522-0756	L-Cube Innov. Solution	(203)378-1343
Ji-Haw.	(310)328-0051	Kepner-Tregoe Inc.	(800)257-0404	La Cie	(800)999-0143
JIAN	(800)346-5426	Key Computers, Inc.	(404)565-0089	Tech Support	(800)288-9919
Tech Support	(415)941-9191	Key Lime Systems	(800)789-5463	LA Computer	(310)533-7177
Jimi Software	(215)628-0840	Tech Support	(407)627-5322	LA Trade	(800)433-3726
Jinco Computers	(800)253-2531	Key Power, Inc.	(310)948-2084	Tech Support	(310)539-0019
Tech Support	(818)309-1103	Key Services Inc	(919)768-4400	Labconco Corporation	(800)821-5525

Labtec Enterprises	(206)896-2000
LacTek USA Company	(714)545-4916
LaFrance Corporation	(215)365-8000
Lahey Computer Sys	(702)831-2500
Lamp Technology	(516)567-1800
LAN Magazine	(415)905-2200
Lan Systems	(212)995-7700
LAN Technology	(415)358-9500
Lan Times	(801)565-1060
LANCAST	(603)880-1833
Landmark	(800)683-6696
Tech Support	(800)683-0854
Lane Service Company	(800)231-0861
Lang Chao Group	(916)638-8900
Language Systems	(703)478-0181
LANpoint Systems	(800)328-2526
LanSource Techn	(416)866-8575
Lantana Tech	(619)565-6400
LANtek Computer	(800)462-0436
Lantell Systems	(800)526-8355
LANWorks	(416)238-5528
Lapis Techn-Focus Tech	(800)538-8865
Tech Support	(800)647-7744
Large Stor. Configs	(800)831-9482
Larson-Davis Info Sys	(801)375-8855
Laser Computer, Inc.	(708)540-8086
Laser Digital Inc	(408)737-2666
Laser Magnetic Storage	(800)777-5764
Laser Master Corp	(800)950-6868
Laser Precision	(800)443-6154
Laser Printers Access	(619)485-8411
Tech Support	(619)486-8411
Laser Source	(315)463-6090
Laser Supply	(800)422-0080
Laser Tek Industries	(800)322-8137
Laser's Edge, Inc.	(515)472-7850
LaserByte	(800)619-9200
LaserCard Systems	(415)969-4428
Laserex Inc	(800)225-5503
LaserGo, Inc.	(619)450-4600
LaserMaster Corp-MAC	(612)944-9330
Tech Support	(612)944-8008
LaserMaster Corp-PC	(619)944-9330
Tech Support	(612)944-9331
LaserTechnics Inc	(505)822-1123
LaserTek	(800)252-7374
LaserTools	(800)767-8004
Tech Support	(510)420-1319
Lattice, Incorporated	(708)769-4060
Laudholm Automation	(207)761-5657
Laura Technologies	(602)940-9800
Lava Computer Mfg	(416)674-5942
Law Cypress Distrib	(800)344-3044
LAWN O'Neill Comm	(908)329-4100
Lawson Associates	(612)379-2633
LCS Industries	(201)778-5588
LCT Technology Inc	(818)575-5000
LDI Retail Services	(800)874-3209
Lead Electronics	(315)699-6099
Lead Technologies	(704)549-5532
Leader Instrument Corp.	(800)645-5104
Leader Technology	(714)757-1787
Tech Support	(505)822-0700
Leading Edge	(800)874-3340
Tech Support	(800)225-2283
League for Prog. Freedom	(617)243-4091

Learning Company	(800)852-2255
LearnKey Inc	(801)224-8210
Leasametric	(800)553-2255
LeCroy Corporation	(800)553-2769
Lectronix Cmptr Serv	(304)736-8035
Lectronix Distrib. & Serv.	(800)325-3348
Lee Data/IIS	(800)533-3282
Legacy Storage Sys	(508)435-4700
Legacy Technology	(800)832-8883
Legend Micro	(800)366-6333
Legent Corporation	(703)734-9494
Legeon Corporation	(714)546-4900
Leisure Products	(408)448-7020
Lek Technologies Inc	(806)355-7900
Lenel Systems Int'l	(716)248-9720
Tech Support	(716)248-9720
Lermer Pkg.Corp	(908)789-0900
LES International	(714)595-7299
Letraset	(800)343-8973
Tech Support	(800)634-3463
Level Computers	(714)974-6427
Leviton Mfg Inc	(206)486-2222
Lexidyne of Penn	(412)661-4526
Lexmark Int'l Inc	(800)453-9872
Tech Support	(606)232-3000
Liant-Ryan McFarland-TX	(800)237-1874
Tech Support	(512)343-1010
Liant-Ryan McFarland-MA	(800)237-1874
Tech Support	(800)833-3678
Liberty Research Grp	(406)771-7736
Liberty Systems Inc	(408)983-1127
Libra Corporation	(800)453-3827
Library Software Review	(203)226-6967
Lifeboat Associates	(908)389-8950
Lifeboat Software Grp	(904)825-0220
Tech Support	(904)825-0220
Light Brigade	(206)251-1240
Light Source	(800)231-7226
Tech Support	(415)461-3030
Lighthorse Tech., Inc	(800)443-3446
Lighthouse Technology	(800)842-8288
Lightning Comm	(714)457-8001
Likom Group	(408)954-8070
Linco Computer	(213)903-1299
Lind Electr. Design	(800)659-5956
Tech Support	(612)927-6303
Link Computer, Inc	(714)993-0800
Link Technologies	(800)448-5465
Tech Support	(800)448-5465
Link-Up	(609)654-6266
Linkon Corporation	(212)753-2544
Linksys	(800)546-5797
Tech Support	(714)261-1288
LIPS Inc	(516)673-2255
Lite-On, Inc.	(408)946-4873
Literature Display Sys	(800)669-4399
Litton Industries	(310)859-5000
Liuski International	(800)347-5454
LJ Enterprises	(800)296-5536
Lion USA Inc	(818)991-4330
Lloyd Bush, Inc	(212)962-4004
LMT Marketing Inc	(805)644-1797
Lockheed	(818)876-2000
Locus Computing	(800)423-2386
Tech Support	(310)337-5995
Logica North America	(617)890-7730

Logical Connection, Inc	(503)585-4174
Tech Support	(503)585-4174
Logical Operations Inc.	(716)482-7700
Logical Sys. Corp.	(813)885-7179
Logicode Technology	(805)388-9000
Tech Support	(805)388-9000
Logicon, Inc	(213)373-0220
Logitech	(800)231-7717
Tech Support	(510)795-8100
Longshine Microsys	(310)903-0899
Longshine Technology	(408)942-1746
LookUp Software	(702)786-4242
Loop Computer Prods	(714)549-5818
Loral Commercial Sys	(313)390-2601
Lortec Power Systems	(800)927-5051
Lotus-Word Processing	(800)831-9679
Tech Support	(404)399-5505
Lotus Devel. Corp	(800)345-1043
Tech Support	(800)223-1662
Lotus Publishing	(617)494-1192
Lousig-Nont & Assoc.	(800)477-3211
Lowry Cmptr Prods	(800)733-0010
LPA Software Inc	(800)248-9602
LSI Logic Corporation	(408)433-8000
LSW Inc	(301)772-8700
Lucas Deeco Corp	(510)471-4700
Lucasey Mfg Corp	(510)534-1435
Lucid	(800)843-4204
Tech Support	(214)994-8101
Lucky Star Int'l	(214)690-1825
Luctor Corporation	(602)582-5503
Lugaru Software	(412)421-5911
Luxor Corporation	(708)244-1800
Lxycon	(818)281-3957
Lyco Cmptr Marketing	(800)233-8760
Tech Support	(717)494-1670
Lynx Technology	(416)886-7315
Lysis Corporation	(404)373-3359
Lyte Optronics Inc	(310)451-8551
Lytec Systems Inc	(801)562-0111
M & P Services	(714)359-6011
M Global	(713)960-0205
M Technology	(408)748-8701
M USA Business Sys	(214)386-6100
Tech Support	(214)490-0100
M&T Publishing	(415)358-9500
M-Test Equipment	(800)334-4293
M-USA Business Sys	(800)933-6872
Tech Support	(214)490-0100
M/A-Com LCS	(800)669-1769
M1 Electronic Industry	(514)956-7834
MA Labs Inc	(408)954-8188
Mac America	(408)434-0433
Tech Support	(800)832-4003
Mace, Paul Software	(503)488-2322
Machine Design	(216)696-7000
Macmillan New Media	(617)225-9023
MacMillan Publish.	(800)428-5331
MacMillan Publishing	(800)428-5331
Tech Support	(800)428-5331
MACRACON SYSTEMS	(510)651-9115
Macromedia	(800)288-4797
Tech Support	(415)252-9080
Macromind	(415)442-0200
Macronix Inc	(408)453-8088
Macrotron Systems	(510)651-9115

INDUSTRY PHONE NUMBERS

MacShack Inc.	(716)344-9230	
Macuser.	(415)378-5600	
Madge Networks	(800)876-2343	
Tech Support	(800)876-2343	
MAG InnoVision Inc	(800)827-3998	
Tech Support	(714)751-2008	
Magee Enterprises, Inc.	(800)662-4330	
Tech Support	(404)662-5387	
Magic RAM	(213)413-9999	
Magic Software Ent.	(714)250-1718	
Magic Solutions, Inc.	(201)529-5533	
Magma Sftwre Solutions	(201)912-0192	
Magna	(408)282-0900	
Tech Support	(408)879-7911	
Magnetic Data, Inc.	(800)328-3441	
Magnetic Recovery Techn.	(805)257-2261	
Magni Systems, Inc.	(503)626-8400	
Magretech Inc.	(805)685-4551	
Magus Data Techn.	(416)513-0823	
MAI Systems	(714)731-0201	
Main Boards	(800)359-0201	
Main Source Electr.	(800)456-6246	
Tech Support	(813)351-8420	
MainLan Inc.	(214)248-0305	
Mainlan, Inc.	(407)331-4400	
Mainline Cmptr Repair	(215)644-0534	
Mainstay Software	(805)484-9400	
Tech Support	(805)484-9400	
Mainstream Software	(214)934-8906	
Maintech	(800)426-8324	
Maintenance Etc.	(713)520-6567	
Maint. Troubleshooting.	(302)738-0532	
Mallard Software	(214)436-0044	
Tech Support	(214)219-0242	
Man & Machine Inc.	(301)277-3760	
Mandax Computer	(206)867-1973	
Manhatttan Electr. Cable	(800)228-6322	
Mannesmann Tally	(206)251-5609	
Mansfield Software Grp.	(203)429-8402	
Mantis Computer Parts	(800)252-9989	
Manugistics	(800)592-0050	
Manusoft Corporation	(818)304-2762	
Manzana Microsystems	(805)968-1387	
Manzanita Sftwr Sys	(800)447-5700	
Tech Support	(800)447-5700	
Maple Systems	(408)456-0355	
Mapinfo Corporation	(518)274-6000	
Marclyn	(408)739-2443	
Marconi Circuit Techn.	(516)293-8686	
Mark IV Industries	(716)689-4972	
Mark of the Unicorn	(617)576-2760	
Market Intelligence	(415)961-9000	
Marlin P. Jones & Assoc.	(407)848-8236	
Marshall Industries	(800)522-0084	
Marstek Inc.	(714)833-7740	
Martin Info Systems	(808)733-2003	
Martin Marietta Corp.	(301)897-6000	
Masque Publishing	(800)765-4223	
Mass Memory Systems.	(800)347-5722	
Mass Micro Systems	(800)522-7970	
Tech Support	(800)522-7970	
Masstor Systems Corp.	(408)955-0160	
Master Bond Inc.	(201)343-8963	
Masterclip Graphics-IMSI.	(305)983-7440	
Tech Support	(305)983-7440	
Mastersoft	(800)624-6107	

Mastertronics	(714)833-8710	
Tech Support	(714)833-8710	
Math Soft Inc.	(800)628-4223	
Mathematica	(813)682-1128	
Tech Support	(813)682-1130	
MathSoft, Inc.	(800)628-4223	
Tech Support	(617)577-1778	
Matrix Digital Prods	(818)566-8567	
Matrox Electronic Sys	(800)663-8765	
Tech Support	(800)663-8765	
Matrox Graphic Inc.	(800)361-1409	
Tech Support	(514)685-0270	
Matter of FAX	(800)433-3329	
Tech Support	(212)431-5426	
Maui Research & Techn.	(800)875-2320	
Max Software Consult.	(301)828-5935	
Max Systems	(407)877-3807	
Maxa	(818)543-1300	
Maxcard	(503)593-6027	
MaxConcepts	(619)530-9062	
Maxell	(800)325-7717	
Tech Support	(800)533-2836	
Maxell Corp/America	(800)533-2836	
Maxi Switch, Inc.	(602)294-5450	
Maxim Technology	(800)755-1008	
Maximus	(800)394-6299	
Tech Support	(800)894-0142	
Maxis Software	(800)366-2947	
Tech Support	(510)253-3755	
Maxoptix Corporation	(800)848-3092	
Maxspeed	(415)345-5447	
Maxtor CO - Miniscribe	(303)651-6000	
Tech Support	(800)356-5333	
Maxtor Corporatio	(800)262-9867	
Tech Support	(800)262-9867	
Maxtron	(818)350-5706	
MAXX Memory Prods.	(800)748-6629	
Maya Electronic Prod.	(915)590-8880	
Mayesys Corporation	(301)961-4899	
Maynard Electronics	(800)821-8782	
Maysteel Corporation	(414)629-5535	
MBS	(800)944-3808	
Tech Support	(301)762-7405	
MBS Technologies	(800)860-8700	
Tech Support	(800)860-8703	
McAfee Associates	(408)988-3832	
McArthur Associatcs	(914)279-8049	
McCarty Associates	(203)388-6994	
MCCI	(408)954-8070	
McClure Consultants	(708)382-6233	
McDonnell Douglas	(314)232-0232	
McGraw Hill	(800)262-4729	
McGraw-Hill TechNet Grp.	(212)512-4604	
McGraw-Hill Cmptr Publ.	(415)513-6800	
McGraw-Hill/Data Comm.	(800)822-8158	
MCI Commun. Corp.	(202)872-1600	
MCM Electronics	(800)543-4330	
McNeil & Associates	(612)428-4068	
MCR Computer Serv	(800)849-9595	
MCR Marketing Inc.	(513)861-3046	
MCSI Technologies, Inc.	(301)495-4444	
McTronic Systems	(713)462-7687	
McWains Chelsea	(201)993-5700	
Mead Training Systems.	(800)621-8711	
Mead-Hatcher, Inc.	(716)877-1185	
Measure. & Control Prod.	(212)662-6012	

Measurex Corporation	(408)255-1500	
MECA Software	(800)820-7458	
Tech Support	(203)255-7562	
MECC (MN)	(612)569-1529	
Tech Support	(612)569-1678	
MECC (CA)	(800)685-6322	
Meckler Corporation	(203)226-6967	
Mectel International.	(800)248-0255	
Media 4 Less	(800)621-6827	
Media Cybernetics	(800)992-4256	
Media Factory	(800)879-9536	
Tech Support	(408)456-9182	
Media Products	(408)432-1711	
Media Resources	(714)256-5048	
Media Source	(800)356-2553	
Media Value	(800)845-3472	
Media Vision Resource	(800)845-5870	
Tech Support	(800)638-2807	
MediaLogic, Inc.	(508)695-2006	
MediaShare Corp.	(619)931-7171	
Medical Sys. & Mgt.	(310)914-1600	
Mega Drive Systems	(800)322-4744	
Tech Support	(310)970-8000	
Mega Drive Systems	(310)847-0006	
Mega PC Technology	(714)850-1044	
Megadata Corporation	(516)589-6800	
MegaHaus	(800)426-0560	
Tech Support	(713)333-1944	
Megahertz	(800)527-8677	
Tech Support	(800)527-8677	
Megasource	(800)473-9728	
Megatel Cmptr Corp	(416)245-2953	
MEI/Micro Center	(800)634-3478	
Meirick Inc.	(800)735-5069	
Melard Technologies	(914)273-4488	
Meltek Inc.	(408)438-4986	
Memorex Cmptr Supp.	(408)957-1000	
Memorex Telex Corp.	(918)627-2333	
Memory Express	(800)877-8188	
Memory Media Prods.	(714)669-1800	
Memory Prods & More	(714)753-1200	
Memory Technology Inc.	(303)786-8080	
Memsoft Inc.	(407)997-6655	
Menai	(415)617-5730	
Mendon Optronics Inc.	(716)248-8480	
Mentor Electronics	(216)951-1884	
Mentor Graphics Corp.	(503)685-7000	
Mentor Market Research.	(408)268-6333	
Merchant Systems	(602)951-9390	
Mercury Cmptr Sys	(508)458-3100	
Mercury Technologies	(514)747-0254	
Mergent International.	(800)688-3227	
Tech Support	(800)688-3227	
Meridian Data	(800)767-2537	
Tech Support	(800)755-8324	
Merisel	(800)542-9955	
Merit Software	(214)385-2353	
Tech Support	(214)385-2957	
Meritec	(216)354-3148	
Merlin Software	(206)361-0093	
Merrill & Bryan Ent.	(619)689-8611	
Merritt Cmptr Prods.	(214)339-0753	
MESA Distribution	(800)388-3339	
Mesa Systems Inc.	(510)462-9491	
Meta Software	(617)576-6920	
Metagraphics	(408)438-1550	

Metc Software	(800)767-6292	
Metcan Info.Techn	(416)881-9955	
Metheus Corporation	(800)638-4387	
Methode Electronics	(800)323-6858	
Metra Info. Systems	(408)730-9188	
Metrix Cust. Supp. Sys.	(414)798-8560	
Metrix Network Sys.	(603)888-7000	
Metro Data-Vac	(914)357-1600	
Metro Software	(602)292-0313	
Metromedia Paging Serv.	(201)462-4966	
Metropolis Software	(415)322-2001	
MetroTel Corporation	(516)937-3420	
MetroVision Microsys.	(800)875-2099	
Metrum Instrumentation	(415)969-5500	
Metz Software	(206)641-4525	
Tech Support	(206)641-4525	
Mextel	(708)595-4146	
MFS Inc.	(800)456-2159	
MGI Group Int'l Inc.	(310)352-3100	
MGV Manufacturing	(205)772-1100	
MIC Media Corp.	(510)226-0606	
Micom Systems, Inc.	(805)583-8600	
Micro 2000 Inc.	(818)547-0125	
Micro Accessories Inc.	(800)777-6687	
Micro Care Corp.	(800)638-0125	
Micro Central	(800)836-4276	
Micro Chan. Devel.Assoc.	(916)222-2262	
Micro Computer Cable	(313)946-9700	
Micro Connectors Inc.	(510)839-8112	
Micro Data	(800)539-0123	
Micro Data Base Sys.	(317)463-2581	
Micro Design Inc.	(215)884-1112	
Micro Design Int'l, Inc.	(800)241-1853	
Micro Display-Ranger Tech.	(612)437-2233	
Micro Electronic Techn.	(800)468-0252	
Micro Electr.WinBook	(800)468-0252	
Micro Exchange Corp.	(201)284-1200	
Micro Fine Int'l Inc.	(718)358-3870	
Micro Focus	(415)856-4161	
Micro House	(800)926-8299	
Tech Support	(303)443-3389	
Micro Industries Corp.	(614)548-7878	
Micro Informatica	(305)377-1930	
Micro League Sports	(302)368-9990	
Micro Mart Inc.	(508)888-2225	
Micro Media Int'l.	(714)588-9882	
Micro Medic Inc.	(714)581-3651	
Micro Medics	(313)759-0231	
Micro Palms Cmptr.	(813)530-0128	
Micro Power Electr.	(800)642-7612	
Micro Professionals	(800)800-8300	
Micro Security Sys.	(801)575-6600	
Micro Service Express	(214)239-7033	
Micro Solutions	(815)756-3411	
Micro Star	(619)731-4949	
Micro Supply	(408)954-0640	
Tech Support	(408)954-0640	
MICRO SUPPLY	(206)885-5420	
Micro Systems	(800)548-5182	
Micro Technology	(201)340-0442	
Micro X-Press	(800)875-9737	
Tech Support	(317)328-5784	
Micro-Integration	(301)777-3307	
Micro-Integration, Inc.	(301)746-5888	
Micro-Term, Inc.	(314)822-4111	
MicroAge Cmptr Ctrs.	(602)929-2416	

Microbase Info. Sys.	(310)479-1239
Microbilt Corporation	(404)955-0313
MicroBiz Corporation	(800)6378268
Tech Support	(914)425-3789
MicroClean Inc.	(408)412-0611
Microcom-Carbon Copy	(800)8228224
Tech Support	(617)551-1414
Microcom-Hardware	(800)822-1125
Tech Support	(617)551-1313
Microcomputer Access	(800)521-8270
Tech Support	(310)645-9400
Microcmptr Concepts	(800)772-3914
Microcmptr Techn. Serv.	(508)796-9912
Microdynamics Inc.	(214)343-1170
Microdyne Corp-LAN	(800)255-3967
Tech Support	(800)255-3967
Microdyne Corp-LAN	(800)255-3967
Tech Support	(800)255-3967
Microfield Graphics	(503)626-9393
MicroGate Corp.	(512)345-7791
Micrografx, Inc.	(800)733-3729
Tech Support	(214)234-2694
MicroId	(408)395-4096
MicroId Research, Inc.	(408)727-6991
Microlink/Micro Filmware	(800)767-5465
Microlog Corporation	(800)333-6564
Micrologic	(201)342-6518
MicroLogic Software	(510)652-5464
Tech Support	(510)652-5464
MicroLogic Systems	(903)561-0007
Microlytics	(800)828-6293
Tech Support	(716)248-9150
MicroMaid Inc.	(800)369-7079
MicroMaps Software	(800)334-4291
Tech Support	(609)397-1611
Micromation Techn.	(408)739-2999
Micromax Distr.	(800)795-6299
Micron Computer	(800)438-3343
Micron Technology	(800)642-7661
Micronet Cmptr Sys.	(714)739-2244
MicroNet Technology	(714)453-6100
Tech Support	(714)453-6060
Micronics Computers	(510)651-2300
Tech Support	(510)651-2322
MicroPen Cmptr Corp.	(408)734-4181
Microplex Systems Ltd.	(604)875-1461
Micropolis Corp.	(818)709-3388
Tech Support	(818)709-3325
Micropost Corporation	(604)682-6258
MicroProcessors Unltd.	(918)267-4961
Tech Support	(918)267-3879
Microprose Software	(800)876-1151
Tech Support	(410)771-1151
Microref/Educat'l Sftwr.	(708)498-3780
Microrim	(800)248-2001
Tech Support	(206)649-9551
Micros Systems, Inc.	(301)210-6000
Microseconds Int'l.	(619)756-0765
Microseeds Publ.	(813)882-8635
MicroScrv Inc.	(800)736-3599
MicroSlate Inc.	(514)444-3680
MicroSoft Corporation	(800)426-9400
Access	(206)635-7050
Auth Train'g Ctr. Prog.	(800)426-9400
Basic PDS	(206)635-7053
CD-ROM Installation	(206)635-7033

Certified Professionals	(800)765-7768
Consulting Services	(800)922-9446
Delta	(206)635-7019
Developer Network	(800)759-5474
Download Serv-USA	(206)935-6735
Excel for Macintosh	(206)635-7080
Excel for Windows/OS/2.	(206)635-7070
Excel SDK	(206)635-7048
Fast Tips,Advanced Sys.	(800)936-4400
Fast Tips, Desktop Apps.	(800)936-4100
Fast Tips, Devel. Tools.	(800)936-4300
Fast Tips, Pers Op Sys.	(800)936-4200
FORTRAN	(206)635-7015
Forum on CompuServe.	(800)848-8199
Fox prods,Macintosh	(206)635-7192
Fox prods,DOS/Win.	(206)635-7191
Hrdwre-Mouse,BPoint.	(206)635-7040
Macro Assembler-MASM.	(206)646-5109
Money	(206)635-7131
MS-DOS 6.0/.2 Upgrades.	(206)646-5104
Multimedia Products	(206)635-7172
Office for Macintosh	(206)635-7055
Office for Windows	(206)635-7058
OnLine-Win Tech Supp	(800)443-4672
PowerPoint	(206)635-7145
Premier Supp/Sales&Info.	(800)936-3500
Priority Comprehensive.	(900)555-2100
Pr. Comprehensive - CC.	(800)935-5900
Pr. Desktop Apps.	(900)555-2000
Pr. Desktop Apps - CC	(800)936-5700
Pr. Develop w/DesktpCC.	(800)936-5800
Pr. Develop w/Desktop.	(900)555-2300
Pr. Personal Op Sys-CC.	(800)936-5700
Pr. Personal Op Sys.	(900)555-2000
Profiler	(206)635-7015
Profit	(800)723-3333
Project	(206)635-7155
Publisher	(206)635-7140
QuickBasic	(206)646-5101
QuickC	(206)635-7010
Schedule	(206)635-7049
Sol. Provider Sales & Info.	(800)426-9400
Supp. Ntwrk Sales & Info.	(800)936-3500
Switcher Line	(206)635-7041
TechNet	(800)344-2121
Test for Windows	(206)635-7052
TT/TDD-Text Telephone.	(206)635-4948
Video for Windows	(206)635-7172
Visual Basic	(206)646-5105
Visual Basic Prof.Toolkt	(206)646-5105
Visual C/C+	(206)635-7007
Win Entertainment Prods.	(206)637-9308
Win NT-Install Supp	(206)635-7018
Win Sftwre Devel. Kit.	(206)635-3329
Win/Win for Workgrp.	(206)637-7098
Word for MS-DOS	(206)635-7210
Word for the Mac	(206)635-7200
Word for Windows	(206)462-9673
Works for the Mac	(206)635-7160
Works for MS-DOS	(206)635-7150
Works for Windows	(206)635-7130
Microsoft Press	(800)426-9400
Tech Support	(206)635-3313
Microsoft Sys Journal	(415)535-8950
Microspeed	(800)232-7888
Tech Support	(800)232-7888

INDUSTRY PHONE NUMBERS

Microspot.........................(800)622-7568
   Tech Support............(408)257-4000
MicroStep Inc. ....(818)336-8991
MicroSupply (WA).........(206)885-5420
MicroSupply (CO) ....(303)792-5474
Microsystems Devel ......(408)296-4000
MicroTac Software.........(800)366-4170
   Tech Support............(619)271-5700
Microtech Conversn Sys...(800)223-3693
Microtech International ..(800)666-9689
   Tech Support............(800)626-4276
Microtek Lab....................(800)654-4160
   Tech Support............(310)297-5100
Microtest.........................(800)526-9675
Microtimes.......................(510)934-3700
MicroTouch Systems .....(800)866-6873
Microtrace Inc..................(317)842-0772
Microvitec Inc..................(404)991-2246
Microvoice Corp.............(714)588-2739
Microware Distributors.(800)777-9511
   Tech Support............(800)888-4797
Microware Techn. Dist...(800)382-2405
MicroWay, Inc...................(508)746-7341
MicroWest Spacesaver...(800)969-9699
MICS Computers Inc.....(310)325-4520
Midern Computer Inc...(818)964-8682
MIDI Land Inc.................(714)595-0708
Midisoft Corporation.....(800)776-6434
   Tech Support............(206)881-7176
Midland ComputerMart.(800)407-0700
   Tech Support............(708)967-0746
Midwest Cmptr Support..(419)259-2600
Midwest Cmptr Works...(800)669-5208
Midwest Micro..............(800)312-8822
   Tech Support............(800)243-0313
Midwestern Diskette.....(800)221-6332
   Tech Support............(515)782-5190
Migraph, Inc..................(206)838-4677
Mikael Blaisdell&Assoc..(510)865-4515
Milan Technology..........(408)752-2770
Miles Tek ....(800)524-7444
Miller Freeman Publ......(415)397-1881
Miltope Corporation .....(516)420-0200
Mind Path Technologies.(214)233-9296
Mind's Eye ....(617)935-2679
Mindflight Technology...(604)434-6463
Mini-Micro Supply Co...(408)456-9500
Minolta Corporaation....(201)825-4000
Minta Technologies Co..(201)329-2020
Minuteman UPS.............(800)238-7272
MIPS Technologies, Inc..(415)960-1980
MIPSI Systems, Inc.........(800)727-6774
Mirage Computer ....(800)666-8098
   Tech Support............(909)598-2602
Miramar Systems............(805)966-2432
   Tech Support............(805)966-2432
Mirror Technologies.......(800)654-5294
   Tech Support............(612)633-2105
Mirus ....(408)944-9770
MIS Computer Systems.(408)730-9188
Misco.............................(908)876-4726
MissionSix Devel Corp..(408)722-9211
Mita Copystar America..(201)806-8444
Mitel Corporation..........(613)592-2122
Mitsuba Corporation .....(714)392-2000
Mitsubishi Electronics...(800)843-2515

Tech Support............(800)344-6352
Mitsubishi Electr Amer..(714)220-2500
Mitsubishi Int'l Corp......(914)997-4960
Mitsubishi Rayon Co......(213)627-7120
Mitsumi Electr Corp-NY.....(516)752-7730
   Tech Support............(408)970-9699
Mitsumi Electr Corp-TX ....(214)550-7300
Mix Software..................(800)333-0330
   Tech Support............(214)783-6001
MM Newman Corp........(617)631-7100
MMB Devel Corp............(310)318-1322
MMC Ad Systems............(408)263-0781
MMF Industries...............(800)445-8293
Mobile Cmptr Recovery ..(800)688-6262
Mod-Tap ....(508)772-5630
Modem Office Techn.....(216)696-7000
Modgraph, Inc...............(617)229-4800
Modumend ....(800)350-5558
Monitech........................(800)332-9349
Moniterm Corporation..(800)343-4969
Monitor Maint. Corp......(617)961-2600
Monogram Media ....(414)887-7744
Monotype Typography ..(800)666-6897
   Tech Support............(800)666-6897
Monster Design ....(415)871-6000
   Tech Support............(415)871-6000
Montech.........................(508)663-5015
Monterey Cmptr Consult..(408)646-1147
Monterey Electronics ....(408)437-5496
Moon Valley Software....(800)473-5509
   Tech Support............(800)473-5509
Moore Bus. Forms & Sys..(708)480-3000
...............................(708)615-6000
Morelli Associates ....(508)543-4105
Morgan Davis Group.....(619)670-0563
Morris Video...................(310)533-4800
   Tech Support............(310)533-4800
Morrow Cmptr Corp.....(800)859-6849
   Tech Support............(212)360-0580
Morse Technology, Inc...(818)854-8688
Mortice Kern Systems...(519)884-2251
   Tech Support............(519)884-2270
Morton Management.....(800)548-5744
Moses Computers..........(408)358-1550
MOST Inc.......................(714)898-9400
Motherboard Warehouse ..(800)486-9975
   Tech Support............(602)829-7751
Motion Works Inc..........(604)685-9975
Motor Management.......(800)548-5744
Motorola Codex.............(508)261-4307
Motorola Inc. (IL)...........(708)576-5304
   Tech Support............(800)311-6456
Motorola Inc. (TX)........(512)891-2000
Motorola Mobile Data....(800)247-2346
MountainGate ....(800)556-0222
Mountain Ntwrk Solution.(800)458-0300
   Tech Support............(408)438-7897
Mouse Systems Corp.....(510)656-1117
   Tech Support............(510)656-1117
Mouser Electronics........(800)346-6873
Movonics........................(415)960-1250
MP Systems....................(214)385-2221
MPS Multimedia..............(800)533-4677
   Tech Support............(602)829-7751
Mr. Software, Inc............(212)947-6272
MSI Data Corporation ...(714)549-6000

MST Distribution ....(216)248-2533
M-Systems ....(408)654-5820
Mueller............................(216)771-5225
Mueller Techn Research.(708)726-0709
Multi Connection Techn...(510)670-0633
Multi-Ad Services...........(800)447-1950
Multi-Dimension Resrch..(818)337-6860
Multi-Industry Tech........(310)921-6669
Multi-Link Inc.................(800)535-4651
Multi-Net Comm.............(503)883-8099
Multi-Tech Systems, Inc.(800)328-9717
MultiLing International..(801)377-7077
Multimedia Direct...........(800)386-3342
Multimedia Warehouse..(800)683-2868
Muliple Zones................(800)258-2088
MultiTech Systems.........(800)328-9717
MultiWriter Software.....(201)833-1333
Murata Business Sys.......(214)403-3300
Mustang Software, Inc...(800)999-9619
   Tech Support............(805)873-2550
Mustek Inc......................(800)468-7835
   Tech Support............(714)250-4880
Mux Lab........................(800)361-1965
Mylex Corporation........(800)776-9539
   Tech Support............(510)796-6100
Myoda Inc......................(708)369-5199
Myried Inc......................(510)659-8782
MySoftware Company...(303)522-3000
   Tech Support............(303)522-3000
Nada Concepts ....(612)623-0711
Nanao USA Corporation ..(213)325-5202
Nantucket Corporation.(310)390-7923
Nashua Corporation.......(800)258-1370
Natl Assoc of Serv Mgr..(708)310-9930
National Micronetics......(914)338-0333
National Advancement..(800)832-4787
Natl Bureau of Standards...(301)975-6776
Natl Business Assoc ....(214)991-5381
Natl Communications ...(201)733-9200
Natl Computer Distrib...(305)967-2397
National Computer Sys.(612)829-3000
Natl Customer Eng.........(619)452-7974
National Data Corp........(404)728-2000
National Datacomputer.(508)663-7677
National Design Inc........(512)329-5055
National Instruments.....(800)433-3488
Natl Inventory Exchange.(800)633-2869
Natl Peripheral Service..(800)628-9025
Natl Semiconductor.......(408)721-5000
   Tech Support............(404)564-5699
Natl Service Network....(206)845-1288
Natl Soft.Testing Labs....(215)941-9600
Natl Standards Institute.(212)642-4900
Natl Technical Info Serv.(703)487-4650
National TeleVAR...........(800)468-1732
Nationwide Cmptr Dist.(800)777-1054
   Tech Support............(201)659-2977
Natl Sftwr Testing Lab....(215)941-9600
Natter Manufacturing....(801)561-9261
Navacor InCorp..............(408)441-6500
NavPress Software.........(719)598-1212
NBI, Inc.........................(303)444-5710
   Tech Support............(800)225-5824
NCI.................................(303)650-5522
NCL America..................(408)734-1006
NCR Corporation...........(316)636-8000

NCR Corp-Ed Services...(800)845-2273
NCR Direct Connect.....(800)627-8076
   Tech Support............(800)531-2222
NCR Microelectronics...(800)334-5454
NCR Wrldwde Serv.Parts...(800)367-1842
NDC Communications..(408)428-9108
   Tech Support............(800)323-7325
Neamco......................(617)269-7600
NEC Technologies Inc...(800)632-4636
   Tech Support............(800)388-8888
Needham's Electronics..(916)924-8037
NEI.............................(714)753-8588
Nesco Battery Systems..(800)423-2664
Net Computers Int'l......(214)386-9310
   Tech Support............(214)386-9337
Net Soft......................(818)572-0607
NET-Source Inc............(408)246-6679
Nctalliance...................(206)637-3305
NetFrame Systems.........(800)737-8377
Netherlands Ch.of Comm.(404)523-4400
Netline........................(703)760-0660
NETS Electronics Inc.....(800)633-7999
Network.......................(508)568-0933
Network Comm. Corp...(800)451-1984
Network Equip Tech......(415)366-4400
Network Express...........(800)33-9899
   Tech Support...........(813)359-2876
Network General...........(708)574-3399
Network Interface Corp..(913)894-2277
Network Security Sys....(800)755-7078
   Tech Support............(800)755-7078
Network Systems Corp.(612)424-4888
Network Technologies..(800)742-8324
Networth.....................(800)544-5255
Neuralytic Systems.........(415)321-3777
Nevada Computer.........(800)654-7762
New England Software..(203)625-0062
New Horizn Cmptr Lrn Ctr.(714)556-1220
New Media Corp...........(714)453-0100
   Tech Support............(714)753-0100
New Media Graphics.....(508)663-0666
New MMI.....................(800)221-4283
New Quest Technology.(801)975-9992
New Vision Technology.(613)727-8184
   Tech Support............(613)727-0884
New World Technology.(800)443-8885
Newer Technology.........(316)685-4904
NewGen Systems Corp.(714)641-8600
   Tech Support............(714)641-8600
NewMedia Magazine......(415)573-5170
Neworg Inc...................(804)358-5626
NewQuest Technology..(613)727-8184
Nexgen Microsystems...(408)435-0202
Next Computer Corp....(415)366-0900
Next Generation Sftwr..(404)365-8258
Nial Systems.................(613)234-4188
Nichimen America Inc...(312)938-8887
Nikon Electr. Imaging....(516)547-4350
Nikon Precision.............(800)446-4566
Nimax Inc.....................(619)566-4800
Ninga Software Corp.....(403)265-6611
Nisca Inc......................(214)242-9696
Nissei Sangyo America ..(617)893-5700
Nissho Electronics -USA.(714)261-8811
Nisus...........................(800)922-2993
   Tech Support............(619)481-1477

Nitek Inc......................(602)285-5662
NMB Technologies.........(818)341-3355
No Hands Software........(800)598-3921
   Tech Support............(415)321-2925
No-Brainer Software......(800)748-4499
Noesis.........................(213)399-8208
Noetic Technologies......(800)780-6343
Noice Cancellat'n Techn..(410)636-8700
   Tech Support............(410)636-8700
Nolo Press...................(800)992-6656
   Tech Support............(800)992-6656
Nomai.........................(800)556-6624
NOMDA/NIA................(816)941-3100
NoRad Corporation.......(800)262-3260
Norcom.......................(907)780-6464
Nordisk Systems ....(805)485-4778
Norick Data Systems.....(405)947-7560
Nortek Computers-ON..(705)474-2058
Nortek Computers-FL...(305)351-4500
North American InfoNet..(707)765-1999
North Hills Electronics..(516)671-5700
North-East Microcmptr..(416)513-6800
Northeast Techn Serv....(800)647-9725
Northeastern Sonics......(800)243-2452
Northern Technologies.(800)727-9119
Northern Telecom Ltd..(416)897-9000
Northgate Cmptr Sys.....(800)548-1993
   Tech Support............(800)446-5037
Northstar Matrix-Serv..(800)969-0009
Norton-Lambert...........(805)964-6767
   Tech Support............(805)964-6767
Noteable Computers.....(800)274-4124
NoteStar Computers......(908)651-8686
Notework Corporation..(617)734-4317
Nova Techn Services......(800)523-2773
Novacor Inc.................(800)486-6682
NovaStor Corporation..(818)707-9900
Novell Desktop Sys........(800)768-9771
Novell Inc. (UT).............(800)638-9273
   Tech Support............(800)453-1267
Novell Inc. (CA)............(800)638-9273
   Tech Support............(800)453-1267
Now Software................(503)274-2800
   Tech Support............(503)274-2800
Noyes Fiber Systems .....(603)528-7780
NPA Systems.................(800)873-6724
NPA West.....................(800)999-4672
NRD Inc.......................(716)773-7634
NRG Data Corporation..(408)727-9700
NRI.............................(202)244-1600
NSM Information Sys.....(516)261-7700
NSSI/Deltek ....(800)755-7078
NSTS..........................(404)923-1383
NTE Electronics Inc.......(800)631-1250
Ntergaid, Inc................(203)368-0632
NTR Computer..............(408)727-4500
Nu Data.......................(908)842-5757
NUIQ Software, Inc.......(914)833-3479
Number 9 Cmptr Corp.(800)438-6463
   Tech Support............(617)674-0009
Numonics Corporation.(215)362-2766
NUS............................(800)247-8818
NUS Training Corp.........(800)848-1717
NView Corporation........(800)736-8439
NYCE..........................(516)997-7170
Nynex Corporation ....(914)741-4700

O'Neill Comm...............(800)624-5296
   Tech Support............(215)957-5408
O.K. Industries...............(914)969-6800
Oakland Group..............(617)491-7311
OAZ Communications ..(408)745-1750
OBI Distributors, Inc......(714)259-1925
Objective Software........(415)324-3333
Occarn Research...........(617)923-3545
   Tech Support............(617)923-3903
Ocean Information Sys..(800)325-2496
Ocean Interface Co.......(714)595-1212
Ocean Isle Software ......(407)770-4777
   Tech Support............(407)770-4777
OCEAN Microsystems...(408)374-8300
OCLI (Opt Coat'g Lab)..(707)545-6440
Ocron, Inc....................(408)980-8900
Octocom Systems Inc....(508)441-2181
Octophase Techn Corp..(408)954-1240
OCTuS Inc....................(619)452-9400
Odestus Corporation.....(708)498-5615
   Tech Support............(708)798-8852
Odetics Inc...................(714)774-6900
Odyssey Development..(303)394-0091
OEM Parts Repair Depot..(800)422-2115
Office Automation Sys...(619)452-9400
Office Publications, Inc..(203)327-9670
OFTI............................(508)695-6606
Oki Semiconductor.......(800)832-6654
Okidata Corporation......(800)654-3282
   Tech Support............(609)273-0300
Okna..........................(201)909-8600
Olduvai........................(800)822-0772
   Tech Support............(305)670-1112
Olicom USA.................(800)654-2661
   Tech Support............(800)654-2661
Olivetti........................(408)996-3867
Olivetti Office USA........(201)526-8200
Olivetti/ISC..................(509)927-5622
Olympus......................(800)347-4027
Omega Techn/Taiwan....(305)597-5564
Omni CEO....................(508)937-5004
Omni Labs....................(800)706-3342
   Tech Support............(415)788-1345
Omni-Data Comms........(800)922-2329
Omnicomp Graphics......(713)464-2990
Omniprint Inc................(800)878-6800
Omnitech Gencorp........(305)599-9898
OmniTel Inc..................(510)490-2202
Omnium Corporation ...(715)268-8500
Omron Electronics, Inc..(708)843-7900
Omron Office Auto Prod..(408)727-1444
On Board Cmptr Serv....(203)881-0555
ON Technology..............(800)767-6683
   Tech Support............(800)767-6683
On Time Mac Service....(415)367-6263
On-Line Data.................(519)579-3930
On-Line Power Co.........(213)721-5017
On-Line Software Int'l...(201)592-0009
On-Line/AAA Power.......(213)721-5017
OnDisk Info Systems.....(800)654-3146
Oneac Corporation........(708)816-6000
Online Press Inc. ....(206)641-3434
Online, USA..................(303)932-1900
Ontrack Computer Sys..(800)752-1333
   Tech Support............(612)937-2121
Opcode Systems............(415)856-3333

INDUSTRY PHONE NUMBERS

Tech Support............(415)369-1676
Open Systems................(800)328-2276
   Tech Support............(800)582-5000
Open Text Corporation.(519)571-7711
Opt-Tech Data Process'g..(702)588-3737
OPTi, Inc......................(408)980-8178
Optibase, Inc................(818)719-6566
Optical Access Int'l........(800)433-5133
Optical Cable Corp........(703)265-0690
Optical Data Systems ....(214)234-6400
Optical Devices, Inc. .....(805)987-8801
Optical Storage Corp.....(310)791-2028
Optical Stor.Trade Assoc..(805)569-2541
Optima Techn Corp......(714)476-0515
Optiquest, Inc. ....(310)948-1185
Opus Computer Prods..(216)248-9264
OR Cmptr Keyboards....(604)879-9815
ORA Electronics.............(818)772-9977
   Tech Support............(818)772-9977
Oracle Corporation ....(415)506-2200
Orange Micro, Inc..........(714)779-2772
Orbit Industries, Inc......(604)582-6301
Orca Technology Corp..(408)441-1111
Orchid Technology........(800)767-2443
   Tech Support............(510)683-0323
Oregon Software............(503)624-6883
Orevox USA Corp..........(818)333-6803
Orientec Corp/America.(818)442-1818
Origin Systems, Inc........(512)328-5490
   Tech Support............(512)328-0282
OS Computer City.........(800)938-6722
OS/2 2.0 Applications ...(800)426-3333
Osborne/McGraw Hill...(800)227-0900
Oscan Electro-Optics.....(613)745-4600
Oscar International........(909)595-0339
OSI Netter, The..............(612)935-2035
Osicom Technologies ....(201)586-2550
Our Business Machines.(818)337-9614
Outbound Systems, Inc..(303)786-9200
Output Tech Corp..........(800)468-8788
   Tech Support............(800)468-8788
Overdrive Systems........(216)292-3425
   Tech Support............(216)292-3410
Overland Data, Inc.........(619)571-5555
Overseas Trade Group...(313)340-0300
Owl International..........(206)747-3203
OWP............................(603)880-5100
P.A. Computer Access....(818)448-9221
P.M. Ware ....(619)738-6633
P.N.Y. Electronics, Inc.....(800)234-4597
   Tech Support............(201)438-6300
PACE Custom Cases......(800)359-6670
Pace Inc.......................(301)490-9860
Pacer Industries.............(800)283-1141
Pacer Software..............(508)454-0565
   Tech Support............(508)898-3300
Pacific Computer Prod..(714)549-7535
Pacific Data Products ...(619)552-0880
   Tech Support............(619)587-4690
Pacific Dataware Inc......(800)234-4734
Pacific Decision Sciences..(714)832-2200
Pacific Electro Data.......(800)676-2468
Pacific Gold Coast Corp..(800)732-3002
Pacific Image Commun.(818)441-0104
Pacific International Ctr...(808)539-1533
Pacific Magnetics Corp..(619)474-8216

Pacific Magtron, Inc.......(408)733-1188
Pacific Micro Data, Inc...(714)838-8900
Pacific Micro Mrktg.......(510)838-0100
Pacific Microelectronics...(415)948-6200
   Tech Support............(415)948-6200
Pacific NW Partnership.(206)682-6900
Pacific Power Source.....(714)898-2691
Pacific Rim Systems.......(800)722-7461
Pacific Telecom, Inc. ......(206)696-0983
Pacific Telesis Group.....(415)394-3000
Packard Bell................(818)865-1555
   Tech Support............(800)733-4433
Packintell Electronics ....(916)635-2784
Padware.......................(617)848-7310
Page Computer.............(800)886-0055
PageAhead Software......(206)441-0340
PagePlus.......................(800)697-3743
Paladin Corporation......(800)272-8665
Palindrome Corp...........(708)505-3300
   Tech Support............(708)505-3300
Palo Alto Design Grp.....(415)327-9444
Palomar Software...........(619)721-7000
   Tech Support............(619)721-7000
Palsoft.........................(512)854-8788
   Tech Support............(512)854-8794
Pam-Pacific Associates ...(818)333-3009
Panacea Inc...................(800)729-7420
Panamax ....(800)472-5555
   Tech Support............(800)472-5555
Panasonic Comm&Sys...(800)742-8086
   Tech Support............(800)222-0584
Panduit Corporation......(800)777-3300
Pantex Computer, Inc....(713)988-1688
Par Technology Corp.....(315)738-0600
Para Systems ....(214)446-7363
Paradigm Systems.........(607)748-5966
Paradise/West. Digital ....(714)932-5000
   Tech Support............(800)832-4778
Paradyne Corporation ...(813)530-2000
Paragon Concepts ....(619)481-1477
Paragon Memory Corp..(714)454-6444
Parallel Peripherals Tech..(714)394-7244
Parana Supplies Corp ....(800)472-7262
   Tech Support............(800)472-7262
Parcplace Systems..........(415)691-6700
   Tech Support............(800)822-8259
Parity Systems...............(408)378-1000
Parker Systems, Inc........(800)458-1049
Parsons Technology......(319)395-7314
   Tech Support............(319)395-7314
Parts Express................(800)377-6543
Parts Now Inc...............(608)276-8688
Parts Port Ltd................(800)253-0515
Passport Designs, Inc.....(415)726-0280
   Tech Support............(415)726-0280
Pastel Development.......(212)431-3421
   Tech Support............(212)941-7500
Patco Electronics Inc.....(407)268-0205
Pathfinder Associates....(408)984-2256
Patton & Patton Sftwr....(800)525-0082
Patton Consultants.......(716)334-2554
Paul Mace Software.......(800)523-0258
   Tech Support............(503)488-0224
Paxr Test Systems..........(800)825-7297
Paychex, Inc..................(716)385-6666
PBS Inc...........................(603)889-6512

PC & C Research Corp..(805)484-1865
PC Amer/General Store.(800)722-6374
   Tech Support............(804)523-6600
PC Catalog....................(402)477-8900
PC CompoNet, Inc........(310)943-9878
PC Cmptr Source Book.(408)446-0551
PC Computing..............(212)503-5449
PC Concepts, Inc...........(818)768-6033
PC Connection.............(800)800-5555
PC Discount Center.......(800)245-7453
   Tech Support............(708)390-7451
PC DOCS, Inc...............(904)942-3627
PC Dynamics, Inc..........(818)889-1741
   Tech Support............(818)889-1742
PC Express, Inc.............(818)307-0288
PC Globe, Inc................(602)730-9000
PC Guardian.................(800)288-8126
PC House......................(213)324-8621
PC Importers................(800)886-5155
   Tech Support............(216)464-5641
PC Laptop Magazine......(310)858-7155
PC Letter......................(415)592-8880
PC Link Corporation......(212)730-8036
PC Logic, Inc................(717)399-2399
PC Magazine.................(212)503-5446
PC Manager, Inc............(703)356-4600
PC Novice.....................(402)477-8900
PC Power & Cooling......(800)722-6555
   Tech Support............(619)931-6988
PC Publishing Inc..........(617)661-8050
PC QUICK CORP.........(503)644-5644
PC Repair Corporation..(800)727-3724
PC Service Source..........(214)406-8583
PC Serviceland Inc.........(404)934-0440
PC Today......................(402)477-8900
PC Week Magazine.......(617)693-3753
PC Weeks Labs..............(617)393-3700
PC Wholesale................(708)307-1700
PC World......................(617)579-0700
PC-Kwik Corporation....(800)274-5945
   Tech Support............(503)644-8827
PC-Sig/Spectra Publ.......(800)245-6717
PC/Nametag..................(608)273-4300
PCI Spec Interest Grp....(800)433-5177
PCMCIA......................(408)720-0107
PCPI............................(800)225-4098
PCR Pers Cmptr Rentals..(800)922-8646
PCs Compleat................(800)669-4727
PCS/Prof Computer.......(408)263-0222
PCUBID Cmptr Techn..(619)793-1328
PDA Engineering............(714)540-8900
PDI.............................(503)646-5024
Peachtree Software........(800)247-3224
   Tech Support............(800)346-5317
Peak Technologies Grp..(800)627-6372
Peaktron Computer.......(404)591-2484
Pearson Technologies....(404)591-2484
PedCom Inc..................(800)733-4488
Pedro Cos....................(800)328-9284
Peed Corporation.........(402)477-8900
Peer Logic ....(415)626-4545
Pelikan, Inc..................(800)874-5898
Pen Magic Software.......(604)988-2616
   Tech Support............(604)988-2616
Pen Systems, Inc...........(714)489-0047
Pengo Cmptr Access......(818)350-4990

Penmagic Software	(604)988-9982
Tech Support	(604)988-2616
Pentax Technologies	(303)460-1600
Pentel of America Ltd.	(310)320-3831
Penton Publishing	(216)696-7000
PenWare, Inc.	(415)858-4920
Tech Support	(415)858-4922
Peoplesmith Software	(617)545-7300
Peradata Techn Corp	(516)588-2216
Perception Technology	(617)921-0320
Perceptive Solutions	(214)954-1774
Perco, Inc.	(503)344-1189
Percom Technology	(510)656-2866
Percon, Inc.	(800)873-7266
PereLine Data Systems	(408)364-2770
Perfect Data Corp	(805)581-4000
Pericomp Corporation	(508)655-7660
Peripheral Cmptr Supp	(408)263-4043
Peripheral Land Inc.	(800)288-8754
Tech Support	(800)288-8754
Periphcral Maintenance	(201)227-8411
Peripheral Parts Supp	(617)890-9101
Peripheral Repair Corp	(800)627-3475
Peripheral Scrv Prods	(800)247-4733
Peripheral Solutions	(408)425-8280
Peripheral Vision	(800)441-0933
Peripherals Plus	(800)444-7369
Tech Support	(908)363-6270
Periscope	(800)722-7006
Perkin-Elmer Corp	(203)762-1000
Perma Power Electr	(800)323-4255
Persoft	(800)368-5283
Tech Support	(608)273-4357
Persona Tcchnologies	(415)871-6000
Personal Cmptr Prods	(619)485-8411
Personal Cmptr Sol	(214)661-8144
Tech Support	(214)661-8144
Personal Cmpting Tools	(800)767-6728
Pers Library Software	(301)926-1402
Personal Publishing	(708)665-1000
Personal Tex	(415)388-8853
Personal Training Sys	(800)832-2499
Tech Support	(800)832-2499
Personal Travel Techn	(516)538-1234
Personics Corporation	(800)445-3311
Tech Support	(508)658-0040
Perspective Software	(313)537-6168
Peter Norton Cmpting	(310)453-4600
Phar Lap Software	(617)661-1510
Pheecom Technology	(714)668-9550
PHIHONG USA	(408)263-2200
Philips PDO Media	(800)235-7373
Phillips Consumer Electr	(615)521-4316
Phillips Corporation	(310)217-1300
Phillips ECG	(800)526-9354
Phillips Key Modules	(714)453-7373
Phillips Labs	(800)628-0363
Philtek Power Corp	(800)727-4877
Phoenix Contact Inc.	(717)944-1300
Phoenix Technologies	(617)551-4000
Physician Micro Sys	(206)441-8490
Physiotronics Corp USA	(212)887-9555
PI Manufacturing Corp	(714)596-3718
Pick Systems	(714)261-7425
Pico Electronics	(800)431-1064
PictureWare, Inc.	(215)667-0880

Piiceon	(800)366-2983
Tech Support	(408)432-8030
Pilot Corp of America	(203)377-8800
Pilot Software Inc.	(800)944-0094
Pine Computer Sys	(619)569-7463
Pinnacle Data Systems	(614)487-1150
Pinnacle Micro	(800)553-7070
Tech Support	(714)727-3300
Pinnacle Publishing	(800)231-1293
Tech Support	(206)251-3513
Pinnacle Software	(514)345-9578
Pinpoint Publishing	(800)788-5236
Pioneer Commun	(201)327-6400
Pioneer Computer, Inc.	(510)623-0808
Pioneer Magnetics	(800)233-1745
Pioneer New Media Tech	(310)952-2111
Tech Support	(310)952-2111
Pioneer Software	(800)876-3101
Pioneer Standard Electr	(216)587-3600
Pitney Bowes Inc	(203)351-7226
Pivar Computing Serv	(800)266-8378
Pixar	(800)888-9856
Tech Support	(800)937-3179
PKware, Inc	(414)354-8699
Plainview Batteries Inc	(800)642-2354
Plamer Systems	(503)690-1100
Plasmaco, Inc.	(914)883-6800
Plasmon Data Systems	(408)432-0570
Plastic Systems Inc	(508)485-7390
Platinum Desktop Sftwr	(714)727-3775
Tech Support	(714)727-2110
Platinum Software	(714)727-1250
Plato Products Inc.	(818)965-8044
Platt Luggage	(800)222-1515
Plesman Publications	(416)497-9562
PLI	(800)288-8754
Tech Support	(800)288-8754
Plotworks	(619)457-5090
Pluma Software	(602)696-9441
Tech Support	(602)969-9441
Plus 5 Engineering Ltd.	(301)977-4048
Plus Developmcnt	(800)624-5545
Tech Support	(900)740-4433
Plustek USA, Inc.	(800)685-8088
PMR Corporation	(800)456-6480
Point 4 Data Corp	(714)259-0777
Polar Instruments	(800)328-0817
Polaris Service Inc.	(800)541-5831
Polaris Software	(800)338-5943
Tech Support	(619)592-7400
Polaroid Corporation	(800)225-2770
Tech Support	(800)225-1618
Policy Mgmt Systems	(803)735-4000
Polygon, Inc	(314)432-4142
Tech Support	(314)432-4142
Polytele Cmptr Prods	(408)745-1540
Polytronics	(318)797-2952
Polywell Computers	(415)583-7222
Popking Sftwr & Sys	(212)571-3434
Popular Programs, Inc	(800)447-6787
Poqet Computer Corp	(800)624-8999
Porelon, Inc.	(615)432-4042
Portable Warehouse	(714)993-1095
Tech Support	(714)993-1096
Portacom Technologies	(415)390-8507
Portfolio Systems	(800)729-3966

Tech Support	(800)434-6300
Positive Software Sol	(310)301-8446
Postcraft International	(805)257-1797
Tech Support	(416)641-0768
Power Clinic Inc.	(214)245-4016
Power Computing	(516)938-0506
Power General	(617)828-6216
Power Integrity Corp	(800)237-6260
Power Line	(800)234-2444
Power Plus	(800)875-5530
Power Pros	(800)788-0070
Power Up! Software	(800)851-2917
Tech Support	(415)345-0551
Powercard Supply	(305)251-5855
Powercom America	(714)252-8241
Powercore Inc.	(800)237-4754
Tech Support	(800)237-4754
PowerPro Software	(415)345-9278
PowerTek Industries	(303)680-9400
Powervar Inc.	(800)369-7179
PQ Systems	(513)885-2255
Practical Peripherals	(800)442-4774
Tech Support	(805)496-7707
PriarieTek Corporation	(800)825-2511
PRC	(703)556-1000
Pre-Owned Electronics	(800)274-5343
Precise Power Corp	(813)746-3515
Precision Data Prods	(800)968-0888
Precision Line Inc.	(612)475-3550
Precision Methods	(703)752-2800
Precision Micro Rsrch	(408)727-9697
Precision Motion	(805)546-8294
Prccision Plus Software	(519)657-0633
Preferred Cmptr Serv	(708)268-9150
Prch Electr. Industries	(708)438-4000
Prema Precision Electr	(800)441-0305
Prentice Hall Cmptr Pub	(317)573-2500
Prentice Hall, Inc	(201)767-5937
Prescience	(415)543-2252
Tech Support	(415)543-2252
Present Techn Comp	(503)641-1370
Prestance Corporation	(206)448-5052
Priam Corporation	(408)946-4600
Priam Systems	(408)441-4180
Prima International	(408)727-2600
Primages Inc.	(516)585-8200
Primavera Systems, Inc.	(800)423-0245
Tech Support	(215)668-3030
Primax Electronics	(800)338-3693
Prime Portable Mfr	(800)966-7237
Prime Solutions	(619)274-5000
Tech Support	(619)272-4000
PrimeService	(508)620-2800
Princeton Technology	(714)847-2477
Principia Products	(215)429-1359
Print Products Int'l	(800)638-2020
Printech Enterprises	(800)346-2618
Printech Ribbons Inc	(514)684-8450
Printer Connection	(800)622-7060
Printer Products	(617)254-1200
Printer Source	(215)538-3188
Printer Systems Corp	(301)258-5060
Printer Works	(800)225-6116
Printers Plus	(800)562-2727
Printers Plus Natl Sales	(800)877-4683
Tech Support	(800)258-2661

INDUSTRY PHONE NUMBERS

Printing Techn Center....(800)285-6496
    Tech Support............(216)524-1291
Printronix, Inc.............(714)863-1900
    Tech Support............(714)863-1900
Prism Imaging Systems..(510)490-9360
Pro Active Software.......(415)691-1500
Pro Tools Inc.................(800)743-4335
Pro-C Ltd.......................(519)725-5173
Pro-Mation, Inc.............(801)566-4655
Pro-Serv Development..(302)234-2733
Pro-Tech Cases.............(800)638-3789
ProTecT Cmptr Prods....(801)295-7739
ProBoard International..(612)537-8655
Processing Telecom Tech...(205)971-8001
Processor Magazine.......(800)247-4880
Processor, The..............(800)247-4880
Procom Technology.......(714)852-1000
    Tech Support............(714)852-1000
Procomp USA, Inc. ....(216)234-6387
Prod-Art Marketing-USA....(516)223-9800
Prodatel Comm..............(800)561-4019
Prodem Techn America.(408)984-2850
Prodigy Services Co.......(800)333-5779
    Tech Support............(800)284-5933
Product Safety Eng........(813)989-2360
Productivity Enhancmnt..(714)348-1011
Productivity Software....(212)818-1144
Professional Cmptr Serv.(404)998-7776
Professional Mgmt Inst..(800)383-1296
Professional MicroCare..(513)223-2348
Profit Press...................(800)843-7990
Profitability of Hawaii....(808)536-6167
Progen Technology Inc..(714)549-5818
Prognostics....................(415)424-8711
Programmer's Paradise..(908)389-8950
Programmer's Shop.......(800)421-8006
Programmer's Wrhse.....(602)443-0580
    Tech Support............(602)443-7667
Progress Software Corp.(617)275-4500
Progressive Cmptr Serv.(504)831-9717
Progressive Micro Sys....(800)220-9888
    Tech Support............(800)220-9898
Progressive Ribbon........(800)800-7426
ProHance Technology....(408)746-0950
Prolink Computer Inc....(213)780-7978
ProMaccomputers Inc...(503)691-0304
Promark Ltd...................(505)345-7701
ProMax Technology.......(800)977-6629
Prometheus Products....(800)477-3473
    Tech Support............(503)692-9601
Promise Technology.......(408)452-0948
ProSoft..........................(818)765-4444
Prosonus ....(800)999-6191
ProSource Power...........(800)949-4797
Protec Microsystems.....(514)630-5832
Protech Inc....................(210)614-1690
Protective Closures Co..(716)876-9855
Protek Inc......................(201)767-7242
Proteon, Inc. ....(800)666-4400
    Tech Support............(508)898-3100
Protolab........................(804)785-5000
Proton Corporation.......(714)952-6900
ProtoView Development.(908)329-8588
ProVUE Development...(714)892-8199
    Tech Support............(714)892-8599
Proworks.......................(503)567-1459

Tech Support............(503)567-8836
Proxim Inc.....................(415)960-1630
    Tech Support............(415)960-1630
Proxima Corporation.....(800)447-7694
    Tech Support............(800)447-7694
PS Solutions, Inc. ....(214)980-2632
PSI Integrations............(800)622-1722
    Tech Support............(800)774-4965
Psion Inc.......................(506)371-0310
PSN..............................(212)696-9476
PSSI Plug-In Stor Solutions.(800)231-5952
Psygnosis Limited.........(800)438-7794
    Tech Support............(617)497-7794
PTI Industries...............(408)438-3900
PTN Publishing.............(516)845-2700
Public Brand Software...(800)426-3475
Public Software Library.(800)242-4775
Publishers Group West..(510)658-3453
Publishing Perfection ....(800)782-5974
Publishing Technology ..(512)246-2835
Pulizzi Engineering Inc..(714)540-4229
Pulse Metric Inc.............(619)546-9461
Pup-Pak........................(310)568-1790
Purart...........................(603)772-9907
Pure Data.....................(800)661-8210
    Tech Support............(800)661-8210
Puretek Industrial Co ....(510)656-8083
Pycon Inc......................(800)949-0349
Pyramid Data.................(800)972-7972
    Tech Support............(415)312-7080
Pyramid Techn. Corp....(415)965-7200
Q/Media Sftwr Corp......(604)679-6886
Qantel Business Sys.......(510)887-7777
QDI Computer Inc.........(310)906-1029
QMS Inc........................(800)523-2696
    Tech Support............(205)633-4500
QSound Ltd...................(403)291-2492
Qtronix Corporation .....(408)954-8040
Qtronix Inc....................(213)383-8068
Quadbase Systems.........(408)738-6989
Quadram Corporation...(404)923-6666
Quadrant Components..(510)656-9988
Quadtel Corporation.....(714)440-8000
Quaid Software Limited.(416)961-8243
Qualitas ....(800)676-8386
    Tech Support............(301)907-7470
Quality Cmptr Access....(818)964-3398
Quality Power Prods.....(800)525-7502
Quality Repair Services.(510)651-8486
Quality Software Prods..(310)410-0303
Quality Systems, Inc. ....(714)731-7171
Qualstar Corporation.....(818)882-5822
Qualtec Data Prods.......(800)628-4413
    Tech Support............(800)628-4413
Quanta..........................(800)682-1738
Quantum Corporation ..(800)345-3377
    Tech Support............(800)826-8022
Quantum Data................(708)888-0450
Quantum Software Sys..(613)591-0931
Quark Inc.......................(303)894-8888
    Tech Support............(303)894-8899
Quarter-Inch Cartr. Dr. Std.(805)963-3853
Quarterdeck Office Sys.(800)354-3260
    Tech Support............(310)392-9701
Quatech, Inc..................(216)434-3154
Que Corporation...........(800)428-5331

Que Sftwr/Prentice Hall..(800)992-0244
    Tech Support............(317)571-3833
Questronics Inc.............(801)262-9923
Quick Comm..................(408)956-8236
Quickpath Systems........(510)440-7288
Quicksoft.......................(800)888-8088
Quintar Comp................(310)320-5700
Quintas Corporation......(800)542-1283
Quixale America Inc......(815)399-3608
Qurnax Corporation.......(408)954-8040
Qume............................(408)262-7700
.....................................(408)942-4140
.....................................(408)942-4000
Quotron Systems, Inc.....(310)827-4600
QVS, Inc. (MI).................(800)622-9606
QVS, Inc. (NV)................(800)344-3371
R & D Business Sys.......(604)872-1118
R & K Supply Co............(800)362-6780
R & R Electronics...........(800)736-3644
    Tech Support............(404)368-1159
R Co..............................(310)441-0447
R Company.....................(310)441-0447
R&K Supply....................(800)362-6780
R's Data Services............(818)700-8766
R.J. Swantek & Assoc .....(203)953-0236
R.R. Software................(608)251-3133
Rabbit Software.............(800)445-4357
Racal-Datacom Inc.........(800)572-2255
Racal-Interlan................(800)526-8255
    Tech Support............(800)526-8255
RaceCom.......................(800)638-8068
Racore Cmptr Prods......(800)635-1274
    Tech Support............(801)596-0265
Radiant Communications .(201)757-7444
Radio Shack...................(817)390-3011
Radiometrics Midwest...(708)932-7262
    Tech Support............(708)932-7262
Radius Inc.....................(800)227-2795
    Tech Support............(408)434-1012
Radix Group Int'l...........(310)338-2525
RAG Electronics Inc. .....(818)998-6500
Raima............................(206)747-5570
    Tech Support............(206)562-2622
Rainbow Technologies ..(800)852-8569
Ralin Wholesaler...........(800)752-9512
RAM Mobile Data...........(212)303-7800
Ram Solutions................(602)759-5520
Ramp Industries.............(607)729-5256
Ramtek Corporation......(408)954-2700
    Tech Support............(408)954-2750
Rancho Technology........(714)987-3966
Rand Information Sys....(415)391-2213
Random House Inc........(301)848-1900
    Tech Support............(301)857-9460
Randomex Inc. ....(310)595-8301
Raosoft Inc....................(206)525-4025
Rapid Systems Inc.........(206)547-8311
Rapid Technology Corp.(716)833-8533
RARE Systems Inc.........(214)991-7273
Raster OPS ....(800)729-2656
    Tech Support............(801)785-5750
Rational Data Systems. ..(415)499-3354
Rational Systems...........(508)653-6194
Ratliff Software ....(818)546-3850
Ray Dream.....................(415)960-0768
    Tech Support............(415)960-0768

INDUSTRY PHONE NUMBERS

Raynet Electronics	(713)578-3802
Rayovac Corporation	(608)275-3340
Raytheon (MA)	(617)862-6600
Raytheon (RI)	(401)847-8000
Rayton Comm-USA	(800)472-9866
Rayven Inc.	(800)627-3776
RC Electronics	(800)882-3475
RCI	(908)874-4072
RDN & Associates	(800)647-6747
Reach Software	(800)624-5356
React Computer Serv	(800)662-9199
Reactor	(312)573-0800
Tech Support	(312)573-0800
Read/Right Prods Div	(201)327-9100
Real Applications Ltd.	(818)226-6600
Realia	(312)346-0642
Reality Technologies	(800)521-2471
Tech Support	(800)521-2471
RealWorld Corporation	(800)678-6336
Tech Support	(603)288-3432
Recognita Corp / America	(408)749-9935
Recognition Equipment	(214)579-6000
Recordex Corporation	(619)467-9068
Recoton	(800)223-6009
Recovery Management	(508)486-8866
Recovery Plus Plan. Prod.	(800)356-7586
Recovery Resources	(407)851-7657
Red Wing Business Sys	(800)732-9464
Redysoft Software	(714)626-4070
Reference Software	(800)872-9933
Tech Support	(415)541-0226
Reflection Systems	(408)432-0943
Reflection Technology	(617)890-5905
Regent Peripherals	(509)662-8848
Relational Courseware	(617)262-4933
Relax Technology	(510)471-6112
Relay Technologies	(203)798-3800
Rlse 1.0/Edventure Hold	(212)924-8800
Relialogic Corporation	(510)770-3990
Relisys	(408)945-9000
REM	(408)655-1111
Remote Control Int'l	(800)992-9952
RenaSonce Group Inc.	(619)287-3348
Renewable Resources	(800)832-1400
Rent-A-Computer	(408)727-7800
Repeat-O-Type Mfg	(800)288-3300
Reply Corporation	(800)955-5295
Reseller Management	(201)292-5100
Reset Inc.	(805)584-4900
ResNova Software Inc.	(714)379-9000
Resource Spectrum	(214)484-9330
Retix	(310)828-3400
Revelation Technology	(800)262-4747
Tech Support	(203)973-1011
Revolution Software	(908)879-7038
Rexon Corporation	(805)583-5255
RFF Electronics	(303)663-5767
RFG Onyx	(800)946-8324
Tech Support	(800)766-2711
RG Software Systems	(602)423-8000
RGB Spectrum	(510)848-0180
Tech Support	(510)848-0180
Ribbon Tek USA	(719)578-0506
Ribbon Tree USA Inc	(800)862-9499
Richmond Technology	(714)794-2111
Ricks RamStar, Inc	(800)327-2303

Ricoh Corporation	(714)259-1310
Tech Support	(714)566-3584
Rimage Corporation	(800)445-8288
Tech Support	(612)934-5432
Rinda Technologies	(312)736-6633
Ring King Visibles, Inc	(800)272-2366
Tech Support	(800)553-9647
Ripe C&C Technology	(408)492-9585
Riser-Bond Instruments	(800)688-8377
RISO, Inc.	(508)777-7377
Rite-Off Inc.	(800)645-5853
River Data	(818)222-7191
Rix Softworks, Inc.	(800)345-9059
RJ Steams Associates	(508)263-3426
RMS Computer Corp	(212)840-8666
RO Associates	(208)772-2781
Road Scholar	(800)243-7623
Tech Support	(713)266-7623
Robec Distributors	(800)223-7087
Robec Distrib-East PA	(800)223-7081
Tech Support	(800)223-7087
Robec Distrib-West	(800)433-5061
Robert J. Victor & Assoc	(201)875-3600
Roberts Express	(800)762-3787
Robitron Software	(404)684-5855
Rochelle Commun	(800)542-8808
Tech Support	(512)794-0088
Rockwell Int'l (IL)	(708)960-8000
Rockwell Int'l (CA)	(714)833-4700
Roctec Electronics Ltd.	(408)379-1713
Tech Support	(408)379-1713
Rodax Inc.	(206)885-9999
Rodime Systems, Inc.	(800)227-4144
Rohde & Schwartz Inc.	(301)459-8800
Roland Corporation US	(213)685-5141
Roland Digital Group	(714)975-0560
Tech Support	(714)975-0670
Rorke Data	(800)328-8147
Rose Electronics	(713)933-7673
ROSH Intelligent Sys	(800)677-7674
Rotating Memory Repair	(714)472-0159
Rotating Memory Serv	(916)939-7500
Tech Support	(916)939-7500
Roundhill	(708)690-3737
Royal Computer	(818)333-7628
Tech Support	(818)330-2717
Royal Seating Corp	(817)697-6421
Roykore Inc.	(415)563-9175
RPA	(800)879-5860
RQDQ Corporation	(315)437-2631
RT&C Systems Inc	(510)655-1993
Rundel Products	(800)547-7061
Rupp Techn Corp-AZ	(602)224-9922
Tech Support	(602)224-9922
Rupp Techn Corp-CA	(800)852-7877
Tech Support	(602)224-0897
Ryan McFarland	(512)343-1010
Rybs Electronics	(303)444-6073
S & W Cmptrs & Electr	(800)874-1235
Tech Support	(212)463-8330
S-MOS Systems Inc.	(408)922-0200
S1 Computers	(800)886-3210
Tech Support	(818)912-0166
S3 Inc	(408)980-5400
Saber Software	(800)338-8754
Tech Support	(800)526-8086

Sabina International	(800)272-2462
Safeware Insure Agency	(800)848-3469
SAG Electronics	(800)989-3475
Tech Support	(800)899-5752
Sager Computer	(800)669-1624
SAIC Imaging Solutions	(800)442-7242
Salient	(800)766-7283
Samna Corporation	(800)831-9679
Tech Support	(404)256-2272
Sampo Corp of America	(404)449-6220
Sampson MIDI Source	(214)328-2730
SAMS	(317)581-3500
Samsonite Corporation	(303)373-2000
Tech Support	(303)373-6666
Samsung	(800)446-0262
Tech Support	(800)446-0262
Samsung Electr America	(800)446-0262
Tech Support	(201)691-6214
Samsung Info Sys America	(800)446-0262
Tech Support	(800)446-0262
Samtron	(714)522-1282
Tech Support	(714)522-1282
Sankyo Seiki (America)	(714)724-1505
Santa Cruz Operations	(408)425-7222
Tech Support	(800)347-4381
Santos Technology Inc.	(310)320-8888
Sanyo Business Systems	(800)524-0048
Tech Support	(201)440-9300
Sanyo Energy Corp	(619)661-6620
Sapro-Impact Software	(800)369-8649
Tech Support	(714)541-2202
SaRonix	(415)856-6900
SAS Electronics Inc	(408)245-5000
SAS Industries	(800)245-4657
SAS Institute, Inc.	(919)677-8000
Tech Support	(919)677-8008
Save Rite Technologies	(800)668-7972
Savin Corporation	(203)967-5000
Sayett Technology, Inc.	(800)836-7730
Tech Support	(800)836-7730
SBE, Inc.	(510)680-7722
Tech Support	(800)827-2245
SBT	(415)331-9900
Tech Support	(415)332-9308
Scan-Optics, Inc.	(800)854-8412
Scandinavian PC Sys	(301)294-7450
Tech Support	(301)294-7453
Scandura Intelligent Sys	(215)664-1207
Scantech Computer Sys	(818)960-2999
Sceptre Technologies	(714)993-9193
Scherrer Resources Inc.	(215)836-1830
Tech Support	(215)836-1805
Schlumberger Ltd.	(212)350-9400
Schlumberger Technology	(800)225-5765
Schnellmann America	(408)441-6026
Scholastic, Inc.	(314)636-5271
SCI Systems, Inc.	(205)882-4755
SCI/CAD Scan Inc.	(505)881-4872
Scicom Data Service	(612)933-4200
Science Lab SW	(800)442-7242
Tech Support	(619)766-7242
Scientific Endeavors	(615)376-4146
Scientific Logics	(408)446-3575
Scientific Micro Systems	(408)954-1633
Scientific Software Inc.	(303)292-1111
Scitor Corporation	(415)570-7700

INDUSTRY PHONE NUMBERS

Scopus Technology Inc. (510)428-0500
Script Systems, Inc.........(201)343-8500
    Tech Support...........(800)724-8400
Sriptel Corporation........(614)276-8402
SCS/Compute, Inc..........(314)966-1040
SDA Corporation............(800)833-5020
SDB Systems ....(813)481-0224
Seagate Technologies......(800)468-3472
    Tech Support...........(408)438-8222
Seagull Scientific Sys......(800)758-2001
Searchlight Software......(216)631-9290
Seco Industries ....(213)726-9721
Sector Computer Serv...(216)524-5858
Secura Technologies......(714)248-1544
Secure Telecom Inc. ......(408)992-0572
Secured Communication..(416)888-1580
Security Microsystems ..(800)345-7390
SEEQ Technology, Inc. ...(408)432-7400
SEI (National FSI Inc.)...(214)689-3200
Seiko Instruments USA .(800)888-0817
    Tech Support...........(800)553-5312
Seiko Instruments USA .(408)922-1917
    Tech Support...........(408)922-1917
Seikosha America Inc. ...(201)327-7227
    Tech Support...........(201)327-7227
Sejin America ....(408)752-8447
Selecterm, Inc. ....(800)877-7586
    Tech Support...........(800)767-7586
Selective Software..........(408)423-3556
    Tech Support...........(800)423-3556
Selectronics & Microlytics.(716)248-9150
SemiTech International.(617)628-8880
Semware.......................(404)641-9002
Sencore Inc. ....(800)736-2673
Seneca Data Distributors ..(800)227-3432
Sensible Software..........(313)528-1950
Sensible Solutions Inc....(508)830-0130
Senstron Electronic Co .(908)561-8585
    Tech Support...........(908)561-8585
Sentinel Cmptr Services....(708)990-8060
Sequel Inc. ....(800)848-8537
Sequent Computer Sys..(503)626-5700
Sequoia Data Corp........(415)696-8750
Sequoia Publishing, Inc. (303)972-4167
Seraph-Foresight............(800)721-7243
Sercomp Corporation....(800)428-2635
    Tech Support...........(800)428-2635
Serif Inc........................(800)697-3743
Serigraph Inc.................(414)335-7200
Serius (Novell) ....(800)876-6847
    Tech Support...........(800)876-6847
Servatek ....(410)760-7337
Server Technology ....(800)835-1515
    Tech Support...........(408)988-0142
Service 2000 ....(800)466-2000
Service InfoSystems.......(716)334-9126
Service Management .....(603)882-7783
Service Management Grp.(410)992-9975
Service Partner Inc. ......(201)770-4949
Service Systems Int'l......(913)661-0190
Serviceland/Upstate NY...(716)427-0880
ServiceScope Corp ....(203)265-2624
ServiceWare ....(716)842-1611
Servicing Sys-Profile Tech..(800)659-9649
Servitech Inc..................(708)620-8750
Servonics Corporation ..(508)295-6372

Set Laboratories.............(503)289-4758
Setpoint, Inc..................(713)584-1000
SGS-Thomson Microelectr.(602)867-6100
Shafer's Full Service Sys.(619)440-5421
    Tech Support...........(619)440-5421
Shaffstaff Corporation ...(800)248-3475
    Tech Support...........(317)842-2077
Shape Corporation ....(403)463-3330
    Tech Support...........(403)463-3330
Shape Electronics Inc....(800)367-5811
Shapeware......................(800)446-3335
Shared Medical Systems.(215)296-6300
Shareware Testing Labs .(317)322-2000
Sharp Electronics Corp.(800)237-4277
Sharpe Systems Corp ....(909)596-0070
Shattuck Industries........(408)336-5145
Shields Bus Machines....(800)759-6161
Shereff Systems, Inc.......(503)626-2022
    Tech Support...........(503)626-2022
Sherwood Kimtron ....(800)777-8755
Shining Technology ....(310)802-3081
Shiva............................(800)458-3550
    Tech Support...........(617)270-8400
Shreve Systems ....(800)227-3971
Shugart Corporation......(714)770-1100
Shuttle Computer Int'l ..(510)623-8876
    Tech Support...........(510)623-8876
SI Dynamics In...............(619)322-2761
Sicon International Inc..(408)432-8585
    Tech Support...........(408)432-8585
Sidco Software Int'l.......(212)627-4475
Sidon Data Systems ......(714)553-1131
Sidus..........................(416)882-1600
Siecor Corporation........(800)633-7432
Siemens Comm.Test Eqp...(704)327-5051
Siemens Nixdorf Info.Sys..(617)273-0480
    Tech Support...........(617)273-0480
Siemon Company ....(203)274-2523
Sierra Computers ....(702)322-6455
Sierra On-Line ....(800)757-7707
    Tech Support...........(209)683-8989
Sigen............................(408)737-3904
Sigma Data ....(800)446-4525
Sigma Designs................(800)845-8086
    Tech Support...........(510)770-0100
Sigma International Inc.(800)658-8893
Sigmatronics, Inc...........(800)852-6322
SIIG, Inc. ....(510)657-8688
    Tech Support...........(510)657-8688
Silcom Mfg Techn. ....(416)438-8822
Silicom ....(201)529-1100
Silicon Beach Software..(619)695-6956
Silicon Graphics ....(415)960-1980
Silicon Graphics, Inc......(800)676-6272
    Tech Support...........(800)676-6272
Silicon Integrated Sys ....(408)735-1362
Silicon Star Int'l Inc. .....(510)623-0500
Silicon Systems, Inc........(714)573-6000
    Tech Support...........(714)731-7110
Silicon Valley Computer..(415)967-1100
Silver-Lisco ....(408)991-6000
Silver Reed (USA) Inc....(800)733-7333
    Tech Support...........(800)733-7333
Silverware....................(214)247-0131
Sim-Trade Company ......(800)435-7482
    Tech Support...........(800)435-7482

Simon&Schuster Sftwr ..(800)624-0023
    Tech Support...........(212)373-8500
Simon&Schuster Sftwr ..(800)922-0579
Simple Foresight Techn.(800)367-7330
Simple Software.............(914)297-5858
    Tech Support...........(914)297-5868
Simplex Tim Recorder....(508)632-2500
Sir-Tech Software...........(315)393-6633
SitBack Technologies.....(913)894-0808
Sitka...........................(800)445-8677
    Tech Support...........(510)769-8711
Sixgraph Computing......(514)332-1331
Skill Dynamics ....(404)835-1969
SkiSoft Publishing.........(617)863-1876
SkyTel..........................(800)759-3375
    Tech Support...........(800)759-3375
SL Waber Inc.................(800)634-1485
    Tech Support...........(800)257-8384
Slate...........................(800)826-8071
    Tech Support...........(602)991-6844
Slinger Sierra................(209)295-5595
SLR Systems ....(412)282-0864
Small Computer Co.......(914)769-3160
Small Cmptrs in Library...(203)226-6967
Smart Modular Techn ....(510)623-1231
Smart Technologies Inc.(403)233-9333
SmartMicro Technology ..(800)766-2467
    Tech Support...........(805)495-1385
SMC............................(800)762-4968
SMH Electronics ....(508)291-7447
Smith Design.................(215)661-9107
Smith Micro Software....(714)362-5800
SMK Electronics Corp...(714)996-0960
SMS Technology, Inc. .....(408)954-1633
SNA Comms Report ......(703)760-0660
Snow Software..............(813)784-8899
Social Software Inc........(212)956-2707
SofNet..........................(800)343-2948
    Tech Support...........(404)984-9958
Sofpak Inc. ....(613)591-1555
Sofsolutions..................(512)735-0746
Soft Cable....................(310)828-2577
Soft Warehouse, Inc. ......(808)734-5801
Soft-Age Publishing........(805)945-0051
    Tech Support...........(805)945-0051
Soft-Com Inc.................(212)242-9595
Soft-Hard Systems..........(818)999-9531
Soft-Letter....................(617)924-3944
Softa Group Inc.,The.....(708)291-4000
    Tech Support...........(800)874-0045
SoftArc, Inc...................(416)299-4723
Softbridge, Inc...............(617)576-2257
    Tech Support...........(617)576-2257
SoftCraft, Inc. ....(800)351-0500
    Tech Support...........(608)257-3300
SofTest Designs Corp ....(210)697-8828
Softfocus ....(416)825-0903
SoftKat ....(800)641-1057
    Tech Support...........(818)700-8061
Softkey International......(800)323-8088
    Tech Support...........(800)323-8088
Softkey Software Prod...(404)426-0008
    Tech Support...........(404)428-0008
Softklone......................(800)634-8670
    Tech Support...........(904)878-8564
SoftLogic Solutions........(603)627-9900

INDUSTRY PHONE NUMBERS

Tech Support............(603)644-5555
SofTouch Systems, Inc...(405)947-8060
Softronics.....................(800)225-8590
   Tech Support............(719)593-9550
SOFTSOULUTIONS.......(801)226-6000
Softsync (in CA).............(800)854-3415
   Tech Support...(800)854-3415
Softsync (outside CA) ...(800)854-5212
   Tech Support...........(800)847-5212
Software Academy, Inc..(619)464-2500
Software Add-Ons.........(800)822-8068
Software AG Systems.....(703)860-5050
SOFTWARE ALLIANCE..(800)443-5152
Software Artistry............(317)876-3042
Software City, Inc...........(800)222-0918
Software Creations, Inc.(800)767-3279
   Tech Support..............(800)767-3279
Sftwr Developer's Co ....(800)421-8006
Sftwr Developmt Factory..(301)666-8129
Software Digest...............(215)878-9300
Software Directions.......(201)584-8466
   Tech Support...........(201)584-3882
Software Factory............(214)490-0835
Software Grove..............(800)793-0040
Software Interphase......(401)397-2340
Software Link.................(404)448-5465
   Tech Support...........(404)263-8676
Software Machine, The..(801)561-9393
Software Magazine ....(508)366-2031
Software Marketing.......(602)893-2400
Software Matters Inc.....(800)253-5274
   Tech Support...........(317)253-8088
Software of the Future..(800)766-7355
   Tech Support...........(214)264-2626
Software Partners..........(415)857-1110
Software Plumbers Inc..(301)963-8423
   Tech Support...........(301)963-8423
Software Plus.................(301)261-0264
Software Products Int'l..(800)937-4774
   Tech Support...........(800)937-4774
Sftwr Publ Association..(800)388-7478
Sftwr Publishers Corp...(800)234-2500
   Tech Support...........(408)988-4005
Software Resource.........(415)883-0600
Software Security Inc....(203)329-8870
Software Shop Systems.(908)938-3200
   Tech Support...........(800)654-8923
Software Solutions, Inc.(404)418-2000
   Tech Support...........(404)418-2000
Software Support...........(800)873-4357
   Tech Support...........(800)873-4357
Sftwr Supp Professionals...(619)674-4864
Software Toolworks.......(800)234-3088
   Tech Support.....(415)883-5157
Software Ventures..........(800)336-6477
   Tech Support...........(510)644-1325
Sola Electric ....(800)289-7652
Solartech......................(800)367-1132
Solder Absorbing Techn ...(413)788-6191
Solea Systems Inc..........(714)768-7736
Solectek Accessories .....(800)437-1518
   Tech Support............(619)450-1220
Solectron Corporation...(408)942-1943
Solidex.........................(800)722-1888
   Tech Support.........(909)599-2666
Solidstate Controls.........(800)635-7300

Tech Support............(800)222-9079
Solomat Instrumentation ..(203)849-3111
Soltec.........................(800)423-2344
Solution Develpmnt Assn..(215)362-2611
Solutions Incorporated..(802)865-9220
   Tech Support...........(802)658-5506
Solutions Systems ....(800)821-2492
   Tech Support...........(800)999-9663
Solutronix Corporation.(800)875-2580
Sonera Technologies......(800)932-6323
Sonic Systems ....(800)535-0725
   Tech Support............(408)736-1900
SonicAir Couriers ....(800)528-6052
Sony (Dealer).................(800)222-7669
   Tech Support............(408)894-0225
Sony (Desktop Library).(800)342-5721
   Tech Support............(800)326-9551
Sony (Serv Ctr Locations)..(800)342-5721
   Tech Support............(408)894-0555
Sony Corp of America ...(800)222-7669
Sony Electronic Publ.....(212)702-2974
   Tech Support............(212)702-2974
Sony Electronics ....(800)352-7669
Sophisticated Circuits....(206)485-7979
   Tech Support...........(206)485-7979
Soricon Corporation .....(303)440-2800
SOS Computer...............(800)767-2554
SOS Cmptr Consultants ..(503)385-0993
Sound Electro Flight......(800)777-3475
   Tech Support...........(805)524-0046
Sound Ideas ....(416)886-5000
Sound Minds Technology.(408)374-7070
Sound Source Unlimited..(800)877-4778
   Tech Support............(805)494-9996
Soundware Corporation ..(800)333-4554
Source & Solution..........(813)962-8911
Source Graphics ....(800)553-5285
Source Service Corp......(800)877-8896
   Tech Support............(415)381-1793
SourceMate Info Sys......(800)877-8896
   Tech Support............(415)381-1793
South East Cmptr Brokers.(305)792-3780
SouthHills Datacom VAR..(800)624-1770
Southdale ....(416)455-9533
Southern Technical........(502)585-5635
Soyo USA Inc.................(818)330-1712
   Tech Support............(818)330-1712
SPA News......................(202)452-1600
Spacepage Inc................(800)332-7243
Spartan Electronics.........(516)499-9500
Spea/Video Seven..........(510)683-6201
Spear Technology Inc.....(800)852-4202
Specialix......................(800)423-5364
   Tech Support............(800)423-5364
Specialix Inc. ....(408)378-7919
Specialized Bus Sols .....(800)359-3458
Specialized Prods Co.....(800)527-5018
Specom Technology Corp..(408)736-7832
Spectra Logic ....(303)449-7759
SpectraFAX..................(800)833-1329
Spectragraphics ....(619)450-0611
Spectrum Cmptr Corp..(800)959-1030
Spectrum Holobyte.......(510)522-1164
   Tech Support............(510)522-1164
Spectrum Info Techn....(516)627-8992
Speedbird Data Sys........(303)440-9983

Spencer Industries.........(812)937-4561
Spider Island Software ..(714)669-9260
Spindrift Laboratories....(708)255-6909
Spinnaker Software ....(800)325-8088
   Tech Support............(800)223-8088
Spirit Technology...........(800)945-5549
Sprague Magnetics ....(800)553-8712
Spring Circle Cmptr......(310)944-2287
   Tech Support............(213)698-5961
Sprite, Inc. ....(408)773-8888
SPSS, Inc......................(800)543-2185
Square D/Topaz.............(619)279-0111
SRW Cmptr Component..(800)547-7766
   Tech Support............(800)547-7766
Stac Electronics-Mac......(619)431-7474
   Tech Support............(619)431-8355
Stac Electronics-OS/2 ....(800)522-7822
   Tech Support............(619)431-8201
Stac Electronics-PC/Win.(800)522-7822
   Tech Support............(619)431-6712
Staco Energy Products...(513)253-1191
Stallion Technologies.....(800)347-7979
   Tech Support............(800)347-7979
Standard Cmptr Corp....(800)662-6111
Standard Microsys Corp..(800)762-4968
   Tech Support............(800)638-5323
Standard Rate&Data Serv...(708)256-6067
Stanley-Vidmar...............(215)797-6600
Star Gate Technologies..(216)349-1860
Star Micronics America..(800)447-4700
   Tech Support............(714)768-3192
Star Path System ....(517)332-1137
   Tech Support............(517)332-1256
Star Software Systems ...(310)533-1190
   Tech Support............(800)443-5737
Star-Tek Inc. ....(508)393-9393
StarGate Computers.......(800)945-0202
Startech Computer.........(519)438-8529
Starware Publishing........(800)354-5353
Stat-Tech International ..(719)543-5005
State Street Discount......(800)212-1519
   Tech Support............(800)242-1519
Static Control Compon..(800)356-2728
Statpower Technology...(604)420-1585
StatSoft ....(918)583-4149
Statx Brands Company..(708)520-0007
STB Systems Inc.............(800)234-4334
   Tech Support............(214)234-8750
Stellar Computer, Inc......(508)369-7666
Stevenson Software ....(206)562-0225
STI-Certified Products....(800)274-3475
Stingray Cmptr Int'l........(615)355-0242
Stockholder Systems......(404)441-3387
Stone & Associates.........(619)459-9173
Stone & Wire.................(617)441-8780
Stonehouse & Co...........(214)960-1566
Storage Concepts, Inc...(800)525-9217
Storage Devices Inc.......(714)562-5500
Storage Dimensions.......(800)765-7895
   Tech Support............(408)894-1325
Storage Solutions ....(800)745-5508
Storage Technology Corp.(303)673-5151
Storage Tek ....(303)673-6761
Storage USA ....(800)538-3475
Storm Technology.........(800)275-5734
   Tech Support............(800)275-5734

INDUSTRY PHONE NUMBERS

StrandWare, Inc.............(715)833-2331
Strata ....(800)678-7282
   Tech Support............(801)628-9751
Strategic Mapping Inc...(800)442-8887
   Tech Support............(800)999-6543
Strategic Simulations.....(408)737-6800
   Tech Support............(408)737-6850
Strategic Solutions.........(203)221-1334
Stratus Computer, Inc....(508)460-2000
Strawberry Tree.............(408)736-8800
Street Electronics............(805)684-4593
   Tech Support............(805)684-4593
Streetwise Software.......(310)829-7827
Stride Software, Inc. ......(213)433-6977
Strohl Systems ....(800)634-2016
Structural Dynamics Rsrch.(513)576-2400
Structured Sftwr Sols.....(214)985-9901
STSC.............(301)984-5000
   Tech Support............(301)984-5489
Studebaker-Worthington...(800)645-7242
Sub Systems.............(617)438-8901
SubLOGIC.............(217)359-8482
   Tech Support............(800)637-4983
Success Trainers Inc......(800)229-4708
Summagraphics ....(800)729-7866
   Tech Support............(800)729-7866
Summatec Computer....(800)335-7573
Summit Memory Sys......(800)523-4767
   Tech Support............(408)438-7897
Summit Micro Design....(408)739-6348
   Tech Support............(408)739-6348
Summus Corporation....(713)492-6611
Sun Country Software...(505)873-2220
Sun Microsytems Techn..(800)643-8300
   Tech Support............(800)872-4786
Sun Moon Star.............(408)452-7811
   Tech Support............(408)452-7811
Sun Remarketing.............(800)821-3221
   Tech Support............(800)992-7631
Sun River Corporation...(512)835-8001
Suncom Technologies....(708)647-4040
   Tech Support............(708)647-4040
SunData Inc.............(404)449-6116
Sundog Software.............(718)855-9141
Sunflex L.P.............(408)522-8850
Sungard Data Systems...(215)341-8700
Sunhill Distributing ....(800)544-1361
Sunny Hill Software.......(800)367-0651
   Tech Support............(206)857-2666
Sunnyvale Memories......(800)262-3475
   Tech Support............(800)262-3475
SunRace Techn. Corp.....(714)468-2955
   Tech Support............(800)872-4786
Sunrise Cmptr Supplies...(813)877-7866
Sunrise Imaging.............(510)657-6250
Sunshine Video/Cmptrs...(800)828-2992
   Tech Support............(407)368-2922
SunSoft.............(415)960-3200
   Tech Support............(800)872-4786
Sunwell Int'l Corp. ....(408)436-9797
   Tech Support............(408)436-1107
Super Computer Inc......(213)532-2133
Super PC Market.............(800)426-6669
Supercom, Inc.............(408)456-8888
Supercomputer Sys ......(715)839-8484
Superior Electric.............(203)582-9561

Superior IS.............(713)662-8500
Superpower Supply.......(310)903-4528
SuperTime Inc. ....(416)499-3288
Support Systems.............(800)777-6269
   Tech Support............(209)734-9090
Support Systems Int'l....(800)777-6269
Supra Corporation.........(800)774-4965
   Tech Support............(800)774-4965
Survivor Software ....(213)410-9527
Sutrasoft.............(713)491-2088
Sutton Designs.............(800)326-8119
SW Training Services.....(609)751-5481
Swifte International.......(800)237-9383
   Tech Support............(302)234-1750
Switchcraft Inc.............(312)792-2700
Sybex, Inc.............(800)227-2346
   Tech Support............(800)227-2346
Sycom Design Software..(313)774-2153
SyDOS.............(800)437-9367
   Tech Support............(800)536-7936
Symantec (Corporate)...(408)253-9600
Symantec.............(800)441-7234
   Tech Support............(408)252-5700
Symbios Logic.............(800)862-7729
Symbol Technologies.....(516)563-2400
Symbolics Inc.............(617)221-1000
Symbologic Corporation..(800)448-9292
   Tech Support............(800)448-9292
Symmetry Software.......(800)624-2485
   Tech Support............(800)624-2485
Symphony Laboratories..(408)986-1701
SymSoft.............(702)832-4300
Symtech ....(619)569-6800
Synchronics ....(901)761-1166
Syncomp Int'l Corp........(213)690-1011
   Tech Support............(213)694-0555
Synergetics Int'l ....(303)678-5200
Synergy Cmptr Services..(416)273-9565
Synergy Software.............(215)779-0522
   Tech Support............(215)779-0522
Synergy Solutions ....(602)545-9797
   Tech Support............(602)545-9797
Synergystex Int'l.............(216)225-3112
Synex.............(800)447-9639
SynOptics Communicatn..(800)776-8023
   Tech Support............(800)473-4911
Syntrex, Inc.............(908)542-1500
Syquest Technology.......(800)245-2278
   Tech Support............(510)226-4000
Sys Technology, Inc........(213)493-6888
Sys-Com.............(800)343-0100
Sysgen, Inc. ....(800)821-2151
Sysgration USA Inc. ....(415)306-7860
   Tech Support............(415)348-5663
SysKonnect ....(800)752-3334
   Tech Support............(408)725-4667
Sysnet Computer Sys.....(800)627-8964
Systat, Inc.............(708)864-5670
Systech Corporation......(619)453-8970
System Connection.........(800)877-1985
System Dynamic Grp.....(800)573-6467
System General Corp ....(408)263-6667
   Tech Support............(408)236-6667
System Industries ....(800)333-2220
System Integrators, Inc..(916)929-9481
System Security Techn...(702)454-7009

Systematics, Inc.............(501)220-5100
   Tech Support............(501)220-5653
Systems & Cmptr Techn..(215)647-5930
Systems and Software....(714)833-1700
   Tech Support............(714)833-1700
Systems Compatability...(800)333-1395
   Tech Support............(312)527-4357
Systems Enhancement ..(314)532-2855
Systems Integration ....(617)964-3030
Sys Integration Assoc.....(312)440-1275
   Tech Support............(312)440-1275
Systems Plus, Inc.............(415)969-7047
Systems Software Assoc..(312)641-2900
Systems Strategies Inc...(212)279-8400
Sytron Corporation.......(800)877-0016
   Tech Support............(508)896-0193
T & T Computer Inc .....(714)594-1420
T/Maker Company ....(415)962-0195
   Tech Support............(415)962-0195
Tab Books/McGraw-Hill..(800)233-1128
Tactic Software ....(305)665-4665
Tadiran ....(408)727-0300
Tadiran Electr Industry..(516)621-4980
Tae II Media ....(510)657-1244
Tagram Systems ....(800)824-7267
Taiwan Mfr Association .(714)393-7712
Tall Tree Systems.............(415)493-1980
Tallgrass Technologies ...(800)825-4727
   Tech Support............(800)825-4727
Tally Systems Corp ....(800)262-3877
Talon Instruments ....(909)599-0690
Tamrac, Inc.............(818)407-9500
Tandberg Data Inc.........(805)495-8384
Tandem Computers.......(800)255-5010
Tandy Corporation.......(817)390-3700
Tangent Computer, Inc..(415)342-9388
   Tech Support............(415)342-9388
Tapette Corporation......(714)638-7960
Tardis Technology Inc. ..(310)490-3150
Target Micro Inc. ....(800)883-8830
Target Systems Corp......(800)223-3493
Targus.............(714)523-5429
   Tech Support............(714)523-5429
Tasco Inc.............(800)999-9952
Tatung Co of America....(800)829-2850
   Tech Support............(800)827-2850
Tatung Science & Techn..(408)435-0140
Tau-Tron ....(800)828-8766
Tauber Electronics Inc. .(619)274-7242
Taxan America, Inc. ....(408)748-0900
Taxan USA Corp ....(408)946-3400
Taylored Graphics ....(813)948-7808
   Tech Support............(813)948-7808
TC Computer.............(800)723-8282
   Tech Support............(800)723-6380
TCE Company ....(800)383-8001
TCF-Techn Cmptr Ind Serv.(510)537-9030
TCS Distributors ....(800)488-0589
TDA/WINK Data Prods.(800)624-2101
TDK Electronics Corp...(516)625-0100
TDX Peripherals, Inc. ....(800)842-0708
   Tech Support............(800)842-0708
TEAC America, Inc.........(213)726-0303
   Tech Support............(213)726-0303
Teachware, Inc. ....(814)696-2530
Team Systems Inc.........(800)338-1981

INDUSTRY PHONE NUMBERS

Tech 101 Off Automatn ...(714)261-5141	Telemart............................(800)537-4735
Tech Assist Inc. ....(800)274-3785	Telematics Int'l...............(305)772-3070
Tech Data Corporation..(800)237-8931	Telenex Corporation-NJ....(609)234-7900
Tech Spray Inc. ....(806)372-8523	Telenex Corporation-VA...(800)368-3261
Tech Tronic Fabrications..(417)745-2195	Telepro Technologies.....(403)341-7826
Tech-Cessories Inc.........(800)637-0909	Telesystems SLW Inc. ....(416)441-9966
Tech-Sa-Port....................(800)543-2233	Teletutor........................(800)542-2242
Techanalysis Corp..........(612)925-5900	Televideo Systems, Inc...(800)345-6050
Techglove Unlimited .....(415)508-9709	Tech Support............(800)345-6050
Tech Support............(415)508-9709	Teleware Inc. ....(201)586-2269
Techmart Inc ....(404)772-9811	Tech Support............(201)586-2269
Techni-Tool Inc...............(215)941-2400	Telex Communications. (612)774-4051
Techn/Logistical Cons....(508)478-8211	Telindus Inc. ....(212)682-2595
Technical Cmptr Supp..(619)792-8216	Telix.............................(919)460-4556
Technical Parts Inc. ....(619)552-2288	Telos Corporation.........(213)450-2424
Technicom Cmptr Serv..(800)621-8229	TelPro Technologies.......(804)442-5865
Techniserv......................(512)289-9060	Teltron Inc. ....(215)582-2711
Techno Inc......................(312)567-9200	Telxon Corporation.......(216)867-3700
Technologic Systems.....(513)644-2230	Tempest Technologies...(703)471-0157
Technology Concepts ...(800)477-3473	Template Garden Sftwr.(800)233-3569
Tech Support............(503)692-9601	Tech Support............(914)337-0982
Technology Congress....(612)420-9800	Temptronic Corp..........(617)969-2501
Tech Support............(612)420-9800	Ten Times Sales...........(602)438-0889
Techn Enhancement Grp..(602)464-4494	Tech Support............(602)438-0889
Techn Integrated Prods.(408)980-5191	Tenera, L.P......................(510)845-5200
Technology Marketing ..(714)863-1100	Tenex............................(219)259-7040
Technology Works........(800)933-6113	Tech Support............(219)358-9603
Tech Support............(800)933-6113	Teradyne, Inc.................(617)482-2700
Technoserv Inc..............(800)553-1984	TeraTech.........................(800)447-9120
TechPlus Electr Corp.....(800)776-8160	Terminal Data Corp.......(805)529-1500
TechSoft Systems...........(800)825-8386	Test Engineering Serv....(800)842-0333
Tecmar............................(800)624-8560	Test Probes Inc. ....(800)368-5719
Tech Support............(800)344-4463	Texas Instruments ....(800)232-3200
Technet Canada Inc.......(604)388-6677	Texas Instruments ....(800)477-8924
Tecnocorp, Inc...............(305)477-5862	Texas Instruments Inc...(800)527-3500
TECRA TOOL.................(303)338-9224	Texas Micro...................(713)933-8050
TECsupport....................(813)540-2775	Texas Microsystems......(713)933-8050
Ted Dasher & Assoc......(800)638-4833	Texel.............................(408)980-1838
Tekcom-Prentice Corp..(408)435-9515	Tech Support............(408)980-1838
Tekelec...........................(818)880-5656	Textronix, Inc................(503)627-7111
Teklogix.........................(800)663-3040	TextWare Corporation...(801)645-9600
Teklogix Inc...................(317)849-1390	Tech Support............(801)645-9600
Teknosys........................(800)873-3494	Texwipe Company........(800)284-5577
Tech Support............(813)620-3494	Thaumaturge Resrce Corp.(317)870-5666
Teknowledge, Inc..........(415)424-0500	The AG Group................(510)937-7900
Tekra Corporation ....(800)448-3572	Tech Support............(510)937-7900
Tekserv..........................(508)459-9480	The Boeing Company ...(206)655-3897
Teksyn, Inc....................(317)875-9750	The Boston Cmptr Society.(617)232-0600
Tech Support............(317)875-9750	The Brimble Grp of Co's.(512)478-6678
Tektronix........................(800)835-6100	The Chair Works............(409)693-7000
Tech Support............(503)682-7300	The Complete PC..........(407)997-9683
Tekworks Inc..................(201)540-1096	Tech Support............(407)997-9683
TEL Electronics Inc........(800)824-7451	The Computer Factory..(914)347-5000
Tech Support............(800)824-7451	The Continuum Co........(512)345-5700
Tel-Tex Cmptr Prods......(713)868-6000	The Foxboro Company.(508)543-8750
Telcor, Inc......................(908)852-7000	The Interface Group......(617)449-6600
Tele-Art Instruments......(516)594-0952	The JLR Group Inc. ....(617)254-9109
Telebit ....(800)835-3248	The Learning Company.(800)852-2255
Tech Support............(800)835-3248	Tech Support............(800)852-2255
Telebyte Technology......(516)423-3232	The Maxximum Co. ......(800)766-6229
Telecommunications Tech..(301)353-1550	The One-Off CD Shop..(800)387-1633
Telecomputer, Inc..........(800)637-9695	The Programmer's Shop..(800)421-8006
TeleDynamics Corp........(800)847-5629	The Protector Corp........(303)939-8100
Teledyne, Inc.................(213)277-3311	The Ryco Company.......(414)963-5967
Teleglobe Communicatn..(508)681-0600	The Sftwr Toolworks.....(415)883-3000
Telegnostics Corp...........(805)544-8588	Tech Support............(415)883-3000

The Stolas Group...........(800)521-7666
The Stone Group...........(408)982-9999
The Techn Congress Ltd ...(612)420-9800
The Ultimate Corp.........(201)877-9222
The Vidicode US, Inc. ....(919)452-5600
The Voyager Company ..(800)446-2001
Tech Support............(914)591-5500
THEOS Software Corp...(510)935-1118
Tech Support............(510)935-1118
Thermalloy, Inc..............(214)243-4321
Thermodyne Int'l Ltd ....(310)603-1976
Thinx Software Inc.........(301)604-2588
Third Party Industries....(510)713-0392
Thirdware Cmptr Prods...(800)446-5987
Tech Support............(800)446-5987
Thomas & Betts Electr...(803)676-2900
Thomas Cmptr Corp......(708)647-0880
Thomas-Conrad Corp....(800)332-8683
Tech Support............(800)344-4112
Thompson & Thompson.(714)855-3838
Thomson Consumr Elect.(609)853-2525
Thought I Could.............(216)673-9724
Tech Support............(216)673-9724
Three Com Corp............(800)876-3266
Thunderware, Inc..........(510)254-6581
Tiara Computer Sys.......(800)638-4272
Tech Support............(800)638-4272
TIE/Communications....(203)888-8000
TIEX..............................(214)392-0647
Tiger Software................(800)888-4437
Tigon Corporation.........(800)962-2330
Timberline Software......(503)626-6775
Time Arts Inc.................(707)576-7722
Time Design Software...(303)693-3425
Time Motion Tools.........(619)679-0303
Timekeeping Systems....(216)361-9995
Timeplex, Inc................(201)391-1111
Timeslips Corporation...(800)285-0999
Tech Support............(508)768-7490
TimeValue Software.......(714)727-1800
Timeworks Inc...............(708)559-1310
Tech Support............(708)559-1331
Titan Corporation..........(619)453-9592
TKC...............................(813)544-2594
TLCSE Inc. ....(408)986-8300
TMC Research Corp......(408)262-0888
TMS Computer Maint....(210)492-8827
TMS Inc..........................(415)903-2252
Todd Enterprises............(800)445-8633
Todd SCI.......................(818)331-7377
Togal InfraLogic, Inc......(714)975-8522
Token Perspectives,The..(612)935-2035
Tokico America Inc........(313)336-5280
Tokyo Electric Co-CA....(510)651-5333
Tokyo Electric Co-MA...(617)235-4422
Tool Kit Specialists........(800)722-1123
Tool Techn Publishing...(415)459-3700
Tools & Techniques.......(800)444-1945
Top Data.......................(800)888-3318
Tech Support............(408)734-9343
Top Microsystems.........(408)980-9813
Top-Link Computers.......(408)263-2200
TOPS Computer Co.......(508)887-5915
Toray Opt Storage Solutns.(800)867-2973
Toshiba.........................(800)999-4273
Tech Support............(800)999-4273

INDUSTRY PHONE NUMBERS

Toshiba Consumer Prods..	(800)999-4273
Tech Support	(800)999-4273
Toshiba Elect. Company..	(800)999-4273
Tech Support	(800)999-4273
Toshiba America, Inc	(800)457-7777
Tech Support	(714)455-0407
Toshiba Facsimilie	(714)583-3580
Tosoh USA, Inc.	(415)588-5200
Total Cmptr Concepts	(206)867-9050
Total Concept Sales	(800)488-0589
Total Maint Concepts	(708)834-7351
Total Multimedia	(805)371-0500
Total Peripheral Repair..	(619)552-2288
Total Peripherals Inc	(508)480-8327
Total Power Int'l	(508)453-1503
Total Software Inc	(204)654-3896
Total Systems Services	(404)649-2387
Total Technologies, Ltd.	(512)328-9284
TouchStone Sftwr Corp	(800)531-0450
Tech Support	(714)969-7746
Toyogo	(800)869-6469
TPS Electronics	(415)856-6833
Trace Products	(800)872-2318
Trade Winds	(818)700-6920
Trade Winners Net Mktg	(206)694-1765
Trans Datacorp	(415)327-2692
Trans Leasing Int'l	(800)323-1180
Trans-Micro Inc.	(407)464-5335
Transamerica Commercl	(510)847-2008
Transcend Information	(714)598-5500
TransComputer, Inc.	(408)747-1355
Transform Logic Corp	(602)948-2600
Transition Engineering	(612)941-7600
Transitional Technology	(714)693-1133
Transtector Systems	(800)829-2901
Trantor Systems, Ltd.	(408)945-8600
Traveling Software	(800)662-2652
Tech Support	(206)483-8088
Travis-Helwig Inc.	(602)745-5452
Treasure Chest Periph	(800)677-9781
Tech Support	(504)468-2010
Tredex California Inc.	(800)338-0939
Tech Support	(310)551-3139
Trellis Communications	(603)668-1213
Trenton Terminals, Inc.	(404)381-6031
Tri State Computer	(800)433-5199
Tech Support	(212)608-2308
Tri-Star Computer Corp.	(800)800-7400
Tech Support	(916)568-1708
Triad Systems Corp	(510)449-0606
Tribe Computer Works..	(510)814-3930
Tech Support	(510)547-7145
Tribeca Peripherals	(800)445-6222
Trident Microsystems	(415)691-9211
TriGem	(800)359-0491
Trilogy Magnetics	(800)873-4323
Trimarchi Inc.	(800)356-6638
TriMark Eng-Doorway	(615)966-3667
Trimm Industries	(800)272-3557
Trinzic/Channel Cmpting	(800)289-0053
Trio Information Sys.	(919)846-4990
Trio Systems	(818)584-9706
Tripp Lite	(312)329-1777
Tech Support	(312)329-1602
Tritech Information Sys.	(408)252-5441
Triton Technologies	(908)855-9440

Tech Support	(908)855-9440
Triwef Corporation	(201)770-2800
Trompeter Electronics	(818)707-2020
TRON Association	(602)249-3388
Tron Computer	(800)397-8909
Tronix Peripherals, Inc.	(408)727-4191
Trosper Consulting	(719)589-0705
True Basic Inc.	(800)872-2742
TrueData Products	(800)635-0300
Tech Support	(508)278-6555
TrueTech	(612)944-8712
Truevision	(317)841-0332
Tech Support	(317)841-0332
TRW Customer Serv Div	(800)722-2736
TS Micro Tech, Inc.	(310)787-1640
TSA Inc.	(800)422-4872
Tseng Laboratories Inc.	(215)968-0502
TSL Holdings, Inc.	(805)582-6119
TSR Systems	(516)331-6336
Tucker Electronics	(800)527-4642
Tulin	(408)432-9025
Turbo Technologies	(310)641-4622
Turbopower Software	(719)260-6641
Turtle Beach Systems	(717)767-0200
Tech Support	(717)767-0200
Tutankhamon Electronics	(800)998-4888
Tech Support	(800)996-4888
TVM Professional Monitor.	(800)822-8168
Twelve Tone Systems	(617)926-2480
Twilight Express	(800)376-4797
Twilight Technologies	(810)695-8933
Twincom	(201)935-8880
Twinhead Corporation	(408)945-0808
TWIX	(800)344-8949
Tyan Computer Corp	(408)720-1200
Tech Support	(408)720-1200
Tyan Computer Corp	(408)956-8000
Tycor International	(403)259-3200
Tyler Corporation	(214)754-7800
Typerite Ribbon Mfg	(800)328-8028
Tystar Electronics Co	(816)842-7900
U S Robotics	(800)342-5877
Tech Support	(800)982-5151
U S West, Inc.	(303)793-6500
U-Lead Systems, Inc.	(800)858-5323
U-Tron Technologies	(800)933-7775
U.S. Computer	(305)477-2288
U.S. Robotics, Inc.	(800)342-5877
Tech Support	(708)982-5151
UDP Data Products	(213)782-9800
UDP Fonts	(310)782-9800
UDS Motorola	(800)451-2369
ULSI Systems (CA)	(408)943-0562
ULSI Systems (TX)	(512)329-8220
Ulta Computers	(800)755-7518
Tech Support	(304)748-1891
Ultima Electronics Corp	(510)659-1580
Ultimate Corporation	(201)887-9222
Ultimedia Tool Series, IBM.	(415)694-3090
Ultra-X Inc.	(800)722-3789
UltraStor Corporation	(714)581-4100
Ungermann-Bass, Inc.	(408)496-0111
Uni-CGS, Inc.	(714)468-1577
Uni-Rep	(619)662-1271
Unibind USA Inc	(800)874-7579
Unicomp Inc.	(714)571-1900

Unicore Software	(800)800-2467
Tech Support	(508)686-2204
Unicorn Software	(702)597-0818
Unidata	(916)362-1239
Uniform Industrial Corp	(510)549-0817
Uniplex	(214)717-0068
Tech Support	(800)338-9940
Unipress Software	(908)985-8000
Uniq Technology, Inc.	(415)226-9988
Tech Support	(415)226-9996
UniQube Corporation	(800)334-4990
Unison Technologies	(714)855-8700
Unisphere	(214)343-3717
UniStor	(800)422-2115
Tech Support	(800)422-2115
Unisys	(800)448-1424
Unit Tech America Inc.	(310)602-2392
United Barcode Ind	(301)210-3000
United Bus Machines	(800)722-7703
Tech Support	(909)279-1298
United Cmptr Express	(800)448-3738
United Cmptr Supply	(714)468-2680
United Innovations	(413)733-3333
United Microelectronics	(408)727-2100
United Networks Inc.	(408)433-0900
United Parcel Service	(404)913-7047
United Software Security	(703)556-0007
United Systems & Sftwr.	(407)875-2120
United Technology Corp.	(203)728-7000
United Telecomm, Inc.	(913)624-3000
Unitek Technology	(800)944-5650
Unitron Computer USA.	(818)333-0280
Universal Computer	(800)457-4433
Tech Support	(305)446-9905
Universal Enterprises	(800)547-5740
Universal Fiber Optics.	(703)389-9844
Univ Memory Products.	(800)678-8648
Universal Rsrch Techn	(713)623-8001
Universal Techn Sys	(815)963-2220
Universal Vectors Corp	(703)435-2500
Unix International	(201)263-8400
Unix Review Magazine.	(415)905-2200
Unlimited Systems Corp	(619)277-3300
Up Time Disaster Recovry.	(800)366-1282
Upgrades Etc.	(800)541-1943
Upsonic	(800)877-6642
Uptime Cmptr Support.	(805)254-3384
URS Information Sys	(508)657-6100
US Computer	(305)477-2288
US Computer Maint	(800)473-8650
US Logic	(619)467-1100
US Paging Corporation.	(201)305-6000
US Technologies	(201)288-8200
USA Electronics	(214)631-1574
Tech Support	(214)631-1693
USA Flex	(800)872-3539
Tech Support	(708)351-7172
USA Microsystems	(800)365-4774
Tech Support	(301)881-8974
Use 'R Computers, Inc.	(800)624-2480
Useful Software Inc.	(818)880-9128
User Friendly Cmptrs	(303)444-0770
USIT	(800)543-2294
UVC Corporation	(714)261-5336
V Communications	(408)296-4224
Valcom, Inc.	(402)392-3900

INDUSTRY PHONE NUMBERS

Valid Logic Systems	(408)432-9400
Valiteck, Inc.	(800)825-4835
Valitek	(413)549-2700
Vallesverd Company	(612)933-0023
Valtron Technologies	(805)257-0333
Valtronix	(714)261-6671
Value Added Inc.	(404)662-5800
ValueStor	(800)873-8258
Van Nostrand Reinhold	(212)254-3232
Vantage Technologies	(800)487-5678
Varbusiness	(516)365-4600
Varta Batteries	(800)468-2782
Vector Automation, Inc.	(301)433-4200
Vector Information Sys.	(203)797-0558
Vektron International	(800)725-0020
Tech Support	(214)606-2843
Ven-Tel Inc.	(800)538-5121
Tech Support	(800)538-5121
Ventek Corporation	(818)991-3866
Ventura Software	(800)772-6735
Tech Support	(313)357-5444
Verbatim	(800)538-8589
Tech Support	(800)538-8589
Verbatim Corporation	(704)547-6500
Verbum	(619)644-9977
Verdix Corporation	(703)378-7600
Verilink Corporation	(408)945-1199
Veritas	(408)727-1222
Verite	(310)326-5040
VeriTest, Inc.	(310)450-0062
Vermont Creative Sftwr	(802)848-7731
Tech Support	(802)848-7571
Vermont Database	(802)253-4437
Vermont Microsystems	(800)354-0055
Tech Support	(800)354-0055
Versacad Corporation	(800)488-7228
Vestronix	(519)745-2700
VI & C Technology	(617)861-8877
VIA Technologies, Inc.	(510)770-0370
ViaGrafix	(918)825-6700
Vic's Computer Service	(800)999-1827
Victor Technologies	(215)251-5000
Tech Support	(800)628-2420
Victory Enterprises Techn.	(800)727-3475
Video Display Corp.	(800)241-5005
Video Electr Standard Assn	(408)435-0333
Video Express Productn	(414)644-7042
Video Seven	(800)238-0101
Tech Support	(800)248-1850
Video Works	(800)838-1031
VideoLogic, Inc.	(617)494-0530
Videomail, Inc.	(408)747-0223
Videomedia, Inc.	(408)227-9977
Videx, Inc.	(503)758-0521
VidTech Microsys, Inc	(800)752-8033
Vienna Sftwr Publishing	(800)392-7724
View Sonic	(714)869-7976
Viewpoint Software	(800)635-5621
Viewsonic	(800)888-8583
Tech Support	(909)869-7976
Viking Acoustical Corp.	(800)328-8385
Viking Components	(714)643-7255
VIP Computer, Inc.	(714)562-6999
VIP Data Systems	(800)352-1150
Viratec Thin Films, Inc.	(507)334-0051
Virgin Games	(714)833-8710

Tech Support	(714)833-1999
Virtual Technologies	(210)787-2443
Visage, Inc.	(508)620-7100
Visalia Cmptr Technology	(209)625-1480
Visi-Tron, Inc.	(609)424-0400
Visible Systems Corp	(617)969-4100
Visiflex Seels	(201)487-8060
Vision Cmptr Remarketers	(800)242-5224
Vision Imaging	(714)965-7122
Visionary Software	(503)246-6200
Tech Support	(503)246-6200
Visionetics Int'l	(310)316-7940
Visionex	(408)954-0640
Visitech Software	(919)676-8474
Vista Microsystems	(508)695-8459
Vistron, Inc.	(408)522-8900
Visual Business Systems	(404)956-0325
Vita Ent Int'l. Corporation	(818)458-0282
Vital Communications	(516)437-4400
Vital Records Inc.	(908)369-6900
Viziflex Seels, Inc.	(201)487-8080
VLSI Technology, Inc.	(602)752-8574
VocalTec Inc.	(201)784-0993
Voice-It Software Inc.	(604)589-1086
VoiceFax Infor Systems	(604)732-9771
Voicetek Corporation	(508)250-9393
Volkswriter, Inc.	(408)648-3000
Volpe, Hank	(410)256-5767
Volt-Guard Inc.	(800)237-0769
Voltura Enterprises	(908)879-5803
Vorex Computer Labs	(800)486-4586
Tech Support	(800)883-8008
Voyager Company	(800)446-2001
Voyetra Technologies	(914)738-4500
VST Power Systems	(508)287-4600
Tech Support	(508)287-4600
Vu-Data Corporation	(619)452-7670
VXibus Associates	(201)299-8321
Vycor Corporation	(800)888-9267
VZ Corporation	(801)595-1352
W Systems	(800)344-8335
Wacom Technology Corp	(800)922-6613
Tech Support	(800)922-6635
Wadsworth	(606)525-2230
Wall Data Inc.	(800)927-8622
Tech Support	(800)927-8622
Wall Street Cmptr Review	(212)869-1300
Wallaby Software Corp	(201)934-9333
Wallace Comp. Serv's	(312)626-2000
Walling Company	(602)838-1277
Wallsoft Systems	(212)406-7026
Walnut Creek CDROM	(800)786-9907
Tech Support	(510)674-0783
Walt Disney Cmptr Sftwr	(818)973-4101
Tech Support	(818)841-3326
Wandel & Goltermann	(800)277-7404
Wang Labs Taiwan Ltd	(212)308-5862
Wang Laboratories, Inc.	(800)225-0654
WangDat, Inc.	(714)753-8900
Wangtek/Wang DAT-CAN	(805)582-3620
Wangtek/Wang DAT-US	(800)992-9916
Wantree Development	(913)441-1336
Warner Computer Sys.	(201)794-4800
Warner Electronics Inc.	(216)661-0304
Warner New Media	(818)955-9999
Tech Support	(818)955-9999

Warrantech	(203)975-1100
Warshawski/Whitney&Co	(312)431-6100
Washburn & Company	(800)836-8026
Watcom Products	(800)265-4555
Watergate Software	(510)596-1770
Waterloo Furn Compnt	(519)748-5060
Watermark Software	(619)229-2600
Tech Support	(619)229-2600
Watson Info Systems	(512)476-4665
Wave Mate, Inc.	(213)533-8190
Wavetek Corporation	(800)223-9885
Wayzata Technology	(218)326-0597
Tech Support	(800)377-7321
WCSC	(800)966-4832
Tech Support	(713)983-9427
Weames Techn Corp	(408)456-8838
Webcorp	(415)331-1449
Weetech Inc.	(800)232-5152
Weitek Corporation	(408)738-8400
Tech Support	(408)735-9348
Welch Allyn	(315)685-8945
Welling Electronics	(402)342-6564
Wen Technology Corp	(914)347-4100
Wescorp	(800)537-7828
Wescorp Statis Control	(800)537-7828
Wespercorp	(714)261-0606
Westbrook Technology	(800)742-2442
Tech Support	(203)399-7111
Western Digital	(800)832-4778
Tech Support	(800)832-4778
Western Eng Consultants	(805)375-4025
Western Micro	(800)634-2248
Western Scientific	(800)443-6699
Western Telematic Inc.	(800)854-7226
Tech Support	(800)854-7226
Western Union Corp	(201)818-5000
Western Wares	(303)327-4898
Westinghouse Electric	(412)244-2000
Westlake Data Corp	(512)328-1041
Tech Support	(512)328-1043
Wetex Int'l (USA)	(800)759-3839
Tech Support	(213)728-3156
Weyerhauser Recovery	(800)654-9347
White Pine Software	(603)886-9050
Tech Support	(603)886-9050
White Plains Software	(603)886-9050
Whitewater Group	(708)328-3800
Wicat Systems, Inc.	(801)224-6400
Wilcom Inc.	(800)222-1898
Williams & Macius	(509)235-2012
Willies Cmptr Software	(800)966-4832
Tech Support	(713)963-9427
Willow Creek Techn	(519)836-1532
Willow Peripherals	(800)444-1585
Tech Support	(800)444-1585
Wilson Laboratories	(714)998-1980
Wilson WindowWare	(206)937-9335
WIN Group	(213)903-1440
Wincom Int'l Network	(909)594-2218
Windows User Mag	(212)302-2626
WindSoft Inc.	(201)586-4400
Windsor Technologies	(415)456-2200
Wink Data Products	(206)742-4145
Winners Only Inc.	(619)549-2249
WinSoft	(800)275-7638
Winsryg Corp, The	(602)431-9118

INDUSTRY PHONE NUMBERS

Wintec Indrustries Inc. ..(510)770-9239
Wintime Corporation....(310)375-5930
WinWare ....(214)458-0540
WIP Technology.............(800)743-2318
Wise Components.........(800)543-4333
Wise-Ware ....(714)556-6523
WIT ....(408)433-0188
Wizardworks.................(612)559-5140
   Tech Support...........(612)544-8581
Wolff Forbes & Assoc ....(914)478-5048
Wolfram Research, Inc...(800)441-6264
Wollongong Group........(415)962-7100
Wonder Corporation.....(617)965-8400
Wonderware ....(714)727-9779
Wong's Int'l USA...........(415)967-1111
Word Star International.(800)227-5609
   Tech Support...........(812)323-8814
Wordata Inc...................(800)543-1922
WordPerfect Corp.........(800)451-5151
   Borland Office ....(800)661-2722
   Competitor's Suite ......(800)861-2721
   ConvertPerfect ....(801)228-9934
   DataPerfect ....(800)861-2132
   Developer's Tool Kit....(801)228-9508
   Edultainment ....(801)228-9939
   Envoy.........................(801)228-9929
   Extend Ann Supp-Classic.(800)861-3380
   Extend Ann Supp-Priority.(800)861-2220
   French........................(800)321-6844
   Gateways.....................(800)861-2135
   Grammatik DOS/WIN.(801)228-9933
   Hard Disk-Gift Shop.....(801)228-3783
   Hard Disk-Kitchen.......(801)228-3788
   Hard Disk-Specials.......(801)228-3780
   Hearing Impaired-TDD...(800)321-3256
   InfoCentral..................(801)228-9938
   Informs.......................(800)861-2133
   InfoShare (FAX)...........(800)228-9960
   Intellitag (DOS)...........(801)228-9925
   Intellitag (UNIX)..........(801)228-9935
   Language Modules.......(800)321-7431
   Letter/Elect/Dict/Clip Art (801)228-9933
   NAS............................(800)321-0034
   NAS, CAP...................(800)228-9505
   Office UNIX.................(800)861-2134
   Office/Priority Service (800)861-2136
   Piracy-BSA...................(801)688-2721
   Piracy-WordPerfect......(800)222-4449
   PlanPerfect.................(800)321-3248
   Presentations (DOS)....(800)861-2060
   Presentations (WIN)....(800)861-2050
   Quattro Pro (DOS) ......(800)861-3773
   Quattro Pro (WIN) ......(800)861-2774
   Sales, French Speaking.(800)321-2318
   Sales, Certification ....(800)993-3700
   Sales, Cust Registration....(801)222-4500
   Sales, Direct Sales.........(800)321-4566
   Sales, Easy Move/Spec Lic.(800)228-5040
   Sales, Hearg Impaird-TDD.(800)321-3256
   Sales, International.......(801)222-4200
   Sales, Mini-Main Info/Ord.(800)321-3280
   Sales, Orders on Acct....(800)321-3220
   Sales, Orders Resolution.(800)321-2319
   Sales, Sftwr Subscriptn (800)282-2892
   Sales, Workgroup/Office..(800)861-2507
   Shell 4.0......................(801)228-9937

Shell 4.0 Macros..........(801)228-9928
Soft Shoppe ....(800)526-6215
Spanish.......................(800)321-8492
Suite Consulting...........(800)861-2721
WP5.1 DOS, Fax...........(800)861-2316
WP5.1 DOS, Features...(800)861-2164
WP5.1 DOS, Graph/Tabl..(800)861-2101
WP5.1 DOS, Installation .(800)861-2055
WP5.1 DOS, Macro/Merg.(800)861-2745
WP5.1 DOS, Network...(800)861-2116
WP5.1 DOS, Prn-Dot Matx(800)861-2333
WP5.1 DOS, Prn-Laser/PS.(800)861-2351
WP5.2 WIN, Features...(800)228-1029
WP5.2 WIN, Graphics..(800)228-6013
WP5.2 WIN, Installatn..(800)228-6076
WP5.2 WIN, Macro/Merg.(800)228-1032
WP5.2 WIN, Networks.(800)228-6066
WP5.2 WIN, Prn-Dot Matx(800)228-1017
WP5.2 WIN, Prn-Laser/PS..(800)228-6076
WP6.0 DOS, Fax..........(800)228-2066
WP6.0 DOS, Features...(800)228-9038
WP6.0 DOS, Graph/Tabl..(800)228-9006
WP6.0 DOS, Installatn..(800)228-9012
WP6.0 DOS, Macro/Merg.(800)228-9013
WP6.0 DOS, Networks.(800)228-9019
WP6.0 DOS, Prn-Dot Matx(800)228-9032
WP6.0 DOS, Prn-Laser/PS.(800)228-9027
WP6.0 WIN, Features...(800)228-9907
WP6.0 WIN, Graph/Tabl..(800)228-8720
WP6.0 WIN, Installatn..(800)228-7610
WP6.0 WIN, Macro/Merg.(800)228-2021
WP6.0 WIN, Networks.(800)228-8807
WP6.0 WIN, Prn-Dot Matx(800)228-6646
WP6.0 WIN, Prnt-Laser/PS.(800)228-1023
WP Communications...(801)228-9915
WP DOS, Fax...............(800)861-2480
WP DOS, Features........(800)861-2410
WP DOS, Graph/Tabl....(800)861-2420
WP DOS, Installation....(800)861-2460
WP DOS, Macro/Merge(800)861-2430
WP DOS, Networks......(800)861-2470
WP DOS, Prn-Dot Matrx..(800)861-2450
WP DOS, Prn-Laser/PS .(800)861-2440
WP MAC 2.1 x.............(800)336-3614
WP MAC 3.0................(800)228-2875
WP MAC French Speak.(800)321-2173
WP Macintosh.............(800)861-2070
WP Magazine, Info.......(800)228-9656
WP Magazine, Subscript..(800)228-9626
WP Mfg, Receptionist ..(801)861-5049
WP Mfg, Research........(800)446-4652
WP Mfg, Research-US...(800)526-6215
WP OS/2.....................(800)321-1230
WP System 370............(801)222-5100
WP UNIX, Features......(800)861-2030
WP UNIX, Print............(800)861-2040
WP UNIX/Xenix Feature.(801)226-5333
WP UNIX/Xenix Print.(801)228-9903
WP VAX/Dec...............(800)861-2010
WP VAX/VMS All in One.(801)226-4180
WP WIN, Features......(800)861-2310
WP WIN, Graph/Tabl...(800)861-2320
WP WIN, Installation....(800)861-2360
WP WIN, Macro/Merg..(800)861-2330
WP WIN, Networks......(800)861-2370
WP WIN, Prn-Dot Matrix.(800)861-2350

WP WIN, Prn-Laser/PS .(800)861-2340
WP Works DOS/WIN...(801)228-9936
WordStar International..(800)227-5609
   Tech Support...........(800)227-5609
Wordstar USA................(617)494-1200
WordTech Systems, Inc. (510)254-0900
WorksWare...................(818)989-2298
   Tech Support...........(818)969-2298
Worlco Data Systems.....(215)630-9500
World Richman Corp ....(708)298-1188
Worldata.......................(407)393-8200
Worldcomm...................(800)472-0438
Worldnet Marketing ......(714)545-7118
Worldwide Cmptr Serv .(201)694-8876
Worldwide Technology .(800)457-6937
   Tech Support...........(215)922-4640
Worldwide Video...........(201)491-5147
Worthington Data Sol....(800)345-4220
Wrist Pro.......................(800)348-8633
WV Computronics ....(304)882-3086
WWIV Software Serv.....(210)631-6090
Wyle Laboratories..........(213)322-1763
Wynit............................(800)999-9648
Wyse Technology...........(800)438-9973
   Tech Support...........(800)800-9973
X Ceed ....(800)642-7661
   Tech Support...........(800)642-7661
X-10 (USA) Inc..............(201)784-9700
X3 Secretariat, CBEMA ..(202)737-8888
XBR Communication ....(514)489-1001
Xcel Computer Systems(508)799-9494
XDB Systems Inc. ....(301)317-6800
Xeltek..........................(800)541-1975
Xentek Inc. ....(619)727-0949
Xerox Corp (CA)...........(800)832-6979
Xerox Corp (CT)...........(203)968-3000
Xerox Corp (NY)...........(716)423-5078
Xerox Imaging Systems.(800)248-6550
   Tech Support...........(800)248-6550
Xerox Int'l Partners.......(415)813-7700
Xerox/X-Soft ....(800)334-6200
Xidex Corporation ....(408)970-6574
Xinetron.......................(408)727-5509
Xircom.........................(800)874-7875
   Tech Support...........(800)874-4428
Xistor...........................(702)824-7777
XL/Datacomp Inc..........(800)323-3289
XOR Corporation ....(612)831-8640
   Tech Support...........(612)831-8640
Xpect Trading Corp.......(800)332-5555
XScribe Corporation .....(619)457-5091
Xtend Micro Products...(800)232-9836
XtraCom Inc. ....(416)427-6612
XTree Co-Central Point .(800)964-2490
   Tech Support...........(800)964-2490
Xtron Cmptr Equipment.(201)798-5000
Xuron Corporation........(207)283-1401
XXCAL, Inc...................(800)879-9225
Xxera Technologies.......(818)286-5569
Xylogics, Inc..................(800)225-3317
   Tech Support...........(617)272-8140
XXQuest.......................(508)671-0888
Y-E Data America Inc. ...(404)446-8655
Y.E.S. Systems Corp........(510)657-8886
Yamaha LSI..................(800)543-7457
Yamaha Sys Technology.(800)543-7457

Yamaichi Electronics.....(408)452-0797
Yangs Int'l Corporation.(510)651-4305
Yokogawa Corp/America.(800)258-2552
Young Micro Systems....(310)946-3450
Yuasa-Exide Inc.............(215)378-0333
Z Soft.........................(404)428-0008
Z-International, Inc ....(816)474-8400
Z-Mar Technology..........(704)841-8845
Z-Ram.........................(800)368-4726
Z-Soft ....(800)444-4780
Z-World.......................(916)753-3722
Z/Max Cmptr Solution..(315)635-1882
Zaptec Int'l Corp...........(714)792-2229
Zedcor.........................(800)482-4567
    Tech Support............(602)881-2310
Zemaitis, Inc.................(408)436-1530
Zenith Data Systems......(800)553-0331
    Tech Support............(800)227-3360
Zenographics, Inc..........(800)366-7494
    Tech Support............(714)851-2191
Zenon Computer Sys ....(800)899-6119
    Tech Support............(800)229-7898
Zentao Corporation.......(708)350-9040
Zentek Storage/America...(408)946-4464
Zeny Cmptr Systems .....(510)659-0386
Zeos International ....(800)423-5891
Zericon, Inc..................(800)727-8380
Zi-Tech Instrument........(415)326-2151
Ziff Davis Techn Info Sys...(617)393-3200
Ziff-Davis Publ Co..........(212)503-5446
Zippertubing.................(310)527-0488
Zirco ....(303)421-2013
Zirco Inc......................(303)421-2013
Zitel Corporation...........(408)946-9600
Zoltrix Inc....................(510)657-1188
Zoom Telephonics ....(617)423-1072
    Tech Support............(617)423-1076
Zom Industries..............(603)894-4950
Zortech........................(617)937-0696
ZSoft Corporation..........(800)444-4780
Ztest Electronics............(416)238-3543
Zykronix Inc..................(303)799-4944
ZyLAB Corporation........(800)544-6339
ZyMOS Corporation.......(408)730-5400
    Tech Support.............(800)422-7369
Zytec Corporation..........(612)941-1100
ZyXEL USA....................(800)255-4101

INDUSTRY PHONE NUMBERS

BULLETIN BOARD SERVICES

Many manufacturers of hard drives and other related computer products maintain computer bulletin boards to provide technical support for their customers. Listed below are bulletin boards that we know about. The ones that we have called all use 8, N, 1, modem parameters. Many of them support modem speeds up to 28.8K baud.

To the best of our knowledge, these numbers are correct, but CSC cannot assume liability for their use.

3Com Corporation......(408)980-8204
3rd Planet Software.....(213)841-2260
Abacus Concepts........(616)698-8106
Abacus Software.........(616)698-8106
Able Soft.....................(804)898-8686
Above Software...........(714)851-5102
Access Software..........(801)364-7449
Accton Technology......(408)452-8828
Acculogic Inc..............(714)454-8124
Acer America...............(408)428-0140
......................................(800)833-8241
Acer Technologies.......(800)833-8241
Activision....................(310)820-1276
Adaptec......................(408)945-7727
Adobe Systems, Inc.....(408)562-6839
Advanced Digital Info..(206)883-3211
Advanced Gravis Cptr.(604)431-5927
Advanced Logic Rsrch.(714)458-6834
Agfa Compugraphics...(508)694-9577
All Computers.............(416)960-8679
Alloy Computer Prods.(508)486-4044
Alpha Software Corp..(617)229-2915
Altsys.........................(214)680-9696
Always Technology......(818)597-0275
Amdek Corporation.....(408)922-4400
American Cybermetic..(602)968-1082
Amer. Small Bus Cptr...(918)825-4878

APCU(Assoc PC Grps) (408)439-9367
Apogee Software.........(508)365-2359
Appian.......................(206)454-0511
Appoint......................(510)803-9018
Arabesque Software....(206)881-0905
Archive Software.........(407)263-3502
Arco Electronics..........(305)925-2791
Areal Technology.........(408)954-0360
Arsenal Computer.......(913)234-9395
Artful Applications......(416)538-3107
Artisoft, Inc................(602)884-8648
Artist Graphics...........(612)631-7669
Ascii Computer Ent.....(209)836-2402
AskSam Systems.........(904)584-8287
Aspen Peripherals.......(503)286-9620
AST Computer............(714)727-4723
AST Research..............(714)727-4132
AST Research Canada..(905)512-8558
Asymetrix....................(206)451-1173
AT&T Computer Sys...(908)769-6397
ATI Technologies.........(905)764-9404
......................................(416)764-9404
Attachmate Corp.........(206)649-6660
Aurora Terra...............(301)230-1214
AutoDesk Inc..............(415)289-2270
Autumn Hill Software.(303)494-8868
Avatar/DCA...............(404)740-9428
Award (BIOS).............(415)968-0249
Award Software Inc....(408)371-3139
Baker & Taylor Labels...(800)775-4200
......................................(415)257-3070
Beagle Bros.................(801)226-1605
Best Power Tech..........(608)565-7424
Bestgift Service...........(813)978-3044
Bethesda Softworks.....(301)990-7552
Big State Doors...........(512)376-5644
Bit Software, Inc.........(510)490-6637
Blackmond Software...(505)589-0319
Boardwatch Magazine.(303)973-4222
Boca Research.............(407)241-1601
Borland......................(408)439-9096
Bottom Line Ind..........(214)394-4170

Bourbaki.....................(208)342-5823
Brightbill Roberts........(315)472-1058
Brightwork Dvlpmnt...(914)667-4759
Broderbund Software..(415)883-5889
Brown Bag Software...(408)371-7654
Bruce Krobusek..........(716)924-4193
BTC Corporation.........(510)657-1859
Buerg.........................(707)778-8944
Buffalo Creek Sftwre...(515)225-8496
Bureau of Elect Publ..(201)808-0085
Button Ware, Inc.........(206)454-7875
C Source.....................(816)478-0944
CalComp....................(714)236-3045
Calera Recognition......(408)773-9068
Campbell Services Inc.(313)559-6434
Canon Computer Sys..(714)438-3325
Capstone....................(305)471-8962
Cardinal Technologies.(717)293-3074
Cardz.........................(604)734-5400
Castelle......................(408)496-1807
Catspaw.....................(719)539-4830
CBIS, Inc...................(404)446-0485
CC:Mail, Inc...............(415)691-0401
CDB Systems, Inc........(303)642-7463
CDC...........................(408)438-8771
Central Point Software (503)690-6650
Certus International....(503)484-6669
CH Products...............(619)598-3224
Cheyenne Software.....(516)484-3445
Chinon.......................(310)320-4160
Chips & Technology....(408)456-0721
ChipSoft Inc. (Intuit)...(619)550-5018
Chwatal Develpment..(318)487-0800
Citizen America..........(310)453-7564
Citrix Systems............(305)346-9004
Clarion Software.........(305)785-2594
Claris Corporation......(408)987-7421
Clark Develpment Co..(801)261-8976
Clary Corporation.......(801)261-8976
Clear Software............(617)965-5406
CMS Enhance.............(714)222-6601
CNet Technology, Inc..(408)954-1787

BULLETIN BOARD SERVICES

Coconut Computing... (619)456-0815	Diagnostic Technlgy.... (905)607-6570	Future Soft Enginr'g....(713)588-6870
Codenoll......................(914)965-1972	DiagSoft Inc............... (408)438-8997	FutureSoft, Inc............(713)588-6870
Colorado Memory Sys..(303)635-0650	Diamond Comptr Sys..(408)524-9301	Galacticomm Inc.........(305)583-7808
Columbia Data Prods.. (407)862-4724	Digiboard, Inc........ (612)943-0812	GammaLink.................(408)745-2216
Compaq Computer..... (713)378-1418	Digicom Systems, Inc..(408)262-1412	Gap Development.......(714)493-3819
Complex, Inc.............(714)630-2570	Digital Dynamics.........(714)529-5313	Gateway 2000.............(605)232-2109
Comprehensive Video..(201)767-7990	Digital Research..........(408)429-7785	Gateway BBS.............(605)232-2109
Compton's NewMedia.(619)929-2597	Digital Theatre...........(404)446-0485	Gazelle Systems.......... (801)375-2548
Compulink Mgmt Ctr..(310)212-5850	Digital Vision..............(617)329-8387	GEcho.......................(316)263-5313
Computer Classifieds..(206)643-2874	Disk Technician Corp..(619)272-9240	General Datacomm.....(202)596-0593
Computer Coverup.....(312)327-9078	Disk Technologies.......(407)671-6099	Genicom.................... (703)949-1576
Computer Design Mag (508)392-2265	Disney Cptr Software..(818)567-4027	GEnie Info Service...... (800)638-8369
Computer Support......(214)404-8652	Dist. Logic Corp..........(407)831-6432	Genoa.......................(408)943-1231
Computers Intl............(213)823-3609	DNA Networks, Inc.....(215)296-9558	Gensoft Development.(206)562-9407
Computone Corp........(404)343-9737	Dove Computer...........(919)343-5616	GeoClock....................(703)241-7980
Comtrol Corporation.. (612)631-8310	DPT(DistProcess Tech) (407)831-6432	GeoWorks...................(510)814-4262
Conner International.. (408)456-4415	DSP Solutions..............(415)494-1621	Gibson Research.........(714)362-8848
Conner Peripherals..... (408)456-4415	DTK Computer (CA)...(818)333-6548	Gigatrend Inc..............(619)931-9469
....................................(407)263-3502	DTK Computer(TX)....(713)568-9941	Gilmore Systems......... (805)379-3450
Core International.......(407)438-8771	Dudley Software......... (615)966-3574	Global Village Comm.. (415)390-8334
Corel Systems, Inc.......(613)728-4752	Dynamic Microprocsr. .(516)462-6638	GoldDisk (AMI)...........(905)602-7534
Cornerstone Imaging..(408)435-8943	E-Machines..................(408)541-6190	GoldDisk (MAC)..........(905)602-7534
Cornerstone Technlgy. .(408)435-8943	E-Tech Research Inc....(408)988-3663	Gold Disk (PC)............(905)602-7534
Corvus Systems, Inc.... (408)972-9154	E-WARE......................(714)236-1388	Gotoless Conversion...(214)625-6905
CoStar........................(203)661-6292	Eagle Technology.........(408)453-0734	Graphic Workshop......(416)729-4609
Creative Labs, Inc........(405)742-6660	Eagle Soft....................(812)479-1310	Great Amer. Software...(603)889-7292
Creative Programming.(214)418-0059	EDS Development.......(812)423-3394	Greenleaf Software...... (214)250-3378
Cross Comm............... (303)444-9003	Elan Software Corp.....(310)459-3443	Gwynn's Comm.......... (703)494-0096
Crosstalk Comm..........(404)740-8428	Elite Business Apps..... (410)987-2335	Hamilton Tel..............(819)682-7771
CrossTies....................(714)732-6754	EMAC/EVEREX............(510)226-9694	Hayes Microcptr Prod..(404)446-6336
Crystal Services...........(604)681-9516	Emerald Systems......... (619)673-4617	....................................(800)874-2937
CSC Tech Support...... (408)541-8455	Emulex Corporation... (714)662-1445	Hazard Soft..................(405)243-3200
CSS Laboratories.........(714)852-9231	Enable Software..........(518)877-6316	HDC Computer Corp..(206)869-2418
CTX International, Inc .(909)594-8973	Envisio.......................(612)633-0051	Headland Technology..(510)656-0503
Cubix Corporation......(702)882-8737	Epson Amer, OEM Div. .(408)946-8777	Helic Software.............(718)392-4054
Cumulus.....................(216)464-3019	Epson Amer, Inc..........(310)782-4531	Helix Software Co.......(718)392-4054
Cyco International...... (404)634-1441	Equinox.....................(305)378-1696	Helix Technology.........(718)392-4054
Cyrix Corporation.......(214)680-3187	Equinox Systems, Inc..(305)791-1633	Hercules Cmptr Tech.. (510)623-7449
DAC Software..............(214)931-6617	Ergo Computing, Inc...(508)535-7228	Hewlett Packard..........(208)344-1691
DacEasy, Inc................ (214)931-6617	ESoft Product Support.(303)699-8222	Hyundai Electronics....(800)955-5432
Dak Industries, Inc......(818)715-7153	ETS Incorporated........(801)265-0919	IBM Corporation(Can).(905)316-4244
Dariana Software.........(714)236-1388	Everex........................(510)226-9694	IBM Microelectronics..(919)517-0001
Darius Technology.......(714)994-7410	Evergreen Technology.(503)757-8869	IBM PC Company........(919)517-0001
Darwin Systems.......... (301)251-9206	Exabyte Corporation...(913)492-8751	IBM PC Users Group...(404)988-2790
Data Access Corp........(305)238-0640	Excalibur.....................(408)244-0813	IBM PS/1 BBS..............(404)835-8230
Data Base Solutions.....(619)270-2042	Excalibur Comm., Inc. .(918)496-8113	Image-In....................(612)888-2324
Data Technology Corp .(408)942-4010	ExperVision Inc...........(408)456-0280	ImageSoft, Inc. .... (516)767-7094
Data Watch..................(919)549-0042	EZX Publishing............(713)280-8180	IMC Networks Corp...(714)724-0930
Datadesk International.(503)691-5199	Family Scrapbook........(904)249-9515	IMSI Software..............(415)454-2893
DataEase International.(203)374-6302	Farallon Computing....(510)865-1321	Incomm Data Systems.(708)459-9331
Dataman.....................(407)649-3159	FCC Public Access.......(301)725-1072	Infinity Comptr Serv... (215)965-8028
Dataproducts...............(818)887-8167	Fifth Generation Sys....(504)295-3344	InfoChip Systems.........(408)727-2496
Datawatch...................(919)549-0042	Fifth Generation Sys....(504)295-3344	InnovativeData Cncpts.(215)357-4183
Dayna Comm..............(801)269-7398	Flytek Technology Co..(408)727-0737	Intel Application Supp .(916)356-3600
DCA............................(404)740-8428	Foresight Resource..... (816)891-8465	Intel Corporation........(503)645-6275
DCA/Crosstalk Comm.(404)740-8428	Frame Technology.......(408)433-4841	Intel Support..............(503)645-6275
DEC PC Support......... (508)496-8800	FreeSoft Company.......(412)846-5312	Intelligent Graphics....(408)441-0386
Dell Computer Corp...(512)728-8528	Frontline Systems........(415)327-7319	InterPlay Productions. (714)252-2822
Delphi........................(800)365-4636	Fujitsu America, Inc.....(408)944-9899	Intacorp.....................(305)378-8793
DeltaComm Devel.......(919)481-9399	Fujitsu Comptr Prods..(408)944-9899	IOMEGA......................(801)778-4400

IQ Software	(206)821-5486	Mergent International. (203)257-4305	Okidata Corporation... (609)234-5344
IQ Technologies	(206)821-5486	Meridian Data	(408)439-9509	Olicom USA	(214)422-9835
Irwin Magnetics	(407)263-3662	Merit Software	(214)702-8641	Omen Technology	(503)621-3746
JET FAX	(415)324-1259	Metagraphics	(408)438-5368	Online USA	(303)932-1400
JetForm Corporation... (613)563-2894	Metz Software	(206)644-3663	Ontrack Cmptr Sys	(612)937-0860
Jovian Logic Corp	(510)651-6989	Micro Help	(404)516-1497	Open Network	(718)638-2239
JTS Corporation-Kalok .(408)734-4258	Micro House	(303)443-9957	OPTI, Inc	(408)980-9774
Kent Marsh	(713)522-8921	Micro Solutions	(815)756-9100	Optima Technology	(714)476-0626
Key Tronic	(509)927-5288	Microcom-Carb. Copy..(617)255-1125	Orchid Technology	(510)683-0327
Keyfile	(603)883-5968	Microcom (Hardware) .(617)255-1125	Origin Systems, Inc	(512)328-8402
Kingston Electronics...(714)435-2636	Microdyne Corp	(703)760-8509	Pacific Data Products..(619)452-6329
Knowledge Adventure (818)248-0166	Microdyne Corp	(408)376-3662	Pacific Microelectrncs. (415)941-9699
Knowledge Dynamics.(512)964-3929	Micrografx, Inc	(214)234-2694	Packard Bell	(818)313-8601
Kodiak Technology	(510)659-0857	Microlink/Micro Frwr..(405)321-3553	Palindrome Corp	(708)505-3336
Kurta	(602)243-9440	Micron Technology	(208)368-4530	Panacea Inc	(603)432-5193
LAN Magazine	(415)267-7640	Micronics	(510)651-6837	Panasonic Comm. Sys..(201)863-7845
LAN Master	(817)771-0233	Micropolis Corp	(818)709-3310	Paperback Corp	(415)644-0782
LANWorks	(416)238-0253	Microprose Software...(410)785-1841	Paradise/Westrn Digitl .(714)753-1234
Laser Master Corp	(612)835-5463	Microrim	(206)649-9836	Pathfinder Associates.. (408)246-0164
LaserGo, Inc	(617)450-9370	Microsoft Corporation .(206)936-6735	Patton & Patton Sftwr. (408)778-9697
LaserMaster Corp	(612)835-5463	Microsoft Corporation .(905)507-3022	Pentax Technology	(303)460-1637
LaserTools, Inc	(510)420-1942	Microsoft Press	(206)936-6735	Peripheral Land Inc	(510)651-5948
Lattice, Inc	(708)916-1200	Microspeed	(510)490-1664	Persoft	(608)273-6595
Leading Edge	(508)836-3971	Microsystems Devel....(408)296-4200	Perspective Software.. (313)255-2466
Lexmark International. (606)232-5238	Microsystems Sftware. (508)875-8009	Phillips (LMSI)	(719)593-4081
Lightning Comm, Inc.. (714)457-9429	Microtech Int'l	(203)469-6430	Phoenix Technologies. (714)453-8619
Link Technologies	(510)623-6680	Microtek Lab	(310)297-5102	Pinnacle Micro	(714)453-8619
Linksys	(714)222-5111	Miniscribe	(303)678-2222	Pinnacle Publishing	(206)251-6217
LianoWare Doors	(805)264-0443	Miramar Systems	(805)963-6951	Pinnacle Software	(514)345-8654
Locus Computing	(310)337-5995	Mitsubishi Electronics.(714)236-6286	Pinpoint Publishing	(707)523-0468
Logical Connection	(504)295-3344	MMB Development	(310)318-5302	Pioneer Software	(919)851-1381
Logitech	(510)795-0408	Morgan Davis Group...(619)670-5379	PKWare (PKZip)	(414)354-8670
Lotus-Word Process'g..(404)395-7707	Mountain Network	(408)438-2665	PLI	(510)651-5948
Lotus Devel. Corp	(617)693-7001	Mouse Systems	(510)683-0617	Plus Development	(408)434-1664
Lucid	(214)994-8125	Multi-Tech Systems	(612)785-9875	Polaris Software	(619)592-2674
Mace, Paul Software	(503)482-7435	Multitech Systems	(800)392-2432	Power Computing	(516)822-7396
MadgeNetworks	(408)955-0262	Mustang Software, Inc. (805)873-2400	Powercore Inc	(815)468-2633
Magee Enterprises	(404)446-6650	Mustek Inc	(714)453-1210	Practical Peripherals... (805)496-4445
Magitronic Techn	(516)454-8262	Mutant Group	(405)372-6621	Priam Systems	(408)434-1646
Magma Software Sys... (201)912-0668	Mylex Corporation	(510)793-3491	Primavera Systems	(215)660-5833
Magnavox/Phillips	(310)532-6436	MySoftware Company..(510)793-3491	Prime Solutions	(619)272-9240
Mainlan	(407)331-7433	National Instruments.. (800)327-3077	ProBoard International (612)537-8659
Mannesmann Tally	(206)251-5513	National Semicndctor..(408)245-0671	Procom Technology	(714)852-1305
Manugistics	(301)984-5222	NCD Distribution	(305)966-6097	Procomp USA, Inc	(216)234-6581
Manx Software Sys	(201)542-2793	NCR Microelectronics..(719)574-0424	Programmer's Wrhse...(602)443-1662
Martek	(714)453-1210	NDC Communications.(408)428-1143	Prometheus Products..(503)691-5199
Mass Micro Systems....(408)522-1248	NEC Technologies, Inc.(508)635-4706	Promise Technology	(714)852-1305
Masterclip Graphics....(305)967-9453	Network Products	(818)441-6933	Proxim	(415)960-2419
Mathematica	(813)683-6840	New Media Corp	(714)453-0214	Proteon, Inc	(508)366-7827
Matrix Technology	(617)569-3787	NewGen Systems	(714)641-3869	Public Brand Software .(317)856-2087
Matrox Graphic Inc....(514)685-6008	Night Owl BBS	(716)881-5688	Pure Data	(214)242-3225
Maxi Host Support	(209)836-2402	Nisca Inc	(214)446-0646	Quantum	(408)894-3214
Maxis Software	(510)254-3869	Northgate Computer...(612)361-5217	Quarterdeck Off Sys....(310)396-3904
Maxtech GVC	(201)579-2380	Norton-Lambert	(805)683-2249	Quercus Systems	(408)867-7488
Maxtor Colorado	(303)678-2020	Norton/Symantec	(408)973-9598	Quess Micro	(719)597-8670
Maxtor Corporation	(303)678-2222	Novell (2400)	(408)649-3443	Quick Comm	(408)956-1358
Maynard Electronics...(407)263-3502	(9600)	(408)649-3696	QuickBBS	(407)896-0494
McAffee Association	(408)988-4004	NUIQ Software, Inc	(914)833-1479	Racal-Interlan	(508)264-4345
Media Vision Resource.(510)770-0968	Ocean Isle Software	(407)778-2407	Race	(305)271-2146
Menai	(415)617-5726	OCR Systems	(215)938-7245	Racore Cmptr Prods... (801)363-8720

BULLETIN BOARD SERVICES

Rams' Island Sftwr.......(303)841-6269	Symantec Corporate... (503)484-6669	Velocity.........................(708)991-0597
Red Wing Bus. Sys.......(612)388-9605	Symantec Tech Supp...(408)973-9598	Ven-Tel, Inc.................(408)922-0988
Reference Software.....(801)225-4444	Synergy Solutions........(602)545-0232	Ventura Software.........(619)673-7691
RelayNet National.......(301)229-5623	Synopsys.....................(408)970-3719	Vermont Creative Soft.(802)848-7581
Remote Control Intl....(619)431-4030	Syquest.....................(510)656-0473	Vermont Microsystem.(802)655-7461
ResNova Software, Inc.(714)379-9004	Sysgen, Inc.................(408)946-5032	Video Seven.............. (510)656-0503
Revelation Technology.(206)641-8110	Systat, Inc...................(708)492-3570	VideoLogic, Inc.......... (617)494-4960
Rix Softworks, Inc.......(714)476-0728	Systems Compatability.(312)670-4239	Viewsonic.................. (909)468-1241
Rodent Labs Software. (801)756-2901	T A G BBS...................(313)582-6671	Virex........................(919)419-1602
Rybs Electronics..........(303)443-7437	Tallgrass Technologies.(913)492-8757	Virgin Games.............(714)833-3305
Saber Software............(214)361-1883	TEAmate.....................(213)318-5302	Virgin Software.........(714)833-3305
Sam Sung Info. Sys...... (408)434-5684	Tech Data....................(813)538-7090	Virtual Technologies... (210)787-8974
Seagate Tech. USA.......(408)438-8771	Technology Concepts. (503)691-5199	Visual Business Syst... .(404)953-1613
Seagate Tech. UK.........44-628-478011	TechnologyWorks.......(512)329-6327	Volkswriter, Inc...........(408)648-3015
Seagate Tech. Germ....49-89-140-9331	Tecmar.......................(216)349-0853	Volpe, Hank..............(410)256-3631
Seagate Tech. Singpore....65-227-2217	Tektronix (OR)............(503)685-4504	Vortex Systems............(412)322-3216
Searchlight Software... (216)631-9285	Tektronixs (CA).......... (408)685-4504	Wacom Technology..... (415)960-0236
Semware.....................(404)641-8968	Telebit.......................(408)745-3861	Walker,Richer & Quinn(206)324-2357
Shiva.........................(617)273-0023	Telepro Technologies..(403)347-3262	Wall Data, Inc..............(206)558-0392
Sierra On-Line............. (209)683-4463	Televideo Systems, Inc (408)954-8231	Wallsoft Systems..........(206)962-1923
Sigma Designs.............(510)770-0111	Telix Support.............. (919)481-9399	W. Disney Cmptr Sftwr (818)567-4027
Silicon Valley Cmptrs. .(415)967-8081	TelPro Technologies....(804)442-5867	Wangtek/Wang DAT.... (805)582-3620
Silverware................. (214)247-2177	Template Garden........ (212)627-5089	Wangtek/Wang DAT-US(805)582-3620
Sitka.........................(510)769-8774	Texas Instruments.......(512)250-6112	Wantree Development(913)441-0595
SLR Systems................ (412)282-2799	The Ryco Company.....(414)962-1097	Wayzata Technology.... (218)326-2939
SMS Technology...........(510)964-5700	TheSoft Programming..(415)581-3019	WCSC........................(713)568-6401
SofNet...................... (404)984-9926	Thomas-Conrad Corp..(512)836-8012	Weitek Corporation.... (408)522-7517
SoftArc, Inc................(416)609-2250	Thumper Technology.. (918)627-0059	Western Digital...........(717)753-1068
Softklone....................(904)878-9884	Thunderbyte USA........(302)732-6399	White Water Systems.. (708)328-9442
SoftLogic Solutions..... (603)644-5556	Tiara Computer Sys.....(415)966-8533	Whitewater Group......(708)328-9442
Softronics...................(719)593-9295	Timeline Software......(415)892-0408	Whole Counsel Mnstry(804)590-1659
Software Products Intl (619)450-2179	Timeslips Corporation.(508)768-7581	Willies Computer Soft.(713)568-6401
Software Security, Inc..(203)329-7263	Tool Technology Publ. (415)289-7414	Willow Peripherals......(718)993-2066
Software Support........ (508)439-9096	Tops Microsystems......(510)769-8774	WordPerfect Corp.......(801)225-4414
Software Ventures....... (510)849-1912	TopSoft Software.........(502)425-9941	WordStar International.(404)514-6332
Solectek Accessories... (619)450-6537	Toshiba America..........(714)837-4408	WordTech Systems, Inc(415)254-1141
Solutions Systems........(617)237-8530	Toshiba America Elec...(714)581-7600	Worldwide Video.........(201)491-5147
Sony (Dealer)..............(408)955-5107	Toshiba America, Inc...(714)837-2116	WWIV Software Serv...(210)631-5841
Sony-Desktop Library..(408)955-5107	Toshiba Printer Prods. .(714)538-3000	Wyse Technology.........(408)922-4400
Sony-Serv. Ctr. Loction..(408)955-5107	TouchStone Software..(714)969-0688	SBR Communication...(514)489-0445
Sound Source Unlmtd.(805)373-8589	Trantor Systems, Ltd....(408)945-7727	Xircom.......................(818)878-7618
Spectrum Holobyte......(510)522-8909	Traveling Software......(206)485-1736	XTree Company...........(805)546-9150
Spider Island Software.(714)730-5785	Trident Microsystems..(415)691-1016	XYQuest.....................(508)667-5669
Stac Electronics...........(619)431-5956	TriMark Eng.-Doorway.(615)675-3282	Z-Soft........................(404)427-1045
Standard Microsystem..(714)707-2481	Trio Information Sys... (919)846-4987	Zenith Data Systems... (708)808-2264
STB Systems, Inc.........(214)437-9615	TriSoft Inc...................(207)941-0805	Zenographics, Inc........(714)851-3860
Storage Dimension......(408)944-1220	Triton Technologies.... (908)855-9609	Zoneware....................(414)461-9702
Streamline Design........(905)793-1411	Trius.........................(508)794-0762	Zoom Telephonics.......(617)423-3733
Summit Memory Sys... (408)439-6774	Truevision...................(317)577-8783	ZyXEL USA.................(714)693-0762
Sun Country Software..(505)877-8354	Tseng Laboratories......(215)579-7536	
SunDisk Corporation.. (408)986-1186	TSR Systems...............(516)331-6682	
Sunrise Software.........(404)256-9525	Turbo Tax...................(619)453-5232	
Sunriver.....................(512)835-8082	TurboCom...................(503)482-2633	
Supermac Software.....(408)541-6190	Turtle Beach Systems..(717)845-4835	
Supra Corporation......(503)967-2444	U.S. Robotics...............(708)982-5092	
Swan Technologies......(814)237-6145	UltraStor Corporation. .(510)623-9091	
Sybex, Inc...................(510)523-3926	Unicom Software........(317)784-2147	
Sycom Design Sftwr...(313)772-6442	UniNova Service Corp.(509)925-3893	
Sydex.........................(503)683-1385	US Sage......................(417)331-7433	
SyDOS........................(408)994-4367	ValueStor.................... (408)945-8376	

DIRECTORY

Accton Technology
1962 Zanker Road
San Jose, CA 95112
(408)452-8900
(408)452-8988 Fax
(408)452-8828 BBS

Ace Technologies, Ltd.
592 Weddell Drive,
Suite 6
Sunnyvale, CA 94089
(408)734-0100
(408)734-3344 Fax
(408)734-8266 BBS
www.acetech.com

Acer America
2641 Orchard Parkway
San Jose, CA 95134
(800)848-ACER
(408)922-2933 Fax
(408)428-0140 BBS
http:\\www.acer.com\aac

Acma Computers, Inc.
47988 Fremont Blvd.
Fremont, CA 94538
(510)249-0560
(510)623-0818 Fax
(510)651-6211 BBS

Adaptec, Inc.
691 South Milpitas Blvd.
Milpitas, CA 95035
(408)945-8600
(408)262-2533 Fax
(408)945-7727 BBS
http:\\www.adaptec.com

Adtron Corporation
3050 S. Country Club Dr.,
Suite 24
Mesa, AZ 85210
(602)926-9324
(602)926-9359

Advanced Digital
Information Corp.
10201 Willows Road
Redmond WA 98052
(800)336-1233
(206)881-8004
(206)881-2296 Fax
(206)883-3211 BBS

Advanced Gravis
Computer Tech, Ltd
1790 Midway Lane
Bellingham WA 98226
(360)733-8472
(360)676-5679 Fax
(604)431-5927 BBSe

Advanced Microdevices
901 Thompson Place
Sunnyvale, CA 94088
(800)538-8450
(408)732-2400
http:\\www.amd.com

Allegro MicroSystems, Inc.
115 Northeast Cutoff,
Box 15036
Worchester, MA 01615
(508)853-5000
(508)853-5049 Fax

Alphatronix, Inc.
4022 Stirrup Creek Drive,
Suite 315
Duram, NC 27713
(919)544-0001
(919)544-4079 Fax

American Megatrends
6145-F Northbelt Pkwy.
Norcross, GA 30071
(770)246-8600
(770)246-8791 Fax
(770)246-8780 BBS
www.megatrends.com

AMP, Inc.
P.O. Box 3608
Mail Stop 38-03
Harrisburg, PA 17105
(800)522-6752
(717)564-0100
(717)986-7575 Fax
(800)522-6752 Faxback

AMS
1460 SW 3rd. Street,
Suite B-8
Pompono Beach, Fl 33069
(305)784-0900
(305)784-0904 Fax
http:\\www.gatenet\~ams

Analogic Corporation
8 Centennial Drive
Peabody, MA 01960
(800)446-8936
(508)977-3000
(508)532-6097 Fax

Ancot Corporation
115 Constitution Drive
Menlo Park, CA 94025
(415)322-5322
(415)322-0455 Fax
help@ancot.com

Antex Electronics Corp.
16100 South Figueroa Street
Gardena, CA 90248
(800)338-4231
(310)532-3092
(310)532-8509 Fax
(310)768-3947 BBS

Apex Data
6624 Owens Drive
Pleasanton, CA 94588-3334
(800)841-APEX
(510)416-5656
(510)416-0909 Fax
(510)416-0809/0814 BBS

Apple Computer, Inc.
20525 Mariani Avenue
Cupertino, CA 95014
(800)877-8221
(408)996-1010
(408)996-0275 Fax
(800)505-0171 Faxback
http://www.apple.com

Applied Concepts, Inc.
9130 S.W. Pioneer Court
Wilsonville, OR 97070
(800)624-6808
(503)685-9300
(503)685-9099 Fax

APS Technologies
6131 Deramus
P.O. Box 4987
Kansas City, MO 64120
(800)235-8935
http://www.apstech.com

Ariel Corporation
433 River Road
Highland Park, NJ 08904
(908)249-2900
(908)249-2123 Fax
(908)249-224 BBS

AST Research, Inc.
16215 Alton Parkway
P.O. Box 19658
Irvine, CA 92718
(800)876-4278
(714)727-4141
(714)727-9355 Fax
(800)926-1278 Faxback
(714)727-4723 BBS

AT&T Global Info Solutions
1700 S. Patterson Blvd.
Dayton, OH 45479
(513)445-5000
(503)445-4732 Fax
(800)692-8872 BBS

DIRECTORY

AT & T Microelectronics
555 Union Blvd.
Allentown, PA 18103
(800)372-2447
(610)712-4106 Fax
(610)712-3771 & 3772BBS
http:\\www.att.com

AT & T Paradyne
8545 126th Avenue N
Largo, Fl 34649
(800)482-3333
(813)530-2103 Fax

Atmel Corporation
2125 O'Neal Drive
San Jose, CA 95131
(408)441-0311
(408)436-4300 Fax

ATTO Technology Inc.
40 Hazelwood Drive,
Suite 106
Amherst, NTY 14228
(716)691-1999
(716)691-9353 Fax

Austin Direct, Inc.
10300 Metric Blvd.
Austin, TX 78758
(800)752-4171
(512)339-3570 Fax
(512)339-3583 BBS
urlhttp://www.ipctechinc.com

Award Software
International
777 Middlefield Road
Mt. View, CA 94043
(415)968-4433
(415)968-0274 Fax
(415)968-0249 BBS

Axonix Corporation
844 South 200 East
Salt Lake City, UT 84111
(800)866-9797
(801)521-9797
(801)521-9798 Fax
(801)521-2084 BBS

Aztech Labs Inc.
47811 Warm Springs Blvd.
Fremont, CA 94539
(800)886-8859
(510)623-8988
(510)623-8989 Fax
(510)623-8933 BBS

B & C Microsystems, Inc.
750 N. Pastoria Avenue
Sunnyvale, CA 94086
(408)730-5511
(408)730-5521 Fax
bcm@cup.portal.com

Belkin Components
1303 Walnut Parkway
Compton, CA 90220
(800)2-BELKIN
(310)898-1100
(310)898-1111 Fax

Berg-Electronics
825 Old Trail Road
Etters, PA 17319
(800)237-2374
(717)938-7620 Fax

Bi-Tech Enterprises Inc.
10 Carlough Road
Bohemia, NY 11716
(516)567-8155
(516)567-8266
(516)567-8267 BBS

Blackhole Tech. Corp.
225 East Street
Winchester, Ma 01890
(800)227-1688
(617)721-7690

Blue Planet
1575 Tenaka Place,
Suite W3
Sunnyvale, CA 94087
(408)732-9935 Fax
b-planet@ix.netcom.com

Boca Research
1377 Clint Moore Road
Boca Raton, FL 33487
(407)997-2163
(407)241-1601 Fax Back

Boca Raton Technical Service
1000 NW 51st Street
Boca Raton, FL 33429
(407)443-2000
(407)982-4288 Fax
(407)241-1601 BBS

Buffalo Inc.
2805 19th Street S.E.
Salem, OR 97302
(800)345-2356
(503)585-3414
(503)585-4505 Fax
(503)585-5797 BBS

BusLogic Inc.
4151 Burton Drive
Santa Clara, CA 95054
(800)707-SCSI
(408)492-9090
(408)492-1542
(408)492-1984 BBS

Calluna Technology
1762 Technology Drive
San Jose, CA 95110
(408)453-4753
(408)453-0427 Fax

Canon U. S. A. Inc.
1 Canon Plaza
Lake Success, NY 11042
(516)488-6700

Carvey DataBook, Inc.
112 Prospect Street
Babcock Hall
Ithaca, NY 11850
(716)889-4204
(716)889-2593 Fax

Catalyst Semiconductor
2231 Calle De Luna
Santa Clara, CA 95054
(408)748-7700
(408)980-8209 Fax

CD Connection
5805 State Bridge Road,
Suite G303
Deluth, GA 30155
(770)446-1332
(770)446-9164 Fax

Centennial Technologies
37 Manning Road, Ste. 1
Billerica, MA 01821
(508)670-0646
(508)670-9025 Fax

Century Microelectronics
4800 Great America Pkwy.,
Suite 308
Santa Clara, CA 95054
(408)748-7788
(408)748-8688 Fax
http:\\www.centurymicro.com

Chaplet Systems USA, Inc.
252 North Wolfe Road
Sunnyvale, CA 94086
(408)732-7950
(408)732-6159 Tech Support
(408)732-6050 Fax

Chinon America, Inc.
615 Hawaii Avenue
Torrence, CA 90503
(800)441-0222
(310)533-0274
(310)533-1727 Fax
(310)320-4160 BBS

CIM Engineering (USA)
1291 E. Hillsdale Blvd.
Foster City, CA 94404
(415)578-9998
(415)578-0259 Fax

Cirrus Logic
3100 W. Warren
Femont, CA 94538
(510)623-8300
(510)226-2180 Fax
(510)440-9080 BBS

CMS Enhancements, Inc.
2722 Michelson
Irvine, CA 92715
(800)555-1671
(714)222-6000
(714)437-0099 Fax

Colorado Memory Systems
800 S. Taft Avenue
Loveland, CO 80537
(303)669-8000
(970)667-0997 Fax
(970)635-0650 BBS
http://www.corp.hp.com

Commstar, Inc.
6440 Flying Cloud Drive
Eden Prairie, MN 55344
(612)941-8188
(612)941-0971 FAX

Computer Age, Inc.
9443 Georgia Avenue
Silver Spring, MD 20910
(800)622-3384
(301)588-6565
(301)587-2132 Fax

Computer Boards
125 High Street
Mansfield, MA 02048
(508)261-1123
(508)261-1094 Fax
info@comp-4.com

Conner Peripherals
3081 Zanker Road
San Jose, CA 95134-2128
(800)4-CONNER
(408)456-4500
(408)456-4501 Fax
(408)456-4415 BBS

Contemporary Cybernetics
11846 Rock Landing
Newport News, VA 23606
(804)873-9000
(804)873-8836 Fax

Control Concepts Inc.
8500 Executive Park Ave.
Fairfax, VA 22031
(800)922-9259
(703)876-6444
(703)876-6416 Fax

Core International
Technical Support
6500 E. Rogers Circle
Boca Raton, FL 33487
(407)997-6033
(407)997-6202 Fax
(407)241-2929 BBS

Corel Corporation
1600 Carling Avenue
Ottawa, Ontario, Canada
K12 8R7
(800)836-7274
(613)728-8200
(613)7728-9790 Fax
(613)728-4752 BBS

Corporate Systems Center
1294 Hammerwood Avenue
Sunnyvale, CA 94089
(408)734-3475
(408)745-1816 Fax
(408)541-8455 BBS
www.corpsys.com

Creative Labs, Inc.
1901 McCarthy Blvd.
Milpitas, CA 95035
(800)998-5227
(408)428-6600
(408)428-6611 Fax
(405)742-6660 BBS

Cristie Electronics Ltd.
Bonds Mill, Stonehouse
Gloucestershire GL10 3RG
United Kingdom
453823611
453825768 Fax

Curtis, Inc.
418 W. County Road D
Saint Paul, MN 55112
(612)631-9512
(612)631-9508 Fax

Cutting Edge
8191 Center Street
La Mesa, CA 91941
(619)667-7888
(619)66707890 Fax
CUT EDGE@eworld.com EMail
www.cuttingedge.com

Data General Corporation
4400 Computer Drive
Westboro, MA 01580
(508)898-5000
(508)336-1319 Fax

Data I/O
10525 Willows Road NE
P.O. Box 97046
Redmond, WA 98073-9746
(800)332-8246
(206)881-6444
(206)881-6856 Fax

Datalight
307 N. Olympic Avenue,
Suite 201
Arlington, WA 98223
(360)435-8086
(360)435-0253 Fax
(360)435-8734 BBS

Datquest
1290 Ridder Park Drive
San Jose, CA 95131
(408)437-8000
(408)437-0292 Fax

Data Technology Corp. (DTC)
1515 Center Point Drive
Milpitas, CA 95035
(408)942-4000
(408)942-4052 Fax
(408)942-4005 Faxback
(408)942-4010 BBS

Denon America, Inc.
222 New Road
Parsippany, NJ 07054
(201)575-7810
(201)808-1608 Fax
(201)575-2532 Fax

Digi-Data Corporation
8580 Dorsey Run Road
Jessup, MD 20794
(301)498-0200
(301)498-0771

Disk Emulation Services
3080 Oak Mead Village Dr.
Santa Clara, CA 95051
(408)727-5497
(408)727-5497 Fax

Disk Technologies, Inc.
925 S. Senoran Blvd.,
Suite 114
Winterpark, FL 32792
(800)553-0337
(407)645-0001
(407)671-6606 Fax
(407)671-6099 BBS

Distr. Processing Technology
(DPT)
140 Candace Drive,
Maitland, FL 32751
(800)322-4378
(407)830-5522
(407)260-5366 Fax
(407)831-6432 BBS

DMA Technologies, Inc.
601 Pine Avenue
Goleta, CA 93117
(800)223-9443
(805)964-0733
(805)964-0734 Fax

ECCS Inc.
One Shelia Drive,
Building 6A
Tinton Falls, NJ 07724
(800)322-7462
(908)747-6995
(908)747-6542 Fax

Enhance Memory Products
18730 Oxnard Street
Tarzana, CA 91356
(800)343-0100
(818)343-3066
(818)343-1436 Fax

Everex Systems Inc.
5020 Brandin Court
Fremont, CA 94538
(800)821-0806
(510)498-1111
(510)683-2800 Faxback
(510)226-9694 BBS

Exabyte Corporation
1685 68th Street
Boulder, CO 80301
(800)EXABYTE
(303)442-4333
(303)447-7170 Fax
(303)447-7100 BBS

EXP Memory
12C Mauchly
Irvine, CA 92718
(714)453-1020
(714)453-1319 Fax
(516)496-3753 BBS

FarPoint Communications
104 East Avenue K4, Ste. F
Lancaster, CA 93535
(805)726-4420
(805)726-4438 Fax
www.fapo.com

FDK America, Inc.
2270 North First Street
San Jose, CA 95131
(408)432-8331
(408)435-7478 Fax

Fintec Peripheral
Solutions
15520 Rockfield Blvd.,
Suite 1
Irvine, CA 92718
(714)768-8219
(714)768-2986 Fax

Flexstar Technology
213 Hammond Avenue
Fremont, CA 94539
(510)440-0170
(510)440-0177 Fax

Focus Microsystems
1735 North First Street,
Suite 307
San Jose, CA 95112
(408)436-2336
(408)436-2348 Fax

FOREX Computer Corp.
1999 Concourse Drive
San Jose, CA 95131
(408)955-9280
(408)955-9611 Fax
(408)955-0938 BBS

Foxconn International, Inc.
930 West Maude Avenue
Sunnyvale, CA 94086
(408)749-1228
(408)749-1266 Fax

Fujitsu America, Inc.
3055 Orchard Drive
San Jose, CA 95134
(408)432-1300
(408)432-1818 Fax

Fuji Electronics Company
47520 Westinghouse
Fremont, CA 94538
(510)438-9700
(510)438-9753 Fax

FutureDomainCorporation
2801 McGaw Avenue
Irvine, CA 92714
(714)253-0400
(714)253-0913 Fax
(714)253-0432 BBS

FWB, Inc.
1555 Adams Drive
Menlo Park, CA 94025
(415)325-4392
(415)833-4622
fwb.com

Gateway 2000
610 Gateway Drive
North Sioux City, SD
57049
(800)846-2000
(605)232-2000
(605)232-2023 Fax

Genoa Systems Corp.
75 East Trimble Road
San Jose, CA 95131
(800)934-3662
(408)432-9090
(408)434-0997 Fax
(408)943-1231 BBS

Greystone Peripherals
130-A Knowles Drive
Los Gatos, CA 95030
(800)600-5710
(408)866-4739
(408)866-8328 Fax
(408)866-6938 BBS

Hayes Microcomputer
P.O. Box 105203
Atlanta, GA 30348
(404)441-1617
(404)441-1213 Fax
(800)429-3739 Fax Back

HCo. Computer Products
16812 Hale Avenue
Irvine, CA 92714
(800)726-2477
(714)833-3222
(714)833-3389 Fax

Hirose Electric, Inc.
2688 Westhill Court
Simi Valley, CA 93065
(805)522-7958
(805)522-3217 Fax

DIRECTORY

IAWA America, Inc.
19850 East Business Pkwy.
Walnut, CA 91789
(909)468-5690
(909)468-1810 Fax

IAWA, Inc.
Sales Office
800 Corporate Drive
Mahwah, NJ 07430
(201)512-3600
(201)512-3704 Fax

IBM Microelectronics
1000 River Street
Essex Junction, VT 05452
(802)769-6774

IBM PC Help Center
Route 100
Somers, NY 10589
(800)772-2227
(800)426-4329 Fax

Industrial Computer Source
9950 Barnes Canyon Road
San Diego, CA 92121
(800)523-2320
(619)271-9340
(619)677-0898 Fax

Intel Corporation
1900 Prairie City Road
Folsom, CA 95630
(800)879-4683
(916)356-5033 Fax

Interface Data Inc.
600 West Cummings Park,
Suite 3100
Woburn, MA 01801
(800)370-DATA
(617)938-6333
(617)938-0626 Fax

Interphase Corporation
13800 Senlac
Dallas, TX 75234
(800)327-8638
(214)919-9000
(214)919-9200
http://www.iphase.com

Iomega Corporation
1821 West 4000 South
Roy, UT 84067
(800)777-4045
(804)778-1000
(801)778-3450 Fax
(801)778-5763 Faxback
(801)392-9819 BBS

JAE Electronics
142 Technology Drive,
Building 100
Irvine, CA 92718-2401
(714)753-2600
(714)753-2699 Fax

Jets Cybernetics
535 Ramona Street,
The Penthouse
Palo Alto, CA 94301
(415)322-7070
(415)327-5387 Fax

Kaitech Engineering
9051 Pelican Avenue
Fountain Valley, CA 92708
(714)964-6405
(714)965-9935 Fax

Kingston Electronics,
Engineering Division
17600 Newhope Street
Fountain Valley, CA 92708
(800)435-0642
(714)435-2699
(714)534-2699 Fax

Kyocera Electronics,
Engineering Division
1321 Harbor Bay Pkwy.
Alameda, CA 94501
(800)245-8979-Tech Support
(800)367-7437
(510)748-6680

La Cie, Ltd
8700 SW Creekside Place
Beaverton, OR 97008
(800)999-0143
(503)520-9000
(503)520-9100 Fax
www.lacie.com/~lacie

Laura Technologies Inc.
106 South 54th Street
Chandler, AZ 85226
(602)940-9800
(602)940-0222 Fax
(602)940-1050 BBS

Legacy Storage Systems Inc.
138 River Road
Andover, MA 01810
(800)966-6442
(508)689-9004 Fax
(905)475-5793 BBS

Liberty Systems
120 Saratoga Avenue,
Suite 82
Santa Clara, CA 95051
(408)983-1127
(408)243-2885 Fax

Linksys
16811A Millikan Avenue
Irvine, CA 92714
(714)261-1288
(714)261-8868 Fax
(714)222-5111/5110 BBS

Logitech Inc.
6505 Kaiser Drive
Fremont, CA 94555
(510)795-8500
(510)792-8901 Fax
(800)245-0000 Faxback
(510)795-0408 BBS

Loviél Computer Corp.
5599 W. 78th Street
Minneapolis, MN 55439
(800)688-3696
(612)828-6881 Fax
http://www.loviel.com/

MagicRAM, Inc.
1850 Beverly Blvd.
Los Angeles, CA 90057
(213)413-9999
(213)413-0828 Fax

Maxell Corporation
22-08 Route 208
Fair Lawn, NJ 07410
(201)794-4900
(201)796-8790 Fax

Maxim Integrated Products
120 San Gabriel Drive
Sunnyvale, CA 94086
(408)737-7600
(408)737-7194 Fax

Maxtech GVC
400 Commons Way
Rockaway, NJ 07876
(201)586-3008
(201)586-3308 Fax

Maxtor Corporation
211 River Oaks Pkwy.
San Jose, CA 95134
(800)2-MAXTOR
(408)432-1700
(408)432-4510 Fax
(303)678-2222 BBS

Media Integration Inc.
3949 Research Park Court
Suite 190
Soquel, CA 95073
(800)824-7385
(408)475-9400
(408)475-0110 Fax

Megabit Communications
90 W. County Road C
St. Paul, MN 55117
(800)886-6778
(612)481-0921
(612)481-1538 Fax

Mega Drive Systems
489 S. Robertson Blvd.
Beverly Hills, CA 90211
(800)322-4744
(310)556-1663
(310)347-8118 Fax

Micro Design International
6985 University Blvd.
Winter Park, FL 32792
(800)228-0891
(407)677-8333
(407)677-8365 Fax
(407)677-4854 BBS

MicroNet Technology Inc.
80 Technology
Irvine, CA 92718
(714)453-6100
(714)453-6101 Fax

Micropolis Corporation
21211 Nordhoff Street
Chatsworth, CA 91311
(800)395-3748
(818)709-3300
(818)709-3325
(818)709-3310 BBS

Mitsubishi Electronics
1050 E. Arques Avenue
Sunnyvale, CA 94086
(408)730-5900
(408)730-4972 Fax

Molex, Inc.
2222 Wellington Court
Lisle, IL 60532
(708)969-4550
(708)969-1352 Fax

Morton Management, Inc.
12079 Tech Road
Silver Spring, MD 20904
(301)622-5600
(301)622-5438 Fax

Motorola NewsCard
(Div. of PCSF)
3301 Quantum Blvd.
Boyton Beach, FL 33426
(800)542-7882
www.mot.com/MIMS/PPG

Motorola UDS
5000 Bradford Drive
Huntsville, AL 35805
(800)451-2369
(205)430-8067
(508)261-1058 BBS

Mountaingate Data Systems
9393 Gateway Drive
Reno, NV 89511
(702)851-9393
(702)851-5533 Fax

Mountain Network Solutions
360 El Pueblo Road
Scotts Valley, CA 95066
(800)458-0300
(408)438-6650
(408)438-7623 Fax
(408)438-2665

Multimedia Systems
(Div. of Hitachi)
401 W. Artesia Blvd.
Compton, CA 90220
(800)369-0422
(310)537-8383

Multitech Design & Test
1152 Morse Avenue
Sunnyvale, CA 94089
(408)734-3222
(408)734-3274

Multitech Systems
2205 Woodale Drive
Mounds View, MN 55112
(800)328-9717
(612)785-3500
(612)785-9874 Fax
(800)392-2432 BBS

Mustek Inc.
1702 McGaw Avenue
Irvine, CA 92714
(714)250-8855
(714)250-3372 Fax
(714)250-4263 BBS

Mylex Corporation
34551 Ardenwood Blvd.
Fremont, CA 94555
(800)77-MYLEX
(510)796-6100
(510)745-7715 Fax
(510)793-3491 BBS

National Instruments
6504 Bridge Point Pkwy.
Austin, TXC 78730-5039
(512)794-0100
(512)794-8411 Fax
(800)327-3077 BBS
www.natnst.com

National Semiconductor
1111 West Bardin Road
Arlington, TX 76017
(800)272-9959
(817)468-6935 Fax
www.natsemi.com

NDC Communications
2180 Bering Drive
San Jose, CA 95131
(408)428-9108
(408)428-9109 Fax
(408)428-1143 BBS

NEC Technologies
1414 Massachusetts Avenue
Boxborough, MA 01719
(800)388-8888
(508)264-8673 Fax
(800)366-0476 FaxBack
(508)635-4706 BBS

New Media Corporation
1 Technology, Building A
Irvine, CA 92718
(800)453-0550
(714)453-0100
(714)453-0114 Fax
(714)789-5212 Faxback
(714)453-0214 BBS
Compuserve:gonewmedia

Novacor, Inc.
1841 Zanker Road
San Jose, CA 95112
(408)441-6500
(408)441-6811 Fax
http//www.novas.com

Ocean Microsystems
246 E. Hacienda Avenue
Campbell, CA 95008
(408)374-8300

Oki Semiconductor
785 North Mary Avenue
Sunnyvale, CA 94086
(408)737-6372
(408)720-1918 Fax

Olson Computer Products
1903 North Austin Street
Seguin, TX 78155
(210)379-7000
(210)379-4921

Optima Technology Corp.
17526 Van Karman
Irvine, CA 92714
(714)476-0515
(714)476-0613 Fax
(714)476-0626 BBS

Orca Technology Corp.
1751 Fox Drive
San Jose, CA 95131
(408)441-1111
(408)441-1102 Fax

Pacific Magtron, Inc.
568-8 Weddell Drive
Sunnyvale, CA 94089
(408)828-2822
(408)744-1188 Fax

Panasonic Industrial Co.
2 Panasonic Way, B7C7
Secaucus, NJ 07094
(800)848-3979
(201)348-5272
(201)392-6361 Fax

Parity Systems Inc.
110 Knowles Drive
Las Gatos, CA 95030
(800)514-4080
(408)378 1000
(408)378-1022

PCs Computer Products
1350 Ridder Park Drive
San Jose, CA 95131
(408)441-6174
(408)453-7667 Fax

Pen National, Inc.
2351 South 2300 West
Salt Lake City, UT 84119
(800)8-PCMCIA
(801)973-6090
(801)973-4550 Fax

Perceptive Solutions Inc.
2700 Flora Street
Dallas, TX 75201
(800)486-3278
(214)954-1774
(214)953-1774 Fax
(214)954-1856 BBS

Peripheral Land Inc. (PLI)
47421 Bayside Parkway
Fremont, CA 94538
(800)288-8754-out of CA
(800)788-9440-in CA
(510)657-2211
(510)683-9713 Fax
(510)651-5948 BBS

Personal Computer
Peripherals Corp. (PCPC)
4710 Eisenhower Blvd.,
Building A-4
Tampa, FL 33634
(800)622-2888

Philips Consumer Electronics
Philips LMS
4425 Arrowswest Drvie
Colorado Springs, CO 80907
(800)777-5674
(719)593-7900
(719)593-4597 Fax
(719)593-4081 BBS

Plexstor Corporation
4255 Burton Drive
Santa Clara, CA 95054
(800)886-3935
(408)980-1838
(408)980-1010 Fax
(408)986-1569 BBS

Prima Storage Solutions
3350 Scott Blvd.,
Building 7
Santa Clara, CA 95054
(800)73-PRIMA
(408)727-2600
(408)727-2435 Fax

Procomp USA Inc.
6777 Engle Road
Cleveland, OH 44130
(216)234-6387
(216)234-2233 Fax
(216)234-6581 BBS

Procom Technology Inc.
2181 Dupont Drive
Irvine, CA 92715
(800)800-8600
(714)852-1000
(714)852-1221 Fax
(714)852-1305 BBS

Quantum
500 McCarthy Blvd.
Milpitas, CA 95035
(408)894-4000
(408)894-3218 Fax
(800)434-7532 Faxback
(408)894-3214 BBS

Relax Technologies Inc.
3101 Whipple Road
Union City, CA 94587
(510)471-6112
(510)471-6267 Fax

DIRECTORY

Relisys Corporation
320 S. Milpitas Blvd.
Milpitas, CA 95035
(800)783-2333
(408)945-9000
(408)945-0587 Fax
(408)946-7027 BBS

SC&T International, Inc.
3837 E. LaSalle Street
Phoenix, AZ 85040
(800)760-9004
(602)470-1334
(602)470-1507 Fax

Seagate Technology Inc.
920 Disc Drive
Scotts Valley, CA 95066
(800)468-DISC
(408)438-6550
(408)429-6356 Fax
(408)438-8771 BBS

Shaffstall Corporation
7901 E. 88th Street
Indianapolis, IN 42656
(317)842-2077
(317)842-8294 Fax

Sony Electronics Inc.
Computer Peripherals Prod.
3300 Zanker Road
San Jose, CA 95134
(408)432-0190
(408)432-0253 Fax
(408)955-5505 Faxback
(408)955-5107 BBS

Storage Dimensions Inc.
1656 McCarthy Blvd.
Milpitas, CA 95035
(408)954-0710
(408)944-1203 Fax
(408)944-1220 BBS

Sun Microsystems, Inc.
2550 Garcia Avenue
Mountain View, CA 94043
(800)USA-4SUN
http://www.sun.com

Symbios Logic Incorporated
1635 Aero Plaza Drive
Colorado Springs, CO 80916
(716)596-5795
(719)573-3289 Fax
(719)573-3562 BBS-driver
(719)574-0424 BBS-SCSI
ftp.hmpd.com

Teac America Inc.
7733 Telegraph Road
Montebello, CA 90640
(213)726-0303
(213)727-7672 Fax
(213)272-7629 Faxback

Tecmar Inc.
6224 Cochran Road
Solon, OH 44139
(800)422-2587
(216)349-0600
(216)349-0851 Fax
(216)349-2997 Faxback
(216)349-0853 BBS

Tekram Technology
(Alpha Research Corp.)
P.O. Box 27140
Austin, TX 78755
(512)418-0220
(512)418-0720 Fax
(512)418-0821 BBS

Tulin Technology
2156-H O'Toole Avenue
San Jose, CA 95131
(408)432-9057
(408)943-0782 Fax

UltraStor Corporation
13766 Alton Parkway,
Suite 144
Irvine, CA 92718
(714)581-4100
(714)581-4102 Fax
(714)581-4541 Faxback
(714)581-4125 BBS

Wangtek Inc.
6225 Cochran Road
Solon, OH 44139
(800)422-2587
(216)349-0600
(216)349-0851 Fax
(216)349-2997 Faxback
(216)349-0853 BBS

Western Automation Labs Inc.
1700 N. 55th Street
Boulder, CO 80301
(800)833-1132
(303)449-6400
(303)939-8844 Fax

Western Digital Corp.
8105 Irvine Center Drive
Irvine, CA 92718
(800)832-4778
(714)932-5000
(714)932-6498 Fax
(714)932-4300 Faxback
(714)753-1038/1234 BBS
http://www.wdc.com

Winchester Systems Inc.
400 W. Cummings Park
Woburn, MA 01801
(617)933-8500
(617)933-6174 Fax

Xirlink Inc.
4118 Clipper Court
Fremont, CA 94538
(510)770-5188
(510)770-5189 Fax
(510)770-5186 BBS

GLOSSARY

A-CABLE   A 50-wire cable used for 8-bit SCSI-1 buses. There are two types of A-cable connectors: high- and low-density. The low-density A-cable connector is also known as a Centronics-type connector.

ACCESS   The process of obtaining data from, or transferring data to a storage device, register or RAM (i.e. accessing a memory location).

ACCESS TIME   Time required to perform an ACCESS. Usages, i.e.: 1) seek to location on a disk, 2) amount of time to read or write to a memory location, 3) the time to position to the correct location in a disk drive. Access time is often defined as the time from the leading edge of the first step pulse received to SEEK COMPLETE (including settling). The additional time required before a read or write is referred to as "latency". A more realistic definition of total access time is the sum of SEEK, LATENCY and SETTLING times.

ACTIVE TERMINATION   A type of termination used to reduce bus noise, particularly on the SCSI bus. Active terminators use less power than passive terminators, and are recommended when using long SCSI cables.

ACTIVE TERMINATOR   A terminator that can compensate for variations in the terminator power supplied by the host adapter through means of a built-in voltage regulator. Also see forced-perfect terminator; passive terminator.

ACTUATOR   The two basic types of actuators are steppers and voice coils. Open-loop steppers are obsolete, except in floppy disks because they cannot achieve positioning accuracy and speed as high as closed-loop voice coil systems. For more information on actuators, see the Basic Drive Operation section. *See* HEAD POSITIONER.

ADAPTER   A card that communicates with and controls a device or system.

ADD-ON   Something added to the computer to expand it's functionality. Commonly refers to cards that are plugged into the computer.

ADDRESS (physical)   A specific location in memory where a byte, or other unit of data like a disk sector is stored. Each area on a disk is given a unique address consisting of three components: cylinder number, sector number, and head number. CYLINDER ADDRESSING is accomplished by assigning numbers to the disk's surface concentric circles (cylinders). The cylinder number specifies the radial address component of the data area. SECTOR ADDRESSING is accomplished by numbering the data records (sectors) from an index that defines the reference angular position of the disks. Index records are then counted by reading their ADDRESS MARKS. HEAD ADDRESSING is accomplished by vertically numbering the disk surfaces, usually starting with the bottom-most disk data surface. For example, the controller might send the binary equivalent of the decimal number 610150 to instruct the drive to access data at cylinder 610, sector 15, and head 0.

ADDRESS MARK   Two byte address at the beginning of both the ID field and the data field of the track format. The first byte is the "A1" data pattern, the second byte is used to specify either an ID field or a data field.

ADJUSTABLE INTERLEAVE   Interleaving permits access to more than one memory module, i.e., if one memory module contains odd-numbered address and another even-numbered address, they can both be accessed simultaneously for storage. If the interleave is adjustable, the user may select which ranges or areas are to be accessed each time.

ADVANCED SCSI PROGRAMMING INTERFACE   Formerly called the Adaptec SCSI Programming Interface, ASPI was developed by Adaptec as a standard way for programs to send commands and data between SCSI host adapters and devices. ASPI standards exist for DOS, Windows, Win 95, Win NT, OS/2 and Novell.

ANSI   American National Standards Institute. The organization that promotes standards for hardware and software including those used in PCs. SCSI is an ANSI standard.

API Application Programming Interface. A software module that provides a consistent set of commands that programs can use to perform tasks. ASPI and CAM are examples of SCSI APIs.

APPLICATION PROGRAM A sequence of programmed instructions that tell the computer how to perform an end task (i.e. accounting, word processing or other work for the computer system user). To use a program, it must first be loaded into MAIN MEMORY from a floppy diskette or hard disk.

AREAL DENSITY Bit density (bits per inch, or BPI) multiplied by track density (tracks per inch, or TPI), or bits per square inch of the disk surface. Bit density is measured around a track (circumference around a disk), and track density is radially measured.

ASCII American Standard for Coded Information Interchange.

ASME American Society of Mechanical Engineers.

ASPI *See* ADVANCED SCSI PROGRAMMING INTERFACE.

ASYNCHRONOUS DATA Data sent usually in parallel mode without a clock pulse. Time intervals between transmitted bits may be of unequal lengths.

ASYNCHRONOUS TRANSFER A method of sending data that requires an acknowledgment from the receiver for each byte of data that is sent before the next on is sent. Asynchronous transfers are slower than synchronous transfers.

AT INTERFACE Disk drive interface on the IBM PC-AT computer and compatibles, sometimes called the IDE (Integrated Drive Electronics Interface).

ATAPI/IDE An extended command set standard which permits CD-ROM drives, tape drives, and other non-hard drive peripherals to share the IDE bus. ATAPI commands are modeled after SCSI standard commands.

AUTOMATIC BACK UP OF FILES This gives a user the security to make changes to a file without worrrying about accidentally destroying it; there is always another copy. One weakness of this method is that files take up twice the room on a disk.

AUTODETECTION   The ability of the computer to check the identity and configuration of a device without user intervention.

AUXILIARY MEMORY   Memory other than main memory; generally a mass storage subsystem, it can include disk drives, backup tape drives, controllers and buffer memory. Typically, AUXILIARY MEMORY is non-volatile.

AUXILIARY STORAGE DEVICE   Devices, generally magnetic tape and magnetic disk, on which data can be stored for use by computer programs. Also known as secondary storage.

AVERAGE ACCESS TIME   Average track access time, calculated from the end of the CONTROLLER   commands to access a drive, to drive Seek complete time averaged over all the possible track locations at the start ACCESS, and over all possible data track ADDRESSES. Typically, the minimum average access time including carriage settling for open loop actuators is less than 85 ms, and for voice coil disk drives is less than 40 ms. As technology improves these times will continue to decrease.

AZIMUTH   The angular distance in the horizontal plane, usually measured as an angle from true track location.

B-CABLE   A 68-wire cable used for 16-bit SCSI-2 buses.

BACKUP DEVICE   Disc or tape drive used with a fixed Winchester disk drive to make copies of files or other data for off line storage, distribution or protection against accidental data deletion from the Winchester drive, or against drive failure.

BACKUP FILE   File copies made on another removable media device (disk, tape or sometimes a remote hard disk system) and kept to ensure recovery of data lost due to equipment failure, human errors, updates, disasters and the like.

BACKWARD COMPATABILITY   The ability of newer technology to work with older technology without any modification.

BAUD RATE   A variable unit of data transmission speed equal to one bit per second.

BBS   *See* BULLETIN BOARD SYSTEM.

BCAI   Byte Count After Index. Used in defect mapping to indicate the position of defects with relation to index.

BDOS   The Basic Disk Operating System (BDOS) controls the organization of data on a disk. BDOS is usually pronounced "B-DOS".

BI-DIRECTIONAL BUS   A bus that may carry information in either direction but not in both simultaneously, i.e. the SCSI data bus.

BINARY   A number system like the decimal numbers, but using 2 as its base and having only the two digits 0 (zero) and 1 (one). It is used in computers because digital logic can only determine one of two states - "OFF" and "ON". Digital data is equivalent to a binary number.

BIOS   Basic Input/Output System. Software stored in a chip used for a variety of purposes. In a PC, the BIOS contains code that communicates with devices such as the floppy drive, keyboard and video output.

BIOS ADDRESS   The memory address that is used to access code stored in the BIOS chip.

BIT   Binary digit. The smallest unit of data used by digital computes and devices. A bit can be either on or off. The two states are referred to as 1 and 0, true and false, high and low, to name a few.

BIT CELL LENGTH   Physical dimension of the bit cell in direction of recording along the disk circumference of a track.

BIT CELL TIME   The time required to pass one bit of information between the controller and the drive. Cell time is the inverse of the drive's data rate; nominally 200 nsec for 5 Mhz drives.

BIT DENSITY   Expressed as "BPI" (Bits Per Inch), bit density defines how many bits can be written onto one inch of track on a disk surface. It is usually specified for "worst case", which is the inner track. Data is the densest in the inner tracks where track circumferences are the smallest.

BIT JITTER   The time difference between the leading edge of read and the center of the data window. A source of errors in hard disks. Bit Jitter is caused by spindle speed variations, electrical noise, and mechanical vibrations.

BIT SHIFT   A data recording effect, which results when adjacent 1's written on magnetic disks repel each other. The "worst case" is at the inner cylinder where bits are closest together. BIT SHIFT is also called pulse crowding.

BLOCK   A group of Bytes handled, stored and accessed as a logical data unit, such as an individual file record. Typically, one block of data is stored as one physical sector of data on a disk drive. Normally a 512 byte sector in most SCSI devices.

BOOT   Transfer of a disk operating system program from storage on diskette or hard disk drive to computer's working memory. Also called BOOTUP.

BUFFER   A temporary data storage area that compensates for a difference in data transfer rates and/or data processing rates between sender and receiver.

BUFFERED SEEK   A feature of the ST412 INTERFACE. In buffered mode head motion is postponed until a string of step pulses can be sent to the drive. These pulses represent the number of tracks that the head is to be stepped over and are sent much faster than the heads can move. The pulses are saved or buffered, then the optimum head movement to the correct track is performed.

BUILT-IN   A peripheral or device that is manufactured as a part of the computer, not added by the user.

BULLETIN BOARD SYSTEM   A computer or group of computers that provide services such as E-Mail and file transfer via modem or the Internet. These are commercial (CompuScrve, America Online, Prodigy) as well as private. Also called BBS.

BURST SPEED   The rate at which data can be transferred for a short period of time. Burst speeds are generally higher than sustained speeds.

BUS   A length of parallel conductors that forms a major interconnection route between the computer system CPU and it's peripheral subsystems. Depending on it's design, a bus may carry data to and from a peripheral's addresses, power and other related signals. ISA, EISA, VL-Bus and PCI are examples of PC buses. SCSI is also a bus.

BUS MASTERING   A method of transferring data through a bus in which the device takes over the bus and directly controls the transfer of data to the computer's memory. Bus mastering is a method of DMA transfer. Also known as first-parity DMA.

BUS SLOTS   Also known as expansion slots or simply slots, bus slots are connectors inside the computer that are used for attaching add-on cards and devices to a bus.

BYTE   A sequence of adjacent BINARY digits or BITS considered as a unit, 8 bits in length. One byte is sufficient to define all the alphanumeric characters. There are 8 BITS in 1 BYTE. The storage capacity of a disk drive is commonly measured in MEGABYTES, which is the total number of bits storable, divided by eight million.

CACHE MEMORY   Cache Memory allows the system to load bytes of frequently used data from the hard disk to memory. The system may then refer to memory for information instead of going back to the hard disk, thereby increasing the processing speed.

CAM   Common Access Method. The proposed ANSI software interface for SCSI devices and a part of the SCSI-3 standard.

CAPACITY   Amount of memory (measured in megabytes) which can be stored in a disk drive. Usually given as formatted. *See* FORMAT OPERATION.

CARRIAGE ASSEMBLY   Assembly which holds read/write heads and roller bearings. It is used to position the heads radially by the actuator, in order to access a track of data.

CASCADING DRIVERS   Drivers that can connect to, and thereby work with, other drivers.

CCS   *See* Common Command Set.

CD   *See* Compact Disk.

CDB   *See* Command Desciptor Block.

CD-R   Compact Disk Recordable. A special type of CD that can be written to once. It is primarily used for making a master disc to be mass-produced.

CD-ROM   Compact Disc Read Only Memory is a standard format for optical disks which stores 650MB per disk and uses a standard software format (ie. High Sierra) which is interchangeable between various platforms.

CENTRAL PROCESSOR UNIT (CPU)   The heart of the computer system that executes programmed instructions. It includes the arithmetic logic unit (ALU) for performing all math and logic operations, a control section for interpreting and executing instructions, fast main memory for temporary (VOLATILE) storage of an application program and its data.

CHANGER   A robotic device which automatically loads disk into a drive. CD-ROM and erasable optical drive changers are the most common.

CHARACTER   An information symbol used to denote a number, letter, symbol or punctuation mark stored by a computer. In a computer a character can be represented in one (1) byte or eight (8) bits of data. There are 256 different one-byte binary numbers, sufficient for 26 lower case alphas, 26 upper case alphas, 10 decimal digits, control codes and error checks.

CHIP   An integrated circuit fabricated on a chip of silicon or other semiconductor material, typically an integrated circuit, a microprocessor, memory device or a digital logic device.

CLOCK RATE   The rate at which bits or words are transferred between internal elements of a computer or to another computer.

CLOSED LOOP   A control system consisting of one or more feedback control loops in which functions of the controlled signals are combined with functions of the command to maintain prescribed relationships between the commands and the controlled signals. This control technique allows the head actuator system to detect and correct off-track errors. The actual head position is monitored and compared to the ideal track position, by reference information either recorded on a dedicated servo surface, or embedded in the inter-sector gaps. A position error is used to produce a correction signal (FEEDBACK) to the actuator to correct the error. *See* TRACK FOLLOWING SERVO.

CLUSTER SIZE   An operating system term describing the number of sectors that the operating system allocates each time disk space is needed. A cluster is the standard group of data which is accessed by the operating system. DOS cluster sizes increase with drive capacity.

CODE   A set of rules specifying the way which digital data is represented as magnetized bits, on a disk drive. The main objectives of coding are to pack the maximum number of binary bits in the smallest space on the disk. MFM and RLL are coding techniques.

COERCIVITY   A measurement in units of orsteads of the minimum amount of magnetic energy required to cause a reversal in the magnetic dipole moments of a recording media.

COMMAND   1) An instruction sent by the central processor unit (CPU) to a controller for execution. 2) English-like commands entered by users to select computer programs or functions. 3) A CPU command, which is a single instruction such as "add two binary numbers" or "output a byte to the display screen".

COMMAND CHAINING   Combining multiple SCSI commands into a single group in order to reduce the overhead of many individual commands.

COMMAND DESCRIPTOR BLOCK (CDB)   A block of SCSI information containing the command, parameter, and address information needed by the target to carry out a certain task.

COMMON ACCESS METHOD   *See* CAM.

COMMON COMMAND SET (CCS)   A standard set of commands for communicating with SCSI devices.

COMPACT DISC   An optical disc capable of storing the equivalent of hundreds of floppy disks. *See* CD-ROM.

CONSOLE (CRT)   A device from which a computer can be operated; often includes a monitor and a keyboard. Also called a terminal.

CONTROLLER CARD   A circuit board that plugs into the motherboard on the computer. Controller cards allow the computer to communicate and control devices. SCSI and IDE cards are examples of hard disk controller cards. Some printers and scanners also require controller cards, called printer controller cards and scanner controller cards, respectively.

CORE   Originally a computer's main memory was made of ferrite rings (CORES) that could be magnetized to contain one or two bits of data each. CORE MEMORY is synonymous with MAIN MEMORY. Main memory today is fabricated from CHIPS, usually DRAM.

CPU   Central Processing Unit. The main microprocessor in a computer. The CPU carries out the primary functions of the computer.

CRASH   A malfunction in the computer hardware or software, usually causing loss of data.

CROSS-PLATFORM   Cross-platform hardware or software can function on more than one type of computer (i.e. PC, Macintosh, or Sun) or operating system (i.e. DOS, Windows, or UNIX).

CROSS SECTION   An illustration that shows what something looks like after being cut.

CROSS TALK   Interference between two wires caused by the signal from one wire appearing on the other.

CYCLIC-REDUNDANCY-CHECK (CRC)   Used to verify data block integrity. In a typical scheme, two CRC bytes are added to each user data block. The two bytes are computed from the user data, by digital logical chips. The mathematical model is polynomials with binary coefficients. When reading back data, the CRC bytes are read and compared to new CRC bytes computed from the read back block to detect a read error. The read back error check process is mathematically equivalent to dividing the read block, including its CRC, by a binomial polynomial. If the division remainder is zero, the data is error free.

CYLINDER   The cylindrical surface formed by identical track numbers on verically stacked discs. In a drive with dedicated servo, at any location of the head positioning arm, all tracks under all heads are the cylinder. Cylinder number is one of the three address components required to find a specific ADDRESS; the other two are head number and sector number.

D-SUB CONNECTOR   A widely used family of connectors probably deriving its name from its "D" shape. Specific connectors are denoted by a letter for its size and a number for its pin configuration. For example, a DB-15 connector is a D-sub connector of size B with pin configuration number 15.

DAISY CHAIN   A way of connecting multiple drives to one controller. The controller drive select signal is routed serially through the drives, and is intercepted by the drive whose number matches. The disk drives have switches or jumpers on them which allow the user to select the drive number desired.

DATA   Information processed by a computer, stored in memory, or fed into a computer.

DATA ACCESS   When the controller has specified all three components of the sector address to the drive, the ID field of the sector brought under the head by the drive is read and compared with the address of the target sector. A match enables access to the data fiedld of the sector.

DATA ADDRESS   To return to the same area on the disk, each area is given a unique address consisting of the three components: cylinder, head and sector numbers. HORIZONTAL: accomplished by assigning numbers to the concentric circles (cylinders) mapped out by the heads as the positioning arm is stepped radially across the surface, starting with 0 for the outermost circle. By specifying the cylinder number the controller sppecifies a horizontal or radial address component of the data area. ROTATIONAL: once a head and cylinder have been addresses, the desired sector around the selected track of the selected surface is found by counting address marks from the index pulse of the track. Remember that each track starts with an index pulse and each sector starts with an address mark. VERTICAL: assume a disk pack with six surfaces, each with its own read/write head, vertical addressing is accomplished by assigning the numbers 00 through XX to the heads, in consecutive order. By specifying the head number, the controller specifies the vertical address component of the data area.

DATA BASE   An organized collection of data stored in DISK FILES, often shared by multiple users. For example the Official Airline Guide, which contains up-to-date schedules for all airlines.

DATA BASE MANAGEMENT SYSTEM (DBMS)   Application program used to manage, access and update files in a data base.

DATA ENCODING   To use a code such as GCR, MFM, RLL, NZR, etc. to represent characters for memory storage.

DATA FIELD   The portion of a sector used to store the user's DIGITAL data. Other fields in each sector include ID, SYNC and CRC which are used to locate the correct data field.

DATA SEPARATOR   Controller circuitry takes the CODED playback pulses and uses the timing information added by the CODE during the write process to reconstruct the original user data record. *See* NZR, MFM and RLL.

DATA TRACK   Any of the circular tracks magnetized by the recording head during data storage.

DATA TRANSFER RATE   A measure of how quickly informatiuon can be passed between the computer and another device or between devices. The higher the data transfer rate, the less you'll have to wait for data to get to where it needs to go.

DECREASE THE FLYING HEIGHT   Since the head core is closer to the media surface, the lines of flux magnetize a smaller area. Thus, more bits can be recorded in a given distance, and higher BPI (bits per inch) is achievable.

DEDICATED SERVO SYSTEM   A complete disk surface is dedicated fpr servo data. This technique offers quicker access times, but less accuracy as it does not provide a method to compensate for thermal warpage of the head stack assembly.

DEFAULT   A particular value of a variable which is used by a computer unless specifically changed, usually via an entry made through a software program.

DENSITY   Generally, bit recording density. *See* AREAL, BIT and STORAGE DENSITY.

DEVICE   Usually refers to equipment that can be connected to the computer, such as printers, hard disks, scanners and modems. Devices can also be interface cards, such as video cards, SCSI cards and sound cards. The computer itself may also be referred to as a device.

DEVICE DRIVER   A software module that communicates with and transfers data to a controller or other device.

DEVICE ID   *See* SCSI ID.

DIFFERENTIAL   A SCSI bus configuration in which each signal is sent on two wires. The signal is derived by taking the difference in voltage between the two wires, effectively eliminating unwanted noise in the wire. *See* SINGLE-ENDED.

DIGITAL   Any system that processes the digital binary signals having only the values of a 1 or 0. An example of a non-digital signal is an analog signal which continuously varies, i.e., TV or audio.

DIGITAL MAGNETIC RECORDING   *See* MAGNETIC RECORDING

DIRECT ACCESS   Generally refers to an AUXILIARY MEMORY device, having all data on-line. I.E., a tape drive without a tape mounted is not direct access, but a WINCHESTER DRIVE is direct access.

DIRECT MEMORY ACCESS   A method of transferring data from a device to the computer's memory without intervention by the CPU. DMA is handled by a DMA controller chip in the computer (third- party DMA) or by the device itself (bus mastering or first-party DMA).

DIRECTORY   A special disk storage area (usually cylinder zero) that is read by a computer operating system to determine the ADDRESSES of the data records that form a DISK FILE.

DISCONNECT/RECONNECT   The ability of a device to remove itself from a bus to perform a task (such as tape drive fast-forwarding) and then connecting itself back to the bus after completion of the task.

DISK CACHE   Memory used to temporarily store data read from and/or written to a floppy or hard disk to increase performance.

DISK FILE   A file of user data, i.e., the company employee list, with all names and information. The data in the file is stored in a set of disk SECTORS (records).

DISK OPERATING SYSTEM   A single-tasking operating system for the PC. The most common version of DOS is developed by Micosoft.

DISK PACK   A number of metal disks package in a canister for removal from the disk drive. WINCHESTER DRIVES do not have disk packs.

DISK PLATTER   For rigid disks, a flat, circular aluminum disk substrate, coated on both sides with a magnetic substance (iron oxide or thin film metal media) for non-VOLATILE data storage. The substrate may consist of metal, plastic or even glass. Surfaces of disks are usually lubricated to minimize wear during drive start-up or power down.

DISK STORAGE   Auxiliary memory system containing disk drives.

DISKETTE   A floppy disk. A plastic (mylar) substrate, coated with magnetic iron oxide, enclosed in a protective jacket.

DLL   *See* DYNAMIC LINK LIBRARY.

DMA   *See* DIRECT MEMORY ACCESS.

DOS   *See* DISK OPERATING SYSTEM.

DOS PROTECTED MODE INTERFACE   An API that allows programs to used memory beyond the 640K limitation imposed by DOS. Also called DPMI.

DOUBLE-CLICK   Pressing a mouse button twice in rapid succession.

DOUBLE-SPEED SCSI   *See* FAST-20.

DOUBLE WIDE SCSI   A 32 bit implementation of the SCSI. Transfers data at 40-80 Mbytes/sec
.

DPMI   *See* DOS PROTECTED MODE INTERFACE.

DRIVE   A computer memory device with moving storage MEDIA (disk or tape).

DRIVER   *See* DEVICE DRIVER.

DRIVE SELECT   An ADDRESS component that selects among a string of drives attached to a disk controller. In the ST 506/412 interface standard, a drive's select code is physically set in the drive to a value between 0 and 3. When the controller activates one of the four drive select code lines in the J1 cable, the selected drive is enabled to respond to access commands from the controller.

DRIVE TYPE   A number representing a standard configuration of physical parameters (cylinders, heads and sectors) of a particular type of disk drive. Each AT system BIOS contains a list of drive types that the system considers "Standard Types". These types are not necessarily the same from one BIOS to the next. That is, drive type 25 on one BIOS may represent a drive that has 615 cylinders, 4 data heads, and 17 sectors per track, while type 25 on another BIOS could be totally different.

DROP-IN/DROP-OUT   Types of disk media defects usually caused by a pin-hole in the disk coating. If the coating is interrupted, the magnetic flux between medium and head is zero. A large interruption will induce two extraneous pulses, one at the beginning and one at the end of the pin-holes (2 DROP-INs). A small coating interruption will result in no playback from a recorded bit (a DROP-OUT).

DRUM   An early form of rotating magnetic storage, utilizing a rotating cylindrical drum and a multiplicity of heads (one per track). Disc stack more compactly than drums.

DYNAMIC LINK LIBRARY   A windows file, that contains code that can be added to a Windows program while it is running.

E-MAIL   Electronic Mail. Messages sent by modem or other electronic means, which enables people to communicate over long distances in minutes as opposed to days. *See* SNAIL-MAIL.

ECC   *See* ERROR CORRECTION CODE.

EIDE   *See* Enhanced IDE.

EISA   *See* Extended Industry Standard Architecture.

ELECTRO-STATIC DISCHARGE   An integrated circuit (CHIP) failure mechanism. Since the circuitry of CHIPs are microscopic in size, they can be damaged or destroyed by small static discharges. People handling electronic equipment should always ground themselves before touching the equipment. Electronic equipment should always be handled by the chassis or frame. Components and printed circuit board edge connectors should never be touched. Also called ESD.

EMBEDDED SERVO SYSTEM   Servo data is embedded or superimposed along with data on every cylinder.

END USER   You. A person who uses hardware and software.

ENHANCED IDE   The second generation of IDE technology that improves the data throughput of IDE hard disks and adds the capacity of connecting CD-ROM drives to the same interface card as hard disks.

ENHANCED SMALL DISK INTERFACE   A high-speed hard disk bus interface used in the 1980's that has been superceded by SCSI due to ESDI's limitation of supporting only hard drives.

ERASE   To remove previously recorded data from magnetic storage media.

ERROR   *See* HARD ERROR and SOFT ERROR.

ERROR CHECKING   Any one of a number of methods used to verify that data sent from one place to another arrives at its destination without errors.

ERROR CORRECTION CODE   A method used on hard disks to detemine if an error has occurred in the data stored on the drive. Also called ECC.

ESCON   An IBM standard interface between mainframes and disk storage units. Also used by Fujitsu, Amdahl, Storage Tech, and Hitachi.

ESDI   *See* Enhanced Small Device Interface.

EVEN PARITY   *See* PARITY CHECKING.

EXCLUSIVE OR   *See* OR and XOR.

EXECUTE   To perform a data processing operation described by an instruction or a program in a computer.

EXTENDED INDUSTRY STANDARD ARCHITECTURE   A 32-bit computer bus introduced in 1988 that enhanced the capabilities and performance of the ISA bus standard.

EXTERNAL CLOCK RATE   The frequency at which peripherals outside the CPU operate.

FCI   *See* FLUX CHANGES PER INCH.

FACE PLATE   The front cover (usually plastic) of a device such as a hard disk or CD-ROM drive.

FAST-20   A SCSI-3 transfer mode that is capable of sending data at 20 MB/sec. Also known as DoubleSpeed SCSI and UltraSCSI.

FAST-40   A SCSI-3 transfer mode that is twice as fast as Fast-20, capable of sending data at 40 MB/sec.

FAST SCSI   A SCSI-2 transfer mode that operates at 10 MB/sec, twice as fast as regular SCSI.

FAST WIDE SCSI   Wide SCSI operating at twice the rate of regular Wide SCSI.

FAULT TOLERANCE   Able to recover from errors or other failures without loss or corruption of data.

FEEDBACK   A closed-loop control system, using the head-to-track positioning signal (from the servo head) to modify the HEAD POSITION-ER signal (to correctly position the head on the track).

FETCH   A CPU read operation from MAIN MEMORY and its related data transfer operations.

FIBRE CHANNEL   A new ANSI standard that specifies high-speed serial communication between devices. Fibre Channel is used as one of the bus architectures in SCSI-3.

FIELDS   Storage units grouped together to make a record are considered to be a field; i.e., a record might be a company's address; a field in the record might be the company's Zip Code.

FILE   A file consists of a group of logically related records that, in turn, are made up of groups of logically related fields. *See* DISK FILE.

FILE ALLOCATION TABLE (FAT)   What the operating system uses to keep track of which clusters are allocated to which files and which are available for use. FAT is usually stored on Track-0.

FILE NAME   Each file has a name, just like the name on the tab of a file folder. When you want DOS to find a file, you give DOS the file name.

FILESERVER   A computer used primarily for storing files on a network.

FIREWIRE   *See* IEEE 1394.

FIRMWARE   A computer program written into a storage medium which cannot be accidentally erased, i.e., ROM. It can also refer to devices containing such programs.

FIRST-PARITY DMA   *See* BUS MASTERING.

FIXED DISK   A disk drive with disks that cannot be removed from the drive by the user, i.e. WINCHESTER DISK DRIVE.

FLAT-RIBBON CABLE   *See* RIBBON CABLE.

FLOPPY DISK   A magnetic disk used to store computer data. FLOPPY DISKS generally exhibit slow ACCESS TIME and smaller CAPACITY compared to WINCHESTER DRIVES, but feature removable disks.

FLUX CHANGE   Location on the data track, where the direction of magnetization reverses in order to define a 1 or 0 bit.

FLUX CHANGES PER INCH   Linear recording density defined as the number of flux changes per inch of data track. Also called FCI.

FM   Frequency modulation CODE scheme, superceded by MFM, which is being superceded by RLL.

FORCED-PERFECT TERMINATOR   A type of terminator containing a sophisticated circuit that can compensate for variations in the power supplied by the host adapter, as well as variations in bus impedance of complex SCSI systems. Also called FPT. *See* PASSIVE TERMINATOR and ACTIVE TERMINATOR.

FORMAT   The purpose of a format is to record "header" data that organize the tracks into sequential sectors on the disk surfaces. This information is never altered during normal read/write operations. Header information identifies the sector number and also contains the head and cylinder ADDRESS in order to detect an ADDRESS ACCESS error.

FORMATTED CAPACITY   Actual capacity available to store user data. The formatted capacity is the gross capacity, less the capacity taken up by the overhead data used is formatting the disks. While the unformatted size may be 24 M bytes, only 20 M bytes of storage may be actually available to the user after formating.

FPI   *See* FLUX CHANGES PER INCH.

FPT   *See* FORCED-PERFECT TERMINATOR.

FREE-AIR CHARACTERISTIC IMPEDANCE   The average impedance of air.

FRICTION   Resistance to relative motion between two bodies in contact; i.e., there is sliding friction between head and disk during drive power up/down.

FRPI   The number of Flux Reversals per inch. *See* FLUX CHANGES PER INCH.

FULL HEIGHT DRIVE   Winchester 5-1/4" drive which fits in the same space as full height mini-floppy drive (called the full-height form factor).

G   A G is a unit of force applied to a body at rest equal to the force exerted on it by gravity. Hard disk drive shock specifications are usually called out in Gs. A shock specification of 40 Gs non-operating means that a drive will not suffer any permanent damage if subjected to a 40 G shock. This is roughly equivalent to a drop of the drive to a hard surface from a distance of 1 inch.

GAP   1) FORMAT: Part of the disk format. Allows mechanical compensations (i.e., spindle motor rotational speed variations) without the last sector on a track overwriting the first sector. 2) HEAD: An interruption in the permeable head material, usually a glass bonding material with high permeability, allowing the flux fields to exit the head structure to read/write data bits in the form of flux changes on the recording media.

GAP LENGTH   Narrowing the head gap length achieves higher bit density because the lines of force magnetize a smaller area where writing data in the form of flux changes on the recording media.

GAP WIDTH   The narrower the gap width, the closer the tracks can be placed. Closer track placement results in higher TPI.

GB   Gigabyte. One gigabyte equals 1,073,741,824 bytes.

GENERIC PACKETIZED PROTOCOL   A method for transferring groups of data that is independent of the type of hardware used, hence the name "Generic". Also referred to as GPP.

GROUP CODE ENCODING   Data encoding method. Also called GCR. *See* the encoding section in "Disk Drive Operation".

GUARD BAND   1) Non-recorded band between adjacent data tracks. 2) For closed loop servo drives, extra servo tracks outside the data band preventing the CARRIAGE ASSEMBLY from running into the crash stop.

HALF HEIGHT DRIVE   A Winchester drive which fits in one half of the space of a full height mini-floppy drive.

HANDSHAKE   The communication that occurs between devices in order to determine the method and speed of data transfer to be used.

HARD DISK DRIVE   Commonly called rigid disk drives, or Winchester disk drives. An electromechanical device that can read rigid disks. Though similar to floppy disk drives, that hard disks have higher bit density and multiple read/write surfaces.

HARD ERROR   An error that occurs repeatedly at the same location on a disk surface. Hard errors are caused by imperfections in the disk surface, called media defects. When formatting hard disk drives, hard error locations, if known, should be spared out so that data is not written to these locations. Most drives come with a hard error map listing the locations of any hard errors by head, cylinder and BFI (bytes from index - or how many bytes from the beginning of the cylinder).

HARD ERROR MAP   Also called defect map, bad spot map, media map. Media defects are avoided by deleting the defective sectors from system use, or assigning an alternative track (accomplished during format operation). The defects are found during formatting, and their locations are stored on a special DOS file on the disk, usually on cylinder 0.

HARD SECTOR MODE   A hardware controlled convention defining a fixed number of sectors per track in any specified zone.

HARDWARE   Computer equipment (as opposed to the computer programs and software).

HDA   *See* HEAD/DISK ASSEMBLY.

HD (HIGH-DENSITY) CONNECTOR   A connector in which the pins are closely packed in order to save space. High-density A-cable connectors have just as many pins as low-density A-cable connectors but are smaller than the low-density ones.

HEAD   An electromagnetic device that can write (record), read (playback) or erase data on magnetic media. There are three types:

Head Type	BPI	TPI	Areal Density
Monolithic	8000	900	10 to 6th
Composite	12000	2000	10 to 8th
Thin-film	25000	3000	10 to 9th

HEAD CRASH   A head landing occurs when the disk drive is turned on or off. This function normally does not damage the disk as the disk has a very thin lubricant on it. A head crash occurs when the head and disk damage each other during landing, handling or because a contaminant particle gets betweem them. Head crash is a catastrophic failure condition and causes permanent damage and loss of data.

HEAD/DISK ASSEMBLY   A sealed Winchester assembly including disks, heads, filter and actuator assembly.

HEAD LANDING AND TAKEOFF   In Winchester drives, the head is in contact with the platter when the drive is not powered. During the power up cycle, the disk begins rotation and an "air bearing" is established as ;thc disk spins up to full RPM (rotations per minute). This air bearing prevents any mechanical contact between head and disk.

HEAD LANDING ZONE   An area of the disk set aside for takeoff and landing of the Winchester heads when the drive is turned on and off.

HEAD POSITIONER   Also known as the ACTUATOR, a mechanism that moves the CARRIAGE ASSEMBLY to the cylinder being accessed.

HEAD SLAP   Similar to a HEAD CRASH but occurs while the drive is turned off. It usually occurs during mishandling or shipping. Head slap can cause permanent damage to a hard disk drive. *See* HEAD CRASH.

HEXADECIMAL (HEX)   A number system based on sixteen, using digits 0 through 9 and letters A through F to represent each digit of the number. (A = 10, B = 20, C = 30, D = 40, E = 50, F = 60).

HOST   The computer that contains the SCSI host adapter.

HOST ADAPTER   The controller card used to communicate with and control devices. A SCSI host adapter is used to attach and communicate with SCSI devices.

ID FIELD   The address portion of a sector. The ID field is written during the Format operation. It includes the cylinder, head and sector number of the current sector. This address information is compared by the disk controller with the desired head, cylinder and sector number before a read or write operation is allowed.

IDE   *See* INTEGRATED DRIVE ELECTRONICS

IEEE   Institute of Electrical and Electronics Engineers. An organization that promotes electrical and electronics standards.

IEEE 1394   Called Firewire by Apple, IEEE 1394 is a serial bus that runs at 100 MB/sec and doesn't require any terminators. A special feature of IEEE 1394 is asynchronous transfer mode.

IMAGE-BACKUP MODE   Used with streaming tpae, image-backup mode records an exact copy of the disk, including unused sectors and bad tracks.

IMPEDANCE   A measure of a material's resistance to the transfer of electricity.

INDEX (PULSE)   The index pulse is the starting point for each disk track. The index pulse provides initial synchronization for sector addressing on each individual track.

INDEX TIME   The time interval between similar edges of the index pulse, which measures the time for the disk to make one revolution. This information is used by a disk drive to verify correct rotational speed of the media.

INDUSTRY STANDARD ARCHITECTURE   An 8-bit computer bus introduced by IBM (International Business Machines) in 1983 and later expanded to 16-bit for the IBM AT computer. The ISA bus is also known as the AT bus.

INITIATOR   A device that is in control of the bus and sends commands to a target.

INPUT   1) Data entered into the computer to be processed. 2) User commands or queries.

INPUT/OUTPUT   The process of entering data into or removing data from a computer system. Also called I/O.

INTEGRATED DRIVE ELECTRONICS   A hard disk technology that puts the communication control and related circuitry on the drive itself (using one microprocessor for both functions saves costs and eliminates the need for an intelligent controller card.). Older technologies such as MFM had some of the electronics on the drive and the rest on the interface card.   Popular electronic interface standard for hard drives used in IBM XT and AT compatable computers. Also called IDE. *See* also EIDE.

INTELLIGENT PERIPHERAL   A peripheral device that contains a processor or microprocessor to enable it to interpret and execute commands, thus relieving the computer for other tasks.

INTERFACE   The protocol data transmitters, data receivers, logic and wiring that link one piece of computer equipment to another, such as a disk drive to a controller or a controller to a system bus. Protocol means a set of rules for operating the physical interface, i.e., don't read or write before SEEK COMPLETE is true.

INTERFACE STANDARD   The interface specifications agreed to by various manufacturers to promote industry-wide interchange ability of products such as disk drives and controllers. An interface standard generally reduces product costs, allows buyers to purchase from more than one source, and allows faster market acceptance of new products.

INTERLEAVE FACTOR   The ratio of physical disk sectors skipped for every sector actually written.

INTERLEAVING   The interleave value tells the controller where the next logical sector is located in relation to the current sector. For example, an interleave value of one (1) specifics that the next logical sector is physically the next sector on the track. Interleave of two (2) specifies every other physical sector, three (3) every third sector and so on.

Interleaving is used to improve the system throughout based on overhead time of the host software, the disk drive and the controller. Thus, if an APPLICATION PROGRAM is processing sequential logical records of a DISK FILE in a CPU time of more than one second but less than two, then the interleave factor of 3 will prevent wasting an entire disk revolution between ACCESSES.

INTERNAL CLOCK RATE   The frequency at which a microprocessor operates internally.

INTERRUPT   A signal, usually from a peripheral device to a CPU, to signify that a commanded operation has been completed or cannot be completed.

INTERRUPT REQUEST   A signal used by devices to indicate that they need attention from the CPU. Computers have several IRQ channels so that many devices can be attached, each one to its own IRQ, and serviced by the CPU.

I/O PROCESSOR   Intelligent processor or controller that handles the input/output operations of a computer.

IRQ   *See* INTERRUPT REQUEST

ISA   *See* INDUSTRY STANDARD ARCHITECTURE.

ISOCHRONOUS TRANSFER   A method of sending data that guarantees that the data will arrive at its destination at a specified period of time. Isochronous transfers are important for sending data such as video and audio, since they are dependent on time.

JUMPER   A small plastic and metal connector used to bridge the gap between two or more pins. Jumpers are commonly used for configuring devices and add-on cards.

KILOBIT   One kilobit equals 1,024 bits of 128 bytes. Also called Kb.

KILOBYTE   1) 1,024 bytes (two to the tenth power, this is the normal definition). 2) 1,000 bytes (this definition is used by disk drive companies to bolster the specified capacity of their drives.

LADDR   *See* LAYERED DEVICE DRIVER.

LAN   Local Area Network.

LANDING ZONE   The landing zone is where the read/write head sits when it is not active. If the system features a dedicated landing zone, the head will rest on the same track each time.

LATENCY (ROTATIONAL)   The time for the disk to rotate the accessed sector under the head for read or write. Average latency is usually slightly more than the time for half a disk revolution.

LAYERED DEVICE DRIVER   A SCSI device driver architecture used in early versions of OS/2. Also called LDD.

L-CABLE   A 110-wire cable used for 32-bit SCSI-3 buses.

LOCAL BUS   A computer bus that allows devices to transfer data directly to the CPU. VL-Bus and PCI are common types of local bus.

LOGIC   Electronic circuitry that switches on and off ("1" and "0") to perform digital operations.

LOGICAL UNIT   Usually the medium used by a device to store or retrieve data. A CD-ROM drive is a device and the disk in the drive is a logical unit.

LOGICAL UNIT NUMBER   A 3-bit value identifying a logical unit in a device. Also called LUN.

LOOKUP   The action of obtaining and displaying data in a file.

LOW LEVEL FORMAT   The first step in preparing a drive to store information after physical installation is complete. The process sets up the "handshake" between the drive and the controller. In an XT system, the low level format is usually done using DOS's debug utility. In an AT system, AT advanced diagnostics is typically used. Other third-party software may also be used to do low level format on both XTs and ATs.

LUN   *See* LOGICAL UNIT NUMBER.

MAGNETIC MEDIA   A disk or tape with a surface layer containing particles of metal or metallic oxides that can be magnetized in different directions to represent bits of data, sounds or other information..

MAGNETIC RECORDING   The use of a head, recording head, recording media (tape or disk) and associated electronic circuitry for storing data, sound or video.

MAGNETO-OPTICAL   A storage medium similar to CD-ROM, except that magneto-optical discs can be erased and rewritten thousands of times. Also called MO.

MAINFRAME COMPUTER   An extremely large (occupying the space of entire rooms) and costly computer used for supporting many users running programs similtaneously. *See* MINICOMPUTER, MICROSOMPUTER and RANDOM-ACCESS MEMORY.

MASTER DRIVE   The primary (or first) IDE drive installed on a system. For example, Drive C:.

MAX OUT   Slang term meaning to use fully.

Mb   *See* MEGABIT.

MB   *See* MEGABYTE.

MCA   Micro Channel Architecture. *See* MICRO CHANNEL.

MEAN TIME BEFORE FAILURE   The average time before a failure will occur. This is not a warranty measurement. MTBF is a calculation taking into consideration the MTBF of each component in a system and is the statistical average operation time between the start of a unit's lifetime and its time of a failure. After a product has been in the field for a few years, the MTBF can become a field proven statistic.

MEAN TIME TO REPAIR   The average time to repair a given unit. Limited to a qualified technician with proper equipment. Also called MTTR.

MEDIA   The magnetic layers of a disk or tape. *See* DISK/PLATTER.

MEDIA DEFECT   A media defect can cause a considerable reduction of the read signal (missing pulse or DROP-OUT), or create an extra pulse (DROP-IN). *See* HARD ERROR MAP.

MEGABIT   One million bits. Not to be confused with megabyte (see below). There are usually 8 bits in a bit.

MEGABYTE   1) 2 to the 20th power (1,024K). This is the industry standard definition. 2) One million bytes (exactly 1,000,000 bytes). This definition is used by disk drive companies.

MEMORY   Any device or storage system capable of storing and retrieving information .

MICRO CHANNEL   A 32-bit computer bus developed by IBM for its PS/2 series of computers.

MICROCOMPUTER   A computer whose central processor unit (CPU) is manufactured as a chip or a small number of chips. The PC and Macintosh arc examples of microcomputers.

MICROINCH   One-millionth of an inch (uin).

MICROSECOND   One-millionth of a second (us).

MILLISECOND   One-thousandth of a second (Msec).

MINICOMPUTER   A computer midway in size and processing power between a MICROCOMPUTER and a MAINFRAME COMPUTER.

MINI-SLIDER HEADS   Manganese/Zinc Ferrite Winchester heads. Smaller, lighter heads with stiffer load arms than standard Winchester heads. They allow smaller flying heights, and therefore higher bit and track density, if they are made with smaller and narrower gaps.

MINI WINCHESTER   A Winchester disk drive with 5-1/4 or 3 1/2 inch diameter disks.

MNEUMONIC   A shortened abbreviation for a series of codes.

MO   *See* MAGNETO-OPTICAL.

MODIFIED FREQUENCY MODULATION   A method of recording digital data, using a particular CODE to get the flux reversal times from the data pattern. MFM recording is self-clocking because the CODE guarantees timing information for the playback process. The controller is thus able to synchronize directly from the data. This method has a maximum of bit of data with each flux reversal. *See* NRZ and RLL.

MOTHERBOARD   The main circuit board in a computer on which the CPU, main memory, system BIOS and any other built-in electronics reside.

MULTIPROCESSOR   A computer containing two or more processors.

MULTITASKING   The ability of a computer system to execute more than one program or program task simultaneously. Windows 95, OS/2 and UNIX are examples of multitasking programs.

MULTIUSER   The ability of a computer system to execute programs for more than one user at a time.

NETWARE   A network operating system developed by Novell Corporation.

NEXUS   The link between initiator, target and logical unit used to identify and I/O process. An I_T_L (initiator, target, logical unit) nexus is the most basic type of SCSI link. To send multiple I/O processes to the same target and logical unit, an I_T_L_Q (initiator, target, logical unit, queue) nexus is used.

NOISE   Unwanted and usually interfering elctrical signals that interfere with information signals (similar to radio static or TV interference). Sources of noise in computers can be power supplies, ground loops, radio interference, cable routing, etc.

NRZ (NON-RETURN TO ZERO)   1) User digital data bits. 2) A method of magnetic recording of digital data in which a flux reversal denotes a one bit, and no flux reversal a zero bit, NRZ recording requires an accompanying or synchronization clock to define each cell time unlike MFM or RLL recording.

ODD PARITY   *See* PARITY CHECKING.

OFF LINE   Processing or peripheral operations performed while not connected to the system CPU via the system bus.

ONE-OFF   A master CD-R usually intended for duplication purposes.

ONLINE   Existing on a BBS.

OPEN COLLECTOR   A type of output structure found in certain bipolar logic families. The device has NPN transistor with grounded emitter that enables it to output to a low voltage level only. When the device is inactive, an external resistor holds the device output at a high voltage level.

OPERATING SYSTEM   An operating system is a program which acts as an interface between the user of a computer and the computer hardware. The purpose of the operating system is to provide an environment in which a user may run programs. The goal of the operating system is to enable the user to conveniently use the computer's resources such as the CPU, memory, storage devices and printers.

OR   A binary operation that compares two bits and yields a 1 if at least one of the bits being compared is set to 1.

OS/2   A multitasking operating system for the PC developed by IBM Corporation.

OUTPUT   Processing data being transferred out of the computer system to peripherals (i.e., disk, printer, etc.). This includes responses to user commands or queries.

OVERHEAD   Time lost during an operation due to error checking or other tasks that hinder the completion of the operation.

PARALLEL   Sending bits in groups. *See* SERIAL.

PARITY   A computer data checking method using an extra bit in which the total number of binary 1's (or 0's) in a byte is always odd or always even; thus, in a odd parity scheme, every byte has eight bits of data and one parity bit. If using odd parity and the number of 1 bits comprising the byte of data is not odd, the 9th or parity bit is set to 1 to create the odd parity. In this way, a byte of data can be checked for accurate transmission by simply counting the bits for an odd parity indication. If the count is ever even, an error is indicated.

PARITY CHECKING   *See* PARITY.

PARKING   Parking the disk drive heads means the recording heads are moved so that they are not over the platter's data area. Many drives have an auto-park feature where the heads are automatically parked when the power to the drive is shut off. Other drives require the user to run some kind of parking software to park the heads.

PARTITIONING   Method for dividing an area on disk drive for use by more than one disk operating system or for dividing large disk drives into areas which the File Allocation Table (FAT) can deal with when in use. The current IBM DOS maximum partition size is 2000MB.

PASSIVE TERMINATION   The most common way of reduceing noise on a cable. Network cables and SCSI cables use resistive passive termination.

PASSIVE TERMINATOR   A terminator that provides a fixed-value impedance match between the end of the SCSI bus and the cable. Passive terminators are comprised only of resistors and are susceptible to variations in the power supplied by the host adapter. *See* ACTIVE TERMINATOR and FORCED-PERFECT TERMINATOR.

PATH   The DOS term "path" has three definitions and each involves directories. A PATH may be defined as: 1) the names of the chain of directories leading to a file; 2) the complete file or directory name; 3) a DOS command.

P-CABLE   A 68-wire cable used for 16-bit SCSI-3 buses. P-cables can be used with Q-cables for 32-bit SCSI-3 buses.

PCI   *See* PERIPHERAL COMPONENT INTERCONNECT.

PERIPHERAL COMPONENT INTERCONNECT   A 32-bit local bus developed by Intel that allows peripherals to communicate directly with the CPU.

PERIPHERAL EQUIPMENT   Auxiliary memory, displays, printers, disk drives and other equipment usually attached to a computer systems' CPU by controllers and cables (they are often packaged together in a desktop computer).

PIO   *See* PROGRAMMED INPUT/OUTPUT.

PIPELINE   A channel used to transfer commands, data or signals.

PLATED THIN FILM DISKS   Magnetic disk memory media having its surface plated with a thin coating of metallic alloy instead of being coated with oxide.

PLATTER   The round magnetic disk surfaces used for read/write operations in a hard disk system.

PLUG-AND-PLAY   An Intel/Microsoft standard for configuring add-on cards and other devices so that user intervention is minimized. No more switches, jumpers and wheels to fiddle with.

PLUG-IN CARD   *See* ADD-ON.

POLLING   A technique that discerns which of several devices on a connection is trying to get the processor's attention.

POSTSCRIPT   A printer language used to describe the text and graphics to be be printed.

PRECOMPENSATION   Applied to write data by the controller in order to partially alleviate bit shift which causes adjacent 1's written on magnetic data physically to move apart. When adjacent 1's are sensed by the controller, precompensation is used to write them closer together on the disk, thus fighting the repelling effect caused by the recording. Precompensation is only required on some oxide media drives.

PREVENTATIVE MAINTENANCE   A method of doing a scheduled routine observation or exchanging a part, prior to a breakdown of a piece of equipment.

PRINTED CIRCUIT BOARD   A circuit board IC and other components, like the one attached to a drive. Also called PCB.

PROCESSING (DATA PROCESSING)   The process of computer handling, manipulating and modifying data such as arithmetic calculation, file lookup and updating, or word processing.

PROGRAM   A sequence of instructions stored in memory and executed by a processor or microprocessor. *See* also APPLICATION PROGRAMS.

PROGRAMMED INPUT/OUTPUT   A method of transferring data from a device to the host computer's memory that requires the CPU to perform the transfer. PIO is slower than DMA.

PROTOCOL   A set of conventions governing the format of messages to be exchanged within a communications system.

P-TO-A TRANSITION CABLE   An adapter used to connect 8-bit SCSI-1 devices using A-cables to a 16- or 32-bit SCSI-3 device using P-cables.

Q-CABLE   A 68-wire cable used in conjunction with a P-cable for 32-bit SCSI-3 buses.

QUARTER-INCH CARTRIDGE (QIC)   A tape format used for backing up data. QIC tape is 1/4 inch.

QUEUING   Grouping a series of commands in order to send them as a single command, thereby reducing data transfer overhead.

RADIAL   A way of connecting multiple drives to one controller. In radial operation, all output signals are active even if the drive is not selected. *See* DAISY CHAIN.

RAID   *See* REDUNDANT ARRAY OF INEXPENSIVE DRIVES.

RAM   *See* RANDOM ACCESS MEMORY.

RAM DISK   A system where part of the computer's random access memory is used to simulate a disk drive. The RAM disk and its contents will disappear if power is lost or the system is restarted. RAM is far faster (microseconds ACCESS TIME) than disks (milliseconds), so APPLICATION PROGRAMS which access the disk run faster.

RANDOM ACCESS MEMORY   Memory where any locatiom can be read from or written to in a random order. Random access memory usually refers to volatile memory where the contents are lost when power is removed. The user addressable memory of a computer is random access memory.

READ   To access a storage location and obtain previously recorded data.

READ-INTENSIVE   A process that requires a lot of reading of data from a device such as a hard disk.

READ-ONLY   Something that can only be read from, not written to.

READ ONLY MEMORY   A chip that can be programmed once with bits of information. This chip retains this information even if the power is turned off. When this information is programmed into the ROM, it is called burning the ROM.

RECALIBRATE   Return to Track Zero. A common disk drive function in which the heads are returned to track 0 (outermost track).

RECORD   A single unit made up of logically related fields.

REDUCED WRITE CURRENT   A signal input (to some older drives) which decreases the amplitude of the write current at the actual drive head. Normally this signal is specified to be used during inner track write operations to lessen the effect of adjacent "bit" crowding. Most drives today provide this internally and do not require controller intervention.

REDUCED WRITECURRENT   To minimize the effects of peak shift, on some drives, the magnitude of the write current is reduced on some of the innermost tracks. When installing a drive in a system, the number requested is the first track number to begin the area of reduced write current, that track and all subsequent tracks will be written with reduced write current.

REDUNDANT ARRAY OF INEXPENSIVE DRIVES   A collection of storage devices configured to provide higher data transfer rates and/or data recovery capability. Also called RAID.

REGULAR SCSI   8-bit SCSI.

RESOLUTION   With regards to magnetic recording, the band width (or frequency response) of the recording heads.

RF   Radio Frequency.

RIBBON CABLE   A group of wires arranged in rows that comprise a single flat cable resembling a ribbon.

RLL   *See* RUN LENGTH LIMITED CODE.

ROM   *See* READ ONLY MEMORY.

ROTATIONAL SPEED   The speed at which the media spins. On 5 1/4" or 3 1/2" Winchester drives it is usually 3600 rpm.

ROUND-ROBIN   A method of guaranteeing that a number of devices will have an opportunity to be serviced. The round-robin method simply requires that every device is serviced in turn. After the last device is serviced, the process begins again with the first one.

RUN LENGTH LIMITED CODE 1) A method of recording digital data, whereby the combinations of flux reversals are coded/decoded to allow greater than one (1) bit of information per flux reversal. This compression of information increases data capacity by approximately 50 percent. 2) A scheme of encoding designed to operate with the ST412 interface at a dial transfer rate of 7.5 megabit/sec. The technical name of this specific RLL CODE used is "two, seven".

SASI Shugart Associates System Interface. The predecessor to SCSI.

SC *See* SELCTOR CHANNEL.

SCAM *See* SCSI CONFIGUREDAUTO-MAGICALLY.

SCO UNIX A version, or flavor, of UNIX developed by Santa Cruz Operations.

SCSI Small Computer Systems Interface. An intelligent bus for transmitting data and commands between a variety of devices. The current "high end" CPU-to-drive interface. See SCSI-II, SCSI III, FAST SCSI, WIDE SCSI, FAST WIDE SCSI, FAST-20 and FAST-40 for various types of SCSIs available.

SCSI-II The second generation of SCSI; includes many improvements to SCSI-I, including FAST SCSI, WIDE SCSI, and mandatory parity checking.

SCSI-III Commonly used to refered to "Wide SCSI", although this is not the correct definition. SCSI-III is the third generation of SCSI; introduces FAST-20 and FAST-40 as improvements to the parallel bus. The standard also includes a number of specifications for high-speed serial bus architecture such as SSA, FIBRE CHANNEL, and IEEE 1394.

SCSI BIOS A chip on the host adapter that contains programs for communicating with the adapter and the bus.

SCSI CONFIGURED AUTO-MAGICALLY A pending standard that will give SCSI devices the ability to automatically select their SCSI IDs.

SCSI ID A number used on SCSI devices to uniquely identify them among other devices on the bus. Also referred to as a device ID.

SECTOR   A sector is a section of a track whose size is determined by formatting. When used as an address component, sector and location refer to the sequence number of the sector around the track. Typically, one sector stores one user record of data. Drives typically are formatted from 17 to 26 sectors per track. Determining how many sectors per track to use depends on the system type, the controller capabilities and the drive encoding method and interface.

SECTOR-SLIP   Sector-slip allows any sector with a defect to be mapped and bypassed. The next contguous sector is given that sector address.

SEEK   The radial movement of the heads to a specified track address.

SEEK COMPLETE   An ST506 interface signal from drive to controller which indicates that read/write heads have settled on the desired track and completed the seek.

SELECTOR CHANNEL   An intelligent bus used on the IBM 360 mainframe.

SEQUENTIAL ACCESS   Writing or reading data in a sequential order, such as reading data blocks stored one after the other on magnetic tape (the opposite of random access).

SERIAL   Sending bits individually, one after the other. *See also* PARALLEL.

SERIAL STORAGE ARCHITECTURE   A high-speed serial communication bus developed by IBM for sending commands, data and status signals between devices.

SERVO TRACK   A prerecorded reference track on the dedicated servo surface of a closed-loop disk drive. All data track positions are compared to their corresponding servo track to determine "off-track/on-track" postition.

Information written on the servo surface that the electronics of the drive uses to position the heads over the correct data track. This information is written on the drive by the servo track writer.

SETUP   Program used by AT type computers to store configuration in CMOS. This program is sometimes found in the system BIOS and can be accessed from the keyboard. On other systems, the program is on diskette.

SHIELDED   Containing a metal cover to keep out unwanted interference from the environment. A shielded connector has a metal cover. A shielded cable has a foil wrapping or braided metal sleeve under the plastic covering.

SHROUDED HEADER CONNECTOR   A device connector with a plastic guard around its perimeter. The shroud ensures that all the pins on a cable are plugged into the device. Shrouded connectors also have a notch on one side so that the cable can only be inserted in one direction.

SILICON   Semiconductor substrate material generally used to manufacture microprocessors and other integrated circuit chips.

SINGLE-ENDED   A SCSI bus configuration in which each signal is carried by a signal wire. Single-ended buses are more susceptible to noice than differential buses.

SINGLE-TASKING   The ability to perform only one process at a time. DOS is a single-tasking operating system.

SKEWING   Some low-level formatting routines may ask for a Head and/or Cylinder Skew value. The value will represent the number of sectors being skewed to compensate for head switching time of the drive and/or track-to-track seek time allowing for continuous read/write operation without losing disk revolutions.

SLAVE DRIVE   The secondary drive installed in a IDE system. For example, drive D:.

SMD (STORAGE MODULE DEVICE)   An 8" mainframe and minicomputer disk drive interface standard.

SMD (SURFACE MOUNTED DEVICE)   A CHIP in a smaller integrated surface package, without connection leads.

SNAIL-MAIL   Regular old, lick the stamp, seal the envelope, and then sit and wait for several days mail. *See* E-MAIL.

SOFT ERROR   A bit error during playback which can be corrected by repeated attempts to read.

SOFT SECTOR MODE   A convention, defined by software, of setting a variable number of sectors per track in direct relationship to the drive's FCI rating in regards to the area of media that passes beneath the head. This scheme takes advantage of the fact that, in actual surface area, the outermost tracks are longer than the innermost.

SOFTWARE APPLICATION PROGRAMS   The Disc Operating System and other programs (as opposed to HARDWARE). The instructions or programs, usually stored on floppy or hard disks, which are used to direct the operations of a computer, or other hardware.

SOFTWARE PATCH   Software modification which allows or adds function not otherwise available using the standard software program.

SOLID-STATE   Electronics not utilizing vacuum tubes.

SOUND CARD   An add-on card used to play and/or record audio.

SPINDLE   The rotating hub structure to which the disks are attached.

SPINDLE MOTOR   The spindle motor is the electro-mechanical part of the disk drive that rotates the platters.

SSA   *See* SERIAL STORAGE ARCHITECTURE.

ST-506/ST-412 INTERFACE   An early industry standard interface between a hard disk and hard disk controller. In the ST-506/St-412 interface, the "intelligence" is on the controller rather than on the drive. *See* INTERFACE STANDARD, ESDI, and SCSI.

STAND-ALONE   Able to operate without support.

STEP   An increment or decrement of the head positioning arm to move the heads in or out, respectively, one track from their current position. In buffered mode (open loop drives), the head motion is postponed until the last of a string of step pulses has been received.

STEPPER MOTOR   The stepper motor is the electro-mechanical part of the disk drive that positions the heads by step pulse on the tracks of the disk to read and write data.

STEP PULSE   The trigger pulse sent from the controller to the stepper motor on the step interface signal line to initiate a step operation.

STEP TIME The time required by the drive to step the heads from the current cylinder position to a target cylinder.

STICTION A slang term used in the drive industry to describe the condition when Winchester heads become "stuck" to a disk. This occurs when the disk lubricant hardens under the head.

STORAGE CAPACITY Amount of data that can be stored in a memory, usually specified in kilobytes (KB) for main memory and floppy disk drives and megabytes (MB) for hard disk and tape drives.

STORAGE DENSITY Usually refers to recording density (BPI, TPI, or their product, AREAL DENSITY).

STORAGE LOCATION A memory location, identified by an ADDRESS, where information is to be read or written.

STORAGE MODULE DRIVE Storage module drive interface. An interface, used in larger disk drives, i.e., 8" & 14" drives.

SUSTAINED SPEED The rate at which data can be transferred continuously. *See* BURST SPEED.

SYNC Shortened form of synchronized. Events that happen at the same time.

SYNCHRONOUS DATA Data sent, usually in serial mode, with a clock pulse.

SYNCHRONOUS TRANSFER A method of sending data that allows many bytes of data to be sent before acknowledgment is received from the target. Only data can be sent in synchronous mode. Commands, messages and status must be transmitted in asynchronous mode.

SYNCHRONOUS TRANSFER NEGOTIATION The process of determining if a target is able to send/receive data using synchronous transfers.

TAPE DRIVE A sequential access memory device whose magnetic media is tape in a cassette, reel or continuous loop.

TARGET A device that responds to commands from a device (initiator).

TERMINAL   A screen and keyboard combination device used to interact with a computer. Terminals are usually used to access a mainframe computer.

TERMINATE AND STAY RESIDENT   A program that resides dormant in the computer's memory until triggered by another program or by a device. Also called TSR.

TERMINATION   A technique used to reduce echoing, ringing, and noise on a transmission line.

TERMINATOR   1) An electrical circuit attached to each end of a SCSI bus to minimize signal reflections and extraneous noise. SCSI defines passive, active and forced-perfect termination schemes. 2) A movie starring Arnold.

TERMPWR   Terminator power.

THIN FILM HEADS   A read/write head whose read/write element is deposited using integrated circuit techniques rather than being manually fabricated by grinding ferrite and hand winding coils.

THIRD-PARTY DMA   *See* DMA.

TPI   Tracks per inch.

TRACK   The radial position of the heads over the disk surface. A track is the circular ring traced over the disk surface by a head as the disk rotates under the heads.

TRACK ACCESS TIME   *See* AVERAGE ACCESS TIME.

TRACK FOLLOWING SERVO   A closed-loop positioner control system that continuously corrects the position of the disk drive's heads by utilizing a reference track and a feedback loop in the head positioning system. *See* also CLOSED LOOP.

TRACK PITCH   Distance from centerline to centerline of adjacent tracks (TPI divided into 1.0). New drives have track pitches approaching 3000 TPI.

TRACKS PER INCH   Track density, number of tracks per inch.

TRACK WIDTH   Width of data track. Also called core width of Read/Write Head.

TRACK ZERO   Track zero is the outermost data track on a disk drive. In the ST-506 interface, the interface signal denotes that the heads are positioned at the outermost cylinder.

TRACK ZERO DETECTOR   An obsolete technology that RECALIBRATES by sensing when infrared beams between an LED and infrared sensitive photo-transistor are blocked by the track zero interrupter (TZI). In newer drives, the track position is encoded in the servo signals.

TRANSLATION   In IDE applications, the conversion from physical head, sector, and track numbers to their logical equivilents.

TRUNCATION   In IDE applications, cylinder truncation can limit drive capacity. This occurs in older machines which do not have a BIOS supporting more than 1024 cylinders.

TSR   *See* TERMINATE AND STAY RESIDENT.

TUNNEL ERASE   An erase scheme where both sides of the recorded data are erased when writing data to elimate track to track interference. This is primarily used on floppy disk drives.

TWISTED PAIR   Two wires twisted together to reduce susceptibility to RF noise.

TWISTED-PAIR FLAT CABLE   A group of twisted pairs of wires arranged in rows that comprise a single flate cable. Twisted-pair flat cables are less susceptible to noise than are ribbon cables.

ULTRASCSI   *See* FAST-20.

UMB   Upper Memory Block. *See* UPPER MEMORY.

UNFORMATTED (CAPACITY)   Drive byte capacity before formatting. Maximum capacity of a disk drive before formatting = (bits per track) x # of heads x # of cylinders. *See* MEGABYTE.

UNIX   A multitasking operating system used on a variety of computer types, including PCs.

UPGRADE PATH   Generally, with disk products, a family having multiple products with varying capacities such that the system storage capacity can increase with changing application requirements simply by using a different disk drive within the product family.

UPPER MEMORY   Memroy in the PC that is between 640K and 1 MB. This memory area is used for BIOS addresses and can be used to store TSRs and other drivers. Upper memory is divided into 64K subsections called upper memory blocks (UMBs).

USENET   A collection of message areas accessed via Internet.

VERIFICATION   This feature lets the computer go back and read what it just wrote to disk to ensure the data was written correctly.

VIDEO ELECTRONICS STANDARDS ASSOCIATION (VESA)   A standards body that promotes video hardware and software specifications. VESA is also the organization governing the VL-BUS.

VL-BUS (VLB)   VESA Local Bus. A 32-bit local bus promoted by VESA for communicating directly to the CPU rather than through the ISA or EISA bus.

VOICE COIL MOTOR   An electro-magnetic positioning motor in the rigid disk drive similar to that used in audio speakers. A wire coil is placed in a stationary magnetic field. When current is passed through the coil, the resultant flux causes the coil to move. In a disk drive, the CARRIAGE ASSEMBLY is attached to the voice coil motor. Either a straight line (linear) or circular (rotary) design may be employed to position the heads on the disk's surface.

VOLATILE MEMORY   Memory that will be erased if power is lost. Typically, MAIN MEMORY is volatile, and AUXILIARY MEMORY is non-volatile and can be used for permanent (but changeable at will) storage fo programs and data.

WAN   Acronym for Wide Area Network.

WEDGE SERVO SYSTEM   A certain part of each TRACK contains servo positioning data. Gaps between each sector contain servo data to maintain head stack position on that cylinder. Identical to EMBEDDED SERVO.

WIDE SCSI   A 16-bit implementation of the SCSI-II standard, commonly referred to as SCSI-III. 68 pin connectors are commonly used with WIDE SCSI. MAximum transfer rates are 20-40Mbytes/sec.

WINCHESTER DRIVE   A disk drive with a Winchester style (floats on air) heads and non-removable (fixed) disks sealed in a containment-free housing.

WINDOWS   A multitasking operating system for the PC developed by Microsoft Corporation.

WINDOWS NT   A high-end, cross-platform, multitasking operating system also developed by Microsoft Corporation.

WORD   Number of bits processed in parallel (in a single operation) by a CPU. Standard word lengths are 8, 16, 32 and 64 bits (1, 2, 4 or 8 bytes).

WORM   *See* WRITE ONCE, READ MANY.

WRITE   To access a storage location and store data on the magnetic surface.

WRITE CURRENT   The amount of electrical current used to drive a magnetic recording head. The amount of write current necessary to saturate the magnetic media in different cell location vary.

WRITE FAULT   Disc drive interface signal to the controller used to inhibit further writing when a condition exists in the drive, which, if not detected, would cause improper writing on the disk. A "Write Fault Error" may occur if an operating system detects this bit is set or is unable to verify data written to a disk.

WRITE-INTENSIVE   A process that requires a lot of writing of data to a device such as a hard disk.

WRITE ONCE, READ MANY   A storage medium that can be written to only once, but read many times. Also called WORM.

XOR   A binary operation that compares two bits and yields a 1 only if the bits being compared are different.

XSMD   Extended storage module drive interface. A popular electrical interface for 8" drives used in minicomputer and mainframe applications.

X3.131-1986   The document describing the specifications of the SCSI-1 standard.

X3.131-1994   The document describing the specifications of the SCSI-2 standard.

X3T10   The ANSI committee responsible for organizing, realizing, and promoting SCSI standards.

ZONED RECORDING (ZBR)   A media optimization technique where the number of sectors per track is dependent upon the cylinder circumference. I.E., tracks on the outside cylinders have more sectors per track than the inside cylinders. ZBR is a trademark of Seagate Technology. Zoned Recording is used to maximize the capacity of all modern hard disk drives. Also referred to as Zone Bit Recording.

INDEX

INDEX

INDEX

INDEX

INDEX

INDEX

NOTES

NOTES

NOTES

NOTES

NOTES